VBSCRIPT SUPERBIBLE

THE COMPLETE REFERENCE TO PROGRAMMING IN MICROSOFT VISUAL BASIC SCRIPTING EDITION

Jinjer L. Simon

WAITE GROUP PRESS™

A Division of Sams Publishing

Corte Madera, CA

PUBLISHER: Mitchell Waite
ASSOCIATE PUBLISHER: Charles Drucker

ACQUISITIONS MANAGER: Jill Pisoni

EDITORIAL DIRECTOR: John Crudo
PROJECT EDITOR: Laura E. Brown
DEVELOPMENTAL EDITOR: Luann Rouff
TECHNICAL EDITORS: Ken Cox and Donald Doherty
COPY EDITOR: Merrilee Eggleston/Creative Solutions

PRODUCTION DIRECTOR: Julianne Ososke
PRODUCTION MANAGER: Cecile Kaufman
PRODUCTION EDITOR: Kate Talbot
SENIOR DESIGNER: Sestina Quarequio
DESIGNERS: Karen Johnston, Jil Weil
COVER IMAGE: © 1996 PhotoDisk, Inc.
ILLUSTRATIONS:
PRODUCTION: Jennifer Dierdorff, Mike Henry, Shawn Ring, Laura A. Smith, Kevin Fulcher

Published by Waite Group Press™, 200 Tamal Plaza, Corte Madera, CA 94925

Waite Group Press™ is a division of Sams Publishing.

Printed in the United States of America
97 98 99 • 10 9 8 7 6 5 4 3 2 1

Library of Congress Cataloging-in-Publication Data
Simon, Jinjer, 1966-
Visual Basic, scripting edition, superbible / Jinjer Simon.
p. cm.
Includes index.
ISBN 1-57169-081-6
1. Microsoft Visual Basic. 2. VBScript (Computer program language)
QA76.73.B3S553 1997 96-45240
005.2'762--dc21 CIP

Dedication

I dedicate this book to my parents.

About the Author

Jinjer L. Simon has been actively involved in the computer industry since 1984, when she was a student at Utah State University. Her involvement in the industry includes various stints in programming, providing software technical support, and end-user training, as well as the development of written and online user documentation, the creation of software tutorials, and the development of Internet Web sites. Jinjer and her husband currently live in Carrollton, Texas with their two children. She is self-employed as an Internet consultant and online documentation developer.

Acknowledgments

I would like to thank Laura Brown for the efficient way she was able to coordinate this project and still keep it enjoyable; Jill Pisoni for providing me the opportunity to be involved; and Mitchell Waite, not only for his dedication to providing the highest quality books on the market, but also for the acquisition of such a great staff to work with.

I would like to thank my content editor, Luann Rouff, and my two technical editors, Ken Cox and Donald Doherty, for helping me perfect the contents of the book. Special thanks to Ken Cox for writing the appendix on server-side scripting.

I also appreciate the great work and dedication of the other members of the Waite Group Press staff who pulled everything together and produced such a sharp-looking book: Mark Nigara, production editor, Merrilee Eggleston, copy editor, and Dan Scherf, who created the CD.

Most of all, I would like to thank my husband Richard, not only for supporting me in this project, but also for helping me to create the best Blackjack game ever developed under VBScript.

Table of Contents

Contents

1

GETTING STARTED

1

GETTING STARTED

Microsoft Visual Basic, Scripting Edition, most commonly referred to as VBScript, is one of the most valuable tools available for Web page development. Not only does it allow you to work with the properties of objects, such as ActiveX controls, it also enables you to perform data verifications directly on the user's machine (the client) without first sending the data back to the Web server.

This chapter provides a brief overview of the VBScript language. It also explains the layout of each chapter in this book.

What Is VBScript?

VBScript is a subset of the popular Visual Basic 4.0 development language. Because of its close link to Visual Basic, VBScript can be easily learned by current Visual Basic programmers. VBScript was developed by Microsoft to provide active scripting on the Web page. Besides being a subset of Visual Basic, VBScript is interpreted at run time. This means that the code can only be used with a browser or other application that knows how to interpret VBScript.

VBScript allows you to add Visual Basic code directly to your HTML document. In order for the browser to interpret this code, you use the HTML **<SCRIPT>** element to identify the code as VBScript code, as illustrated below.

```
<SCRIPT LANGUAGE = VBSCRIPT>

MsgBox "Hello"

</SCRIPT>
```

VBScript provides a vast array of new features to the HTML Web development world. These new features include items such as the ability to validate data on the client side and inform the user if the wrong data was entered, and modify the properties of ActiveX controls and Java applets.

Array Handling

VBScript provides the ability to work with single-dimensional and multidimensional arrays. Use of arrays allows you to work with and store related data values more efficiently. For more information about working with arrays, refer to Chapter 6, Array Handling.

Control Flow

Using the flow control statements provided by VBScript, you design a conditional statement in which a certain statement, or series of statements, are executed as long as a condition is true. There are other statements that can be used to determine if a certain condition exists; the following code illustrates how to use a `Select Case` statement to check for a value. For more information about controlling the flow of your VBScript code, refer to Chapter 2, VBScript Basics.

```
Select Case UserValue
  Case 1
    MsgBox "You selected the first item"
  Case 2
    MsgBox "You selected the second item"
  Case 3
    MsgBox "You selected the third item"
End Select
```

Data Conversions

Because VBScript has only one data type, a variant, it is often necessary to convert the data to the desired subtype before using certain functions. For example, if you are going to add two values, you should convert them to numeric values, such as integers, prior to performing the mathematical calculation. For more information about converting data, refer to Chapter 7, Data Conversion.

Dates and Times

VBScript provides the ability to work with date and time values. The system date and time can be captured from the user's system, and then displayed on the Web page, as illustrated in Figure 1-1. For more information about date and time functions, refer to Chapter 5, Date and Time Values.

Data Validation

One extremely important reason for using VBScript is to validate the user's input on his or her machine prior to returning the data to the Web server. By checking the validity of data on the client side, you can greatly increase the efficiency of your Web site. The following code illustrates how to check a variable to make sure it can be converted to a numeric value. For more information about data validation, refer to Chapter 4, Data Validation.

Figure 1-1 The system date and time can be captured from the user's machine

```
If Not IsNumeric(InputValue) Then
  MsgBox "You must type a numeric value."
End If
```

User Interaction

VBScript provides functions that allow you to interact with the user. These functions allow you to display messages to the user and request additional information from the user, as illustrated in Figure 1-2. For more information about interacting with the user, refer to Chapter 10, User Interaction.

Mathematical Calculations

VBScript lets you manipulate numeric values by providing a vast array of mathematical operators and several trigonometric functions. For more information about mathematical operators, refer to Chapter 2, VBScript Basics. For information about using trigonometric functions, refer to Chapter 8, Computing Values.

Working with Objects

One of the best reasons for using VBScript is its ability to work directly with objects such as ActiveX controls and Java applets. In HTML you can embed an object, but you cannot alter any of its properties. With VBScript you can easily modify the properties

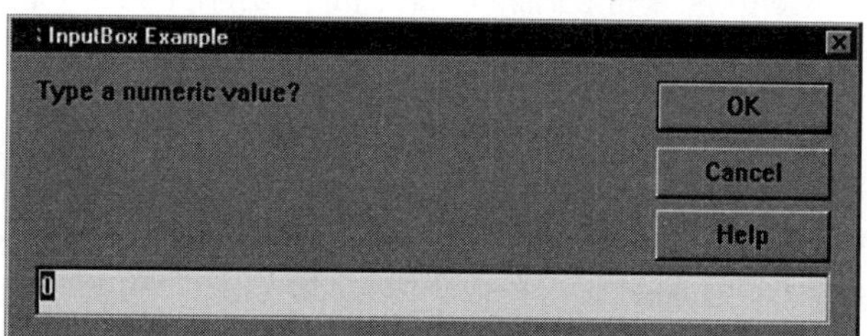

Figure 1-2 The `InputBox()` function allows you to request information from the user

of an object while a user is viewing your Web page. For example, if you have an ActiveX control that graphs values, you could request the values from the user and then pass new values to the control using VBScript. For more information about working with objects, refer to Chapter 12, Adding Objects, and Chapter 13, Advanced VBScript Programming.

String Manipulation

VBScript also provides several functions that can be used to work with string data. For example, you make sure that a password field always contains lowercase characters by using the `LCase()` function as illustrated in the following code. For more information about working with strings, refer to Chapter 9, String Manipulation.

```
Sub GetPassword()
  Dim UserValue
  Dim Password

  UserValue = InputBox(Type your password)

  Password = LCase(UserValue)

End Sub
```

Use of VBScript

VBScript is becoming a widely used scripting language for several Microsoft products. The functionality of the language is essentially the same in all of the products; the main difference is how VBScript is embedded in the code.

This book focuses on the use of VBScript with HTML 3.0 and Internet Explorer 3.0, although the concepts covered in this book can be used in any environment where VBScript is available.

Differences Between VBScript and Visual Basic 4.0

Because of the design of VBScript, there are some Visual Basic elements that are not needed when working with VBScript. Table 1-1 has been provided as a reference for Visual Basic programmers so that they can easily see the elements of Visual Basic that are not used in VBScript. It is important to note that VBScript does not use any of the **$** functions found in Visual Basic.

Table 1-1 Visual Basic features not used in VBScript

Category	Feature
Array handling	`Option Base` statement
	Declaring arrays with a lower bound <> 0
Clipboard	`Clipboard` object, `Clear` method, `GetFormat` method, `GetData` method, `SetData` method, `GetText` method, `SetText` method

Category	Feature
Collection	Add, Count, Item, Remove
	Access to collections using ! character (for example, CollectionOne!Foo)
Conditional compilation	#Const statement, #If...Then...#Else statement
Constants/literals	Const statement, all intrinsic constants
	Exponent-based real number (for example, 1.2345E+100)
	Trailing data-type characters (for example, 256&)
Control flow	DoEvents function
	GoSub ... Return statement, GoTo statement, On Error GoTo statement, On ... GoSub statement, On ... GoTo statement, Line numbers, Line labels, With ... End With statement
Conversion	Chr$ function, Hex$ function, Oct$ function, CCur function, CVar function, CVDate function, Format function, Format$ function, Str$ function
Data types	All intrinsic data types except variant, Type ... End Type statement
Date/time	Date statement, Time statement, Date$ function, Time$ function, Timer function
DDE	LinkExecute method, LinkPoke method, LinkRequest method, LinkSend method
Debugging	Debug.Print, End statement, Stop statement
Declaration	Declare statement (for declaring DLLs), Property Get statement, Property Let statement, Property Set statement, Public keyword, Private keyword, ParamArray statement, Optional statement, New statement
Error handling	Erl function, Error function, Error$ function
File input/output	All functions except MsgBox and InputBox
Financial	All financial functions
Graphics	Cls method, Circle method, Line method, Point method, PSet method, Scale method, Print method, Spc method, Tab method, TextHeight method, TextWidth method, LoadPicture statement, SavePicture statement, QBColor function, RGB function
Manipulating objects	Arrange property, ZOrder method, SetFocus method, InputBox$ function, Drag method, Hide method, Show method, Load method, Unload method, Move method, PrintForm method, Refresh method, AddItem method, RemoveItem method
Miscellaneous	Environ function, Environ$ function, SendKeys statement, Command function, Command$ function, AppActivate statement, Shell function, Beep statement
Object manipulation	GetObject function, TypeOf statement
Operators	Like operator
Optional arguments	IsMissing function
Options	deftype statement, Option Base statement, Option Compare statement, Option Private Module statement
Printing	TextHeight method, TextWidth method, EndDoc method, NewPage method, PrintForm method
Strings	All fixed-length strings, LCase$ function, UCase$ function, LSet statement, RSet statement, Space$ function, String$ function, Format function, Format$ function, Left$ function, Mid$ function, Right$ function, Mid statement, Trim$ function, LTrim$ function, RTrim$ function, StrConv function
Using classes	TypeName function

Acquiring VBScript

Microsoft is distributing VBScript, free of charge, with Internet Explorer 3.0. Because of this wide distribution of the product and its ease of use, it will have mass appeal as a developmental platform for adding active scripts to Web pages.

The CD included with this book contains a copy of Internet Explorer 3.0 that should be installed if you do not currently have a browser that supports VBScript. When Internet Explorer is installed on your system, the appropriate .dlls are also installed so that you can view Web pages that contain VBScript code.

Using This Book

Visual Basic Scripting Edition SuperBible is a comprehensive reference to the VBScript language. This book is designed so that it can be used as a reference, both by those already familiar with Visual Basic 4.0 and by those who have not used Visual Basic in the past. Each chapter provides a discussion of a specific topic with an alphabetical listing of the related functions, statements, operators, methods, and objects. Following is a description of the information that is covered in each chapter of this book.

Chapter 1, Getting Started

This chapter provides a brief introduction to VBScript and an overview of the information covered in this book. The layout of each chapter is also discussed.

Chapter 2, VBScript Basics

This chapter provides a description of how to incorporate VBScript into your Web pages. It describes the basic statements used for laying out your code, program flow, and conditional situations, with examples of how to use each one. It also provides examples and descriptions of each of the operators used with VBScript.

Chapter 3, VBScript Data Types and Variables

This chapter outlines the different subtypes of the variant and how to declare and work with variables and constants in VBScript.

Chapter 4, Data Validation

This chapter describes each of the functions used to validate data on the client machine. The project at the end of the chapter demonstrates how to use the validation functions to ensure that the user has entered the requested type of data.

Chapter 5, Date and Time Values

This chapter describes the functions that can be used to capture and manipulate date and time values on a Web page. The project at the end of the chapter illustrates how to use the date and time functions in the chapter to determine the amount of time that will elapse between two events.

Chapter 6, Array Handling

This chapter describes the functions and statements used for dealing with arrays. The project at the end of the chapter illustrates how to create a dynamic array and then sort the values in the array.

Chapter 7, Data Conversion

This chapter describes the functions that are used to convert data. For example, you would use the `CInt()` function to convert a value to an integer value. The project at the end of the chapter illustrates how to use the conversion functions to convert the data typed by the user so that you can make the appropriate calculations.

Chapter 8, Computing Values

This chapter describes the functions used to compute values. For example, the `Rnd()` function is used to create a random number. The project at the end of the chapter uses the functions in this chapter to create a scientific calculator.

Chapter 9, String Manipulation

This chapter describes the functions that are used to work with string data. For example, the `Len()` function allows you to determine the number of characters in a string. The project at the end of this chapter uses the functions in the chapter to create a simple word game.

Chapter 10, User Interaction

This chapter describes the two VBScript functions, `MsgBox()` and `InputBox()`, that are used to gather input from the user. The project at the end of the chapter uses these functions to create a simple game in which the user can practice adding, multiplying, subtracting, and dividing numbers. The program generates random numbers and displays an equation for the user in an input box. The message box function displays the results.

Chapter 11, Error Handling

This chapter discusses the error handling methods that are available in VBScript and describes the `On Error` statement as well as the `Err` object and its properties and methods. The project at the end of the chapter is designed to illustrate how to use the error handling methods that are available in VBScript.

Chapter 12, Adding Objects

This chapter discusses how to add and work with objects using VBScript. It provides examples of how to work with ActiveX controls and Java applets. The project at the end of the chapter illustrates how to use VBScript to modify the properties of an ActiveX control by allowing the user to change the values of a graph and specify the graph type.

Chapter 13, Advanced VBScript Programming

This chapter uses the VBScript functionality covered in other chapters to create an interactive blackjack game. The project illustrates how to use VBScript to interact with several ActiveX controls.

Chapter 14, HTML Features Supported by Internet Explorer 3.0

This chapter provides an alphabetical listing of the HTML elements supported by Internet Explorer 3.0. This chapter is intended to be used as a reference while creating your Web pages.

Chapter 15, Internet Explorer Object Model for Scripting

This chapter provides descriptions of each of the objects that make up the Internet Explorer document, and their related properties, methods, and events.

Appendix A, VBScript in Server-Side Scripts

This appendix provides a brief overview of how server-side scripting compares to client-side scripting.

Appendix B, Newly Released VBScript Functions

This appendix provides a description of the new functions that will be added to the next VBScript version released with the next version of Internet Explorer. These functions are also used with the ActiveX Server.

Appendix C, Microsoft Internet Explorer 3.0: A Field Guide

This appendix chapter provides licensing information for the Microsoft Internet Explorer 3.0 included on the CD with this book.

Chapter Organization

With the exception of Chapters 1–3, 14, and 15, the chapters in this book are all designed using the popular Waite Group SuperBible format. Chapters 4 through 12 consist of three parts: a topic overview, an alphabetically arranged section of language reference entries, and a chapter project that encompasses the information discussed in the chapter. Chapter 13 provides an overview of the chapter and then a chapter project.

Chapters 1 through 3 are designed to provide an introduction to the VBScript language by providing detailed information and examples of the basic statements and operators available. You will also find information about the variant data type and its various subtypes. Chapters 14 and 15 provide additional HTML and Internet Explorer information that you may need when developing your Web pages.

Topic Overview

The first section of each chapter provides an introduction to the topic and identifies the purpose for using the information covered in the chapter. At the end of each of these sections, you will find a table listing all of the functions, statements, objects, and methods discussed in the chapter.

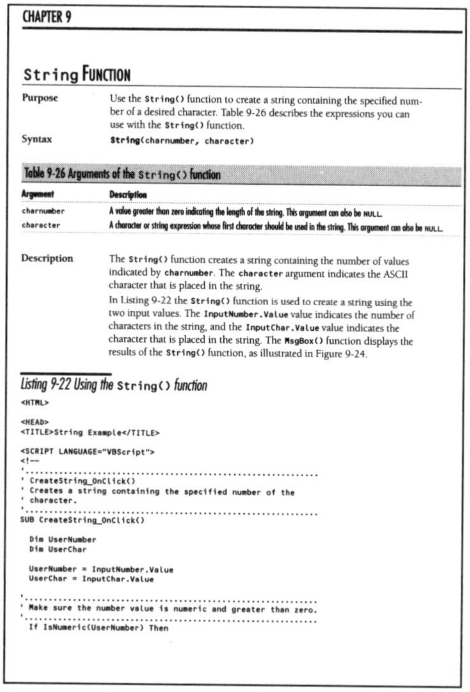

CHAPTER 9

String FUNCTION

Purpose Use the `String()` function to create a string containing the specified number of a desired character. Table 9-26 describes the expressions you can use with the `String()` function.

Syntax `String(charnumber, character)`

Table 9-26 Arguments of the `String()` function

Argument	Description
charnumber	A value greater than zero indicating the length of the string. This argument can also be NULL.
character	A character or string expression whose first character should be used in the string. This argument can also be NULL.

Description The `String()` function creates a string containing the number of values indicated by `charnumber`. The `character` argument indicates the ASCII character that is placed in the string.

In Listing 9-22 the `String()` function is used to create a string using the two input values. The `InputNumber.Value` value indicates the number of characters in the string, and the `InputChar.Value` value indicates the character that is placed in the string. The `MsgBox()` function displays the results of the `String()` function, as illustrated in Figure 9-24.

Listing 9-22 Using the `String()` *function*

```
<HTML>

<HEAD>
<TITLE>String Example</TITLE>

<SCRIPT LANGUAGE="VBScript">
<!--
'............................................................
' CreateString_OnClick()
' Creates a string containing the specified number of the
' character.
'............................................................
SUB CreateString_OnClick()

  Dim UserNumber
  Dim UserChar

  UserNumber = InputNumber.Value
  UserChar = InputChar.Value

'............................................................
' Make sure the number value is numeric and greater than zero.
'............................................................
  If IsNumeric(UserNumber) Then
```

Figure 1-3 A detailed description is provided for each VBScript element

Reference Entries

The main section of each chapter consists of alphabetically arranged entries (see Figure 1-3 for a sample) for each of the VBScript elements that are related to the subject of the chapter. For example, in Chapter 4, Data Validation, this section contains detailed descriptions and examples of all the functions that are used to validate data. The entries are structured as follows:

- *Name* - The name of the function, statement, operator, object, method, or property. This is the name referenced in the index.
- *Purpose* - A short statement that identifies the purpose for using the specified item.
- *Syntax* - A template that illustrates how to use the item. If the item has attributes, they are listed in a table under the syntax.
- *Description* - A detailed description of the item and how it is used. If a sample of the item has been placed in this section, a description of how the sample code works will be included.
- *Listing* - Sample code that illustrates how the item is used.

- *Example* - A description of how this item is used in the chapter project.
- *Comments* - Points out some unique information about the specified item. This may include special circumstances when the item should be used.

Chapter Projects

Chapters 4 through 13 each have a detailed project at the end that illustrates how to use the information discussed in that chapter, as shown in Figure 1-4. These projects are designed to illustrate how the features discussed in the chapter can be applied to a Web page's development. Each project section is made up of the following four elements:

- *Introductory Text* - Provides a broad description of the project and the features that are used in it.
- *Building the Project* - A detailed tutorial that illustrates how to assemble the project. These steps include not only the VBScript code, but also the HTML code needed to create the page.
- *How It Works* - Describes in more detail the way the features of the project work.
- *Complete Source Code* - Provides the complete source code for the project. This source is also located on the CD in the directory for the corresponding chapter.

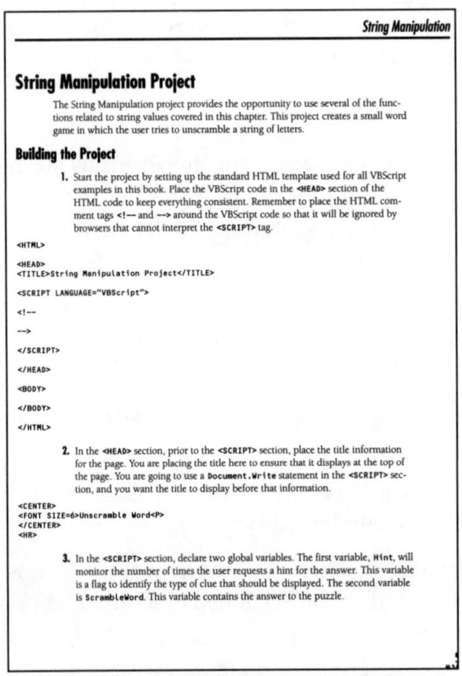

String Manipulation

String Manipulation Project

The String Manipulation project provides the opportunity to use several of the functions related to string values covered in this chapter. This project creates a small word game in which the user tries to unscramble a string of letters.

Building the Project

1. Start the project by setting up the standard HTML template used for all VBScript examples in this book. Place the VBScript code in the <HEAD> section of the HTML code to keep everything consistent. Remember to place the HTML comment tags <!-- and --> around the VBScript code so that it will be ignored by browsers that cannot interpret the <SCRIPT> tag.

```
<HTML>

<HEAD>
<TITLE>String Manipulation Project</TITLE>

<SCRIPT LANGUAGE="VBScript">

<!--

-->

</SCRIPT>

</HEAD>

<BODY>

</BODY>

</HTML>
```

2. In the <HEAD> section, prior to the <SCRIPT> section, place the title information for the page. You are placing the title here to ensure that it displays at the top of the page. You are going to use a Document.Write statement in the <SCRIPT> section, and you want the title to display before that information.

```
<CENTER>
<FONT SIZE=6>Unscramble Word<P>
</CENTER>
<HR>
```

3. In the <SCRIPT> section, declare two global variables. The first variable, Hint, will monitor the number of times the user requests a hint for the answer. This variable is a flag to identify the type of clue that should be displayed. The second variable is ScrambleWord. This variable contains the answer to the puzzle.

Figure 1-4 A detailed project is provided at the end of each chapter

CD Installation

The CD included with this book contains all the examples created in the book, organized by chapters. The examples are actual Web pages that can be viewed with any browser capable of interpreting VBScript. To view the actual source for the page, simply select the Source option for the browser you are using. If you are using Internet Explorer 3.0, this option is located on the View menu.

The following illustrates how to copy files from the companion CD-ROM to your hard drive in Windows 3.1, Windows 95, and Windows NT.

> **Note:**
> **For the following PC examples, the installation instructions assume that the CD-ROM drive you want to copy files *from* is the D: drive and the hard drive you want to copy files *to* is the C: drive. If your system is set up differently, please substitute the appropriate drive letters.**

Windows 3.1

Perform the following steps to install the sample programs onto your hard drive.

1. Open the File Manager.
2. In File Manager, locate the drive you want to copy to and click on it.
3. If you have a directory to copy the files to, skip to step 4. Otherwise, create a new directory by selecting the Create Directory option on the File menu and then type

```
vbscript
```

   or type a directory name of your choice and press ENTER or click on the OK button.
4. Click on the new directory you created.
5. Double-click on the D: drive icon. Then double-click the Source directory. You should see chapter directories. Drag the contents of the Source directory to the new directory you created on the destination drive. If you only want to copy a few directories, Control-click on the directories and drag the selection to the destination drive.

> **Note:**
> When Windows copies a CD-ROM, it does not change the Read-only attribute for the files it copies. You can view the files, but you cannot edit them until you remove this attribute. To change this, select the top-most directory with the files in it. In File Manager, select File, Properties and click on the Read-only checkbox to deselect it and click OK.

Windows 95/Windows NT 4.0

The easiest way to copy files using Windows 95 and Windows NT 4.0 is by using the Desktop.

1. Double-click on the My Computer icon. Your drives display in a window on the desktop.
2. Double-click on your hard drive and create a new folder, such as VBScript Source, by selecting File, New, Folder from the window menu. A folder called New Folder is created on your hard drive with the name highlighted. To specify the folder name, type the desired name and press the ENTER key.
3. Go back to your drive window and double-click on the icon that represents your CD-ROM. You will see a window that has three folders in it. Double-click the Source folder to display a window that has the chapter folders in it.
4. Select the directories you want to copy (Control-click on the folders if you're not copying all of them) and drag your selection to the directory you created on your hard drive. You might need to reposition your windows to make the window for your hard drive visible.

> **Note:**
> When Windows copies a CD-ROM, it does not change the Read-only attribute for the files it copies. You can view the files, but you cannot edit them until you remove this attribute. To change this, select the top-most directory with the files in it. In the folder, right-click on the file or folder and select Properties; click on the Read-only checkbox to deselect it and click OK.

Additional Software on CD

The CD also includes copies of Internet Explorer 3.0 and the Microsoft ActiveX Control Pad. Each of these products is currently being distributed for free by Microsoft. They are included on the CD for your convenience.

The Internet Explorer, or another Web browser that supports VBScript, must be installed on your system before viewing any of the examples on the CD. When you run the installation program for the Internet Explorer, it will also install the files needed to work with VBScript code. Appendix C provides information about installing Internet Explorer 3.0 on your operating system.

The Microsoft ActiveX Control Pad is a tool developed by Microsoft that allows you to easily place ActiveX controls in your HTML code. If desired, this tool can be used as the development environment for your entire Web page. The ActiveX Control Pad also includes several ActiveX controls that are installed on your system. Some of these controls are used in the project in Chapter 13, Advanced VBScript Programming. Therefore, before running that project you will need to install the ActiveX Control Pad.

The ActiveX Control Pad can be installed on your Windows 95 or Windows NT system. Perform the following steps to install it on your system:

1. Double-click on the My Computer icon. Your drives display in a window on the desktop.
2. Go back to your drive window and double-click on the icon that represents your CD-ROM. You will see a window that has three folders in it. Double-click the Ctrlpad folder to display a window that has the install file in it.
3. Double-click the Setuppad icon to run the install program for the ActiveX Control Pad. The installation program will step you through the process of installing the software on your system.

2

VBSCRIPT BASICS

2

VBSCRIPT BASICS

VBScript provides you with the ability to activate your Web site. It features several functions that allow you to validate user input before it is returned to your Web server, calculate values, or even modify the properties of an object, such as an ActiveX control or a Java applet.

This chapter outlines the basics of using VBScript, including placing VBScript code directly within your HTML code. This chapter also covers the basic statements and operators available for use with your VBScript code.

Placing VBScript in HTML

HTML 3.0 allows you to include a script directly within your code. By using a scripting language, you are able to add features to your Web page that are not available by simply using HTML. These features include the ability to manipulate data typed by the user, modify objects, or even simply validate the input values.

The browser that is displaying the Web page must know how to interpret the script. To eliminate potential errors caused by a browser that does not know how to interpret a particular scripting language, the HTML standard is to place the scripting language within two `<SCRIPT>` tags. If a browser does not recognize VBScript, the code between the two `<SCRIPT>` tags is simply ignored. To ensure that the code is ignored by browsers that do not recognize the `<SCRIPT>` tag, use HTML comment tags around your VBScript code. One comment tag is placed after the `<SCRIPT>` tag and the other before the `</SCRIPT>` tag, as illustrated in the following code. The initial `<SCRIPT>` tag must include the `LANGUAGE` property to indicate which type of scripting code is included within the `<SCRIPT>` tags. The `LANGUAGE` property identifies the scripting language that the browser should use to interpret the code.

```
<SCRIPT LANGUAGE = "VBSCRIPT">
<!--
```

continued on next page

continued from previous page

```
.
.
.

->
</SCRIPT>
```

The server-side version of VBScript (code-named "Denali") adds the **RUNAT** property to indicate the location where the code should run. You can specify that the code run either at the server or at the client. The syntax for declaring a server-side script is **<SCRIPT LANGUAGE="VBSCRIPT" RUNAT="SERVER">**. When you embed server-side scripts in an HTML file, you can use the **<%** and **%>** tags around the VBScript code. For more information about server-side scripting, refer to Appendix A, VBScript in Server-Side Scripts.

Standard Layout for an HTML Page

Although it is possible to place your VBScript code in both the **<HEAD>** and **<BODY>** sections of the HTML page, for purposes of consistency and clarity the best location for the code is in the **<HEAD>** section. Placing the code in the **<HEAD>** section ensures that all of the VBScript code is together and makes it easier to read; the **<BODY>** section will only contain the HTML tags needed to lay out the page.

Listing 2-1 illustrates the suggested HTML template to use with your VBScript code. This template has been included on the CD in the directory for Chapter 2. The file is named **Layout**. If desired, you can use this file as a standard when you create your VBScript programs. You will notice that it was used to create all the samples in this book.

Listing 2-1 Layout of an HTML page with VBScript code

```
<HTML>

<HEAD>
<TITLE>Layout Example</TITLE>

<SCRIPT LANGUAGE="VBScript">
<!--

Rem This is where you place your VBScript Code.
-->

</SCRIPT>
</HEAD>

<BODY>

<!--
  This section contains HTML tags for designing your page.
-->

</BODY>

</HTML>
```

Remember that the `<SCRIPT>` tags are always placed around the VBScript code. The HTML comment tags `<!--` and `-->` are always used within the `<SCRIPT>` tags to ensure that your VBScript code is ignored by any browser that cannot interpret it.

VBScript Code Elements

VBScript provides several different functions, statements, and operators that can be used to develop your code. Each of these elements is covered in detail in this book. This chapter covers each of the basic statements available in VBScript that are used to design the flow of your program, although some of the more specific statements, such as the **Randomize** statement, are covered with related functions in other chapters. The operators available in VBScript are also covered in detail in this chapter.

All of the VBScript functions have been grouped according to their functionality and placed in the appropriate chapter later in this book.

VBScript Layout Statements

VBScript provides five different basic statements that are used in almost all programs. These statement are used for inserting comments in your code, identifying user-defined functions and procedures, and calling functions and procedures. Each of these statements is listed in Table 2-1. A detailed description of each statement follows the table.

Table 2-1 VBScript layout statements

Statement	Description
`Call`	Used to call a user-defined function or procedure
`Function`	Identifies a user-defined function
`Option Explicit`	Indicates that all variables must be defined
`Rem`	Identifies a comment in the source code
`Sub`	Identifies a user-defined procedure
`'`	Identifies a comment in the source code

`Call` STATEMENT

Purpose Use the **Call** statement to transfer the control to a user-defined function or procedure. Table 2-2 describes the expressions you can use with the **Call** statement.

Syntax `Call procedurename argumentlist`

Table 2-2 Arguments of the `Call` statement

Argument	Description
`procedurename`	The name of the procedure or function to call.
`argumentlist`	A comma-delimited list of variables, arrays, or expressions to pass to the function or procedure specified by the `procedurename` argument. Each value passed in the `argumentlist` can be preceded with the `ByVal` keyword to indicate that it is being passed by the value. If the `ByVal` keyword is not specified for an argument, assignment to the argument within the procedure or function is not allowed.

Description The `Call` statement allows you to pass control to another user-defined function or procedure within your VBScript code. When you use the `Call` statement, you specify the name of the function or procedure that should be executed. You can also specify values, such as variables, arrays, and expressions, that should be passed to the specified function or procedure. If you want to change the value of a variable that you are passing to a procedure within that procedure, you need to use the keyword `ByVal` in front of the variable name.

The `Call` statement is optional when calling a function or procedure. However, if you use the `Call` statement to call a procedure that requires arguments, the `argumentlist` must be enclosed in parentheses. If you omit the `Call` statement, you also must omit the parentheses around the `argumentlist`.

Listing 2-3, under the `Sub` statement description in this chapter, uses the `Call` statement to call a procedure from within another procedure. The procedure, `SubtractValues()`, is called with two arguments.

`Function` STATEMENT

Purpose Use the `Function` statement to declare a `Function` procedure. Table 2-3 describes the expressions you can use with the `Function` statement.

Syntax

```
Function name (argumentlist)
  statements
  name = expression
End Function
```

Table 2-3 Arguments of the `Function` statement

Argument	Description
`name`	The name of the `Function`.
`argumentlist`	A list of variables representing arguments that are passed to the `Function` procedure when it is called. If the list contains multiple variables, they are separated by commas.

Argument	Description
`statements`	A group of statements that is executed within the body of the `Function` procedure.
`expression`	The value returned by the `Function`. The `name = expression` is an optional statement that can be used to assign a return value for the function.

Description

The **`Function`** statement is used to indicate the start of a function within your code. The statement declares the name, arguments, and statements that make up the function. The **`ByVal`** keyword can be used in the argument list for the function to ensure that only the value of the argument is passed to the function.

When you declare a function, it is public. In other words, the function is visible to all other procedures and functions within your VBScript code. Any variables declared within a function are private to that function and cannot be used by other procedures.

Unlike the **`Sub`** statement, you can call a **`Function`** procedure on the right side of an expression in the same way you use any intrinsic function, such as **`Sqr()`**, **`Cos()`**, or **`Chr()`**. By calling the function from the right side of an expression, you can return a value from the function to the variable on the left side of the expression. This process of calling a function is illustrated in Figure 2-1.

Listing 2-2 uses the **`Function`** statement to identify a function used to add the two values typed by the user. When the user clicks the Add the values

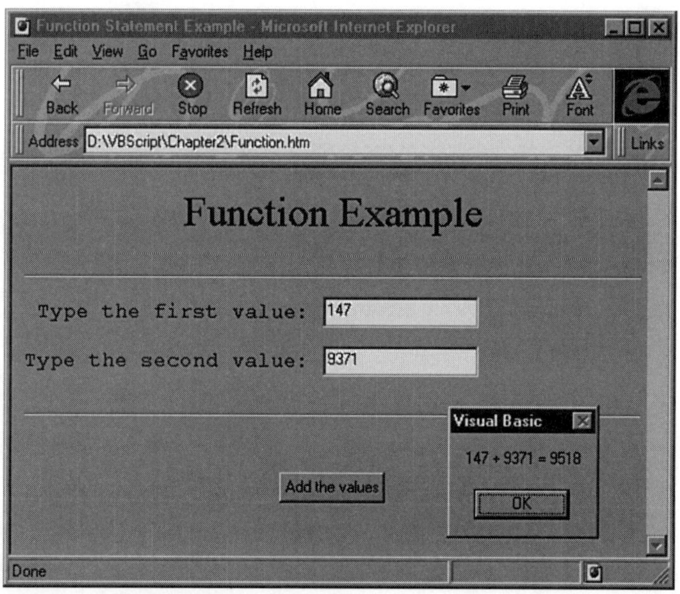

Figure 2-1 The **`Function`** statement identifies a function that adds the input values

button, the **CheckValues_OnClick()** procedure is called to make sure both of the values are numeric. If the values are numeric, the **AddValues()** function is called by assigning the results of the function to a variable called **Results**. The function adds the two numbers and passes the sum back to the procedure. The procedure uses the **MsgBox()** function to display a dialog box that contains the results of the function.

Listing 2-2 Using the Function statement

```
<HTML>

<HEAD>
<TITLE>Function Statement Example</TITLE>

<SCRIPT LANGUAGE="VBScript">
<!--
Option Explicit
'.......................................................
' CheckValues_OnClick()
' This procedure is called when the user selects the
' Add the values button. This makes sure both values typed
' are numeric and then calls the AddValues() function to
' sum the values.
'.......................................................
Sub CheckValues_OnClick()

  Dim UserValue1
  Dim UserValue2
  Dim Result

  UserValue1 = InputValue1.Value
  UserValue2 = InputValue2.Value

  If (IsNumeric(UserValue1)) and (IsNumeric(UserValue2)) Then

'...............................................................
' If both values are numeric, call the AddValues() function and
' assign the return value of the function to the Result
' variable.
'...............................................................
     Result = AddValues(UserValue1, UserValue2):

'...............................................................
' Displays the results from the AddValues() function.
'...............................................................
     MsgBox UserValue1 & " + " & UserValue2 & " = " & Result
  End If

End Sub
'.............................................................
' AddValues()
' Adds the two values typed by the user.
'.............................................................
Function AddValues (ByVal Value1, ByVal Value2)
  Dim Sum
```

```
  Sum = CDbl(Value1) + CDbl(Value2)

'.............................................................
' Assigns the sum of the two numbers to the function as the
' return value for the function.
'.............................................................
  AddValues = Sum

END Function
-->

</SCRIPT>
</HEAD>

<BODY>

<CENTER>

<FONT SIZE=6>Function Example<P>
</CENTER>
<HR>

<FONT SIZE=4>

<PRE> Type the first value: <INPUT NAME=InputValue1 SIZE=20>

Type the second value: <INPUT NAME=InputValue2 SIZE=20>

<HR>
<CENTER>
<INPUT TYPE=BUTTON VALUE="Add the values" NAME="CheckValues">
</CENTER>

</FONT>

</BODY>

</HTML>
```

Comments

You can use a function recursively, meaning that the function can call itself. Be aware that recursion can cause stack overflow.

You can use the `Exit Function` statement to terminate the execution of the statements within a function if a specific condition exists.

`Option Explicit` Statement

Purpose

Use the `Option Explicit` statement to ensure that all variables are explicitly declared before they are used.

Syntax

`Option Explicit`

Description

The `Option Explicit` statement can be used to ensure that all variables are explicitly declared within your VBScript code. If the Option Explicit statement is used, the variables must be declared using the `Dim`, `Private`, `Public`, and `ReDim` statements before they are used. Use of the `Option`

`Explicit` statement ensures that you do not mistype a variable name in one location. If you attempt to use a variable that has not been declared, a run-time error will occur. This statement is normally used to maintain consistency within the code.

Listing 2-2 uses the `Option Explicit` statement to ensure that all variables are declared within the code.

Comments Use the `Option Explicit` statement to avoid incorrectly typing the name of an existing variable or to avoid risking confusion in code where the scope of the variable is not clear.

Rem OR ' STATEMENT

Purpose Use either the `Rem` or `'` (single quote mark) statements to identify a comment within your VBScript code. Table 2-4 outlines the type of expression that can be used with the `Rem` or `'` statements.

Syntax

```
Rem expression
```

or

```
' expression
```

Table 2-4 Arguments of both the Rem and ' statements

Argument	Description
`expression`	Any expression

Description The `Rem` and `'` statements are used within your VBScript code to provide comments about the code. Any information placed following either of these statements is ignored by the run-time compiler. Use of these statements is good programming practice. They allow you to provide detailed information about the code so that someone can easily understand and modify it at a later date.

Listing 2-3, under the `Sub` statement description, uses both the `Rem` and `'` statements to indicate comments within the source code.

Comments You can use a single quotation mark, or apostrophe (`'`), instead of the `Rem` keyword. If the `Rem` statement follows other statements on a line, it must be separated from the statements by a colon. However, when you use a single quotation mark, the colon is not required after other statements. There must be a space between the `Rem` statement and the comment text.

Sub STATEMENT

Purpose

Use the **Sub** statement to declare a **Sub** procedure. Table 2-5 describes the expressions you can use with the **Sub** statement.

Syntax

```
Sub name (argumentlist)
 statements
 name = expression
End Sub
```

Table 2-5 Arguments of the Sub statement

Argument	Description
name	The name of the procedure.
argumentlist	A list of variables representing arguments that are passed to the procedure when it is called. If the list contains multiple variables, they are separated by commas.
statements	A group of statements that is executed within the body of the procedure.

Description

The **Sub** statement is used to indicate the start of a procedure within your code. The statement declares the name, arguments, and statements that make up the procedure. The **ByVal** keyword can be used in the argument list for the procedure, to ensure that only the value of the argument is passed to the procedure.

When you declare a procedure, it is public. In other words, the procedure is visible to all other procedures and functions within your VBScript code. Any variables declared within a procedure are private to that procedure and cannot be used by other procedures.

Listing 2-3 uses the **Sub** statement to call the **SubtractValues()** procedure from within the **CheckValues()** procedure. The two values typed by the user are passed to the **SubtractValues()** procedure. The procedure subtracts one value from the other, and then uses the **MsgBox()** function to display a dialog box with the results, as illustrated in Figure 2-2.

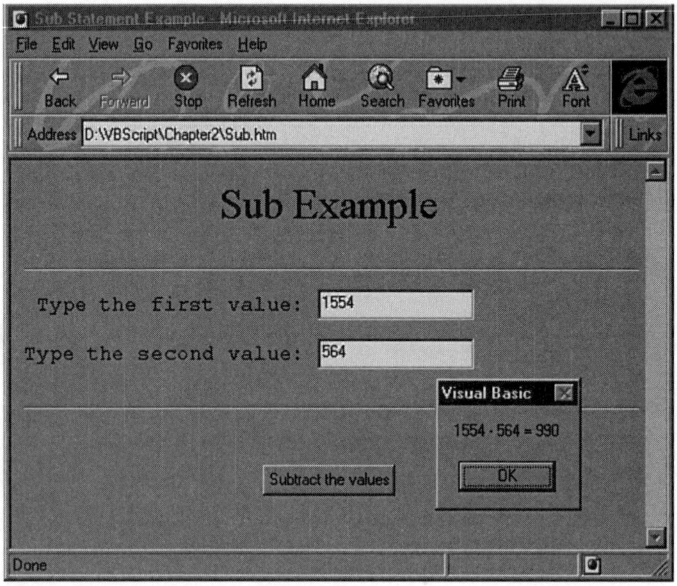

Figure 2-2 The `Sub` statement calls a specific procedure

Listing 2-3 Using the `Sub` statement

```
<HTML>

<HEAD>
<TITLE>Sub Statement Example</TITLE>

<SCRIPT LANGUAGE="VBScript">
<!--
Option Explicit
'.............................................................
' CheckValues_OnClick()
' This procedure is called when the user selects the Subtract
' the values button. This procedure makes sure both of the
' values are numeric. Then it calls the SubtractValues()
' procedure.
'.............................................................
Sub CheckValues_OnClick()

  Dim UserValue1
  Dim UserValue2
  Dim Result

  UserValue1 = InputValue1.Value
  UserValue2 = InputValue2.Value

'.............................................................
' Make sure both values are numeric.
'.............................................................
  If (IsNumeric(UserValue1)) and (IsNumeric(UserValue2)) Then
```

```
Rem Call the SubtractValues() procedure.

     Call SubtractValues(UserValue1, UserValue2)

  End If

End Sub
'............................................................
' SubtractValues()
' Subtracts the first value from the second value.
'............................................................
Sub SubtractValues (ByVal Value1, ByVal Value2)
  Dim Total

  Total = CDbl(Value1) - CDbl(Value2)

  MsgBox Value1 & " - " & Value2 & " = " & Total

END Sub
-->

</SCRIPT>
</HEAD>

<BODY>

<CENTER>

<FONT SIZE=6>Sub Example<P>
</CENTER>
<HR>

<FONT SIZE=4>

<PRE> Type the first value: <INPUT NAME=InputValue1 SIZE=20>

Type the second value: <INPUT NAME=InputValue2 SIZE=20>

<HR>
<CENTER>
<INPUT TYPE=BUTTON VALUE="Subtract the values" NAME="CheckValues">
</CENTER>

</FONT>

</BODY>

</HTML>
```

Comments

You can use a procedure recursively, meaning that it can call itself. Be aware that recursion can cause stack overflow.

You can use the `Exit Sub` statement to terminate the execution of the statements within a procedure if a specific condition exists.

Program Flow Statements

VBScript provides several statements that you can use to control the flow of your code. These statements can be grouped into two different types: looping statements and conditional statements.

Looping statements are designed to repeat a series of statements a specific number of times or while a specific condition is **TRUE**. The looping statements available in VBScript are listed in Table 2-6. A detailed description of each statement appears in alphabetical order after the table.

Table 2-6 VBScript looping statements

Use This Statement...	To Do This...
`Do Loop`	Repeat a group of statements while or until a condition is `TRUE`.
`Exit`	Exit a function, procedure, `Do` loop, or `For` loop.
`For Next`	Repeat a group of statements a specified number of times.
`While Wend`	Repeat a group of statements while a specified condition is `TRUE`.

Conditional statements provide the capability to specify a statement or series of statements that only execute if the specified condition is **TRUE**. For example, you could use a conditional statement to see if the user typed a numeric value in a field and, if they did, perform a mathematical calculation; but if they typed a string value, you would not want to perform the same calculation. Table 2-7 lists each of the conditional statements that can be used in VBScript.

Table 2-7 VBScript conditional statements

Use This Statement...	To Do This...
`If Then Else`	Execute a group of statements if a condition is `TRUE`.
`Select Case`	Execute different groups of statements for each value of a variable expression.

Do Loop Statement

Purpose Use the `Do Loop` statement to repeat a group of statements either while a specific condition is `TRUE`, or until the condition is `TRUE`. Table 2-8 describes the arguments of the `Do Loop` statement.

Syntax

```
Do While condition
  statements
Loop
```

or

```
Do Until condition
  statements
Loop
```

or

```
Do
  statements
Loop While condition
```

or

```
Do
  statements
Loop Until condition
```

Table 2-8 Arguments of the Do Loop statement

Argument	Description
condition	Any expression that has a Boolean value of TRUE or FALSE. If the expression has a NULL value, it is treated as a FALSE value.
statements	One or more statements that are repeated either while or until the specified condition is TRUE.

Description

The **Do Loop** statement is used when you want to repeat a series of statements either as long as (**While**) or until (**Until**) a specific condition is **TRUE**. For example, you may want to continue to add a series of numbers until the user selects a button. The **Do Loop** statement would check to see if the button had been pressed. This looping statement is probably the most versatile one in VBScript because it provides four different versions: **Do While**, **Do Until**, **Loop While**, and **Loop Until**.

You can use either the keyword **While** or **Until** with the **Do Loop**. One of these two keywords always precedes the condition of the loop. The **While** keyword causes a series of statements to execute as long as the specified condition is **TRUE**. The **Until** keyword causes the series of statements to execute until a specified condition is **TRUE**; as long as the condition is **FALSE**, the loop continues.

As illustrated in the Syntax section, you can either place the keywords (**While** and **Until**) at the beginning of the loop, after the **Do**, or at the end of the loop, after the **Loop**. If the keyword and condition arguments are placed at the beginning of the loop, a **Do While** or **Do Until** statement, the condition is checked before executing the series of statements for the first time. If the exit condition for the loop is met at the beginning, the statements within the loop will never be executed.

If the keyword and condition are at the end of the loop, the series of statements in the loop execute at least once before the condition is checked.

The statements always execute with the `Loop While` and the `Loop Until` statements.

Listing 2-4 uses the `Do Loop` statement to total the user-typed numeric value ten times. The program takes the value typed by the user in the `InputValue` field and continues to add that value to the `Sum` variable until the `Counter` variable equals `10`. When the loop is exited, the `MsgBox()` function displays the results of the loop, as illustrated in Figure 2-3.

Listing 2-4 Using the `Do Loop` *statement*

```
<HTML>

<HEAD>
<TITLE>Do Loop Statement Example</TITLE>

<SCRIPT LANGUAGE="VBScript">
<!--
'.......................................................
' DoLoopSum_OnClick()
' Totals the numeric value typed ten times. Then the
' sum of the number is displayed.
'.......................................................
SUB DoLoopSum_OnClick()
```

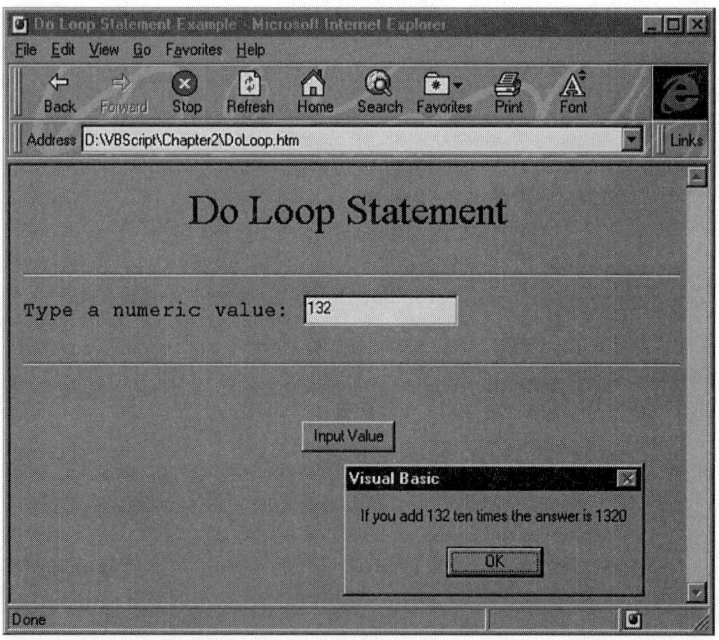

Figure 2-3 The `Do Loop` statement executes a series of statements until a condition is met

```
  Dim UserValue
  Dim Counter
  Dim Sum

  UserValue = InputValue.Value
  Counter = 1
  Sum = 0

'.....................................................
' Perform these statements as long as the Counter value
' is less than or equal to 10.
'.....................................................
  Do While (Counter <= 10)

'.....................................................
' Make sure a numeric value was typed, if not exit the
' loop.
'.....................................................
    If Not IsNumeric(UserValue) Then

       MsgBox UserValue & " is not a numeric value"
       Exit Do

    End If

'.....................................................
' Add the value to the Sum variable. Increase the
' counter variable each time the loop executes.
'.....................................................
    Sum = Sum + UserValue

    Counter = Counter + 1

  Loop

'......................................................
' Indicate the sum that was generated by the Do Loop
'......................................................
  MsgBox "If you add " & UserValue & " ten times the answer is " & Sum

END SUB
-->

</SCRIPT>
</HEAD>

<BODY>

<CENTER>

<FONT SIZE=6>Do Loop Statement<P>
</CENTER>
<HR>

<FONT SIZE=4>

<PRE>Type a numeric value: <INPUT NAME=InputValue SIZE=20>
```

continued on next page

continued from previous page

```
<HR>
<CENTER>
<INPUT TYPE=BUTTON VALUE="Input Value" NAME="DoLoopSum">
</CENTER>

</FONT>

</BODY>

</HTML>
```

Comments You can use the **Exit** statement to exit a loop instead of waiting for the condition of the loop to be met. For example, in Listing 2-4 the **Exit** statement was used to exit the loop when a nonnumeric value was typed. The **Exit** statement is normally used with an **If** statement that is checking for a certain condition. If the condition is not correct, the **Exit** statement transfers the control to the statement immediately following the loop.

Exit Statement

Purpose Use the **Exit** statement to exit out of a function, procedure, **Do Loop** statement, or **For Next Loop** statement. When an **Exit** statement is encountered, none of the other statements in the function, procedure, or loop are executed. Table 2-9 describes the keywords you can use with the **Exit** statement.

Syntax `Exit keyword`

Table 2-9 Keywords for the Exit statement

Keyword	Description
Function	Exit the current function.
Sub	Exit the current procedure.
Do	Exit the current Do Loop statement.
For	Exit the current For Next statement.

Description The **Exit** statement allows you to alter the flow of your code by exiting the current function, procedure, **Do Loop** statement, or **For Next** statement. This statement is normally used with an **If** statement that checks to see if a condition exists. For example, if your procedure determines that the specified delivery date has already passed, you would want to exit the procedure without processing the order that lists that date. You can use the **Exit** statement to leave the procedure without completing the processing of the order, and then prompt the user to specify a new delivery date.

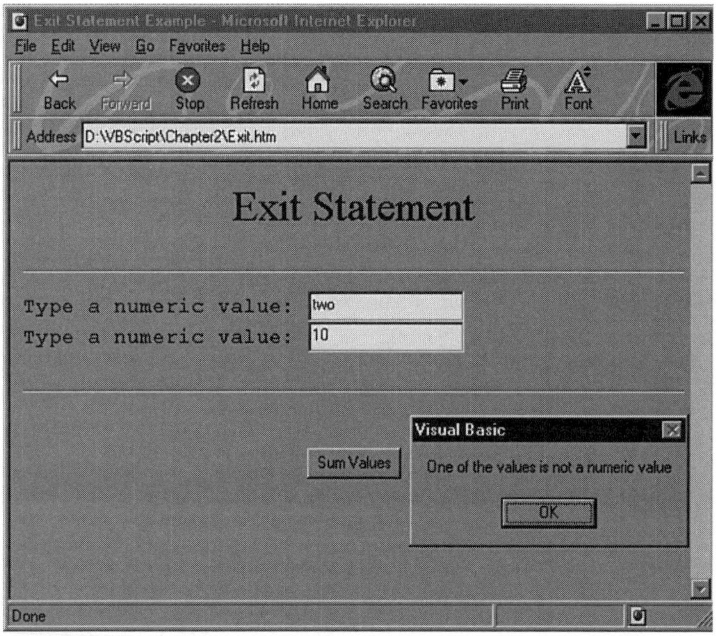

Figure 2-4 The **Exit** statement exits out of the current procedure if the wrong type of value is entered

Listing 2-5 uses the **Exit** statement to exit out of the procedure if the user types a nonnumeric value in one of the fields. The **MsgBox()** function displays a message indicating that a nonnumeric value was typed, as illustrated in Figure 2-4.

Listing 2-5 Using the `Exit` *statement*

```
<HTML>

<HEAD>
<TITLE>Exit Statement Example</TITLE>

<SCRIPT LANGUAGE="VBScript">
<!--
'.........................................
' SumValues_OnClick()
' Sums the values if they are both numeric.
'.........................................
SUB SumValues_OnClick()

  Dim UserValue1
  Dim UserValue2
  Dim Sum
```

continued on next page

continued from previous page

```
  UserValue1 = InputValue1.Value
  UserValue2 = InputValue2.Value
  Sum = 0


'.....................................................
' Make sure a numeric value was typed, if not exit the
' procedure.
'.....................................................
    If Not (IsNumeric(UserValue1)) Or Not (IsNumeric(UserValue2)) Then

       MsgBox "One of the values is not a numeric value"
       Exit Sub

    End If

'.....................................................
' Sum the input values
'.....................................................
    Sum = CDbl(UserValue1) + CDbl(UserValue2)


  MsgBox "The sum of " & UserValue1 & " + " & UserValue2 & " is " & Sum

END SUB
-->

</SCRIPT>
</HEAD>

<BODY>

<CENTER>

<FONT SIZE=6>Exit Statement<P>
</CENTER>
<HR>

<FONT SIZE=4>

<PRE>Type a numeric value: <INPUT NAME=InputValue1 SIZE=20>
<PRE>Type a numeric value: <INPUT NAME=InputValue2 SIZE=20>

<HR>
<CENTER>
<INPUT TYPE=BUTTON VALUE="Sum Values" NAME="SumValues">
</CENTER>

</FONT>

</BODY>

</HTML>
```

Comments A conditional statement, such as an `If` statement, is normally used before an `Exit` statement. This conditional statement checks to see if a condition exists that make it inappropriate to execute the remainder of the function, procedure, or loop.

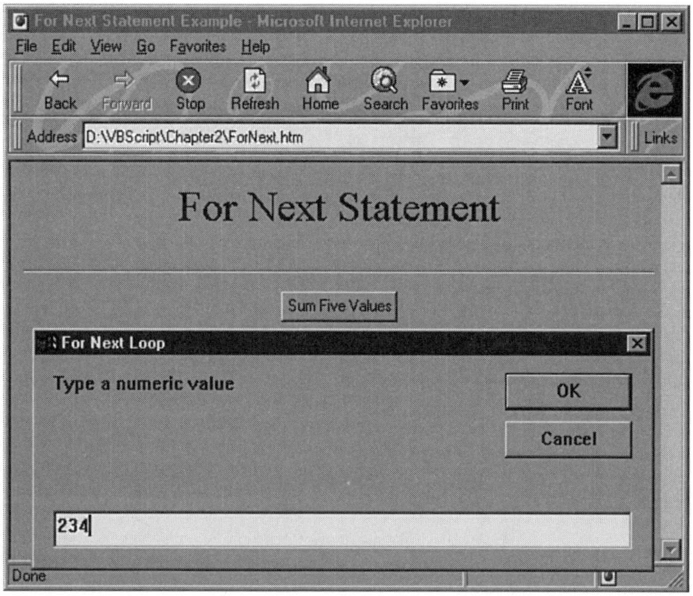

Figure 2-5 The `For Next` statement executes a series of statements a specified number of times

`For Next` STATEMENT

Purpose

Use the `For Next` statement to repeat a group of statements a specific number of times. Table 2-10 describes the arguments of the `For Next` statement.

Syntax

```
For counter = start To end Step step
 statements
Next
```

Table 2-10 Arguments of the `For Next` statement

Argument	Description
`counter`	A numeric variable that is used as the counter for the loop. The variable can't be an array element or an element of a user-defined type.
`start`	The initial value for the `counter` variable.
`end`	The final value for the `counter` variable.
`step`	This value, along with the `Step` keyword, is optional with the `For Next` statement. If this value is used, it is the amount that the `counter` variable is incremented each time the loop executes. If the value is omitted, the default is to step or increment one.
`statements`	One or more statements that are repeated until the `counter` variable is the size specified by the `end` value.

Description

The `For Next` statement allows you to design a loop that executes a series of statements a specified number of times. Each time the statements between the `For` and the `Next` are executed, the value of the `counter` variable is incremented by the step value. If the step value is omitted, the `counter` variable is incremented by one.

Listing 2-6 uses the `For Next` statement to sum five different values from the user. The `InputBox()` function is used to request each value from the user, as illustrated in Figure 2-5. Each time the statements in the loop execute, the `Count` variable is incremented by two. Since the start value is set at `2` and the end value at `10`, the loop will execute five times.

Listing 2-6 Using the `For Next` *statement*

```
<HTML>

<HEAD>
<TITLE>For Next Statement Example</TITLE>

<SCRIPT LANGUAGE="VBScript">
<!--
'.........................................
' SumValues_OnClick()
' Sums the values if they are all numeric.
'.........................................
SUB SumValues_OnClick()

  Dim UserValue
  Dim Count
  Dim Sum

  Sum = 0

'.....................................................
' Use a For Next loop with a start value of 2, an
' end value of 10, and a step value of 2. This will
' request 5 values.
'.....................................................
    For Count = 2 To 10 Step 2

      UserValue = InputBox("Type a numeric value" , "For Next Loop")

'.....................................................
' If a non-numeric value was typed, instruct the user
' to enter a numeric value
'.....................................................
      While Not IsNumeric(UserValue)

        MsgBox "You must type a numeric value."

        UserValue = InputBox("Type a numeric value", "For Next Loop")

      Wend
```

```
'.....................................................
' Sum the input values
'.....................................................
     Sum = Sum + CDbl(UserValue)

   Next

  MsgBox "The sum of the five numbers is " & Sum

END SUB
-->

</SCRIPT>
</HEAD>

<BODY>

<CENTER>

<FONT SIZE=6>For Next Statement<P>
</CENTER>
<HR>

<FONT SIZE=4>

<CENTER>
<INPUT TYPE=BUTTON VALUE="Sum Five Values" NAME="SumValues">
</CENTER>

</FONT>

</BODY>

</HTML>
```

Comments

`For Next` statements can be nested together so that one statement executes inside of another statement. If you use nested `For Next` statements, make sure that you use a different counter variable for each loop.

You can use the `Exit` statement to exit a loop instead of waiting for the condition of the loop to be met. The `Exit` statement is normally used with an `If` statement that is checking for a certain condition. If the condition is not correct, the `Exit` statement transfers control to the statement immediately following the loop.

If Then Else STATEMENT

Purpose

Use the `If Then Else` statement to execute a series of statements if a specific condition is `TRUE`. Table 2-11 describes the expressions you can use with the `If Then Else` statement.

Syntax

```
If condition Then
  statements
```

```
End If
```

or

```
If condition Then
  statements
Else
  elsestatements
End If
```

or

```
If condition Then
  statements
ElseIf condition2
  elseifstatements
Else
  elsestatements
End If
```

Table 2-11 Arguments of the `If Then Else` statement

Argument	Description
`condition`	An expression with a value of either `TRUE` or `FALSE`. If the value of the expression is `NULL`, it is treated as `FALSE`.
`statements`	One or more statements that are separated by colons. The statements are executed if the value of the `condition` argument is `TRUE`.
`condition2`	This is an optional argument that is used only if the `ElseIf` keyword is used with the statement. It is an expression with a value of either `TRUE` or `FALSE`. If the value of the expression is `NULL`, it is treated as `FALSE`.
`elseifstatements`	This is an optional argument that is used only if the `ElseIf` keyword is used with the statement. It is one or more statements separated by colons. The statements are executed if the value of the `condition2` argument is `TRUE`.
`elsestatements`	This is an optional argument that is used only if the `Else` keyword is used with the statement. It is one or more statements that are separated by colons. The statements are executed only if neither the `condition` nor the `condition2` argument is `TRUE`.

Description

The `If Then Else` statement is used when you have a statement or a group of statements that should only be executed when a certain condition exists. The `Else` keyword specifies the statements that should be executed if the condition specified by the `If` does not exist. The `Else` keyword is optional.

The `ElseIf` keyword can be used to specify another condition that may exist if the first condition is `FALSE`. This is also an optional keyword, but it can be used multiple times within the `If Then Else` statement to express several options.

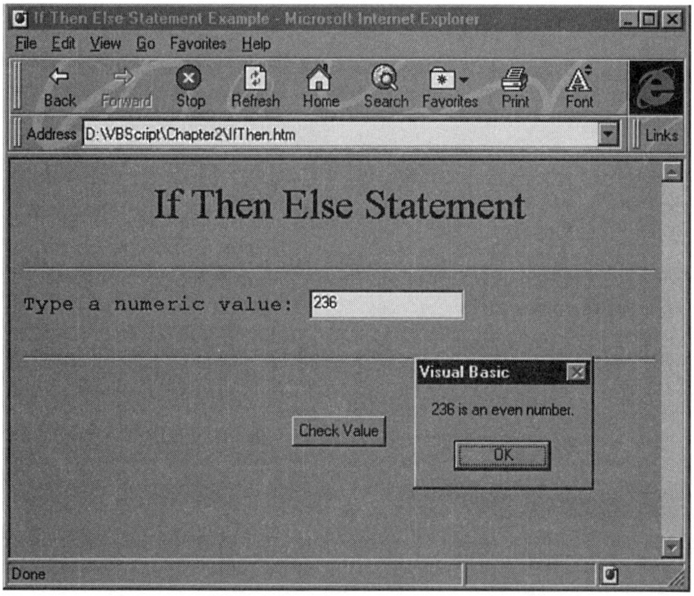

Figure 2-6 The `If Then Else` statement executes a series of instructions if a specific condition is `TRUE`

Listing 2-7 uses the `If Then Else` statement to determine whether the value typed by the user is an odd or even value. Before the value is checked, it is converted to an integer value. The `MsgBox()` function shown in Figure 2-6 displays a dialog box with the results of the `If Then Else` statement.

Listing 2-7 Using the `If Then Else` statement

```
<HTML>

<HEAD>
<TITLE>If Then Else Statement Example</TITLE>

<SCRIPT LANGUAGE="VBScript">
<!--
'..........................................................
' CheckValue_OnClick()
' Determines if the value typed by the user is an odd
'or even number.
'...........................................................
SUB CheckValue_OnClick()

  Dim UserValue

  UserValue = CInt(InputValue.Value)
```

continued on next page

continued from previous page

```
'.........................................
' If the value is an even number display the
' first message, otherwise display the
' second message.
'.........................................
  If (UserValue MOD 2 = 0) Then

     MsgBox UserValue & " is an even number."

  Else

     MsgBox UserValue & " is an odd number."

  End If


END SUB
-->

</SCRIPT>
</HEAD>

<BODY>

<CENTER>

<FONT SIZE=6>If Then Else Statement<P>
</CENTER>
<HR>

<FONT SIZE=4>

<PRE>Type a numeric value: <INPUT NAME=InputValue SIZE=20>

<HR>
<CENTER>
<INPUT TYPE=BUTTON VALUE="Check Value" NAME="CheckValue">
</CENTER>

</FONT>

</BODY>

</HTML>
```

Comments

The condition of the `If Then Else` statement can be an expression of the form `TypeOf objectname Is objecttype`. The `objectname` is any object reference and `objecttype` is any valid object type. The expression is `TRUE` if `objectname` is of the object type specified by `objecttype`; otherwise, the expression is `FALSE`.

`Select Case` STATEMENT

Purpose

Use the `Select Case` statement to execute one or a series of statements depending upon the value of an expression. Table 2-12 describes the expressions you can use with the `Select Case` statement.

Syntax

```
Select Case expression
  Case expressionvalue
    statements
  Case Else expressionvalue
    elsestatements
End Select
```

Table 2-12 Arguments of the `Select Case` statement

Argument	Description
`expression`	Any expression.
`expressionvalue`	One value or a delimited list of values for the specified `expression`.
`statements`	One or more statements that are executed if the `expression` equals the specified `expressionvalue`.
`elsestatements`	This is an optional argument that is used only if the `Case Else` keyword is used with the statement. It is one or more statements that are executed only if the `expression` does not match the `expressionvalue` argument.

Description

The `Select Case` statement executes a statement or group of statements based upon the value of the condition variable. This statement is useful if you have a series of different options that should be performed based on the value of a certain variable. For example, you may need to perform one series of statements if the user selects a Yes button, another group with a No button, and other statements if the Cancel button is selected.

The `Case` keyword can be used multiple times within the `Select Case` statement, as illustrated in Listing 2-8. The `Else Case` statement is optional and can be used to identify statements that should be executed if none of the other `Case` values match.

Listing 2-8 uses the `Select Case` statement to determine which message is displayed to the user. The program is designed to help the user practice Spanish numbers between 1 and 10. The user types the number he or she wants to practice in the input field. The `Select Case` statement uses the value of the `UserValue` variable as the condition of the statement. If the user types a `1`, the dialog box displays the Spanish word *Uno*. A different dialog box displays for each value of the `UserValue` variable, as illustrated in Figure 2-7.

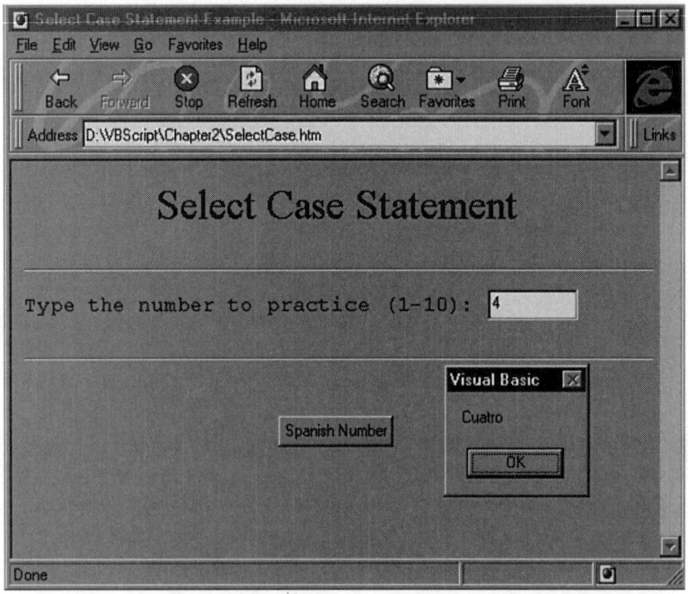

Figure 2-7 The `Select Case` statement performs a statement depending upon the value of the condition variable

Listing 2-8 Using the `Select Case` *statement*

```
<HTML>

<HEAD>
<TITLE>Select Case Statement Example</TITLE>

<SCRIPT LANGUAGE="VBScript">
<!--
'.............................................................
' PracticeNumbers_OnClick()
' Displays the Spanish word for the number typed.
'..............................................................
SUB PracticeNumbers_OnClick()

  Dim UserValue

  UserValue = InputValue.Value

'.............................................................
' Make sure value typed is numeric and between 1 and 10.
'.............................................................
  If IsNumeric(UserValue) Then

    If (UserValue > 0) And (UserValue <= 10) Then

'.............................................................
' Use the Select Case statement to determine the value
' displayed based on the value typed by the user.
'.............................................................
```

```
        Select Case UserValue

          Case 1
            MsgBox "Uno"

          Case 2
            MsgBox "Dos"

          Case 3
            MsgBox "Tres"

          Case 4
            MsgBox "Cuatro"

          Case 5
            MsgBox "Cinco"

          Case 6
            MsgBox "Seis"

          Case 7
            MsgBox "Siete"

          Case 8
            MsgBox "Ocho"

          Case 9
            MsgBox "Nueve"

          Case 10
            MsgBox "Diez"

        End Select

     Else

       MsgBox "Type a value between 1 and 10"
     End If

   Else

     MsgBox "Type a numeric value between 1 and 10"

   End If

END SUB
-->

</SCRIPT>
</HEAD>

<BODY>

<CENTER>

<FONT SIZE=6>Select Case Statement<P>
</CENTER>
<HR>
```

continued on next page

continued from previous page

```
<FONT SIZE=4>

<PRE>Type the number to practice (1-10): <INPUT NAME=InputValue SIZE=10>

<HR>
<CENTER>
<INPUT TYPE=BUTTON VALUE="Spanish Number" NAME="PracticeNumbers">
</CENTER>

</FONT>

</BODY>

</HTML>
```

Comments The `Select Case` statements can be nested. Each nested `Select Case` statement must have a matching `End Select` statement.

`While Wend` STATEMENT

Purpose Use the `While Wend` statement to perform a series of statements as long as the specified condition is `TRUE`. Table 2-13 describes the expressions you can use with the `While Wend` statement.

Syntax

```
While condition
 statements
Wend
```

Table 2-13 Arguments of the `While Wend` statement

Argument	Description
`condition`	Any expression that evaluates to a Boolean value of `TRUE` or `FALSE`. If the expression has a `NULL` value, it is treated as a `FALSE` value.
`statements`	One or more statements that are repeated either while or until the specified condition is `TRUE`.

Description The `While Wend` statement performs a series of statements as long as the expression specified for the `condition` argument is `TRUE`. When the `While` is encountered, the condition expression is checked; if it is `TRUE`, the statements between the `While` and `Wend` are executed. When the `Wend` is encountered, the program control returns to the `While`. This process continues until the condition expression is a `FALSE` value.

Listing 2-9 uses the `While Wend` statement to process statements as long as the user continues to select the Yes button on the dialog box. Since the `MsgBox()` function returns a value of `6` if the Yes button is selected, a user response value of `6` is used as the condition for the loop. The dialog box is displayed each time the number is added to itself to see if the user wants to continue the addition, as illustrated in Figure 2-8.

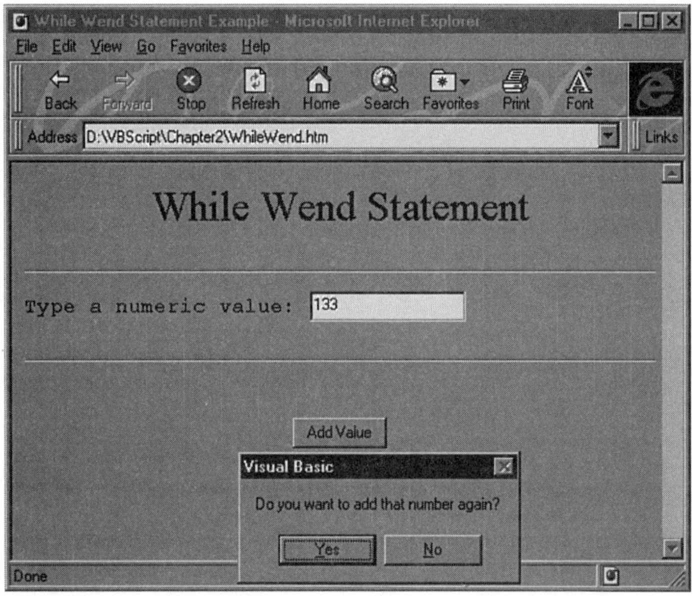

Figure 2-8 The `While Wend` statement continues as long as the condition specified is `TRUE`

Listing 2-9 Using the `While Wend` statement

```
<HTML>

<HEAD>
<TITLE>While Wend Statement Example</TITLE>

<SCRIPT LANGUAGE="VBScript">
<!--
'...........................................................
' SumWhile_OnClick()
' Totals the numeric value until the user selects the No
' button on the dialog box.
'...........................................................
SUB SumWhile_OnClick()

  Dim UserValue
  Dim Response
  Dim Sum

  UserValue = InputValue.Value

'...........................................................
' Set the inital values for the Response variable and
' Sum variable.
'...........................................................
  Response = 6
  Sum = 0
```

continued on next page

continued from previous page

```
'.......................................................
' Execute the statements as long as the user wants to
' continue. When they select the Yes button a value of 6 is
' returned by the MsgBox() function.
'.......................................................
  While (Response = 6)

    Sum = Sum + UserValue

    Response = MsgBox("Do you want to add that number again? ", 4)

  Wend

  MsgBox "The sum  is " & Sum

END SUB
-->

</SCRIPT>
</HEAD>

<BODY>

<CENTER>

<FONT SIZE=6>While Wend Statement<P>
</CENTER>
<HR>

<FONT SIZE=4>

<PRE>Type a numeric value: <INPUT NAME=InputValue SIZE=20>

<HR>
<CENTER>
<INPUT TYPE=BUTTON VALUE="Add Value" NAME="SumWhile">
</CENTER>

</FONT>

</BODY>

</HTML>
```

Comments `While Wend` statements can be nested together so that one statement executes inside of another statement, as illustrated in the following sample code.

```
While i < 5

  While j < 5

    MsgBox CStr(i) & "," CStr(j)

  Wend

Wend
```

VBScript Operators

VBScript provides several different operators that can be used when comparing values. There are basically four different types of operators available, as described in Table 2-14. Each type of operator and the associated operators for that type are discussed in detail later in this chapter.

Table 2-14 VBScript operator types

Operator Type	Purpose
Computation	Perform mathematical calculations.
Comparison	Compare two values.
Logical	Perform logical operations.
Concatenation	Combine string expressions.

Operator Precedence

When VBScript encounters an expression that contains several different operators, a basic precedence order is followed to evaluate the expression. This predetermined order of evaluating operators is known as operator precedence. Since the portions of an expression that are placed within parentheses are evaluated first, you can use parentheses within your expression to override the operator precedence and force some portions of your expression to be evaluated before other portions. Within the parentheses, however, VBScript maintains normal operator precedence.

When expressions contain operators from more than one category, computational operators are evaluated first, concatenation operators are evaluated next, then comparison operators are evaluated, and logical operators are evaluated last. Comparison operators all have equal precedence; that is, they are evaluated in the left-to-right order in which they appear. Arithmetic and logical operators are evaluated in order of precedence. Table 2-15 shows the order of precedence for VBScript operators.

Table 2-15 Precedence of operators in VBScript

Operator	Description
`()`	Parentheses.
`^`	Exponentiation.
`-`	Negation.
`*, /`	Multiplication and division operators. These have the same precedence; they are evaluated from right to left.
`\`	Integer division.
`Mod`	Modulo arithmetic.
`+, -`	Addition and subtraction operators. These have the same precedence; they are evaluated from right to left.

continued on next page

continued from previous page

&	String concatenation.
<, >,=, <>, <=, >=	Comparison operators. These have the same precedence order; they are evaluated right to left.
`Is`	Compare object references.
`Not`	Negate the result of an expression.
`And`	Join the result of two expressions.
`Or`	Perform a logical disjunction of two expressions.
`Xor`	Perform a logical exclusion of two expressions.
`Eqv`	Perform a logical equivalence of two expressions.
`Imp`	Perform a logical implication of two expressions.

Operators for Computing Values

VBScript provides a variety of operators that you can use when computing numeric values. For example, if you want to determine the sum of two variables, you can use the addition (+) operator. Each of the computational operators available in VBScript is listed in Table 2-16. A description of how to use each operator follows the table.

Table 2-16 VBScript computational operators

Use This Operator...	To Do This...
+	Add two values.
-	Either subtract two values or negate a value.
*	Multiply two numeric values.
^	Raise a value to the specified exponential value.
/	Divide two numbers and return a floating-point number as the result.
\	Divide two numbers and return an integer result.
`Mod`	Divide two numbers and return an integer result.

+ Operator

Purpose Use the + (addition) operator to add two numbers. This operator can also be used to concatenate two strings (that is, add the contents of one string to the end of another string). Table 2-17 describes the expressions you can use with the addition operator.

Syntax `expression1 + expression2`

Table 2-17 Arguments of the addition operator

Argument	Description
`expression1`	Any expression
`expression2`	Any expression

Description

The addition operator (+) is used to add two values together. The operator can also be used to concatenate two string values, although the `&` operator is normally used for concatenation. Since all values in VBScript are variants, it is important to determine the subtype of the data prior to using the `+` operator. If the values are nonnumeric, you need to convert them to numeric values prior to using the operator; otherwise, the values will be concatenated instead of being added.

Listing 2-10 uses the `+` operator to add the two values typed in the `InputValue1` and `InputValue2` fields. Before adding the values, the `IsNumeric()` function verifies that both values are numeric. If the values are numeric, they are converted to a numeric function using the `CDbl()` function. The `CDbl()` function is used to allow for the largest size of a numeric value. Any numeric conversion function could be used. The values are added and the results are then displayed using the `MsgBox()` function, as illustrated in Figure 2-9.

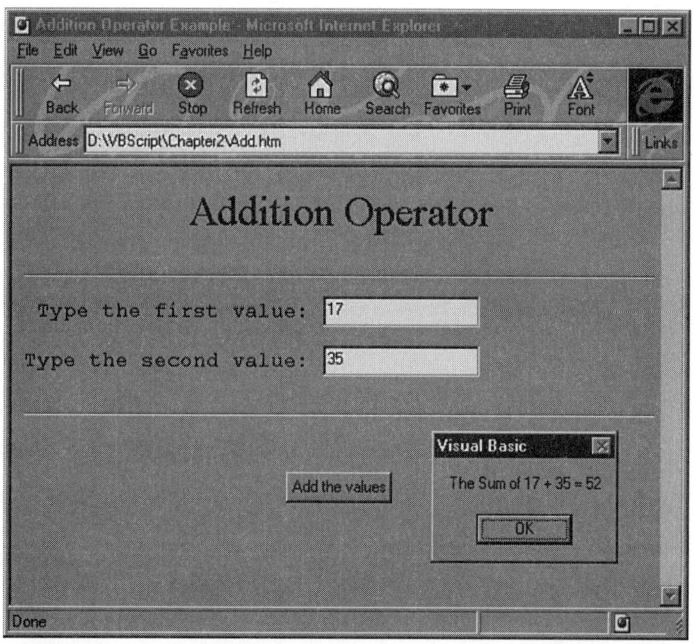

Figure 2-9 The + operator adds the values typed in the two input fields

In Listing 2-10, if at least one of the values typed in the fields is a string, the two values are both considered strings and concatenated, as illustrated in Figure 2-10.

Listing 2-10 Using the addition operator

```
<HTML>

<HEAD>
<TITLE>Addition Operator Example</TITLE>

<SCRIPT LANGUAGE="VBScript">
<!--
'.............................................................
' AddValues_OnClick()
' Adds the two values typed by the user.
'.............................................................
SUB AddValues_OnClick()

  Dim UserValue1
  Dim UserValue2
  Dim Sum

  UserValue1=InputValue1.Value
  UserValue2=InputValue2.Value

'.............................................................
' Find out if the values are numeric; if they are, convert
' them to numeric values so that the operator will add them.
'.............................................................
  If IsNumeric(UserValue1) and IsNumeric(UserValue2) Then

     Sum = CDbl(UserValue1) + CDbl(UserValue2)
    MsgBox "The Sum of " & UserValue1 & " + " & UserValue2 & " = " & Sum
  Else
'.............................................................
' If the values are not both numeric, concatentate the values
' using the addition operator.
'.............................................................

    Sum = UserValue1 + UserValue2

    MsgBox "The Sum of " & UserValue1 & " + " & UserValue2 & " = " & Sum

  End If

END SUB
-->

</SCRIPT>
</HEAD>

<BODY>

<CENTER>
```

```
<FONT SIZE=6>Addition Operator<P>
</CENTER>
<HR>

<FONT SIZE=4>

<PRE> Type the first value: <INPUT NAME=InputValue1 SIZE=20>

Type the second value: <INPUT NAME=InputValue2 SIZE=20>

<HR>
<CENTER>
<INPUT TYPE=BUTTON VALUE="Add the values" NAME="AddValues">
</CENTER>

</FONT>

</BODY>

</HTML>
```

Comments

Since the **+** operator either adds two numeric values or concatenates two values, if one is a string, it is important to know what type of value the variable contains before using the **+** operator. To make sure both values are numeric before using the operator, use the **IsNumeric()** function. For more information about the **IsNumeric()** function, refer to Chapter 4, Data Validation.

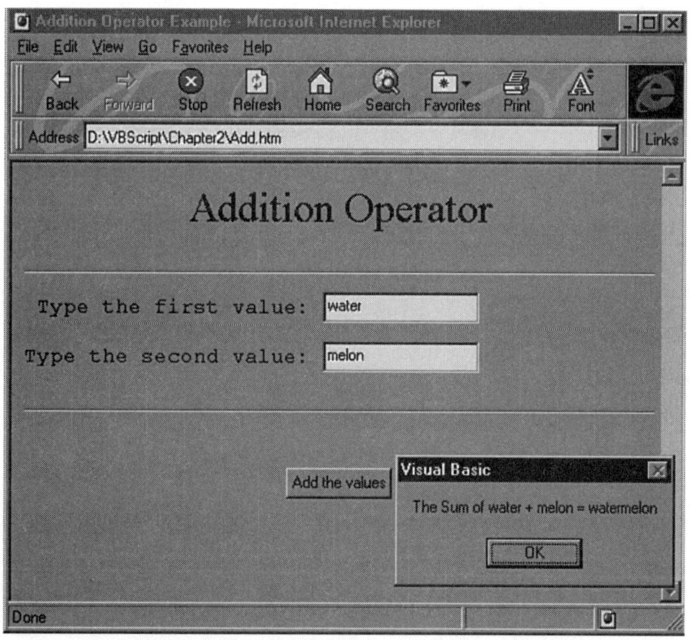

Figure 2-10 The **+** operator concatenates two strings

Although both the **+** and **&** operators can be used to concatenate two strings (hook one string value onto the end of another string value), the preferred method is to use the **&** operator when you intend to concatenate two strings. This will ensure that strings containing only numeric values will also be concatenated properly.

– Operator

Purpose

The **-** (subtraction) operator is used to either subtract one value from another value, or to negate the value of a variable. When you negate a value, if it is a positive value, it becomes a negative value; if it is a negative value, it becomes a positive value. Table 2-18 describes the expressions you can use with the **-** operator.

Syntax

```
expression1 - expression2
```

or

```
- expression1
```

Table 2-18 Arguments of the – operator

Argument	Description
`expression1`	Any numeric expression
`expression2`	Any numeric expression

Description

The **-** operator is used to either subtract one numeric expression from another numeric expression or to negate the value of a numeric expression.

Listing 2-11 uses the **-** operator to subtract the value typed in the **InputValue2** field from the value in the **InputValue1** field. Before subtracting the values, the **IsNumeric()** function verifies that both values are numeric. If both values are numeric, they are subtracted and the results are then displayed using the **MsgBox()** function, as illustrated in Figure 2-11.

Listing 2-11 Using the subtraction operator

```
<HTML>

<HEAD>
<TITLE>Subtraction Operator Example</TITLE>

<SCRIPT LANGUAGE="VBScript">
<!--
'..........................................................
' SubValues_OnClick()
```

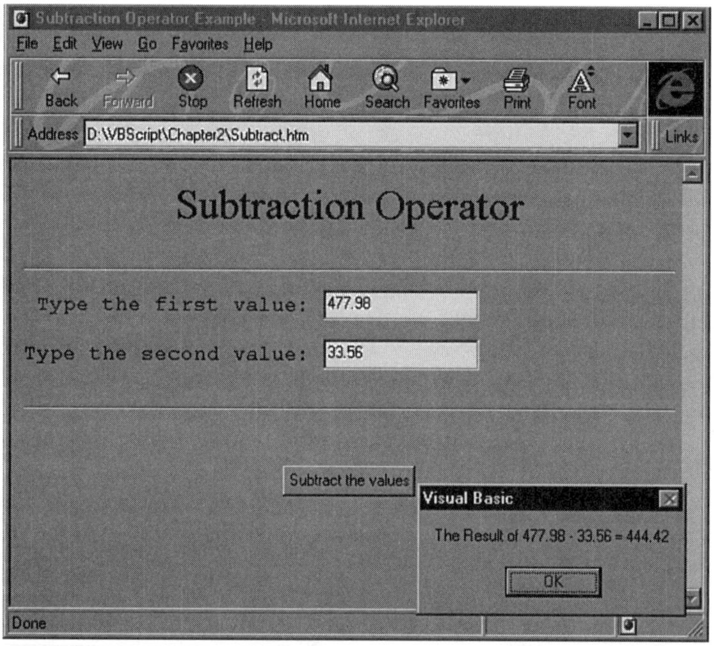

Figure 2-11 The – operator subtracts the second value from the value in the first input field

```
' Subtracts the second value from the first value.
'..............................................................
SUB SubValues_OnClick()

  Dim UserVal1
  Dim UserVal2
  Dim Result

  UserVal1=InputValue1.Value
  UserVal2=InputValue2.Value

'..............................................................
' Find out if the values are numeric; if they are, convert
' them to numeric values so that the operator will subtract them.
'..............................................................
  If IsNumeric(UserVal1) and IsNumeric(UserVal2) Then

   Result = UserVal1 - UserVal2
   MsgBox "The Result of " & UserVal1 & " - " & UserVal2 & " = " & Result
Else

   MsgBox "One of the values is not numeric."
  End If

END SUB
-->
```

continued on next page

continued from previous page

```
</SCRIPT>
</HEAD>

<BODY>

<CENTER>

<FONT SIZE=6>Subtraction Operator<P>
</CENTER>
<HR>

<FONT SIZE=4>

<PRE> Type the first value: <INPUT NAME=InputValue1 SIZE=20>

Type the second value: <INPUT NAME=InputValue2 SIZE=20>

<HR>
<CENTER>
<INPUT TYPE=BUTTON VALUE="Subtract the values" NAME="SubValues">
</CENTER>

</FONT>

</BODY>

</HTML>
```

Comments

When you use the `-` operator to subtract one numeric expression from another, if one or both of the specified expressions are `NULL` expressions, the result is a `NULL` value. If one of the two expressions is `Empty`, that expression is treated as if it were `0`.

To make sure both values are numeric before using the `-` operator, use the `IsNumeric()` function. For more information about the `IsNumeric()` function, refer to Chapter 4, Data Validation.

* OPERATOR

Purpose

Use the `*` (multiplication) operator to multiply two numbers. Table 2-19 describes the expressions you can use with the multiplication operator.

Syntax

`expression1 * expression2`

Table 2-19 Arguments of the multiplication operator

Argument	Description
expression1	Any numeric expression
expression2	Any numeric expression

Description

The * operator is used to multiply two values. Since the * operator only works with numeric expressions, it is important to make sure the values are numeric before using this operator.

Listing 2-12 uses the * operator to multiply the two values typed in the `InputValue1` and `InputValue2` fields. Before multiplying the values, the `IsNumeric()` function verifies that both values are numeric. If the values are numeric, they are multiplied and the results are then displayed using the `MsgBox()` function, as illustrated in Figure 2-12.

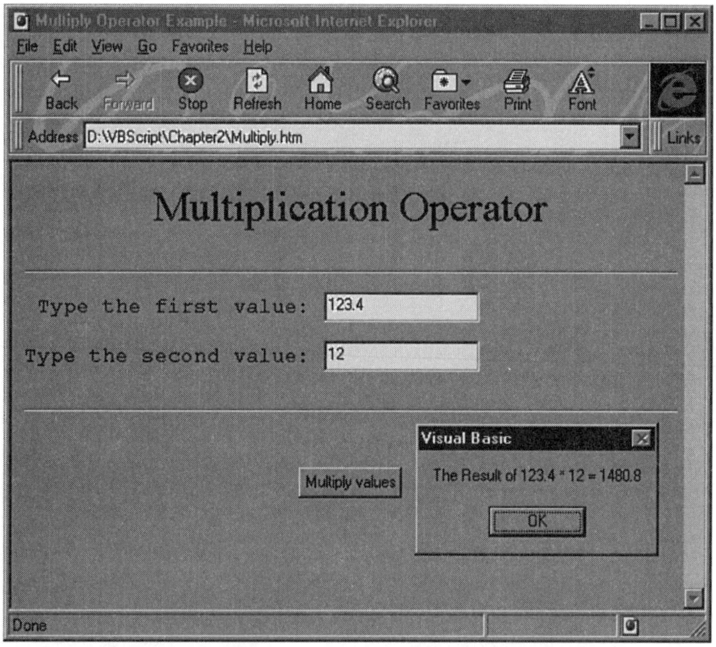

Figure 2-12 The * operator multiplies the two input values

Listing 2-12 Using the multiplication operator

```
<HTML>

<HEAD>
<TITLE>Multiply Operator Example</TITLE>

<SCRIPT LANGUAGE="VBScript">
<!--
'.........................................................
' MultiplyVal_OnClick()
' Multiplies the two input values.
'..........................................................
SUB MultiplyVal_OnClick()

  Dim UserVal1
  Dim UserVal2
  Dim Result

  UserVal1=InputValue1.Value
  UserVal2=InputValue2.Value

'............................................................
' Find out if the values are numeric before multiplying.
'............................................................
  If IsNumeric(UserVal1) and IsNumeric(UserVal2) Then

    Result = UserVal1 * UserVal2

    MsgBox "The Result of " & UserVal1 & " * " & UserVal2 & " = " & Result
  Else

    MsgBox "One of the values is not numeric."
  End If

END SUB
-->

</SCRIPT>
</HEAD>

<BODY>

<CENTER>

<FONT SIZE=6>Multiplication Operator<P>
</CENTER>
<HR>

<FONT SIZE=4>

<PRE> Type the first value: <INPUT NAME=InputValue1 SIZE=20>

Type the second value: <INPUT NAME=InputValue2 SIZE=20>

<HR>
<CENTER>
<INPUT TYPE=BUTTON VALUE="Multiply values" NAME="MultiplyVal">
```

```
</CENTER>
</FONT>
</BODY>
</HTML>
```

Comments

When you use the * operator to multiply two numeric expressions, if one or both of the specified expressions are `NULL` expressions, the result is a `NULL` value. If one of the two expressions is `Empty`, that expression is treated as if it were `0`.

To make sure both values are numeric before using the * operator, use the `IsNumeric()` function. For more information about the `IsNumeric()` function, refer to Chapter 4, Data Validation.

^ Operator

Purpose

Use the ^ (exponentiation) operator to raise a numeric expression to an exponential. Table 2-20 describes the expressions you can use with the exponentiation operator.

Syntax

`expression1 ^ expression2`

Table 2-20 Arguments of the exponentiation operator

Argument	Description
expression1	Any numeric expression
expression2	Any numeric expression

Description

The exponentiation operator is used to raise a numeric expression to the specified exponential power. If the value of `expression1` is negative, the value of `expression2` must be an integer value. If your expression contains more than one exponentiation operator, the operators are evaluated from left to right.

Listing 2-13 uses the exponentiation operator to raise the value typed in the `InputValue1` field to the power specified in the `InputValue2` field. Before adding the values, the `IsNumeric()` function verifies that both values are numeric. The result is displayed using the `MsgBox()` function, as illustrated in Figure 2-13.

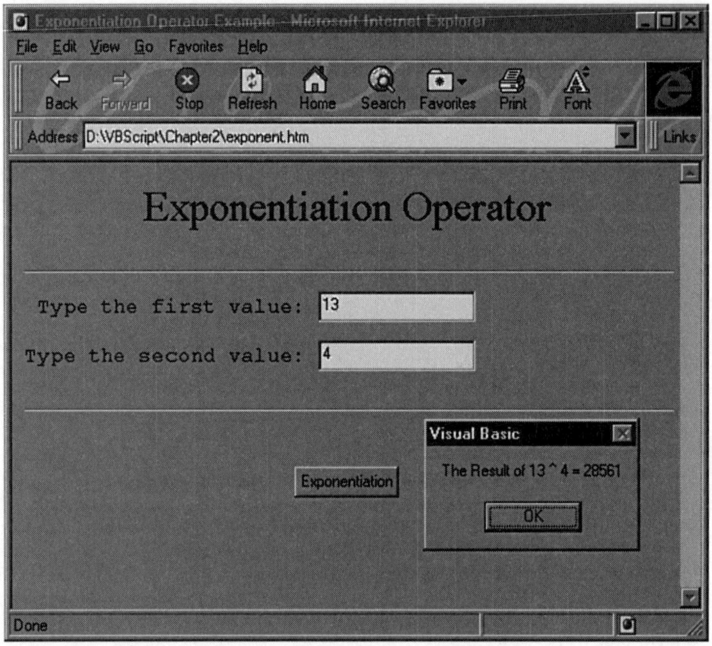

Figure 2-13 The exponentiation operator raises the first value to the value typed in the second field

Listing 2-13 Using the exponentiation operator

```
<HTML>

<HEAD>
<TITLE>Exponentiation Operator Example</TITLE>

<SCRIPT LANGUAGE="VBScript">
<!--
'.........................................................
' ExponentValues_OnClick()
' Raises the first value to the second value.
'..........................................................
SUB ExponentValues_OnClick()

  Dim UserVal1
  Dim UserVal2
  Dim Result
  Dim TestInput

  UserVal1=InputValue1.Value
  UserVal2=InputValue2.Value

'..........................................................
' Find out if the values are numeric.
'..........................................................
  If IsNumeric(UserVal1) and IsNumeric(UserVal2) Then
```

```
'.........................................................
' If the first value is negative, the second must be an
' integer. If the user types a decimal value convert it to
' an integer.
'.........................................................
    If UserVal1 < 0 Then

      UserVal2 = CInt(UserVal2)

    End If

'.........................................................
' Calculate the result of the expression.
'.........................................................
   Result = UserVal1 ^ UserVal2

   MsgBox "The Result of " & UserVal1 & " ^ " & UserVal2 & " = " & Result
  Else

   MsgBox "One of the values is not numeric."
  End If

END SUB
-->

</SCRIPT>
</HEAD>

<BODY>

<CENTER>

<FONT SIZE=6>Exponentiation Operator<P>
</CENTER>
<HR>

<FONT SIZE=4>

<PRE> Type the first value: <INPUT NAME=InputValue1 SIZE=20>

Type the second value: <INPUT NAME=InputValue2 SIZE=20>

<HR>
<CENTER>
<INPUT TYPE=BUTTON VALUE="Exponentiation" NAME="ExponentValues">
</CENTER>

</FONT>

</BODY>

</HTML>
```

Comments To make sure both values are numeric before using the `^` operator, use the `IsNumeric()` function. For more information about the `IsNumeric()` function, refer to Chapter 4, Data Validation.

/ OPERATOR

Purpose Use the / (division) operator to divide one value by another value and return a floating-point value. Table 2-21 describes the expressions you can use with the division operator.

Syntax `expression1 / expression2`

Table 2-21 Arguments of the division operator

Argument	Description
expression1	Any numeric expression
expression2	Any numeric expression

Description The division operator is used to divide one numeric expression by another numeric expression. When the division operator is used, a floating-point value is returned for the result. This means that a decimal value is returned that expresses the exact value when one number is divided by the other number. For example, if you divide 15 by 6, the resulting answer is 2.5.

Listing 2-14 uses the division operator to divide the first value typed by the user, `InputValue1`, by the second value, `InputValue2`. Before dividing the values, the `IsNumeric()` function verifies that both values are numeric. If they are both numeric, the values are divided and the results are then displayed using the `MsgBox()` function, as illustrated in Figure 2-14.

Listing 2-14 Using the division operator

```
<HTML>

<HEAD>
<TITLE>Division Operator Example</TITLE>

<SCRIPT LANGUAGE="VBScript">
<!--
'..........................................................
' DivideValues_OnClick()
' Divides the second value into the first value.
'...........................................................
SUB DivideValues_OnClick()

  Dim UserVal1
  Dim UserVal2
  Dim Result

  UserVal1=InputValue1.Value
  UserVal2=InputValue2.Value

'...........................................................
```

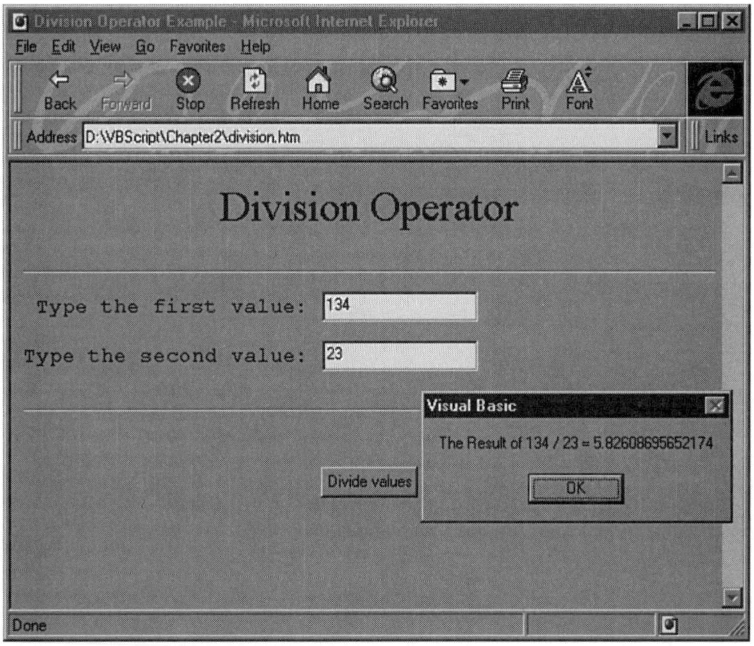

Figure 2-14 The division operator divides the value typed in the first field by the value in the second field

```
' Find out if the values are numeric before dividing.
'..............................................................
  If IsNumeric(UserVal1) and IsNumeric(UserVal2) Then

'..............................................................
' The second value cannot equal zero or there will be a
' divide by zero error.
'..............................................................
   If UserVal2 = 0 Then

     MsgBox "You cannot divide by zero. Type a new value."

     Exit Sub

   End If

'..............................................................
' Divide the values and display the result.
'..............................................................

   Result = UserVal1 / UserVal2

   MsgBox "The Result of " & UserVal1 & " / " & UserVal2 & " = " & Result
  Else

   MsgBox "One of the values is not numeric."
  End If
```

continued on next page

continued from previous page

```
END SUB
-->

</SCRIPT>
</HEAD>

<BODY>

<CENTER>

<FONT SIZE=6>Division Operator<P>
</CENTER>
<HR>

<FONT SIZE=4>

<PRE> Type the first value: <INPUT NAME=InputValue1 SIZE=20>

Type the second value: <INPUT NAME=InputValue2 SIZE=20>

<HR>
<CENTER>
<INPUT TYPE=BUTTON VALUE="Divide values" NAME="DivideValues">
</CENTER>

</FONT>

</BODY>

</HTML>
```

Comments When you use the division operator to divide two numeric expressions, if one or both of the specified expressions are `NULL` expressions, the result is a `NULL` value. If one of the two expressions is `Empty`, that expression is treated as if it were `0`.

To make sure both values are numeric before using the operator, use the `IsNumeric()` function. For more information about the `IsNumeric()` function, refer to Chapter 4, Data Validation.

\ Operator

Purpose Use the `\` (integer division) operator to divide one value by another value and only return the integer portion of the result. Table 2-22 describes the expressions you can use with the integer division operator.

Syntax `expression1 \ expression2`

Table 2-22 Arguments of the integer division operator

Argument	Description
`expression1`	Any numeric expression
`expression2`	Any numeric expression

Description

The integer division operator is used to divide one numeric expression by another numeric expression and return only the integer portion of the result.

Listing 2-15 uses the integer division operator to divide the value in the first input field, `InputValue1`, by the value in the second input field, `InputValue2`. Before dividing the values, the `IsNumeric()` function verifies that both values are numeric. If both values are numeric, the first is divided by the second and the results are then displayed using the `MsgBox()` function, as illustrated in Figure 2-15.

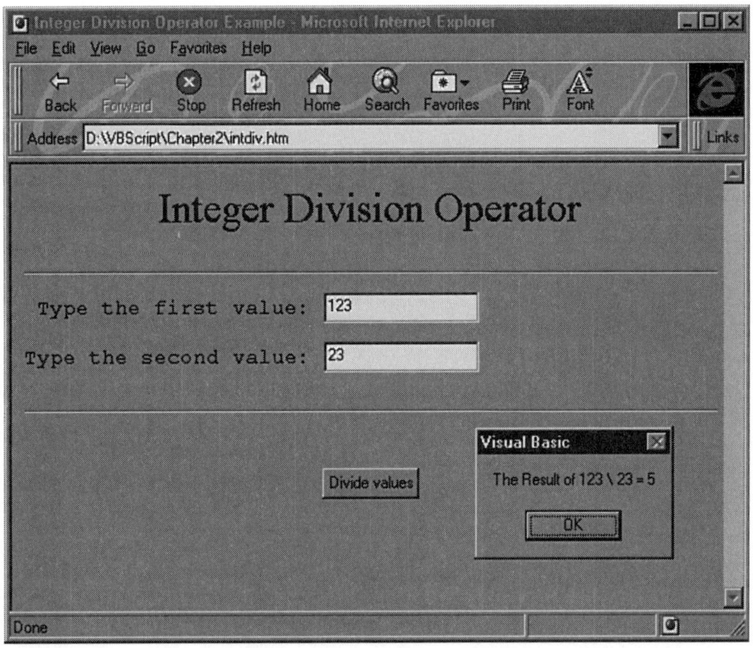

Figure 2-15 The integer division operator divides the two values and returns only the integer portion of the result

Listing 2-15 Using the integer division operator

```
<HTML>

<HEAD>
<TITLE>Integer Division Operator Example</TITLE>

<SCRIPT LANGUAGE="VBScript">
<!--
'...........................................................
' DivideValues_OnClick()
' Divides the second value into the first value.
'...........................................................
SUB DivideValues_OnClick()

  Dim UserVal1
  Dim UserVal2
  Dim Result

  UserVal1=InputValue1.Value
  UserVal2=InputValue2.Value

'...........................................................
' Find out if the values are numeric before dividing.
'...........................................................
  If IsNumeric(UserVal1) and IsNumeric(UserVal2) Then

'...........................................................
' The second value cannot equal zero or there will be a
' divide by zero error.
'...........................................................
   If UserVal2 = 0 Then

     MsgBox "You cannot divide by zero. Type a new value."

     Exit Sub

   End If

'...........................................................
' Divide the values and display the result.
'...........................................................
   Result = UserVal1 \ UserVal2

   MsgBox "The Result of " & UserVal1 & " \ " & UserVal2 & " = " & Result
  Else

   MsgBox "One of the values is not numeric."
  End If

END SUB
-->

</SCRIPT>
</HEAD>

<BODY>
```

```
<CENTER>

<FONT SIZE=6>Integer Division Operator<P>
</CENTER>
<HR>

<FONT SIZE=4>

<PRE> Type the first value: <INPUT NAME=InputValue1 SIZE=20>

Type the second value: <INPUT NAME=InputValue2 SIZE=20>

<HR>
<CENTER>
<INPUT TYPE=BUTTON VALUE="Divide values" NAME="DivideValues">
</CENTER>

</FONT>

</BODY>

</HTML>
```

Comments

When you use the integer division operator to divide one numeric expression by another, if one or both of the specified expressions are **NULL** expressions, the result is a **NULL** value. If one of the two expressions is **Empty**, that expression is treated as if it were **0**.

To make sure both values are numeric before using the operator, use the **IsNumeric()** function. For more information about the **IsNumeric()** function, refer to Chapter 4, Data Validation.

Mod Operator

Purpose

Use the **Mod** operator to divide one value by another and return the remainder. Table 2-23 describes the expressions you can use with the **Mod** operator.

Syntax

`expression1 Mod expression2`

Table 2-23 Arguments of the Mod operator

Argument	Description
expression1	Any numeric expression
expression2	Any numeric expression

Description

The Mod, or modulo arithmetic, operator allows you to determine the remainder when one number is divided by another number. The operator uses integer division to divide one value by the other; once an integer value is determined, the value that remains is what the **Mod** operator returns. Of course if the number divides into the other number evenly, the remainder would be 0. But if, for example, you divide 3 into 10, you would have a remainder of 1.

Listing 2-16 uses the **Mod** operator to divide the first value, the **InputValue1** field, by the second value, the **InputValue2** field, and determine the remainder. Before dividing the values, the **IsNumeric()** function verifies that both values are numeric. If the values are numeric, they are divided and the results are then displayed using the **MsgBox()** function, as illustrated in Figure 2-16.

Listing 2-16 Using the **Mod** *operator*

```
<HTML>

<HEAD>
<TITLE>Mod Operator Example</TITLE>

<SCRIPT LANGUAGE="VBScript">
<!--
'.............................................................
' ModValues_OnClick()
' Divides the second value into the first value and returns
' the remainder.
'.............................................................
SUB ModValues_OnClick()

  Dim Val1
  Dim Val2
  Dim Result

  Val1=InputValue1.Value
  Val2=InputValue2.Value

'.............................................................
' Find out if the values are numeric before dividing.
'.............................................................
  If IsNumeric(Val1) and IsNumeric(Val2) Then

    Result = Val1 Mod Val2

    MsgBox "The Result of " & Val1 & " Mod " & Val2 & " is " & Result
  Else

    MsgBox "One of the values is not numeric."
  End If

END SUB
-->

</SCRIPT>
</HEAD>

<BODY>

<CENTER>
```

```
<FONT SIZE=6>Mod Operator<P>
</CENTER>
<HR>

<FONT SIZE=4>

<PRE> Type the first value: <INPUT NAME=InputValue1 SIZE=20>

Type the second value: <INPUT NAME=InputValue2 SIZE=20>

<HR>
<CENTER>
<INPUT TYPE=BUTTON VALUE="Mod values" NAME="ModValues">
</CENTER>

</FONT>

</BODY>

</HTML>
```

Comments

When you use the **Mod** operator to divide one numeric expression by another, if one or both of the specified expressions are **NULL** expressions, the result is a **NULL** value. If one of the two expressions is **Empty**, that expression is treated as if it were **0**.

To make sure both values are numeric before using the operator, use the **IsNumeric()** function. For more information about the **IsNumeric()** function, refer to Chapter 4, Data Validation.

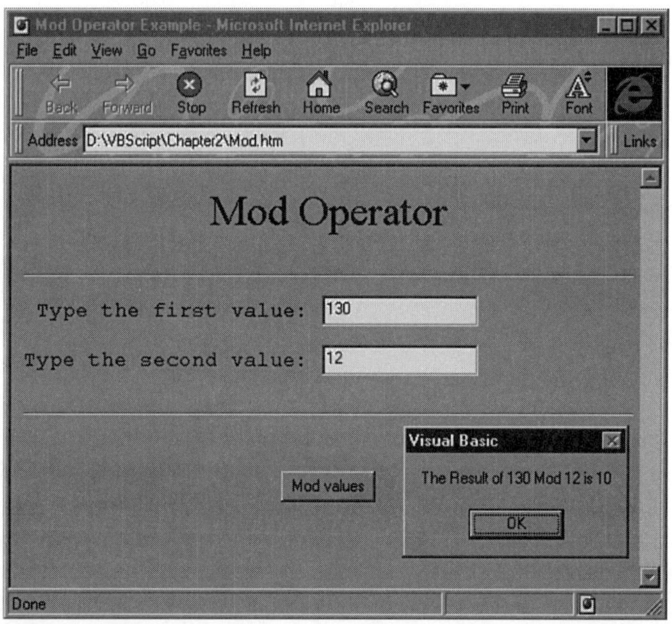

Figure 2-16 The **Mod** operator divides two values and returns the remainder

Operators for Comparing Values

VBScript provides a variety of operators that you can use when comparing values. For example, if you want to determine if one value is larger than another value, you would use the greater than (>) operator. Each of the comparison operators available in VBScript is listed in Table 2-24. A description of how to use each operator follows the table.

Table 2-24 VBScript comparison operators

Use This Operator...	To Determine If...
<	One expression is less than another expression.
>	One expression is greater than another expression.
<=	One expression is less than or equal to another expression.
>=	One expression is greater than or equal to another expression.
=	Two expressions are equal.
<>	Two expressions are not equal.
`Is`	Two variables reference the same object.

< Operator

Purpose

Use the **<** (less than) operator to determine if one numeric expression is less than another numeric expression. Table 2-25 describes the expressions you can use with the less than operator.

Syntax

```
expression1 < expression2
```

Table 2-25 Arguments of the less than operator

Argument	Description
`expression1`	Any numeric expression
`expression2`	Any numeric expression

Description

The less than operator compares two different numeric expressions and returns a Boolean value of **`TRUE`** if the first expression is less than the second expression; otherwise, the operator returns a value of **`FALSE`**.

Listing 2-17 uses the less than operator to determine if the value typed in the **`InputValue1`** field is less than the value typed in the **`InputValue2`** field. Before the operator is used, the **`IsNumeric()`** function makes sure both of the input fields contain values that can be converted to numeric values. The **`MsgBox()`** function displays a message indicating whether or not the first value was less than the second value, as illustrated in Figure 2-17.

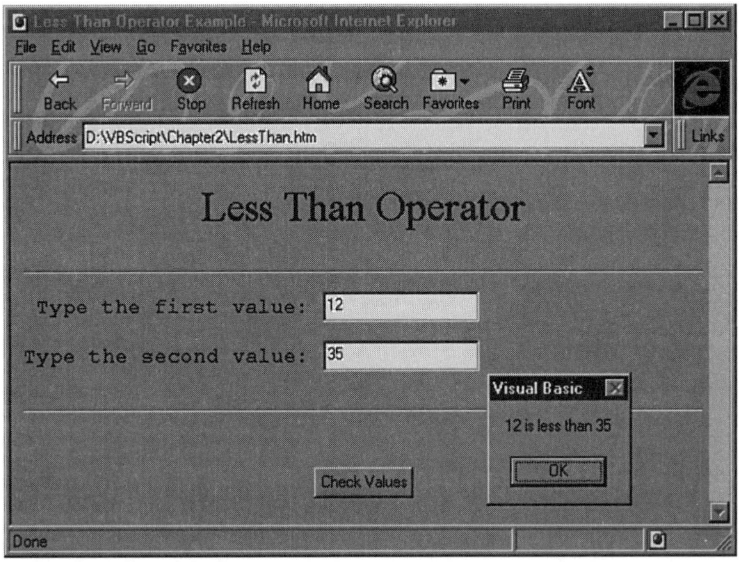

Figure 2-17 The less than operator determines if the first value is less than the second value

Listing 2-17 Using the less than operator

```
<HTML>

<HEAD>
<TITLE>Less Than Operator Example</TITLE>

<SCRIPT LANGUAGE="VBScript">
<!--
'............................................................
' CheckLessThan_OnClick()
' Determines whether or not the first value is less than the
' second value.
'.............................................................
SUB CheckLessThan_OnClick()

  Dim UserValue1
  Dim UserValue2

  UserValue1=InputValue1.Value
  UserValue2=InputValue2.Value

'.............................................................
' Make sure both expressions are numeric.
'.............................................................
  If IsNumeric(UserValue1) And IsNumeric(UserValue2) Then

'.............................................................
' Check to see if the value is less than the second value.
' Display a message that indicates the results of the
```

continued on next page

continued from previous page

```
' comparison.
'..............................................................
    If CDbl(UserValue1) < CDbl(UserValue2) Then

      MsgBox UserValue1 & " is less than " & UserValue2

    Else

      MsgBox UserValue1 & " is not less than " & UserValue2

    End If

  Else

    MsgBox "Type numeric values in the field"

  End If
END SUB
-->

</SCRIPT>
</HEAD>

<BODY>

<CENTER>

<FONT SIZE=6>Less Than Operator<P>
</CENTER>
<HR>

<FONT SIZE=4>

<PRE> Type the first value: <INPUT NAME=InputValue1 SIZE=20>

Type the second value: <INPUT NAME=InputValue2 SIZE=20>

<HR>
<CENTER>
<INPUT TYPE=BUTTON VALUE="Check Values" NAME="CheckLessThan">
</CENTER>

</FONT>

</BODY>

</HTML>
```

Comments

To make sure both values are numeric before accepting the values, use the **IsNumeric()** function. Before comparing the values, use the **CDbl()** function to convert the strings to numeric values. For more information about the **IsNumeric()** function, refer to Chapter 4, Data Validation.

> OPERATOR

Purpose Use the > (greater than) operator to determine if one numeric expression is greater than another numeric expression. Table 2-26 describes the expressions you can use with the greater than operator.

Syntax `expression1 > expression2`

Table 2-26 Arguments of the greater than operator

Argument	Description
expression1	Any numeric expression
expression2	Any numeric expression

Description The greater than operator compares two different numeric expressions and returns a Boolean value of `TRUE` if the first expression is larger than the second expression; otherwise, the operator returns a value of `FALSE`.

Listing 2-18 uses the greater than operator to determine if the value typed in the `InputValue1` field is larger than the value typed in the `InputValue2` field. Before the operator is used, the `IsNumeric()` function makes sure both of the input fields contain values that can be converted into numeric values. The `MsgBox()` function displays a message indicating whether or not the first value was greater than the second value, as illustrated in Figure 2-18.

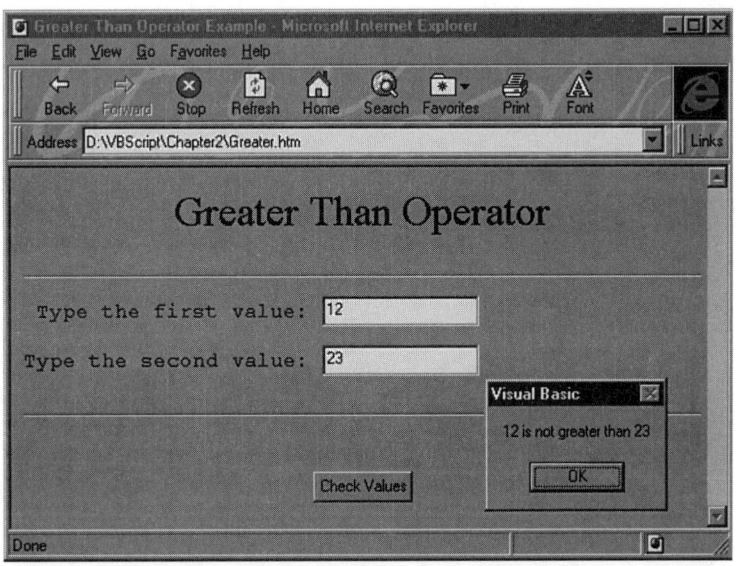

Figure 2-18 The greater than operator determines if the first value is larger than the second value

Listing 2-18 Using the greater than operator

```
<HTML>

<HEAD>
<TITLE>Greater Than Operator Example</TITLE>

<SCRIPT LANGUAGE="VBScript">
<!--
'..............................................................
' CheckGreaterThan_OnClick()
' Determines whether or not the first value is greater than
' the second value.
'..............................................................
SUB CheckGreaterThan_OnClick()

  Dim UserValue1
  Dim UserValue2

  UserValue1=InputValue1.Value
  UserValue2=InputValue2.Value

'..............................................................
' Make sure both expressions are numeric.
'..............................................................
  If IsNumeric(UserValue1) And IsNumeric(UserValue2) Then

'..............................................................
' Check to see if the value is greater than the second value.
' Display a message that indicates the results of the
' comparison.
'..............................................................
    If CDbl(UserValue1) > CDbl(UserValue2) Then

      MsgBox UserValue1 & " is greater than " & UserValue2

    Else

      MsgBox UserValue1 & " is not greater than " & UserValue2

    End If

  Else

    MsgBox "Type numeric values in the field"

  End If
END SUB
-->

</SCRIPT>
</HEAD>

<BODY>

<CENTER>

<FONT SIZE=6>Greater Than Operator<P>
</CENTER>
```

```
<HR>

<FONT SIZE=4>

<PRE> Type the first value: <INPUT NAME=InputValue1 SIZE=20>

Type the second value: <INPUT NAME=InputValue2 SIZE=20>

<HR>
<CENTER>
<INPUT TYPE=BUTTON VALUE="Check Values" NAME="CheckGreaterThan">
</CENTER>

</FONT>

</BODY>

</HTML>
```

Comments To make sure both values are numeric before accepting the values, use the **IsNumeric()** function. Before comparing the values, use the **CDbl()** function to convert the strings to numeric values. For more information about the **IsNumeric()** function, refer to Chapter 4, Data Validation.

<= Operator

Purpose Use the **<=** (less than or equal to) operator to determine if one numeric expression is either less than or equal to another numeric expression. Table 2-27 describes the expressions you can use with the less than or equal to operator.

Syntax `expression1 <= expression2`

Table 2-27 Arguments of the less than or equal to operator

Argument	Description
expression1	Any numeric expression
expression2	Any numeric expression

Description The less than or equal to operator compares two different numeric expressions and returns a Boolean value of **TRUE** if the first expression is either less than or equal to the second expression; otherwise, the operator returns a value of **FALSE**.

Listing 2-19 uses the less than or equal to operator to determine if the value typed in the **InputValue1** field is either less than or equal to the value typed in the **InputValue2** field. Before the operator is used, the **IsNumeric()** function makes sure both of the input fields contain values that can be converted into numeric values. The **MsgBox()** function displays a message indicating the results of the comparison, as illustrated in Figure 2-19.

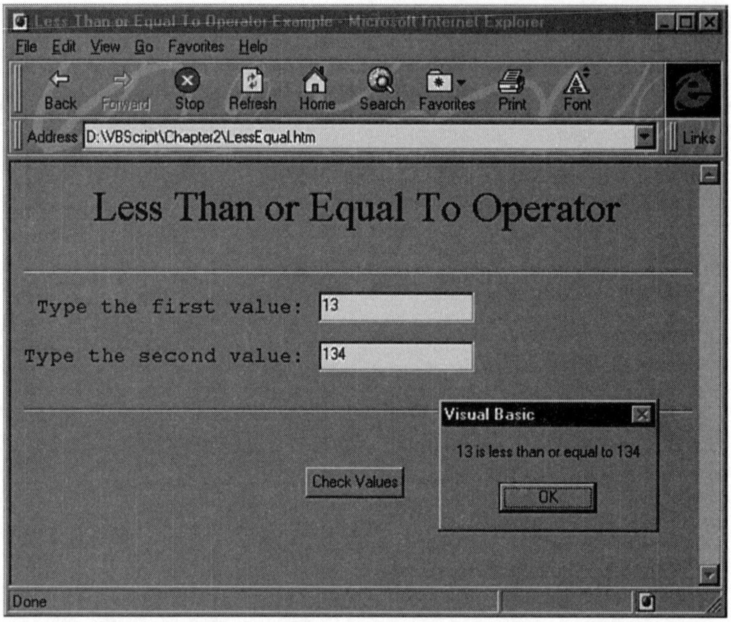

Figure 2-19 The less than or equal to operator determines if the first value is less than or equal to the second value

Listing 2-19 Using the less than or equal to operator

```
<HTML>

<HEAD>
<TITLE>Less Than or Equal To Operator Example</TITLE>

<SCRIPT LANGUAGE="VBScript">
<!--
'..........................................................
' CheckLessEqual_OnClick()
' Determines whether or not the first value is less than or
' equal to the second value.
'..........................................................
SUB CheckLessEqual_OnClick()

  Dim UserValue1
  Dim UserValue2

  UserValue1=InputValue1.Value
  UserValue2=InputValue2.Value

'..........................................................
' Make sure both expressions are numeric.
'..........................................................
  If IsNumeric(UserValue1) And IsNumeric(UserValue2) Then

'..........................................................
' Check to see if the value is less than or equal to the
```

```
' second value. Display a message that indicates the results
' of the comparison.
'..............................................................
    If CDbl(UserValue1) <= CDbl(UserValue2) Then

      MsgBox UserValue1 & " is less than or equal to " & UserValue2

    Else

      MsgBox UserValue1 & " is not less than or equal to " & UserValue2

    End If

  Else

    MsgBox "Type numeric values in the field"

  End If
END SUB
-->

</SCRIPT>
</HEAD>

<BODY>

<CENTER>

<FONT SIZE=6>Less Than or Equal To Operator<P>
</CENTER>
<HR>

<FONT SIZE=4>

<PRE> Type the first value: <INPUT NAME=InputValue1 SIZE=20>

Type the second value: <INPUT NAME=InputValue2 SIZE=20>

<HR>
<CENTER>
<INPUT TYPE=BUTTON VALUE="Check Values" NAME="CheckLessEqual">
</CENTER>

</FONT>

</BODY>

</HTML>
```

Comments

To make sure both values are numeric before accepting the values, use the `IsNumeric()` function. Before comparing the values, use the `CDbl()` function to convert the strings to numeric values. For more information about the `IsNumeric()` function, refer to Chapter 4, Data Validation.

>= Operator

Purpose Use the **>=** (greater than or equal to) operator to determine if one numeric expression is either greater than or equal to another numeric expression. Table 2-28 describes the expressions you can use with the greater than or equal to operator.

Syntax `expression1 >= expression2`

Table 2-28 Arguments of the greater than or equal to operator

Argument	Description
`expression1`	Any numeric expression
`expression2`	Any numeric expression

Description The greater than or equal to operator compares two different numeric expressions and returns a Boolean value of **TRUE** if the first expression is either greater than or the equal to the second expression; otherwise, the operator returns a value of **FALSE**.

Listing 2-20 uses the greater than or equal to operator to determine if the value typed in the **InputValue1** field is either greater than or equal to the value typed in the **InputValue2** field. Before the operator is used, the

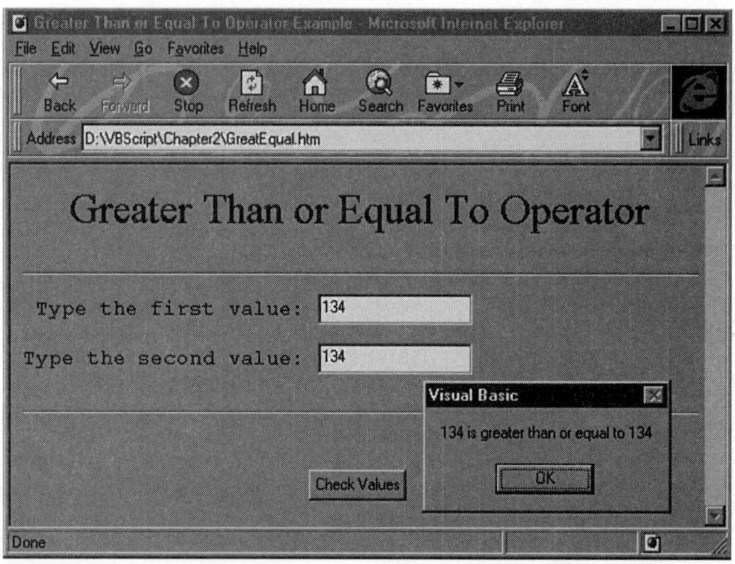

Figure 2-20 The greater than or equal to operator determines if the first value is greater than or equal to the second value

IsNumeric() function makes sure both of the input fields contain values that can be converted into numeric values. The **MsgBox()** function displays a message indicating the results of the comparison, as illustrated in Figure 2-20.

Listing 2-20 Using the greater than or equal to operator

```
<HTML>

<HEAD>
<TITLE>Greater Than or Equal To Operator Example</TITLE>

<SCRIPT LANGUAGE="VBScript">
<!--
'..........................................................
' CheckGreaterEqual_OnClick()
' Determines whether or not the first value is greater than
' or equal to the second value.
'..........................................................
SUB CheckGreaterEqual_OnClick()

  Dim UserValue1
  Dim UserValue2

  UserValue1=InputValue1.Value
  UserValue2=InputValue2.Value

'..........................................................
' Make sure both expressions are numeric.
'..........................................................
  If IsNumeric(UserValue1) And IsNumeric(UserValue2) Then

'..........................................................
' Check to see if the value is greater than or equal to the
' second value. Display a message that indicates the results
' of the comparison.
'..........................................................
    If CDbl(UserValue1) >= CDbl(UserValue2) Then

      MsgBox UserValue1 & " is greater than or equal to " & UserValue2

    Else

     MsgBox UserValue1 & " is not greater than or equal to " & UserValue2

    End If

  Else

    MsgBox "Type numeric values in the field"

  End If
END SUB
-->
```

continued on next page

continued from previous page

```
</SCRIPT>
</HEAD>

<BODY>

<CENTER>

<FONT SIZE=6>Greater Than or Equal To Operator<P>
</CENTER>
<HR>

<FONT SIZE=4>

<PRE> Type the first value: <INPUT NAME=InputValue1 SIZE=20>

Type the second value: <INPUT NAME=InputValue2 SIZE=20>

<HR>
<CENTER>
<INPUT TYPE=BUTTON VALUE="Check Values" NAME="CheckGreaterEqual">
</CENTER>

</FONT>

</BODY>

</HTML>
```

Comments To make sure both values can be evaluated as numeric values, use the `IsNumeric()` function. To convert the string values to numeric values, use the `CDbl()` function. For more information about the `IsNumeric()` function, refer to Chapter 4, Data Validation.

= OPERATOR

Purpose Use the = (equals) operator to determine if one expression is equivalent to another expression. Table 2-29 describes the expressions you can use with the equals operator.

Syntax `expression1 = expression2`

Table 2-29 Arguments of the equals operator

Argument	Description
expression1	Any expression
expression2	Any expression

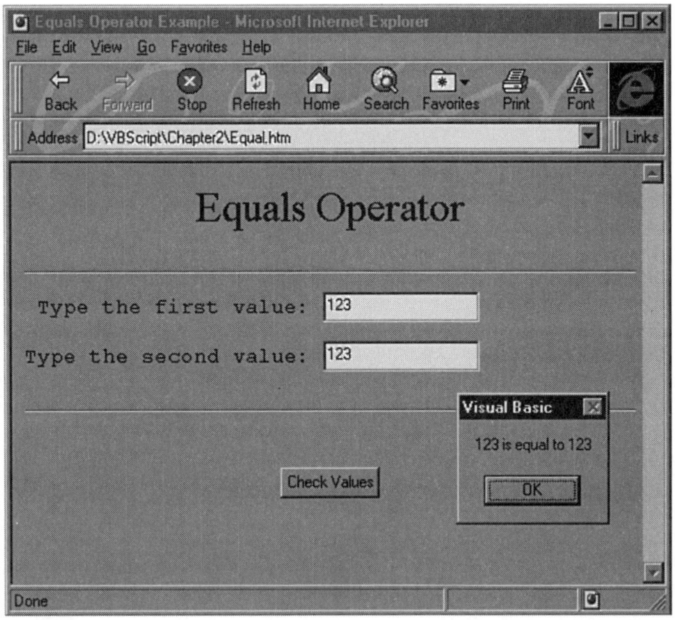

Figure 2-21 The equals operator determines if the first value is the same as the second value

Description

The equals operator compares two different expressions and returns a Boolean value of **TRUE** if both expressions are the same; otherwise, the operator returns a value of **FALSE**. If both expressions contain string values, they must be the same case (all uppercase or all lowercase) in order to return a **TRUE** value. For example, if one string contains the characters "ABC" and another contains the string characters "abc", the equals operator will return a value of **FALSE**, because one string expression is in uppercase characters, and the other is in lowercase characters.

Listing 2-21 uses the equals operator to determine if the value typed in the **InputValue1** field is the same as the value typed in the **InputValue2** field. The **MsgBox()** function displays a message indicating the results of the operation, as illustrated in Figure 2-21.

Listing 2-21 Using the equals operator

```
<HTML>

<HEAD>
<TITLE>Equal Operator Example</TITLE>

<SCRIPT LANGUAGE="VBScript">
<!--
'.......................................................
```

continued on next page

continued from previous page

```
' CheckEqual_OnClick()
' Determines whether or not the first value is equal to the
' second value.
'............................................................
SUB CheckEqual_OnClick()

  Dim UserValue1
  Dim UserValue2

  UserValue1=InputValue1.Value
  UserValue2=InputValue2.Value

'............................................................
' Check to see if the value is equal to the second value.
' Display a message that indicates the results
' of the comparison.
'............................................................
    If UserValue1 = UserValue2 Then

      MsgBox UserValue1 & " is equal to " & UserValue2

    Else

      MsgBox UserValue1 & " is not equal to " & UserValue2

    End If

END SUB
-->

</SCRIPT>
</HEAD>

<BODY>

<CENTER>

<FONT SIZE=6>Equals Operator<P>
</CENTER>
<HR>

<FONT SIZE=4>

<PRE> Type the first value: <INPUT NAME=InputValue1 SIZE=20>

Type the second value: <INPUT NAME=InputValue2 SIZE=20>

<HR>
<CENTER>
<INPUT TYPE=BUTTON VALUE="Check Values" NAME="CheckEqual">
</CENTER>

</FONT>

</BODY>

</HTML>
```

Comments The equals operator will compare any type of value. If you are working with string values, you may want to ensure that all characters of the strings are either uppercase or lowercase. The `UCase()` function can be used to convert all characters in a string to uppercase characters, and the `LCase()` function can be used to convert all characters in a string to lowercase characters. For more information about the `UCase()` and `LCase()` functions, refer to Chapter 9, String Manipulation.

<> Operator

Purpose Use the **<>** (not equal to) operator to determine if one expression is not equal to another expression. Table 2-30 describes the expressions you can use with the not equal to operator.

Syntax

```
expression1 <> expression2
```

Table 2-30 Arguments of the not equal to operator

Argument	Description
`expression1`	Any expression
`expression2`	Any expression

Description The not equal to operator compares two different expressions and returns a Boolean value of `TRUE` if the expressions are not the same; otherwise, the operator returns a value of `FALSE`. If both expressions contain string values, the same characters, and are the same case (all uppercase or all lowercase), the operator returns a `FALSE` value. For example, if one string contains the characters "ABC" and another string contains the characters "abc", the not equal to operator will return a value of `TRUE`, because one string expression is in uppercase characters and the other is in lowercase characters.

Listing 2-22 uses the not equal to operator to determine if the value typed in the `InputValue1` field is different from the value typed in the `InputValue2` field. The `MsgBox()` function displays a message indicating results of the operation, as illustrated in Figure 2-22.

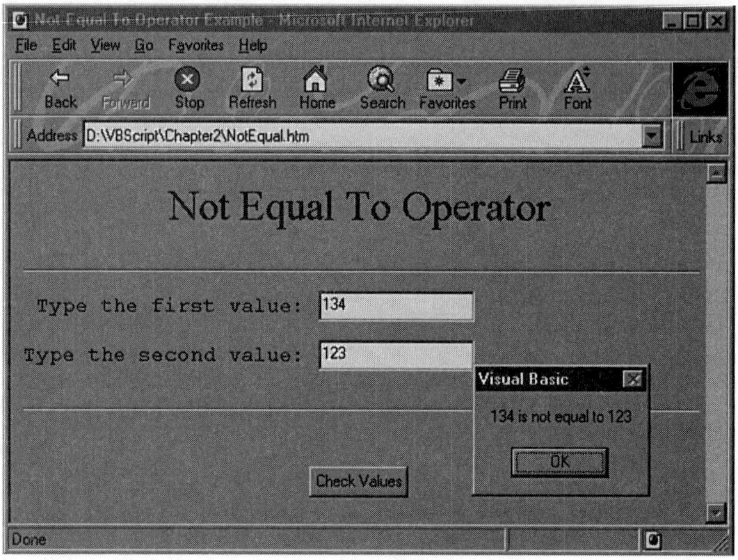

Figure 2-22 The not equal to operator determines if the first value is different from the second value

Listing 2-22 Using the not equal to operator

```
<HTML>

<HEAD>
<TITLE>Not Equal To Operator Example</TITLE>

<SCRIPT LANGUAGE="VBScript">
<!--
'............................................................
' CheckNotEqual_OnClick()
' Determines whether or not the first value is equal to the
' second value.
'.............................................................
SUB CheckNotEqual_OnClick()

  Dim UserValue1
  Dim UserValue2

  UserValue1=InputValue1.Value
  UserValue2=InputValue2.Value

'.............................................................
' Check to see if the value is not equal to the second value.
' Display a message that indicates the results
' of the comparison.
'.............................................................
    If UserValue1 <> UserValue2 Then

      MsgBox UserValue1 & " is not equal to " & UserValue2
```

```
    Else

      MsgBox UserValue1 & " is equal to " & UserValue2

    End If

END SUB
-->

</SCRIPT>
</HEAD>

<BODY>

<CENTER>

<FONT SIZE=6>Not Equal To Operator<P>
</CENTER>
<HR>

<FONT SIZE=4>

<PRE> Type the first value: <INPUT NAME=InputValue1 SIZE=20>

Type the second value: <INPUT NAME=InputValue2 SIZE=20>

<HR>
<CENTER>
<INPUT TYPE=BUTTON VALUE="Check Values" NAME="CheckNotEqual">
</CENTER>

</FONT>

</BODY>

</HTML>
```

Comments The not equal to operator will compare any type of values. If you are working with string values, you may want to ensure that all characters of the strings are either uppercase or lowercase. The **UCase()** function can be used to convert all characters in a string to uppercase characters, and the **LCase()** function can be used to convert all characters in a string to lowercase characters. For more information about the **UCase()** and **LCase()** functions, refer to Chapter 9, String Manipulation.

Is Operator

Purpose Use the **Is** operator to determine if two variables reference the same object. Table 2-31 describes the expressions you can use with the **Is** operator.

Syntax `expression1 Is expression2`

Table 2-31 Arguments of the `Is` operator

Argument	Description
`expression1`	Any expression that references a valid object
`expression2`	Any expression that references a valid object

Description

The **`Is`** operator compares two expressions and returns a Boolean value of **`TRUE`** if they both reference the same object; otherwise, the operator returns a value of **`FALSE`**.

Listing 2-23 uses the **`Is`** operator to determine if the value of a variable is the same as the **`ID`** value of the object. If the values are the same, the value typed by the user in the input field is used to rotate the text of the object, as illustrated in Figure 2-23.

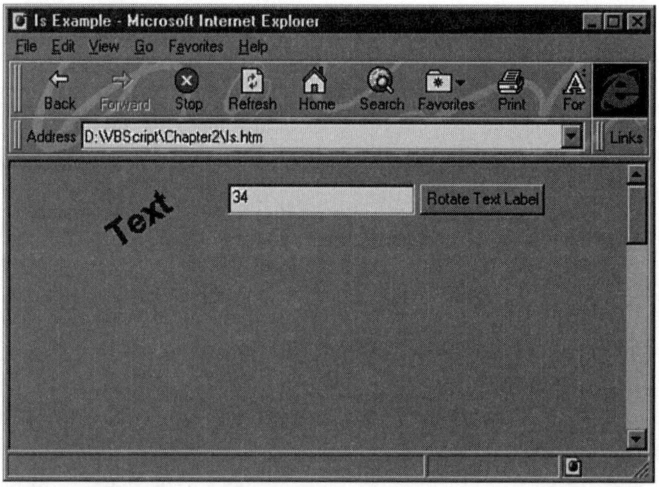

Figure 2-23 The **`Is`** operator determines if two expressions reference the same object

Listing 2-23 Using the `Is` operator

```
<HTML>

<HEAD>

<TITLE>Is Example</TITLE>

<SCRIPT LANGUAGE="VBScript">
<!--
'.........................................................
' RotText_OnClick()
'
' Checks to make sure there is a valid object referenced;
' if so, rotates the text.
'........................................................

SUB RotText_OnClick()
  Dim EntryForm

  Set EntryForm=Document.ActiveXLabel

  Set Object1 = lblActiveLbl

'.........................................................
' Make sure a numeric value was typed.
'.........................................................
  If IsNumeric(EntryForm.txtNewText.Value) Then

'..........................................................
' Use Is operator to see if Object1 references the
' correct object.
'..........................................................
    If Object1 Is lblActiveLbl Then
      Object1.Angle = EntryForm.txtNewText.Value
    End If

  Else
    MsgBox "Enter a Numeric Value"
  End If

END SUB

</SCRIPT>

<OBJECT
       classid="clsid:99B42120-6EC7-11CF-A6C7-00AA00A47DD2"
       id=lblActiveLbl
       width=100
       height=850
       align=left
       hspace=20
       vspace=0
>
<PARAM NAME="_extentX" VALUE="550">
<PARAM NAME="_extentY" VALUE="700">
<PARAM NAME="Angle" VALUE="45">
```

continued on next page

continued from previous page

```
<PARAM NAME="Alignment" VALUE="2">
<PARAM NAME="BackStyle" VALUE="0">
<PARAM NAME="Caption" VALUE="Text">
<PARAM NAME="FontName" VALUE="Arial">
<PARAM NAME="FontSize" VALUE="20">
<PARAM NAME="FontBold" VALUE="1">
<PARAM NAME="FrColor" VALUE="0">
</OBJECT>

</HEAD>

<BODY>

<FORM NAME="ActiveXLabel">

<INPUT TYPE="TEXT" NAME="txtNewText" SIZE=25>
<INPUT TYPE="BUTTON" NAME="RotText" VALUE="Rotate Text Label">

</FORM>

</BODY>

</HTML>
```

Comments

Listing 2-23 also uses the `IsNumeric()` function to make sure the value typed by the user is numeric before modifying the properties of the object. For more information about the `IsNumeric()` function, refer to Chapter 4, Data Validation.

Operators for Logical Operations

VBScript provides a variety of operators that you can use when performing logical operations. For example, if you want to use an `If` statement that is `TRUE` if two statements are `TRUE`, you would use the `And` operator to combine the statements (`If (A = B) And (C > D) Then`). Each of the logical operators available in VBScript is listed in Table 2-32. Descriptions of how to use each operator follow the table.

Table 2-32 VBScript logical operators

Use This Operator...	To Do This...
`And`	Join the results of either two Boolean expressions or two bit values.
`Eqv`	Determine if the results of either two Boolean expressions or two bit values are the same.
`Imp`	Perform a logical implication of either two Boolean expressions or two bit values.
`Not`	Negate the value of either a Boolean expression or a bit value.
`Or`	Perform a logical disjunction of either two Boolean expressions or two bit values.
`Xor`	Perform a logical exclusion of either two Boolean expression or two bit values.

And Operator

Purpose Use the **And** operator to perform a logical conjunction of two expressions. These expressions can either be Boolean expressions that evaluate as **TRUE** or **FALSE**, or bitwise expressions that have a value of either **0** or **1**. Table 2-33 describes the expressions you can use with the **And** operator.

Syntax `expression1 And expression2`

Table 2-33 Arguments of the And operator

Argument	Description
expression1	Any expression with either a Boolean value of TRUE or FALSE or a bitwise value of 0 or 1
expression2	Any expression with either a Boolean value of TRUE or FALSE or a bitwise value of 0 or 1

Description The **And** operator combines the results of two Boolean expressions. The result of each individual expression determines whether or not the combined expression formed using the **And** operator is **TRUE** or **FALSE**. For example, if results of both expressions are **TRUE**, the combined result is **TRUE**. Table 2-34 outlines the results of the expression created when the **And** operator is used to combine two Boolean expressions.

Table 2-34 Results of a Boolean expression with the And operator

If expression1 Is...	And expression2 Is...	The Result Is...
TRUE	TRUE	TRUE
TRUE	FALSE	FALSE
FALSE	TRUE	FALSE
FALSE	FALSE	FALSE
NULL	TRUE	NULL
NULL	FALSE	NULL
TRUE	NULL	NULL
FALSE	NULL	NULL
NULL	NULL	NULL

Listing 2-24 uses the **And** operator to determine if the specified values were typed in both the **InputValue1** and **InputValue2** fields. Since each field requires a different value, the value in each field is checked and the **And** operator combines the results of the two fields to determine if both responses were correct. The **MsgBox()** function displays a message indicating the results of the operation, as illustrated in Figure 2-24.

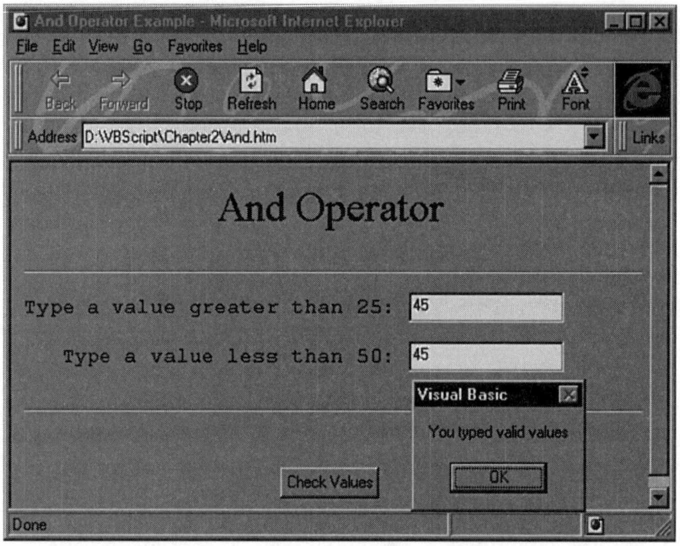

Figure 2-24 The **And** operator combines the results of two Boolean expressions

Listing 2-24 Using the **And** *operator*

```
<HTML>

<HEAD>
<TITLE>And Operator Example</TITLE>

<SCRIPT LANGUAGE="VBScript">
<!--
'..........................................................
' UseAnd_OnClick()
' Determines user typed the appropriate values.
'..........................................................
SUB UseAnd_OnClick()

  Dim UserValue1
  Dim UserValue2

  UserValue1=InputValue1.Value
  UserValue2=InputValue2.Value

'..........................................................
' Check to see if the value is equal to the second value.
' Display a message that indicates the results
' of the comparison.
'..........................................................

  If (UserValue1 > 25) And (UserValue2 < 50) Then

    MsgBox "You typed valid values"
```

```
  Else

   MsgBox "At least one of the values is not in the right range"

  End If

END SUB
-->

</SCRIPT>
</HEAD>

<BODY>

<CENTER>

<FONT SIZE=6>And Operator<P>
</CENTER>
<HR>

<FONT SIZE=4>

<PRE>Type a value greater than 25: <INPUT NAME=InputValue1 SIZE=20>

   Type a value less than 50: <INPUT NAME=InputValue2 SIZE=20>

<HR>
<CENTER>
<INPUT TYPE=BUTTON VALUE="Check Values" NAME="UseAnd">
</CENTER>

</FONT>

</BODY>

</HTML>
```

Comments The And expression is also used to perform a bitwise comparison of two identically positioned bits in two different numeric expressions. When the comparison is made, the corresponding bit is set in the result based on the values in Table 2-35.

Table 2-35 Results of a bitwise comparison with the And operator

If Bit in expression1 Is...	And Bit in expression2 Is...	The Result Is...
1	1	1
1	0	0
0	1	0
0	0	0

Eqv Operator

Purpose Use the **Eqv** operator to perform a logical equivalence of two expressions. These expressions can either be Boolean expressions that evaluate as **TRUE** or **FALSE**, or bitwise expressions that have a value of either **0** or **1**. Table 2-36 describes the expressions you can use with the **Eqv** operator.

Syntax `expression1 Eqv expression2`

Table 2-36 Arguments of the Eqv operator

Argument	Description
expression1	Any expression with either a Boolean value of TRUE or FALSE or a bitwise value of 0 or 1
expression2	Any expression with either a Boolean value of TRUE or FALSE or a bitwise value of 0 or 1

Description The **Eqv** operator compares the logical results of two Boolean expressions. If the results of each expression are the same, both **TRUE** or both **FALSE**, the result of the expression formed with the **Eqv** operator is **TRUE**. Table 2-37 outlines the results of the expression created when the **Eqv** operator is used with two Boolean expressions.

Table 2-37 Results of Boolean expressions with the Eqv operator

If expression1 Is...	And expression2 Is...	The Result Is...
TRUE	TRUE	TRUE
TRUE	FALSE	FALSE
FALSE	TRUE	FALSE
FALSE	FALSE	TRUE
NULL	TRUE	NULL
NULL	FALSE	NULL
TRUE	NULL	NULL
FALSE	NULL	NULL
NULL	NULL	NULL

Listing 2-25 uses the **Eqv** operator to determine if the values typed in both the **InputValue1** and **InputValue2** fields are either both **TRUE** or both **FALSE**. The **MsgBox()** function displays a message indicating the results of the operation, as illustrated in Figure 2-25.

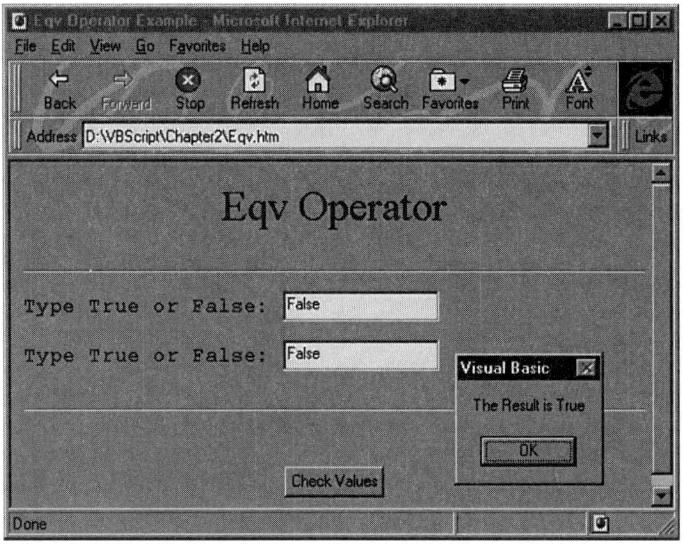

Figure 2-25 The **Eqv** operator compares the results of two Boolean expressions

Listing 2-25 Using the `Eqv` operator

```
<HTML>

<HEAD>
<TITLE>Eqv Operator Example</TITLE>

<SCRIPT LANGUAGE="VBScript">
<!--
'..........................................................
' UseEqv_OnClick()
' Determines if both values are either True or False.
'...........................................................
SUB UseEqv_OnClick()

  Dim UserValue1
  Dim UserValue2

  UserValue1=InputValue1.Value
  UserValue2=InputValue2.Value

  MsgBox "The Result is " & (UserValue1 Eqv UserValue2)


END SUB
-->

</SCRIPT>
</HEAD>
```

continued on next page

continued from previous page

```
<BODY>

<CENTER>

<FONT SIZE=6>Eqv Operator<P>
</CENTER>
<HR>

<FONT SIZE=4>

<PRE>Type True or False: <INPUT NAME=InputValue1 SIZE=20>

Type True or False: <INPUT NAME=InputValue2 SIZE=20>

<HR>
<CENTER>
<INPUT TYPE=BUTTON VALUE="Check Values" NAME="UseEqv">
</CENTER>

</FONT>

</BODY>

</HTML>
```

Comments The **`Eqv`** expression is also used to perform a bitwise comparison of two identically positioned bits in two different numeric expressions. When the comparison is made, the corresponding bit is set in the result based on the values in Table 2-38.

Table 2-38 Results of a bitwise comparison with the `Eqv` operator

If Bit in `expression1` Is...	And bit in `expression2` Is...	The Result Is...
1	1	1
1	0	0
0	1	0
0	0	1

`Imp` OPERATOR

Purpose Use the **`Imp`** operator to perform a logical implication of two expressions. These expressions can either be Boolean expressions that evaluate as **`TRUE`** or **`FALSE`**, or bitwise expressions that have a value of either **`0`** or **`1`**. Table 2-39 describes the expressions you can use with the **`Imp`** operator.

Syntax `expression1 Imp expression2`

Table 2-39 Arguments of the `Imp` operator

Argument	Description
`expression1`	Any expression with either a Boolean value of `TRUE` or `FALSE` or a bitwise value of `0` or `1`
`expression2`	Any expression with either a Boolean value of `TRUE` or `FALSE` or a bitwise value of `0` or `1`

Description

The **`Imp`** operator combines the results of two Boolean expressions. The result of each individual expression determines whether or not the combined expression formed using the **`Imp`** operator is **`TRUE`** or **`FALSE`**. This operator has somewhat strange results; the only time the result of the expression is **`FALSE`** is when the first expression is **`TRUE`** and the second expression is **`FALSE`**. The result is **`NULL`** only if the first expression is either **`TRUE`** or **`NULL`** and the second expression is **`NULL`**. Table 2-40 outlines the results of the expression created when the **`Imp`** operator is used to combine two Boolean expressions.

Table 2-40 Results of a Boolean expression with the `Imp` operator

If `expression1` Is...	And `expression2` Is...	The Result Is...
TRUE	TRUE	TRUE
TRUE	FALSE	FALSE
FALSE	TRUE	TRUE
FALSE	FALSE	TRUE
NULL	TRUE	TRUE
NULL	FALSE	NULL
TRUE	NULL	NULL
FALSE	NULL	TRUE
NULL	NULL	NULL

Listing 2-26 uses the **`Imp`** operator to evaluate the **`TRUE`** or **`FALSE`** values typed in both the **`InputValue1`** and **`InputValue2`** fields. The **`MsgBox()`** function displays a message indicating the results of the operation, as illustrated in Figure 2-26.

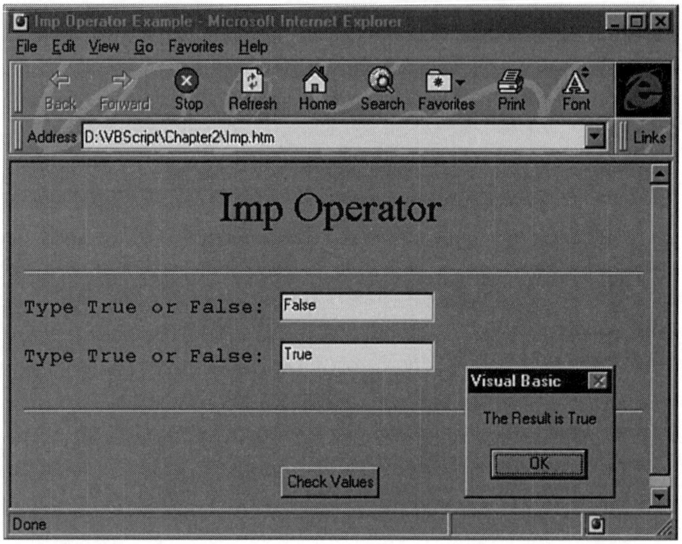

Figure 2-26 The **Imp** operator evaluates the results of two Boolean expressions

Listing 2-26 Using the `Imp` *operator*

```
<HTML>

<HEAD>
<TITLE>Imp Operator Example</TITLE>

<SCRIPT LANGUAGE="VBScript">
<!--
'.................................................................
' UseImp_OnClick()
' Evaluate both values and return either True or False.
'.................................................................
SUB UseImp_OnClick()

  Dim UserValue1
  Dim UserValue2

  UserValue1=InputValue1.Value
  UserValue2=InputValue2.Value

  MsgBox "The Result is " & (UserValue1 Imp UserValue2)


END SUB
-->

</SCRIPT>
</HEAD>

<BODY>
```

```
<CENTER>

<FONT SIZE=6>Imp Operator<P>
</CENTER>
<HR>

<FONT SIZE=4>

<PRE>Type True or False: <INPUT NAME=InputValue1 SIZE=20>

Type True or False: <INPUT NAME=InputValue2 SIZE=20>

<HR>
<CENTER>
<INPUT TYPE=BUTTON VALUE="Check Values" NAME="UseImp">
</CENTER>

</FONT>

</BODY>

</HTML>
```

Comments The `Imp` operator is also used to perform a bitwise comparison of two identically positioned bits in two different numeric expressions. When the comparison is made, the corresponding bit is set in the result based on the values in Table 2-41. Using the `Imp` operator is basically the same as using the `^` operator with the bit values.

Table 2-41 Results of a bitwise comparison with the `Imp` operator

If Bit in `expression1` Is...	And Bit in `expression2` Is...	The Result Is...
1	1	1
1	0	0
0	1	1
0	0	1

Not OPERATOR

Purpose Use the `Not` operator to perform a logical negation of the value of an expression. The expression can either be a Boolean expression that evaluates as `TRUE` or `FALSE`, or a bitwise expression that has a value of either `0` or `1`. Table 2-42 describes the expressions you can use with the `Not` operator.

Syntax `Not expression1`

Table 2-42 Argument of the Not operator

Argument	Description
expression1	Any expression with either a Boolean value of TRUE or FALSE or a bitwise value of 0 or 1

Description

The **Not** operator takes the result of a Boolean expression and negates the value. Therefore, if the result of the expression is **TRUE**, the **Not** operator causes a **FALSE** value to be returned. Table 2-43 outlines the results of the expression created when the **Not** operator is used with Boolean expressions.

Table 2-43 Results of a Boolean expression with the Not operator

If expression1 Is...	The Result Is...
TRUE	FALSE
FALSE	TRUE
NULL	NULL

Listing 2-27 uses the **Not** operator to perform a logical negation of the value typed in the **InputValue1** field. The **MsgBox()** function displays a message indicating the results of the operation, as illustrated in Figure 2-27.

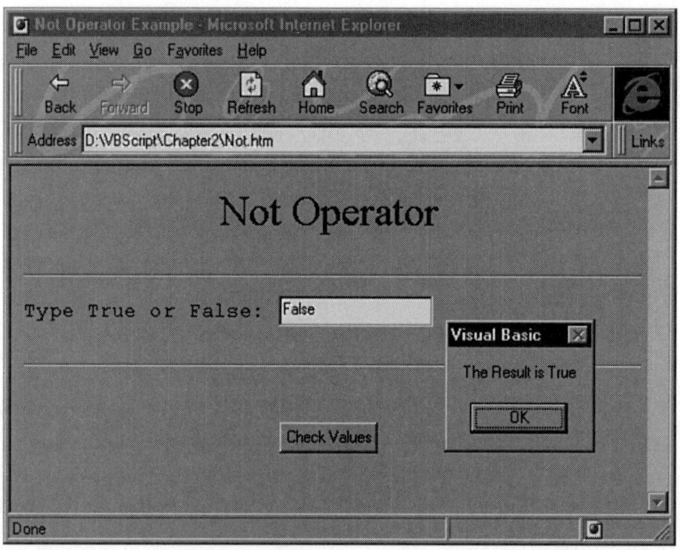

Figure 2-27 The **Not** operator performs a logical negation of a value

Listing 2-27 Using the `Not` operator

```
<HTML>

<HEAD>
<TITLE>Not Operator Example</TITLE>

<SCRIPT LANGUAGE="VBScript">
<!--
'.........................................................
' UseNot_OnClick()
' Return the opposite value, either True or False.
'..........................................................
SUB UseNot_OnClick()

  Dim UserValue1

  UserValue1=InputValue1.Value

  MsgBox "The Result is " & (Not UserValue1)


END SUB
-->

</SCRIPT>
</HEAD>

<BODY>

<CENTER>

<FONT SIZE=6>Not Operator<P>
</CENTER>
<HR>

<FONT SIZE=4>

<PRE>Type True or False: <INPUT NAME=InputValue1 SIZE=20>

<HR>
<CENTER>
<INPUT TYPE=BUTTON VALUE="Check Values" NAME="UseNot">
</CENTER>

</FONT>

</BODY>

</HTML>
```

Comments The **`Not`** operator is also used to invert a bit value of an expression. When the **`Not`** operator is used, the corresponding bit is set in the result based on the values in Table 2-44.

Table 2-44 Results of a bit value with the `Not` operator

If Bit in `expression1` Is...	The Result Is...
1	0
0	1

`Or` OPERATOR

Purpose Use the `Or` operator to perform a logical disjunction of two expressions. This means that if one of the expressions is `TRUE`, the entire expression is `TRUE`. These expressions can either be Boolean expressions that evaluate as `TRUE` or `FALSE`, or bitwise expressions that have a value of either `0` or `1`. Table 2-45 describes the expressions you can use with the `Or` operator.

Syntax `expression1 Or expression2`

Table 2-45 Arguments of the `Or` operator

Argument	Description
`expression1`	Any expression with either a Boolean value of `TRUE` or `FALSE` or a bitwise value of `0` or `1`
`expression2`	Any expression with either a Boolean value of `TRUE` or `FALSE` or a bitwise value of `0` or `1`

Description The `Or` operator looks at the results of two Boolean expressions; if at least one of the expressions is `TRUE`, the `Or` operator returns a value of `TRUE`. Table 2-46 outlines the results of the expression created when the `Or` operator is used with two Boolean expressions.

Table 2-46 Results of a Boolean expression with the `Or` operator

If `expression1` Is...	And `expression2` Is...	The Result Is...
TRUE	TRUE	TRUE
TRUE	FALSE	TRUE
FALSE	TRUE	TRUE
FALSE	FALSE	FALSE
NULL	TRUE	TRUE
NULL	FALSE	NULL
TRUE	NULL	TRUE
FALSE	NULL	NULL
NULL	NULL	NULL

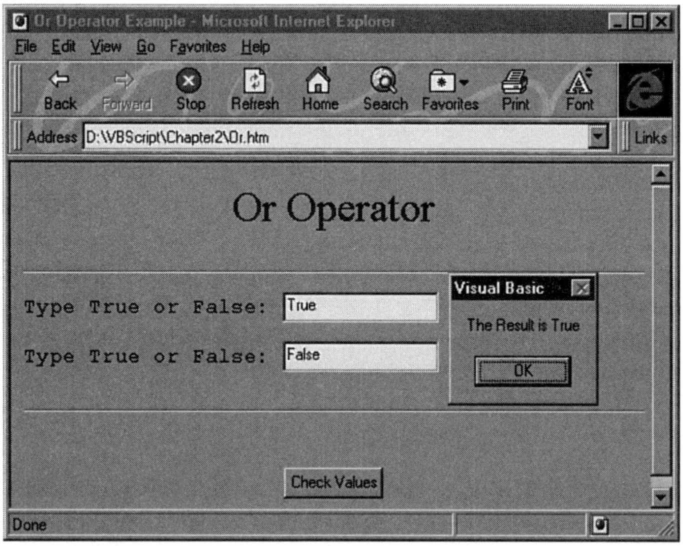

Figure 2-28 The `Or` operator compares the results of two Boolean expressions

Listing 2-28 uses the `Or` operator to compare the specified values typed in both the `InputValue1` and `InputValue2` fields. The `MsgBox()` function displays a message indicating the results of the operation, as illustrated in Figure 2-28.

Listing 2-28 Using the `Or` operator

```
<HTML>

<HEAD>
<TITLE>Or Operator Example</TITLE>

<SCRIPT LANGUAGE="VBScript">
<!--
'..........................................................
' UseOr_OnClick()
' Evaluate both values and return either True or False.
'..........................................................
SUB UseOr_OnClick()

  Dim UserValue1
  Dim UserValue2

  UserValue1=InputValue1.Value
  UserValue2=InputValue2.Value

  MsgBox "The Result is " & (UserValue1 Or UserValue2)
```

continued on next page

continued from previous page

```
END SUB
-->

</SCRIPT>
</HEAD>

<BODY>

<CENTER>

<FONT SIZE=6>Or Operator<P>
</CENTER>
<HR>

<FONT SIZE=4>

<PRE>Type True or False: <INPUT NAME=InputValue1 SIZE=20>

Type True or False: <INPUT NAME=InputValue2 SIZE=20>

<HR>
<CENTER>
<INPUT TYPE=BUTTON VALUE="Check Values" NAME="UseOr">
</CENTER>

</FONT>

</BODY>

</HTML>
```

Comments The `Or` expression is also used to compare two identically positioned bits in two different numeric expressions. When the comparison is made, the corresponding bit is set in the result based on the values in Table 2-47.

Table 2-47 Results of a bitwise comparison with the `Or` operator

If Bit in `expression1` Is...	And Bit in `expression2` Is...	The Result Is...
1	1	1
1	0	1
0	1	1
0	0	0

`Xor` Operator

Purpose Use the `Xor` operator to perform a logical exclusion of two expressions. These expressions can either be Boolean expressions that evaluate as `TRUE` or `FALSE`, or bitwise expressions that have a value of either `0` or `1`. Table 2-48 describes the expressions you can use with the `Xor` operator.

Syntax `expression1 Xor expression2`

Table 2-48 Arguments of the Xor operator

Argument	Description
expression1	Any expression with either a Boolean value of TRUE or FALSE or a bitwise value of 0 or 1
expression2	Any expression with either a Boolean value of TRUE or FALSE or a bitwise value of 0 or 1

Description

The Xor operator combines the results of two Boolean expressions, and if only one of the expressions evaluates to TRUE, the result of the Xor operator is TRUE; otherwise, the result is FALSE. However, if either one or both of the expressions have a NULL value, the result is NULL. Table 2-49 outlines the results of the expression created when the Xor operator is used to combine two Boolean expressions.

Table 2-49 Results of a Boolean expression with the Xor operator

If expression1 Is...	And expression2 Is...	The Result Is...
TRUE	TRUE	FALSE
TRUE	FALSE	TRUE
FALSE	TRUE	TRUE
FALSE	FALSE	FALSE
NULL	TRUE	NULL
NULL	FALSE	NULL
TRUE	NULL	NULL
FALSE	NULL	NULL
NULL	NULL	NULL

Listing 2-29 uses the Xor operator to combine the values typed in both the InputValue1 and InputValue2 fields and determine if one of the values is TRUE. The MsgBox() function displays a message indicating the results of the operation, as illustrated in Figure 2-29.

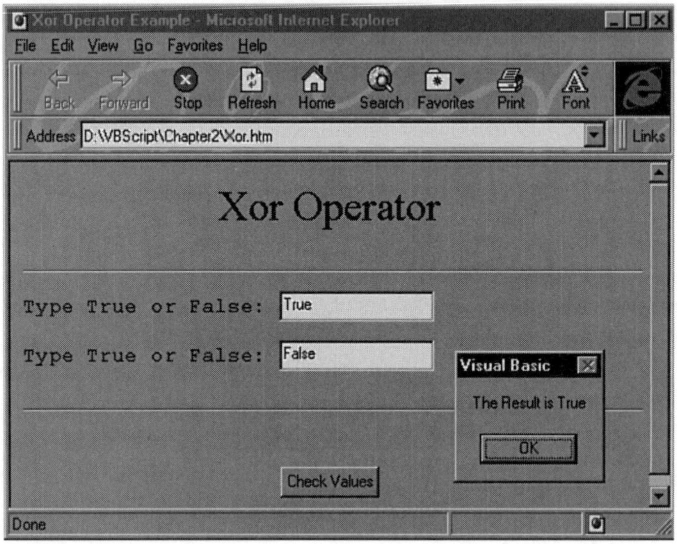

Figure 2-29 The **Xor** operator combines the results of two Boolean expressions

Listing 2-29 Using the `Xor` *operator*

```
<HTML>

<HEAD>
<TITLE>Xor Operator Example</TITLE>

<SCRIPT LANGUAGE="VBScript">
<!--
'.........................................................
' UseXor_OnClick()
' Evaluate both values and return either True or False.
'.........................................................
SUB UseXor_OnClick()

  Dim UserValue1
  Dim UserValue2

  UserValue1=InputValue1.Value
  UserValue2=InputValue2.Value

  MsgBox "The Result is " & (UserValue1 Xor UserValue2)


END SUB
-->

</SCRIPT>
</HEAD>

<BODY>
```

```
<CENTER>

<FONT SIZE=6>Xor Operator<P>
</CENTER>
<HR>

<FONT SIZE=4>

<PRE>Type True or False: <INPUT NAME=InputValue1 SIZE=20>

Type True or False: <INPUT NAME=InputValue2 SIZE=20>

<HR>
<CENTER>
<INPUT TYPE=BUTTON VALUE="Check Values" NAME="UseXor">
</CENTER>

</FONT>

</BODY>

</HTML>
```

Comments The `Xor` expression is also used to compare two identically positioned bits in two different numeric expressions. When the comparison is made, the corresponding bit is set in the result based on the values in Table 2-50.

Table 2-50 Results of a bitwise comparison with the `Xor` operator

If Bit in `expression1` Is...	And Bit in `expression2` Is...	The Result Is...
1	1	0
1	0	1
0	1	1
0	0	0

Operators for Concatenating Strings

VBScript provides two operators that you can use to concatenate, or join, two string values. Each of the concatenation operators available in VBScript is listed in Table 2-51. Although the **+** operator can be used to concatenate two strings, the **&** operator is preferred. The **+** operator was covered earlier in the chapter.

Table 2-51 VBScript concatenation operators

Use This Operator...	To Do This...
&	Concatenate two strings.
+	Concatenate two strings, or add two numeric expressions.

& OPERATOR

Purpose Use the & (concatenation) operator to join two expressions together. This operator adds the contents of one string to the end of another string. Table 2-52 describes the expressions you can use with the concatenation operator.

Syntax `expression1 & expression2`

Table 2-52 Arguments of the concatenation operator

Argument	Description
expression1	Any expression
expression2	Any expression

Description The concatenation operator is used to join two expressions together. When the strings are joined, the contents of the second string are added to the end of the first string. For example, if you have a string that contains the value `Air` and another string with the value `port`, using the concatenation operator will result in `Airport`. If the expressions are numeric, they are still joined; the value of `12` and `34` becomes `1234`.

Listing 2-30 uses the `&` operator to join the two expressions typed in the `InputValue1` and `InputValue2` fields. The results are displayed using the `MsgBox()` function, as illustrated in Figure 2-30.

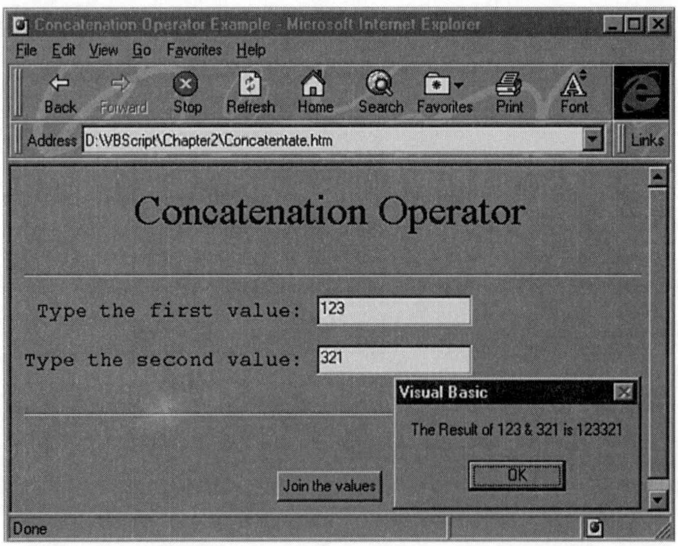

Figure 2-30 The concatenation operator joins two expressions

Listing 2-30 Using the concatenation operator

```
<HTML>

<HEAD>
<TITLE>Concatenation Operator Example</TITLE>

<SCRIPT LANGUAGE="VBScript">
<!--
'..............................................
' JoinValues_OnClick()
' Joins the two expressions typed by the user.
'..............................................
SUB JoinValues_OnClick()

  Dim Val1
  Dim Val2

  Val1=InputValue1.Value
  Val2=InputValue2.Value

'...............................................
' The & operator not only joins two expressions,
' but it can be used with functions, such as
' the MsgBox function, to join strings and
' variables that should display in the dialog
' box.
'................................................
  MsgBox "The Result of " & Val1 & " & " & Val2 & " is " & Val1 & Val2

END SUB
-->

</SCRIPT>
</HEAD>

<BODY>

<CENTER>

<FONT SIZE=6>Concatenation Operator<P>
</CENTER>
<HR>

<FONT SIZE=4>

<PRE> Type the first value: <INPUT NAME=InputValue1 SIZE=20>

Type the second value: <INPUT NAME=InputValue2 SIZE=20>

<HR>
<CENTER>
<INPUT TYPE=BUTTON VALUE="Join the values" NAME="JoinValues">
```

continued on next page

continued from previous page

```
</CENTER>

</FONT>

</BODY>

</HTML>
```

Comments

Although both the **+** and **&** operators can be used to concatenate two strings (that is, hook one string value onto the end of another string value), the preferred method is to use the **&** operator when you intend to concatenate two strings. This will ensure that strings containing only numeric values will also be concatenated properly.

3

VBSCRIPT DATA TYPES AND VARIABLES

3

VBSCRIPT DATA TYPES AND VARIABLES

Unlike other versions of Visual Basic, VBScript provides only one data type, a variant. This data type has several different subtypes that can be used to work with different types of data. This chapter outlines the different subtypes of the variant, and how to declare and work with variables and constants.

What Is a Variant?

A variant has the ability to store all types of data. The type of data that it stores is determined by how it is used. Also, because there is only one data type in VBScript, the data returned by a function is also a variant.

Basically, a variant contains either numeric data or string information. VBScript treats a variant as a number when you use it in a numeric context and as a string when you use it in a string context. In other words, if you are working with data that contains only numbers, VBScript assumes that you want the value treated as a numeric value. If the data contains alpha characters, VBScript automatically treats it as string data. If you want to ensure that numeric values are treated as a string, you can enclose them in quotation marks.

Variant Subtypes

Beyond the simple numeric or string classifications, a variant can make further distinctions about the specific nature of numeric information. For example, you can have numeric information that represents a date or a time. When this numeric information is used with other date or time data, the result is always expressed as a date or a time. You can also have numeric information that ranges in size from Boolean values to huge floating-point numbers. The different types, or categories, of information that can be contained in a variant are called subtypes. Table 3-1 outlines each of the different variant subtypes.

Most of the time, you can simply put the kind of data you want in a variant and VBScript treats the variant in the most appropriate way based on the data it contains. If you want to ensure that the data is treated appropriately, you can use one of the conversion functions outlined in Chapter 7, Data Conversion, to convert the value to the appropriate subtype. For example, you can use the `CInt()` function to make sure the value is treated as an integer value. You can also use the `VarType()` function to determine what type of information is stored in the variant. Refer to Chapter 4, Data Validation, for more information about the `VarType()` function.

Table 3-1 Variant subtypes

Subtype	Description
Boolean	A Boolean value of `TRUE` or `FALSE`.
Byte	An integer value in the range of 0 to 255.
Date	A date value in the range of January 1, 100, to December 31, 9999, for Microsoft Windows. Other platforms may have different date ranges.
Double	A double-precision, floating-point number in the range -1.79769313486232E308 to -4.94065645841247E-324 for negative values; or 4.94065645841247E-324 to 1.79769313486232E308 for positive values.
Empty	A variable that has not been initialized.
Error	An error number.
Integer	An integer value in the range -32,768 to 32,767.
Long	An integer value in the range -2,147,483,648 to 2,147,483,647.
Null	A variable does not contain valid data.
Object	An OLE automation object.
Single	A single-precision, floating-point number in the range -3.402823E38 to -1.401298E-45 for negative values; 1.401298E-45 to 3.402823E38 for positive values.
String	A string of variable length. The maximum length is approximately two billion characters.

Using Variables

A variable allows you to specify a location for a specific value. When you declare a variable, a placeholder for the value is created in the computer's memory. When a value is assigned to the variable, it is placed in the specified memory location.

Variables are widely used in all programming. They allow you to create the program without knowing the exact value that the variable will contain. For example, if you want users to specify the number of items they want to order, you would create a variable called `NumOrder`, where VBScript can place the number specified by the user.

VBScript has the following rules that must be followed when creating a variable:

- A variable name must begin with an alphabetic character (this can be either an uppercase or lowercase character, A through Z).
- The remaining characters in the variable name can be either alphabetic characters (A through Z), numbers (0–9), or underscores (_).
- A variable name cannot contain an embedded period.
- The name cannot be longer than 255 characters.
- The variable name cannot be a VBScript reserved word. The reserved words include the names of functions, operators, properties, statements, and keywords.
- The variable must be unique in the scope in which it is declared. For example, if it is declared within a function, it must be the only variable in that function with that name. You can have a variable in another function with the same name, as long as both variables are procedure level (only available within the procedure where they are declared).

Be aware that variable names are not case sensitive. Therefore, although you may use any combination of uppercase and lowercase characters, if they are the same characters, VBScript will treat them as the same variable. For example, if you have the variable names `Test`, `test`, and `TEST`, they would all be considered to be referencing the same variable.

Variable Declaration Statements

VBScript does not require a variable to be declared before it can be used. This is called an implicitly declared variable. The danger with using this type of variable declaration is that run-time errors can occur because a variable name was misspelled at one location within the code. In order to ensure that all variables are declared before they are used, you can place the `Option Explicit` statement at the beginning of your VBScript code. If a variable that was not initially declared is referenced, an error will occur.

There are two types of variable declarations that can be made in VBScript. If you declare a variable within a procedure, only the code within that procedure can access or change the value of that variable. A variable declared within a procedure has local scope and is known as a procedure-level variable. The value of this variable is only available as long as the procedure is running.

There are times when you may need to use a variable whose value is available to all the procedures within the same script. If you declare a variable outside a procedure, you make it recognizable to all the procedures in your script. A variable declared outside of all procedures is a script-level variable. The value of this variable is available as long as your script is running.

Figure 3-1 illustrates the difference between script-level and procedure-level variables. As illustrated by the drawing, the script-level variables are available for all portions of your VBScript code, whereas procedure-level variables are only available within a limited portion of the code (the procedure where they are declared).

VBScript provides two different statements that are used when declaring a variable. Each of these statements is listed in Table 3-2. A detailed description of each statement follows the table.

Table 3-2 VBScript declaration statements

Statement	Description
`Dim`	Declares either a script-level or procedure-level variable
`Set`	Assigns an object reference to a variable or property

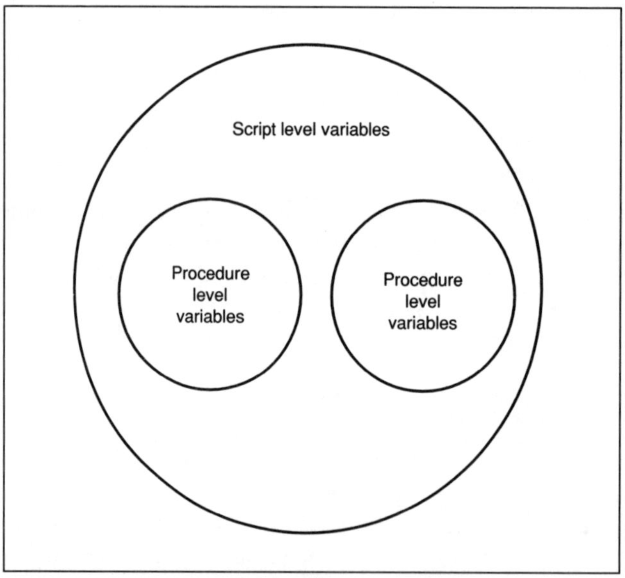

Figure 3-1 Script-level versus procedure-level variables

Dim STATEMENT

Purpose Use the `Dim` statement to declare variables. Use of this statement is required if you have used the `Option Explicit` statement at the beginning of the VBScript code. Table 3-3 describes the expressions you can use with the `Dim` statement.

Syntax `Dim variablename(subscript)`

Table 3-3 Argument of the `Dim` statement

Argument	Description
`variablename`	A unique variable name that starts with an alphabetic character. The name must be less than 256 characters in length.
`subscript`	This argument is only used if `variablename` is the name of an array; otherwise, the parentheses are omitted. This argument specifies the dimensions of an array variable, declared as the `variablename` argument. You can declare a variable with up to 60 multiple dimensions. The lower bound of an array is always `0`; therefore, you are specifying the upper bound or limit for the array.

Description The `Dim` statement is used to declare variables. When you declare a variable, the system allocates storage space for the specified variable. This statement can be used at either the script level, outside of any procedures or functions, or at the procedure level. If a variable is declared at the script level, it is available within all procedures and functions. If it is declared within a procedure or function, it can only be used within that procedure or function.

When using the `Dim` statement, a numeric variable is initialized with a value of `0`, and a string variable is initialized with a zero-length string (`" "`). You can declare a dynamic array by using empty parentheses with the declaration. After declaring a dynamic array, you can use the `ReDim` statement to specify the number of dimensions and elements in the array. For more information about the `ReDim` statement, refer to Chapter 6, Array Handling.

The `Dim` statement is used in most of the examples in this book. Listing 3-1 uses the `Dim` statement to demonstrate how to declare a dynamic array. The `ReDim` statement is later used to change the size of the array to contain the number of elements specified by the user. Figure 3-2 illustrates the dialog box that displays indicating the number of elements in the array.

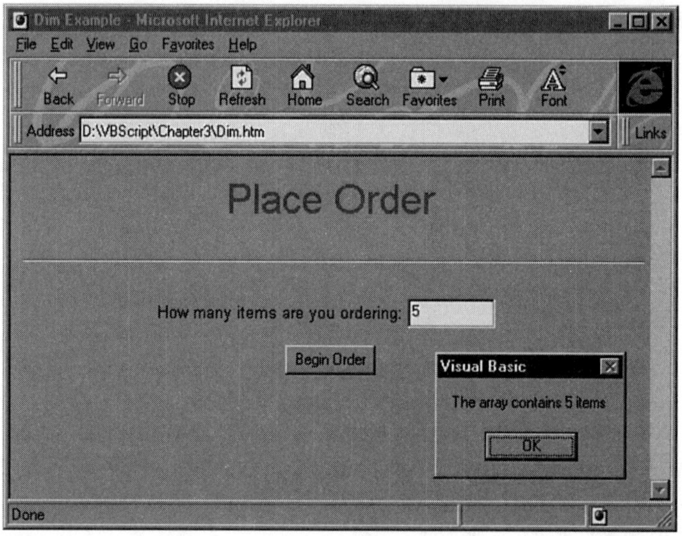

Figure 3-2 The `Dim` statement is used to declare a dynamic array

Listing 3-1 Using the `Dim` statement

```
<HTML>

<HEAD>
<TITLE>Dim Example</TITLE>
</HEAD>


<SCRIPT LANGUAGE="VBScript">
<!--
'..................................................
' ProcOrder_OnClick()
'
' Creates an array with the number of elements
' specified by the user. Fills the array with items.
'..................................................

SUB ProcOrder_OnClick()
  Dim OrderArray()
  Dim InputValue
  Dim Counter

'..................................................
' Assigns the input value to a variable.
'..................................................
  InputValue=UserValue.Value

'..................................................
' Makes sure the value entered is numeric; if it is,
' it is used to specify the number of elements in
' the array.
'..................................................
```

```
  If IsNumeric(InputValue) Then

    ReDim OrderArray(InputValue)

'.....................................................
' Requests the number of items specified in the
' input field. Places each value in the array.
'.....................................................
    For Counter = 0 To InputValue-1

      OrderArray(Counter)=InputBox("Type item number " & Counter+1)

    Next


    MsgBox "The array contains " & Counter & " items "

'......................................................
' Message sent when a non-numeric value was entered.
'......................................................
  Else
    MsgBox "Type a numeric value in the field."
  End If

END SUB

-->
</SCRIPT>

<BODY>

<FONT FACE="Arial" SIZE=2>
<FONT COLOR=Fushia>

<CENTER>
   <FONT SIZE=6>Place Order<P>

</CENTER>

  <HR>

  <FONT FACE="Arial" SIZE=2>
  <FONT COLOR=BLACK>

  <BR>
  <CENTER>
  How many items are you ordering: <INPUT NAME=UserValue SIZE=10>

  <BR>
  <BR>
  <INPUT TYPE=BUTTON VALUE="Begin Order" NAME="ProcOrder">

  </CENTER>

</BODY>

</HTML>
```

Comments Remember, when you declare an array, the lower bound of the array is always `0`. Therefore, if you want an array of 10 elements, you need to declare an upper bound of `9` for the `subscript` argument. If you declare an upper bound of `10`, you will have 11 elements in the array.

Set Statement

Purpose Use the `Set` statement to assign an object reference to either a variable or a property. Table 3-4 describes the expressions you can use with the `Set` statement.

Syntax

```
Set objectvar = expression Nothing
```

Table 3-4 Arguments of the `Set` statement

Argument	Description
`objectvar`	The name of the variable or property that is being assigned.
`expression`	An expression that identifies the object to be assigned, this expression consists of the name of an object, another declared variable of the same object type, or a function or method that returns an object of the same object type. This argument is omitted if the `Nothing` keyword is used in the statement.
`Nothing`	An optional keyword used to discontinue the association of a variable specified by the `objectvar` argument with any specific object. Assigning the `objectvar` argument to `Nothing` releases all the system and memory resources associated with the previously referenced object if there is not another variable that refers to the same object.

Description The `Set` statement is used to assign an object to a variable. The object can be an HTML object such as a form or an OLE automation object such as an ActiveX control. When you use the `Set` statement, a reference to the object is assigned to the specified variable. More than one variable can reference the same object. Since the variables only reference the object, if the object changes, the changes are reflected in all of the variables that reference it.

Before you can use the `Set` statement, you should declare the variable using either the `Dim`, `Private`, or `Public` statements.

Listing 3-2 uses the `Set` statement to both assign the document and form name to a variable and to assign the reference to an OLE object to a variable. Both of these variables are declared first using the `Dim` statement. (Since this sample code uses only one routine, the `Private` and `Public` statements could have also been used.) The rotation value of the object is changed to the value typed by the user, as illustrated in Figure 3-3.

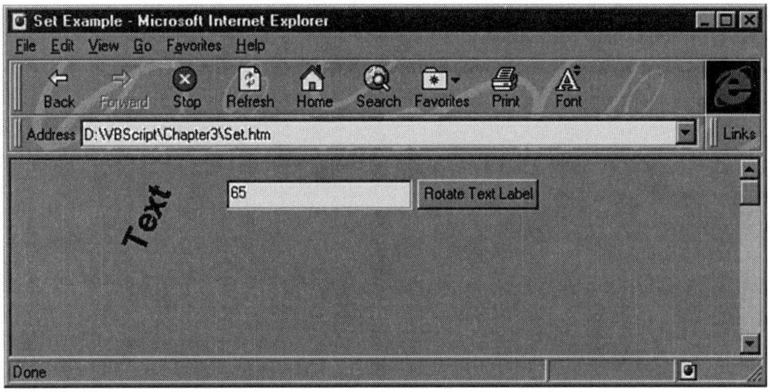

Figure 3-3 The **Set** statement assigns a variable to an object reference

Listing 3-2 Using the `Set` statement

```
<HTML>

<HEAD>

<TITLE>Set Example</TITLE>

<SCRIPT LANGUAGE="VBScript">
<!--
'..........................................................
' RotText_OnClick()
'
' Checks to make sure there is a valid object referenced;
' if so, rotates the text.
'.........................................................

SUB RotText_OnClick
  Dim EntryForm
  Dim Object1

  Set EntryForm=Document.ActiveXLabel

  Set Object1 = lblActiveLbl

'..........................................................
' Make sure a numeric value was typed.
'..........................................................
  If IsNumeric(EntryForm.txtNewText.Value) Then

'..........................................................
' Changes the rotation of the text
'..........................................................
    Object1.Angle = EntryForm.txtNewText.Value
```

continued on next page

continued from previous page

```
  Else
    MsgBox "Enter a Numeric Value"
  End If

END SUB

</SCRIPT>

<OBJECT
       classid="clsid:99B42120-6EC7-11CF-A6C7-00AA00A47DD2"
       id=lblActiveLbl
       width=100
       height=850
       align=left
       hspace=20
       vspace=0
>
<PARAM NAME="_extentX" VALUE="550">
<PARAM NAME="_extentY" VALUE="700">
<PARAM NAME="Angle" VALUE="45">
<PARAM NAME="Alignment" VALUE="2">
<PARAM NAME="BackStyle" VALUE="0">
<PARAM NAME="Caption" VALUE="Text">
<PARAM NAME="FontName" VALUE="Arial">
<PARAM NAME="FontSize" VALUE="20">
<PARAM NAME="FontBold" VALUE="1">
<PARAM NAME="FrColor" VALUE="0">
</OBJECT>

</HEAD>

<BODY>

<FORM NAME="ActiveXLabel">

<INPUT TYPE="TEXT" NAME="txtNewText" SIZE=25>
<INPUT TYPE="BUTTON" NAME="RotText" VALUE="Rotate Text Label">

</FORM>

</BODY>

</HTML>
```

Assigning Values to a Variable

Once a variable is declared, values are assigned to the variable by simply using the equal sign (=). The variable is placed on the left side of the equal sign and the new value is placed on the right side of the equal sign, as illustrated in this example code:

```
TestVariable = "Test"
```

Creating Constants

A constant is a name used to refer to a variable containing a value that never changes during the execution of the program. A constant is declared just like any other variable by using either the `Dim`, `Private`, or `Public` statement. Once the constant variable has been declared, you assign a value to the variable using the equal sign (=), just as you do with any other variable. Basically, as far as VBScript is concerned, a constant variable is just another variable.

4

DATA VALIDATION

4

4

DATA VALIDATION

One of the most important features of VBScript is its ability to validate data entered by the user on the client machine prior to sending it to the Web server. This feature of VBScript can greatly increase the efficiency of any Web site due to the elimination of most server validation requirements.

Client Validation Versus Server Validation

In the current HTML world, if a user enters a value on a form, the value must be sent back to the Web server for verification. If the wrong type of value was entered, a message is then returned to the user requesting a new value, and the cycle continues until the user returns the desired data type. Depending on the access rate of the user and the speed of the Web server, this process, performed for each field on a form, greatly decreases the efficiency of the Web page.

Using VBScript, user input can be verified prior to sending the data to the server. This simple validation process, when performed on the client machine, greatly increases the speed of a Web site without the need to change the access rate of the user.

Using VBScript to Validate User Data

Using VBScript, you can quickly perform the form processing that is done on a server under HTML. This provides you with the ability to check data entered by a user before it is sent to the Web server. For example, if a field requires a date value, VBScript can check the value typed in that field by the user and make sure it is a valid date. If the value entered is not a date, a request is sent to the user to enter a valid date value. All of this validation processing occurs on the user's own machine. Once a valid date is entered, the date is then sent to the Web server to make sure it is a feasible delivery date based upon the corporate schedule.

Not only can data be validated on the client machine, but with VBScript most data calculations can also be performed on the client machine. Since all variables in VBScript are variants, it is important to check the subtype of a variable before performing a data calculation or conversion. For example, the **IsDate()** function provides the ability to make sure a variable contains a valid date before processing, as illustrated in the following code. Figure 4-1 illustrates a message that displays when the incorrect data type is entered.

```
Sub CheckDate

  If IsDate(DateEntered) Then
     ProcessDate
   Else
     MsgBox "Enter a Valid Date. ", 0, "Date Validation"
  End If

End Sub
```

Elimination of Runtime Data Errors

With the data manipulation capabilities that VBScript brings to HTML, the user is much more likely to receive runtime errors as the result of entering an improper value. Proper use of the data validation functions can eliminate most, if not all, data errors.

For example, if VBScript attempts a mathematical calculation on a nonnumeric value, the user could receive a runtime error indicating a type mismatch, as illustrated in Figure 4-2.

By simply using the **IsNumeric()** function before attempting to convert or manipulate data entered by the user, as illustrated in the following code, you would immediately know if the user has entered the correct type of data.

```
SUB ValidateNumValue

  Dim TotalValue

  If IsNumeric(UserValue) Then
      TotalValue = TotalValue + Cint(UserValue)
  Else
      MsgBox "Type a numeric value in the field"
  End If

END SUB
```

Figure 4-1 The **IsDate()** function checks for a valid date from the user

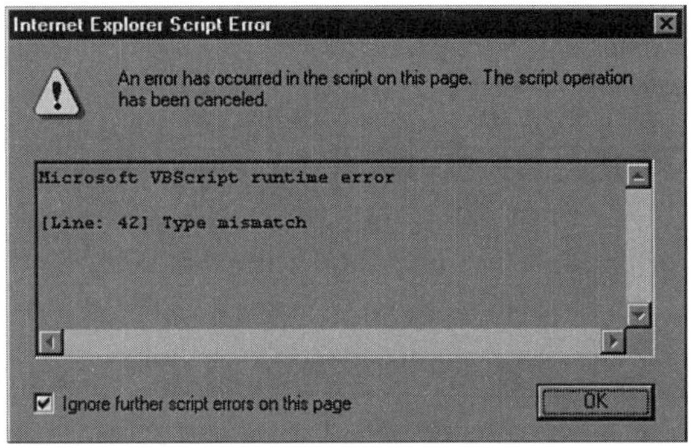

Figure 4-2 Runtime error due to an attempt to add a nonnumeric value

Summary of Data Validation Functions

Table 4-1 summarizes the main functions used to validate data on a client machine. Although there are other related functions that can also be used in the validation process, this table outlines the major functions. Detailed descriptions of each function follow the table, with sample syntax that illustrates the function's use. The Data Validation project at the end of the chapter demonstrates how to use these functions to validate user data on a form.

Table 4-1 Data validation function summary

Use...	To Do This...
`IsArray`	Determine whether a variable is an array.
`IsDate`	Determine whether the specified variable is a date or time value.
`IsEmpty`	Determine whether a variable has been initialized.
`IsNull`	Make sure a variable does not contain a `NULL` value.
`IsNumeric`	Determine whether a variable contains a numeric value.
`IsObject`	Determine whether a variable references an OLE object.
`VarType`	Determine the subtype of a variant.

`IsArray` FUNCTION

Purpose Use the `IsArray()` function to determine whether a specific variant expression is an array of values. Table 4-2 describes the expressions that can be used with the `IsArray()` function.

Syntax `IsArray(expression)`

Table 4-2 Argument of the `IsArray()` function

Argument	Description
`expression`	Any unique variable can be used with this function.

Description

The `IsArray()` function returns a Boolean value of `TRUE` if the specified variable is an array; otherwise `FALSE` is returned.

In the example in Listing 4-1, the user enters a value that specifies the variable selected to be passed to the `CheckArray()` function. If the array is passed, `IsArray()` returns a `TRUE` value; otherwise, `FALSE` is returned. Figure 4-3 shows a Web page created by Listing 4-1.

Listing 4-1 Using the `IsArray()` function

```
<HTML>

<HEAD>
<TITLE>IsArray Example</TITLE>
</HEAD>

<FONT FACE="Arial" SIZE=2>
<FONT COLOR=Fuchsia>

<CENTER>
   <FONT SIZE=4>Locate an Array<P>
</CENTER>

<SCRIPT LANGUAGE="VBScript">
<!--
'...................................
' Submit_OnClick()
' Determines the type of value selected
' by the user.
'...................................

SUB Submit_OnClick()
Dim Test1(3)
Dim Test2

If UserValue.Value=1 Then
   CheckArray(Test1)
Else
   CheckArray(Test2)
End If

END SUB
'....................................................
' CheckArray()
' Tells the user whether an array was selected.
'....................................................

Function CheckArray(SampleValue)

   If IsArray(SampleValue) Then
```

```
      MsgBox "You selected an array", 0, "Array Check"
   Else
      MsgBox "This is not an array", 0, "Array Check"
   End If
End Function

-->
</SCRIPT>

<BODY>

  <HR>

  <FONT FACE="Arial" SIZE=2>
  <FONT COLOR=BLACK>

  <BR>
  <CENTER>
  Type a Value (1 or 2): <INPUT NAME=UserValue SIZE=10>

  <BR>
  <BR>
  <INPUT TYPE=BUTTON VALUE="Submit Value" NAME="Submit">

  </CENTER>

</BODY>

</HTML>
```

Example

The Data Validation project at the end of this chapter uses the **IsArray()** function to determine whether the value passed to a function is an array. If the function receives an array, the values within the array are totaled to determine the customer cost.

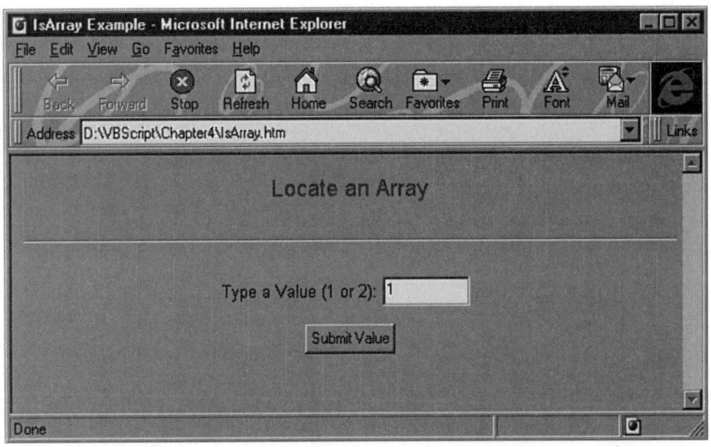

Figure 4-3 The **IsArray()** function determines whether value is an array

Comments The `IsArray()` function is especially useful when working with arrays in VBScript. Since all variables are of the same data type, variant, `IsArray()` verifies that an argument passed to a function contains an array.

For more information about working with arrays, refer to Chapter 6, Array Handling.

See Also `IsEmpty()`, `IsNull()`, `IsNumeric()`, `IsObject()`, `LBound()`, `UBound()`, `VarType()`

IsDate Function

Purpose Use the `IsDate()` function to determine whether the selected expression can be converted to a date or time expression. Table 4-3 describes the expressions that can be used with the `IsDate()` function. Table 4-4 indicates the values returned based upon expression type.

Syntax `IsDate(expression)`

Table 4-3 Argument of the `IsDate()` function

Argument	Description
`expression`	Any date or string expression that can be converted to a valid time or date value

Description A Boolean value of `TRUE` is returned if the specified variable can be converted to a date or time expression; otherwise, a `FALSE` value is returned.

In Listing 4-2, the `IsDate()` function verifies that a user has entered a valid date or time string in a field, as illustrated in Figure 4-4. The user can enter the date and time values in a variety of formats, as indicated in Table 4-4. The `IsDate()` function returns a `TRUE` value as long as the expression can be evaluated as either a date or time value. You should use the `IsDate()` function to make sure a valid date and time has been entered before continuing to process the string. In Listing 4-2, if the user enters an invalid date and the `IsDate()` returns a `FALSE` value, he or she is prompted to enter a valid date value, as illustrated in Figure 4-5.

Listing 4-2 Using the `IsDate()` function

```
<HTML>

<HEAD>
<TITLE>Cyber Clean</TITLE>
</HEAD>

<FONT FACE="Arial" SIZE=2>
<FONT COLOR=Fuchsia>
```

```
<CENTER>
   <FONT SIZE=6>Cyber Clean<P>

   <FONT COLOR=Black>
   <FONT SIZE=4><I>Let Cyber Clean schedule your next house cleaning</I><P>
</CENTER>

<SCRIPT LANGUAGE="VBScript">
<!--
'..................................................
' CheckDate_OnClick()
' If the date entered by user is a valid date, checks
' to see if date is greater than today.
'..................................................

SUB CheckDate_OnClick()
   Dim CleanDate

   CleanDate=CleaningDate.Value

   If IsDate(CleanDate) Then
      If CDate(CleanDate) > Date Then
         MsgBox "Your cleaning has been scheduled.", 0, "Cyber Clean"
      Else
         MsgBox "Please enter a date greater than today.", 0, "Cyber Clean"
      End If
  Else
      MsgBox "Enter a Valid Date.", 0, " Cyber Clean"
  End If

END SUB

-->
</SCRIPT>

<BODY>

<HR>

<FONT FACE="Arial" SIZE=2>
<FONT COLOR=BLACK>

   <BR>
   <CENTER>
    Cleaning Date: <INPUT NAME=CleaningDate SIZE=20>
   <BR><BR>
   <INPUT TYPE=BUTTON VALUE="Schedule" NAME="CheckDate">
   <BR><BR>

   </CENTER>

</BODY>

</HTML>
```

Figure 4-4 The `IsDate()` function verifies that a valid date was entered

Figure 4-5 The `IsDate()` function returns a `FALSE` value if an invalid date is entered

Table 4-4 Boolean values returned by the `IsDate()` function

If the `expression` Is...	The `IsDate()` Function Returns...
hh:mm (`2:00`)	`TRUE`
mm-dd-yy (`05-19-96`)	`TRUE`
mm-dd-yyyy (`05-10-1996`)	`TRUE`
mm/dd/yy (`06/19/96`)	`TRUE`
mm/dd/yyyy (`06/19/1996`)	`TRUE`
Numeric (112296)	`FALSE`
Other string expression	`FALSE`
String that resembles a date (`May 16, 1996`)	`TRUE`

Example The Data Validation project at the end of this chapter uses the `IsDate()` function to verify that the value entered by the customer in the Delivery Date field is a valid date. If `IsDate()` returns a value of `FALSE`, the project prompts the customer to enter a valid date value.

Comments When working in Microsoft Windows, the valid date range is January 1, 100, to December 31, 9999. This range may vary on other operating systems. For more information about dealing with date and time values, refer to Chapter 5, Date and Time Values.

See Also `CDate()`, `IsArray()`, `IsEmpty()`, `IsNull()`, `IsNumeric()`, `IsObject()`, `VarType()`

IsEmpty FUNCTION

Purpose Use the `IsEmpty()` function to determine whether the selected expression has been initialized. Table 4-5 indicates the expressions that can be used with the `IsEmpty()` function.

Syntax `IsEmpty(expression)`

Table 4-5 Argument of the `IsEmpty()` function

Argument	Description
expression	Any single expression

Description The `IsEmpty()` function returns a Boolean value of `TRUE` whether the specified expression has not been initialized; otherwise, a value of `FALSE` is returned if it has been initialized, was explicitly set to empty, or if the expression contains more than one value.

In the example in Listing 4-3, the `IsEmpty()` function checks to see whether the user typed a value in the CleaningDate value field before attempting to process the date. Figure 4-6 illustrates the message that displays on the screen when the user did not type a date in the field.

Listing 4-3 Using the `IsEmpty()` function

```
<HTML>

<HEAD>
<TITLE>Cyber Clean</TITLE>

<FONT FACE="Arial" SIZE=2>
<FONT COLOR=Fuchsia>

<CENTER>
   <FONT SIZE=6>Cyber Clean<P>
   <FONT COLOR=Black>
   <FONT SIZE=4><I>Let Cyber Clean schedule your next house cleaning</I><P>
</CENTER>

<SCRIPT LANGUAGE="VBScript">
<!--
```

continued on next page

continued from previous page

```
'..............................................
' CheckDate_OnClick()
'
' Checks to see that date is greater than today and
' schedule is empty so cleaning can be scheduled.
'..............................................

SUB CheckDate_OnClick()
Dim CleanDate
Dim Schedule

      CleanDate=CleaningDate.Value
      If IsDate(CleanDate) AND IsEmpty(Schedule) Then
         If CDate(CleanDate) > Date Then
            MsgBox "Your cleaning has been scheduled.", 0, "Cyber Clean"
            Schedule=CleanDate
         Else
            MsgBox "Please enter a date greater than today.", 0, "Cyber Clean"
         End If
      Else
         MsgBox "Type a date before selecting the Schedule button", 0, " Date Validation"
      End If

END SUB
-->
</SCRIPT>

</HEAD>

<BODY>

<HR>

<FONT FACE="Arial" SIZE=2>
<FONT COLOR=BLACK>

<BR>
   <CENTER>
    Cleaning Date: <INPUT NAME=CleaningDate SIZE=20>
   <BR><BR>
   <INPUT TYPE=BUTTON VALUE="Schedule" NAME="CheckDate">
   <BR><BR>
   </CENTER>

</BODY>

</HTML>
```

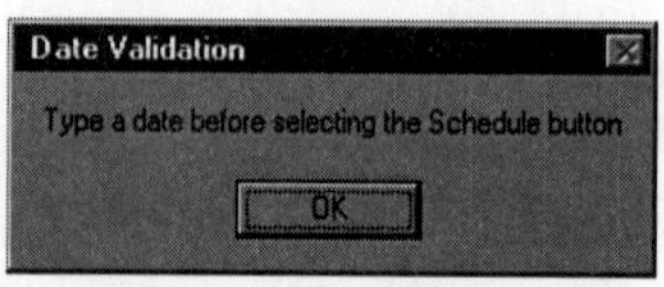

Figure 4-6 The `IsEmpty()` function verifies that a field contains a value

Example The Data Validation project at the end of this chapter uses the `IsEmpty()` function to determine whether a variable has been initialized. The variable `SelOption` is used as a flag to indicate the option selected by the user. If the variable has not been initialized, then the user receives a message requesting a selection.

Comments The `IsEmpty()` function can only check a single variable expression. To see whether multiple expressions have been initialized, call the `IsEmpty()` function for each expression.

The `IsEmpty()` function does not check values returned from HTML `<INPUT>` controls. Even though the field may have been left blank by the user, it still assumes the field has been initialized. To check values returned from these controls, use the `IsNumeric()` function to check for a numeric value, or the `IsDate()` function to check for a date or time value.

See Also `IsArray()`, `IsDate()`, `IsNull()`, `IsNumeric()`, `IsObject()`, `VarType()`

IsNull Function

Purpose Use the `IsNull()` function to determine whether an expression contains a `NULL` value. A `NULL` value means that the expression does not contain valid data. Table 4-6 describes the expressions that can be used with the `IsNull()` function.

Syntax `IsNull(expression)`

Table 4-6 Argument of the `IsNull()` function

Argument	Description
`expression`	Any unique variable can be used with this function.

Description The `IsNull()` function returns a Boolean value of `TRUE` if the specified variable contains a `NULL` value; otherwise, a value of `FALSE` is returned.

In Listing 4-4, the `IsNull()` function checks a variable to see whether it contains a `NULL` variable. The variable is initially set to `NULL` when it is declared. The value of the variable changes when the user enters the correct value. By explicitly setting the value of the variable to `NULL`, the variable becomes a flag that indicates when a specific condition changes, as illustrated in Figure 4-7.

Listing 4-4 Using the `IsNull()` function

```
<HTML>

<HEAD>
<TITLE>IsNull Example</TITLE>
```

continued on next page

continued from previous page

```
<FONT FACE="Arial" SIZE=2>
<FONT COLOR=Fuchsia>

<CENTER>
   <FONT SIZE=6>Positive Number<P>
</CENTER>

<SCRIPT LANGUAGE="VBScript">
<!--

'..................................................
' CheckValue_OnClick()
'
' Uses the Null Value as a Flag to determine if the
' user entered the desired value.
'
'..................................................

SUB CheckValue_OnClick()

  Dim PositiveValue

  PositiveValue=NULL

 If IsNumeric(Number.Value) And Number.Value > 0 Then
   MsgBox "Valid Number", 0, "Positive Number"
   PositiveValue=Number.Value
 End If

 If IsNull(PositiveValue) Then
    MsgBox "Type a Number Larger Than Zero", 0, "Positive Number"
 End If
END SUB
-->
</SCRIPT>

</HEAD>

<BODY>

<HR>

<FONT FACE="Arial" SIZE=2>
<FONT COLOR=BLACK>

<BR>
   <CENTER>
    Enter a Positive Number: <INPUT NAME=Number SIZE=20>
   <BR><BR>
   <INPUT TYPE=BUTTON VALUE="Submit Value" NAME="CheckValue">
   <BR><BR>
   </CENTER>

</BODY>

</HTML>
```

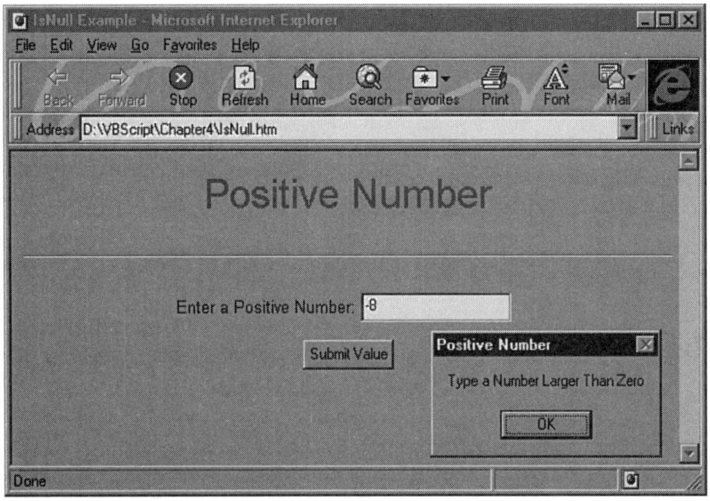

Figure 4-7 The `IsNull()` function checks a variable for a `NULL` value

Example The Data Validation project at the end of this chapter uses the `IsNull()` function to see whether the value of a variable has changed. The variable is initially set to `NULL`. If the value of a field changes in the form, the variable value is changed.

Comments A `NULL` value indicates that the variable does not contain valid data. A `NULL` value is not the same as an empty variable (a variable that has not yet been initialized). It is also not the same as a zero-length string, which is sometimes referred to as a null string.

See Also `IsArray()`, `IsDate()`, `IsEmpty()`, `IsNumeric()`, `IsObject()`, `VarType()`

`IsNumeric` FUNCTION

Purpose Use the `IsNumeric()` function to determine whether an expression can be treated as a numeric value. Table 4-7 describes the expressions that can be used with the `IsNumeric()` function.

Syntax `IsNumeric(expression)`

Table 4-7 Argument of the `IsNumeric()` function

Argument	Description
`expression`	Any unique expression

Description The `IsNumeric()` function allows you to verify that a variable contains a numeric value before you attempt to perform any type of calculation. In

Listing 4-5, the **IsNumeric()** function verifies that a variable contains a numeric value. The function returns a Boolean value of **TRUE** if the specified variable can be converted to a number; otherwise, a value of **FALSE** is returned. The value of each variable is checked before the cost is calculated. If **IsNumeric()** returns **FALSE**, the user is prompted to enter a valid numeric value, as in Figure 4-8.

Listing 4-5 Using the IsNumeric() *function*

```
<HTML>
<HEAD>
<TITLE>Meal Net</TITLE>
<FONT FACE="Arial" SIZE=2>
<FONT COLOR=Aqua>

<CENTER>
   <FONT SIZE=6>Meal Net<P>
   <FONT COLOR=Black>
   <FONT SIZE=4><I>Avoid the long lines - Let us deliver.</I><P>
</CENTER>

<SCRIPT LANGUAGE="VBScript">
<!--
'.........................................................
' ValidateOrder_OnClick()
' Calls each procedure to determine the cost of each item.
'.........................................................

SUB ValidateOrder_OnClick()
   Call HamburgerOrder()
   Call FrenchFriesOrder()
   Call SoftDrinkOrder()
END SUB
'.......................................................
' HamburgerOrder(), FrenchFriesOrder(), SoftDrinkOrder()
'
' Determines if value entered is numeric.  If it
' is, returns a total for it.
'.......................................................

SUB HamburgerOrder()

     If IsNumeric(Burger.Value) Then
       BurgerSum.Value=Burger.Value * 1.25
     Else
       MsgBox "Enter a Number in the Hamburger field.", 0, "Meal Net"
     End If

END SUB

SUB FrenchFriesOrder()

   If IsNumeric(Fries.Value) Then
     FriesSum.Value=Fries.Value * .75
   Else
```

```
    MsgBox "Enter a Number in the French Fries field.", 0, "Meal Net"
  End If

END SUB

SUB SoftDrinkOrder()

  If IsNumeric(Soda.Value) Then
    SodaSum.Value=Soda.Value * .95
  Else
    MsgBox "Enter a Number in the Soft Drink field.", 0, "Meal Net"
  End If

END SUB
-->
</SCRIPT>
</HEAD>

<BODY>

<HR>

<FONT FACE="Times Roman" SIZE=5>
<FONT COLOR=BLACK>
<BR>

  <PRE> <INPUT NAME=Burger VALUE=0 SIZE=10> Hamburger   ($1.25 each)   <INPUT⇐
NAME=BurgerSum VALUE="$0.00" SIZE=10<P> </PRE>
  <PRE> <INPUT NAME=Fries VALUE=0 SIZE=10> French Fries ($0.75 each)  <INPUT⇐
NAME=FriesSum VALUE="$0.00" SIZE=10<P> </PRE>
  <PRE> <INPUT NAME=Soda VALUE=0 SIZE=10> Soft Drink  ($0.95 each)   <INPUT⇐
NAME=SodaSum VALUE="$0.00" SIZE=10<P> </PRE>

  <CENTER>
  <BR><BR>
      <INPUT TYPE=BUTTON VALUE="Order Meal" NAME="ValidateOrder">
  </CENTER>

</BODY>
</HTML>
```

Example

The Data Validation project at the end of this chapter uses the `IsNumeric()` function to verify that numeric values have been entered in fields on the form.

Comments

The `IsNumeric()` function will return a value of `FALSE` if the expression is a date expression.

To avoid runtime errors, it is important to verify that a variable contains a numeric value before attempting to perform any type of mathematical calculations with the value. The variable may also need to be converted. Refer to Chapter 7, Data Conversion, for more information about data conversion.

See Also

`IsArray()`, `IsDate()`, `IsEmpty()`, `IsNull()`, `IsObject()`, `VarType()`

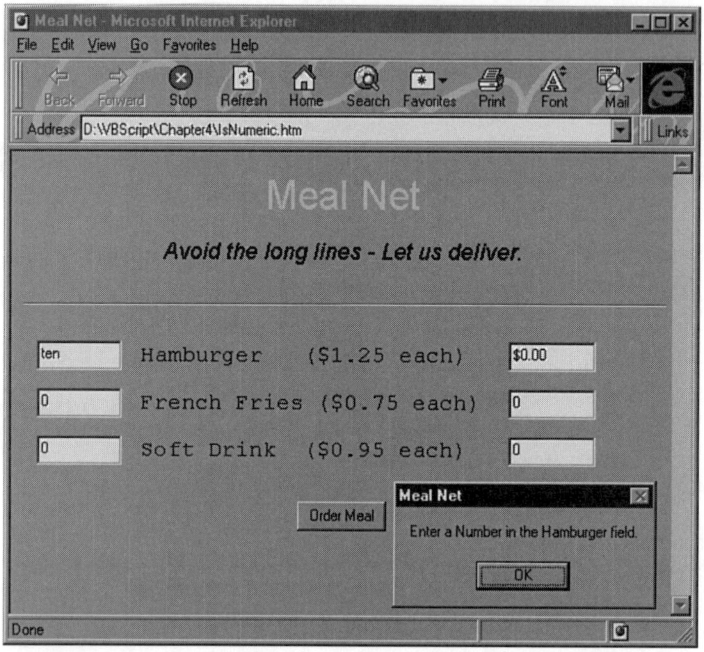

Figure 4-8 The `IsNumeric()` function verifies that numeric values are entered in each field; a message displays when a nonnumeric value is entered

`IsObject` FUNCTION

Purpose Use the `IsObject()` function to determine whether an expression references a valid OLE automation object. Table 4-8 describes the expressions that can be used with the `IsObject()` function.

Syntax `IsObject(expression)`

Table 4-8 Argument of the `IsObject()` function

Argument	Description
`expression`	Any unique variant expression

Description The `IsObject()` function returns a Boolean value of `TRUE` if the specified variant expression has an object subtype or is a user-defined object; otherwise, a value of `FALSE` is returned. This function is used to make sure an object resides on a client machine before attempting to access it.

In Listing 4-6, the `IsObject()` checks for an object before VBScript attempts to modify its settings. Figure 4-9 illustrates the result when a valid object is referenced.

Listing 4-6 Using the `IsObject()` function

```
<HTML>

<HEAD>

<TITLE>IsObject Example</TITLE>

<SCRIPT LANGUAGE="VBScript">
<!--
'...........................................................
' RotText_OnClick()
'
' Checks to make sure there is a valid object referenced;
' if so, rotates the text.
'..........................................................

SUB RotText_OnClick()
  Dim EntryForm
  Set EntryForm=Document.ActiveXLabel

  If IsNumeric(EntryForm.txtNewText.Value) Then
    If IsObject(lblActiveLbl) Then
      lblActiveLbl.Angle = EntryForm.txtNewText.Value
    End If
  Else
    MsgBox "Enter a Numeric Value"
  End If
END SUB
-->
</SCRIPT>

<OBJECT
       classid="clsid:99B42120-6EC7-11CF-A6C7-00AA00A47DD2"
       id=lblActiveLbl
       width=100
       height=850
       align=left
       hspace=20
       vspace=0
>
<PARAM NAME="_extentX" VALUE="550">
<PARAM NAME="_extentY" VALUE="700">
<PARAM NAME="Angle" VALUE="45">
<PARAM NAME="Alignment" VALUE="2">
<PARAM NAME="BackStyle" VALUE="0">
<PARAM NAME="Caption" VALUE="Text">
<PARAM NAME="FontName" VALUE="Arial">
<PARAM NAME="FontSize" VALUE="20">
<PARAM NAME="FontBold" VALUE="1">
<PARAM NAME="FrColor" VALUE="0">
</OBJECT>

</HEAD>

<BODY>
```

continued on next page

continued from previous page

```
<FORM NAME="ActiveXLabel">

<INPUT TYPE="TEXT" NAME="txtNewText" SIZE=25>
<INPUT TYPE="BUTTON" NAME="RotText" VALUE="Rotate Text Label">

</FORM>
</BODY>
</HTML>
```

Comments For more information about dealing with objects, refer to Chapter 12, Adding Objects.

See Also `IsArray()`, `IsDate()`, `IsEmpty()`, `IsNull()`, `IsNumeric()`, `VarType()`

`VarType` FUNCTION

Purpose Use the `VarType()` function to determine the subtype of the specified variant expression. Table 4-9 describes the argument for this function. Table 4-10 outlines the return values for the `VarType()` function.

Syntax `VarType(expression)`

Table 4-9 Argument of the `VarType()` function

Argument	Description
`expression`	Any variant expression can be used with this function.

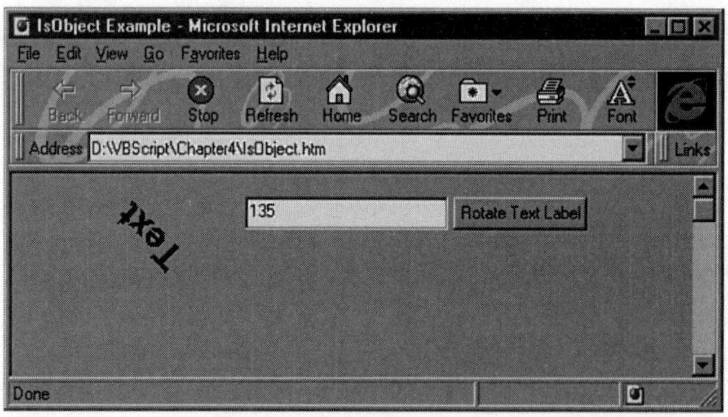

Figure 4-9 The `IsObject()` makes sure the object referenced is valid

Table 4-10 Return values for the `VarType()` function

If Subtype of...	`VarType` Returns...	Description
Empty	0	Variable has not been initialized.
Null	1	Variable does not contain valid data.
Integer	2	Integer value in the range -2,147,483,648 to 2,147,483,647.
Long	3	Integer value in the range -2,147,483,648 to 2,147,483,647.
Single	4	Single-precision, floating-point number in the range -3.402823E38 to -1.401298E-45 for negative values; 1.401298E-45 to 3.402823E38 for positive values.
Double	5	Double-precision, floating-point number in the range -1.79769313486232E308 to -4.94065645841247E-324 for negative values; 4.94065645841247E-324 to 1.79769313486232E308 for positive values.
Currency	6	Currency value.
Date	7	Date value in the range of January 1, 100, to December 31, 9999, for Microsoft Windows. Other platforms may have different date ranges.
String	8	String of variable length. The maximum length is approximately two billion characters.
Object	9	An OLE automation object.
Error	10	An error number.
Boolean	11	A Boolean value of `TRUE` or `FALSE`.
Variant	12	Used with an array of variants.
Non-OLE object	13	An non-OLE automation object.
Byte	14	Integer value in the range of 0 to 255.
Array	8192	An array.

Description The `VarType()` function checks the subtype of a variant expression and returns one of the values in Table 4-10 indicating the expression's subtype.

In Listing 4-7, the `VarType()` function determines the value type of an expression passed to the `CheckValue()` function. The user receives a message indicating the subtype of the selected expression, as illustrated in Figure 4-10.

Listing 4-7 Using the `VarType()` function

```
<HTML>

<HEAD>
<TITLE>VarType Example</TITLE>

<SCRIPT LANGUAGE="VBScript">
<!--
'..................................................
' SpecifyVal() Procedures
```

continued on next page

continued from previous page

```
' Sets selection value and calls CheckValue function
'...............................................

SUB SpecifyVal1()
Dim Val1

 Val1="One Hundred Dollars"
 Call CheckValue(Val1)

END SUB

SUB SpecifyVal2()
Dim Val2

 Val2=100
 Call CheckValue(Val2)

END SUB

SUB SpecifyVal3()
Dim Val3

 Val3=125.35
 Call CheckValue(Val3)

END SUB

SUB SpecifyVal4()
Dim Val4

 Val4= 02/15/96
 Call CheckValue(Val4)

END SUB

'..........................
' CheckValue()
' Determines the type of
' value selected.
'..........................

Function CheckValue(SelVal)

   If VarType(SelVal) = 0 Then MsgBox "Variable is Empty"
   If VarType(SelVal) = 1 Then MsgBox "Null Value"
   If VarType(SelVal) = 2 Then MsgBox "Integer Value"
   If VarType(SelVal) = 3 Then MsgBox "Long Integer Value"
   If VarType(SelVal) = 4 Then MsgBox "Single-Precision Floating Point"
   If VarType(SelVal) = 5 Then MsgBox "Double-Precision Floating Point"
   If VarType(SelVal) = 6 Then MsgBox "Currency Value"
   If VarType(SelVal) = 7 Then MsgBox "Date Value"
   If VarType(SelVal) = 8 Then MsgBox "String"
   If VarType(SelVal) = 9 Then MsgBox "OLE Object"
   If VarType(SelVal) = 10 Then MsgBox "Error"
   If VarType(SelVal) = 11 Then MsgBox "Boolean Value"
   If VarType(SelVal) = 12 Then MsgBox "Variant Array"
   If VarType(SelVal) = 13 Then MsgBox "Non-OLE object"
   If VarType(SelVal) = 14 Then MsgBox "Byte"
```

```
  If VarType(SelVal) = 8192 Then MsgBox "An Array"

End Function
-->

</SCRIPT>
</HEAD>

<BODY>

<FONT FACE="Arial" SIZE=2>
<FONT COLOR=Fuchsia>

<CENTER>
   <FONT SIZE=6>Select an Expression<P>
</CENTER>
<HR>

<FONT FACE="Arial" SIZE=2>
<FONT COLOR=BLACK>

<TABLE XBORDER=1 WIDTH=725 ALIGN=MIDDLE>
<TR><TD> <INPUT TYPE="RADIO" NAME="VarExp" OnClick="SpecifyVal1"></TD>
       <TD>One Hundred Dollars</TD></TR>
<TR><TD> <INPUT TYPE="RADIO" NAME="VarExp" OnClick="SpecifyVal2"></TD>
       <TD>100</TD></TR>
<TR><TD> <INPUT TYPE="RADIO" NAME="VarExp" OnClick="SpecifyVal3"></TD>
       <TD>125.35</TD></TR>
<TR><TD> <INPUT TYPE="RADIO" NAME="VarExp" OnClick="SpecifyVal4"></TD>
       <TD>2/15/96</TD></TR>
</TABLE>

</BODY>

</HTML>
```

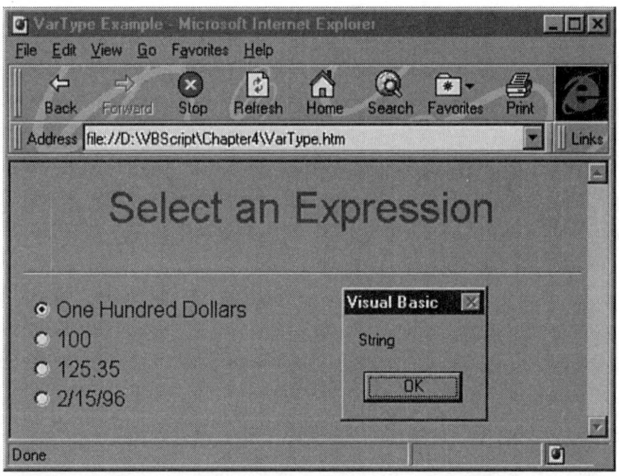

Figure 4-10 The `VarType()` function determines the type of data stored in a variable

Comments

If the VarType() function encounters an array value, it returns a value that is the array value of 8192 plus another value indicating the type of elements in the array. For example, if VarType() finds an array of integers, the value 8194 (8192 + 2) is returned. If an object has a default property, VarType(object) returns the type of its default property.

Because the values passed to VBScript from an HTML <INPUT> control are always strings, the VarType() function will always return a value of 8 when used to check these controls. This function is designed to check values within the VBScript code.

See Also

IsArray(), IsDate(), IsEmpty(), IsNull(), IsNumeric(), IsObject()

Data Validation Project

The Data Validation project demonstrates the concepts of validating user input on the client machine. The project takes you step by step through the process of designing an entry form that validates user data using the functions described in this chapter.

Building the Project

1. Start the project by setting up the standard HTML template used for all VBScript examples in this book. The VBScript code is placed in the <HEAD> section of the HTML code to keep everything consistent. Remember to place the HTML comment tags <!-- and --> around the VBScript code so that it will be ignored by browsers that cannot interpret the <SCRIPT> tag.

```
<HTML>

<HEAD>
<TITLE>Data Validation Project</TITLE>

<SCRIPT LANGUAGE="VBScript">

<!--

-->

</SCRIPT>

</HEAD>

<BODY>

</BODY>

</HTML>
```

2. In the <BODY> section, place the desired title information for the Web page. For this example, you are creating a Web page where customers can order a box of chocolates, so this information is indicated by the titles.

```
<BODY>

<CENTER>
   <FONT FACE="Arial" SIZE=6>
   <FONT COLOR="Brown">Chocolate Express<P>

   <FONT COLOR="White">
   <FONT SIZE=3>Order a Box of 12 Chocolates

</CENTER>
```

3. Design an HTML form containing a table for receiving the user input. Create a table containing radio buttons allowing customers to select either a standard or a custom box of chocolates, as illustrated in Figure 4-11.

```
<FORM Name="OrderForm">

<TABLE XBORDER=1 WIDTH=725 ALIGN=MIDDLE>
   <TR><TD> <INPUT TYPE="RADIO" NAME="CHOCBOX" OnClick="SelStandardBox"></TD>
       <TD WIDTH=10><B>Standard</B></TD>
       <TD><I>(Contains 2 of each flavor  $11.25/box)</TD></I></TR>
<TR><TD><INPUT TYPE="RADIO" NAME="CHOCBOX" OnClick="SelCustomBox"></TD>
    <TD WIDTH=10><B>Custom</B></TD>
    <TD><I>(Indicate desired amount of each flavor - 12 total)</I></TD></TR>
</TABLE>
```

4. Enter the VBScript code in the <HEAD> section to determine which radio button the user selects. This example is designed to use a global flag, **SelOption**, that keeps track of whether or not the user has selected a box of chocolates.

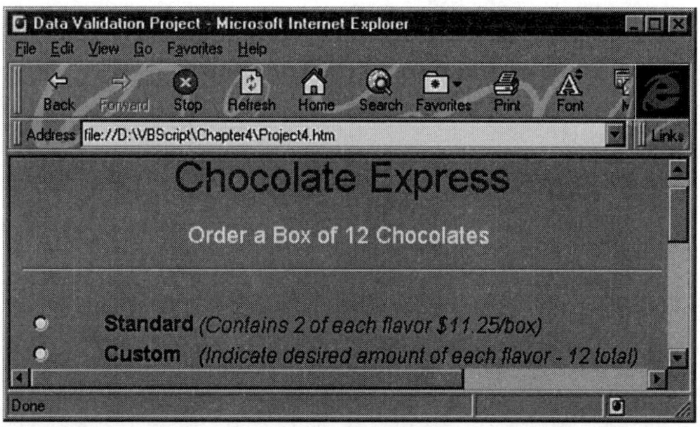

Figure 4-11 Radio buttons allowing user to select one of the boxes of chocolates

```
<SCRIPT LANGUAGE="VBScript">
<!--
Dim SelOption

SUB SelStandardBox()

 SelOption = 0

END SUB

SUB SelCustomBox()

   SelOption = 1

END SUB
```

5. In the <BODY> section, create table rows that contain the flavors that can be selected for the custom box of chocolate. The user types a value in the field next to the description that indicates the number of each flavor that he or she would like in the custom box.

```
<TR><TD></TD><TD WIDTH=10><INPUT NAME=Caramel VALUE=0 SIZE=3></TD>
<TD><B>Caramel</B>       ($1.00/each)</TD></TR>
<TR><TD></TD><TD WIDTH=10><INPUT NAME=Cherry VALUE=0 SIZE=3></TD>
    <TD><B>Cherry</B>     ($1.25/each)</TD></TR>
<TR><TD></TD><TD WIDTH=10><INPUT NAME=Mint VALUE=0 SIZE=3></TD>
    <TD><B>Mint</B>       ($0.95/each) </TD></TR>
<TR><TD></TD><TD WIDTH=10><INPUT NAME=Strawberry VALUE=0 SIZE=3></TD>
    <TD><B>Strawberry</B> ($1.15/each)</TD></TR>
<TR><TD></TD><TD WIDTH=10><INPUT NAME=Truffle VALUE=0 SIZE=3></TD>
    <TD><B>Truffle</B>    ($1.30/each)</TD></TR>
<TR><TD></TD><TD WIDTH=10><INPUT NAME=Solid VALUE=0 SIZE=3></TD>
    <TD><B>Solid</B>      ($0.75/each)</TD>
```

6. In the <BODY> section, add a field that informs the user of the total cost of the box of chocolates that he or she has selected. This field is changed when the user selects the Calculate Box Cost button. The field is added to the table so that it displays on the last row. The Calculate Box Cost button displays centered below the table. Figure 4-12 illustrates how the input fields and Calculate Box Cost button display on the page.

```
<TD><B>Box Cost = </B><INPUT NAME=BoxCost VALUE="$0.00" SIZE=10></TD></TR>
</TABLE>

<!--
<CENTER>
<INPUT TYPE=BUTTON VALUE="Calculate Box Cost" Name="CalcTotalCost">
</CENTER>
```

7. In the <HEAD> section, create a procedure that performs the necessary calculations to place the total cost of the box of chocolates in the Box Cost field. Use the `IsEmpty()` function to make sure that the user selects a box type. If none is selected, send a message that instructs the user to select a type. If the user selects

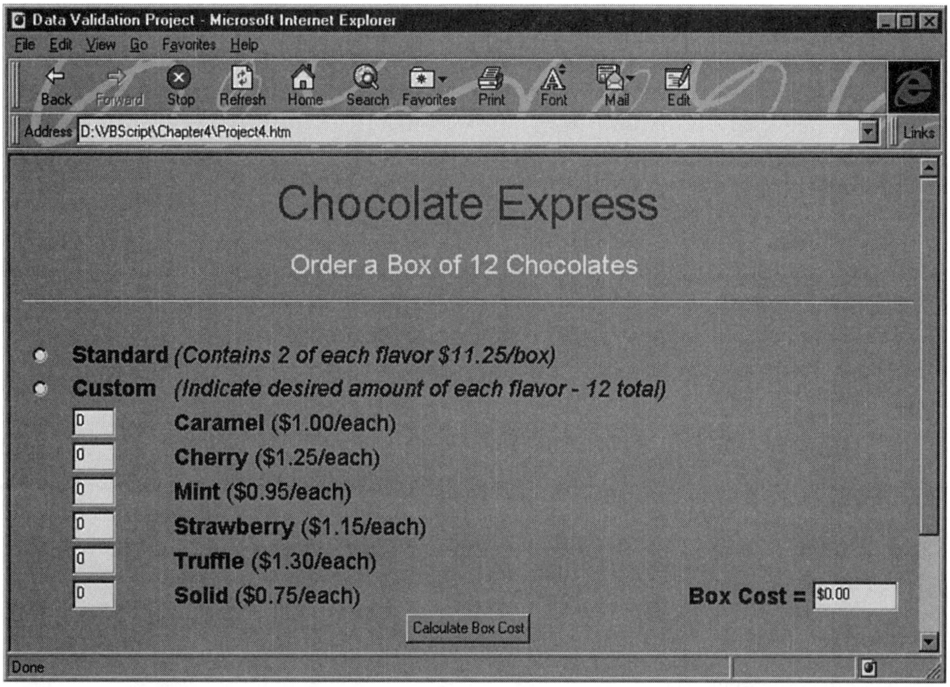

Figure 4-12 The input fields allow the user to indicate the desired number of each flavor

a Standard box, the procedure calls the **`CalcCost()`** function with a value of $11.25.

If the user selects a Custom box, the **`IsNumeric()`** function verifies that a numeric value was typed in each flavor field. If the field contains a numeric value, multiply the value by the cost of that chocolate flavor and assign the flavor cost to the appropriate element of the **`CustCost`** array. Determine the cost of each flavor and pass the **`CustCost`** array to the **`CalcCost()`** function.

```
SUB CalcTotalCost_OnClick()
 Dim StanCost
 Dim CustCost(6)
 Dim ChocForm

 Set ChocForm = Document.OrderForm

   If IsEmpty(SelOption) Then
      MsgBox "Select a box type (Standard or Custom)"
   End If

   If SelOption = 0 Then
      StanCost=11.25
      Call CalcCost(StanCost)
   End If
```

continued on next page

continued from previous page

```
   If SelOption = 1 Then
      If IsNumeric(ChocForm.Caramel.Value) Then
         CustCost(0) = ChocForm.Caramel.Value * 1.00
      End If

      If IsNumeric(ChocForm.Cherry.Value) Then
         CustCost(1) = ChocForm.Cherry.Value * 1.25
      End If

      If IsNumeric(ChocForm.Mint.Value) Then
         CustCost(2) = ChocForm.Mint.Value * .95
      End If

      If IsNumeric(ChocForm.Strawberry.Value) Then
         CustCost(3) = ChocForm.Strawberry.Value * 1.15
      End If

      If IsNumeric(ChocForm.Truffle.Value) Then
         CustCost(4) = ChocForm.Truffle.Value * 1.30
      End If

      If IsNumeric(ChocForm.Solid.Value) Then
         CustCost(5) = ChocForm.Solid.Value * .75
      End If

      CalcCost(CustCost)
    End If

END SUB
```

8. Create a function called **CalcCost()** that determines the box cost and places the value in the Box Cost field. Use the **IsArray()** function to determine whether **CalcCost()** received an array value. If **BoxValue** is an array, create a **For** loop to calculate the total cost of the box by adding the values in the array and placing the total cost in the Total Cost field. If **BoxValue** is not an array, place its value in the Total Cost field.

```
Function CalcCost(BoxValue)
Dim TotalCost
 Dim Count

 If IsArray(BoxValue) Then

   For Count = 0 To 5
      TotalCost=TotalCost + CSng(BoxValue(Count))
   Next

   Document.OrderForm.BoxCost.Value = "$" + CStr(TotalCost)

 Else
   Document.OrderForm.BoxCost.Value = "$" + CStr(BoxValue)
 End If

End Function
```

9. In the <BODY> section, create a field where the user can specify the desired delivery date for the chocolates. A horizontal rule is placed above the date to separate it from the table.

```
<HR>
<FONT SIZE=3>Delivery Date: <INPUT NAME="DelDate" SIZE=10>
```

10. Create a button that the user presses when the order is complete and ready for processing.

```
<CENTER>

<INPUT TYPE=BUTTON VALUE="Place Chocolate Order" NAME="CheckDate">

</CENTER>
<BR>
```

11. Create a procedure that uses that `IsDate()` function to make sure a valid date was typed in the Delivery Date field. Create an `If` statement that makes sure a chocolate box has been specified by checking the Box Cost field. If it contains a value, a flag is set. Use the `IsNull()` function to check the flag to make sure a box has been selected before accepting the order.

```
SUB CheckDate_OnClick()

 Dim CheckSel

 CheckSel = NULL

 If (Document.OrderForm.BoxCost.Value) <> "$0.00" Then
    CheckSel = 1
 End If

 If IsDate(Document.OrderForm.DelDate.Value) Then
    If NOT IsNull(CheckSel) Then
       MsgBox "Order has been processed"
    Else
       MsgBox "Select a box of chocolates before ordering"
    End If
 Else
    MsgBox "You must enter a delivery date before your order can be processed"
 End If

END SUB
```

How It Works

The Data Validation project provides the ability to select either a custom or standard box of chocolates. If a custom box is selected, the user indicates the quantity of each flavor that he or she wants in the box. Once a box type is selected, the Calculate Box Cost button determines the cost of the box of chocolates.

If the user is satisfied with the cost, he or she types a delivery date in the Delivery Date field and selects the Place Chocolate Order button. VBScript verifies that a box

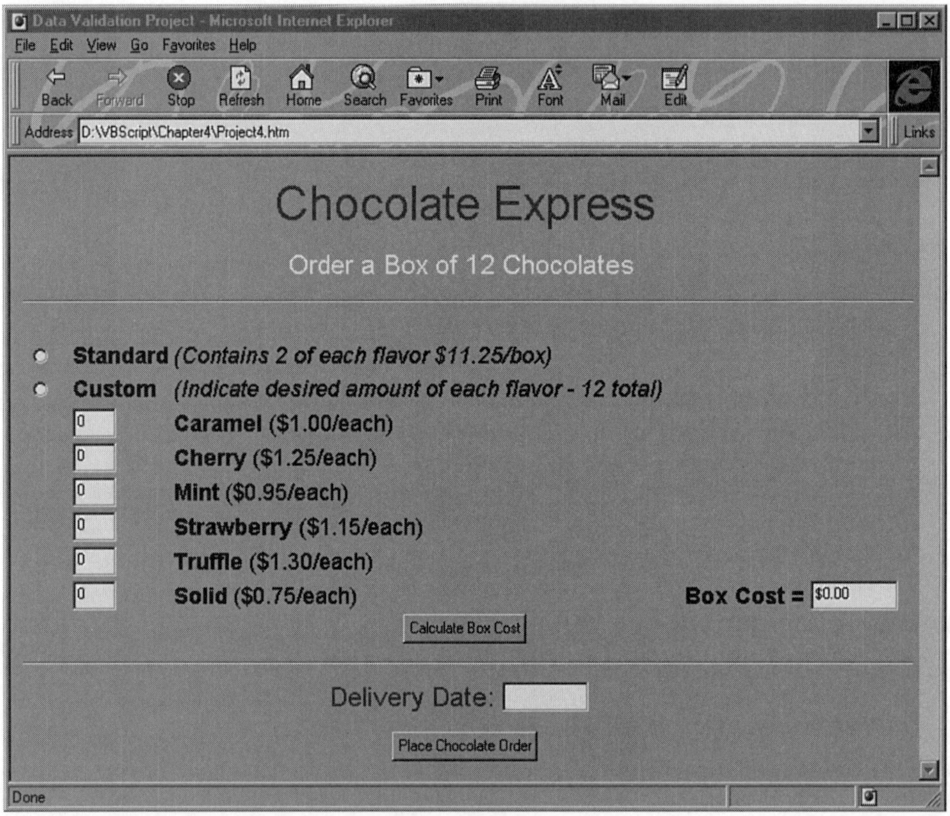

Figure 4-13 The completed Data Validation project

was selected and a valid date was entered. If the order is valid, the user receives a message indicating that the order has been placed; otherwise, he or she is instructed to make the necessary changes to the order. Figure 4-13 illustrates the completed Data Validation project, and Listing 4-8 contains the complete source code.

Listing 4-8 Complete source for the Data Validation project

```
<HTML>

<HEAD>
<TITLE>Data Validation Project</TITLE>

<SCRIPT LANGUAGE="VBScript">
<!--
'.........................................................................
' SelOption
' global variable that keeps track of whether the user has selected a box type
'.........................................................................
Dim SelOption
'............................................................
```

```
' SelStandardBox()
' Called when user selects a Standard box to set SelOption to 0
'..............................................................

SUB SelStandardBox()

 SelOption = 0

END SUB
'............................................................
' SelCustomBox()
' Called when user selects a Custom box to set SelOption to 1
'............................................................

SUB SelCustomBox()

   SelOption = 1

END SUB

'..............................................................................
' CalcTotalCost_OnClick()
' Based on box type selected determines the value passed to the CalcCost
' function.
'..............................................................................

SUB CalcTotalCost_OnClick()
 Dim StanCost
 Dim CustCost(6)
 Dim ChocForm

 Set ChocForm = Document.OrderForm

'.....................................
' Make sure box type was selected
'.....................................
   If IsEmpty(SelOption) Then
      MsgBox "Select a box type (Standard or Custom)"
   End If

'......................................................................
' If Standard box selected, passes value of 11.25 to CalcCost function.
'......................................................................

   If SelOption = 0 Then
      StanCost=11.25
      Call CalcCost(StanCost)
   End If

'..........................................................................
' If Custom Cost selected, checks each flavor field for a numeric value,
' calculates the cost of each flavor, and places the costs in an array that
' is passed to the CalcCost function.
'..........................................................................

   If SelOption = 1 Then
      If IsNumeric(ChocForm.Caramel.Value) Then
         CustCost(0) = ChocForm.Caramel.Value * 1.00
```

continued on next page

continued from previous page

```
      Else
         MsgBox "Type a numeric Value in the Caramel field"
      End If

      If IsNumeric(ChocForm.Cherry.Value) Then
         CustCost(1) = ChocForm.Cherry.Value * 1.25
      End If

      If IsNumeric(ChocForm.Mint.Value) Then
         CustCost(2) = ChocForm.Mint.Value * .95
      End If

      If IsNumeric(ChocForm.Strawberry.Value) Then
         CustCost(3) = ChocForm.Strawberry.Value * 1.15
      End If

      If IsNumeric(ChocForm.Truffle.Value) Then
         CustCost(4) = ChocForm.Truffle.Value * 1.30
      End If

      If IsNumeric(ChocForm.Solid.Value) Then
         CustCost(5) = ChocForm.Solid.Value * .75
      End If

      CalcCost(CustCost)
    End If

END SUB

'....................................................
' CalcCost()
' Determines the value placed in the Box Cost field.
'....................................................

Function CalcCost(BoxValue)
Dim TotalCost
 Dim Count

'..................................................................
' If value passed is an array, the values in the array are totaled.
'..................................................................

 If IsArray(BoxValue) Then

   For Count = 0 To 5
      TotalCost=TotalCost + CSng(BoxValue(Count))
   Next

   Document.OrderForm.BoxCost.Value = "$" + CStr(TotalCost)

'.......................................................
' If the value passes was not an array, it is the cost.
'.......................................................
Else
   Document.OrderForm.BoxCost.Value = "$" + CStr(BoxValue)
 End If

End Function
```

```
'.....................................................................
' CheckDate_OnClick()
' Makes sure a valid delivery date was entered and that a box of
' chocolates has been selected. Places the order, if everything is valid.
'.....................................................................

SUB CheckDate_OnClick()

 Dim CheckSel

 CheckSel = NULL

 If (Document.OrderForm.BoxCost.Value) <> "$0.00" Then
    CheckSel = 1
 End If

 If IsDate(Document.OrderForm.DelDate.Value) Then
    If NOT IsNull(CheckSel) Then
       MsgBox "Order has been processed"
    Else
       MsgBox "Select a box of chocolates before ordering"
    End If
 Else
    MsgBox "You must enter a delivery date before your order can be processed"
 End If

END SUB
-->
</SCRIPT>
</HEAD>
<BODY>

<CENTER>
   <FONT FACE="Arial" SIZE=6>
   <FONT COLOR="Brown">Chocolate Express<P>

   <FONT COLOR="White">
   <FONT SIZE=3>Order a Box of 12 Chocolates
</CENTER>

<HR>

<FONT SIZE=2>
<FONT COLOR="Brown">

<FORM Name="OrderForm">

<TABLE XBORDER=1 WIDTH=725 ALIGN=MIDDLE>
 <TR><TD> <INPUT TYPE="RADIO" NAME="CHOCBOX" OnClick="SelStandardBox"></TD>
       <TD WIDTH=10><B>Standard</B></TD>
       <TD><I>(Contains 2 of each flavor  $11.25/box)</TD></I></TR>
 <TR><TD><INPUT TYPE="RADIO" NAME="CHOCBOX" OnClick="SelCustomBox"></TD>
    <TD WIDTH=10><B>Custom</B></TD>
    <TD><I>(Indicate desired amount of each flavor - 12 total)</I></TD></TR>
 <TR><TD></TD><TD WIDTH=10><INPUT NAME=Caramel VALUE=0 SIZE=3></TD>
    <TD><B>Caramel</B>      ($1.00/each)</TD></TR>
 <TR><TD></TD><TD WIDTH=10><INPUT NAME=Cherry VALUE=0 SIZE=3></TD>
    <TD><B>Cherry</B>     ($1.25/each)</TD></TR>
```

continued on next page

continued from previous page

```
 <TR><TD></TD><TD WIDTH=10><INPUT NAME=Mint VALUE=0 SIZE=3></TD>
    <TD><B>Mint</B>       ($0.95/each) </TD></TR>
 <TR><TD></TD><TD WIDTH=10><INPUT NAME=Strawberry VALUE=0 SIZE=3></TD>
    <TD><B>Strawberry</B> ($1.15/each)</TD></TR>
 <TR><TD></TD><TD WIDTH=10><INPUT NAME=Truffle VALUE=0 SIZE=3></TD>
    <TD><B>Truffle</B>    ($1.30/each)</TD></TR>
 <TR><TD></TD><TD WIDTH=10><INPUT NAME=Solid VALUE=0 SIZE=3></TD>
    <TD><B>Solid</B>      ($0.75/each)</TD>
    <TD><B>Box Cost = </B><INPUT NAME=BoxCost VALUE="$0.00" SIZE=10></TD></TR>
</TABLE>

<CENTER>
<INPUT TYPE=BUTTON VALUE="Calculate Box Cost" NAME="CalcTotalCost">
</CENTER>

<HR>
<FONT SIZE=3>Delivery Date: <INPUT NAME="DelDate" SIZE=10>

<CENTER>
<INPUT TYPE=BUTTON VALUE="Place Chocolate Order" NAME="CheckDate">
</CENTER>

</FORM>

</BODY>
</HTML>
```

5

DATE AND TIME VALUES

5

DATE AND TIME VALUES

Developing a Web site that requires you to keep track of date and time values is quite common. These values may be supplied by the user or the system. VBScript provides several functions that allow you to easily capture and manipulate dates and times.

VBScript Date and Time Values

Since all variables in VBScript are variants, date and time values are stored as variants with a subtype of date. When a date or time value is captured from HTML, VBScript treats it as a string until it is converted to a date, using either the **DateValue()** function for a date, or the **TimeValue()** function for a time expression.

It is important to make sure that a variable contains a valid date before attempting to convert or manipulate it. Using the **IsDate()** function, covered in Chapter 4, Data Validation, you can quickly check a date value. The following code illustrates how to make sure a variable contains a date value.

```
SUB CheckDate

  If IsDate(UserDate) Then
    Call ProcessDate
  Else
    MsgBox "Enter a Valid Date"
  End If

END SUB
```

Valid Date and Time Expressions

VBScript can work with date and time expressions in a variety of formats. The date and time formats that can be used with each function are described in this chapter. Table 5-1 provides a list of the basic formats that can be used with most time and date functions.

Table 5-1 Time and date formats for VBScript

Format	Example
hh:mm:ss	2:32:45
hh:mm:ss AM	2:34:45 AM
hh:mm:ss (military)	14:34:45
hh:mm:ss pm	2:32:45 pm
mm-dd-yy	6-12-96
mm-dd-yyyy	6-12-1996
mm/dd/yy	6/12/96
mm/dd/yyyy	6/12/1996
month dd, yyyy	June 12, 1996

Acceptable Date Ranges

VBScript allows you to work with dates within the range of January 1, 100, through December 31, 9999. Any dates outside of this range are considered invalid.

If a year value is entered between 00 and 99, Visual Basic converts it to a year value within the twentieth century (1900–1999). This is an important point to note as we approach the year 2000. Any dates entered with a two-digit year of 00 will be considered to be the year 1900. It is important to inform users that they need to type all four digits of the year if it exceeds the year 1999.

Summary of Date and Time Values Functions

Table 5-2 summarizes the date and time functions provided by VBScript. The chapter contains a detailed description of each function with sample syntax that illustrates the function's use. The Date and Time Values project at the end of the chapter demonstrates how to use most of these functions to work with date and time values from the system and user.

Table 5-2 Date and time values function summary

Use...	To Do This...
`Date`	Return the system date
`DateSerial`	Create a date value in the mm/dd/yyyy format
`DateValue`	Convert a string to a variant of subtype of date in an mm/dd/yyyy format
`Day`	Determine the day of the month
`Hour`	Determine the hour of the day based on military time format (0 to 23)
`IsDate`	Determine whether the specified variable is a date or time value
`Minute`	Determine the minute portion of a time expression
`Month`	Return the month value from a date expression
`Now`	Return the system date and time
`Second`	Determine the second portion of a time expression
`Time`	Return the system time
`TimeSerial`	Obtain a time value in the format hh:mm:ss based on the values supplied for the hour, minutes, and seconds
`TimeValue`	Convert a string that expresses a time to a variant with a date subtype
`Weekday`	Return a value between 1 and 7 that represents the day of the week
`Year`	Return the year value from a date expression

`Date` FUNCTION

Purpose Use the `Date()` function to capture the current system date.

Syntax `Date()`

Description The `Date()` function allows you to capture the current system date from the user's machine. This function helps to ensure that the user's current date displays on the screen.

In Listing 5-1, the `Date()` function captures and displays the system date on the screen. The `Document.Write` method is used to display the date on the document page, as illustrated in Figure 5-1. Use of this method allows VBScript to place information directly onto the document. For more information about the `Document` object, refer to Chapter 15, Internet Explorer Object Model for Scripting.

Listing 5-1 Using the `Date()` function

```
<HTML>

<HEAD><TITLE>Date Example</TITLE></HEAD>

<BODY BGCOLOR="White">

<FONT SIZE=10>
```

continued on next page

continued from previous page

```
<SCRIPT LANGUAGE="VBScript">
<!--
'.......................................................
' Since this VBScript code resides in the body of the
' HTML document, it automatically executes when the
' page is loaded. The system date is checked and written
' to the page by referencing the HTML Document object.
'.......................................................

   Document.Write "Today's date is... "
   Document.Write Date()

-->

</SCRIPT>

</FONT>

</BODY>

</HTML>
```

Example The project at the end of this chapter uses the `Date()` function to capture the system date. The date is placed on the screen using the `Document` object method. The `Date()` function is also used to capture the system date and compare it to the date typed in the Departure Date field by the user.

See Also `CDate()`, `Now()`, `Time()`

DateSerial FUNCTION

Purpose Use the `DateSerial()` function to obtain a date value in the format mm/dd/yyyy based on values supplied for the month, day, and year. Table 5-3 describes the expressions that can be used with the `DateSerial()` function.

Syntax `DateSerial( YearValue, MonthValue, DayValue )`

Figure 5-1 The `Date()` function captures the system date

Table 5-3 Arguments of the DateSerial() function

Argument	Description
YearValue	Any numeric expression between 0 and 9999. Values in the range of 0 through 99 are interpreted by VBScript as the years 1900 through 1999.
MonthValue	Any numeric expression.
DayValue	Any numeric expression.

Description The **DateSerial()** function returns a date expression in the range of 1/1/100 through 12/31/9999. In Listing 5-2, the **DateSerial()** function uses the values entered into the document to create a date value. The new date value is returned using the **MsgBox()** function, as illustrated in Figure 5-2.

Listing 5-2 Using the DateSerial() *function*

```
<HTML>

<HEAD>

<TITLE>DateSerial Example</TITLE>

<SCRIPT LANGUAGE="VBScript">
<!--
'..........................................................
' CreateDate_OnClick()
' Creates a date using the values input by the user. The
' function is called when the user clicks the Create Date
' button on the screen.
'..........................................................
SUB CreateDate_OnClick()

 Dim UserDate

 UserDate=DateSerial(UserYear.Value,UserMonth.Value,UserDay.Value)

 MsgBox "The Date is " & UserDate

END SUB
-->

</SCRIPT>
</HEAD>

<BODY>

<CENTER>

<FONT SIZE=6>Date Creation<P>
</CENTER>
<HR>
```

continued on next page

continued from previous page

```
<FONT SIZE=4>

<PRE>Enter Month: <INPUT NAME=UserMonth SIZE=10>
<BR>
  Enter Day: <INPUT NAME=UserDay SIZE=10>
<BR>
 Enter Year: <INPUT NAME=UserYear SIZE=10></PRE>

<HR>
<CENTER>
<INPUT TYPE=BUTTON VALUE="Create Date" NAME="CreateDate">
</CENTER>

</FONT>

</BODY>

</HTML>
```

Comments The **DateSerial()** function uses the date December 31, 1899, as a basis for all dates created. Therefore, if a negative value is typed for any of the three expressions (month, day, year), the **DateSerial()** function uses the base date values of **12/31/1899** to calculate the desired date. For example, if the month value is **-2**, the day **20**, and the year **1994**, the **DateSerial()**

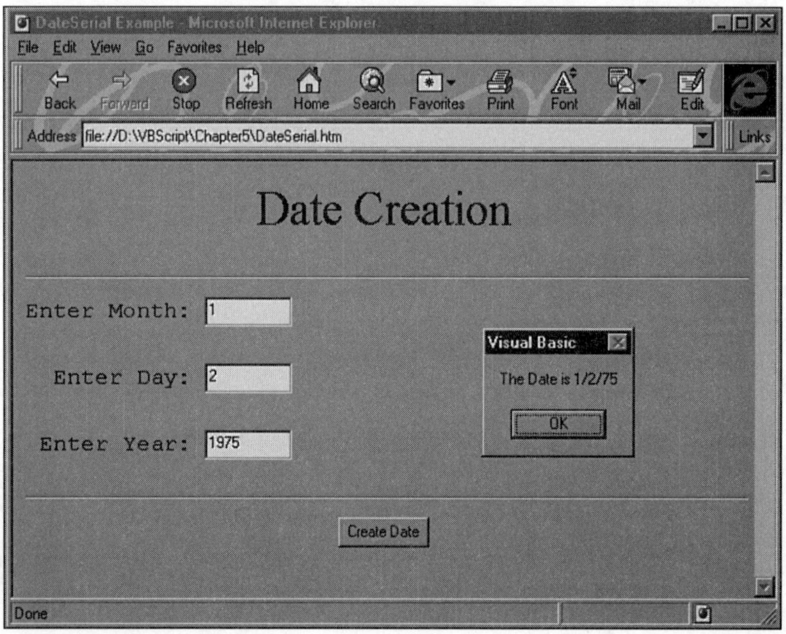

Figure 5-2 The **DateSerial()** function combines the values typed for month, day, and year

function returns the date 10/20/94. Since the function receives a value of -2, it uses the base month value of 12 and subtracts 2 to return a value of 10.

Probably the most useful feature of this function is the ability to use a variable expression to calculate a portion of the date. In the following example code, each date expression is calculated based on the values of variables.

```
<SCRIPT LANGUAGE = "VBScript">

Dim NewMonth, NewYear, NewDay

NewMonth = 10
NewYear = 1984
NewDay = 6

DateSerial (NewYear-3, NewMonth+2, NewDay+1)

</SCRIPT>
```

If a value of the date expression exceeds the acceptable range for the unit, the next unit is incremented. For example, if a value of 14 is received in the month expression, the year expression is incremented by one and the month expression is incremented by two.

See Also `Date()`, `DateValue()`, `Day()`, `Month()`, `Now()`, `TimeSerial()`, `TimeValue()`, `Weekday()`, `Year()`

DateValue FUNCTION

Purpose Use the `DateValue()` function to convert a date string to a variant with a date subtype. Table 5-4 describes the expressions that can be used with the `DateValue()` function.

Syntax `DateValue(expression)`

Table 5-4 Argument of the DateValue() function

Argument	Description
expression	Any string expression that represents a date within the range of January 1, 100, through December 31, 9999. Refer to Table 5-5 for more information about the valid string expressions for the DateValue() function.

Description The expression used with the `DateValue()` function can be any string expression that represents a date, as outlined in Table 5-5. If the expression is a time, the `DateValue()` function considers it valid, but it does not return the time value. It returns a value of 12:00 AM, indicating a time value was passed to the function.

Table 5-5 Valid expressions for the `DateValue()` function

An Expression in Format...	Is...
hh:mm (2:00)	Valid, but the `DateValue()` function will not return the expression
mm-dd-yy (05–19–96)	Valid
mm-dd-yyyy (05–10–1996)	Valid
mm/dd/yy (06/19/96)	Valid
mm/dd/yyyy (06/19/1996)	Valid
Numeric (112296)	Not valid
Other string expression	Not valid
String that resembles a date ("May 16, 1996")	Valid

In Listing 5-3, the **DateValue()** function interprets the string entered by the user and returns a date value if the string is valid. The **MsgBox()** function displays the results of the **DateValue()** function, as illustrated in Figure 5-3.

Listing 5-3 Using the `DateValue()` *function*

```
<HTML>

<HEAD>
<TITLE>DateValue Example</TITLE>

<SCRIPT LANGUAGE="VBScript">
<!--
'........................................................
' CreateDate_OnClick()
' Creates from the string entered by the user.
'........................................................
SUB CreateDate_OnClick()

 Dim UserDate

 UserDate=DateValue(ConvertDate.Value)

 MsgBox "The Date is " & UserDate

END SUB
-->

</SCRIPT>
</HEAD>

<BODY>

<CENTER>

<FONT SIZE=6>Date Creation<P>
</CENTER>
<HR>
```

```
<FONT SIZE=4>

<PRE>Type Date to Convert: <INPUT NAME=ConvertDate SIZE=20>

<HR>
<CENTER>
<INPUT TYPE=BUTTON VALUE="Create Date" NAME="CreateDate">
</CENTER>

</FONT>

</BODY>

</HTML>
```

Example The Date and Time Values project at the end of this chapter uses the `DateValue()` function to convert the date string typed by the user in the Departure Date field to a variant with a subtype of date.

Comments The `DateValue()` function only looks for date information. Therefore, if it encounters a valid time, it recognizes it as a time, but does not return its value. If it encounters an invalid time, such as `34:21`, it returns an error.

The `DateValue()` function determines the month, day, and year order of the values it receives based on the short-date format that is currently established for your system.

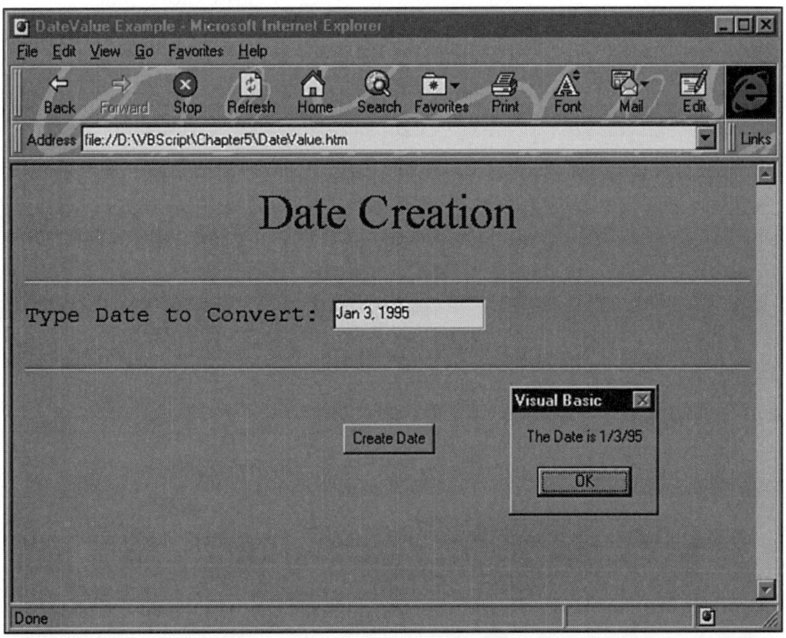

Figure 5-3 The `DateValue()` function converts the string to a valid date

If the year is omitted from the date string it receives, the **DateValue()** function uses the current year based on that computer's system date. Year values of **0** through **99** are interpreted as the years 1900 through 1999.

See Also **CDate()**, **DateSerial()**, **Day()**, **Month()**, **Now()**, **TimeSerial()**, **TimeValue()**, **Weekday()**, **Year()**

Day Function

Purpose Use the **Day()** function to determine the numeric value that corresponds to the day of the month. Table 5-6 describes the expressions that can be used with the **Day()** function.

Syntax **Day(expression)**

Table 5-6 Argument of the Day() function

Argument	Description
expression	Any expression that represents a date, or a NULL value

Description The **Day()** function returns a numeric value in the range of 1 to 31 that represents the day of the month. If it receives a **NULL** value, it returns a **NULL** value. Table 5-7 identifies the types of expressions that the **Day()** function can evaluate.

Table 5-7 Valid date expressions

An Expression in Format...	Is...
hh:mm (2:00)	Not valid
mm-dd-yy (05-19-96)	Valid
mm-dd-yyyy (05-10-1996)	Valid
mm/dd/yy (06/19/96)	Valid
mm/dd/yyyy (06/19/1996)	Valid
String that resembles a date ("May 16, 1996")	Valid
Other string expression	Not valid
Numeric (112296)	Not valid

In Listing 5-4, the **Day()** function evaluates the expression typed in the input field and returns a numeric value that represents the day of the month portion of the expression, as illustrated in Figure 5-4.

Listing 5-4 Using the `Day()` *function*

```
<HTML>

<HEAD>
<TITLE>Day Example</TITLE>

<SCRIPT LANGUAGE="VBScript">
<!--
'..............................................................
' FindDay_OnClick()
' Determines day of week from the string entered by the user.
'..............................................................
SUB FindDay_OnClick()

 Dim UserDay

 UserDay=Day(InputDate.Value)

 MsgBox "The day of the month is " & UserDay

END SUB
-->

</SCRIPT>
</HEAD>

<BODY>

<CENTER>

<FONT SIZE=6>Day Locator<P>
</CENTER>
<HR>

<FONT SIZE=4>

<PRE>Enter a date: <INPUT NAME=InputDate SIZE=20>

<HR>
<CENTER>
<INPUT TYPE=BUTTON VALUE="Find Day" NAME="FindDay">
</CENTER>

</FONT>

</BODY>

</HTML>
```

Example

The `Day()` function is used in the Date and Time Values project at the end of this chapter to determine the day portion of both the system date and the date entered in the Departure Date field. Once the values are determined, the days in the current date are subtracted from the vacation date to determine the number of days until the event occurs.

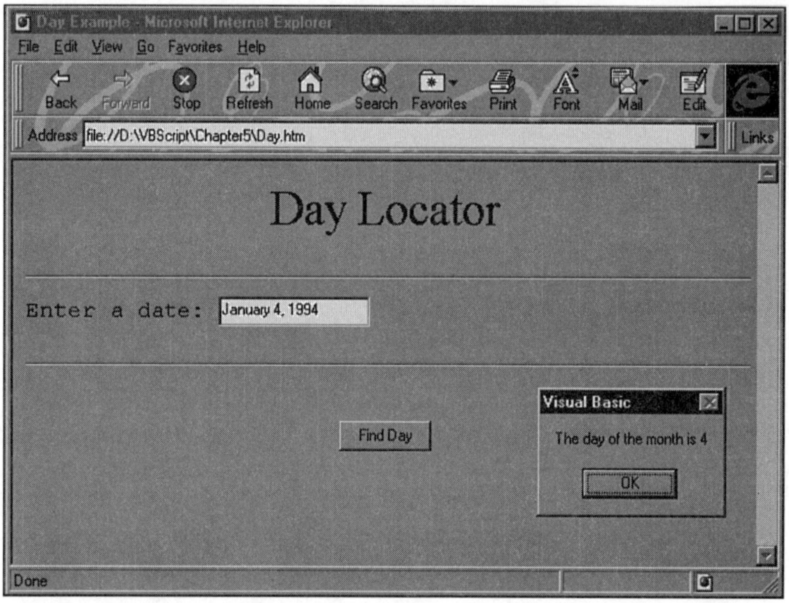

Figure 5-4 The `Day()` function returns a numeric value that represents the day

Comments The `Day()` function is normally used with the `Month()` and `Year()` functions to construct a date in the desired format.

See Also `Date()`, `Hour()`, `Minute()`, `Month()`, `Now()`, `Second()`, `Weekday()`, `Year()`

Hour FUNCTION

Purpose Use the `Hour()` function to return a numeric value between 0 and 23 that represents the hour of the day. Table 5-8 describes the expressions that can be used with the `Hour()` function.

Syntax `Hour(expression)`

Table 5-8 Argument of the `Hour()` function

Argument	Description
`expression`	Any expression that represents a time, or a `NULL` value

Description The `Hour()` function returns a numeric value in the range of 0 to 23 that represents the hour of the day in military time. If it receives a `NULL` value, it returns a `NULL` value. The function can interpret times that are followed by A.M. or P.M. values. These time values are also converted to a military time format; for example, if the **Hour()** function receives the value **3:00 PM**, it returns a **15**. Table 5-9 identifies the types of expressions that the **Hour()** function can evaluate.

Table 5-9 Valid time expressions

An Expression in Format...	Is...
hh:mm (11:34)	Valid
hh:mm:ss (11:34:56)	Valid
hh:mm PM (3:45 PM)	Valid
hh:mm am (4:54 am)	Valid
mm-dd-yy (05-19-96)	Valid; returns a value of 0
mm-dd-yyyy (05-10-1996)	Valid; returns a value of 0
mm/dd/yy (06/19/96)	Valid; returns a value of 0
NULL	Valid; returns a NULL value
Numeric (1122)	Not valid
Other string expression	Not valid
String that resembles a time ("Three o'clock")	Not valid

In Listing 5-5, the **Hour()** function evaluates the expression typed in the input field and returns a numeric value that represents the hour portion of the expression. The **MsgBox()** function displays the results of the **Hour()** function, as illustrated in Figure 5-5.

Listing 5-5 Using the Hour() *function*

```
<HTML>

<HEAD>
<TITLE>Hour Example</TITLE>

<SCRIPT LANGUAGE="VBScript">
<!--
'..........................................................
' FindHour_OnClick()
' Returns the hour value from the string entered by the user.
'..........................................................
SUB FindHour_OnClick()

 Dim UserTime

 UserTime=Hour(InputTime.Value)

 MsgBox "The hour of the day is " & UserTime

END SUB
-->
```

continued on next page

continued from previous page

```
</SCRIPT>
</HEAD>

<BODY>

<CENTER>

<FONT SIZE=6>Hour Locator<P>
</CENTER>
<HR>

<FONT SIZE=4>

<PRE>Enter a Time: <INPUT NAME=InputTime SIZE=20>

<HR>
<CENTER>
<INPUT TYPE=BUTTON VALUE="Find Hour" NAME="FindHour">
</CENTER>

</FONT>

</BODY>

</HTML>
```

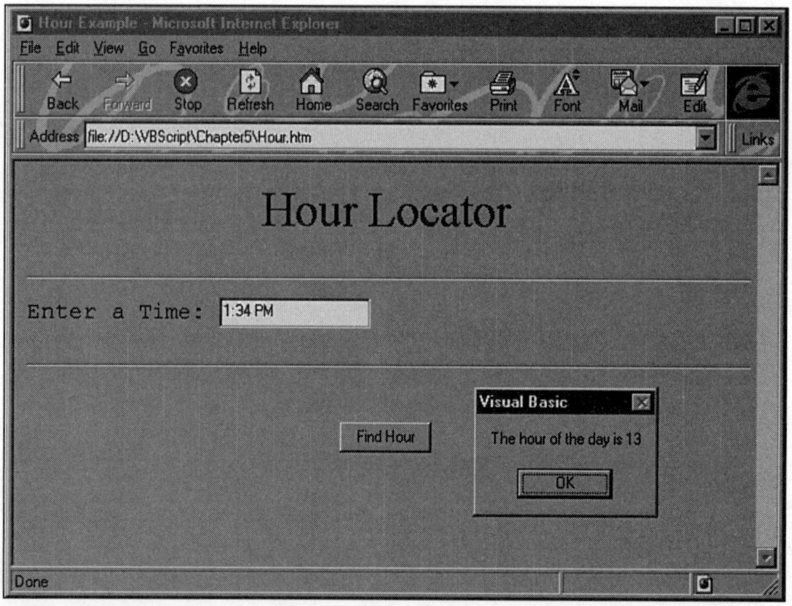

Figure 5-5 The `Hour()` function converts P.M. time values to appropriate military values

Example The `Hour()` function is used in the Date and Time Values project at the end of the chapter to determine the hour portion of both the system time and the time entered in the Time field. Once the values are determined, the hours in the current time are subtracted from the vacation time to determine the number of hours until the event occurs.

Comments The `Hour()` function is normally used with the `Minute()` and `Second()` functions to provide the ability to customize the time display.

See Also `Day()`, `Minute()`, `Now()`, `Second()`, `Time()`

IsDate FUNCTION

Purpose Use the `IsDate()` function to determine if the selected expression can be converted to a date or time expression. Table 5-10 describes the expressions that can be used with the `IsDate()` function.

Syntax `IsDate(expression)`

Table 5-10 Argument of the `IsDate()` function

Argument	Description
expression	Any date or string expression that can be converted to a valid time or date value

Description The `IsDate()` function returns a Boolean value of `TRUE` if the specified variable expression can be converted to a date or time value; otherwise, `FALSE` is returned.

Refer to Chapter 4, Data Validation, for more detailed information about the `IsDate()` function.

Minute FUNCTION

Purpose Use the `Minute()` function to return a numeric value between 0 and 59 that represents the minute portion of the time. Table 5-11 describes the expressions that can be used with the `Minute()` function.

Syntax `Minute(expression)`

Table 5-11 Argument of the `Minute()` function

Argument	Description
expression	Any expression that represents a time, or a `NULL` value

Description The `Minute()` function returns a numeric value in the range of 0 to 59 that represents the minute portion of the time expression. If the function receives a **NULL** value, it returns a **NULL** value. Table 5-9 identifies the types of expressions that the **Minute()** function can evaluate.

In Listing 5-6, the **Minute()** function evaluates the expression typed in the input field and returns a numeric value that represents the minute portion of the expression. The **MsgBox()** function displays the results of the **Minute()** function, as illustrated in Figure 5-6.

Listing 5-6 Using the `Minute()` *function*

```
<HTML>

<HEAD>
<TITLE>Minute Example</TITLE>

<SCRIPT LANGUAGE="VBScript">
<!--
'............................................................
' FindMinute_OnClick()
' Returns the minute value from the string entered by the user.
'............................................................
SUB FindMinute_OnClick()

 Dim UserTime

 UserTime=Minute(InputTime.Value)

 MsgBox "The minute of the hour is " & UserTime

END SUB
-->

</SCRIPT>
</HEAD>

<BODY>

<CENTER>

<FONT SIZE=6>Minute Locator<P>
</CENTER>
<HR>

<FONT SIZE=4>

<PRE>Enter a Time: <INPUT NAME=InputTime SIZE=20>

<HR>
<CENTER>
<INPUT TYPE=BUTTON VALUE="Find Minutes" NAME="FindMinute">
</CENTER>

</FONT>

</BODY>

</HTML>
```

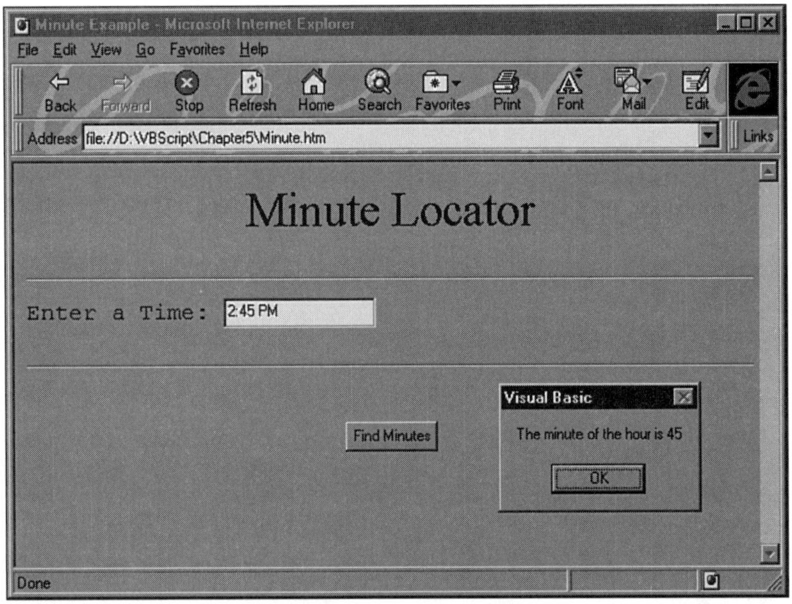

Figure 5-6 The `Minute()` function returns the minute portion of a time expression

Example The `Minute()` function is used in the Date and Time Values project at the end of the chapter to determine the minute portion of both the system time and the time entered in the Time field. Once the values are determined, the minutes in the current time are subtracted from the vacation time to determine the number of minutes until the event occurs.

Comments The `Minute()` function is normally used with the `Hour()` and `Second()` functions to provide the ability to customize the time display.

See Also `Day()`, `Hour()`, `Now()`, `Second()`, `Time()`

Month FUNCTION

Purpose Use the `Month()` function to retrieve the numeric value that corresponds to the month in a date expression. Table 5-12 describes the expressions that can be used with the `Month()` function.

Syntax `Month(expression)`

Table 5-12 Argument of the `Month()` function

Argument	Description
`expression`	Any expression that represents a date, or a `NULL` value

Description

The `Month()` function returns a numeric value in the range of 1 to 12 that represents the month in the specified date expression. If the function receives a `NULL` value, it returns a `NULL` value.

In Listing 5-7, the `Month()` function evaluates the expression typed by the user and returns a numeric value indicating the month portion of the date. The `MsgBox()` function displays the results of the `Month()` function, as illustrated in Figure 5-7.

Listing 5-7 Using the `Month()` *function*

```
HTML>

<HEAD>
<TITLE>Month Example</TITLE>

<SCRIPT LANGUAGE="VBScript">
<!--
'.........................................................
' FindMonth_OnClick()
' Retrieves the month from the string entered by the user.
'.........................................................
SUB FindMonth_OnClick()

 Dim UserMonth

 UserMonth=Month(InputDate.Value)

 MsgBox "The month of the year is " & UserMonth

END SUB
-->

</SCRIPT>
</HEAD>

<BODY>

<CENTER>

<FONT SIZE=6>Month Locator<P>
</CENTER>
<HR>

<FONT SIZE=4>

<PRE>Enter a date: <INPUT NAME=InputDate SIZE=20>

<HR>
<CENTER>
<INPUT TYPE=BUTTON VALUE="Find Month" NAME="FindMonth">
</CENTER>

</FONT>

</BODY>

</HTML>
```

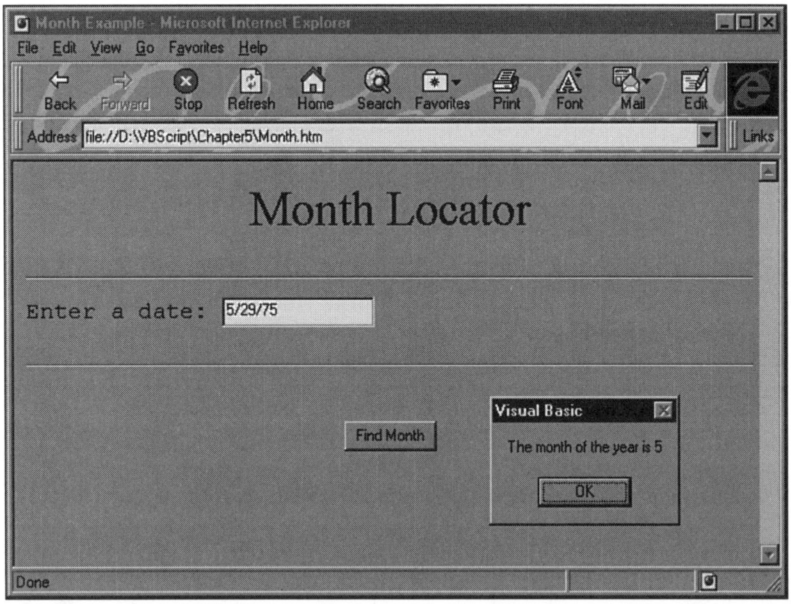

Figure 5-7 The **Month()** function interprets all valid date expressions

Example The **Month()** function is used in the Date and Time Values project at the end of the chapter to determine the month portion of both the system date and the date entered in the Departure Date field. Once the values are determined, the months in the current date are subtracted from the vacation date to determine the number of months until the event occurs.

Comments The **Month()** function can interpret string expressions that are valid representations of a month. For example, it recognizes both the word *November* and the abbreviation *Nov*. For more information about the valid expressions that can be used with the **Month()** function, refer to Table 5-7.

See Also **Date()**, **Day()**, **Now()**, **Weekday()**, **Year()**

Now Function

Purpose Use the **Now()** function to determine the current system date and time.

Syntax **Now()**

Description The **Now()** function does not have any arguments. It simply retrieves the date and time values of the system when the code is executed. Use of this function ensures that the user's current date and time are displayed on the screen.

In Listing 5-8, the **Now()** function captures and displays the system date and time on the screen. Similar to the example for the **Date()** function, the **Document** object is referenced by VBScript so that the value can be written directly to the screen, as illustrated in Figure 5-8. For more information about the **Document** object, refer to Chapter 15, Internet Explorer Object Model for Scripting.

Listing 5-8 Using the `Now()` *function*

```
<HTML>

<HEAD><TITLE>Now Example</TITLE></HEAD>

<BODY BGCOLOR="White">

<FONT SIZE=6>

<SCRIPT LANGUAGE="VBScript">
<!--
'.......................................................
' Since this VBScript code resides in the body of the
' HTML document, it automatically executes when the
' page is loaded. The system date and time are checked
' and written to the page by referencing the HTML
' Document object.
'.......................................................

   Document.Write "It is currently... "
   Document.Write Now()

-->

</SCRIPT>

</FONT>

</BODY>

</HTML>
```

See Also `Date()`, `Day()`, `Hour()`, `Minute()`, `Month()`, `Second()`, `Time()`, `Weekday()`, `Year()`

Second FUNCTION

Purpose Use the **Second()** function to return a value between 0 and 59 that represents the second portion of the time expression. Table 5-13 describes the expressions that can be used with the **Second()** function.

Syntax **Second**(*expression*)

Table 5-13 Argument of the `Second()` function

Argument	Description
`expression`	Any expression that represents a time, or a NULL value

Figure 5-8 The `Now()` function returns the current system date and time values

Description

The `Second()` function returns a numeric value in the range 0 through 59 that represents the number of seconds in the time expression. If the function receives a `NULL` value, it returns a `NULL` value.

In Listing 5-9, the `Second()` function evaluates the expression typed in the input field and returns a numeric value that represents the number of seconds in the time expression. The `MsgBox()` function displays the value returned by the `Second()` function, as illustrated in Figure 5-9.

Listing 5-9 Using the `Second()` *function*

```
<HTML>

<HEAD>
<TITLE>Second Example</TITLE>

<SCRIPT LANGUAGE="VBScript">
<!--
'..........................................................
' FindSecond_OnClick()
' Returns the second value from the string entered by the user.
'..........................................................
SUB FindSecond_OnClick()

 Dim UserTime

 UserTime=Second(InputTime.Value)

 MsgBox "The second value is " & UserTime

END SUB
-->

</SCRIPT>
</HEAD>

<BODY>
```

continued on next page

continued from previous page

```
<CENTER>

<FONT SIZE=6>Second Locator<P>
</CENTER>
<HR>

<FONT SIZE=4>

<PRE>Enter a Time: <INPUT NAME=InputTime SIZE=20>

<HR>
<CENTER>
<INPUT TYPE=BUTTON VALUE="Find Seconds" NAME="FindSecond">
</CENTER>

</FONT>

</BODY>

</HTML>
```

Example

The **Second()** function is used in the Date and Time Values project at the end of the chapter to determine the second portion of both the system time and the time entered in the Time field. Once the values are determined, the seconds in the current time are subtracted from the vacation time to determine the number of seconds until the event occurs.

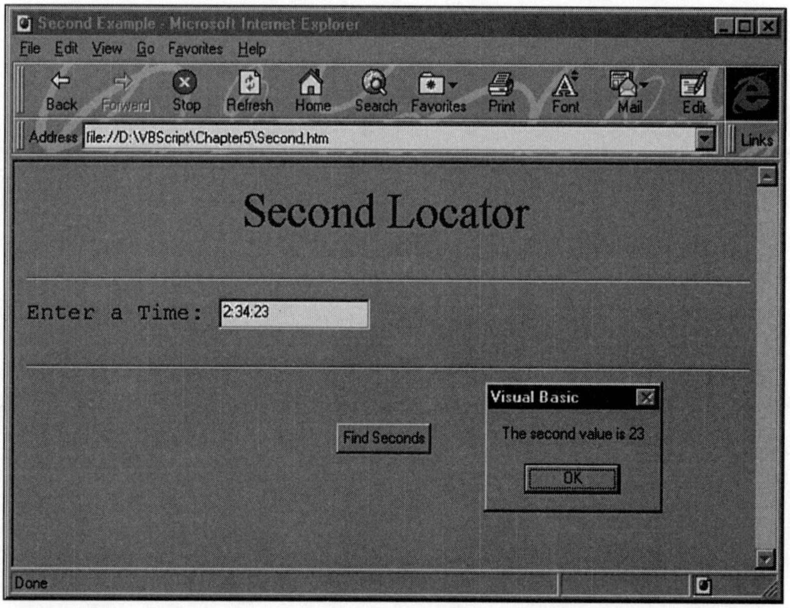

Figure 5-9 The **Second()** function captures the second portion of a time expression

Comments The `Second()` function is normally used with the `Hour()` and `Minute()` functions to provide the ability to customize the time display.

See Also `Day()`, `Hour()`, `Minute()`, `Now()`, `Time()`

Time FUNCTION

Purpose Use the `Time()` function to capture the current system time.

Syntax `Time()`

Description The `Time()` function does not have any arguments. It simply retrieves the current time value of the system when the code is executed.

In Listing 5-10, the `Time()` function captures system time, which is then displayed on the screen using the `Document` object. By referencing the `Document` object, VBScript writes the time expression directly to the screen, as illustrated in Figure 5-10. For more information about the `Document` object, refer to Chapter 15, Internet Explorer Object Model for Scripting.

Listing 5-10 Using the `Time()` function

```
<HTML>

<HEAD><TITLE>Time Example</TITLE></HEAD>

<BODY BGCOLOR="White">

<FONT SIZE=6>

<SCRIPT LANGUAGE="VBScript">
<!--
'.......................................................
' Since this VBScript code resides in the body of the
' HTML document, it automatically executes when the
' page is loaded. The system time is checked and written
' to the page by referencing the HTML Document object.
'.......................................................

   Document.Write "The current time is... "
   Document.Write Time()

-->

</SCRIPT>

</FONT>

</BODY>

</HTML>
```

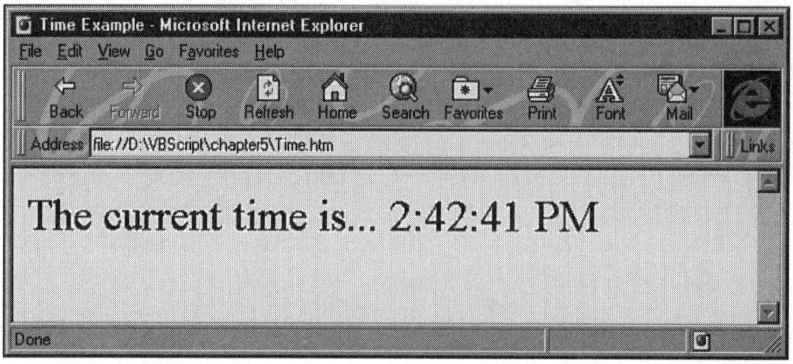

Figure 5-10 The `Time()` function captures the current system time

Example The Date and Time Values project at the end of the chapter uses the `Time()` function to capture the system time. The time is placed on the screen using the `Document` object method. The `Time()` function is also used to capture the system time and compare it to the time typed in the Time field by the user.

See Also `Date()`, `Now()`

`TimeSerial` Function

Purpose Use the `TimeSerial()` function to obtain a time value in the format hh:mm:ss based on the values supplied for the hour, minutes, and seconds. Table 5-14 describes the expressions that can be used with the `TimeSerial()` function.

Syntax `TimeSerial(HourValue, MinuteValue, SecondValue)`

Table 5-14 Arguments of the `TimeSerial()` function

Argument	Description
`HourValue`	Any numeric expression whose value is between 0 and 23
`MinuteValue`	Any numeric expression
`SecondValue`	Any numeric expression

Description The `TimeSerial()` function returns a variant value with a subtype of date in the range of 00:00:00 (12:00 a.m.) to 23:59:59 (11:59 p.m.). In Listing 5-11, the `TimeSerial()` function combines the values entered on the document and creates a time value. VBScript displays the results of the `TimeSerial()` function using the `MsgBox()` function, as illustrated in Figure 5-11.

Listing 5-11 Using the `TimeSerial()` *function*

```
<HTML>

<HEAD><TITLE>TimeSerial Example</TITLE>

<SCRIPT LANGUAGE="VBScript">
<!--
'.......................................................
' CreateTime_OnClick()
' Creates the time using the values input by the user
'.......................................................
SUB CreateTime_OnClick()

 Dim UserTime

 UserTime=TimeSerial(UserHour.Value,UserMinute.Value,UserSecond.Value)

 MsgBox "The Time is " & UserTime

END SUB
-->

</SCRIPT>
</HEAD>

<BODY>

<CENTER>

<FONT SIZE=6>Time Creation<P>
</CENTER>
<HR>

<FONT SIZE=4>

<PRE>     Enter Hour: <INPUT NAME=UserHour SIZE=10>
<BR>
  Enter Minutes: <INPUT NAME=UserMinute SIZE=10>
<BR>
  Enter Seconds: <INPUT NAME=UserSecond SIZE=10></PRE>

<HR>
<INPUT TYPE=BUTTON VALUE="Create Time" NAME="CreateTime">

</FONT>

</BODY>

</HTML>
```

Comments Probably the most useful feature of this function is the ability to use a variable expression to calculate a portion of the time. In the following example code, the time expression is calculated based on the values of variables.

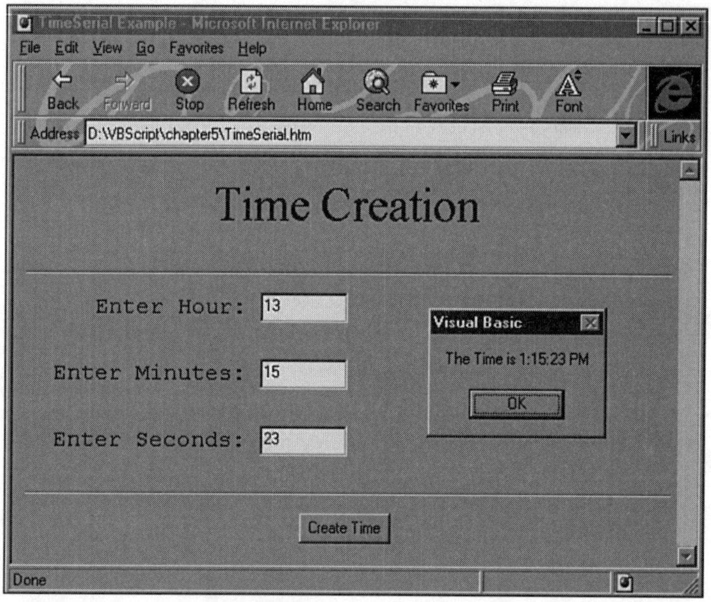

Figure 5-11 The `TimeSerial()` function combines the time values to form a valid date expression

```
<SCRIPT LANGUAGE = "VBScript">

  Dim NewHour, NewMinute, NewSecond

  NewHour = 10
  NewMinute = 12
  NewSecond = 16

  TimeSerial (NewHour-2, NewMinute+4, NewSecond+10)

</SCRIPT>
```

If a value of the time expression exceeds the acceptable range for the unit, the next unit is incremented. For example, if a value of **64** is received in the minute expression, the hour expression is incremented by one and the minute expression is incremented by four.

See Also `DateSerial()`, `DateValue()`, `Hour()`, `Minute()`, `Second()`, `TimeValue()`

TimeValue FUNCTION

Purpose Use the `TimeValue()` function to convert a string that expresses a time to a variant with a date subtype. Table 5-15 describes the expressions that can be used with the `TimeValue()` function.

Syntax `TimeValue(expression)`

Table 5-15 Argument of the `TimeValue()` function

Argument	Description
`expression`	Any string expression that represents a time, or a `NULL` value. Refer to Table 5-16 for more information about the valid string expressions for the `TimeValue()` function.

Description

The `TimeValue()` function converts the expression to a variant with a subtype of date. The expression used with the `TimeValue()` function can be any string expression that represents a valid date, as outlined in Table 5-16. If the expression contains a date, but not a time value, the `TimeValue()` function considers the expression valid but it does not return the date value. It returns a value of `12:00:00 AM`.

Table 5-16 Valid expressions for the `TimeValue()` function

An Expression in Format...	Is...
hh:mm (`4:34`)	Valid
hh:mm:ss (`9:23:12`)	Valid
hh:mm (military time, `14:23`)	Valid
hh:mm pm (`5:23 pm`)	Valid
hh:mm AM (`4:56 AM`)	Valid
mm-dd-yy (`05-19-96`)	Valid, but expression is not returned
mm-dd-yyyy (`05-10-1996`)	Valid, but expression is not returned
mm/dd/yy (`06/19/96`)	Valid, but expression is not returned
mm/dd/yyyy (`06/19/1996`)	Valid, but expression is not returned
Numeric (`1022`)	Not valid
Other string expression	Not valid
String that contains date and time (`"May 1, 1996 2:34"`)	Valid
String that resembles a date (`"May 16, 1996"`)	Valid, but expression is not returned

In Listing 5-12, the `TimeValue()` function interprets the string typed by the user and returns a time value if the string is a valid time. The `MsgBox()` function displays the results of the `TimeValue()` function, as illustrated in Figure 5-12.

Listing 5-12 Using the `TimeValue()` function

```
<HTML>

<HEAD>
<TITLE>TimeValue Example</TITLE>

<SCRIPT LANGUAGE="VBScript">
```

continued on next page

continued from previous page

```
<!--
'.................................................
' CreateTime_OnClick()
' Creates time from the string entered by the user.
'.................................................
SUB CreateTime_OnClick()

 Dim UserTime

 UserTime=TimeValue(ConvertTime.Value)

 MsgBox "The Time is " & UserTime

END SUB
-->

</SCRIPT>
</HEAD>

<BODY>

<CENTER>

<FONT SIZE=6>Time Creation<P>
</CENTER>
<HR>

<FONT SIZE=4>

<PRE>Type Time to Convert: <INPUT NAME=ConvertTime SIZE=20>

<HR>
<CENTER>
<INPUT TYPE=BUTTON VALUE="Create Time" NAME="CreateTime">
</CENTER>

</FONT>

</BODY>

</HTML>
```

Example The Date and Time Values project at the end of this chapter uses the `TimeValue()` function to convert the time string typed by the user in the Time field to a variant with a subtype of date.

Comments The `TimeValue()` function looks for time information only. Therefore, if it encounters a valid date, it recognizes it as a date, but does not return its value. If it encounters an invalid time, such as 13/4/1997, it returns an error.

See Also `DateSerial()`, `DateValue()`, `Hour()`, `Minute()`, `Now()`, `Second()`, `TimeSerial()`

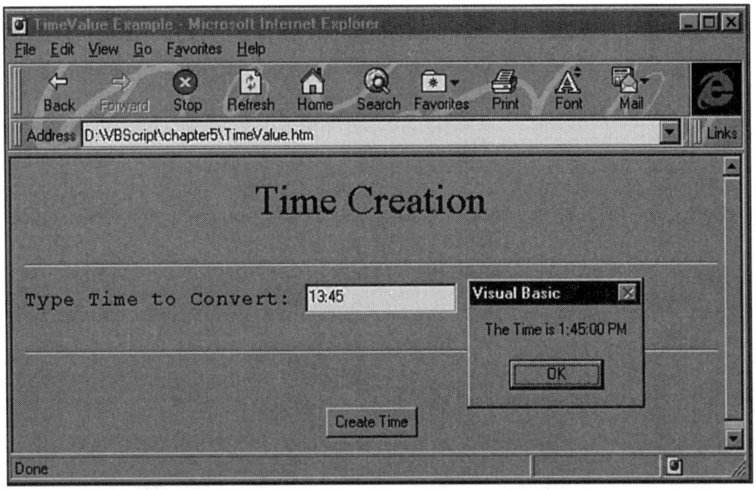

Figure 5-12 The `TimeValue()` function converts the string to a valid time expression

`Weekday` FUNCTION

Purpose Use the **`Weekday()`** function to return a value between 1 and 7 that represents the day of the week. Table 5-17 describes the expressions that can be used with the **`Weekday()`** function.

Syntax **`Weekday`**`(DateValue, FirstDay)`

Table 5-17 Arguments of the `Weekday()` function

Argument	Description
`DateValue`	Any expression that represents a valid date, or a `NULL` value
`FirstDay`	A constant between 0 and 7 that specifies the first day of the week. Refer to Table 5-18 for a description of these constant values.

Description The **`Weekday()`** function returns a value between 1 and 7 that indicates the day of the week specified by the date expression. The value returned is based on the value indicated as the **`FirstDay`** argument. For example, if the date entered is **6/10/96** and the **`FirstDay`** argument is **1**, a value of **2** is returned, because **6/10/96** is a Monday and the **`FirstDay`** argument indicated that Sunday was the first day of the week. If the **`FirstDay`** argument is **3**, the return value is **7**, indicating that **6/10/96** is the last day of the week. If the **`FirstDay`** argument is omitted, a value of **1**, indicating that Sunday is the first day of the week, is used. Table 5-18 contains the possible values for the **`FirstDay`** argument.

Table 5-18 Constants for the `FirstDay` argument of the `Weekday()` function

Value	First Day of the Week
0	Uses the NLS API setting
1	Sunday
2	Monday
3	Tuesday
4	Wednesday
5	Thursday
6	Friday
7	Saturday

If the `DateValue` argument of the `Weekday()` function contains a `NULL` value, the `Weekday()` function returns a `NULL` value. Table 5-19 describes the return values of the `Weekday()` function.

Table 5-19 Return values of the `Weekday()` function

A Return Value of..	Indicates the Date Expression Is the...
1	First day of the week
2	Second day of the week
3	Third day of the week
4	Fourth day of the week
5	Fifth day of the week
6	Sixth day of the week
7	Seventh day of the week
NULL	Contains a `NULL` expression

In the example in Listing 5-13, the `Weekday()` function uses `Inputdate.Value` as the `DateValue` argument and `Inputday.Value` as the `FirstDay` argument. The `MsgBox()` function displays the value returned by the `Weekday()` function, as illustrated in Figure 5-13. As indicated above, even though the same date is entered, the return value changes depending upon the value of the `FirstDay` argument.

Listing 5-13 Using the `Weekday()` function

```
<HTML>

<HEAD>
<TITLE>Weekday Example</TITLE>

<SCRIPT LANGUAGE="VBScript">
```

```
<!--
'.......................................................
' FindWeekday_OnClick()
' Determines the weekday based on the date and first day
' of week values entered.
'.......................................................
SUB FindWeekday_OnClick()

 Dim DayofWeek

 DayofWeek=Weekday(InputDate.Value, InputDay.Value)

 MsgBox "The day of the week is " & DayofWeek

END SUB
-->

</SCRIPT>
</HEAD>

<BODY>

<CENTER>

<FONT SIZE=6>Weekday Locator<P>
</CENTER>
<HR>

<FONT SIZE=4>

<PRE>     Enter a date: <INPUT NAME=InputDate SIZE=20>
<PRE>First day of week: <INPUT NAME=InputDay SIZE=20>

<HR>
<INPUT TYPE=BUTTON VALUE="Day of Week" NAME="FindWeekday">

</FONT>

</BODY>

</HTML>
```

Example The Date and Time Values project at the end of this chapter uses the `Weekday()` function to determine the current day of the week based upon the system date. The value returned by the `Weekday()` function is converted to a string that identifies the day of the week using a `Select Case` statement.

Comments Remember that the `FirstDay` argument has a large impact on the value returned by the `Weekday()` function. To maintain consistency and reduce confusion, you may want to use the same value for that argument.

See Also `Date()`, `Day()`, `Month()`, `Now()`, `Year()`

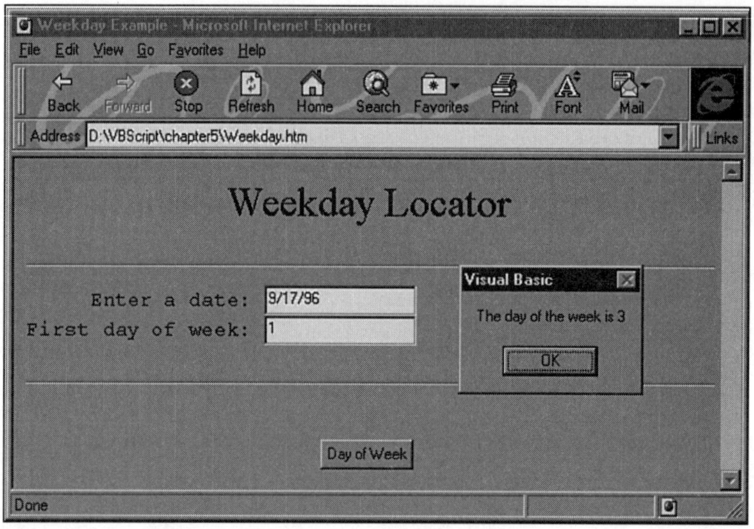

Figure 5-13 The `Weekday()` function returns a value that indicates the day of the week

`Year` FUNCTION

Purpose Use the `Year()` function to return the year value of a date expression. Table 5-20 describes the expressions that can be used with the `Year()` function.

Syntax `Year(expression)`

Table 5-20 Argument of the `Year()` function

Argument	Description
`expression`	Any expression that represents a date, or a `NULL` expression

Description The `Year()` function returns a numeric value between 100 and 9999 that represents the year portion of the date expression. If the function receives a `NULL` value, it returns a `NULL` value. If the function receives a value between 0 and 99, it returns a value between 1900 and 1999. In other words, the function assumes that any value between 0 and 99 corresponds to a date within the twentieth century (1900s). Table 5-21 contains the valid date expressions that the `Year()` function can evaluate.

Table 5-21 Valid expressions for the Year() function

An Expression in Format...	Is...
hh:mm (2:00)	Not valid
mm-dd-yy (05-19-96)	Valid
mm-dd-yyyy (05-10-1996)	Valid
mm/dd/yy (06/19/96)	Valid
mm/dd/yyyy (06/19/1996)	Valid
Numeric (112296)	Not valid
Other string expression	Not valid
String that resembles a date ("May 16, 1996")	Valid

In Listing 5-14, the **Year()** function evaluates the expression in **Inputdate.Value** and returns a value that indicates the date portion of the expression. The **MsgBox()** function displays the results of the **Year()** function, as illustrated in Figure 5-14.

Listing 5-14 Using the Year() function

```
<HTML>

<HEAD>
<TITLE>Year Example</TITLE>

<SCRIPT LANGUAGE="VBScript">
<!--
'...............................................
' FindYear_OnClick()
' Retrieves the year from the date string entered
' by the user.
'...............................................
SUB FindYear_OnClick()

 Dim UserYear

 UserYear=Year(InputDate.Value)

 MsgBox "The year is " & UserYear

END SUB
-->

</SCRIPT>
</HEAD>

<BODY>

<CENTER>

<FONT SIZE=6>Year Locator<P>
</CENTER>
```

continued on next page

continued from previous page

```
<HR>

<FONT SIZE=4>

<PRE>Enter a date: <INPUT NAME=InputDate SIZE=20>

<HR>
<INPUT TYPE=BUTTON VALUE="Find Year" NAME="FindYear">

</FONT>

</BODY>

</HTML>
```

Example The `Year()` function is used in the Date and Time Values project at the end of this chapter to determine the year portion of both the system date and the date entered in the Departure Date field. Once the values are determined, the years in the current date are subtracted from the vacation date to determine the number of years until the event occurs.

Comments The `Year()` function is normally used with the `Month()` and `Day()` functions to construct a date in the desired format.

See Also `Date()`, `Day()`, `Month()`, `Now()`, `Weekday()`

Date and Time Values Project

The Date and Time Values project demonstrates the concepts of working with both system dates and time expressions received from the user or another portion of the program. The project takes you step by step through the process of designing a screen

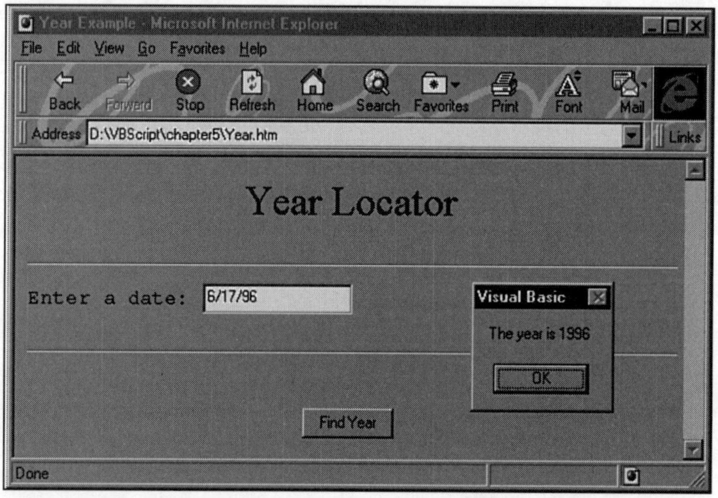

Figure 5-14 The `Year()` function converts a value of **96** to **1996**

that calculates the amount of time between the current date and the future vacation date entered by the user. This project uses most of the functions described in this chapter.

Building the Project

1. Start the project by setting up the standard HTML template used for all VBScript examples in this book. The VBScript code is placed in the **<HEAD>** section of the HTML code to keep everything consistent. Remember to place the HTML comment tags **<!--** and **-->** around the VBScript code so that it will be ignored by browsers that cannot interpret the **<SCRIPT>** tag.

```
<HTML>

<HEAD>
<TITLE>Data and Time Project</TITLE>

<SCRIPT LANGUAGE="VBScript">

<!--

-->

</SCRIPT>

</HEAD>

<BODY>

</BODY>

</HTML>
```

2. In the **<HEAD>** section, place any text that should appear at the top of the screen. You are placing the title here so that it will display before the system date and time information described in step 3. The second font size statement changes the font for the date and time information in step 3.

```
<CENTER>
<FONT SIZE=6>Vacation Countdown<P>
</FONT>
</CENTER>

<HR>

<FONT SIZE=4>
<FONT COLOR="White">
```

3. In the VBScript portion of the HTML code, place the following statements to write the system date and time directly on the document using the HTML **Document** object **Write** method, as illustrated in Figure 5-15. All document methods must be called when the document is loaded. By placing these command lines at the beginning of the VBScript code, they are called as the page loads. The **DetermineDay()** procedure is called to determine the day of the week.

```
<SCRIPT LANGUAGE="VBScript">
<!--
Document.Write "Currently it is... "
   Document.Write Time() & " on "
   Call DetermineDay()
   Document.Write Date()
```

4. Create a procedure called **DetermineDay()** that returns a string value for the day of the week based upon the value returned by the **Weekday()** function. This procedure uses a **Select Case** statement and states that if a value of **1** is returned, the day is Sunday; a **2** indicates a Monday, and so on.

```
Sub DetermineDay()
  Dim DayofWeek

  Select Case Weekday(Date,1)
    Case 1
      Document.Write "Sunday "
    Case 2
      Document.Write "Monday "
    Case 3
      Document.Write "Tuesday "
    Case 4
      Document.Write "Wednesday "
    Case 5
      Document.Write "Thursday "
    Case 6
      Document.Write "Friday "
    Case 7
      Document.Write "Saturday "
  End Select

End Sub
```

5. In the **<BODY>** section, create an input field for the vacation date, an input field for the vacation time, and a button to be pressed when the fields contain the date values to be processed, as illustrated in Figure 5-16.

Figure 5-15 System date and time display using **Document** object properties

```
<BODY>

<FONT SIZE=4>
<FONT COLOR="Blue">
<BR>
<BR>

Departure Date: <INPUT NAME=VacDate SIZE=20>
Time: <INPUT NAME= VacTime SIZE=10>
<INPUT TYPE=BUTTON VALUE="Submit Date" NAME="VacationDate">

<HR>

</FONT>
```

6. In the VBScript section, create a procedure called **VacationDate_OnClick()**. This procedure executes when the Submit Date button is pressed on the screen. The procedure first uses the **IsDate()** function to verify that the date is valid. If the date is valid, it is converted to a date subtype and copied to the **UserDate** variable. If the date is not valid, the user receives a message asking for a valid date.

```
Sub VacationDate_OnClick()
  Dim UserDate
  Dim UserTime

  If IsDate(VacDate.Value) Then

    UserDate=DateValue(VacDate.Value)

  Else

    MsgBox "Type a Valid Date"

  End If

End Sub
```

Figure 5-16 The user types the vacation date and time, and then presses the button

7. The first **If** statement might return a **TRUE** value, and another **If** statement might verifiy that the date entered is not before the current date. If so, a message is sent to the user requesting a new date. If the date is okay (the current date or later), the appropriate functions are called to calculate the number of years, months, days, hours, minutes, and seconds until the anticipated vacation.

```
Sub VacationDate_OnClick()
  Dim UserDate
  Dim UserTime

  If IsDate(VacDate.Value) Then

    UserDate=DateValue(VacDate.Value)

    If UserDate<DateValue(Date) Then
      MsgBox "The Date you typed is already past"
    Else

      Call CalcYear(UserDate)
      Call CalcMonth(UserDate)
      Call CalcDay(UserDate)

      UserTime=TimeValue(VacTime.Value)

      Call CalcHour(UserTime)
      Call CalcMinute(UserTime)
      Call CalcSecond(UserTime)

    End If

  Else
    MsgBox "Type a Valid Date"
  End If

End Sub
```

8. In the **<BODY>** section, create a table where the number of years, months, days, hours, minutes, and seconds are displayed, as illustrated in Figure 5-17.

```
<B>Your Vacation is in...</B>
<BR>
<TABLE>
<TR><TD><INPUT NAME=Years SIZE=5 VALUE=0></TD> <TD>Years</TD></TR>
<TR><TD><INPUT NAME=Months SIZE=5 VALUE=0></TD> <TD>Months</TD></TR>
<TR><TD><INPUT NAME=Days SIZE=5 VALUE=0></TD> <TD>Days</TD></TR>
<TR><TD><INPUT NAME=Hours SIZE=5 VALUE=0></TD> <TD>Hours </TD></TR>
<TR><TD><INPUT NAME=Minutes SIZE=5 VALUE=0></TD> <TD>Minutes</TD></TR>
<TR><TD><INPUT NAME=Seconds SIZE=5 VALUE=0></TD> <TD>Seconds</TD></TR>

</TABLE>
```

9. In the VBScript section, create a function called **CalcYear()** that determines the number of years between the current date and the date entered in the Departure Date field.

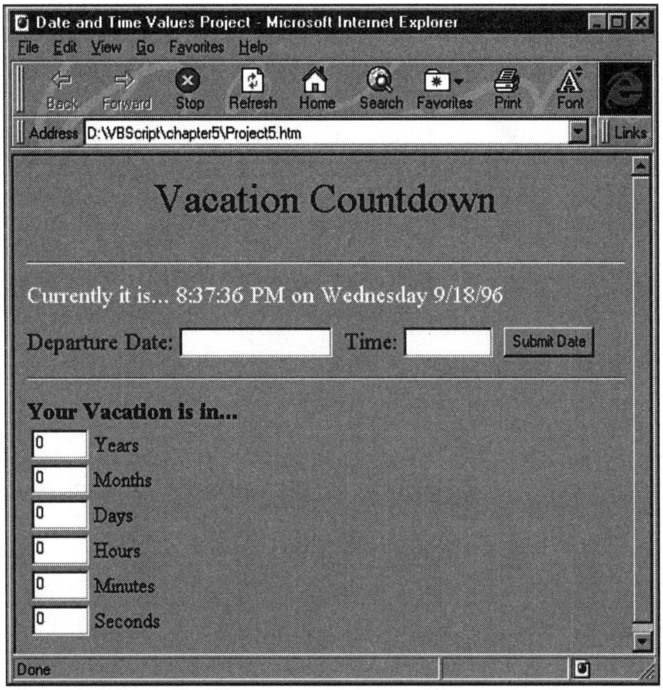

Figure 5-17 A table is created to contain the values for each time element

```
Function CalcYear(YearDate)
   Dim NumYears

  NumYears=Year(YearDate)-Year(Date)

  If NumYears>0 Then
    Years.Value=NumYears
  End If

End Function
```

10. Create a function called `CalcMonth()` that determines the number of months between the current date and the date entered in the Departure Date field. If the number of months is greater than zero, the value is placed in the Months field. If the value is negative, the number of years is reduced by one, and the negative value is subtracted from 12 months. Since the value is already negative, for simplicity it is added to `12` to accomplish the same thing.

```
Function CalcMonth(MonthDate)
  Dim NumMonths

  NumMonths=Month(MonthDate)-Month(Date)

  If NumMonths>0 Then
```

continued on next page

continued from previous page

```
    Months.Value=NumMonths
  Else
    If NumMonths<0 And Years.Value>0 Then
      Years.Value=Years.Value-1
      Months.Value=12+NumMonths
    End If
  End If

End Function
```

11. Create a function called `CalcDay()` that determines the number of days between the current date and the date entered in the Departure Date field. If the number of days is greater than zero, the value is placed in the Days field. If the value is negative, the number of months is reduced by one, and the function `DaysInMonth()` is called to determine the number of days. If the days value is negative and the months value equals zero, the year value is reduced by one, the months value becomes `11`, and then the `DaysInMonth()` function is called to determine the number of days.

```
Function CalcDay(DayDate)
  Dim NumDays

  NumDays=Day(DayDate)-Day(Date)

  If NumDays>0 Then
    Days.Value=NumDays
  Else
      If NumDays<0 And Months.Value=0 Then
      Years.Value=Years.Value-1
      Months.Value=11
      Call DaysInMonth(NumDays)
     End If

     If NumDays<0 And Months.Value>0 Then
      Months.Value=Months.Value-1
      Call DaysInMonth(NumDays)
     End If

  End If

End Function
```

12. Create a procedure called `DaysInMonth()` that determines the number of days for the Days field if the `CalcDays()` function returns a negative value. Since each month in the year has a different number of days, this function is necessary to determine the correct month and then perform the necessary calculation to determine the correct number of days. Once the correct number of days is determined for the month, the number of days in the current month is subtracted from that value and then the number of days in the vacation month is added to the value.

```
Function DaysInMonth(NegDays)
 Dim CalendarDays
 Dim MonthToUse
```

```
 MonthToUse=Month(VacDate.Value)-1
 Select Case MonthToUse
    Case 1
      CalendarDays=31
    Case 2
      CalendarDays=28
    Case 3
      CalendarDays=31
    Case 4
      CalendarDays=30
    Case 5
      CalendarDays=31
    Case 6
      CalendarDays=30
    Case 7
      CalendarDays=31
    Case 8
      CalendarDays=31
    Case 9
      CalendarDays=30
    Case 10
      CalendarDays=31
    Case 11
      CalendarDays=30
    Case 12
      CalendarDays=31
 End Select

 Days.Value=(CalendarDays-Day(Date))+Day(VacDate.Value)

End Function
```

13. Create a function called `CalcHour()` that determines the number of hours between the current date and the date and time entered in the Departure Date field. If the number of hours is greater than zero, the value is placed in the Hours field. If the value is negative, the number of days is reduced by one, and the negative value is subtracted from 24 hours. Since the value is already negative, for simplicity it is added to `24` to accomplish the same thing.

```
Function CalcHour(HourTime)
  Dim NumHours

  NumHours=Hour(HourTime)-Hour(Time)

  If NumHours>0 Then
    Hours.Value=NumHours
  Else
    If NumHours<0 and Days.Value>0 Then
      Days.Value=Days.Value-1
      Hours.Value=24+NumHours
    End If
  End If
End Function
```

14. Create a function called `CalcMinute()` that determines the number of minutes between the current date and the date and time entered in the Departure Date field. If the number of minutes is greater than zero, the value is placed in the

Minutes field. If the value is negative, the number of hours is reduced by one, and the negative value is subtracted from 60 minutes. Since the value is already negative, for simplicity it is added to **60** to accomplish the same thing.

```
Function CalcMinute(MinTime)
  Dim NumMinutes

  NumMinutes=Minute(MinTime)-Minute(Time)

  If NumMinutes>0 Then
    Minutes.Value=NumMinutes
  Else
    If NumMinutes<0 and Hours.Value>0 Then
      Hours.Value=Hours.Value-1
      Minutes.Value=60+NumMinutes
    End If
  End If
End Function
```

15. Create a function called **CalcSecond()** that determines the number of seconds between the current date and the date and time entered in the Departure Date field. If the number of seconds is greater than zero, the value is placed in the Seconds field. If the value is negative, the number of minutes is reduced by one, and the negative value is subtracted from 60 seconds. Since the value is already negative, for simplicity it is added to **60** to accomplish the same thing.

```
Function CalcSecond(SecTime)
  Dim NumSeconds

  NumSeconds=Second(SecTime)-Second(Time)

    If NumSeconds>0 Then
      Seconds.Value=NumSeconds
    Else
      If NumSeconds<0 and Minutes.Value>0 Then
        Minutes.Value=Minutes.Value-1
        Seconds.Value=60+NumSeconds
      End If
    End If
End Function
```

How It Works

The Date and Time Values project provides the ability to calculate the amount of time that will elapse between the current date and time and an event in the future, such as a vacation. The project uses the **Date()** and **Time()** functions to display the current date and time on the page. The Departure Date and Time fields are provided so the user can type a specific date and time in the future and then select the Submit Date button. When the button is selected, VBScript calculates the number of years, months, days, hours, minutes, and seconds from the current date to the date entered by the user.

This project provides a good opportunity to see how the various date and time functions, covered in this chapter, can be used to manipulate dates and times received from users and the system. Figure 5-18 illustrates the completed Date and Time Values project, and Listing 5-15 provides the complete source code.

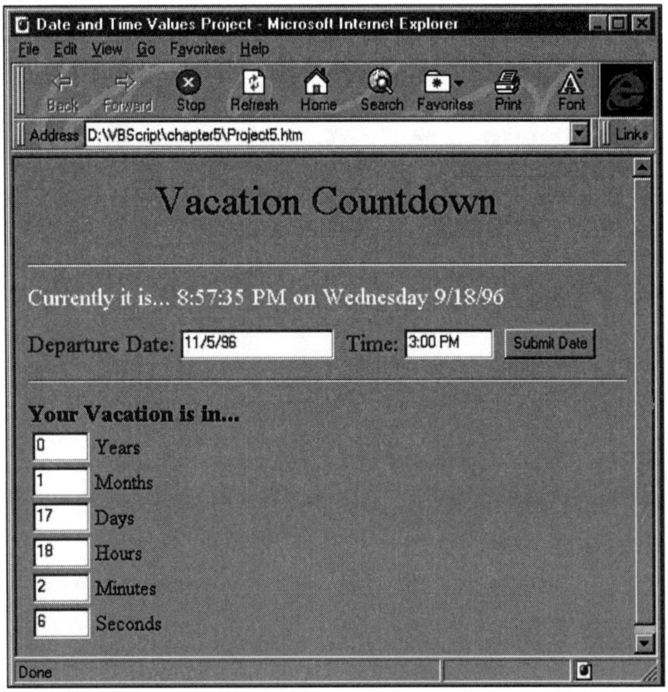

Figure 5-18 The Vacation Countdown project

Listing 5-15 Complete source for the Date and Time Values project

```
<HTML>

<HEAD><TITLE>Date and Time Values Project</TITLE>

<!--.................................................
   This title is placed in the HTML header so that it
   will be placed at the top of the document when the
   page is loaded. This is required since VBScript is
   placing the current date and time on the page when
   it loads.
   ................................................
-->

<CENTER>
<FONT SIZE=6>Vacation Countdown<P>
</FONT>
</CENTER>

<HR>

<FONT SIZE=4>
<FONT COLOR="White">
<SCRIPT LANGUAGE="VBScript">
<!--
```

continued on next page

continued from previous page

```
'.......................................................
' These VBScript statements execute as the page is
' loaded. This is due to the fact that HTML only allows
' you to access the Document object during the loading
' of the page. By placing these statements here, the
' current date and time information are written directly
' to the screen.
'.......................................................

   Document.Write "Currently it is... "
   Document.Write Time() & " on "
   Call DetermineDay()
   Document.Write Date()

'.......................................................
' DetermineDay()
'
' Determines the string equivalent for the numeric value
' returned by the Weekday() function. The string value is
' written to the document.
'.......................................................

Sub DetermineDay()
  Dim DayofWeek

  Select Case Weekday(Date,1)
    Case 1
      Document.Write "Sunday "
    Case 2
      Document.Write "Monday "
    Case 3
      Document.Write "Tuesday "
    Case 4
      Document.Write "Wednesday "
    Case 5
      Document.Write "Thursday "
    Case 6
      Document.Write "Friday "
    Case 7
      Document.Write "Sunday "
  End Select

End Sub

'.......................................................
' VacationDate_OnClick()
'
' This procedure is called when the Submit Date button is
' pressed. It verifies that a valid date was typed in the
' Departure Date field, converts the string to a variant
' date subtype using the DateValue() function, converts the
' time using the TimeValue() function, and calls functions
' to determine the year, month, day, hour, minute, and
' second values.
'.......................................................

Sub VacationDate_OnClick()
  Dim UserDate
  Dim UserTime
```

```
'.........................................................
' Verify that the date is a valid date.
'.........................................................
  If IsDate(VacDate.Value) Then

    UserDate=DateValue(VacDate.Value)

'.........................................................
' If date is valid, make it is not less than the current
' date. Call functions to determine year, month, and day
' values.
'.........................................................
    If UserDate<DateValue(Date) Then
      MsgBox "The Date you typed is already past"
    Else

      Call CalcYear(UserDate)
      Call CalcMonth(UserDate)
      Call CalcDay(UserDate)

'.........................................................
' Call time functions for hour, minute, and second.
'.........................................................
      UserTime=TimeValue(VacTime.Value)

      Call CalcHour(UserTime)
      Call CalcMinute(UserTime)
      Call CalcSecond(UserTime)

    End If
'.........................................................
' Notify user if they typed a date that was not valid.
'.........................................................
  Else
    MsgBox "Type a Valid Date"
  End If

End Sub

'.........................................................
' CalcYear()
'
' Determines the number of years between current date and
' the vacation date.
'.........................................................
Function CalcYear(YearDate)
   Dim NumYears

  NumYears=Year(YearDate)-Year(Date)

  If NumYears>0 Then
    Years.Value=NumYears
  End If

End Function

'.........................................................
' CalcMonth()
```

continued on next page

continued from previous page

```
'
' Determines the number of months between current date and
' the vacation date. If the number of months is a negative
' number but the number of years is greater than 0, the
' number of years is reduced by one and the number of
' months is subtracted from 12. Since it is a negative
' value it is added to 12 to accomplish the result of
' subtraction.
'.......................................................
Function CalcMonth(MonthDate)
  Dim NumMonths

  NumMonths=Month(MonthDate)-Month(Date)

  If NumMonths>0 Then
    Months.Value=NumMonths
  Else
    If NumMonths<0 And Years.Value>0 Then
      Years.Value=Years.Value-1
      Months.Value=12+NumMonths
    End If
  End If

End Function

'.......................................................
' CalcDay()
'
' Determines the number of days. If the number is negative
' but the number of months is greater than 0, the
' number of months is reduced by one and the number of
' days is calculated by calling DaysInMonth. If the number
' of months is zero, 1 is subtracted from the years, months
' are 11, and DaysInMonth() is called.
'.......................................................
Function CalcDay(DayDate)
  Dim NumDays

  NumDays=Day(DayDate)-Day(Date)

  If NumDays>0 Then
    Days.Value=NumDays
  Else
      If NumDays<0 And Months.Value=0 Then
      Years.Value=Years.Value-1
      Months.Value=11
      Call DaysInMonth(NumDays)
     End If

     If NumDays<0 And Months.Value>0 Then
      Months.Value=Months.Value-1
      Call DaysInMonth(NumDays)
     End If

  End If

End Function
```

```
'.......................................................
' DaysInMonth
'
' Determines number of days if a negative day value
' was calculated by CalcDay().
'.......................................................
Function DaysInMonth(NegDays)
 Dim CalendarDays
 Dim MonthToUse

 MonthToUse=Month(VacDate.Value)-1
 Select Case MonthToUse
    Case 1
      CalendarDays=31
    Case 2
      CalendarDays=28
    Case 3
      CalendarDays=31
    Case 4
      CalendarDays=30
    Case 5
      CalendarDays=31
    Case 6
      CalendarDays=30
    Case 7
      CalendarDays=31
    Case 8
      CalendarDays=31
    Case 9
      CalendarDays=30
    Case 10
      CalendarDays=31
    Case 11
      CalendarDays=30
    Case 12
      CalendarDays=31
 End Select

'.......................................................
' Days equal the number of days in the month prior to
' vacation month minus the days in the current date
' plus the days in the vacation month.
'.......................................................
 Days.Value=(CalendarDays-Day(Date))+Day(VacDate.Value)

End Function

'.......................................................
' CalcHour()
'
' Determines the number of hours. If the number is negative
' but the number of days is greater than 0, the
' number of days is reduced by one and the number of
' hours is adjusted by adding the negative day value to 24.
'.......................................................
Function CalcHour(HourTime)
  Dim NumHours

  NumHours=Hour(HourTime)-Hour(Time)
```

continued on next page

continued from previous page

```
  If NumHours>0 Then
    Hours.Value=NumHours
  Else
    If NumHours<0 and Days.Value>0 Then
      Days.Value=Days.Value-1
      Hours.Value=24+NumHours
    End If
  End If
End Function

'..........................................................
' CalcMinute()
'
' Determines the number of minutes. If the number is negative
' but the number of hours is greater than 0, the
' number of hours is reduced by one and the negative
' minute value is added to 60.
'..........................................................
Function CalcMinute(MinTime)
  Dim NumMinutes

  NumMinutes=Minute(MinTime)-Minute(Time)

  If NumMinutes>0 Then
    Minutes.Value=NumMinutes
  Else
    If NumMinutes<0 and Hours.Value>0 Then
      Hours.Value=Hours.Value-1
      Minutes.Value=60+NumMinutes
    End If
  End If
End Function

'..........................................................
' CalcSecond()
'
' Determines the number of seconds. If the number is negative
' but the number of minutes is greater than 0, the
' number of minutes is reduced by one and the negative
' second value is added to 24.
'..........................................................
Function CalcSecond(SecTime)
  Dim NumSeconds

  NumSeconds=Second(SecTime)-Second(Time)

    If NumSeconds>0 Then
      Seconds.Value=NumSeconds
    Else
      If NumSeconds<0 and Minutes.Value>0 Then
        Minutes.Value=Minutes.Value-1
        Seconds.Value=60+NumSeconds
      End If
    End If
End Function

-->
```

```
</SCRIPT>

</FONT>

</HEAD>

<BODY>

<FONT SIZE=4>
<FONT COLOR="Blue">
<BR>
<BR>

Departure Date: <INPUT NAME=VacDate SIZE=20>
Time: <INPUT NAME= VacTime SIZE=10>
<INPUT TYPE=BUTTON VALUE="Submit Date" NAME="VacationDate">

<HR>
</FONT>

<B>Your Vacation is in...</B>
<BR>
<TABLE>
<TR><TD><INPUT NAME=Years SIZE=5 VALUE=0></TD> <TD>Years</TD></TR>
<TR><TD><INPUT NAME=Months SIZE=5 VALUE=0></TD> <TD>Months</TD></TR>
<TR><TD><INPUT NAME=Days SIZE=5 VALUE=0></TD> <TD>Days</TD></TR>
<TR><TD><INPUT NAME=Hours SIZE=5 VALUE=0></TD> <TD>Hours </TD></TR>
<TR><TD><INPUT NAME=Minutes SIZE=5 VALUE=0></TD> <TD>Minutes</TD></TR>
<TR><TD><INPUT NAME=Seconds SIZE=5 VALUE=0></TD> <TD>Seconds</TD></TR>

</TABLE>

</BODY>

</HTML>
```

6

ARRAY HANDLING

6

ARRAY HANDLING

With VBScript, you can use arrays to store related data values. These array handling capabilities, covered in this chapter, add more flexibility to the way data values are handled in VBScript.

What Is an Array?

An array gives you a way to store a group of common values together in the same location so that they can easily be accessed by referencing their common value. When you declare an array, you have one variable that contains several related elements. For example, if you have a Web page that describes your company, you can use an array to store the names of the different departments within the company, as the following code illustrates. The variable is first declared as an array; then a department name is assigned to each element of the array.

```
DIM Departments(4)

  Department(0) = "Information Systems"
  Department(1) = "Finance"
  Department(2) = "Customer Service"
  Department(3) = "Sales"
  Department(4) = "Housekeeping"
```

When values are added to an array, they are added in sequential order. This means that the first value is placed in the first element of the array, the second in the second element, and so on. With this in mind, a specific element in the array can be accessed by simply knowing its place in the order.

An array is made up of two pieces, the array name and the array subscript. The name is the unique identifier, like any variable name, that distinguishes the values from other values within the program. The subscript indicates the highest index value for the elements (related pieces of data) within the array. VBScript creates zero-based arrays, where the first element of the array has an index value of zero. Because of this, in the sample code above we used a subscript value of 4 to get the five elements (0-4).

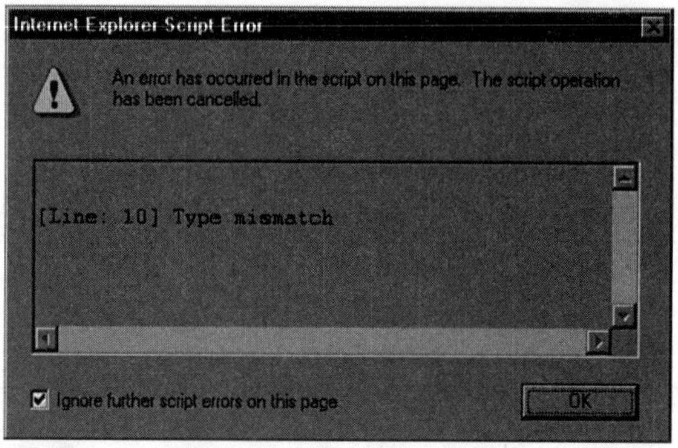

Figure 6-1 Run-time error due to inconsistent data types

All elements of an array should be of the same variant subtype. For example, they should all be integer values, or string values. Since all values in VBScript are the same type, variant, it is possible to store different types of data in an array. But this is not recommended unless it is a multidimensional array and the different value types are stored in different dimensions of the array. For example, you would not store the name of one department and the number of people in another department in the same single-dimensional array. The main reason for maintaining consistent data types is to eliminate potential errors during the processing of the data. If the program anticipates a numeric value and one element contains a string, the user will receive some sort of a run-time error, as shown in Figure 6-1.

Declaring Arrays

Before an array can be used, it first must be declared. Arrays, like all other variables, are normally declared at the beginning of the VBScript code, for global arrays, or at the beginning of a function or procedure, for local arrays. A global array is an array that can be used by all functions and procedures, whereas a local array is available only within the array where it is declared.

The **`Dim`** statement is used to declare all VBScript array types: single-dimensional, multidimensional, static, and dynamic. A brief description of the **`Dim`** statement follows this paragraph. For more detailed information about using this statement to declare a variable, refer to Chapter 3, VBScript Data Types and Variables.

`Dim` STATEMENT

Purpose Use the **`Dim`** statement to allocate the memory needed for storage of the specified array. Table 6-1 describes the expressions that can be used with the **`Dim`** statement.

Syntax `Dim ArrayName(SubscriptValue)`

Table 6-1 Arguments of the `Dim` statement	
Argument	**Description**
`ArrayName`	Any unique variable name.
`SubscriptValue`	A numeric value that indicates the number of elements in the array dimension within the array. An array can have multiple dimensions.

Description The `Dim` statement is used to declare array values. This statement can be used at the beginning of the code to declare a global variable that can be referenced by all procedures and functions, or within a function or procedure to declare a local variable that can only be used within that same function or procedure.

For more detailed information about declaring arrays, refer to Chapter 3, VBScript Data Types and Variables.

Multidimensional Arrays

A multidimensional array is an array that contains more than one dimension, that is, more than one set of subscript values. For example, if you have a two-dimensional array, it is similar to a table with rows and columns. If you add a third dimension, you gain depth in the table, similar to Figure 6-2. The array illustrated in this figure would be declared as follows:

```
Dim CubeArray(2,2,1)
```

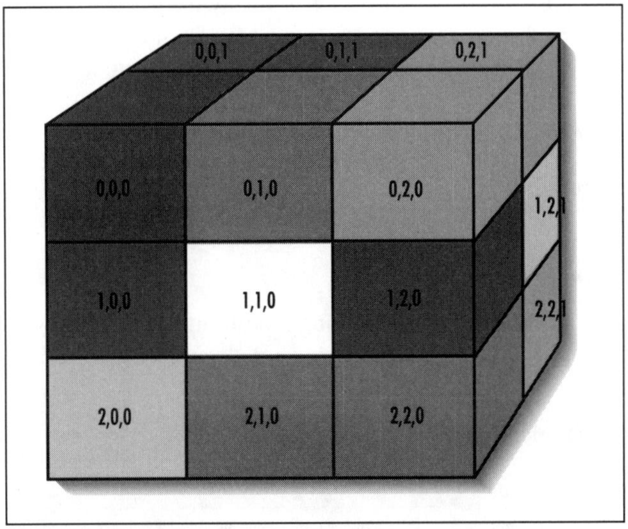

Figure 6-2 A three-dimensional array is similar to a cube

VBScript allows you to declare arrays with up to 60 dimensions. When declaring arrays with more than one dimension, keep in mind that not only does this add to the complexity of the program, but large multidimensional arrays consume more memory.

Multidimensional arrays are useful when storing related types of data. For example, by keeping all of the information about an employee in one array, it can be easier to access the information.

Static Versus Dynamic Arrays

VBScript also provides the flexibility of declaring either a static array or a dynamic array. A static array has a specific number of elements declared using the **Dim** statement. The size of a static array cannot be altered at run time.

A dynamic array provides the flexibility of resizing the array to the appropriate size during run time. Since quite often it is impossible to know during development the number of items that will be added to an array, using a dynamic array makes your program more flexible. For example, you may have an array that stores the items a customer would like to order, and it is impossible to anticipate the exact number of items that each customer will order.

A multidimensional array is first declared without a subscript value. The **ReDim** statement is used to size the array to the appropriate size.

```
Dim SampleArray()

ReDim SampleArray(10)
```

The **ReDim** statement can be used multiple times within the program. However, each time the **ReDim** statement is used, the existing elements in the array are cleared. You can eliminate this erasure of items in the array by using the **Preserve** keyword. When the **Preserve** keyword is used with the **ReDim** statement, the existing elements remain in the array. For more information about the **ReDim** statement, refer to the description in the following section.

```
Dim SampleArray()

ReDim Preserve SampleArray(10)
```

Changing Array Values

VBScript provides two statements for making modifications to an array, as outlined in Table 6-2. These statements are described in more detail following the table.

Table 6-2 Statements used to change the declaration of an array

Statement	Description
Erase	Reinitializes the elements in a static array or reallocates memory for a dynamic array
ReDim	Allocates or reallocates the size (number of elements) of a dynamic array

Erase STATEMENT

Purpose Use the **Erase** statement to either reinitialize the elements in a static array, or reallocate memory originally assigned to a dynamic array. Table 6-3 describes the expressions that can be used with the **Erase** statement.

Syntax **Erase** ArrayName

Table 6-3 Argument of the Erase statement

Argument	Description
ArrayName	Any unique variable name that identifies an existing array

Description The **Erase** statement produces different results depending on whether it is used with a static (fixed-size) or dynamic array. When you use it with a static array, the elements in the array are cleared as outlined in Table 6-4.

Table 6-4 Effects of the Erase statement on a static array

If the Array Contains...	In the Erase Statement...
Numeric values	Each element is set to 0.
Objects	Each element is set to the value of Nothing, indicating that the element is not associated with an actual object.
String values	Each element is set to zero-length.

When the **Erase** statement is used with a dynamic array, it frees the memory that was allocated for the array using the **ReDim** statement. Before the array can be accessed again, it needs to be reallocated using the **ReDim** statement again. It is not necessary to use the **Erase** statement with a dynamic array before using the **ReDim** statement to resize the array.

ReDim STATEMENT

Purpose Use the **ReDim** statement in a function or procedure to allocate or reallocate the number of elements in a dynamic array. Table 6-5 describes the expressions that can be used with the **ReDim** statement.

Syntax **ReDim Preserve** ArrayName(SubscriptValue)

Table 6-5 Arguments of the ReDim statement

Argument	Description
Preserve	This is an optional keyword. If the Preserve keyword is used, the data in the array is maintained during the ReDim statement.

continued on next page

continued from previous page

Argument	Description
`ArrayName`	Any unique variable name.
`SubscriptValue`	A numeric value that indicates the number of elements in the array dimension within the array. An array can have multiple dimensions.

Description

The `ReDim` statement is used to size or resize a dynamic array that was declared as a dynamic array using a `Private`, `Public`, or `Dim` statement with empty parentheses. The `ReDim` statement can be used multiple times within a program to change the number of elements and dimensions in an array.

It is important to remember that resizing the array using the `ReDim` statement will erase the existing elements in the array unless the `Preserve` keyword is used with the `ReDim` statement. However, if you use the `Preserve` keyword with a multidimensional array, you can resize only the last array dimension, and you can't change the number of dimensions in the array. If your array has only one dimension, you can resize that dimension, because it is the last and only dimension. But if your array has two or more dimensions, you can modify only the last dimension and still preserve the contents in the array.

Be careful when resizing arrays; if you resize the array to a smaller size than it was sized originally, data in the eliminated elements is lost.

Summary of Array Handling Functions

Table 6-6 summarizes the array handling functions covered in this chapter. These functions are valuable when working with arrays in VBScript. A detailed description of each function follows this table, and each function is used in the Array Handling project at the end of this chapter.

Table 6-6 Array handling function summary

Use...	To Do This...
`IsArray`	Determine if a specific variant expression is an array of values.
`LBound`	Identify the smallest subscript value for the specified dimension of an array.
`UBound`	Identify the largest subscript value for the specified dimension of an array.

IsArray FUNCTION

Purpose Use the `IsArray()` function to determine if a specific variant expression is an array of values. Table 6-7 describes the expressions that can be used with the `IsArray()` function.

Syntax `IsArray(expression)`

Table 6-7 Argument of the `IsArray()` function

Argument	Description
`expression`	Any unique variable can be used with this function.

Description The `IsArray()` function returns a Boolean value of `TRUE` if the specified variable is an array; otherwise, `FALSE` is returned.

Refer to Chapter 4, Data Validation, for more detailed information about the `IsArray()` function.

LBound FUNCTION

Purpose Use the `LBound()` function to determine the smallest subscript value for the specified dimension of an array. Table 6-8 describes the expressions that can be used with the `LBound()` function.

Syntax `LBound(arrayname, dimension)`

Table 6-8 Arguments of the `LBound()` function

Argument	Description
`arrayname`	The name of a valid array.
`dimension`	This is an optional argument for the `LBound()` function. If specified, it is a whole number that indicates the dimension of the array whose lowest subscript value should be returned.

Description The `LBound()` function returns a numeric value that represents the lowest subscript value of the specified array dimension. The default lowest subscript value for an array is `0`.

The `LBound()` function uses the `dimension` argument to determine which array dimension should be checked. The dimension should be referenced with a numeric value, with the first dimension being `1`, the second `2`, and so on. Therefore, if the `dimension` argument is omitted, a `dimension` argument value of `1` is used, and the `LBound()` function looks at the first array dimension.

The example in Listing 6-1 uses the `LBound()` function to identify the first subscript in a single-dimension array. Once the subscript is identified, that value is used to display the first item in the array, as illustrated in Figure 6-3. This example also illustrates how to create a dynamic array by having the user indicate the number of items that should be placed in the array.

Listing 6-1 Using the `LBound()` *function*

```
<HTML>

<HEAD>
<TITLE>LBound Example</TITLE>
</HEAD>


<SCRIPT LANGUAGE="VBScript">
<!--
'...............................................
' ProcOrder_OnClick()
' Creates an array with the number of elements
' specified by the user. Fills the array with items.
'...............................................

SUB ProcOrder_OnClick()
  Dim OrderArray()
  Dim InputValue
  Dim Counter
  Dim FirstDim
  Dim ArrayDim

'...............................................
' Assigns the input value to a variable.
'...............................................
  InputValue=UserValue.Value

'...............................................
' Makes sure the value entered is numeric; if it is,
' it is used to specify the number of elements in
' the array.
'...............................................
  If IsNumeric(InputValue) Then

'...............................................
' Set the array dimension value to one less than the
' number requested by the user. This is to account
' for the fact that VBScript uses zero-based
' arrays.
'...............................................
    ArrayDim = InputValue - 1
    ReDim OrderArray(ArrayDim)
'...............................................
' Requests the number of items specified in the
' input field. Places each value in the array.
'...............................................
```

```
    For Counter = 0 To ArrayDim

      OrderArray(Counter)=InputBox("Type item number " & Counter+1)

    Next

'.................................................
' LBound() determines the first subscript value. This
' value is used to identify the first value entered.
'.................................................
    FirstDim=LBound(OrderArray)

    MsgBox "The first item is " & OrderArray(FirstDim)

'.................................................
' Message sent when a non-numeric value was entered.
'.................................................
  Else
    MsgBox "Type a numeric value in the field."
  End If

END SUB

-->
</SCRIPT>

<BODY>

<FONT FACE="Arial" SIZE=2>
<FONT COLOR=Fushia>

<CENTER>
   <FONT SIZE=6>Place Order<P>

</CENTER>

  <HR>

  <FONT FACE="Arial" SIZE=2>
  <FONT COLOR=BLACK>

  <BR>
  <CENTER>
  How many items are you ordering: <INPUT NAME=UserValue SIZE=10>

  <BR>
  <BR>
  <INPUT TYPE=BUTTON VALUE="Begin Order" NAME="ProcOrder">

  </CENTER>

</BODY>

</HTML>
```

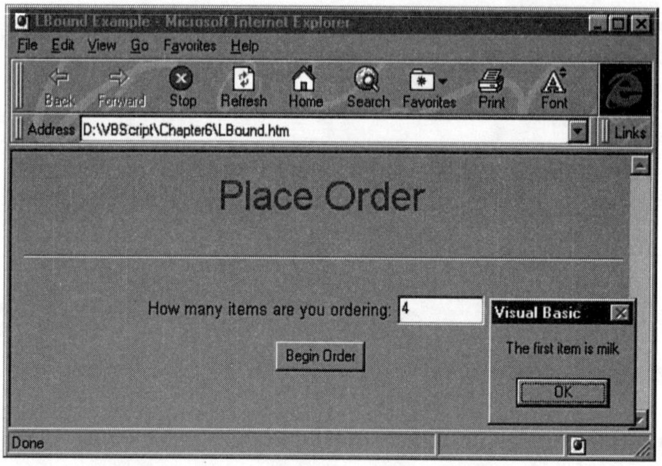

Figure 6-3 The `LBound()` function identifies the subscript of the first element; that value is used to display the first value in the array

Example The Array Handling project at the end of this chapter uses the `LBound()` function to locate the smallest value in an array. The values in the array are sorted prior to calling the `LBound()` function, so the first element of the array contains the smallest value.

Comments The `LBound()` function is normally used with the `UBound()` function to identify the upper and lower limits of a dynamic array. Once these subscript values are determined, you can quickly determine the number of elements in the array by subtracting the lower subscript value (the value returned by `LBound()`) from the upper subscript value (the value returned by `UBound()`) and adding one.

See Also `IsArray()`, `UBound()`

UBound Function

Purpose Use the `UBound()` function to determine the largest subscript value for the specified dimension of an array. Table 6-9 describes the expressions that can be used with the `UBound()` function.

Syntax `UBound(arrayname, dimension)`

Table 6-9 Arguments of the `UBound()` function

Argument	Description
`arrayname`	The name of a valid array.
`dimension`	This is an optional argument for the `UBound()` function. If specified, it is a whole number that indicates the dimension of the array whose highest subscript value should be returned.

Description

The **UBound()** function returns a numeric value that represents the highest subscript value of the specified array dimension. The default lowest subscript value for an array is **0**. Therefore, if the array has 10 elements, the highest subscript value is **9**.

The **UBound()** function uses the **dimension** argument to determine which array dimension should be checked. The dimension should be referenced with a numeric value, with the first dimension being **1**, the second **2**, and so on. Therefore, if the **dimension** argument is omitted, a **dimension** argument value of **1** is used, and the **UBound()** function looks at the first array dimension.

The example in Listing 6-2 uses the **UBound()** function to identify the last subscript in a single-dimension array. Once the subscript is identified, that value is used to display the last item in the array, as illustrated in Figure 6-4. This example also illustrates how to create a dynamic array by having the user indicate the number of items that should be placed in the array.

Listing 6-2 Using the UBound() *function*

```
<HTML>

<HEAD>
<TITLE>UBound Example</TITLE>
</HEAD>


<SCRIPT LANGUAGE="VBScript">
<!--
'.................................................
' ProcOrder_OnClick()
'
' Creates an array with the number of elements
' specified by the user. Fills the array with items.
'.................................................

SUB ProcOrder_OnClick()
  Dim OrderArray()
  Dim InputValue
  Dim Counter
  Dim ArrayDim
  Dim LastDim

'.................................................
' Assigns the input value to a variable.
'.................................................
  InputValue=UserValue.Value

'.................................................
' Makes sure the value entered is numeric; if it is,
' it is used to specify the number of elements in
' the array.
'.................................................
```

continued on next page

continued from previous page

```
  If IsNumeric(InputValue) Then
'...............................................
' Set the array dimension value to one less than the
' number requested by the user. This is to account
' for the fact that VBScript uses zero-based
' arrays.
'...............................................
    ArrayDim = InputValue - 1
    ReDim OrderArray(ArrayDim)
'...............................................
' Requests the number of items specified in the
' input field. Places each value in the array.
'...............................................
    For Counter = 0 To InputValue-1

      OrderArray(Counter)=InputBox("Type item number " & Counter+1)

    Next

'................................................
' UBound() determines the last subscript value. This
' value is used to identify the last value entered.
'................................................
    LastDim=UBound(OrderArray)

    MsgBox "The last item ordered is " & OrderArray(LastDim)

'................................................
' Message sent when a non-numeric value was entered.
'................................................
  Else
    MsgBox "Type a numeric value in the field."
  End If

END SUB

-->
</SCRIPT>

<BODY>

<FONT FACE="Arial" SIZE=2>
<FONT COLOR=Fushia>

<CENTER>
   <FONT SIZE=6>Place Order<P>

</CENTER>

  <HR>

  <FONT FACE="Arial" SIZE=2>
  <FONT COLOR=BLACK>

  <BR>
  <CENTER>
  How many items are you ordering: <INPUT NAME=UserValue SIZE=10>
```

```
  <BR>
  <BR>
  <INPUT TYPE=BUTTON VALUE="Begin Order" NAME="ProcOrder">

  </CENTER>

</BODY>

</HTML>
```

Example The Array Handling project at the end of this chapter uses the `UBound()` function to locate the highest value in an array. The values in the array are sorted prior to calling the `UBound()` function, so the last element of the array contains the largest value.

Comments The `UBound()` function is normally used with the `LBound()` function to identify the upper and lower limits of a dynamic array. Once these subscript values are determined, you can quickly determine the number of elements in the array by subtracting the lower subscript value (the value returned by `LBound()`) from the upper subscript value (the value returned by `UBound()`) and adding one.

See Also `IsArray()`, `LBound()`

Array Handling Project

The Array Handling project demonstrates the concepts of working with arrays using the statements and functions covered in this chapter. This project creates a page that places values entered by the user into an array. When the user finishes entering values,

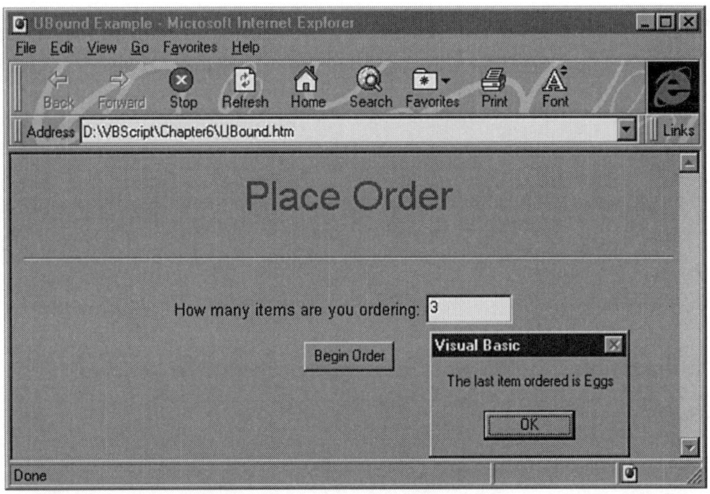

Figure 6-4 The `UBound()` function identifies the subscript of the last element; that value is used to display the last value in the array

the array is sorted and the LBound() and UBound() functions are used to identify the lowest and highest values in the array.

Building the Project

1. Start the project by setting up the standard HTML template used for all VBScript examples in this book. The VBScript code is placed in the <HEAD> section of the HTML code to keep everything consistent. Remember to place the HTML comment tags <!-- and --> around the VBScript code so that it will be ignored by browsers that cannot interpret the <SCRIPT> tag.

```
<HTML>

<HEAD>
<TITLE>Array Handling Project</TITLE>

<SCRIPT LANGUAGE="VBScript">

<!--

-->

</SCRIPT>

</HEAD>

<BODY>

</BODY>

</HTML>
```

2. In the <BODY> section, place the desired title information for the Web page. For this example, you are creating a Web page that sorts a series of numeric values, so this is described in the titles at the beginning of the <BODY> section.

```
<BODY>

<FONT FACE="Arial">
<FONT COLOR=Fuchsia>

   <CENTER>
   <FONT SIZE=6>Number Sorting<P>

   </CENTER>
   <FONT COLOR=White>
   <FONT SIZE=4>To sort numeric values, type each value in field and
   press Input Value button. When all values are entered press
   the Perform Sort button.

  <HR>
```

3. At the beginning of the VBScript code, in the <HEAD> section, create the following global variable definitions. These variables are declared at this location so that

they can be accessed by both procedures. Also, by declaring their initial values outside of the procedures, the values are only set when the page loads. The **OrderArray** variable is initially allocated 10 elements; this allows values to be added to the array. If additional values need to be added, the program has checks to see if the array is full, and if so, increases its subscript value. The **Counter** variable is used to keep track of the number of subscripts used within the array. The **ArrayDim** variable keeps track of the number of elements that can be added to the array.

```
Dim OrderArray()
  Dim Counter
  Dim ArrayDim

  ReDim OrderArray(9)
  Counter=0
  ArrayDim=10
```

4. In the **<BODY>** section, add an input field named **UserItem** where the user can input each value to be added to the array.

```
<FONT SIZE=2>
  <FONT COLOR=BLACK>

  <BR>
  <CENTER>
  Type a Numeric Value: <INPUT NAME=UserItem SIZE=10>

<FONT SIZE=2>
  <FONT COLOR=BLACK>
```

5. Add a button named Input Value that can be pressed to accept each value that is typed in the **UserItem()** field. When the button is pressed, a VBScript procedure named **AcceptValue.OnClick()** will be called.

```
<INPUT TYPE=BUTTON VALUE="Input Value" NAME="AcceptValue">
```

6. In the VBScript section, create a procedure called **AcceptValue_OnClick()** that is called each time the Input Value button is pressed. In this procedure, first verify that a numeric value was typed in the **UserItem** field. If the field does not contain a numeric value, display a message instructing the user to type a numeric value, as illustrated in Figure 6-5. Next, make sure that the array is large enough to receive a new value by comparing the **Counter** value with the **ArrayDim** value. If the **ArrayDim** value is smaller than the **Counter**, increase its value and reallocate the size of the array. Remember to use the **Preserve** keyword to maintain the values in the array. Convert the new item to a variant value with a subtype of double (use the **CDbl()** function) and place the value in the appropriate element of the array.

```
SUB AcceptValue_OnClick()

  If Not IsNumeric(UserItem.Value) Then
```

continued on next page

continued from previous page

```
    MsgBox "Type a Numeric Value in the field"
  Else

If Counter > ArrayDim Then

      ArrayDim = ArrayDim + 1

      ReDim Preserve OrderArray(ArrayDim)
    End If

OrderArray(Counter) = CDbl(UserItem.Value)
    Counter=Counter+1

  End If

END SUB
```

7. Add a button named Perform Sort that is pressed when all of the desired items have been typed in the **UserItem** field. When the button is pressed, a VBScript procedure named **SortOrder.OnClick()** will be called.

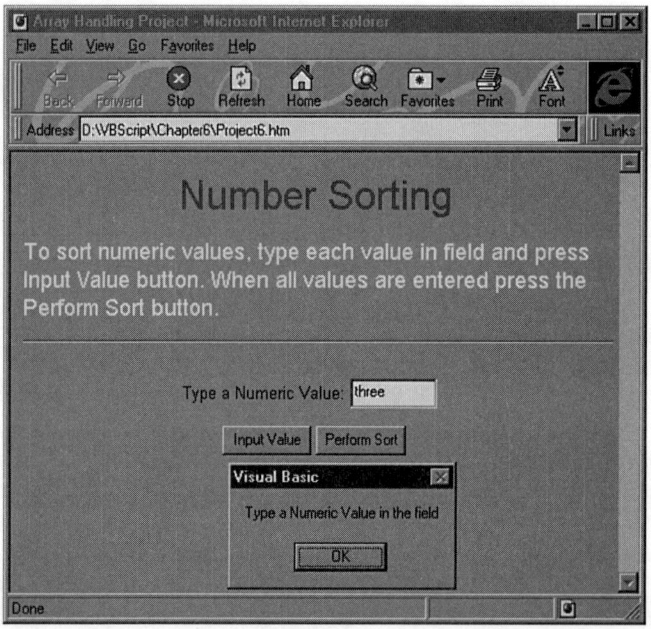

Figure 6-5 The **IsNumeric()** function verifies that a numeric value was typed

```
<INPUT TYPE=BUTTON VALUE="Perform Sort" NAME="SortOrder">

  </CENTER>

</BODY>

</HTML>
```

8. In the VBScript section, create a procedure called **SortOrder_OnClick()** that is called when the Perform Sort button is pressed. In this procedure, first set the **Counter** variable to the appropriate value by subtracting one. This is necessary because one is added to this variable at the end of the **AcceptValue_OnClick()** procedure to prepare it for the next time the procedure is called. Next create an **If** statement that checks to see if any elements of the array are empty. If so, resize the array so that the empty elements are removed. Create a sort routine that sorts the array in ascending order. Use the variable **MinIndex** to keep track of the subscript of the lowest value in each loop.

```
SUB SortOrder_OnClick()

  Dim TempVar
  Dim MinIndex
  Dim Counter2
  Dim Counter3

  Counter=Counter-1

  If Counter < ArrayDim Then

    ReDim Preserve OrderArray(Counter)

  End If

  For Counter2 = 0 To Counter

    MinIndex=Counter2

     For Counter3 = Counter2+1 To Counter

       If OrderArray(Counter3) < OrderArray(MinIndex) Then
         MinIndex=Counter3
       End If

    Next

    TempVar=OrderArray(MinIndex)
    OrderArray(MinIndex)=OrderArray(Counter2)
    OrderArray(Counter2)=TempVar

   Next
```

9. At the bottom of the SortOrder_OnClick() procedure, add one MsgBox() line that indicates the smallest value that was entered. Since the value was sorted to the top of the array, use the LBound() function to return the smallest value, as illustrated in Figure 6-6. Add a MsgBox() line that uses the UBound() function to return the largest value in the array (the sort moved it to the end of the array), as illustrated in Figure 6-7.

```
    MsgBox "The smallest numeric value is " & OrderArray(LBound(OrderArray))
    MsgBox "The largest numeric value is " & OrderArray(UBound(OrderArray))

END SUB

-->
</SCRIPT>
```

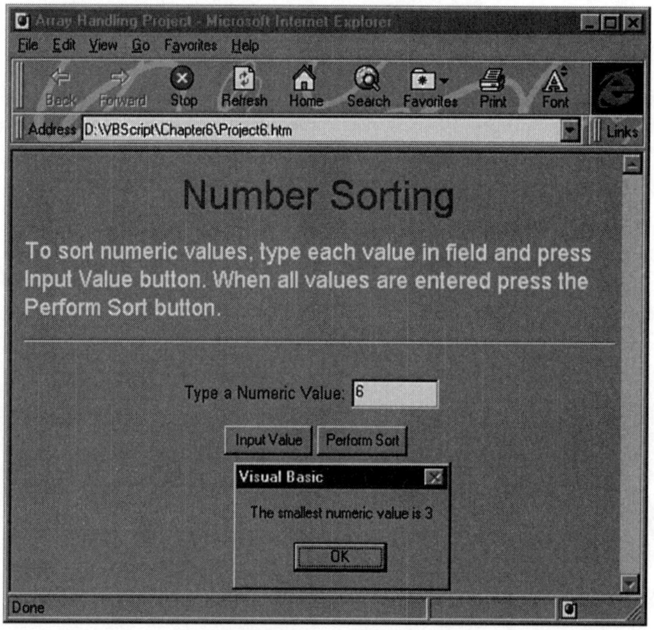

Figure 6-6 The LBound() function determines the first value in the array

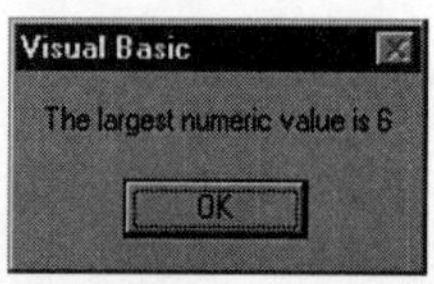

Figure 6-7 The UBound() function determines the last value in the array

How It Works

The Array Handling project illustrates some of the basic capabilities of a dynamic array. It creates a dynamic array that accepts numeric values entered by the user. If the number of values entered exceeds the original size of the array, the size of the array is redeclared to be one element larger. This process continues until the user enters all of the desired values. Conversely, once all of the values have been entered, if the declared size of the array is greater than the number of values added, the array is redeclared to the appropriate size.

After all values have been added by the user, the `SortOrder_OnClick()` procedure sorts the entire array in ascending order. This is accomplished using two `For` loops: one that contains a variable that keeps track of the lowest subscript value and another that contains a variable used to move values.

When the array is sorted, the `LBound()` function is used with the `MsgBox()` function to display the lowest value that was typed. The `LBound()` function can be used to locate the value because it has been sorted to the top of the array. The `UBound()` function is used to locate the largest value in the array, and the `MsgBox()` function displays that value.

This project provides a good opportunity to see how to use the various array functions covered in this chapter. Listing 6-3 contains the complete source code for the project.

Listing 6-3 Complete source for the Array Handling project

```
<HTML>

<HEAD>
<TITLE>Array Handling Project</TITLE>
</HEAD>


<SCRIPT LANGUAGE="VBScript">
<!--
'..................................................
' These variables are declared globally so that they
' can be used by both procedures, and so that the
' values are reset only when the page is loaded.
' The OrderArray array variable is a dynamic array; it
' is initially allocated with a subscript value of
' 10. The program later checks to see if the array
' needs more values, if it has been only partially
' filled.
'..................................................
  Dim OrderArray()
  Dim Counter
  Dim ArrayDim

  ReDim OrderArray(10)
  Counter=0
  ArrayDim=9
```

continued on next page

continued from previous page

```
'..................................................
' AcceptValue_OnClick()
'
' This procedure is called each time the Input Value
' button is pressed. The value typed in the field is
' first checked to make sure it is a numeric value. If
' the value is not numeric, the user receives a message;
' otherwise, the processing continues.
'..................................................
SUB AcceptValue_OnClick()

  If Not IsNumeric(UserItem.Value) Then

    MsgBox "Type a Numeric Value in the field"
  Else

'.........................................................
' This If statement makes sure the array has enough
' subscript values to accept a new value. If it is
' too small, a new subscript value is added. The Preserve
' keyword is used to maintain the values that are currently
' in the array.
'.........................................................
    If Counter > ArrayDim Then

      ArrayDim = ArrayDim + 1

      ReDim Preserve OrderArray(ArrayDim)
    End If

'.............................................................
' The value in the input field is converted to a variant value
' with a subtype of double and copied to the appropriate
' element of the array. The counter variable is increased by
' one so that the next time the procedure is called, the next
' value will be written to the next element of the array.
'.............................................................
    OrderArray(Counter) = CDbl(UserItem.Value)
    Counter=Counter+1

  End If

END SUB

'.................................................................
' SortOrder_OnClick()
'
' This procedure is called when the Perform Sort button is pressed.
' The values in the array are sorted in ascending order, and the
' minimum and maximum values are displayed on the screen.
'.................................................................
SUB SortOrder_OnClick()

  Dim TempVar
  Dim MinIndex
  Dim Counter2
  Dim Counter3
```

```
'..............................................................
' Since the last time the AcceptValue_OnClick() procedure was run, the
' Counter was increased by one; this subtracts one to indicate the
' actual number of items entered.
'...............................................................
  Counter=Counter-1

'.........................................
' Removes any unused elements from the array.
'.........................................
  If Counter < ArrayDim Then

    ReDim Preserve OrderArray(Counter)

  End If

'..............
' Sort Routine
' .............
  For Counter2 = 0 To Counter

    MinIndex=Counter2

'......................................
' Locates the smallest value in the array.
'......................................
    For Counter3 = Counter2+1 To Counter

      If OrderArray(Counter3) < OrderArray(MinIndex) Then
        MinIndex=Counter3
      End If

    Next
'........................................
' Moves the smallest values to the top of
' the array
'........................................
    TempVar=OrderArray(MinIndex)
    OrderArray(MinIndex)=OrderArray(Counter2)
    OrderArray(Counter2)=TempVar

   Next
'...................................................
' Writes the smallest and largest values to the screen.
'...................................................
   MsgBox "The smallest numeric value is " & OrderArray(LBound(OrderArray))
   MsgBox "The largest numeric value is " & OrderArray(UBound(OrderArray))

END SUB

-->
</SCRIPT>

<BODY>

<FONT FACE="Arial">
<FONT COLOR=Fuchsia>
```

continued on next page

continued from previous page

```
   <CENTER>
   <FONT SIZE=6>Number Sorting<P>

   </CENTER>
   <FONT COLOR=White>
   <FONT SIZE=4>To sort numeric values, type each value in field and
   press Input Value button. When all values are entered press
   the Perform Sort button.

  <HR>

  <FONT SIZE=2>
  <FONT COLOR=BLACK>

  <BR>
  <CENTER>
  Type a Numeric Value: <INPUT NAME=UserItem SIZE=10>

  <BR>
  <BR>

<!-- Calls the AcceptValue_OnClick() procedure to add the value to the array -->
  <INPUT TYPE=BUTTON VALUE="Input Value" NAME="AcceptValue">

<!-- Calls the SortOrder_OnClick() procedure to sort values in the array -->
  <INPUT TYPE=BUTTON VALUE="Perform Sort" NAME="SortOrder">

  </CENTER>

</BODY>

</HTML>
```

7

DATA CONVERSION

7

DATA CONVERSION

Unlike other versions of Visual Basic, VBScript has only one data type, but it provides twelve subtypes to apply when using functions that rely upon a specific type of data. Such data values should be converted to the appropriate format before calling functions to perform specific calculations.

VBScript Values

VBScript's single data type, variant, allows you to store either numeric or string information within the same variable. Although the use of one data type provides ease in transferring data from one variable to another, it can also provide run-time error problems if the data is not properly converted before performing any type of calculation.

To help eliminate calculation errors, a variant value should be converted to the appropriate subtype before performing calculations. The functions described in this chapter give you the means to convert a variable to the necessary subtype. Table 7-1 outlines the variant subtypes available within VBScript.

Table 7-1 Variant subtypes

Subtype	Description
Boolean	A Boolean value of TRUE or FALSE.
Byte	Integer value in the range of 0 to 255.
Error	An error number.
Empty	Variable has not been initialized.
Date	Date value in the range of January 1, 100, to December 31, 9999, for Microsoft Windows. Other platforms may have different date ranges.
Double	Double-precision, floating-point number in the range -1.79769313486232E308 to -4.94065645841247E-324 for negative values; 4.94065645841247E-324 to 1.79769313486232E308 for positive values.

continued on next page

continued from previous page

Subtype	Description
Integer	Integer value in the range -32,768 to 32,767.
Long	Integer value in the range -2,147,483,648 to 2,147,483,647.
Null	Variable does not contain valid data.
Object	An OLE automation object.
Single	Single-precision, floating-point number in the range -3.402823E38 to -1.401298E-45 for negative values; 1.401298E-45 to 3.402823E38 for positive values.
String	String of variable length. The maximum length is approximately two billion characters.

Standard, Hexadecimal, and Octal Notations

The VBScript functions normally return values using standard (base 10) notation. This is the form of counting that we all learned in grade school, using the digits 0–9.

Quite often, systems require numeric values in other formats, such as binary, hexadecimal, or octal notations. A binary number uses 0s and 1s to express the desired value. A hexadecimal number uses 16 digits, 0–9 and A–F to express the desired number. An octal number uses 8 digits, 0–7, to express a value. These types of notation are quite often required when dealing with system resources, such as memory locations.

VBScript provides the functions needed to convert a value to either hexadecimal or octal notation. These functions are the `Hex()` and `Oct()` functions. Each of these functions is described in more detail later in this chapter.

Errors During Conversion

Before performing a data conversion, it is important to make sure that the variable contains the appropriate type of value for the conversion function. Failure to check the value can cause users to receive a run-time error when they access your Web page.

Several methods can be used to check the value. If you want to find out whether a string value can be converted to a numeric value, you will want to use the `IsNumeric()` function. To check the range of values, you will need to use an `If()` statement to make sure it is within the desired range.

For more information about data validation functions, refer to Chapter 4, Data Validation.

Summary of Data Conversion Functions

Table 7-2 summarizes the data conversion functions covered in this chapter. A detailed description of each function follows this table. Each of these functions is demonstrated in the data conversion project at the end of the chapter.

Table 7-2 Data conversion function summary

Use...	To Do This...
`Abs`	Determine the absolute value of a numeric expression.
`CBool`	Convert a variant expression so it has a subtype of Boolean.
`CByte`	Convert a variant expression so it has a subtype of byte.
`CDate`	Convert a variant expression so it has a subtype of date.
`CDbl`	Convert a variant expression so it has a subtype of double.
`CInt`	Convert a variant expression so it has a subtype of integer.
`CLng`	Convert a variant expression so it has a subtype of long.
`CSng`	Convert a variant expression so it has a subtype of single.
`CStr`	Convert a variant expression so it has a subtype of string.
`Fix`	Truncate the decimal portion of a number and return only the integer portion.
`Hex`	Convert the numeric expression to a hexadecimal value.
`Int`	Truncate the decimal portion of a number and return only the integer portion.
`Oct`	Convert the numeric expression to octal (base 8) notation.
`Sgn`	Determine whether the numeric expression is positive, negative, or equal to zero.

Abs Function

Purpose

Use the `Abs()` function to determine the absolute value of a numeric expression. This is useful when working with numeric values to ensure that the value is always positive. Table 7-3 describes the expressions you can use with the `Abs()` function. Table 7-4 indicates the values returned based upon expression type.

Syntax

`Abs(expression)`

Table 7-3 Argument of the `Abs()` function

Argument	Description
`expression`	A valid numeric expression, or a `NULL` value

Table 7-4 Values returned by the `Abs()` function

If the Expression Is...	The `Abs` Function Returns...
A positive value (`45`)	A positive value (`45`)
A positive decimal value (`45.23`)	A positive decimal value (`45.23`)
A negative value (`-45`)	A positive value (`45`)

continued on next page

continued from previous page

If the Expression Is...	The Abs Function Returns...
A negative decimal value (-45.23)	A positive decimal value (45.23)
NULL	NULL

Description

As illustrated in Table 7-4, the **Abs()** function returns the unsigned, or positive value of the numeric expression. Therefore, both **Abs(-245)** and **Abs(245)** return the value **245**, even though **-245** is a negative value.

Listing 7-1 uses the **Abs()** function to determine the absolute value of the numeric value typed by the user. The **MsgBox()** function displays the value returned by the **Abs()** function on the screen, as illustrated in Figure 7-1.

Listing 7-1 Using the Abs() *function*

```
<HEAD>
<TITLE>Abs Example</TITLE>

<SCRIPT LANGUAGE="VBScript">
<!--
'.........................................................
' AbsoluteValue_OnClick()
' Determines the absolute value for the value typed in
' the field by the user.
'.........................................................
SUB AbsoluteValue_OnClick()

 Dim UserValue

 UserValue=InputValue.Value

'.........................................................
' Use the IsNumeric() function to make sure the expression
' is a numeric value, before calling the Abs function.
'.........................................................
 If IsNumeric(UserValue) Then

  MsgBox "The Absolute Value is " & Abs(UserValue)

 Else

  MsgBox "Type a numeric value in the field"

 End If

END SUB
-->

</SCRIPT>
</HEAD>

<BODY>

<CENTER>
```

```
<FONT SIZE=6>Absolute Value<P>
</CENTER>
<HR>

<FONT SIZE=4>

<PRE>Type a value: <INPUT NAME=InputValue SIZE=20>
<HR>
<CENTER>
<INPUT TYPE=BUTTON VALUE="Determine Absolute Value" NAME="AbsoluteValue">
</CENTER>
</FONT>

</BODY>

</HTML>
```

Example The Data Conversion project at the end of this chapter uses the `Abs()` function to determine the absolute value of the value typed in the Enter Value to Convert field. The `Abs()` function is called when the checkbox next to the Absolute Value field is selected. The absolute value displays in the field next to the description.

Comments The `Abs()` function only evaluates numeric expressions. If it receives a nonnumeric expression, a run-time error is returned. To eliminate errors, use the `IsNumeric()` function prior to calling the `Abs()` function. For more information about the `IsNumeric()` function, refer to Chapter 4, Data Validation.

See Also `Sgn()`

CBool FUNCTION

Purpose Use the `CBool()` function to convert a variant expression so it has a subtype of Boolean. Converting the value allows you to work with it as a Boolean value of either `TRUE` or `FALSE`. Table 7-5 describes the types of expressions you can use with the `CBool()` function. Table 7-6 indicates the values returned based upon the type of expression passed to the `CBool()` function.

Syntax `CBool(expression)`

Table 7-5 Argument of the `CBool()` function

Argument	Description
`expression`	Any valid expression

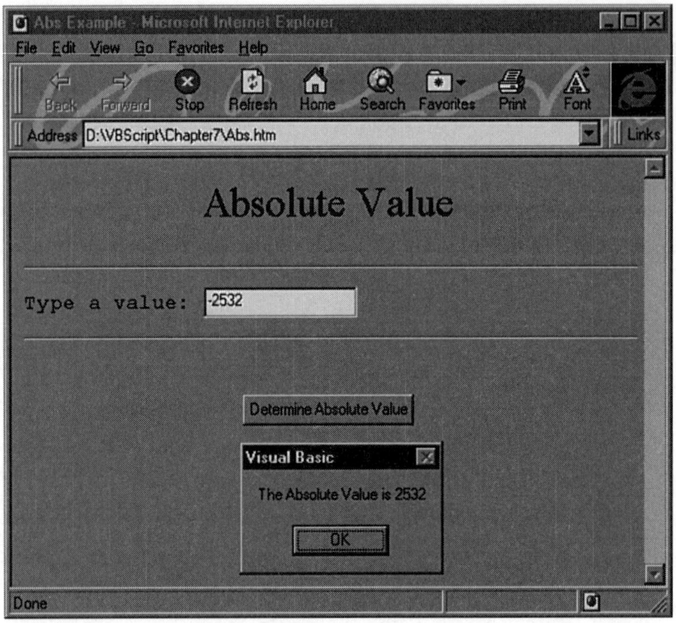

Figure 7-1 The `Abs()` function returns a positive value indicating the absolute value of the expression

Table 7-6 Values returned by the `CBool()` function

If the Expression Contains...	`CBool` Returns...
0	`FALSE`
Numeric value (other than 0)	`TRUE`
String expression `TRUE`	`TRUE`
String expression `FALSE`	`FALSE`
Any other string expression	Run-time error
Valid mathematical expression	`TRUE` or `FALSE` based on value of expression
Time expression (`12:00`)	Run-time error
Date expression (`6/19/96`)	Run-time error

Description The `CBool()` function evaluates the expression it receives and returns a Boolean value. As illustrated in Table 7-6, the function can only evaluate numeric expressions or the actual string value of `TRUE` or `FALSE`. If the `CBool()` function cannot interpret the expression, a run-time error is returned.

The example in Listing 7-2 uses the `CBool()` function to convert the expression typed in the `InputValue` field to a Boolean expression. The ConvertBoolean_OnClick() function captures the expression for the `CBool()` function and uses the `MsgBox()` function to display the results of the `CBool()` function, as illustrated in Figure 7-2.

To demonstrate the fact that the `CBool()` function not only evaluates numeric expressions but also interprets the strings **TRUE** and **FALSE**, the example in Listing 7-2 does not perform any type of data validation on the input expression.

Listing 7-2 Using the `CBool()` *function*

```
<HTML>

<HEAD>
<TITLE>CBool Example</TITLE>

<SCRIPT LANGUAGE="VBScript">
<!--
'.....................................................
' ConvertBoolean_OnClick()
' Converts the value typed by the user to a Boolean value.
'.....................................................
SUB ConvertBoolean_OnClick()

 Dim UserValue

 UserValue= CBool(InputValue.Value)

  MsgBox "The Boolean Value of " & InputValue.Value & " is " & UserValue

END SUB
-->

</SCRIPT>
</HEAD>

<BODY>

<CENTER>

<FONT SIZE=6>Boolean Value Conversion<P>
</CENTER>
<HR>

<FONT SIZE=4>

<PRE>Type a value: <INPUT NAME=InputValue SIZE=20>
<HR>
<CENTER>
<INPUT TYPE=BUTTON VALUE="Return Boolean Value" NAME="ConvertBoolean">
</CENTER>
</FONT>

</BODY>

</HTML>
```

Figure 7-2 The `MsgBox()` function displays the results of the `CBool()` function

Example The Data Conversion project at the end of this chapter uses the `CBool()` function to determine the Boolean value of the value typed in the Enter Value to Convert field. The `CBool()` function is called when the checkbox next to the Boolean Value field is selected. The Boolean value displays in the field next to the description.

Before displaying the value in the field, the `CStr()` function is used to convert the value to a string.

Comments To eliminate run-time errors, it is best to allow only numeric expressions to be passed to the `CBool()` function. You can use the `IsNumeric()` function to check an expression before calling the `CBool()` function. For more information about the `IsNumeric()` function, refer to Chapter 4, Data Validation.

See Also `CByte()`, `CDate()`, `CDbl()`, `CInt()`, `CLng()`, `CSng()`, `CStr()`

CByte Function

Purpose Use the `CByte()` function to convert a variant expression so it has a subtype of byte. Table 7-7 describes the types of expressions you can use with the `CByte()` function.

Syntax `CByte(expression)`

Table 7-7 Argument of the `CByte()` function

Argument	Description
`expression`	Any expression whose value is between 0 and 255

Description

Use the **`CByte()`** function to convert a value to a byte value between 0 and 255. If the value of the expression is greater than 255, the **`CBool()`** function returns an overflow message at run time. This function is normally used to convert currency, single-precision, or double-precision values to byte values.

When the **`CByte()`** function encounters a decimal value, it rounds the value to the closest integer value. For example, **`CByte(22.23)`** returns a value of **22**, whereas **`CByte(22.89)`** returns a value of **23**.

The **`CByte()`** function also provides conversions from any other international data type recognized by your system to a byte subtype. For example, different values are used for decimal separators depending upon the locale settings for your computer.

Listing 7-3 uses the **`CByte()`** function to return a byte value for the expression typed in the **`InputValue`** field, as illustrated in Figure 7-3. The **`IsNumeric()`** function verifies that the field contains a numeric expression; then the range of the value is checked to make sure it is between 0 and 255.

Listing 7-3 Using the `CByte()` function

```
<HTML>

<HEAD>
<TITLE>CByte Example</TITLE>

<SCRIPT LANGUAGE="VBScript">
<!--
'......................................................
' ConvertByte_OnClick()
' Converts the value typed by the user to a byte value.
'......................................................
SUB ConvertByte_OnClick()

  Dim UserValue

  UserValue = InputValue.Value

'......................................................
' Use the IsNumeric() function to make sure a numeric value
' was typed.
'......................................................
  If IsNumeric(UserValue) Then
```

continued on next page

continued from previous page

```
'.....................................................
' Make sure the value typed is between 0 and 255 to avoid
' an overflow message at run time.
'.....................................................
    If (UserValue >= 0) AND (UserValue <= 255) Then

      MsgBox "The Byte Value of " & InputValue.Value & " is " & CByte(UserValue)

    Else

      MsgBox "Type a value greater than 0 or less than 255"

    End If

  Else

    MsgBox "Type a numeric value between 0 and 255"

  End If

END SUB
-->

</SCRIPT>
</HEAD>

<BODY>

<CENTER>

<FONT SIZE=6>Byte Value Conversion<P>
</CENTER>
<HR>

<FONT SIZE=4>

<PRE>Type a value: <INPUT NAME=InputValue SIZE=20>

<HR>
<INPUT TYPE=BUTTON VALUE="Return Byte Value" NAME="ConvertByte">

</FONT>

</BODY>

</HTML>
```

Example

The Data Conversion project at the end of this chapter uses the **`CByte()`** function to determine the byte value of the value typed in the Enter Value to Convert field. The **`CByte()`** function is called when the checkbox next to the Byte Value field is selected. The byte value displays in the field next to the description.

The appropriate data validation is performed to make sure the value is numeric and within the allowable range of 0 to 255 for a byte value.

Comments To help eliminate run-time data errors, use the `IsNumeric()` function to check an expression before calling the `CByte()` function. For more information about the `IsNumeric()` function, refer to Chapter 4, Data Validation. It is also a good idea to make sure the expression is within the acceptable range for a byte value, between 0 and 255. This can be accomplished by using an `If` statement, as demonstrated in Listing 7-3.

See Also `CBool()`, `CDate()`, `CDbl()`, `CInt()`, `CLng()`, `CSng()`, `CStr()`

CDate FUNCTION

Purpose Use the `CDate()` function to convert a variant expression so it has a subtype of date. If you intend to use the other time and date functions covered in Chapter 5, Date and Time Values, it is important that the value be converted to a subtype of date before calling most of the functions covered in that chapter. Table 7-8 describes the types of expressions you can use with the `CDate()` function. Table 7-9 describes the values returned by the `CDate()` function.

Syntax `CDate(expression)`

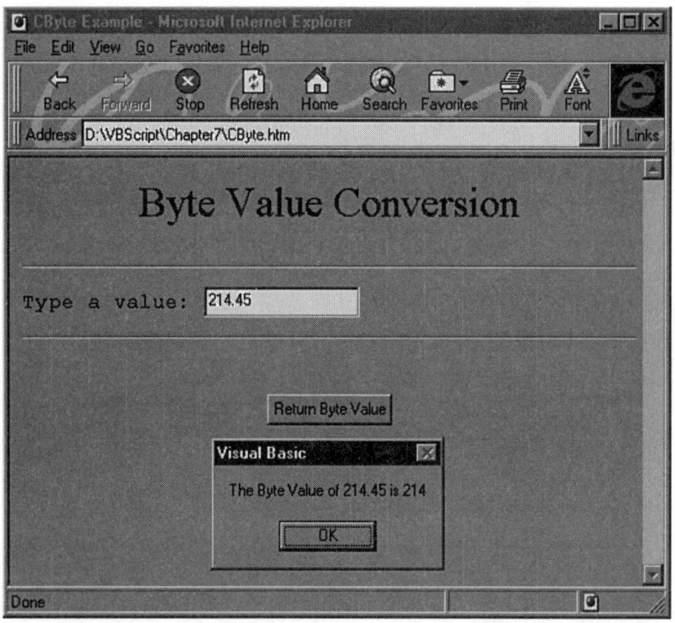

Figure 7-3 The `CByte()` function returns a byte value for the expression typed

Table 7-8 Argument of the `CDate()` function

Argument	Description
`expression`	Any expression that can be converted to a valid date or time. This includes numeric values in the range of -657,434 through 2,958,465.

Table 7-9 Return values for the `CDate()` function

If Expression Is...	`CDate` Returns...
Date and time expression	A date and time value.
Decimal value	A time value that corresponds to the portion of the day represented by the decimal value. For example, `CDate(.5)` returns `12:00 PM` and `CDate(.25)` returns `6:00 AM`. If the decimal value is included with a numeric value in the valid range of -657,434 to 2,958,465, both the date and time are returned. For example, `CDate(1000.25)` returns the value of `9/26/02 6:00 AM`
Numeric value > 2,958,465	Run-time error.
Numeric value < -657,434	Run-time error.
Numeric value in range of -657,434 to 2,958,465	A date expression in the range of 1/1/100 through 12/31/9999. The base date value of 12/30/1899 is used to calculate the date. The date is calculated as the number of days prior to (negative value) or since (positive value) 12/30/1899. Therefore, `CDate(2)` returns `1/1/00`, and `CDate(-2)` returns `12/28/1899`.
Other string expression	Run-time error.
String expression that represents a date	A date expression.
Valid date	A date expression.
Valid time	A time expression.

Description

The `CDate()` function converts time and date expressions to variant expressions with a subtype of date, as indicated in Table 7-8. This also includes numeric values in the range of -657,434 to 2,958,465. When the `CDate()` function receives a value within this range, it converts it to either the number of days prior to 12/30/1899 (if the value is negative) or the number of days since 12/30/1899 (if the value is positive).

If the expression includes a decimal value, the decimal value is converted to a time that represents the portion of the day expressed by the decimal value. For example, if the `CDate()` function receives a decimal value of `.25`, it returns `6:00 AM`, because 6:00 a.m. is one quarter of the 24 hours in a day.

Listing 7-4 uses the **CDate()** function to convert the expression typed in the **InputValue** field. The **MsgBox()** function displays the results of the **CDate()** function. Figure 7-4 illustrates the value returned by the **CDate()** function when a string expression is typed in the **InputValue** field.

Listing 7-4 Using the `CDate()` *function*

```
<HTML>

<HEAD>
<TITLE>CDate Example</TITLE>

<SCRIPT LANGUAGE="VBScript">
<!--
'.......................................................
' ConvertDate_OnClick()
' Converts the value typed by the user to a date or time
' value with a subtype of date.
'.......................................................
SUB ConvertDate_OnClick()

  Dim UserValue

  UserValue = InputValue.Value

  MsgBox "The Date Value is " & CDate(UserValue)

END SUB
-->

</SCRIPT>

</HEAD>

<BODY>

<CENTER>

<FONT SIZE=6>Date Value Conversion<P>
</CENTER>
<HR>

<FONT SIZE=4>

<PRE>Type a value: <INPUT NAME=InputValue SIZE=20>

<HR>
<CENTER>
<INPUT TYPE=BUTTON VALUE="Return Date Value" NAME="ConvertDate">
</CENTER>
</FONT>

</BODY>

</HTML>
```

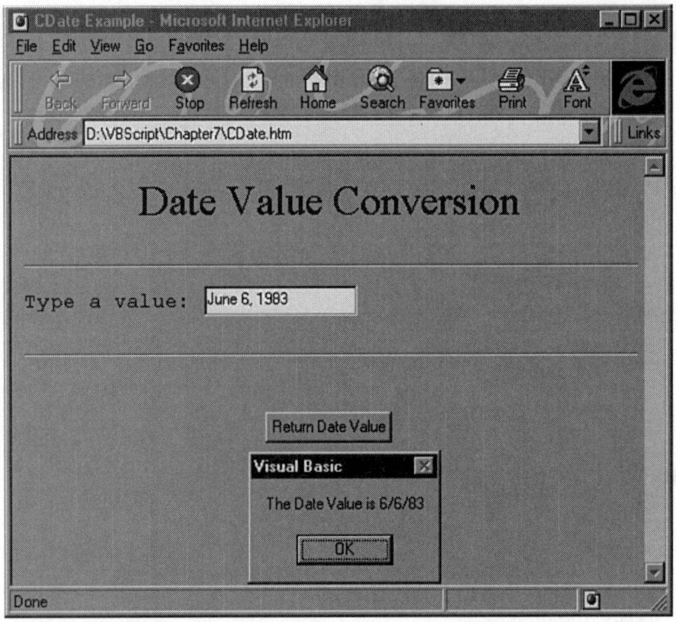

Figure 7-4 The `CDate()` function returns a date expression for a string expression

Example The Data Conversion project at the end of this chapter uses the `CDate()` function to determine the date and time value of the value typed in the Enter Value to Convert field. The `CDate()` function is called when the checkbox next to the Date Value field is selected. The date value displays in the field next to the description.

Comments To eliminate run-time errors, it is important to perform some type of range checking on the values prior to using the `CDate()` function. The `IsDate()` function can be used to check for a valid date or time expression. For more information about the `IsDate()` function, refer to Chapter 4, Data Validation. If you are designing your code to allow numeric values for the `CDate()` function, you will need to perform some type of validation to make sure the value is within the accepted range of -657,434 to 2,958,465. If VBScript receives a value outside this range, the user will receive an overflow message at run time.

See Also `IsDate()`

CDbl Function

Purpose Use the `CDbl()` function to convert a variant expression so it has subtype of double. This conversion is necessary to perform mathematical functions that involve values VBScript needs to recognize as double-precision floating-point numbers. Table 7-10 describes the types of expressions you can use with the `CDbl()` function.

Syntax `CDbl(expression)`

Table 7-10 Argument of the `CDbl()` function

Argument	Description
`expression`	Any numeric expression can be used with this function.

Description The `CDbl()` function converts a variant expression so it has a subtype of double. A subtype of double means that the expression is a double-precision floating-point number whose value is in the range of -1.79769313486232E308 to -4.94065645841247E-324 for negative values and 4.94065645841247E-324 to 1.79769313486232E308 for positive values.

The example in Listing 7-5 illustrates how to use the `CDbl()` function to convert an expression typed in the `InputValue` field. Figure 7-5 illustrates the return value of the `CDbl()` function displayed on the screen using the `MsgBox()` function.

Listing 7-5 Using the `CDbl()` function

```
<HTML>

<HEAD>
<TITLE>CDbl Example</TITLE>

<SCRIPT LANGUAGE="VBScript">
<!--
'..............................................................
' ConvertDouble_OnClick()
' Converts the value typed by the user to a double-precision
' floating-point value with a subtype of double.
'..............................................................
SUB ConvertDouble_OnClick()

  Dim UserValue
```

continued on next page

continued from previous page

```
  UserValue = InputValue.Value

  If IsNumeric(UserValue) Then

    MsgBox "The Value is " & CDbl(UserValue)

  Else

    MsgBox "Type a numeric value in the field"

  End If

END SUB
-->

</SCRIPT>

</HEAD>

<BODY>

<CENTER>

<FONT SIZE=6>Double Conversion<P>
</CENTER>
<HR>

<FONT SIZE=4>

<PRE>Type a value: <INPUT NAME=InputValue SIZE=50>

<HR>
<CENTER>
<INPUT TYPE=BUTTON VALUE="Convert to Double-Precision" NAME="ConvertDouble">
</CENTER>
</FONT>

</BODY>

</HTML>
```

Example

The Data Conversion project at the end of this chapter uses the `CDbl()` function to determine the double-precision floating-point value of the value typed in the Enter Value to Convert field. The `CDbl()` function is called when the checkbox next to the Double-Precision Floating-Point Value field is selected. The double-precision floating-point value displays in the field next to the description.

The appropriate data validation is performed using the `IsNumeric()` function to make sure the value is numeric.

Comments

The `CDbl()` function properly converts an international expression to a double subtype. Depending upon the locale setting used by your system, the decimal and thousands separators will vary. Use of the `CDbl()` function ensures that the proper separators are recognized.

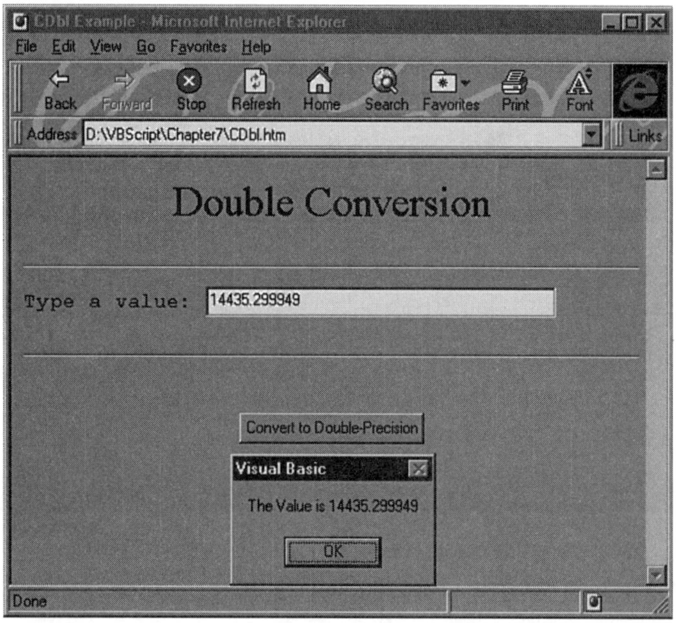

Figure 7-5 The `CDbl()` function converts the input value to a double-precision floating-point number

To help eliminate run-time data errors, use the `IsNumeric()` function to check an expression before calling the `CDbl()` function. For more information about the `IsNumeric()` function, refer to Chapter 4, Data Validation.

See Also `CBool()`, `CByte()`, `CDate()`, `CInt()`, `CLng()`, `CSng()`, `CStr()`

`CInt` FUNCTION

Purpose Use the `CInt()` function to convert a variant expression so it has a subtype of integer. This conversion is necessary to perform mathematical functions that require VBScript to recognize a value as an integer. Table 7-11 describes the types of expressions you can use with the `CInt()` function.

Syntax `CInt(expression)`

Table 7-11 Argument of the `CInt()` function

Argument	Description
`expression`	Any numeric expression can be used with this function.

Description

The `CInt()` function converts a variant expression so it has a subtype of integer. When the value is converted, if it contains a decimal, the value is rounded to the nearest integer value. For example, `CInt(32.34)` returns the value `32`, but `CInt(32.56)` returns the value `33`. If the value is negative, `CInt(-32.34)` returns the value `-32` and `CInt(-32.56)` returns the value `-33`.

Listing 7-6 illustrates how to use the `CInt()` function to convert an expression typed in the `InputValue` field so it has an integer subtype. Figure 7-6 illustrates the return value of the `CInt()` function displayed on the screen using the `MsgBox()` function.

A subtype of integer means that the values must be within the range of -32,768 to 32,767. A value outside that range will cause a run-time error to occur. To avoid a run-time error due to a value out of range, perform some sort of range checking as shown in Listing 7-6. Figure 7-7 illustrates the message displayed when the value typed is outside of the acceptable range for an integer.

Listing 7-6 Using the `CInt()` *function*

```
<HTML>

<HEAD>
<TITLE>CInt Example</TITLE>

<SCRIPT LANGUAGE="VBScript">
<!--
'.............................................................
' ConvertInteger_OnClick()
' Converts the value typed by the user to an integer value.
'.............................................................
SUB ConvertInteger_OnClick()

  Dim UserValue

  UserValue = InputValue.Value

'.............................................................
' Use the IsNumeric() function to make sure the field contains
' a numeric value. Convert the value to a double so you can
' check the range.
'.............................................................
  If IsNumeric(UserValue) Then

    UserValue = CDbl(UserValue)
```

```
'.........................................................
' Make sure the value is within the acceptable range for an
' integer value.
'.........................................................
    If (UserValue >= -32768) AND (UserValue <= 32767) Then

       MsgBox "The Integer Value of " & InputValue.Value & " is " & CInt(UserValue)

    Else

      MsgBox "Type a value between -32,768 and 32,767"

    End If

  Else

    MsgBox "Type a numeric value in the field"

  End If

END SUB
-->

</SCRIPT>

</HEAD>

<BODY>

<CENTER>

<FONT SIZE=6>Integer Conversion<P>
</CENTER>
<HR>

<FONT SIZE=4>

<PRE>Type a value: <INPUT NAME=InputValue SIZE=20>

<HR>
<CENTER>
<INPUT TYPE=BUTTON VALUE="Convert to Integer" NAME="ConvertInteger">
</CENTER>
</FONT>

</BODY>

</HTML>
```

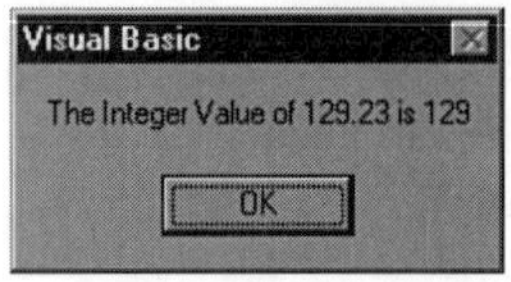

Figure 7-6 The `CInt()` function converts the input value to an integer value

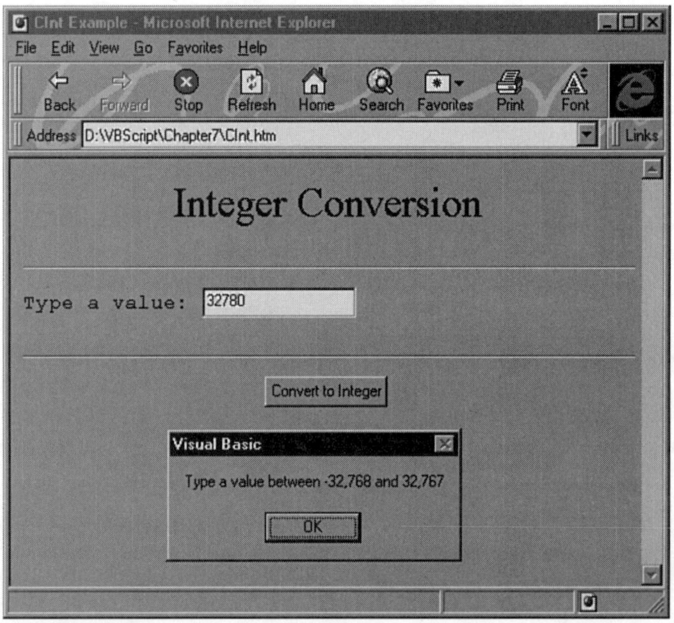

Figure 7-7 The `CInt()` function requires a value within the range of -32,768 to 32,767

Example

The Data Conversion project at the end of this chapter uses the `CInt()` function to determine the integer value of the value typed in the Enter Value to Convert field. The `CInt()` function is called when the checkbox next to the Integer Value (CInt Function) field is selected. The integer value displays in the field next to the description.

The appropriate data validation is performed to make sure the value is numeric and within the allowable range of -32,768 to 32,767 for an integer value.

Comments

The `CInt()` function properly converts an international expression to an integer subtype. Depending upon the locale setting used by your system, the decimal and thousands separators will vary. Use of the `CInt()` function ensures that the proper separators are recognized.

To help eliminate run-time data errors, use the `IsNumeric()` function to make sure an expression contains a numeric value before calling the `CInt()` function. For more information about the `IsNumeric()` function, refer to Chapter 4, Data Validation.

The `CInt()` function produces results different from those of the `Fix()` and `Int()` functions, which truncate the fractional portion of the expression. The `CInt()` function rounds the fractional portion to the nearest whole number. If the fractional part is exactly `.5`, the `CInt()` function rounds to the nearest even number. For example, `CInt(2.5)` returns a value of `2`, but `CInt(3.5)` returns a value of `4`. Table 7-12 illustrates the differences between the `Fix()`, `Int()`, and `CInt()` functions.

Table 7-12 Comparing the `CInt()` function to the `Int()` and `Fix()` functions

Value	`CInt(value)`	`Int(value)`	`Fix(value)`
3.6	4	3	3
3.2	3	3	3
3	3	3	3
-3.6	-4	-4	-3
-3.2	-3	-4	-3

See Also `CBool()`, `CByte()`, `CDate()`, `CDbl()`, `CLng()`, `CSng()`, `CStr()`, `Fix()`, `Int()`

CLng Function

Purpose Use the `CLng()` function to convert a variant expression so it has a subtype of long. This conversion is necessary to perform mathematical functions that require VBScript to recognize a value as a long integer. Table 7-13 describes the type of expressions you can use with the `CLng()` function.

Syntax `CLng(expression)`

Table 7-13 Argument of the `CLng()` function

Argument	Description
`expression`	Any numeric expression can be used with this function.

Description The `CLng()` function converts a variant expression so it has a subtype of long. A variant with a subtype of long is a long integer with an acceptable range of values from -2,147,483,648 to 2,147,483,647.

When the value is converted by the `CLng()` function, if it contains a decimal, the value is rounded to the nearest integer value. For example, `CLng(33,323.34)` returns the value **33,323**, but `CLng(33,323.56)` returns the value **33,324**. If the value is negative, `CLng(-33,323.34)` returns the value **-33,323**, and `CLng(-33,323.56)` returns the value **-33,324**.

Listing 7-7 illustrates how to use the `CLng()` function to convert an expression typed in the `InputValue` field so it has a long subtype. Figure 7-8 illustrates the return value of the `CLng()` function displayed on the screen using the `MsgBox()` function.

As previously stated, a subtype of long means that the values must be within the range of -2,147,483,648 to 2,147,483,647. A value outside that range will cause a run-time error to occur. To avoid a run-time error due to a value out of range, perform some sort of range checking, as shown in Listing 7-7.

Listing 7-7 Using the `CLng()` *function*

```
<HTML>

<HEAD>
<TITLE>CLng Example</TITLE>

<SCRIPT LANGUAGE="VBScript">
<!--
'..............................................................
' ConvertLong_OnClick()
' Converts the value typed by the user to a long integer value.
'..............................................................
SUB ConvertLong_OnClick()

  Dim UserValue

  UserValue = InputValue.Value

'.............................................................
' Use the IsNumeric function to make sure the field contains
' a numeric value. Convert value to a double so you can check
' the range.
'.............................................................
   If IsNumeric(UserValue) Then

     UserValue = CDbl(UserValue)

'.............................................................
' Make sure the value is within the acceptable range for a
' long integer value.
'.............................................................
     If (UserValue >= -2147483648) AND (UserValue <= 2147483647) Then

       MsgBox "The Long Value of " & InputValue.Value & " is " & CLng(UserValue)

     Else

       MsgBox "Type a value between -2,147,483,648 and 2,147,483,647"
```

```
      End If

    Else

      MsgBox "Type a numeric value in the field"

    End If

END SUB
-->

</SCRIPT>

</HEAD>

<BODY>

<CENTER>

<FONT SIZE=6>Long Integer Conversion<P>
</CENTER>
<HR>

<FONT SIZE=4>

<PRE>Type a value: <INPUT NAME=InputValue SIZE=20>

<HR>
<INPUT TYPE=BUTTON VALUE="Convert to a Long Integer" NAME="ConvertLong">

</FONT>

</BODY>

</HTML>
```

Example

The Data Conversion project at the end of this chapter uses the `CLng()` function to determine the long integer value of the value typed in the Enter Value to Convert field. The `CLng()` function is called when the checkbox next to the Long Integer Value field is selected. The long integer value displays in the field next to the description.

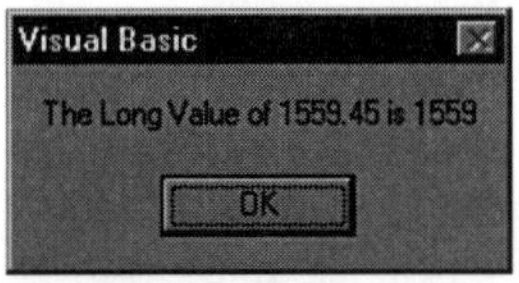

Figure 7-8 The `CLng()` function converts the input value to a long integer

The appropriate data validation is performed to make sure the value is numeric and within the allowable range of -2,147,483,648 to 2,147,483,647 for a long integer value.

Comments The `CLng()` function properly converts an international expression to a long subtype. Depending upon the locale setting used by your system, the decimal and thousands separators will vary. Use of the `CLng()` function ensures that the proper separators are recognized.

To help eliminate run-time data errors, use the `IsNumeric()` function to make sure an expression contains a numeric value before calling the `CLng()` function. For more information about the `IsNumeric()` function, refer to Chapter 4, Data Validation.

The `CLng()` function produces results different from those of the `Fix()` and `Int()` functions, which truncate the decimal portion of the expression. The `CLng()` function rounds the decimal portion to the nearest whole number. If the fractional part is exactly `.5`, the `CLng()` function rounds to the nearest larger even number. For example, `Int(2.5)` returns a value of `2`, but `CLng(3.5)` returns a value of `4`.

See Also `CBool()`, `CByte()`, `CDate()`, `CDbl()`, `CInt()`, `CSng()`, `CStr()`, `Fix()`, `Int()`

CSng Function

Purpose Use the `CSng()` function to convert a variant expression so it has a subtype of single. This conversion is necessary to perform mathematical functions that require VBScript to recognize a value as a single-precision floating-point number. Table 7-14 describes the type of expressions you can use with the `CSng()` function.

Syntax `CSng(expression)`

Table 7-14 Argument of the `CSng()` function

Argument	Description
`expression`	Any numeric expression can be used with this function.

Description The `CSng()` function converts a variant expression so it has a subtype of single. A subtype of single means that it is a single-precision floating-point number whose value is in the range of -3.402823E38 to -1.401298E-45 for negative values and 1.401298E-45 to 3.402823E38 for positive values.

Listing 7-8 illustrates how to use the `CSng()` function to convert an expression typed in the `InputValue` field to a single-precision floating-point value. Figure 7-9 illustrates the return value of the `CSng()` function displayed on the screen using the `MsgBox()` function.

Listing 7-8 Using the `CSng()` function

```
<HTML>

<HEAD>
<TITLE>CSng Example</TITLE>

<SCRIPT LANGUAGE="VBScript">
<!--
'.............................................................
' ConvertSingle_OnClick()
' Converts the value typed by the user to a single-precision
' floating-point value with a subtype of single.
'.............................................................
SUB ConvertSingle_OnClick()

  Dim UserValue

  UserValue = InputValue.Value

  If IsNumeric(UserValue) Then

    MsgBox "The Value is " & CSng(UserValue)

  Else

    MsgBox "Type a numeric value in the field"

  End If

END SUB
-->

</SCRIPT>

</HEAD>

<BODY>

<CENTER>

<FONT SIZE=6>Single-Precision Conversion<P>
</CENTER>
<HR>

<FONT SIZE=4>

<PRE>Type a value: <INPUT NAME=InputValue SIZE=50></PRE>

<HR>
<CENTER>
<INPUT TYPE=BUTTON VALUE="Convert to Single-Precision" NAME="ConvertSingle">
</CENTER>
</FONT>

</BODY>

</HTML>
```

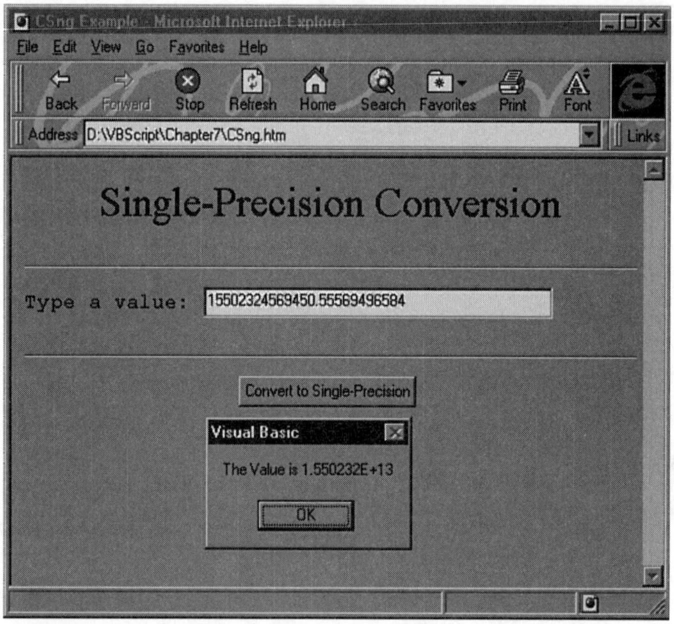

Figure 7-9 The `CSng()` function converts the input value to a single-precision floating-point number

Example

The Data Conversion project at the end of this chapter uses the `CSng()` function to determine the single-precision floating-point value of the value typed in the Enter Value to Convert field. The `CSng()` function is called when the checkbox next to the Single-Precision Floating-Point Value field is selected. The single-precision value displays in the field next to the description.

The appropriate data validation is performed using the `IsNumeric()` function to make sure the value is numeric.

Comments

The `CSng()` function properly `converts` an international expression to a single subtype. Depending upon the locale setting used by your system, the decimal and thousands separators will vary. Use of the `CSng()` function ensures that the proper separators are recognized.

To help eliminate run-time data errors, use the `IsNumeric()` function to check an expression before calling the `CSng()` function. For more information about the `IsNumeric()` function, refer to Chapter 4, Data Validation.

See Also

`CBool()`, `CByte()`, `CDate()`, `CDbl()`, `CInt()`, `CLng()`, `CStr()`

CStr Function

Purpose Use the CStr() function to convert a variant expression so it has a subtype of string. Table 7-15 describes the types of expressions you can use with the CStr() function.

Syntax `CStr(expression)`

Table 7-15 Argument of the CStr() function

Argument	Description
expression	Any expression can be used with this function.

Description The CStr() function converts a variant expression so it has a subtype of string. This is a valuable function to use when you want to ensure that the data is handled as a string.

The type of data passed to the CStr() function determines the return value of the function. Table 7-16 outlines the return values of the CStr() function.

Table 7-16 Values returned by the CStr() function

If the Expression Received Is...	The CStr Function Returns...
Boolean	A string containing a value of TRUE or FALSE indicating the value of the Boolean expression
Date	A string containing a date using the Short Date format of your system
Null	A run-time error
Empty	A zero-length string ("")
Error	A string containing the word Error followed by the error number
Numeric value	A string containing the number
String	A string containing the information

Listing 7-9 illustrates how to use the CStr() function to convert a variant value to a string. The MsgBox() function displays the results of the CStr() function, as illustrated in Figure 7-10.

Listing 7-9 Using the `CStr()` *function*

```
<HTML>

<HEAD>
<TITLE>CStr Example</TITLE>

<SCRIPT LANGUAGE="VBScript">
<!--
'..............................................................
' ConvertString_OnClick()
' Converts the value typed by the user to a string.
'..............................................................
SUB ConvertString_OnClick()

  Dim UserValue

  UserValue = InputValue.Value

    MsgBox "The Value is " & CStr(UserValue)

END SUB
-->

</SCRIPT>

</HEAD>

<BODY>

<CENTER>

<FONT SIZE=6>String Conversion<P>
</CENTER>
<HR>

<FONT SIZE=4>

<PRE>Type a value: <INPUT NAME=InputValue SIZE=50><PRE>

<HR>
<CENTER>
<INPUT TYPE=BUTTON VALUE="Convert String" NAME="ConvertString">
</CENTER>
</FONT>

</BODY>

</HTML>
```

Example

The Data Conversion project at the end of this chapter uses the `CStr()` function twice. The first time, it is used to convert the results of the `CBool()` function to a string. The second time, the `CStr()` function is used to convert the value typed in the Enter Value to Convert field to a string.

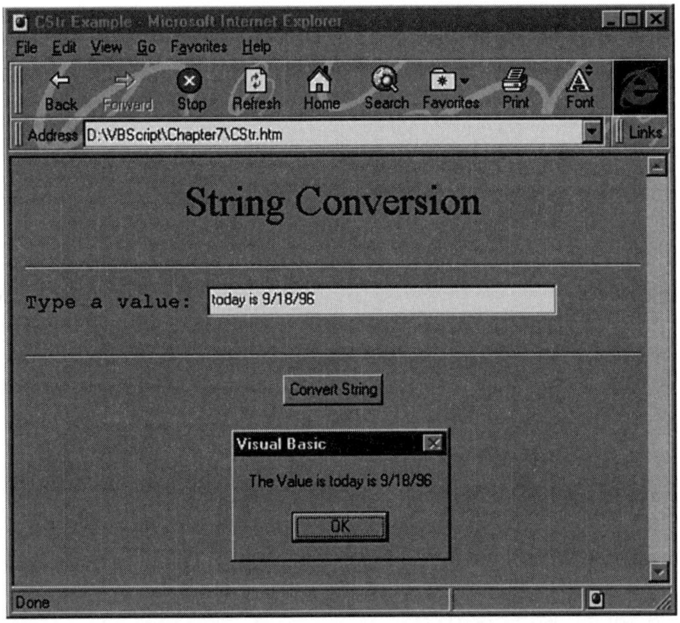

Figure 7-10 The `CStr()` function converts the input value to a string

The `CStr()` function is called when the checkbox next to the String Value field is selected. The string value displays in the field next to the description.

Comments The `CStr()` function properly converts an international expression a string. Depending upon the locale setting used by your system, the decimal and thousands separators will vary. Use of the `CStr()` function ensures that the proper separators are recognized.

See Also `CBool()`, `CByte()`, `CDate()`, `CDbl()`, `CInt()`, `CLng()`, `CSng()`

`Fix` FUNCTION

Purpose Use the `Fix()` function to return the integer portion of a number. Use this function when you want to truncate any decimal values and use only the whole number. Table 7-17 outlines the valid expressions for the `Fix()` function.

Syntax `Fix(expression)`

Table 7-17 Argument of the `Fix()` function

Argument	Description
`expression`	Any numeric expression, or a `NULL` value

Description

The `Fix()` function only returns the integer portion of the numeric expression it receives. Any decimal portion of the number is truncated. For example, `Fix(10.2)` returns a value of `10`, and `Fix(10.7)` also returns a value of `10`. If the numeric value is negative, the `Fix()` function truncates the decimal portion and returns the negative integer value. For example, `Fix(-4.2)` returns a value of `-4`.

Listing 7-10 uses the `Fix()` function to return an integer value for the value typed in the `InputValue` field. The `MsgBox()` function displays the value returned by the `Fix()` function, as illustrated in Figure 7-11.

Since the `Fix()` function only accepts integer values, all values passed to the function must be within the range of -32,768 to 32,767. A value outside that range will cause a run-time error to occur. To avoid a run-time error due to a value out of range, perform some sort of range checking as shown in Listing 7-10.

Listing 7-10 Using the `Fix()` function

```
<HTML>

<HEAD>
<TITLE>Fix Example</TITLE>

<SCRIPT LANGUAGE="VBScript">
<!--
'..........................................................
' FixInteger_OnClick()
' Converts the value typed by the user to an integer value.
'..........................................................
SUB FixInteger_OnClick()

  Dim UserValue

  UserValue = InputValue.Value

'..........................................................
' Use the IsNumeric function to make sure the field contains
' a numeric value. Convert the value to a double so you can
' check its range.
'..........................................................
  If IsNumeric(UserValue) Then

    UserValue = CDbl(UserValue)

'..........................................................
' Make sure the value is within the acceptable range for an
```

```
' integer value.
'.........................................................
    If (UserValue >= -32768) AND (UserValue <= 32767) Then

      MsgBox "The Integer Value of " & InputValue.Value & " is " & Fix(UserValue)

    Else

      MsgBox "Type a value between -32,768 and 32,767"

    End If

  Else

    MsgBox "Type a numeric value in the field"

  End If

END SUB
-->

</SCRIPT>

</HEAD>

<BODY>

<CENTER>

<FONT SIZE=6>Integer Conversion<P>
</CENTER>
<HR>

<FONT SIZE=4>

<PRE>Type a value: <INPUT NAME=InputValue SIZE=20></PRE>

<HR>
<CENTER>
<INPUT TYPE=BUTTON VALUE="Convert to Integer" NAME="FixInteger">
</CENTER>
</FONT>

</BODY>

</HTML>
```

Example

The Data Conversion project at the end of this chapter uses the `Fix()` function to determine the integer value of the value typed in the Enter Value to Convert field. The `Fix()` function is called when the checkbox next to the Integer Value (Fix Function) field is selected. The integer value displays in the field next to the description.

The appropriate data validation is performed to make sure the value is numeric and within the allowable range of -32,768 to 32,767 for an integer value.

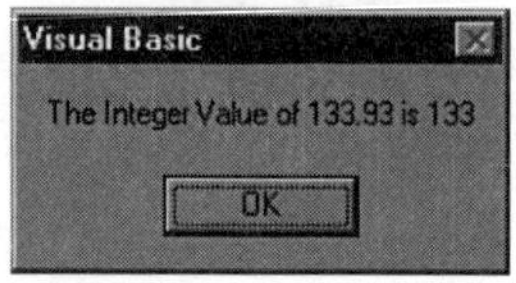

Figure 7-11 The `Fix()` function truncates the decimal portion of a number

Comments The `Fix()` function is similar to the `Int()` and `CInt()` functions. Both the `Fix()` and `Int()` functions truncate the decimal portion of the number. The difference between the `Fix()` function and the `Int()` function is in how each one deals with negative values that contain decimals. The `Fix()` function truncates the decimal portion of the number, while the `Int()` function returns the next whole number smaller than the negative value. Unlike the `Int()` and `Fix()` functions, the `CInt()` function rounds the decimal portions to the nearest whole number. Table 7-18 illustrates the differences between the `Fix()`, `Int()`, and `CInt()` functions.

Table 7-18 Comparing the `Fix()` function to the `Int()` and `CInt()` functions

Value	`Fix(value)`	`Int(value)`	`CInt(value)`
3.6	3	3	4
3.2	3	3	3
3	3	3	3
-3.6	-3	-4	-4
-3.2	-3	-4	-3

To help eliminate run-time data errors, use the `IsNumeric()` function to make sure an expression contains a numeric value before calling the `Fix()` function. For more information about the `IsNumeric()` function, refer to Chapter 4, Data Validation.

See Also `CInt()`, `Int()`

Hex FUNCTION

Purpose Use the `Hex()` function to convert a numeric value to the equivalent hexadecimal value. By using a hexadecimal number, you are able to store larger numeric values using fewer digits. The maximum size of a hexadecimal number is eight bytes. Table 7-19 indicates the types of expressions that can be used with the `Hex()` function.

Syntax `Hex(expression)`

Table 7-19 Argument of the `Hex()` function

Argument	Description
`expression`	Any numeric expression within the range of -2,147,483,648 to 2,147,483,647

Description

The `Hex()` function allows you to convert a number from standard (base 10) format to hexadecimal (base 16) format. Hexadecimal format uses 16 different characters to form numeric values. The characters used are 0–9 and A–F. By using 16 digits, you can store larger numbers using fewer bytes. For example, the number 100 would be stored as 64 in hexadecimal format.

The range for hexadecimal numbers is the same as for a long integer, -2,147,483,648 to 2,147,483,647. The resulting hexadecimal range is 8000000 to FFFFFFFF for negative values and 0 to 7FFFFFFF for positive values. Table 7-20 illustrates the difference between standard and hexadecimal values for positive values; Table 7-21 illustrates how negative values compare.

Table 7-20 Hexadecimal conversions for positive numbers

Standard (Base 10)	Hexadecimal (Base 16)
1	1
5	5
8	8
10	A
12	C
15	F
16	10
17	11
25	19
30	1E
50	32
100	64
150	96
500	1F4

continued on next page

continued from previous page

Standard (Base 10)	Hexadecimal (Base 16)
1000	3E8
500,000	7A120
1,000,000	F4240
2,147,483,647	7FFFFFFF

Table 7-21 Hexadecimal conversions for negative numbers

Standard (Base 10)	Hexadecimal (Base 16)
0	0
-1	FFFFFFFF
-10	FFFFFFF6
-100	FFFFFF9C
-750	FFFFFD12
-5000	FFFFEC78
-200,000	FFFCF2C0
-1,000,000	FFF0BDC0
-2,147,483,648	800000000

You can pass a hexadecimal value to the **Hex()** function by preceding the value with **&H**. For example, **&H10** represents the number 16.

The example in Listing 7-11 uses the **Hex()** function to convert the input value into a hexadecimal value. The **MsgBox()** function displays the results of the **Hex()** function on the screen, as illustrated in Figure 7-12.

Listing 7-11 Using the Hex() *function*

```
<HTML>

<HEAD>
<TITLE>Hex Example</TITLE>

<SCRIPT LANGUAGE="VBScript">
<!--
'..............................................................
' ConvertToHex_OnClick()
' Converts the value typed by the user to a hexadecimal value.
'..............................................................
SUB ConvertToHex_OnClick()

  Dim UserValue

  UserValue = InputValue.Value
```

```
'.........................................................
' Use the IsNumeric() function to make sure the field contains
' a numeric value. Convert UserName to a double so you can
' check its range.
'.........................................................
  If IsNumeric(UserValue) Then

    UserValue = CDbl(UserValue)

'.........................................................
' Make sure the value is within the acceptable range for a
' hexadecimal value. This is the same range used for a
' long integer.
'.........................................................
    If (UserValue >= -2147483648) AND (UserValue <= 2147483647) Then

      MsgBox "The Hexadecimal Value of " & InputValue.Value & " is " & Hex(UserValue)

    Else

      MsgBox "Type a value between -2,147,483,648 and 2,147,483,647"

    End If

  Else

    MsgBox "Type a numeric value in the field"

  End If

END SUB
-->

</SCRIPT>

</HEAD>

<BODY>

<CENTER>

<FONT SIZE=6>Hexadecimal Conversion<P>
</CENTER>
<HR>

<FONT SIZE=4>

<PRE>Type a value: <INPUT NAME=InputValue SIZE=20></PRE>

<HR>
<CENTER>
<INPUT TYPE=BUTTON VALUE="Convert to a Hexadecimal Value" NAME="ConvertToHex">
</CENTER>
</FONT>

</BODY>

</HTML>
```

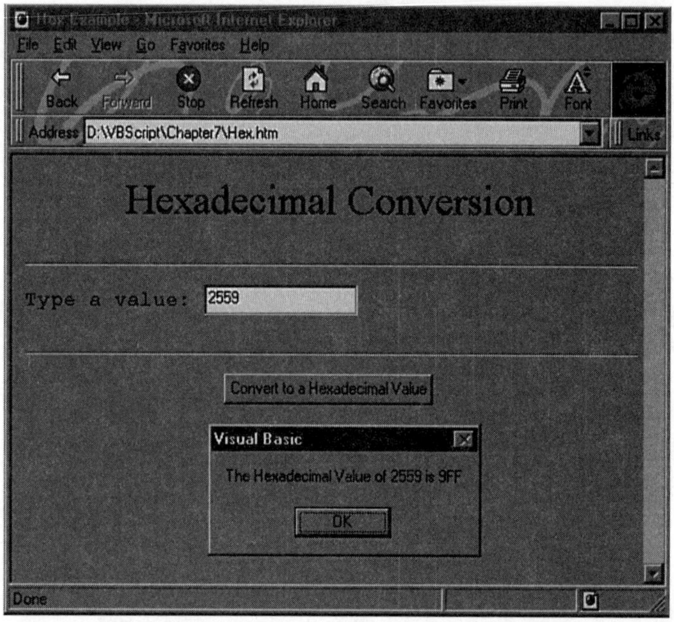

Figure 7-12 The `Hex()` function converts a numeric value to a hexadecimal value

Example

The Data Conversion project at the end of this chapter uses the `Hex()` function to determine the hexadecimal value of the value typed in the Enter Value to Convert field. The `Hex()` function is called when the checkbox next to the Hexadecimal Value field is selected. The hexadecimal value displays in the field next to the description.

The appropriate data validation is performed to make sure the value is numeric and within the allowable range of -2,147,483,648 to 2,147,483,647 for a hexadecimal value.

Comments

Hexadecimal notation is essentially a way of counting using 16 digits. It is quite often used when dealing with system resources, such as memory locations, because it easily converts to binary format (0s and 1s).

If the `Hex()` function is passed a value that contains a decimal or fractional portion, the value is rounded to the nearest whole number before it is converted to a hexadecimal value.

To avoid run-time errors, it is important to make sure that the value passed to the `Hex()` function is numeric. You can use the `IsNumeric()`

function to check for a numeric value. For more information about the `IsNumeric()` function, refer to Chapter 4, Data Validation.

It is also a good idea to check the range of the value passed to the `Hex()` function, as in the example in the Listing 7-11. In this example, an `If` statement is used to make sure the value is within the acceptable range for a hexadecimal conversion.

See Also `Oct()`

`Int` Function

Purpose Use the `Int()` function to return the integer portion of a number. Use this function when you want to truncate the decimal portion of the number and use only the whole number. Table 7-22 outlines the valid expressions for the `Int()` function.

Syntax `Int(expression)`

Table 7-22 Argument of the `Int()` function

Argument	Description
`expression`	Any numeric expression, or a `NULL` value

Description The `Int()` function only returns the integer portion of the numeric expression it receives. Any decimal portion of the number is truncated. For example, `Int(10.2)` returns a value of `10`, and `Int(10.7)` also returns a value of `10`. If the numeric value is negative, the `Int()` function truncates the decimal portion and returns the next negative integer value smaller than the value passed. For example, `Int(-4.2)` returns a value of `-5`.

The example in Listing 7-12 uses the `Int()` function to return an integer value for the value typed in the `InputValue` field. The `MsgBox()` function displays the value returned by the `Int()` function, as illustrated in Figure 7-13.

Since the `Int()` function only accepts integer values, all values passed to the function must be within the range of -32,768 to 32,767. A value outside that range will cause a run-time error to occur. To avoid a run-time error due to a value out of range, perform some sort of range checking, as shown in Listing 7-12.

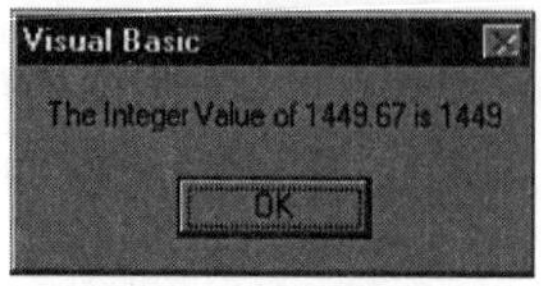

Figure 7-13 The `Int()` function truncates the decimal portion of a number

Listing 7-12 Using the `Int()` *function*

```
<HTML>

<HEAD>
<TITLE>Int Example</TITLE>

<SCRIPT LANGUAGE="VBScript">
<!--
'...........................................................
' ConvertInteger_OnClick()
' Converts the value typed by the user to an integer value.
'...........................................................
SUB ConvertInteger_OnClick()

  Dim UserValue

  UserValue = InputValue.Value

'...........................................................
' Use the IsNumeric() function to make sure the field contains
' a numeric value. Convert UserName to a double so you can
' check its range.
'...........................................................
  If IsNumeric(UserValue) Then

    UserValue = CDbl(UserValue)

'...........................................................
' Make sure the value is within the acceptable range for an
' integer value.
'...........................................................
    If (UserValue >= -32768) AND (UserValue <= 32767) Then

       MsgBox "The Integer Value of " & InputValue.Value & " is " & Int(UserValue)

    Else

      MsgBox "Type a value between -32,768 and 32,767"

    End If

  Else
```

```
    MsgBox "Type a numeric value in the field"

  End If

END SUB
-->

</SCRIPT>

</HEAD>

<BODY>

<CENTER>

<FONT SIZE=6>Integer Conversion<P>
</CENTER>
<HR>

<FONT SIZE=4>

<PRE>Type a value: <INPUT NAME=InputValue SIZE=20></PRE>

<HR>
<CENTER>
<INPUT TYPE=BUTTON VALUE="Convert to Integer" NAME="ConvertInteger">
</CENTER>
</FONT>

</BODY>

</HTML>
```

Example

The Data Conversion project at the end of this chapter uses the `Int()` function to determine the integer value of the value typed in the Enter Value to Convert field. The `Int()` function is called when the checkbox next to the Integer Value (Int Function) field is selected. The integer value displays in the field next to the description.

The appropriate data validation is performed to make sure the value is numeric and within the allowable range of -32,768 to 32,767 for an integer value.

Comments

The `Int()` function is similar to the `Fix()` and `CInt()` functions. Both the `Fix()` and `Int()` functions truncate the decimal portion of the number. The difference between the `Fix()` function and the `Int()` function is in how each one deals with negative values that contain decimals. The `Fix()` function truncates the decimal portion of the number, while the `Int()` function returns the next whole number smaller than the negative value. Unlike the `Int()` and `Fix()` functions, the `CInt()` function rounds the decimal portions to the nearest whole number. Table 7-23 illustrates the differences between the `Int()`, `Fix()`, and `CInt()` functions.

Table 7-23 Comparing the `Int()` function to the `Fix()` and `CInt()` function

Value	Int(*value*)	Fix(*value*)	CInt(*value*)
3.6	3	3	4
3.2	3	3	3
3	3	3	3
-3.6	-4	-3	-4
-3.2	-4	-3	-3

To help eliminate run-time data errors, use the **`IsNumeric()`** function to make sure an expression contains a numeric value before calling the **`Int()`** function. For more information about the **`IsNumeric()`** function, refer to Chapter 4, Data Validation.

See Also `CInt()`, `Fix()`

Oct Function

Purpose Use the **`Oct()`** function to convert a numeric value to the equivalent octal value. The maximum size of an octal number is 11 bytes. Table 7-24 indicates the types of expressions that can be used with the **`Oct()`** function.

Syntax **`Oct(expression)`**

Table 7-24 Argument of the `Oct()` function

Argument	Description
`expression`	Any numeric expression within the range of -2,147,483,648 to 2,147,483,647

Description The **`Oct()`** function allows you to convert a number from standard (base 10) format to octal (base 8) format. Octal format uses eight different characters to form numeric values. The characters used are 0–7. Octal notation is not as commonly used as hexadecimal (base 16) and binary (base 2), although some computers systems require it for addressing memory locations.

The range for octal numbers is the same as for a long integer, -2,147,483,648 to 2,147,483,647. The resulting hexadecimal range is 20000000000 to 37777777777 for negative values and 0 to 17777777777 for positive values. Table 7-25 illustrates the difference between standard (base 10) values and octal (base 8) values for positive values; Table 7-26 illustrates how negative values compare.

Table 7-25 Octal conversions for positive numbers

Standard (Base 10)	Octal (Base 8)
1	1
5	5
8	10
10	12
15	17
16	20
17	21
25	31
30	36
50	62
100	144
150	226
500	764
1000	1750
500,000	1720440
1,000,000	3641100
2,147,483,647	17777777777

Table 7-26 Octal conversions for negative numbers

Standard (Base 10)	Octal (Base 8)
0	0
-1	37777777777
-10	37777777766
-100	37777777634
-750	37777776422
-5000	37777766170
-200,000	37777171300
-1,000,000	37774136700
-2,147,483,648	20000000000

You can pass an octal value to the `Oct()` function by preceding the value with `&O`. For example, `&O20` represents the number 16.

Listing 7-13 uses the `Oct()` function to convert the input value into an octal value. The `MsgBox()` function displays the results of the `Oct()` function on the screen, as illustrated in Figure 7-14.

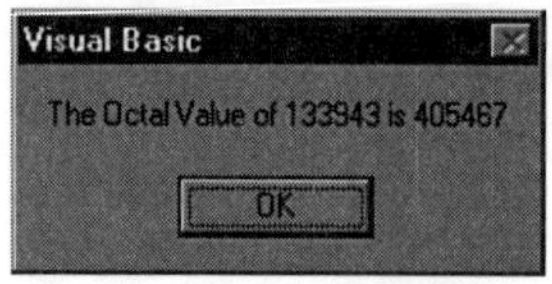

Figure 7-14 The `Oct()` function converts a numeric value to an octal value

Listing 7-13 Using the `Oct()` *function*

```
<HTML>

<HEAD>
<TITLE>Oct Example</TITLE>

<SCRIPT LANGUAGE="VBScript">
<!--
'..............................................................
' ConvertToOct_OnClick()
' Converts the value typed by the user to an octal value.
'..............................................................
SUB ConvertToOct_OnClick()

  Dim UserValue

  UserValue = InputValue.Value

'............................................................
' Use the IsNumeric() function to make sure the field contains
' a numeric value. Convert UserName to a double so you can
' check its range.
'............................................................
   If IsNumeric(UserValue) Then

     UserValue = CDbl(UserValue)

'............................................................
' Make sure the value is within the acceptable range for a
' Hexadecimal value. This is the same range used for a
' long integer.
'............................................................
     If (UserValue >= -2147483648) AND (UserValue <= 2147483647) Then

       MsgBox "The Octal Value of " & InputValue.Value & " is " & Oct(UserValue)

     Else

       MsgBox "Type a value between -2,147,483,648 and 2,147,483,647"
```

```
      End If

   Else

      MsgBox "Type a numeric value in the field"

   End If

END SUB
-->

</SCRIPT>

</HEAD>

<BODY>

<CENTER>

<FONT SIZE=6>Octal Conversion<P>
</CENTER>
<HR>

<FONT SIZE=4>

<PRE>Type a value: <INPUT NAME=InputValue SIZE=20></PRE>

<HR>
<CENTER>
<INPUT TYPE=BUTTON VALUE="Convert to an Octal Value" NAME="ConvertToOct">
</CENTER>
</FONT>

</BODY>

</HTML>
```

Example

The Data Conversion project at the end of this chapter uses the `Oct()` function to determine the octal value of the value typed in the Enter Value to Convert field. The `Oct()` function is called when the checkbox next to the Octal Value field is selected. The octal value displays in the field next to the description.

The appropriate data validation is performed to make sure the value is numeric and within the allowable range of -2,147,483,648 to 2,147,483,647 for an octal value.

Comments

Octal notation is essentially a way of counting using eight digits. It is used by some systems when dealing with system resources, such as memory locations, because it easily converts to binary format (zeroes and ones).

If the `Oct()` function is passed a value that contains a decimal or fractional portion, the value is rounded to the nearest whole number before it is converted to an octal value.

To avoid run-time errors, it is important to make sure the value passed to the `Oct()` function is numeric. You can use the `IsNumeric()` function to check for a numeric value. For more information about the `IsNumeric()` function, refer to Chapter 4, Data Validation.

It is also a good idea to check the range of the value passed to the `Oct()` function, as shown in Listing 7-13. In this example, an `If` statement is used to make sure the value is within the acceptable range for an octal conversion. Figure 7-15 illustrates the message that displays when the user types a value outside of the acceptable range for the `Oct()` function.

See Also `Hex()`

Sgn FUNCTION

Purpose Use the `Sgn()` function to determine the sign of a numeric value. This function is useful when you need to determine whether a positive or negative value was returned by a procedure. Table 7-27 outlines the valid expressions that can be used with the `Sgn()` function.

Syntax `Sgn(expression)`

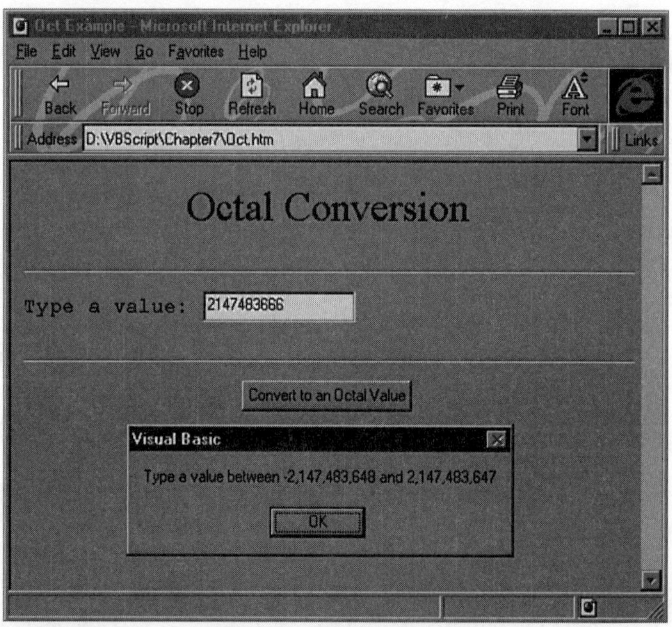

Figure 7-15 The `Oct()` function accepts the range of values between -2,147,483,648 and 2,147,483,647

Table 7-27 Argument of the `Sgn()` function

Argument	Description
`expression`	Any valid numeric expression

Description

The `Sgn()` function allows you to determine whether a variable contains a positive, negative, or zero value. This can be very useful when performing numeric calculations. The `Sgn()` function returns one of the values in Table 7-28.

Table 7-28 Return values for the `Sgn()` function

`Sgn` Returns...	If It Receives...
1	A positive numeric expression
0	A value of zero
–1	A negative numeric expression

The example in Listing 7-14 uses the `Sgn()` function to evaluate the value typed in the `InputValue` field. A `Select Case` statement is used to evaluate the return value of the `Sgn()` function and display a message indicating the type of value typed in the field, as illustrated in Figure 7-16.

Listing 7-14 Using the `Sgn()` function

```
<HTML>

<HEAD>
<TITLE>Sgn Example</TITLE>

<SCRIPT LANGUAGE="VBScript">
<!--
'.............................................................
' DetermineSign_OnClick()
' Determines whether the value typed by the user is positive,
' negative, or equal to zero.
'.............................................................
SUB DetermineSign_OnClick()

  Dim UserValue
   Dim ValueSign

  UserValue = InputValue.Value
```

continued on next page

continued from previous page

```
'..........................................................
' Use the IsNumeric() function to make sure the field contains
' a numeric value.
'..........................................................
   If IsNumeric(UserValue) Then

'..............................................................
' Assign the integer value that specifies the case of the
' input value to ValueSign. Use the Select Case statement to
' determine the message to display on the screen.
'..............................................................
     ValueSign = Sgn(UserValue)

     Select Case ValueSign

       Case 1
         MsgBox "The value is positive"

       Case 0
         MsgBox "The value is zero"

       Case -1
         MsgBox "The value is negative"

     End Select

   Else

     MsgBox "Type a numeric value in the field"

   End If

END SUB
-->

</SCRIPT>

</HEAD>

<BODY>

<CENTER>

<FONT SIZE=6>Determine Sign of Value<P>
</CENTER>
<HR>

<FONT SIZE=4>

<PRE>Type a value: <INPUT NAME=InputValue SIZE=20></PRE>

<HR>
```

```
<CENTER>
<INPUT TYPE=BUTTON VALUE="Determine Sign" NAME="DetermineSign">
</CENTER>
</FONT>

</BODY>

</HTML>
```

Example The Data Conversion project at the end of this chapter uses the `Sgn()` function to determine the sign of the value typed in the Enter Value to Convert field. The `Sgn()` function is called when the checkbox next to the Sign of Value field is selected. A `Select Case` statement converts the return value of the `Sgn()` function so that a string is returned indicating whether the value is positive, negative, or zero.

Comments Since the `Sgn()` function only evaluates numeric expressions, it is important to check the value before passing it to the `Sgn()` function. The `IsNumeric()` function can be used to make sure the value is numeric. For more information about the `IsNumeric()` function, refer to Chapter 4, Data Validation.

See Also `Abs()`

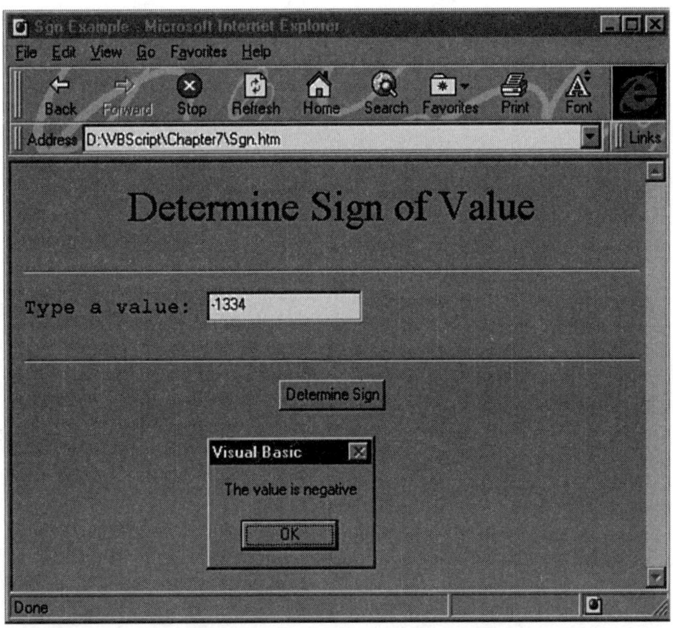

Figure 7-16 The `Sgn()` function determines whether the input value is positive, negative, or zero

Data Conversion Project

The Data Conversion project demonstrates the use of the data conversion functions described in this chapter.

Building the Project

1. Start the project by setting up the standard HTML template used for all VBScript examples in this book. The VBScript code is placed in the **<HEAD>** section of the HTML code to keep everything consistent. Remember to place the HTML comment tags **<!--** and **-->** around the VBScript code so that it will be ignored by browsers that cannot interpret the **<SCRIPT>** tag.

```
<HTML>

<HEAD>
<TITLE>Data Conversion</TITLE>

<SCRIPT LANGUAGE="VBScript">

<!--

-->

</SCRIPT>

</HEAD>

<BODY>

</BODY>

</HTML>
```

2. In the **<BODY>** section, place the desired title information for the Web page. For this example, you are creating a Web page in which the user can select the data conversions that he or she would like to perform, so this is described in the titles at the beginning of the **<BODY>** section.

```
<BODY>

<FONT FACE="Arial" SIZE=6>
<FONT COLOR=NAVY>
```

```
<CENTER>
   <FONT SIZE=5>Data Conversion Project<P>
</CENTER>

<HR>
```

3. Design an HTML form containing a table for receiving the user input. In the first row of the table, place an input field where the user specifies the value that should be converted. Figure 7-17 illustrates the field where the user types the input value.

```
<FORM Name="DataConversionForm">

<TABLE>

   <TR><TD><I>Enter Value to Convert</I></TD>
       <TD><INPUT NAME=InputValue SIZE=20></TD></TR>
```

4. In the table in the **<BODY>** section, add the titles for the conversion types and return values. Change the background color of each table cell to navy blue and the text to white so that these titles stand out on the page. Figure 7-17 illustrates the titles placed on the page with the background color changed for each cell.

```
<TR><TD BGCOLOR=NAVY ALIGN=CENTER><FONT COLOR=WHITE><B>Select Conversion</B></TD>
    <TD BGCOLOR=NAVY ALIGN=CENTER><FONT COLOR=WHITE><B>Result</B></TD></TR>
```

Figure 7-17 The Data Conversion project uses the value typed in the Enter Value to Convert field

5. Also in the table, create checkbox options for each data conversion that can be selected. Add an input field in the cell next to each conversion type that will display the result of the conversion.

```
<TR><TD><INPUT TYPE=CHECKBOX NAME=AbsoluteValue>Absolute Value</TD>
    <TD><INPUT NAME=ResultAbValue SIZE=20></TR>
   <TR><TD><INPUT TYPE=CHECKBOX NAME=ConvertBoolean>Boolean Value</TD>
       <TD><INPUT NAME=ResultBoolValue SIZE=20></TR>
   <TR><TD><INPUT TYPE=CHECKBOX NAME=ConvertByte>Byte Value</TD>
       <TD><INPUT NAME=ResultByteValue SIZE=20></TR>
   <TR><TD><INPUT TYPE=CHECKBOX NAME=ConvertDate>Date Value</TD>
       <TD><INPUT NAME=ResultDateValue SIZE=20></TR>
   <TR><TD><INPUT TYPE=CHECKBOX NAME=ConvertDouble>Double-Precision Floating Point⇐
Value</TD>
       <TD><INPUT NAME=ResultDblValue SIZE=20></TR>
   <TR><TD><INPUT TYPE=CHECKBOX NAME=ConvertInteger>Integer Value (CInt Function)</TD>
       <TD><INPUT NAME=ResultCIntValue SIZE=20></TR>
   <TR><TD><INPUT TYPE=CHECKBOX NAME=ConvertLong>Long Integer Value</TD>
       <TD><INPUT NAME=ResultLngValue SIZE=20></TR>
   <TR><TD><INPUT TYPE=CHECKBOX NAME=ConvertSingle>Single-Precision Floating-Point⇐
Value</TD>
       <TD><INPUT NAME=ResultSngValue SIZE=20></TR>
   <TR><TD><INPUT TYPE=CHECKBOX NAME=ConvertString>String Value</TD>
       <TD><INPUT NAME=ResultStrValue SIZE=20></TR>
   <TR><TD><INPUT TYPE=CHECKBOX NAME=FixInteger>Integer Value (Fix Function)</TD>
      <TD><INPUT NAME=ResultFixValue SIZE=20></TR>
   <TR><TD><INPUT TYPE=CHECKBOX NAME=ConvertToHex>Hexadecimal Value</TD>
       <TD><INPUT NAME=ResultHexValue SIZE=20></TR>
   <TR><TD><INPUT TYPE=CHECKBOX NAME=ConvertInt>Integer Value (Int Function)</TD>
       <TD><INPUT NAME=ResultIntValue SIZE=20></TR>
   <TR><TD><INPUT TYPE=CHECKBOX NAME=ConvertToOct>Octal Value</TD>
       <TD><INPUT NAME=ResultOctValue SIZE=20></TR>
   <TR><TD><INPUT TYPE=CHECKBOX NAME=DetermineSign>Sign of Value</TD>
       <TD><INPUT NAME=ResultSgnValue SIZE=20></TR>

</TABLE>

</FORM>

</BODY>

</HTML>
```

6. In the `<HEAD>` section, create a procedure called `AbsoluteValue_OnClick()` that uses the `Abs()` function to determine the absolute value of the input value. The function is called when the checkbox next to the Absolute Value field is selected. Remember to use the `IsNumeric()` function to make sure a numeric value was entered before calling the `Abs()` function. If the user types a value that is not numeric, display a message, as illustrated in Figure 7-18.

```
SUB AbsoluteValue_OnClick()

  Dim UserValue
  Dim ConvertForm
```

```
  Set ConvertForm = Document.DataConversionForm

  UserValue = ConvertForm.InputValue.Value

  If IsNumeric(UserValue) Then

    ConvertForm.ResultAbValue.Value = Abs(UserValue)

  Else

    MsgBox "Type a numeric value in the field to determine Absolute Value", 0, "Absolute⇐
Value Function"

  End If

END SUB
```

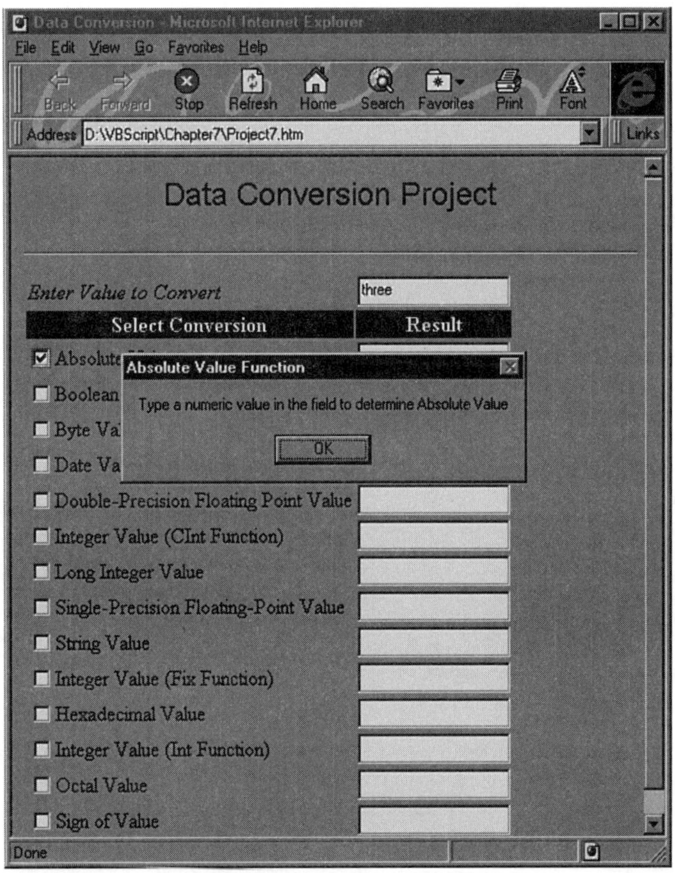

Figure 7-18 The `Abs()` function requires a numeric value

7. Create a procedure called **ConvertBoolean_OnClick()** that uses the **CBool()** function to determine the Boolean value of the input value. The function is called when the checkbox next to the Boolean Value field is selected. Use the **CBool()** function to convert the input value to a Boolean value. When you write the value to the result field, use the **CStr()** function to convert the value to a string so that the appropriate value in placed in the field.

```
SUB ConvertBoolean_OnClick()

 Dim UserValue
 Dim ConvertForm

  Set ConvertForm = Document.DataConversionForm

  UserValue = CBool(ConvertForm.InputValue.Value)

  Document.DataConversionForm.ResultBoolValue.Value = CStr(UserValue)

END SUB
```

8. Create a procedure called **ConvertByte_OnClick()** that uses the **CByte()** function to determine the byte value of the input value. The function is called when the checkbox next to the Byte Value field is selected. Remember to use the **IsNumeric()** function to make sure the input value is numeric. Also, use an **If** statement to make sure the value is within the appropriate range for a byte (0 to 255). If the input value does not meet the appropriate criteria, display a message indicating the problem, as illustrated in Figure 7-19.

```
SUB ConvertByte_OnClick()

  Dim UserValue
  Dim ConvertForm

  Set ConvertForm = Document.DataConversionForm

  UserValue = ConvertForm.InputValue.Value

  If IsNumeric(UserValue) Then

    If (UserValue >= 0) AND (UserValue <= 255) Then

      ConvertForm.ResultByteValue.Value = CByte(UserValue)
```

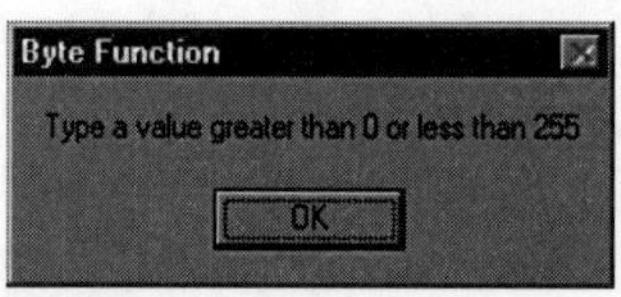

Figure 7-19 Use an **If** statement to make sure the input value is between 0 and 255

```
    Else

      MsgBox "Type a value greater than 0 or less than 255",0, "Byte Function"

    End If

  Else

    MsgBox "Type a numeric value between 0 and 255",0,"Byte Function"

  End If

END SUB
```

9. Create a procedure called `ConvertDate_OnClick()` that uses the `CDate()` function to convert the input value to the appropriate date and time value. The function is called when the checkbox next to the Date Value field is selected.

```
SUB ConvertDate_OnClick()

  Dim UserValue
  Dim ConvertForm

  Set ConvertForm = Document.DataConversionForm

  UserValue = ConvertForm.InputValue.Value

  ConvertForm.ResultDateValue.Value=CDate(UserValue)

END SUB
```

10. Create a procedure called `ConvertDouble_OnClick()` that uses the `CDbl()` function to convert the input value to a double-precision floating-point value. The function is called when the checkbox next to the Double-Precision Floating-Point Value field is selected. Remember to use the `IsNumeric()` function to make sure the input field contains a numeric value.

```
SUB ConvertDouble_OnClick()

  Dim UserValue
  Dim ConvertForm

  Set ConvertForm = Document.DataConversionForm

  UserValue = ConvertForm.InputValue.Value

  If IsNumeric(UserValue) Then

    ConvertForm.ResultDblValue.Value = CDbl(UserValue)

  Else

    MsgBox "Type a numeric value in the field", 0, "Double-Precision Function"

  End If

END SUB
```

11. Create a procedure called **ConvertInteger_OnClick()** that uses the **CInt()** function to convert the input value to an integer value. The function is called when the checkbox next to the Integer Value (CInt Function) field is selected. Remember to use the **IsNumeric()** function to make sure the input field contains a numeric value. Also, use an **If** statement to make sure the input value is within the appropriate range of -32,768 to 32,767 for an integer.

```
SUB ConvertInteger_OnClick()

  Dim UserValue
  Dim ConvertForm

  Set ConvertForm = Document.DataConversionForm

  UserValue = ConvertForm.InputValue.Value

  If IsNumeric(UserValue) Then

    If (UserValue >= -32768) AND (UserValue <= 32767) Then

       ConvertForm.ResultCIntValue.Value = CInt(UserValue)

    Else

      MsgBox "Type a value between -32,768 and 32,767", 0, "Convert Integer Function"

    End If

  Else

    MsgBox "Type a numeric value in the field", 0, "Convert Integer Function"

  End If

END SUB
```

12. Create a procedure called **ConvertLong_OnClick()** that uses the **CLng()** function to convert the input value to a long integer value. The function is called when the checkbox next to the Long Integer Value field is selected. Remember to use the **IsNumeric()** function to make sure the input field contains a numeric value. Also, use an **If** statement to make sure the input value is within the appropriate range of -2,147,483,648 to 2,147,483,647 for a long integer.

```
SUB ConvertLong_OnClick()

  Dim UserValue
  Dim ConvertForm

  Set ConvertForm = Document.DataConversionForm

  UserValue = ConvertForm.InputValue.Value
```

```
    If IsNumeric(UserValue) Then

      If (UserValue >= -2147483648) AND (UserValue <= 2147483647) Then

        ConvertForm.ResultLngValue.Value = CLng(UserValue)

      Else

        MsgBox "Type a value between -2,147,483,648 and 2,147,483,647", 0, "Long Integer⇐
Function"

      End If

    Else

      MsgBox "Type a numeric value in the field", 0, "Long Integer Function"

    End If

END SUB
```

13. Create a procedure called `ConvertSingle_OnClick()` that uses the `CSng()` function to convert the input value to a single-precision floating-point value. The function is called when the checkbox next to the Single-Precision Floating-Point Value field is selected.

```
SUB ConvertSingle_OnClick()

  Dim UserValue
  Dim ConvertForm

  Set ConvertForm = Document.DataConversionForm

  UserValue = ConvertForm.InputValue.Value

  If IsNumeric(UserValue) Then

    ConvertForm.ResultSngValue.Value = CSng(UserValue)

  Else

    MsgBox "Type a numeric value in the field", 0, "Single-Precision Function"

  End If

END SUB
```

14. Create a procedure called `ConvertString_OnClick()` that uses the `CStr()` function to convert the input value to a string value. The function is called when the checkbox next to the String Value field is selected.

```
SUB ConvertString_OnClick()

  Dim UserValue
  Dim ConvertForm

  Set ConvertForm = Document.DataConversionForm

  UserValue = ConvertForm.InputValue.Value

  ConvertForm.ResultStrValue.Value = CStr(UserValue)

END SUB
```

15. Create a procedure called `FixInteger_OnClick()` that uses the `Fix()` function to convert the input value to an integer value. The function is called when the checkbox next to the Integer Value (Fix Function) field is selected. Remember to use the `IsNumeric()` function to make sure the input field contains a numeric value. Also, use an `If` statement to make sure the input value is within the appropriate range of -32,768 to 32,767 for an integer.

```
SUB FixInteger_OnClick()

  Dim UserValue
  Dim ConvertForm

  Set ConvertForm = Document.DataConversionForm

  UserValue = ConvertForm.InputValue.Value

  If IsNumeric(UserValue) Then

    If (UserValue >= -32768) AND (UserValue <= 32767) Then

       ConvertForm.ResultFixValue.Value = Fix(UserValue)

    Else

      MsgBox "Type a value between -32,768 and 32,767", 0, "Fix Integer Function"

    End If

  Else

    MsgBox "Type a numeric value in the field", 0, "Fix Integer Function"

  End If

END SUB
```

16. Create a procedure called `ConvertToHex_OnClick()` that uses the `Hex()` function to convert the input value to a hexadecimal value. The function is called when the checkbox next to the Hexadecimal Value field is selected. Remember to use the `IsNumeric()` function to make sure the input field contains a numeric value.

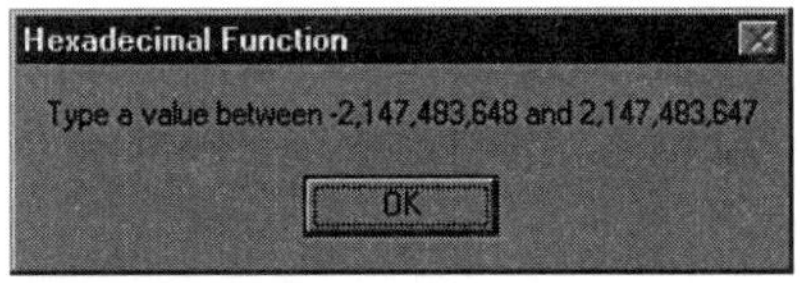

Figure 7-20 Make sure the input value is within the range for a hexadecimal conversion

Also, use an **If** statement to make sure the input value is within the appropriate range of -2,147,483,648 to 2,147,483,647 for a hexadecimal value. If the value in not within the range for a hexadecimal value, use the **MsgBox()** function to display a message, as illustrated in Figure 7-20.

```
SUB ConvertToHex_OnClick()

  Dim UserValue
  Dim ConvertForm

  Set ConvertForm = Document.DataConversionForm

  UserValue = ConvertForm.InputValue.Value

   If IsNumeric(UserValue) Then

     If (UserValue >= -2147483648) AND (UserValue <= 2147483647) Then

       ConvertForm.ResultHexValue.Value = Hex(UserValue)

     Else

       MsgBox "Type a value between -2,147,483,648 and 2,147,483,647", 0, "Hexadecimal⇐
Function"

     End If

   Else

     MsgBox "Type a numeric value in the field", 0, "Hexadecimal Function"

   End If

END SUB
```

17. Create a procedure called **ConvertInt_OnClick()** that uses the **Int()** function to convert the input value to an integer value. The function is called when the checkbox next to the Integer Value (Int Function) field is selected. Remember to use the **IsNumeric()** function to make sure the input field contains a numeric value. Also, use an **If** statement to make sure the input value is within the appropriate range of -32,768 to 32,767 for an integer.

continued on next page

continued from previous page

```
SUB ConvertInt_OnClick()

  Dim UserValue
  Dim ConvertForm

  Set ConvertForm = Document.DataConversionForm

  UserValue = ConvertForm.InputValue.Value

  If IsNumeric(UserValue) Then

    If (UserValue >= -32768) AND (UserValue <= 32767) Then

       ConvertForm.ResultIntValue.Value = Int(UserValue)

    Else

      MsgBox "Type a value between -32,768 and 32,767", 0, "Int Function"

    End If

  Else

    MsgBox "Type a numeric value in the field", 0, "Int Function"

  End If

END SUB
```

18. Create a procedure called `ConvertToOct_OnClick()` that uses the `Oct()` function to convert the input value to an octal value. The function is called when the checkbox next to the Octal Value field is selected. Remember to use the `IsNumeric()` function to make sure the input field contains a numeric value. Also, use an `If` statement to make sure the input value is within the appropriate range of -2,147,483,648 to 2,147,483,647 for an octal value.

```
SUB ConvertToOct_OnClick()

  Dim UserValue
  Dim ConvertForm

  Set ConvertForm = Document.DataConversionForm

  UserValue = ConvertForm.InputValue.Value

  If IsNumeric(UserValue) Then

    If (UserValue >= -2147483648) AND (UserValue <= 2147483647) Then

       ConvertForm.ResultOctValue.Value = Oct(UserValue)

     Else
```

```
        MsgBox "Type a value between -2,147,483,648 and 2,147,483,647", 0, "Octal Function"

      End If

    Else

      MsgBox "Type a numeric value in the field", 0, "Octal Function"

    End If

END SUB
```

19. Create a procedure called `DetermineSign_OnClick()` that uses the `Sgn()` function to determine whether the input value is positive, negative, or zero. The function is called when the checkbox next to the Sign of Value field is selected. Use a `Select Case` statement to display a description of the value in the result field next to the checkbox. Display Positive, if `Sgn()` returns a `1`, Negative if `Sgn()` returns a `-1`, or Zero if `Sgn()` returns a `0`.

```
SUB DetermineSign_OnClick()

  Dim UserValue
  Dim ValueSign
  Dim ConvertForm

  Set ConvertForm = Document.DataConversionForm

  UserValue = ConvertForm.InputValue.Value

  If IsNumeric(UserValue) Then

    ValueSign = Sgn(UserValue)

    Select Case ValueSign

       Case 1
         ConvertForm.ResultSgnValue.Value = "Positive"

       Case 0
        ConvertForm.ResultSgnValue.Value = "Zero"

       Case -1
        ConvertForm.ResultSgnValue.Value = "Negative"

     End Select

  Else

    MsgBox "Type a numeric value in the field", 0, "Sign Function"

  End If

END SUB
```

How It Works

The Data Conversion project is designed so that the user can enter a value and then make selections to view the different conversions for that value on the screen. Each conversion is performed when the checkbox is selected. The appropriate results for the conversion display in the input box next to the conversion description.

Each of the data conversion functions covered in this chapter is used in the project. Since each function has limits that govern the type of data it can receive, the appropriate data validation is performed before calling each function.

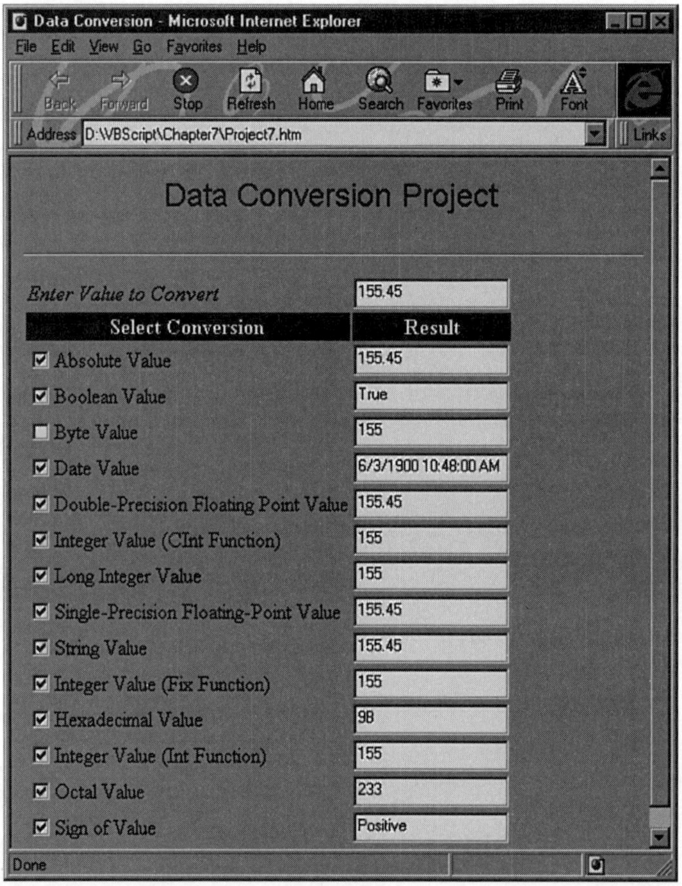

Figure 7-21 The Data Conversion project screen

Figure 7-21 illustrates how the Data Conversion project converts a value typed in the Enter Value to Convert field, and Listing 7-15 contains the complete source code.

Listing 7-15 Complete source for the Data Conversion project

```
<HTML>
<HEAD>
<TITLE>Data Conversion</TITLE>


<SCRIPT LANGUAGE="VBScript">
<!--
'.........................................................
' AbsoluteValue_OnClick()
' Determines the absolute value for the value typed in
' the field by the user.
'.........................................................
SUB AbsoluteValue_OnClick()

  Dim UserValue
  Dim ConvertForm

  Set ConvertForm = Document.DataConversionForm

  UserValue = ConvertForm.InputValue.Value

  If IsNumeric(UserValue) Then

    ConvertForm.ResultAbValue.Value = Abs(UserValue)

  Else

    MsgBox "Type a numeric value in the field to determine Absolute Value", 0, "Absolute⇐
Value Function"

  End If

END SUB

'.........................................................
' ConvertBoolean_OnClick()
' Converts the value typed by the user to a Boolean value.
'.........................................................
SUB ConvertBoolean_OnClick()

 Dim UserValue
 Dim ConvertForm

  Set ConvertForm = Document.DataConversionForm

  UserValue = CBool(ConvertForm.InputValue.Value)

  Document.DataConversionForm.ResultBoolValue.Value = CStr(UserValue)

END SUB
```

continued on next page

continued from previous page

```
'.........................................................
' ConvertByte_OnClick()
' Converts the value typed by the user to a byte value.
'.........................................................
SUB ConvertByte_OnClick()

  Dim UserValue
  Dim ConvertForm

  Set ConvertForm = Document.DataConversionForm

  UserValue = ConvertForm.InputValue.Value

'..................  ....................................
' Use the IsNumeric() function to make sure a numeric value
' was typed.
'.........................................................
  If IsNumeric(UserValue) Then

'....................  ..................................
' Make sure the value typed is between 0 and 255 to avoid
' an Overflow message at run time.
'.........................................................
    If (UserValue >= 0) AND (UserValue <= 255) Then

      ConvertForm.ResultByteValue.Value = CByte(UserValue)

    Else

      MsgBox "Type a value greater than 0 or less than 255",0, "Byte Function"

    End If

  Else

    MsgBox "Type a numeric value between 0 and 255",0,"Byte Function"

  End If

END SUB

'.........................................................
' ConvertDate_OnClick()
' Converts the value typed by the user to a date or time
' value with a subtype of date.
'.........................................................
SUB ConvertDate_OnClick()

  Dim UserValue
  Dim ConvertForm

  Set ConvertForm = Document.DataConversionForm

  UserValue = ConvertForm.InputValue.Value

  ConvertForm.ResultDateValue.Value=CDate(UserValue)

END SUB
```

```
'............................................................
' ConvertDouble_OnClick()
' Converts the value typed by the user to a double-precision
' floating-point value with a subtype of double.
'............................................................
SUB ConvertDouble_OnClick()

  Dim UserValue
  Dim ConvertForm

  Set ConvertForm = Document.DataConversionForm

  UserValue = ConvertForm.InputValue.Value

  If IsNumeric(UserValue) Then

    ConvertForm.ResultDblValue.Value = CDbl(UserValue)

  Else

    MsgBox "Type a numeric value in the field", 0, "Double-Precision Function"

  End If

END SUB

'............................................................
' ConvertInteger_OnClick()
' Converts the value typed by the user to an integer value.
'............................................................
SUB ConvertInteger_OnClick()

  Dim UserValue
  Dim ConvertForm

  Set ConvertForm = Document.DataConversionForm

  UserValue = ConvertForm.InputValue.Value

'............................................................
' Use the IsNumeric() function to make sure the field contains
' a numeric value.
'............................................................
  If IsNumeric(UserValue) Then

'............................................................
' Make sure the value is within the acceptable range for an
' integer value.
'............................................................
    If (UserValue >= -32768) AND (UserValue <= 32767) Then

       ConvertForm.ResultCIntValue.Value = CInt(UserValue)

    Else

      MsgBox "Type a value between -32,768 and 32,767", 0, "Convert Integer Function"
```

continued on next page

continued from previous page

```
    End If

  Else

    MsgBox "Type a numeric value in the field", 0, "Convert Integer Function"

  End If

END SUB

'..............................................................
' ConvertLong_OnClick()
' Converts the value typed by the user to a long integer value.
'..............................................................
SUB ConvertLong_OnClick()

  Dim UserValue
  Dim ConvertForm

  Set ConvertForm = Document.DataConversionForm

  UserValue = ConvertForm.InputValue.Value

'............................................................
' Use the IsNumeric() function to make sure the field contains
' a numeric value.
'............................................................
   If IsNumeric(UserValue) Then

'............................................................
' Make sure the value is within the acceptable range for a
' long integer value.
'............................................................
     If (UserValue >= -2147483648) AND (UserValue <= 2147483647) Then

       ConvertForm.ResultLngValue.Value = CLng(UserValue)

     Else

       MsgBox "Type a value between -2,147,483,648 and 2,147,483,647", 0, "Long Integer⇐
Function"

     End If

   Else

     MsgBox "Type a numeric value in the field", 0, "Long Integer Function"

   End If

END SUB

'............................................................
' ConvertSingle_OnClick()
' Converts the value typed by the user to a single-precision
' floating-point value with a subtype of single.
'............................................................
```

```
SUB ConvertSingle_OnClick()

  Dim UserValue
  Dim ConvertForm

  Set ConvertForm = Document.DataConversionForm

  UserValue = ConvertForm.InputValue.Value

  If IsNumeric(UserValue) Then

    ConvertForm.ResultSngValue.Value = CSng(UserValue)

  Else

    MsgBox "Type a numeric value in the field", 0, "Single-Precision Function"

  End If

END SUB

'.............................................................
' ConvertString_OnClick()
' Converts the value typed by the user to a string.
'.............................................................
SUB ConvertString_OnClick

  Dim UserValue
  Dim ConvertForm

  Set ConvertForm = Document.DataConversionForm

  UserValue = ConvertForm.InputValue.Value

  ConvertForm.ResultStrValue.Value = CStr(UserValue)

END SUB

'.............................................................
' FixInteger_OnClick()
' Converts the value typed by the user to an integer value.
'.............................................................
SUB FixInteger_OnClick()

  Dim UserValue
  Dim ConvertForm

  Set ConvertForm = Document.DataConversionForm

  UserValue = ConvertForm.InputValue.Value

'.............................................................
' Use the IsNumeric() function to make sure the field contains
' a numeric value.
'.............................................................
  If IsNumeric(UserValue) Then
```

continued on next page

continued from previous page

```
'...........................................................
' Make sure the value is within the acceptable range for an
' integer value.
'...........................................................
    If (UserValue >= -32768) AND (UserValue <= 32767) Then

       ConvertForm.ResultFixValue.Value = Fix(UserValue)

    Else

      MsgBox "Type a value between -32,768 and 32,767", 0, "Fix Integer Function"

    End If

  Else

    MsgBox "Type a numeric value in the field", 0, "Fix Integer Function"

  End If

END SUB

'.............................................................
' ConvertToHex_OnClick()
' Converts the value typed by the user to a hexadecimal value.
'.............................................................
SUB ConvertToHex_OnClick()

  Dim UserValue
  Dim ConvertForm

  Set ConvertForm = Document.DataConversionForm

  UserValue = ConvertForm.InputValue.Value

'...........................................................
' Use the IsNumeric() function to make sure the field contains
' a numeric value.
'...........................................................
   If IsNumeric(UserValue) Then

'...........................................................
' Make sure the value is within the acceptable range for a
' hexadecimal value. This is the same range used for a
' long integer.
'...........................................................
     If (UserValue >= -2147483648) AND (UserValue <= 2147483647) Then

       ConvertForm.ResultHexValue.Value = Hex(UserValue)

     Else

       MsgBox "Type a value between -2,147,483,648 and 2,147,483,647", 0, "Hexadecimal⇐
Function"

     End If

   Else
```

```
      MsgBox "Type a numeric value in the field", 0, "Hexadecimal Function"

    End If

END SUB

'............................................................
' ConvertInt_OnClick()
' Converts the value typed by the user to an integer value.
'............................................................
SUB ConvertInt_OnClick()

  Dim UserValue
  Dim ConvertForm

  Set ConvertForm = Document.DataConversionForm

  UserValue = ConvertForm.InputValue.Value

'............................................................
' Use the IsNumeric() function to make sure the field contains
' a numeric value.
'............................................................
  If IsNumeric(UserValue) Then

'............................................................
' Make sure the value is within the acceptable range for an
' integer value.
'............................................................
    If (UserValue >= -32768) AND (UserValue <= 32767) Then

       ConvertForm.ResultIntValue.Value = Int(UserValue)

    Else

      MsgBox "Type a value between -32,768 and 32,767", 0, "Int Function"

    End If

  Else

    MsgBox "Type a numeric value in the field", 0, "Int Function"

  End If

END SUB

'..............................................................
' ConvertToOct_OnClick()
' Converts the value typed by the user to an octal value.
'..............................................................
SUB ConvertToOct_OnClick()

  Dim UserValue
  Dim ConvertForm
```

continued on next page

continued from previous page

```
  Set ConvertForm = Document.DataConversionForm

  UserValue = ConvertForm.InputValue.Value

'.........................................................
' Use the IsNumeric() function to make sure the field contains
' a numeric value.
'.........................................................
   If IsNumeric(UserValue) Then

'.........................................................
' Make sure the value is within the acceptable range for an
' octal value. This is the same range used for a
' long integer.
'.........................................................
     If (UserValue >= -2147483648) AND (UserValue <= 2147483647) Then

       ConvertForm.ResultOctValue.Value = Oct(UserValue)

     Else

       MsgBox "Type a value between -2,147,483,648 and 2,147,483,647", 0, "Octal Function"

     End If

   Else

     MsgBox "Type a numeric value in the field", 0, "Octal Function"

   End If

END SUB

'.............................................................
' DetermineSign_OnClick()
' Determines whether the value typed by the user is positive,
' negative, or equal to zero.
'.............................................................
SUB DetermineSign_OnClick()

  Dim UserValue
  Dim ValueSign
  Dim ConvertForm

  Set ConvertForm = Document.DataConversionForm

  UserValue = ConvertForm.InputValue.Value

'.........................................................
' Use the IsNumeric() function to make sure the field contains
' a numeric value.
'.........................................................
   If IsNumeric(UserValue) Then

'.........................................................
' Assign the integer value that specifies the case of the
' input value to ValueSign. Use the Select Case statement to
' determine the message to display on the screen.
'.........................................................
```

```
      ValueSign = Sgn(UserValue)

      Select Case ValueSign

        Case 1
          ConvertForm.ResultSgnValue.Value = "Positive"

        Case 0
         ConvertForm.ResultSgnValue.Value = "Zero"

        Case -1
         ConvertForm.ResultSgnValue.Value = "Negative"

      End Select

    Else

      MsgBox "Type a numeric value in the field", 0, "Sign Function"

    End If

END SUB


-->

</SCRIPT>

</HEAD>

<BODY>

<FONT FACE="Arial" SIZE=6>
<FONT COLOR=NAVY>

<CENTER>
   <FONT SIZE=5>Data Conversion Project<P>
</CENTER>

<HR>

<FONT FACE="Times New Roman" SIZE=2>
<FONT COLOR=NAVY>

<FORM Name="DataConversionForm">

<TABLE>

   <TR><TD><I>Enter Value to Convert</I></TD><TD><INPUT NAME=InputValue SIZE=20></TD></TR>

   <TR><TD BGCOLOR=NAVY ALIGN=CENTER><FONT COLOR=WHITE><B>Select Conversion</B></TD><TD⇐
BGCOLOR=NAVY ALIGN=CENTER><FONT COLOR=WHITE><B>Result</B></TD></TR>
   <TR><TD><INPUT TYPE=CHECKBOX NAME=AbsoluteValue>Absolute Value</TD>
       <TD><INPUT NAME=ResultAbValue SIZE=20></TR>
   <TR><TD><INPUT TYPE=CHECKBOX NAME=ConvertBoolean>Boolean Value</TD>
       <TD><INPUT NAME=ResultBoolValue SIZE=20></TR>
```

continued on next page

continued from previous page

```
    <TR><TD><INPUT TYPE=CHECKBOX NAME=ConvertByte>Byte Value</TD>
        <TD><INPUT NAME=ResultByteValue SIZE=20></TR>
    <TR><TD><INPUT TYPE=CHECKBOX NAME=ConvertDate>Date Value</TD>
        <TD><INPUT NAME=ResultDateValue SIZE=20></TR>
    <TR><TD><INPUT TYPE=CHECKBOX NAME=ConvertDouble>Double-Precision Floating Point⇐
Value</TD>
        <TD><INPUT NAME=ResultDblValue SIZE=20></TR>
    <TR><TD><INPUT TYPE=CHECKBOX NAME=ConvertInteger>Integer Value (CInt Function)</TD>
        <TD><INPUT NAME=ResultCIntValue SIZE=20></TR>
    <TR><TD><INPUT TYPE=CHECKBOX NAME=ConvertLong>Long Integer Value</TD>
        <TD><INPUT NAME=ResultLngValue SIZE=20></TR>
    <TR><TD><INPUT TYPE=CHECKBOX NAME=ConvertSingle>Single-Precision Floating-Point⇐
Value</TD>
        <TD><INPUT NAME=ResultSngValue SIZE=20></TR>
    <TR><TD><INPUT TYPE=CHECKBOX NAME=ConvertString>String Value</TD>
        <TD><INPUT NAME=ResultStrValue SIZE=20></TR>
    <TR><TD><INPUT TYPE=CHECKBOX NAME=FixInteger>Integer Value (Fix Function)</TD>
        <TD><INPUT NAME=ResultFixValue SIZE=20></TR>
    <TR><TD><INPUT TYPE=CHECKBOX NAME=ConvertToHex>Hexadecimal Value</TD>
        <TD><INPUT NAME=ResultHexValue SIZE=20></TR>
    <TR><TD><INPUT TYPE=CHECKBOX NAME=ConvertInt>Integer Value (Int Function)</TD>
        <TD><INPUT NAME=ResultIntValue SIZE=20></TR>
    <TR><TD><INPUT TYPE=CHECKBOX NAME=ConvertToOct>Octal Value</TD>
        <TD><INPUT NAME=ResultOctValue SIZE=20></TR>
    <TR><TD><INPUT TYPE=CHECKBOX NAME=DetermineSign>Sign of Value</TD>
        <TD><INPUT NAME=ResultSgnValue SIZE=20></TR>

</TABLE>

</FORM>

</BODY>

</HTML>
```

8

COMPUTING VALUES

8

COMPUTING VALUES

VBScript provides a variety of functions that can be used to compute numeric values for information on your Web page. These functions include calculating the size of the angles and sides in a triangle, working with logarithms, generating random numbers, and determining the square root of a value. By using the functions discussed in this chapter, you will be able to perform almost all of the advanced math calculations found on today's scientific calculators.

Working with Right Triangles

Trigonometry is a branch of mathematics that deals with the measurements of sides and angles in triangles. VBScript provides four functions used to perform the trigonometric functions of determining the size of the sides and angles within right triangles.

A right triangle always has one angle that equals 90 degrees, and the sum of the three angles is 180 degrees. Figure 8-1 illustrates a right triangle with a 90 degree angle (angle C). In order to use the trigonometric functions provided by VBScript, you must know either the size of two sides of the triangle, or the size of one side and one angle (other than the right angle). With this information you can easily determine the other side(s) and angles.

The `Atn()`, `Cos()`, `Sin()`, and `Tan()` functions are provided by VBScript for working with right triangles. Each of these functions is covered in detail in this chapter. In order to provide a more accurate value, each function uses a radian value to compute the size of the angle instead of the standard degree value.

Additional trigonometric functions can be derived using these basic functions. For example, cosecant(A) is equal to `1/Sin(A)`. Table 8-1 describes the additional trigonometric functions that can be derived using the functions covered in this chapter.

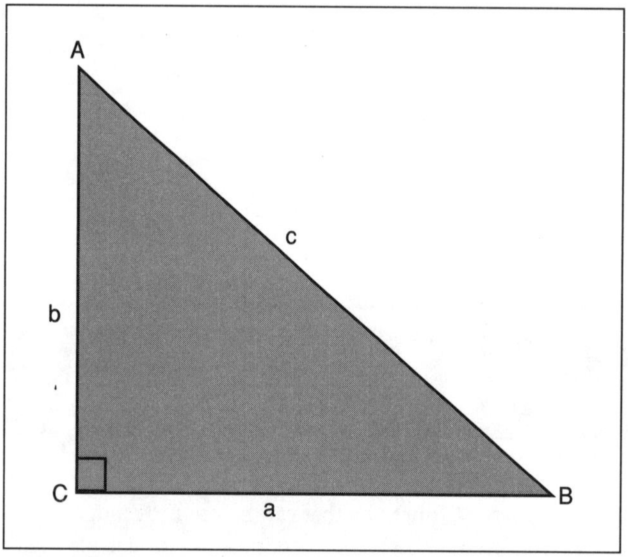

Figure 8-1 A right triangle has one angle that is 90 degrees

Radians Versus Degrees

A radian value is used to express the value of an angle for each of the trigonometric functions provided by VBScript. If the value of an angle is expressed in degrees, it must be converted to a radian value before working with the VBScript trigonometric functions.

To convert a degree measurement to radians, simply multiply it by pi (3.14159) and divide the result by 180. To convert radians to degrees, multiply the radian value by 180 and divide the result by pi.

Deriving Math Functions

As mentioned above, although VBScript only provides four trigonometric functions, most other trigonometric functions can be derived by combining those four with the mathematical operators (see Chapter 2, VBScript Basics) and the other functions covered in this chapter. Table 8-1 provides a list of these additional trigonometric functions and describes how to derive each one. Each of these derived trigonometric functions is used in the project at the end of this chapter.

Table 8-1 Derived trigonometric functions

The Trigonometric Function...	Is Derived by...
Cosecant (Cosec)	`1/Sin(A)`
Cotangent (Cotan)	`1/Tan(A)`
Hyperbolic cosecant (HCosec)	`2 / (Exp(A) + Exp(-A)`
Hyperbolic cosine (HCos)	`(Exp(A) + Exp(-A) / 2`
Hyperbolic cotangent (Hcotan)	`(Exp(A) + Exp(-A)) / (Exp(A) - Exp(-A))`
Hyperbolic secant (HSec)	`2 / (Exp(A) + Exp(-A)`
Hyperbolic sine (HSin)	`(Exp(A) - Exp(-A)) / 2`
Hyperbolic tangent (HTan)	`(Exp(A) - Exp(-A) / (Exp(A) + Exp(-A)`
Inverse cosecant (Arccosec)	`Atn(A / Sqr(A * A - 1)) + (Sgn(A) - 1) * (2 * Atn(1))`
Inverse cosine (Arccos)	`Atn(-A / Sqr (-A * A +1)) + 2 * Atn(1)`
Inverse cotangent (Arccotan)	`Atn(A) + 2 * Atn(1)`
Inverse secant (Arcsec)	`Atn(A / Sqr(A * A - 1)) + Sgn((A) -1) * (2 * Atn(1))`
Inverse sine (Arcsin)	`Atn(A / Sqr (-A * A + 1))`
Inverse hyperbolic cosecant (HArccosec)	`Log((Sgn(A) * Sqr(A * A + 1) + 1) / A`
Inverse hyperbolic cosine (HArccos)	`Log(A + Sqr(A * A - 1))`
Inverse hyperbolic cotangent (HArccotan)	`Log((A + 1) / (A - 1) / 2`
Inverse hyperbolic secant (HArcsec)	`Log((Sqr(- A * A + 1) + 1) / A`
Inverse hyperbolic sine (HArcsin)	`Log(A + Sqr(A * A + 1))`
Inverse hyperbolic tangent (HArctan)	`Log((1 + A) / (1 - A )) / 2`
Secant (Sec)	`1/Cos(A)`

Working with Logarithms

A logarithm is used when working with exponentiation. We all learned that the formula $X = Y^Z$ means take the value Y and multiply it by itself the number of times specified by Z. For example, $2^3 = 8$ (2*2*2). The value Z is the exponential value of the equation. As long as you know what the Y and Z values are in the equation, it is easy to calculate the value of X.

Unfortunately, you may not always know the value of Y and Z. How do you determine Z if you know the value of X and Y? This is when you use a logarithm. A logarithm is the exponent value that indicates the number of times the value Y needs to be multiplied by itself to get the value X. The value that is multiplied (Y) is considered to be the base of the formula.

There are two basic types of logarithms: common and natural. A common logarithm uses a value 10 as the base value. Therefore, in the basic formula for exponentiation above, $X = Y^Z$, the value of Y is 10, and Z is the number of times that Y needs to be multiplied by itself to return the value indicated by X.

Natural logarithms use a base value of approximately 2.71828182845905, normally referred to as e. VBScript provides two functions for working with logarithms: **Exp()** and **Log()**. Each of these functions assumes that the base value is e. These functions are covered in more detail in this chapter, but the **Log()** function returns the natural logarithm of the supplied numeric expression, and the **Exp()** function raises the supplied numeric expression to e.

It is possible to use these functions if you have a different base value by using a simple formula. By dividing the natural log of the desired number (X) by the natural log of the desired base (Y), you can determine the desired logarithm value (Z):
Z = Log(X) / Log(Y)

Generating Random Numbers

You may, on occasion, have the need to create random numbers. Unfortunately, when dealing with computers it is impossible to have a truly random number. In order to generate random numbers, the system requires a value (often called a seed number) to use as a basis for the number generation.

In VBScript you can use the **Randomize** statement to generate the seed number for the series. If the **Randomize** statement is called without a value, the system timer value containing the number of seconds that have elapsed since midnight is used as the seed for the random number generator. If you specify a value for the **Randomize** statement, the series of numbers generated will always be the same.

The **Randomize** statement should be used before calling the **Rnd()** function. The **Rnd()** function returns random numbers in the range of 0 to 1 based on the seed created by the **Randomize** statement. You can create random numbers within any desired range by using a formula to specify the range. Also with this formula you can specify the type of the numbers that are created (integer, double-precision, floating-point, and so on). For this formula the **CInt()** function is used to ensure that the random numbers generated are all integer values:

```
CInt((UpperRange - LowerRange + 1) * Rnd + LowerRange)
```

Randomize STATEMENT

Purpose Use the **Randomize** statement to create the seed to be used by the **Rnd()** function to generate a series of random numbers. Table 8-2 indicates the expressions that can be used with the **Randomize** statement.

Syntax **Randomize(expression)**

Table 8-2 Argument of the Randomize statement

Argument	Description
expression	Any numeric expression. This argument is optional and can be omitted.

Description The `Randomize` statement creates the seed value that is used by the `Rnd()` function to generate random numbers. This statement can be called with or without an expression. If the expression is omitted, the system timer value that identifies the number of seconds that have passed since midnight is used to create the seed.

The example in Listing 8-5 illustrates how to use the `Randomize` statement with the `Rnd()` function to generate a series of random numbers.

See Also `Rnd()`

Summary of Computing Values Functions

Table 8-3 summarizes the computing values functions covered in this chapter. A detailed description of each function follows this table. Each of the functions is also used in the Computing Values project at the end of the chapter.

Table 8-3 Computing values function summary

Use...	To Do This...
`Atn`	Determine the arctangent value of an angle in a right triangle.
`Cos`	Determine the cosine value of an angle in a right triangle.
`Exp`	Raise the natural logarithm to the specified power.
`Log`	Return the exponential power for the natural logarithm.
`Rnd`	Generate a random number.
`Sin`	Determine the sine value of an angle in a right triangle.
`Sqr`	Determine the square root of a numeric expression.
`Tan`	Determine the tangent value of an angle in a right triangle.

`Atn` Function

Purpose Use the `Atn()` function to determine the arctangent of an angle in a right triangle. Table 8-4 describes the expressions you can use with the `Atn()` function.

Syntax `Atn(expression)`

Table 8-4 Argument of the `Atn()` function

Argument	Description
`expression`	Any numeric expression that identifies the ratio of two sides of a triangle

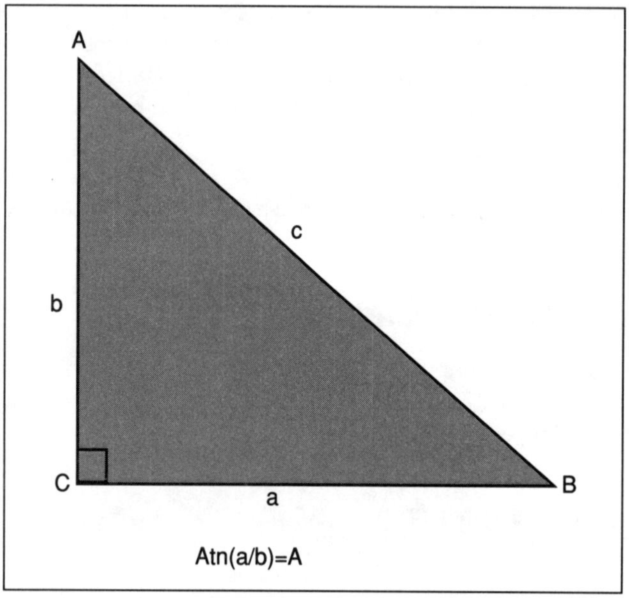

Figure 8-2 The arctangent of the opposite side divided by the adjacent side is the radian value of the angle

Description

The `Atn()` function evaluates the size of an angle in radians and returns a value that indicates the ratio of two sides of a right triangle. The ratio is the length of the side adjacent to the specified angle (the side between the specified angle and right angle) divided by the length of the side opposite the right angle (the hypotenuse). Figure 8-2 illustrates the ratio value that is passed to the `Atn()` function. For example, the arctangent of side a divided by side b is the radian value of angle A.

The value returned by the `Atn()` function is always in the range of -pi/2 to pi/2 radians.

Listing 8-1 illustrates how to use the `Atn()` function to determine the value of an angle in a triangle. The ratio of the two sides of the triangle is typed in the input field. The `Atn()` function uses this value to determine the size of the angle in radians. The radian value is also converted to degrees, and the `MsgBox()` function displays both the radian and degree value of the angle as illustrated in Figure 8-3.

Listing 8-1 Using the `Atn()` function

```
<HTML>

<HEAD>
<TITLE>Atn Example</TITLE>
```

```
<SCRIPT LANGUAGE="VBScript">
<!--
'..............................................................
' ArcTangent_OnClick()
' Determines the arctangent of the value typed by the user.
'..............................................................
SUB ArcTangent_OnClick()

  Dim UserValue
  Dim Degrees
  Dim Radians

  UserValue=InputValue.Value

'..............................................................
' Make sure the value typed by the user is numeric.
'..............................................................
  If IsNumeric(UserValue) Then

'..............................................................
' Calculate the size of the angle in radians and degrees.
'..............................................................
    Radians = Atn(UserValue)

    Degrees = (Radians * 180) / 3.14159265358979

    MsgBox "The Arctangent is " & Radians & " radians " & " or " & Degrees & " degrees"

  Else

'..............................................................
' Display this message if the value passed is not numeric.
'..............................................................
    MsgBox "Type a numeric value in the field"

  End If

END SUB
-->

</SCRIPT>
</HEAD>

<BODY>

<CENTER>

<FONT SIZE=6>Arctangent Value<P>
</CENTER>
<HR>

<FONT SIZE=4>

<PRE>Type a value: <INPUT NAME=InputValue SIZE=20></PRE>

<HR>
<CENTER>
<INPUT TYPE=BUTTON VALUE="Determine the Arctangent" NAME="ArcTangent">
```

continued on next page

continued from previous page

```
</CENTER>
</FONT>

</BODY>

</HTML>
```

Example

The Computing Values project at the end of this chapter uses the **Atn()** function to determine the arctangent value for the value in the **InputValue** field. The function is also used when determining the inverse sine, inverse cosine, inverse secant, inverse cosecant, and inverse tangent.

Comments

To convert a value from radians to degrees, multiply the radian value by 180 and divide the result by pi (3.14159). To convert a value from degrees to radians, multiply the degree value by pi and divide by 180. For example, if you want to convert 45 degrees to radians, multiply 45 by pi to get a result of 141.3717. Divide 141.3717 by 180 to get a radian value of 0.7854.

Remember that the **Atn()** function is the inverse trigonometric function of the **Tan()** function. The **Tan()** function takes the radian value of the angle

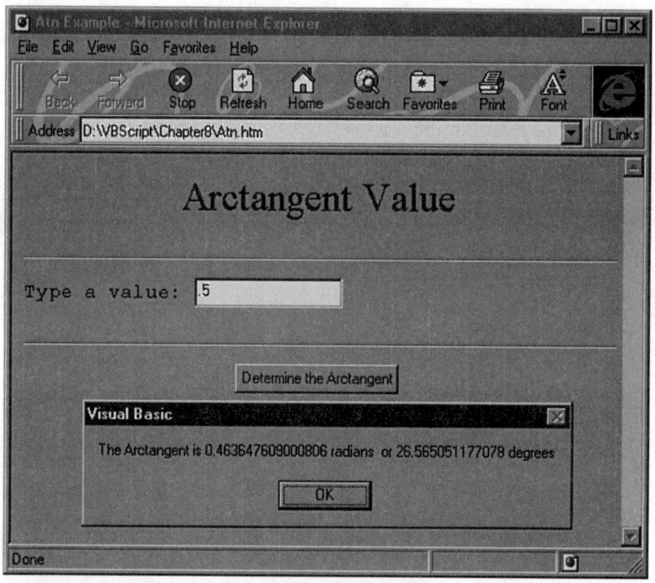

Figure 8-3 The **MsgBox()** function is used to display the value of the angle in radians and degrees

and returns the ratio of the two sides. The `Atn()` function takes the ratio of the two sides and returns the radian value of the angle.

The `Atn()` function only evaluates numeric expressions; if it receives a nonnumeric expression, a run-time error is returned. To eliminate errors, use the `IsNumeric()` function to make sure the value is numeric prior to calling the `Atn()` function. For more information about the `IsNumeric()` function, refer to Chapter 4, Data Validation.

See Also `Cos()`, `Sin()`, `Tan()`

Cos Function

Purpose Use the `Cos()` function to determine the cosine of an angle in a right triangle. Table 8-5 describes the expressions you can use with the `Cos()` function.

Syntax `Cos(expression)`

Table 8-5 Argument of the `Cos()` function

Argument	Description
`expression`	Any numeric expression that describes the size of an angle in radians

Description The `Cos()` function evaluates the size of an angle in radians and returns a value that indicates the ratio of two sides of a right triangle. The ratio is the length of the side adjacent to the specified angle (the side between the specified angle and right angle) divided by the length of the side opposite the right angle (the hypotenuse).

For example, the cosine of angle A in Figure 8-4 is equal to length of side b divided by the length of side c.

The value returned by the `Cos()` function is always in the range of -1 to 1.

Listing 8-2 illustrates how to use the `Cos()` function to determine the cosine of the numeric expression. The `MsgBox()` function is used to display the results of the `Cos()` function on the screen, as illustrated in Figure 8-5.

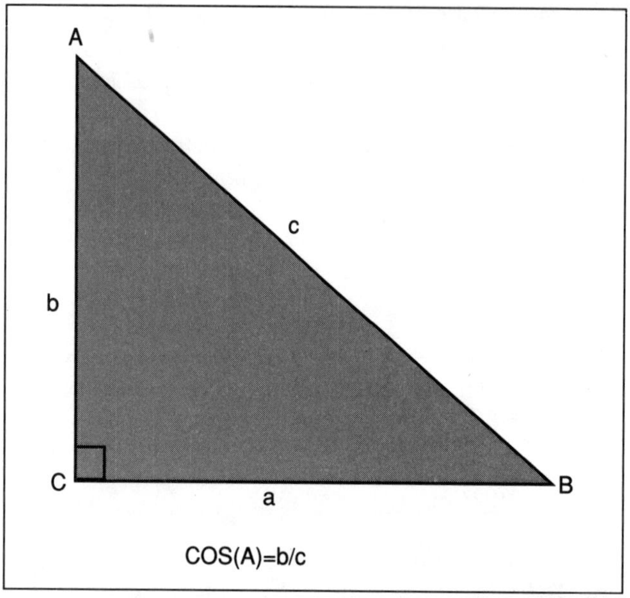

Figure 8-4 The cosine of an angle is the length of the adjacent side divided by the length of the hypotenuse of the triangle

Listing 8-2 Using the `Cos()` *function*

```
<HTML>

<HEAD>
<TITLE>Cos Example</TITLE>

<SCRIPT LANGUAGE="VBScript">
<!--
'.............................................................
' Cosine_OnClick()
' Determines the cosine of the value typed by the user.
'.............................................................
SUB Cosine_OnClick()

  Dim UserValue

  UserValue=InputValue.Value

'.............................................................
' Make sure the value typed by the user is numeric.
'.............................................................
  If IsNumeric(UserValue) Then

     MsgBox "The Cosine is " & Cos(UserValue)
```

```
  Else

'.............................................................
' Display this message if the value passed is not numeric.
'.............................................................
    MsgBox "Type a numeric value in the field"

  End If

END SUB
-->

</SCRIPT>
</HEAD>

<BODY>

<CENTER>

<FONT SIZE=6>Cosine Value<P>
</CENTER>
<HR>

<FONT SIZE=4>

<PRE>Type a value: <INPUT NAME=InputValue SIZE=20></PRE>

<HR>
<CENTER>
<INPUT TYPE=BUTTON VALUE="Determine the Cosine" NAME="Cosine">
</CENTER>
</FONT>

</BODY>

</HTML>
```

Example The Computing Values project at the end of this chapter uses the **`Cos()`** function to determine the cosine value for the value in the **`InputValue`** field. The function is also used when determining the secant value.

Comments To convert a value from radians to degrees, multiply the radian value by 180 and divide the result by pi (3.14159). To convert a value from degrees to radians, multiply the degree value by pi and divide by 180. For example, if you want to convert 45 degrees to radians, multiply 45 by pi to get a result of 141.3717. Divide 141.3717 by 180 to get a radian value of 0.7854.

The **`Cos()`** function only evaluates numeric expressions; if it receives a nonnumeric expression, a run-time error is returned. To eliminate errors, use the **`IsNumeric()`** function to make sure the value is numeric prior to calling the **`Cos()`** function. For more information about the **`IsNumeric()`** function, refer to Chapter 4, Data Validation.

See Also **`Atn()`**, **`Sin()`**, **`Tan()`**

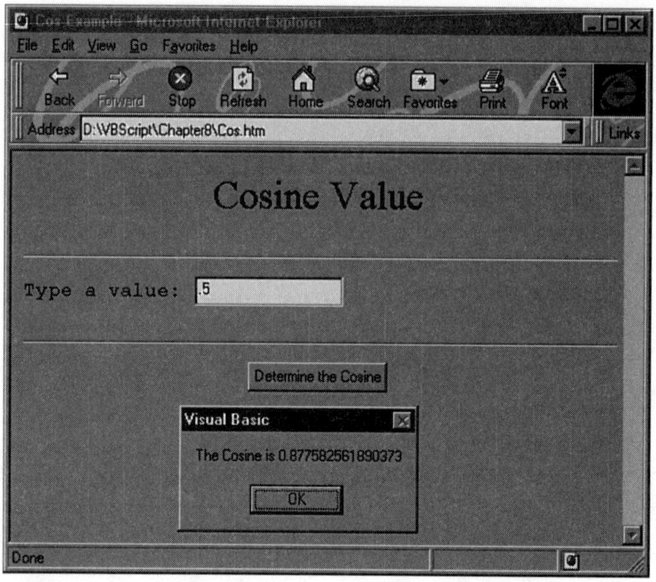

Figure 8-5 The `Cos()` function returns the cosine of the numeric expression

Exp FUNCTION

Purpose Use the `Exp()` function to determine the value of the natural logarithm (e) raised to the specified power. Table 8-6 describes the expressions you can use with the `Exp()` function.

Syntax `Exp(expression)`

Table 8-6 Argument of the `Exp()` function

Argument	Description
`expression`	Any valid numeric expression less than 709.782712893

Description The `Exp()` function returns the result of the natural logarithm raised to the specified exponential power. The natural logarithm, normally referred to as e, is approximately 2.718282. The numeric expression used with the `Exp()` function should not be larger than 709.782712893, or a run-time error will occur.

Listing 8-3 uses the `Exp()` function to determine the exponential value by using the value typed in the `InputValue` field. The `IsNumeric()` function is used to make sure a numeric value was typed in the field. An `If` statement is also used to make sure the value is not larger than

709.782712893. The **MsgBox()** function displays the result of the **Exp()** function, as illustrated in Figure 8-6.

Listing 8-3 Using the Exp() *function*

```
<HTML>

<HEAD>
<TITLE>Exp Example</TITLE>

<SCRIPT LANGUAGE="VBScript">
<!--
'..........................................................
' ExponentValue_OnClick()
' Determines the value of e raised to the specified value.
'..........................................................
SUB ExponentValue_OnClick()

  Dim UserValue

  UserValue = InputValue.Value

'..........................................................
' Make sure the value entered is numeric.
'..........................................................
  If IsNumeric(UserValue) Then

'..........................................................
' Make sure the value is not larger than 709.782712893
'..........................................................
    If UserValue <= 709.782712893 Then

          MsgBox "The value is " & Exp(UserValue)

    Else

      MsgBox "Type a number in the field that is less than 709.782712893"

    End If

  Else

    MsgBox "Type a numeric value in the field"

  End If


END SUB
-->

</SCRIPT>
</HEAD>

<BODY>

<CENTER>
```

continued on next page

continued from previous page

```
<FONT SIZE=6>Exponential Value<P>
</CENTER>
<HR>

<FONT SIZE=4>

Enter the Value: <INPUT NAME=InputValue SIZE=10>

<HR>
<CENTER>
<INPUT TYPE=BUTTON VALUE="Determine Exponent Value" NAME="ExponentValue">
</CENTER>
</FONT>

</BODY>

</HTML>
```

Example

The Computing Values project at the end of this chapter uses the `Exp()` function to determine the exponential value for the value in the `InputValue` field. The function is also used when determining the hyperbolic sine, hyperbolic cosine, hyperbolic tangent, hyperbolic secant, hyperbolic cosecant, and hyperbolic cotangent.

Comments

The `Exp()` function performs basically the reverse of the `Log()` function and is sometimes referred to as the antilogarithm. The `Log()` function

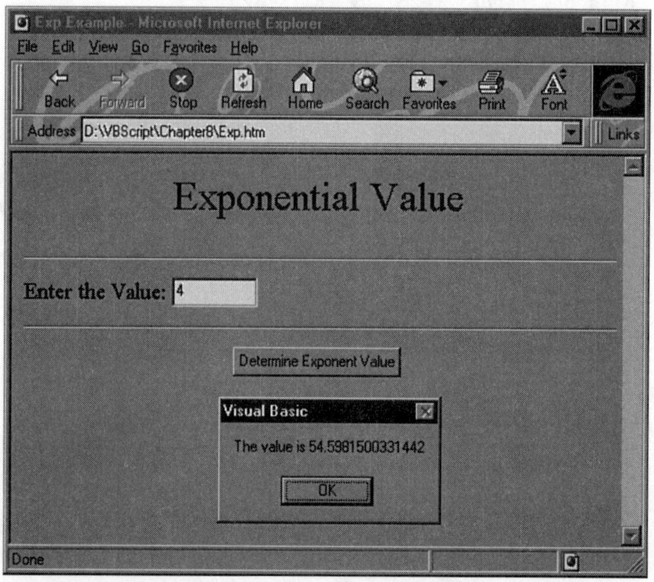

Figure 8-6 The `Exp()` function determines the value of the natural logarithm raised to the value typed by the user

returns the exponential power used to raise the natural log to return the specified value.

Note that the natural logarithm should not be confused with the common logarithm. The common logarithm has a base value of 10.

The `Exp()` function only evaluates numeric expressions; if it receives a nonnumeric expression, a run-time error is returned. To eliminate errors, use the `IsNumeric()` function to make sure the value is numeric prior to calling the `Exp()` function. For more information about the `IsNumeric()` function, refer to Chapter 4, Data Validation.

See Also `Log()`

Log Function

Purpose Use the `Log()` function to return the natural logarithm of the specified number. Table 8-7 describes the expressions you can use with the `Log()` function.

Syntax `Log(expression)`

Table 8-7 Argument of the `Log()` function

Argument	Description
`expression`	Any valid numeric expression greater than zero

Description The `Log()` function returns the exponential value needed to raise the natural logarithm so that it equals the specified value. In other words, it indicates the number of times the natural logarithm needs to be multiplied by itself to return the value specified in the numeric expression. The natural logarithm, normally referred to as e, is approximately 2.718282. The numeric expression used with the `Log()` function must be greater than zero.

You can use the `Log()` function to determine the log value even if you have a different base value, such as 5, by using the following formula: `X = Log(ResultValue) / Log(BaseValue)`. For example, if you know the base is 5 and the numeric expression (desired logarithm value) is 75, take the `Log(75)/Log(5)`. By dividing the natural log of the desired number by the natural log of the desired base, you can determine the desired logarithm value.

In Listing 8-4, the `Log()` function is used to determine the log value of the value typed in the `InputValue` field. Since the value must be numeric and greater than zero, both conditions are checked prior to calling the `Log()` function. The `MsgBox()` function displays the results of the `Log()` function, as illustrated in Figure 8-7.

Listing 8-4 Using the `Log()` *function*

```
<HTML>

<HEAD>
<TITLE>Log Example</TITLE>

<SCRIPT LANGUAGE="VBScript">
<!--
'.............................................................
' LogValue_OnClick()
' Determines the log value based on the value typed by the
' user in the InputValue field.
'.............................................................
SUB LogValue_OnClick()

  Dim UserValue

  UserValue = InputValue.Value

'.............................................................
' Make sure the value entered is numeric.
'.............................................................
  If IsNumeric(UserValue) Then

'.............................................................
' Make sure the value is greater than zero.
'.............................................................
    If UserValue > 0 Then

          MsgBox "The log value is " & Log(UserValue)

    Else

      MsgBox "Type a number that is greater than zero"

    End If

  Else

    MsgBox "Type a numeric value in the field"

  End If

END SUB
-->

</SCRIPT>
</HEAD>

<BODY>

<CENTER>

<FONT SIZE=6>Log Value<P>
</CENTER>
<HR>
```

```
<FONT SIZE=4>

Enter the Value: <INPUT NAME=InputValue SIZE=10>

<HR>
<CENTER>
<INPUT TYPE=BUTTON VALUE="Determine Log Value" NAME="LogValue">
</CENTER>
</FONT>

</BODY>

</HTML>
```

Example

The Computing Values project at the end of this chapter uses the `Log()` function to determine the natural logarithm value for the value in the `InputValue` field. The function is also used when determining the inverse hyperbolic sine, inverse hyperbolic cosine, inverse hyperbolic tangent, inverse hyperbolic secant, inverse hyperbolic cosecant, inverse hyperbolic cotangent, and the logarithm to base 10.

Comments

The `Exp()` function performs basically the reverse of the `Log()` function and is sometimes referred to as the antilogarithm.

Remember that the natural logarithm should not be confused with the common logarithm. The common logarithm has a base value of 10.

The `Log()` function only evaluates numeric expressions; if it receives a nonnumeric expression, a run-time error is returned. To eliminate errors,

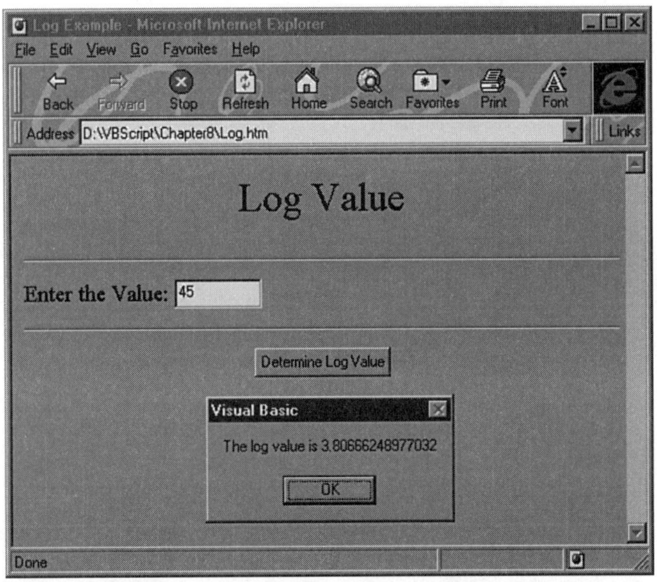

Figure 8-7 The `Log()` function determines the log value based on the value typed in the field

use the **IsNumeric()** function to make sure the value is numeric prior to calling the **Log()** function. For more information about the **IsNumeric()** function, refer to Chapter 4, Data Validation.

See Also `Exp()`

Rnd Function

Purpose Use the **Rnd()** function to generate a random number. Table 8-8 describes the expressions you can use with the **Rnd()** function. The value of the expression passed to the **Rnd()** function determines the type of random number generated, as illustrated in Table 8-9.

Syntax `Rnd(expression)`

Table 8-8 Argument of the Rnd() function

Argument	Description
expression	Any numeric value. The expression is optional and can be omitted.

Table 8-9 Random number values returned by the Rnd() function

If the Expression Is ...	The Rnd Function Returns...
Negative	The same number every time, using negative expression as the seed
Omitted	The next random number in the sequence
Positive	The next random number in the sequence
Zero	The most recently generated number

Description The **Randomize** statement should be used prior to calling the **Rnd()** function to create a seed to be used to generate random numbers. The **Rnd()** function uses the seed created by the **Randomize** statement to create random numbers. The numbers created by the **Rnd()** function are in the range of 0 to 1. You can create random numbers within any desired range by using the following formula:

```
CInt((UpperRange - LowerRange + 1) * Rnd + LowerRange)
```

Depending on the type of numeric values (integers, single-precision floating-point, or double-precision floating-point) you can use any of the numeric conversion functions. For the example formula above, **CInt()** is used to create integer values.

Listing 8-5 uses the **Rnd()** function along with the **Randomize** statement to create random numbers. The number of random numbers created and the range of the numbers are specified on the screen by the user, as illustrated in Figure 8-8. The **IsNumeric()** function makes sure that the values typed by the user are numeric before calling the **Rnd()** function. The **MsgBox()** function displays each random number requested on the screen, as illustrated in Figure 8-9.

Listing 8-5 Using the Rnd() function

```
<HTML>

<HEAD>
<TITLE>Rnd Example</TITLE>

<SCRIPT LANGUAGE="VBScript">
<!--
'.............................................................
' GenerateRandom_OnClick()
' Determines the specified number of random numbers within
' the range specified.
'.............................................................
SUB GenerateRandom_OnClick()

  Dim RandomNumber(10)
  Dim Count
  Dim I
  Dim UpperLimit
  Dim LowerLimit

  Count = RandomCount.Value
  UpperLimit = InputUpper.Value
  LowerLimit = InputLower.Value

'.............................................................
' The Randomize statement creates the seed for the random
' number.
'.............................................................
  Randomize

'.............................................................
' Make sure the upper and lower range values are numeric.
'.............................................................
  If IsNumeric(UpperLimit) and IsNumeric(LowerLimit) Then

'.............................................................
' Make sure the value specifying the number of random number
' values is numeric.
'.............................................................
    If IsNumeric(Count) Then

'.............................................................
' Use a For Next statement to generate the specified number
' of random numbers.
'.............................................................
      For I = 1 to Count
```

continued on next page

continued from previous page

```
        RandomNumber(I) = CInt((UpperLimit - LowerLimit + 1) * Rnd + LowerLimit)

        MsgBox "Random Number " & I & " is " & RandomNumber(I)

      Next

    Else

      MsgBox "Type a number in the field specifying the number of random numbers"

    End If

  Else

    MsgBox "Type numeric values for the limits"

  End If

END SUB
-->

</SCRIPT>
</HEAD>

<BODY>

<CENTER>

<FONT SIZE=6>Random Number Generator<P>
</CENTER>
<HR>

<FONT SIZE=4>

How many random numbers do you want? <INPUT NAME=RandomCount SIZE=10>

<BR><BR>


Specify the range for the random numbers.

<BR>

Lower Limit: <INPUT NAME=InputLower SIZE=10>
<BR>
Upper Limit: <INPUT NAME=InputUpper SIZE=10>


<HR>
<CENTER>
<INPUT TYPE=BUTTON VALUE="Generate Random Numbers" NAME="GenerateRandom">
</CENTER>
</FONT>

</BODY>

</HTML>
```

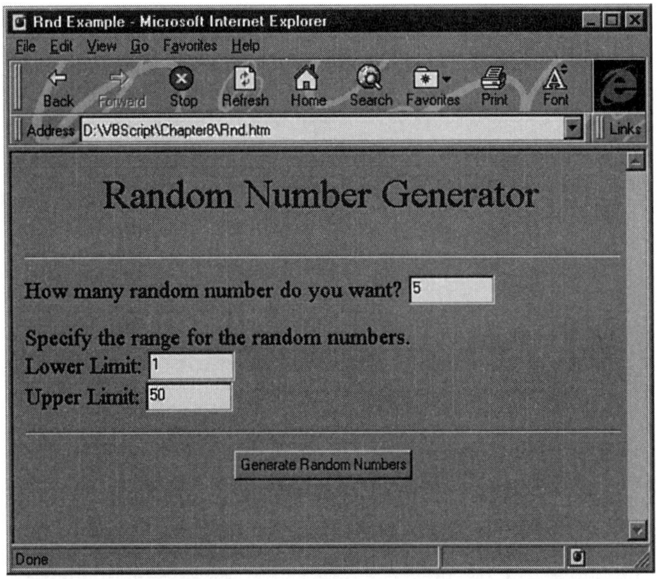

Figure 8-8 The Random Number Generator screen requests the number of random numbers desired and the range for the numbers

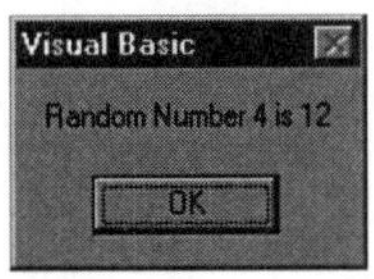

Figure 8-9 The `MsgBox()` function displays each random number generated

Comments

To repeat a sequence of random numbers, call the `Rnd()` function with a negative argument immediately before using the `Randomize` statement with a numeric argument. Simply using the `Randomize` statement with the same value for the argument does not repeat the previous sequence of random numbers.

The `Rnd()` function only evaluates numeric expressions; if it receives a nonnumeric expression, a run-time error is returned. To eliminate errors, use the `IsNumeric()` function to make sure the value is numeric prior to calling the `Rnd()` function. For more information about the `IsNumeric()` function, refer to Chapter 4, Data Validation.

`Sin` FUNCTION

Purpose Use the **`Sin()`** function to determine the sine of an angle in a right triangle. Table 8-10 describes the expressions you can use with the **`Sin()`** function.

Syntax **`Sin(expression)`**

Table 8-10 Argument of the `Sin()` function

Argument	Description
`expression`	Any numeric expression that describes the size of an angle in radians

Description The **`Sin()`** function evaluates the size of an angle in radians and returns a value that indicates the ratio of two sides of a right triangle. The ratio is the length of the side opposite the specified angle (the side that does not touch the desired angle) divided by the length of the side opposite the right angle (the hypotenuse). For example, the sine of angle A in Figure 8-10 is equal to the length of side a divided by the length of side c.

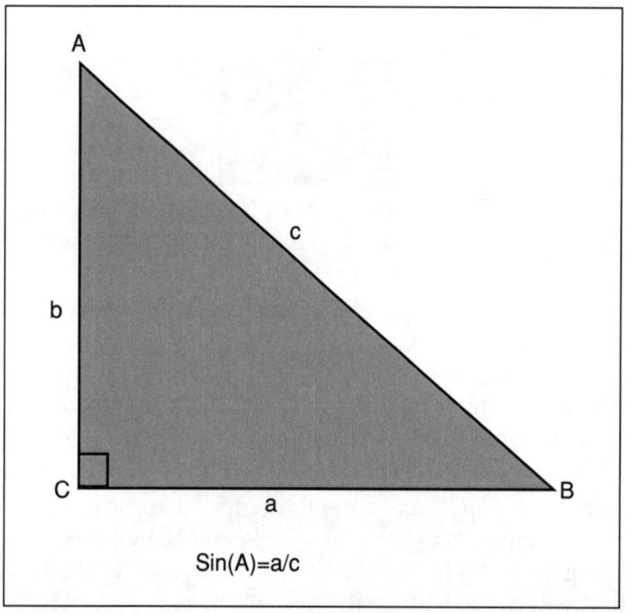

Figure 8-10 The sine of an angle is the length of the opposite side divided by the length of the hypotenuse of the triangle

The value returned by the `Sin()` function is always in the range of -1 to 1. Listing 8-6 illustrates how to use the `Sin()` function to determine the sine of the expression typed in the `InputValue` field. The `MsgBox()` function displays the value returned by the `Sin()` function on the screen, as illustrated in Figure 8-11.

Listing 8-6 Using the `Sin()` function

```
<HTML>

<HEAD>
<TITLE>Sin Example</TITLE>

<SCRIPT LANGUAGE="VBScript">
<!--
'.............................................................
' Sine_OnClick()
' Determines the sine of the value typed by the user.
'..............................................................
SUB Sine_OnClick()

  Dim UserValue

  UserValue=InputValue.Value

'..............................................................
' Make sure the value typed by the user is numeric.
'..............................................................
  If IsNumeric(UserValue) Then

     MsgBox "The Sine is " & Sin(UserValue)

  Else

'.............................................................
' Display this message if the value passed is not numeric.
'.............................................................
    MsgBox "Type a numeric value in the field"

  End If

END SUB
-->

</SCRIPT>
</HEAD>

<BODY>

<CENTER>

<FONT SIZE=6>Sine Value<P>
</CENTER>
<HR>
```

continued on next page

continued from previous page

```
<FONT SIZE=4>

<PRE>Type a value: <INPUT NAME=InputValue SIZE=20></PRE>

<HR>
<CENTER>
<INPUT TYPE=BUTTON VALUE="Determine the Sine" NAME="Sine">
</CENTER>
</FONT>

</BODY>

</HTML>
```

Example The Computing Values project at the end of this chapter uses the `Sin()` function to determine the sine value for the value in the `InputValue` field. The function is also used when determining the secant value.

Comments To convert a value from radians to degrees, multiply the radian value by 180 and divide the result by pi (3.14159). To convert a value from degrees to radians, multiply the degree value by pi and divide by 180. For example, if you want to convert 45 degrees to radians, multiply 45 by pi to get a result of 141.3717. Divide 141.3717 by 180 to get a radian value of 0.7854.

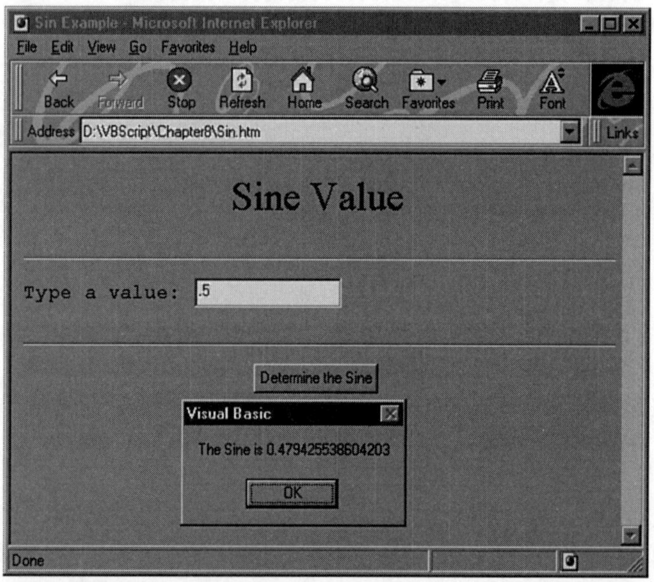

Figure 8-11 The `Sin()` function returns a value between -1 and 1 indicating the sine of the expression

The `Sin()` function only evaluates numeric expressions; if it receives a nonnumeric expression, a run-time error is returned. To eliminate errors, use the `IsNumeric()` function to make sure the value is numeric prior to calling the `Sin()` function. For more information about the `IsNumeric()` function, refer to Chapter 4, Data Validation.

See Also `Atn()`, `Cos()`, `Tan()`

Sqr FUNCTION

Purpose Use the `Sqr()` function to determine the square root of a number. This should be used with any numeric value that is greater than or equal to zero. Table 8-11 describes the expressions you can use with the `Sqr()` function.

Syntax `Sqr(expression)`

Table 8-11 Argument of the `Sqr()` function

Argument	Description
`expression`	Any numeric expression that is greater than or equal to zero

Description The `Sqr()` function returns the square root of the numeric expression. The numeric expression must be a nonnegative value. If you take the square root of the numeric expression and multiply it by itself, the resulting value is the numeric expression. For example, the square root of 64 is 8; thus, 8 multiplied by 8 equals 64. In other words, 8^2 equals 64. When you take the square root of an expression, you are determining the value that when multiplied by itself would give you the specified numeric expression.

Listing 8-7 uses the `Sqr()` function to determine the square root of the numeric expression typed in the `InputValue()` field. The `IsNumeric()` function makes sure that the expression is numeric. If the expression is numeric, an `If` statement is used to make sure the value is greater than or equal to zero. After verifying that the expression is valid, the `MsgBox()` function displays the results of the `Sqr()` function, as illustrated in Figure 8-12.

Listing 8-7 Using the `Sqr()` function

```
<HTML>

<HEAD>
<TITLE>Sqr Example</TITLE>

<SCRIPT LANGUAGE="VBScript">
```

continued on next page

continued from previous page

```
<!--
'..............................................................
' SquareRoot_OnClick()
' Determines the square root of the value typed by the user.
'..............................................................
SUB SquareRoot_OnClick()

  Dim UserValue

  UserValue=InputValue.Value

'..............................................................
' First make sure the value typed by the user is numeric,
' then check to make sure the value is greater than zero.
'..............................................................
  If IsNumeric(UserValue) Then

    If UserValue >= 0 Then


      MsgBox "The Square Root of " & InputValue.Value & " is " & Sqr(UserValue)

    Else

'..............................................................
' Display this message if the value typed is negative.
'..............................................................
      MsgBox "Type a value greater than zero"

    End If

  Else

'..............................................................
' Display this message if the value passed is not numeric.
'..............................................................
    MsgBox "Type a numeric value in the field"

  End If

END SUB
-->

</SCRIPT>
</HEAD>

<BODY>

<CENTER>

<FONT SIZE=6>Square Root<P>
</CENTER>
<HR>

<FONT SIZE=4>

<PRE>Type a value: <INPUT NAME=InputValue SIZE=20></PRE>
```

```
<HR>
<CENTER>
<INPUT TYPE=BUTTON VALUE="Determine Square Root" NAME="SquareRoot">
</CENTER>
</FONT>

</BODY>

</HTML>
```

Example

The Computing Values project at the end of this chapter uses the `Sqr()` function to determine the square root value for the value in the `InputValue` field. The function is also used when determining the inverse sine, inverse cosine, inverse secant, inverse cosecant, inverse hyperbolic sine, inverse hyperbolic cosine, inverse hyperbolic secant, and inverse hyperbolic cosecant.

Comments

The `Sqr()` function requires a positive expression, because it is impossible to multiply a number by itself and return a negative value. A negative value multiplied by a negative value returns a positive value, and a positive value multiplied by a positive value returns a positive value. For example, -3 multiplied by -3 equals 9. Therefore, the square root of a number can be a positive or negative number.

The `Sqr()` function only evaluates numeric expressions; if it receives a nonnumeric expression, a run-time error is returned. To eliminate errors,

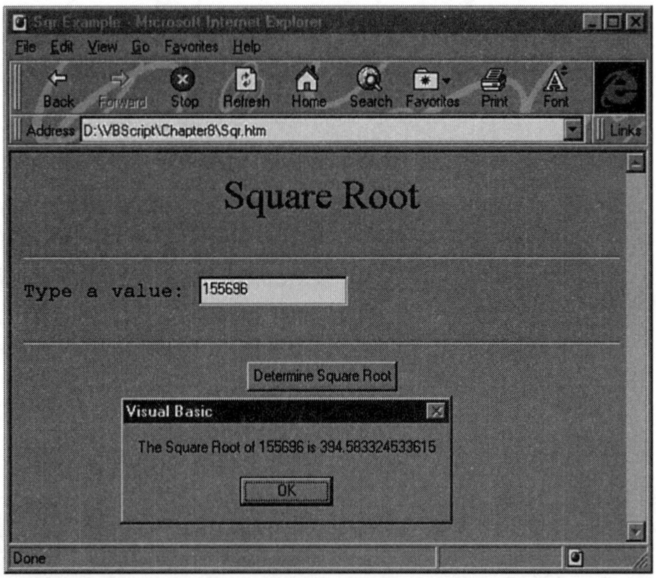

Figure 8-12 The `Sqr()` function returns the square root of the numeric expression

use the `IsNumeric()` function to make sure the value is numeric prior to calling the `Sqr()` function. For more information about the `IsNumeric()` function, refer to Chapter 4, Data Validation.

You will also want to perform an additional check to make sure the expression passed to the `Sqr()` function is not negative. This check can be accomplished using an `If` statement, as demonstrated in Listing 8-7.

Tan Function

Purpose Use the `Tan()` function to determine the tangent of an angle in a right triangle. Table 8-12 describes the expressions you can use with the `Tan()` function.

Syntax `Tan(expression)`

Table 8-12 Argument of the `Tan()` function

Argument	Description
`expression`	Any numeric expression that describes the size of an angle in radians

Description The `Tan()` function evaluates the size of an angle in radians and returns a value indicating the ratio of two sides of a right triangle. The ratio is the length of the side opposite the specified angle (the side that does not touch the specified angle) divided by the length of the side adjacent to the angle (not the hypotenuse of the triangle). For example, the tangent of angle A in Figure 8-13 is equal to length of side a divided by the length of side b.

Listing 8-8 illustrates how to use the `Tan()` function to determine the tangent of the specified angle. The `Tan()` function takes the radian value of the angle from the `InputValue` field and returns the tangent value. The `MsgBox()` function is used to display the results of the `Tan()` function, as illustrated in Figure 8-14.

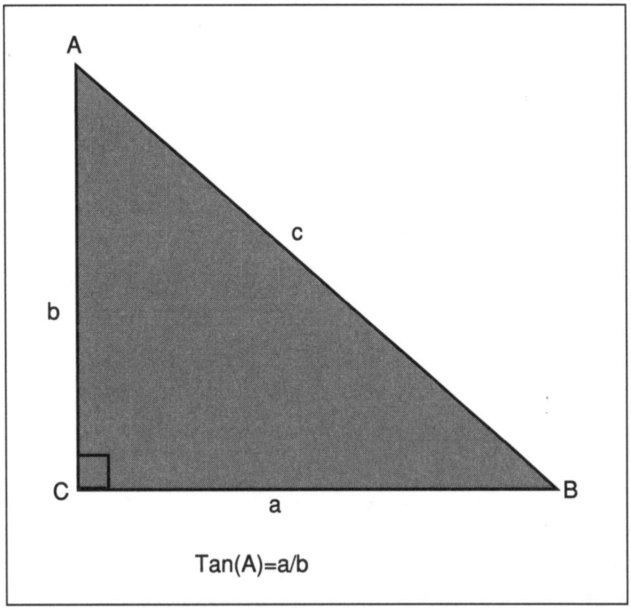

Figure 8-13 The tangent of an angle is the length of the opposite side divided by the length of the adjacent side

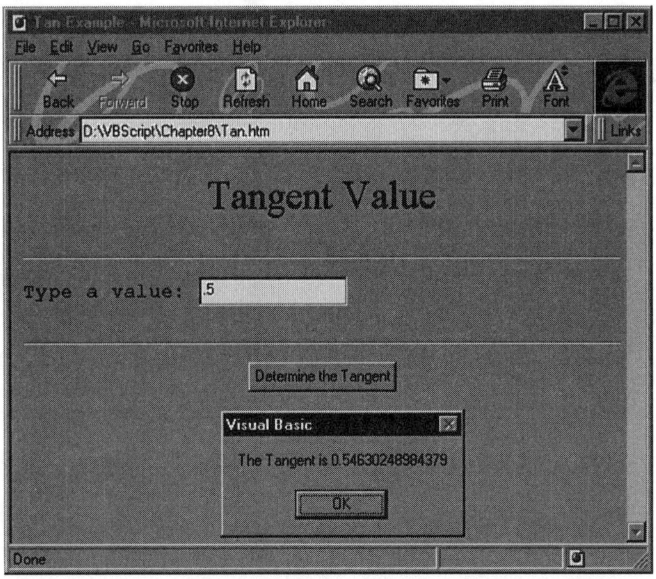

Figure 8-14 The `Tan()` function returns the tangent of the specified angle

Listing 8-8 Using the `Tan()` *function*

```
<HTML>

<HEAD>
<TITLE>Tan Example</TITLE>

<SCRIPT LANGUAGE="VBScript">
<!--
'..........................................................
' Tangent_OnClick()
' Determines the tangent of the value typed by the user.
'...........................................................
SUB Tangent_OnClick()

  Dim UserValue

  UserValue=InputValue.Value

'...........................................................
' Make sure the value typed by the user is numeric.
'...........................................................
  If IsNumeric(UserValue) Then

     MsgBox "The Tangent is " & Tan(UserValue)

  Else

'..........................................................
' Display this message if the value passed is not numeric.
'..........................................................
    MsgBox "Type a numeric value in the field"

  End If

END SUB
-->

</SCRIPT>
</HEAD>

<BODY>

<CENTER>

<FONT SIZE=6>Tangent Value<P>
</CENTER>
<HR>

<FONT SIZE=4>

<PRE>Type a value: <INPUT NAME=InputValue SIZE=20>

<HR>
<INPUT TYPE=BUTTON VALUE="Determine the Tangent" NAME="Tangent">
```

```
</FONT>

</BODY>

</HTML>
```

Example The Computing Values project at the end of this chapter uses the `Tan()` function to determine the tangent value for the value in the `InputValue` field. The function is also used when determining the cotangent value.

Comments To convert a value from radians to degrees, multiply the radian value by 180 and divide the result by pi (3.14159). To convert a value from degrees to radians, multiply the degree value by pi and divide by 180. For example, if you want to convert 45 degrees to radians, multiply 45 by pi (3.14159) to get a result of 141.3717. Divide 141.3717 by 180 to get a radian value of 0.7854.

The `Tan()` function only evaluates numeric expressions; if it receives a nonnumeric expression, a run-time error is returned. To eliminate errors, use the `IsNumeric()` function to make sure the value is numeric prior to calling the `Tan()` function. For more information about the `IsNumeric()` function, refer to Chapter 4, Data Validation.

See Also `Atn()`, `Cos()`, `Sin()`

Computing Values Project

The Computing Values project uses the functions covered in this chapter to create a scientific calculator. Not only are each of the functions used, but the nonintrinsic trigonometric functions covered in Table 8-1 are also used in this project.

Building the Project

1. Start the project by setting up the standard HTML template used for all VBScript examples in this book. Place the VBScript code in the `<HEAD>` section of the HTML code to keep everything consistent. Remember to place the HTML comment tags `<!--` and `-->` around the VBScript code so that it will be ignored by browsers that cannot interpret the `<SCRIPT>` tag.

```
<HTML>

<HEAD>
<TITLE>Computing Values Project</TITLE>

<SCRIPT LANGUAGE="VBScript">

<!--

-->

</SCRIPT>
```

continued on next page

continued from previous page

```
</HEAD>

<BODY>

</BODY>

</HTML>
```

2. In the <BODY> section, place the desired title information for the Web page. For this example, you are creating a Web page with a scientific calculator that computes the values of several mathematical functions.

```
</SCRIPT>
</HEAD>

<BODY>

<CENTER>

<FONT SIZE=6>Computing Values Calculator<P>
</CENTER>
<HR>

<FONT SIZE=4>
```

3. You are going to use an HTML table to design your calculator. Create a table with a border value of `10`. This will give the table a 3D look on the screen.

```
<TABLE BORDER=10>
```

4. In the first row of the table, place the `InputValue` field. This is where the user can type the value to be computed. The results of the computation are also placed in this field. Use the `COLSPAN` table element to have the cell take up the entire first row of the table, as illustrated in Figure 8-15.

```
<TR><TD COLSPAN=4 ALIGN=RIGHT><INPUT NAME=InputValue SIZE=30></TD></TR>
```

5. Add a button for each of the functions that will be available in your calculator. Remember to use the <TR> and </TR> tags to indicate the beginning and end of each row. You are creating a table with seven rows containing four columns; therefore, the <TR> and </TR> tags are placed around each four elements. Figure 8-15 illustrates the layout of the table.

```
<TR><TD><INPUT TYPE=BUTTON VALUE="Cos" NAME="GetCos"></TD>
    <TD><INPUT TYPE=BUTTON VALUE="Sin" NAME="GetSin"></TD>
    <TD><INPUT TYPE=BUTTON VALUE="Tan" NAME="GetTan"></TD>
    <TD><INPUT TYPE=BUTTON VALUE="Atn" NAME="GetAtn"></TD>
</TR>
```

```
<TR><TD><INPUT TYPE=BUTTON VALUE="Sec" NAME="GetSec"></TD>
    <TD><INPUT TYPE=BUTTON VALUE="Cosec" NAME="GetCosec"></TD>
    <TD><INPUT TYPE=BUTTON VALUE="Cotan" NAME="GetCotan"></TD>
    <TD><INPUT TYPE=BUTTON VALUE="Arccos" NAME="GetArccos"></TD>
</TR>

<TR><TD><INPUT TYPE=BUTTON VALUE="Arcsin" NAME="GetArcsin"></TD>
    <TD><INPUT TYPE=BUTTON VALUE="Arccotan" NAME="GetArccotan"></TD>
    <TD><INPUT TYPE=BUTTON VALUE="Arcsec" NAME="GetArcsec"></TD>
    <TD><INPUT TYPE=BUTTON VALUE="Arccosec" NAME="GetArccosec"></TD>
</TR>

<TR><TD><INPUT TYPE=BUTTON VALUE="HCos" NAME="GetHCos"></TD>
    <TD><INPUT TYPE=BUTTON VALUE="HSin" NAME="GetHSin"></TD>
    <TD><INPUT TYPE=BUTTON VALUE="HTan" NAME="GetHTan"></TD>
    <TD><INPUT TYPE=BUTTON VALUE="HCotan" NAME="GetHCotan"></TD>
</TR>

<TR><TD><INPUT TYPE=BUTTON VALUE="HSec" NAME="GetHSec"></TD>
    <TD><INPUT TYPE=BUTTON VALUE="HCosec" NAME="GetHCosec"></TD>
    <TD><INPUT TYPE=BUTTON VALUE="HArccos" NAME="GetHArccos"></TD>
    <TD><INPUT TYPE=BUTTON VALUE="HArcsin" NAME="GetHArcsin"></TD>
</TR>

<TR><TD><INPUT TYPE=BUTTON VALUE="HArctan" NAME="GetHArctan"></TD>
    <TD><INPUT TYPE=BUTTON VALUE="HArcsec" NAME="GetHArcsec"></TD>
    <TD><INPUT TYPE=BUTTON VALUE="HArccosec" NAME="GetHArccosec"></TD>
    <TD><INPUT TYPE=BUTTON VALUE="HArccotan" NAME="GetHArccotan"></TD>
</TR>

<TR><TD><INPUT TYPE=BUTTON VALUE="Exp" NAME="GetExp"></TD>
    <TD><INPUT TYPE=BUTTON VALUE="Log" NAME="GetLog"></TD>
    <TD><INPUT TYPE=BUTTON VALUE="Log 10" NAME="GetLog10"></TD>
    <TD><INPUT TYPE=BUTTON VALUE="Sqr" NAME="GetSqr"></TD>
</TR>

</TABLE>

</FONT>

</BODY>

</HTML>
```

6. In the `<HEAD>` section, create a procedure called `GetCos_OnClick()`. This procedure determines the cosine of the value typed in the `InputValue` field. The procedure is called when the Cos button is selected.

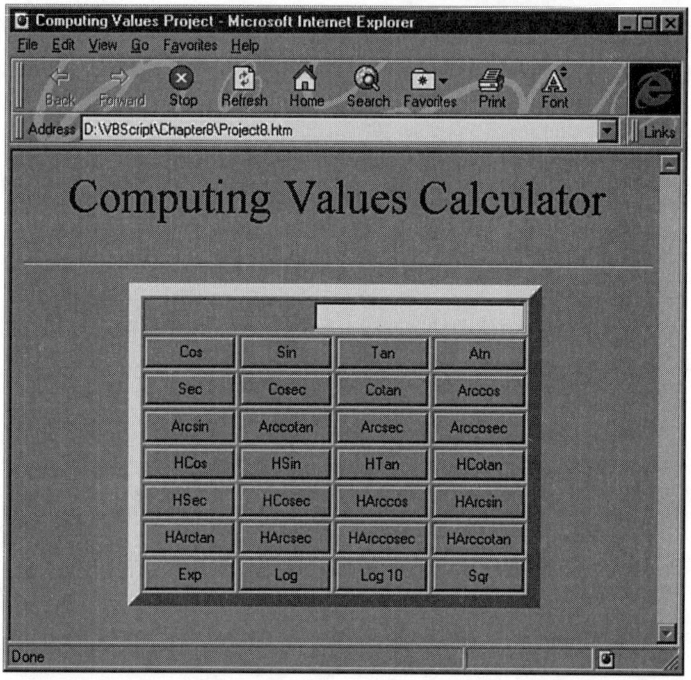

Figure 8-15 The table contains seven rows and four columns of buttons, with the `InputValue` field spanning the last two columns at the top of the table

```
SUB GetCos_OnClick()
  Dim UserValue
  UserValue=InputValue.Value
If IsNumeric(UserValue) Then
     InputValue.Value = Cos(UserValue)
  Else
MsgBox "Type a numeric value in the field"
  End If
END SUB
```

7. Create a procedure called `GetSin_OnClick()` that determines the sine of the value typed in the `InputValue` field. The procedure is called when the Sin button is selected.

```
SUB GetSin_OnClick()
  Dim UserValue
```

```
  UserValue=InputValue.Value
If IsNumeric(UserValue) Then
     InputValue.Value = Sin(UserValue)
  Else
MsgBox "Type a numeric value in the field"
  End If
END SUB
```

8. Create a procedure called **GetTan_OnClick()** that determines the tangent of the value typed in the **InputValue** field. The procedure is called when the Tan button is selected.

```
SUB GetTan_OnClick()
  Dim UserValue
  UserValue=InputValue.Value
  If IsNumeric(UserValue) Then
     InputValue.Value = Tan(UserValue)
  Else
    MsgBox "Type a numeric value in the field"
  End If
END SUB
```

9. Create a procedure called **GetAtn_OnClick()** that determines the arctangent of the value typed in the **InputValue** field. The procedure is called when the Atn button is selected.

```
SUB GetAtn_OnClick()
  Dim UserValue
  UserValue=InputValue.Value
  If IsNumeric(UserValue) Then
    InputValue.Value = Atn(UserValue)
  Else
    MsgBox "Type a numeric value in the field"
  End If
END SUB
```

10. Create a procedure called `GetSec_OnClick()` that determines the secant of the value typed in the `InputValue` field. The procedure is called when the Sec button is selected. The secant is equal to 1 divided by the cosine of the value; therefore, use the formula `1/Cos(UserValue)` to determine the secant of the value typed in the field.

```
SUB GetSec_OnClick()

  Dim UserValue

  UserValue=InputValue.Value

  If IsNumeric(UserValue) Then

     InputValue.Value = 1/Cos(UserValue)

  Else

    MsgBox "Type a numeric value in the field"

  End If

END SUB
```

11. Create a procedure called `GetCosec_OnClick()` that determines the cosecant of the value typed in the `InputValue` field. The procedure is called when the Cosec button is selected. The cosecant is equal to 1 divided by the sine of the value; therefore, use the formula `1/Sin(UserValue)` to determine the cosecant of the value typed in the field.

```
SUB GetCosec_OnClick()

  Dim UserValue

  UserValue=InputValue.Value

If IsNumeric(UserValue) Then

     InputValue.Value = 1/Sin(UserValue)

  Else

    MsgBox "Type a numeric value in the field"

  End If

END SUB
```

12. Create a procedure called `GetCotan_OnClick()` that determines the cotangent of the value typed in the `InputValue` field. The procedure is called when the Cotan button is selected. The cotangent is equal to 1 divided by the tangent of the value; therefore, use the formula `1/Tan(UserValue)` to determine the cotangent of the value typed in the field.

```
SUB GetCotan_OnClick()

  Dim UserValue

  UserValue=InputValue.Value

If IsNumeric(UserValue) Then

     InputValue.Value = 1/Tan(UserValue)

  Else

MsgBox "Type a numeric value in the field"

  End If

END SUB
```

13. Create a procedure called `GetArcsin_OnClick()` that determines the inverse sine of the value typed in the `InputValue` field. The procedure is called when the Arcsin button is selected. The inverse sine is calculated using the formula `Arcsin(A) = Atn(A/Sqr(-A * A + 1))`. In order to simplify the formula, create a variable called `ResultValue` that determines the square root portion of the formula. Then take the arctangent of the value typed divided by the `ResultValue` to determine the inverse sine value. An inverse sine value must be between -1 and 1, so use an `If` statement to check the range of the value typed in the field. If the value is not within the range of -1 to 1, use the `MsgBox()` function to display a message to the user, as illustrated in Figure 8-16.

```
SUB GetArcsin_OnClick()

  Dim UserValue
  Dim ResultValue

  UserValue=InputValue.Value

If IsNumeric(UserValue) Then

   If (UserValue > -1) AND (UserValue < 1) Then

     ResultValue = Sqr(-UserValue*UserValue + 1)

     InputValue.Value = Atn(UserValue/ResultValue)

   Else

     MsgBox "The value for the Arcsin function must be between -1 and 1."

   End If

 Else

    MsgBox "Type a numeric value in the field"

  End If

END SUB
```

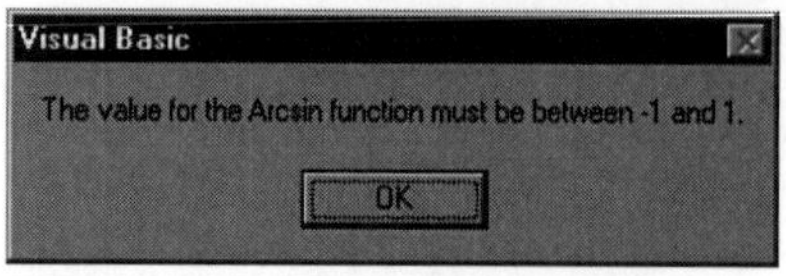

Figure 8-16 The `Arcsin()` function requires a value within the range of -1 to 1

14. Create a procedure called `GetArccos_OnClick()` that determines the inverse cosine of the value typed in the `InputValue` field. The procedure is called when the Arccos button is selected. The inverse cosine is calculated using the formula `Arccos(A) = Atn(-A / Sqr(-A * A + 1)) + 2 * Atn(1)`. In order to simplify the formula, create a variable called `ResultValue` that determines the square root portion of the formula. Then take the arctangent of the value typed divided by the `ResultValue`, add 2 and multiply by the arctangent of 1 to determine the inverse sine value. An inverse sine value must be between -1 and 1, so use an `If` statement to check the range of the value typed in the field.

```
SUB GetArccos_OnClick()

  Dim UserValue
  Dim ResultValue

  UserValue=InputValue.Value

If IsNumeric(UserValue) Then

   If (UserValue > -1) AND (UserValue < 1) Then

     ResultValue = Sqr(-UserValue*UserValue + 1)

     InputValue.Value = Atn(UserValue/ResultValue) + 2 * Atn(1)

   Else

     MsgBox "The value for the Arccos function must be between -1 and 1"

   End If

 Else

  MsgBox "Type a numeric value in the field"

  End If

END SUB
```

15. Create a procedure called `GetArccotan_OnClick()` that determines the inverse cotangent of the value typed in the `InputValue` field. The procedure is called when the Arccotan button is selected. The inverse cotangent is calculated using the formula `Arccotan(A) = Atn(A) + 2 * Atn(1)`. Take the arctangent of the value typed, add 2, and multiply by the arctangent of 1 to determine the inverse tangent value.

```
SUB GetArccotan_OnClick()

  Dim UserValue

  UserValue=InputValue.Value

If IsNumeric(UserValue) Then

   InputValue.Value = Atn(UserValue) + 2 * Atn(1)

  Else

    MsgBox "Type a numeric value in the field"

  End If

END SUB
```

16. Create a procedure called `GetArcsec_OnClick()` that determines the inverse secant of the value typed in the `InputValue` field. The procedure is called when the Arcsec button is selected. The inverse secant is calculated using the formula `Arcsec(A) = Atn(A / Sqr(A * A - 1)) + Sgn((A) -1) * (2 * Atn(1))`. To simplify the formula, create two variables, `ResultValue` and `ResultValue2`. Use `ResultValue` to calculate the square root portion of the formula. Use the `ResultValue2` variable to determine the remaining portion of the formula. Finally, take the arctangent of the value typed divided by the `ResultValue` variable and add `ResultValue2`.

```
SUB GetArcsec_OnClick()

  Dim UserValue
  Dim ResultValue
  Dim ResultValue2

  UserValue=InputValue.Value

If IsNumeric(UserValue) Then

   ResultValue = Sqr(UserValue*UserValue - 1)

   ResultValue2 = Sgn((UserValue) - 1) * (2 * Atn(1))

   InputValue.Value = Atn(UserValue/ResultValue) + ResultValue2

  Else

MsgBox "Type a numeric value in the field"

  End If

END SUB
```

17. Create a procedure called `GetArccosec_OnClick()` that determines the inverse cosecant of the value typed in the `InputValue` field. The procedure is called when the Arccosec button is selected. The inverse cosecant is calculated using the formula `Arccosec(A) = Atn(A / Sqr(A * A - 1)) + (Sgn(A) - 1) * (2 * Atn(1))`. To simplify the formula, create two variables, `ResultValue` and `ResultValue2`. Use `ResultValue` to calculate the square root portion of the formula. Use the `ResultValue2` variable to determine the remaining portion of the formula. Finally, take the arctangent of the value typed divided by the `ResultValue` variable and add `ResultValue2`.

```
SUB GetArccosec_OnClick()

  Dim UserValue
  Dim ResultValue
  Dim ResultValue2

  UserValue=InputValue.Value

If IsNumeric(UserValue) Then

   ResultValue = Sqr(UserValue * UserValue - 1)

   ResultValue2 = Sgn((UserValue) - 1) * (2 * Atn(1))

   InputValue.Value = Atn(UserValue/ResultValue) + ResultValue2

  Else

MsgBox "Type a numeric value in the field"

  End If

END SUB
```

18. Create a procedure called `GetHSin_OnClick()` that determines the hyperbolic sine of the value typed in the `InputValue` field. The procedure is called when the HSin button is selected. The hyperbolic sine is calculated using the formula `HSin(A) = (Exp(A) - Exp(-A)) / 2`.

```
SUB GetHSin_OnClick()

  Dim UserValue

  UserValue=InputValue.Value

  If IsNumeric(UserValue) Then

   InputValue.Value = (Exp(UserValue) - Exp(-UserValue))/2

  Else

  MsgBox "Type a numeric value in the field"

  End If

END SUB
```

19. Create a procedure called `GetHCos_OnClick()` that determines the hyperbolic cosine of the value typed in the `InputValue` field. The procedure is called when the HCos button is selected. The hyperbolic cosine is calculated using the formula `HCos(A) = (Exp(A) + Exp(-A)) / 2`.

```
SUB GetHCos_OnClick()

  Dim UserValue

  UserValue=InputValue.Value

If IsNumeric(UserValue) Then

   InputValue.Value = (Exp(UserValue) + Exp(-UserValue))/2

  Else

MsgBox "Type a numeric value in the field"

  End If

END SUB
```

20. Create a procedure called `GetHTan_OnClick()` that determines the hyperbolic tangent of the value typed in the `InputValue` field. The procedure is called when the HTan button is selected. The hyperbolic tangent is calculated using the formula `HTan(A) = (Exp(A) - Exp(-A)) / (Exp(A) + Exp(-A))`. To simplify the formula, create two variables called `ResultValue` and `ResultValue2`. Use these variables to calculate each portion of the formula. Then divide the two variable values.

```
SUB GetHTan_OnClick()

  Dim UserValue
  Dim ResultValue
  Dim ResultValue2

  UserValue=InputValue.Value

If IsNumeric(UserValue) Then

   ResultValue = (Exp(UserValue) - Exp(-UserValue))

   ResultValue2 = (Exp(UserValue) + Exp(-UserValue))

   InputValue.Value = ResultValue/ResultValue2

  Else

MsgBox "Type a numeric value in the field"

  End If

END SUB
```

21. Create a procedure called `GetHSec_OnClick()` that determines the hyperbolic secant of the value typed in the `InputValue` field. The procedure is called when the HSec button is selected. The hyperbolic secant is calculated using the formula `HSec(A) = 2 / (Exp(A) + Exp(-A))`.

```
SUB GetHSec_OnClick()
  Dim UserValue
  UserValue=InputValue.Value
If IsNumeric(UserValue) Then
   InputValue.Value = 2/(Exp(UserValue) + Exp(-UserValue))
  Else
MsgBox "Type a numeric value in the field"
  End If
END SUB
```

22. Create a procedure called `GetHCosec_OnClick()` that determines the hyperbolic cosecant of the value typed in the `InputValue` field. The procedure is called when the HCosec button is selected. The hyperbolic cosecant is calculated using the formula `HCosec(A) = 2 / (Exp(A) - Exp(-A))`.

```
SUB GetHCosec_OnClick()
  Dim UserValue
  UserValue=InputValue.Value
If IsNumeric(UserValue) Then
   InputValue.Value = 2/(Exp(UserValue) - Exp(-UserValue))
  Else
MsgBox "Type a numeric value in the field"
  End If
END SUB
```

23. Create a procedure called `GetHCotan_OnClick()` that determines the hyperbolic cotangent of the value typed in the `InputValue` field. The procedure is called when the HCotan button is selected. The hyperbolic cotangent is calculated using the formula `HCotan(A) = (Exp(A) + Exp(-A)) / (Exp(A) - Exp(-A))`. To simplify the formula, create two variables called `ResultValue` and `ResultValue2`. Use these variables to calculate each portion of the formula. Then divide the two variable values.

```
SUB GetHCotan_OnClick()

  Dim UserValue
  Dim ResultValue
  Dim ResultValue2

  UserValue=InputValue.Value

If IsNumeric(UserValue) Then

   ResultValue = (Exp(UserValue) + Exp(-UserValue))

   ResultValue2 = (Exp(UserValue) - Exp(-UserValue))

   InputValue.Value = ResultValue/ResultValue2

  Else

    MsgBox "Type a numeric value in the field"

  End If

END SUB
```

24. Create a procedure called `GetHArcsin_OnClick()` that determines the inverse hyperbolic sine of the value typed in the `InputValue` field. The procedure is called when the HArcsin button is selected. The inverse hyperbolic sine is calculated using the formula `HArcsin(A) = Log(A + Sqr(A * A + 1))`.

```
SUB GetHArcsin_OnClick()

  Dim UserValue

  UserValue=InputValue.Value

If IsNumeric(UserValue) Then

   InputValue.Value = Log(UserValue + Sqr(UserValue * UserValue + 1))

  Else

  MsgBox "Type a numeric value in the field"

  End If

END SUB
```

25. Create a procedure called `GetHArccos_OnClick()` that determines the inverse hyperbolic cosine of the value typed in the `InputValue` field. The procedure is called when the HArccos button is selected. The inverse hyperbolic cosine is calculated using the formula `HArcsin(A) = Log(A + Sqr(A * A - 1))`.

```
SUB GetHArccos_OnClick()

  Dim UserValue
```

continued on next page

continued from previous page

```
  UserValue=InputValue.Value

If IsNumeric(UserValue) Then

   InputValue.Value = Log(UserValue + Sqr(UserValue * UserValue - 1))

  Else

MsgBox "Type a numeric value in the field"

  End If

END SUB
```

26. Create a procedure called **GetHArctan_OnClick()** that determines the inverse hyperbolic tangent of the value typed in the **InputValue** field. The procedure is called when the HArctan button is selected. The inverse hyperbolic tangent is calculated using the formula **HArctan(A) = Log((1 + A) / (1 - A)) / 2**. To simplify the formula, create a variable called **ResultValue** that you can use to calculate **(1 + UserValue)** divided by **(1-UserValue)**. Then take the log of **ResultValue** and divide it by 2. Since the value passed to the formula must be between -1 and 1, make sure you check the value before beginning the calculations.

```
SUB GetHArctan_OnClick()

  Dim UserValue
  Dim ResultValue

  UserValue=InputValue.Value

If IsNumeric(UserValue) Then

   If (UserValue > -1) AND (UserValue < 1) Then

     ResultValue = (1 + UserValue)/(1 - UserValue)
     InputValue.Value = Log(ResultValue) / 2

   Else

     MsgBox "The value for the HArctan function must be between -1 and 1."

   End If

 Else

  MsgBox "Type a numeric value in the field"

 End If

END SUB
```

27. Create a procedure called `GetHArcsec_OnClick()` that determines the inverse hyperbolic secant of the value typed in the `InputValue` field. The procedure is called when the HArcsec button is selected. The inverse hyperbolic secant is calculated using the formula `HArcsec(A) = Log((Sqr(-A * A + 1) + 1) / A)`. To simplify the formula, create a variable called `ResultValue` that you can use to calculate the square root portion of the formula. Then take the log of `ResultValue` and divide the value typed. Since the value passed to the formula must be between -1 and 1, make sure you check the value before beginning the calculations.

```
SUB GetHArcsec_OnClick()

  Dim UserValue
  Dim ResultValue

  UserValue=InputValue.Value

If IsNumeric(UserValue) Then

   If (UserValue > -1) AND (UserValue < 1) Then

     ResultValue = Sqr(-UserValue * UserValue + 1)
     InputValue.Value = Log(ResultValue +1) / UserValue

   Else

     MsgBox "The value for the HArcsec function must be between -1 and 1."

   End If

 Else

  MsgBox "Type a numeric value in the field"

  End If

END SUB
```

28. Create a procedure called `GetHArccosec_OnClick()` that determines the inverse hyperbolic cosecant of the value typed in the `InputValue` field. The procedure is called when the HArccosec button is selected. The inverse hyperbolic cosecant is calculated using the formula `HArccosec(A) = Log((Sgn(A) * Sqr(A * A + 1) +1) / A)`. To simplify the formula, create a variable called `ResultValue` that you can use to calculate the square root portion of the formula. Then take the log of the sign of the input value, multiply it by `ResultValue`, add 1 and divide the total by the input value.

```
SUB GetHArccosec_OnClick()

  Dim UserValue
  Dim ResultValue
```

continued on next page

continued from previous page

```
  UserValue=InputValue.Value

If IsNumeric(UserValue) Then

   ResultValue = Sqr(UserValue * UserValue + 1)
   InputValue.Value = Log(Sgn(UserValue) * ResultValue +1) / UserValue

 Else

  MsgBox "Type a numeric value in the field"

  End If

END SUB
```

29. Create a procedure called **`GetHArccotan_OnClick()`** that determines the inverse hyperbolic cotangent of the value typed in the **`InputValue`** field. The procedure is called when the HArccotan button is selected. The inverse hyperbolic cotangent is calculated using the formula **`HArccotan(X) = Log((X + 1) / (X - 1)) / 2`**. To simply the formula, create a variable called **`ResultValue`** that you can use to calculate **`(UserValue + 1)`** divided by **`(UserValue - 1)`**. Then take the log of **`ResultValue`** and divide it by 2.

```
SUB GetHArccotan_OnClick()

  Dim UserValue
  Dim ResultValue

  UserValue=InputValue.Value

 If IsNumeric(UserValue) Then

   ResultValue = (UserValue + 1)/ (UserValue - 1)
   InputValue.Value = Log(ResultValue) / 2

 Else

    MsgBox "Type a numeric value in the field"

  End If

END SUB
```

30. Create a procedure called **`GetExp_OnClick()`** that determines the value of the natural logarithm (e) raised to the input value. The procedure is called when the Exp button is selected. Make sure the input value is less than 709.782712893; if the input value is too large, use the **`MsgBox()`** function to display a message, as illustrated in Figure 8-17.

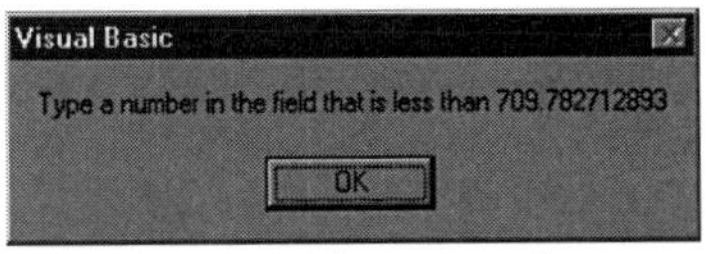

Figure 8-17 The `Exp()` function requires a value that is smaller than 709.782712893

```
SUB GetExp_OnClick()
  Dim UserValue
  UserValue = InputValue.Value
If IsNumeric(UserValue) Then
If UserValue <= 709.782712893 Then
      InputValue.Value = Exp(UserValue)
    Else
      MsgBox "Type a number in the field that is less than 709.782712893"
    End If
  Else
    MsgBox "Type a numeric value in the field"
  End If

END SUB
```

31. Create a procedure called `GetLog_OnClick()` that determines the natural log value of the input value. The procedure is called when the Log button is selected. Make sure the input value is greater than zero.

```
SUB GetLog_OnClick()
  Dim UserValue
  UserValue = InputValue.Value
If IsNumeric(UserValue) Then
```

continued on next page

continued from previous page

```
If UserValue > 0 Then
          InputValue.Value = Log(UserValue)
    Else
      MsgBox "Type a number that is greater than zero"
    End If
  Else
    MsgBox "Type a numeric value in the field"
  End If
END SUB
```

32. Create a procedure called **GetLog10_OnClick()** that determines the base 10 log value of the input value. The procedure is called when the Log10 button is selected. Make sure the input value is greater than zero; if the input value is negative, use the **MsgBox()** function to display a message, as illustrated in Figure 8-18.

```
SUB GetLog10_OnClick()
  Dim UserValue
  UserValue = InputValue.Value
  If IsNumeric(UserValue) Then
    If UserValue > 0 Then
      InputValue.Value = Log(UserValue) / Log(10)
    Else
      MsgBox "Type a number that is greater than zero"
    End If
  Else
    MsgBox "Type a numeric value in the field"
  End If
END SUB
```

33. Create a procedure called **GetSqr_OnClick()** that determines the square root of the input value. The procedure is called when the Sqr button is selected. Make sure the input value is greater than zero.

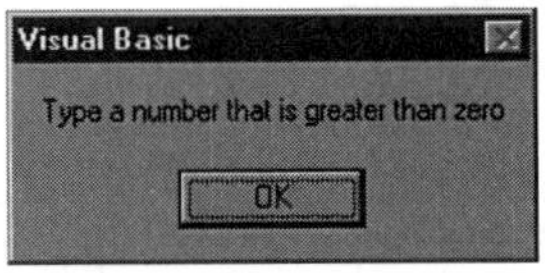

Figure 8-18 The formula that calculates the base 10 log requires a value that is greater than zero

```
SUB GetSqr_OnClick()

  Dim UserValue

  UserValue=InputValue.Value

  If IsNumeric(UserValue) Then

    If UserValue >= 0 Then

     InputValue.Value = Sqr(UserValue)

    Else

    MsgBox "Type a value greater than zero"

    End If

  Else

    MsgBox "Type a numeric value in the field"

  End If

END SUB
```

How It Works

The Computing Values project creates a scientific calculator, as illustrated in Figure 8-19. The user types a value in the input field at the top of the table, and then presses the button that indicates the type of function he or she wishes to perform. VBScript executes the procedure that corresponds to the button selected and places the results in the input field.

Since several of the functions used in this project are not available in VBScript, formulas were used to get the appropriate results. The formulas used are based on the information in Table 8-1.

Each function requires different ranges of input data, so the appropriate range checking is performed for each procedure.

Listing 8-9 contains the code needed to create the Computing Values project.

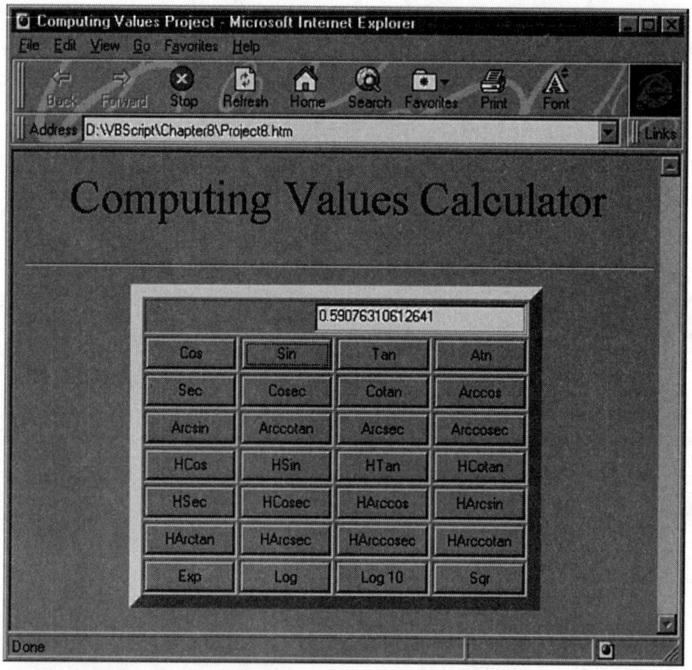

Figure 8-19 The Computing Values project creates a scientific calculator to compute several mathematical functions

Listing 8-9 Complete source for the Computing Values project

```
<HTML>

<HEAD>
<TITLE>Computing Values Project</TITLE>

<SCRIPT LANGUAGE="VBScript">
<!--

'.............................................................
' GetCos_OnClick()
' Determines the cosine of the value in the Input.Value field.
'.............................................................
SUB GetCos_OnClick()

  Dim UserValue

  UserValue=InputValue.Value

'.............................................................
' Make sure the value typed by the user is numeric.
'.............................................................
  If IsNumeric(UserValue) Then
```

```
    InputValue.Value = Cos(UserValue)

  Else

'..............................................................
' Display this message if the value passed is not numeric.
'..............................................................
    MsgBox "Type a numeric value in the field"

  End If

END SUB

'....................................................................
' GetSin_OnClick()
' Determines the sine of the value typed in the InputValue field.
'....................................................................
SUB GetSin_OnClick()

  Dim UserValue

  UserValue=InputValue.Value

'..............................................................
' Make sure the value typed by the user is numeric.
'..............................................................
  If IsNumeric(UserValue) Then

    InputValue.Value = Sin(UserValue)

  Else

'..............................................................
' Display this message if the value passed is not numeric.
'..............................................................
    MsgBox "Type a numeric value in the field"

  End If

END SUB

'..............................................................
' GetTan_OnClick()
' Determines the tangent of the value in the InputValue field.
'..............................................................
SUB GetTan_OnClick()

  Dim UserValue

  UserValue=InputValue.Value

'..............................................................
' Make sure the value typed by the user is numeric.
'..............................................................
  If IsNumeric(UserValue) Then

    InputValue.Value = Tan(UserValue)
```

continued on next page

continued from previous page

```
  Else

'............................................................
' Display this message if the value passed is not numeric.
'............................................................
    MsgBox "Type a numeric value in the field"

  End If

END SUB

'..................................................................
' GetAtn_OnClick()
' Determines the arctangent of the value in the InputValue field.
'..................................................................
SUB GetAtn_OnClick()

  Dim UserValue

  UserValue=InputValue.Value

'............................................................
' Make sure the value typed by the user is numeric and
' determine the arctangent value.
'............................................................
  If IsNumeric(UserValue) Then

    InputValue.Value = Atn(UserValue)

  Else

'............................................................
' Display this message if the value passed is not numeric.
'............................................................
    MsgBox "Type a numeric value in the field"

  End If

END SUB

'............................................................
' GetSec_OnClick()
' Determines the secant of the value in the Input.Value field.
'............................................................
SUB GetSec_OnClick()

  Dim UserValue

  UserValue=InputValue.Value

'............................................................
' Make sure the value typed by the user is numeric.
'............................................................
  If IsNumeric(UserValue) Then

    InputValue.Value = 1/Cos(UserValue)
```

```
  Else

'...........................................................
' Display this message if the value passed is not numeric.
'...........................................................
    MsgBox "Type a numeric value in the field"

  End If

END SUB

'.................................................................
' GetCosec_OnClick()
' Determines the cosecant of the value typed in the InputValue field.
'.................................................................
SUB GetCosec_OnClick()

  Dim UserValue

  UserValue=InputValue.Value

'............................................................
' Make sure the value typed by the user is numeric.
'............................................................
  If IsNumeric(UserValue) Then

     InputValue.Value = 1/Sin(UserValue)

  Else

'...........................................................
' Display this message if the value passed is not numeric.
'...........................................................
    MsgBox "Type a numeric value in the field"

  End If

END SUB

'.............................................................
' GetCotan_OnClick()
' Determines the cotangent of the value in the InputValue field.
'.............................................................
SUB GetCotan_OnClick()

  Dim UserValue

  UserValue=InputValue.Value

'............................................................
' Make sure the value typed by the user is numeric.
'............................................................
  If IsNumeric(UserValue) Then

     InputValue.Value = 1/Tan(UserValue)

  Else
```

continued on next page

continued from previous page

```
'.............................................................
' Display this message if the value passed is not numeric.
'.............................................................
    MsgBox "Type a numeric value in the field"

  End If

END SUB

'......................................................................
' GetArcsin_OnClick()
' Determines the inverse sine of the value in the InputValue field.
'......................................................................
SUB GetArcsin_OnClick()

  Dim UserValue
  Dim ResultValue

  UserValue=InputValue.Value

'.............................................................
' Make sure the value typed by the user is numeric.
'.............................................................
 If IsNumeric(UserValue) Then

   If (UserValue > -1) AND (UserValue < 1) Then

     ResultValue = Sqr(-UserValue*UserValue + 1)

     InputValue.Value = Atn(UserValue/ResultValue)

   Else

     MsgBox "The value for the Arcsin function must be between -1 and 1."

   End If

 Else

'.............................................................
' Display this message if the value passed is not numeric.
'.............................................................
    MsgBox "Type a numeric value in the field"

  End If

END SUB

'......................................................................
' GetArccos_OnClick()
' Determines the inverse cosine of the value in the InputValue field.
'......................................................................
SUB GetArccos_OnClick()

  Dim UserValue
  Dim ResultValue
```

```
  UserValue=InputValue.Value

'..............................................................
' Make sure the value typed by the user is numeric.
'..............................................................
 If IsNumeric(UserValue) Then

   If (UserValue > -1) AND (UserValue < 1) Then

     ResultValue = Sqr(-UserValue*UserValue + 1)

     InputValue.Value = Atn(UserValue/ResultValue) + 2 * Atn(1)

   Else

     MsgBox "The value for the Arccos function must be between -1 and 1"

   End If

 Else

'..............................................................
' Display this message if the value passed is not numeric.
'..............................................................
    MsgBox "Type a numeric value in the field"

  End If

END SUB

'..........................................................................
' GetArccotan_OnClick()
' Determines the inverse cotangent of the value in the InputValue field.
'..........................................................................
SUB GetArccotan_OnClick()

  Dim UserValue

  UserValue=InputValue.Value

'..............................................................
' Make sure the value typed by the user is numeric.
'..............................................................
 If IsNumeric(UserValue) Then

   InputValue.Value = Atn(UserValue) + 2 * Atn(1)

  Else

'..............................................................
' Display this message if the value passed is not numeric.
'..............................................................
    MsgBox "Type a numeric value in the field"

  End If

END SUB
```

continued on next page

continued from previous page

```
'.................................................................
' GetArcsec_OnClick()
' Determines the inverse secant of the value in the InputValue field.
'.................................................................
SUB GetArcsec_OnClick()

  Dim UserValue
  Dim ResultValue
  Dim ResultValue2

  UserValue=InputValue.Value

'.........................................................
' Make sure the value typed by the user is numeric.
'.........................................................
 If IsNumeric(UserValue) Then

   ResultValue = Sqr(UserValue*UserValue - 1)

   ResultValue2 = Sgn((UserValue) - 1) * (2 * Atn(1))

   InputValue.Value = Atn(UserValue/ResultValue) + ResultValue2

  Else

'.........................................................
' Display this message if the value passed is not numeric.
'.........................................................
    MsgBox "Type a numeric value in the field"

  End If

END SUB

'.................................................................
' GetArccosec_OnClick()
' Determines the inverse cosecant of the value in the InputValue field.
'.................................................................
SUB GetArccosec_OnClick()

  Dim UserValue
  Dim ResultValue
  Dim ResultValue2

  UserValue=InputValue.Value

'.........................................................
' Make sure the value typed by the user is numeric.
'.........................................................
 If IsNumeric(UserValue) Then

   ResultValue = Sqr(UserValue * UserValue - 1)

   ResultValue2 = Sgn((UserValue) - 1) * (2 * Atn(1))

   InputValue.Value = Atn(UserValue/ResultValue) + ResultValue2
```

```
  Else

'.............................................................
' Display this message if the value passed is not numeric.
'.............................................................
    MsgBox "Type a numeric value in the field"

  End If

END SUB

'......................................................................
' GetHSin_OnClick()
' Determines the hyperbolic sine of the value in the InputValue field.
'......................................................................
SUB GetHSin_OnClick()

  Dim UserValue

  UserValue=InputValue.Value

'.............................................................
' Make sure the value typed by the user is numeric.
'.............................................................
 If IsNumeric(UserValue) Then

   InputValue.Value = (Exp(UserValue) - Exp(-UserValue))/2

  Else

'.............................................................
' Display this message if the value passed is not numeric.
'.............................................................
    MsgBox "Type a numeric value in the field"

  End If

END SUB

'......................................................................
' GetHCos_OnClick()
' Determines the hyperbolic cosine of the value in the InputValue field.
'......................................................................
SUB GetHCos_OnClick()

  Dim UserValue

  UserValue=InputValue.Value

'.............................................................
' Make sure the value typed by the user is numeric.
'.............................................................
 If IsNumeric(UserValue) Then

   InputValue.Value = (Exp(UserValue) + Exp(-UserValue))/2

  Else
```

continued on next page

continued from previous page

```
'............................................................
' Display this message if the value passed is not numeric.
'............................................................
    MsgBox "Type a numeric value in the field"

  End If

END SUB

'..........................................................................
' GetHTan_OnClick()
' Determines the hyperbolic tangent of the value in the InputValue field.
'...........................................................................
SUB GetHTan_OnClick()

  Dim UserValue
  Dim ResultValue
  Dim ResultValue2

  UserValue=InputValue.Value

'.............................................................
' Make sure the value typed by the user is numeric.
'.............................................................
 If IsNumeric(UserValue) Then

   ResultValue = (Exp(UserValue) - Exp(-UserValue))

   ResultValue2 = (Exp(UserValue) + Exp(-UserValue))

   InputValue.Value = ResultValue/ResultValue2

  Else

'............................................................
' Display this message if the value passed is not numeric.
'............................................................
    MsgBox "Type a numeric value in the field"

  End If

END SUB

'..........................................................................
' GetHSec_OnClick()
' Determines the hyperbolic secant of the value in the InputValue field.
'...........................................................................
SUB GetHSec_OnClick()

  Dim UserValue

  UserValue=InputValue.Value

'.............................................................
' Make sure the value typed by the user is numeric.
'.............................................................
 If IsNumeric(UserValue) Then
```

```
   InputValue.Value = 2/(Exp(UserValue) + Exp(-UserValue))

  Else

'..........................................................
' Display this message if the value passed is not numeric.
'..........................................................
    MsgBox "Type a numeric value in the field"

  End If

END SUB

'.......................................................................
' GetHCosec_OnClick()
' Determines the hyperbolic cosecant of the value in the InputValue field.
'.......................................................................
SUB GetHCosec_OnClick()

  Dim UserValue

  UserValue=InputValue.Value

'..........................................................
' Make sure the value typed by the user is numeric.
'..........................................................
 If IsNumeric(UserValue) Then

   InputValue.Value = 2/(Exp(UserValue) - Exp(-UserValue))

  Else

'..........................................................
' Display this message if the value passed is not numeric.
'..........................................................
    MsgBox "Type a numeric value in the field"

  End If

END SUB

'.......................................................................
' GetHCotan_OnClick()
' Determines the hyperbolic cotangent of the value in the InputValue field.
'.......................................................................
SUB GetHCotan_OnClick()

  Dim UserValue
  Dim ResultValue
  Dim ResultValue2

  UserValue=InputValue.Value

'..........................................................
' Make sure the value typed by the user is numeric.
'..........................................................
 If IsNumeric(UserValue) Then
```

continued on next page

continued from previous page

```
    ResultValue = (Exp(UserValue) + Exp(-UserValue))

    ResultValue2 = (Exp(UserValue) - Exp(-UserValue))

    InputValue.Value = ResultValue/ResultValue2

  Else

'............................................................
' Display this message if the value passed is not numeric.
'............................................................
     MsgBox "Type a numeric value in the field"

  End If

END SUB

'...............................................................................
' GetHArcsin_OnClick()
' Determines the inverse hyperbolic sine of the value in the InputValue field.
'...............................................................................
SUB GetHArcsin_OnClick()

  Dim UserValue

  UserValue=InputValue.Value

'............................................................
' Make sure the value typed by the user is numeric.
'............................................................
 If IsNumeric(UserValue) Then

   InputValue.Value = Log(UserValue + Sqr(UserValue * UserValue + 1))

  Else

'............................................................
' Display this message if the value passed is not numeric.
'............................................................
     MsgBox "Type a numeric value in the field"

  End If

END SUB

'...............................................................................
' GetHArccos_OnClick()
' Determines the inverse hyperbolic cosine of the value in the InputValue field.
'...............................................................................
SUB GetHArccos_OnClick()

  Dim UserValue

  UserValue=InputValue.Value

'............................................................
' Make sure the value typed by the user is numeric.
'............................................................
```

```
 If IsNumeric(UserValue) Then

   InputValue.Value = Log(UserValue + Sqr(UserValue * UserValue - 1))

  Else

'..........................................................
' Display this message if the value passed is not numeric.
'..........................................................
    MsgBox "Type a numeric value in the field"

  End If

END SUB

'...............................................................................
' GetHArctan_OnClick()
' Determines the inverse hyperbolic tangent of the value in the InputValue field.
'...............................................................................
SUB GetHArctan_OnClick()

  Dim UserValue
  Dim ResultValue

  UserValue=InputValue.Value

'..........................................................
' Make sure the value typed by the user is numeric.
'..........................................................
 If IsNumeric(UserValue) Then

   If (UserValue > -1) AND (UserValue < 1) Then

     ResultValue = (1 + UserValue)/(1 - UserValue)
     InputValue.Value = Log(ResultValue) / 2

   Else

     MsgBox "The value for the HArctan function must be between -1 and 1."

   End If

 Else

'..........................................................
' Display this message if the value passed is not numeric.
'..........................................................
    MsgBox "Type a numeric value in the field"

 End If

END SUB

'...............................................................................
' GetHArcsec_OnClick()
' Determines the inverse hyperbolic secant of the value in the InputValue field.
'...............................................................................
SUB GetHArcsec_OnClick()
```

continued on next page

continued from previous page

```
  Dim UserValue
  Dim ResultValue

  UserValue=InputValue.Value

'.............................................................
' Make sure the value typed by the user is numeric.
'.............................................................
 If IsNumeric(UserValue) Then

   If (UserValue > -1) AND (UserValue < 1) Then

     ResultValue = Sqr(-UserValue * UserValue + 1)
     InputValue.Value = Log(ResultValue +1) / UserValue

   Else

     MsgBox "The value for the HArcsec function must be between -1 and 1."

   End If

 Else

'.............................................................
' Display this message if the value passed is not numeric.
'.............................................................
    MsgBox "Type a numeric value in the field"

  End If

END SUB

'.................................................................................
' GetHArccosec_OnClick()
' Determines the inverse hyperbolic cosecant of the value in the InputValue field.
'.................................................................................
SUB GetHArccosec_OnClick()

  Dim UserValue
  Dim ResultValue

  UserValue=InputValue.Value

'.............................................................
' Make sure the value typed by the user is numeric.
'.............................................................
 If IsNumeric(UserValue) Then

   ResultValue = Sqr(UserValue * UserValue + 1)
   InputValue.Value = Log(Sgn(UserValue) * ResultValue +1) / UserValue

 Else

'.............................................................
' Display this message if the value passed is not numeric.
'.............................................................
    MsgBox "Type a numeric value in the field"
```

```
  End If

END SUB

'.............................................................................
' GetHArccotan_OnClick()
' Determines the inverse hyperbolic tangent of the value in the InputValue field.
'.............................................................................
SUB GetHArccotan_OnClick()

  Dim UserValue
  Dim ResultValue

  UserValue=InputValue.Value

'..........................................................
' Make sure the value typed by the user is numeric.
'..........................................................
 If IsNumeric(UserValue) Then

   ResultValue = (UserValue + 1)/ (UserValue - 1)
   InputValue.Value = Log(ResultValue) / 2

 Else

'..........................................................
' Display this message if the value passed is not numeric.
'..........................................................
    MsgBox "Type a numeric value in the field"

  End If

END SUB

'..........................................................
' GetExp_OnClick()
' Determines the value of e raised to the specified value.
'..........................................................
SUB GetExp_OnClick()

  Dim UserValue

  UserValue = InputValue.Value

'..........................................................
' Make sure the value entered is numeric.
'..........................................................
  If IsNumeric(UserValue) Then

'..........................................................
' Make sure the value is not larger than 709.782712893
'..........................................................
    If UserValue <= 709.782712893 Then

      InputValue.Value = Exp(UserValue)

    Else
```

continued on next page

continued from previous page

```
      MsgBox "Type a number in the field that is less than 709.782712893"

    End If

  Else

    MsgBox "Type a numeric value in the field"

  End If


END SUB

'..........................................................
' GetLog_OnClick()
' Determines the log value based on the value typed by the
' user in the InputValue field.
'..........................................................
SUB GetLog_OnClick()

  Dim UserValue

  UserValue = InputValue.Value

'..........................................................
' Make sure the value entered is numeric.
'..........................................................
  If IsNumeric(UserValue) Then

'..........................................................
' Make sure the value is greater than zero.
'..........................................................
    If UserValue > 0 Then

          InputValue.Value = Log(UserValue)

    Else

      MsgBox "Type a number that is greater than zero"

    End If

  Else

    MsgBox "Type a numeric value in the field"

  End If

END SUB

'..........................................................
' GetLog10_OnClick()
' Determines the log base 10 value based on the value typed
' by the user in the InputValue field.
'..........................................................
SUB GetLog10_OnClick()

  Dim UserValue
```

```
  UserValue = InputValue.Value

'..........................................................
' Make sure the value entered is numeric.
'..........................................................
  If IsNumeric(UserValue) Then

'..........................................................
' Make sure the value is greater than zero.
'..........................................................
    If UserValue > 0 Then

      InputValue.Value = Log(UserValue) / Log(10)

    Else

      MsgBox "Type a number that is greater than zero"

    End If

  Else

    MsgBox "Type a numeric value in the field"

  End If

END SUB

'............................................................
' GetSqr_OnClick()
' Determines the square root of the value typed by the user.
'............................................................
SUB GetSqr_OnClick()

  Dim UserValue

  UserValue=InputValue.Value

'............................................................
' First make sure the value typed by the user is numeric,
' then check to make sure the value is greater than zero.
'............................................................
  If IsNumeric(UserValue) Then

    If UserValue >= 0 Then


     InputValue.Value = Sqr(UserValue)

    Else

'..........................................................
' Display this message if the value typed is negative.
'..........................................................
      MsgBox "Type a value greater than zero"

    End If
```

continued on next page

continued from previous page

```
  Else

'.....................................................
' Display this message if the value passed is not numeric.
'.....................................................
    MsgBox "Type a numeric value in the field"

  End If

END SUB

-->

</SCRIPT>
</HEAD>

<BODY>

<CENTER>

<FONT SIZE=6>Computing Values Calculator<P>
</CENTER>
<HR>

<FONT SIZE=4>

<CENTER>

<TABLE BORDER=10>

<TR><TD COLSPAN=4 ALIGN=RIGHT><INPUT NAME=InputValue SIZE=30></TD></TR>

<TR><TD><INPUT TYPE=BUTTON VALUE="Cos" NAME="GetCos"></TD>
    <TD><INPUT TYPE=BUTTON VALUE="Sin" NAME="GetSin"></TD>
    <TD><INPUT TYPE=BUTTON VALUE="Tan" NAME="GetTan"></TD>
    <TD><INPUT TYPE=BUTTON VALUE="Atn" NAME="GetAtn"></TD>
</TR>

<TR><TD><INPUT TYPE=BUTTON VALUE="Sec" NAME="GetSec"></TD>
    <TD><INPUT TYPE=BUTTON VALUE="Cosec" NAME="GetCosec"></TD>
    <TD><INPUT TYPE=BUTTON VALUE="Cotan" NAME="GetCotan"></TD>
    <TD><INPUT TYPE=BUTTON VALUE="Arccos" NAME="GetArccos"></TD>
</TR>

<TR><TD><INPUT TYPE=BUTTON VALUE="Arcsin" NAME="GetArcsin"></TD>
    <TD><INPUT TYPE=BUTTON VALUE="Arccotan" NAME="GetArccotan"></TD>
    <TD><INPUT TYPE=BUTTON VALUE="Arcsec" NAME="GetArcsec"></TD>
    <TD><INPUT TYPE=BUTTON VALUE="Arccosec" NAME="GetArccosec"></TD>
</TR>

<TR><TD><INPUT TYPE=BUTTON VALUE="HCos" NAME="GetHCos"></TD>
    <TD><INPUT TYPE=BUTTON VALUE="HSin" NAME="GetHSin"></TD>
    <TD><INPUT TYPE=BUTTON VALUE="HTan" NAME="GetHTan"></TD>
    <TD><INPUT TYPE=BUTTON VALUE="HCotan" NAME="GetHCotan"></TD>
</TR>

<TR><TD><INPUT TYPE=BUTTON VALUE="HSec" NAME="GetHSec"></TD>
    <TD><INPUT TYPE=BUTTON VALUE="HCosec" NAME="GetHCosec"></TD>
```

```
    <TD><INPUT TYPE=BUTTON VALUE="HArccos" NAME="GetHArccos"></TD>
    <TD><INPUT TYPE=BUTTON VALUE="HArcsin" NAME="GetHArcsin"></TD>
</TR>

<TR><TD><INPUT TYPE=BUTTON VALUE="HArctan" NAME="GetHArctan"></TD>
    <TD><INPUT TYPE=BUTTON VALUE="HArcsec" NAME="GetHArcsec"></TD>
    <TD><INPUT TYPE=BUTTON VALUE="HArccosec" NAME="GetHArccosec"></TD>
    <TD><INPUT TYPE=BUTTON VALUE="HArccotan" NAME="GetHArccotan"></TD>
</TR>

<TR><TD><INPUT TYPE=BUTTON VALUE="Exp" NAME="GetExp"></TD>
    <TD><INPUT TYPE=BUTTON VALUE="Log" NAME="GetLog"></TD>
    <TD><INPUT TYPE=BUTTON VALUE="Log 10" NAME="GetLog10"></TD>
    <TD><INPUT TYPE=BUTTON VALUE="Sqr" NAME="GetSqr"></TD>
</TR>

</TABLE>

</CENTER>

</FONT>

</BODY>

</HTML>
```

9

STRING MANIPULATION

9

STRING MANIPULATION

Strings are used to work with textual information, such as names, titles, street addresses, and so on. VBScript provides several functions that you can use to manipulate the information in a string variable.

Working with Strings

When you work with strings, you can store text, numeric data, or a combination of both. If you store numeric values in a string, you should convert the string to a numeric variable type before attempting to perform data calculations. For example, an attempt to add two strings that contain numeric values concatenates the strings instead of adding them. Concatenation means the strings are joined together end to end. Therefore, as string values, `67 + 13` would return a value of `6713`; as numeric values, they would return `80`.

Changing the Case of a String

When working with strings you will probably find that it is easier to compare two strings if the letters in each string are either all uppercase or all lowercase. VBScript provides two functions that can be used to convert a string to either uppercase or lowercase.

The `LCase()` function converts all characters in a string to lowercase characters. Any lowercase or numeric characters in the string are not changed.

The `UCase()` function converts all characters in a string to uppercase characters. Any uppercase or numeric characters in the string are not changed.

Identifying Specific Characters in a String

Quite often it is necessary to only return a specific character or series of characters in a string, such as the first character or the last character. For example, you might want to display a person's initials. This could be accomplished by simply returning the first character from his or her first, middle, and last names.

VBScript provides three functions that can be used to capture specific characters from a string: `Left()`, `Right()`, and `Mid()`. The `Left()` function returns a specified number of characters from the beginning of a string. The `Right()` function returns a specified number of characters from the end of a string.

The `Mid()` function provides more flexibility; it allows you to not only specify the number of characters that you would like to return, but also the character location, in the string, where you would like to start capturing the characters.

There are also three functions, `LeftB()`, `RightB()`, and `MidB()`, that allow you to work with byte locations instead of character locations. If you use these functions, you will receive the specified number of bytes from the string. Since all characters are 2 bytes long, you need to request at least 2 bytes when you use these functions.

Comparing Strings

There are three VBScript functions that you can use to compare two strings. The first two, `Instr()` and `InstrB()`, check to see if the first string contains the second string. The difference between these functions is that the `Instr()` function returns a character location of the second string within the first string and the `InstrB()` function returns the byte location of the second string within the first string.

The other function, `StrComp()`, simply checks to see if the values contained in the two strings are identical. If the strings match, a value of `0` is returned; otherwise, a value of `-1` or `1` is returned, indicating the larger string.

With each of these functions you can indicate whether you want to perform a binary or textual comparison of the strings. If you perform a binary comparison, the function not only looks for the same characters, but also the same case (uppercase or lowercase). A textual comparison simply compares the letters. For example, if you compare `CAT` and `cat`, a binary comparison will determine that the strings do not match, but a textual comparison will say they do match.

Summary of String Manipulation Functions

Table 9-1 summarizes the string manipulation functions covered in this chapter. A detailed description of each function follows this table. Many of these functions are also used in the string manipulation project at the end of the chapter.

Table 9-1 String manipulation function summary

Use...	To Do This...
`Asc`	Determine the ANSI character code for the first character in a string.
`AscB`	Determine the byte value of the first character in a string.
`AscW`	Determine the Unicode value for the first character in a string.
`Chr`	Determine the character associated with an ANSI character code.
`ChrB`	Determine the character associated with a byte value.
`ChrW`	Determine the character associated with a Unicode value.
`Instr`	Identify the character location of one string within another string.
`InstrB`	Identify the byte location of one string within another string.
`LCase`	Convert a specified string to all lowercase characters.
`Left`	Return a specific number of characters from the left side of a string.
`LeftB`	Return a specific number of bytes from the left side of a string.
`Len`	Determine the number of characters in the specified string.
`LenB`	Determine the number of bytes in the specified string.
`LTrim`	Remove the leading spaces from the specified string.
`Mid`	Return a specific number of characters starting at the specified location within the string.
`MidB`	Return a specific number of bytes starting at the specified location within the string.
`Right`	Return a specific number of characters from the right side of the string.
`RightB`	Return a specific number of bytes from the right side of the string.
`RTrim`	Remove the trailing spaces at the end of the specified string.
`Space`	Create a string containing the specified number of spaces.
`StrComp`	Compare two strings.
`String`	Create a string containing a specific number of the specified character.
`Trim`	Remove the leading and trailing spaces from a string.
`UCase`	Convert a specified string to all uppercase characters.

`Asc` Function

Purpose Use the `Asc()` function to determine the ANSI character code for the first character in the specified string. Table 9-2 describes the expressions that you can use with the `Asc()` function.

Syntax `Asc(expression)`

Table 9-2 Argument of the `Asc()` function

Argument	Description
`expression`	Any valid string expression

Description

The **Asc()** function returns the ANSI character code value for the first character in a string. This function returns an error if it receives an empty variable; therefore, it is important to check the value of the variable to make sure it contains a value prior to calling the **Asc()** function.

Listing 9-1 uses the **Asc()** function to determine the ANSI character code for the first character in the string typed in the **InputValue** field. The **MsgBox()** function displays the results of the **Asc()** function, as illustrated in Figure 9-1. The **Left()** function retrieves the first character in the string.

Listing 9-1 Using the `Asc()` *function*

```
<HTML>

<HEAD>
<TITLE>Asc Example</TITLE>

<SCRIPT LANGUAGE="VBScript">
<!--
'.........................................................
' ANSIChar_OnClick()
' Determines the ANSI character value of the first element
' in the string typed in the InputValue field.
'..........................................................
SUB ANSIChar_OnClick()

  Dim UserValue

  UserValue=InputValue.Value

'..........................................................
' First make sure a value was typed in the InputValue field.
' Then use the Left function to retrieve the first character
' in the string and display the ANSI character code.
'..........................................................
   If Not IsNull(InputValue.Value) Then

      MsgBox "The ANSI value of " & Left(InputValue.Value, 1) & " is " & Asc(UserValue)

   Else

'.........................................................
' Display this message if the field is empty.
'.........................................................
      MsgBox "Type a value in the field"

    End If

END SUB
-->

</SCRIPT>
</HEAD>
```

```
<BODY>

<CENTER>

<FONT SIZE=6>ANSI Value<P>
</CENTER>
<HR>

<FONT SIZE=4>

<PRE>Type a value: <INPUT NAME=InputValue SIZE=20></PRE>

<HR>
<CENTER>
<INPUT TYPE=BUTTON VALUE="Determine ANSI Character" NAME="ANSIChar">
</CENTER>

</FONT>

</BODY>

</HTML>
```

Example

The String Manipulation project, at the end of this chapter, uses the **Asc()** function to determine the character value for the first character in the string. The value is displayed using the **MsgBox()** function.

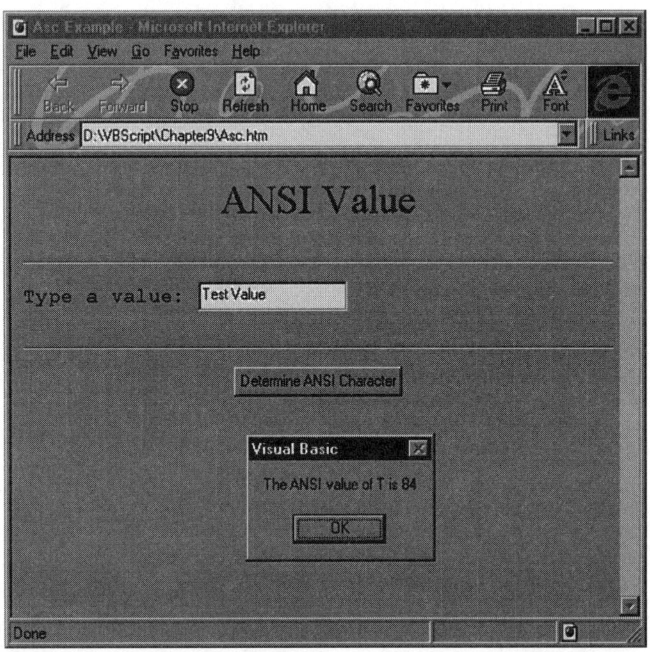

Figure 9-1 The **Asc()** function returns the ANSI character code of the first character in a string

Comments You can use the `IsNull()` function to verify that the variable contains a string value prior to calling the `Asc()` function. For more information about the `IsNull()` function, refer to Chapter 4, Data Validation.

See Also `AscB()`, `AscW()`

AscB Function

Purpose Use the `AscB()` function to determine the byte value for the first character of the selected string. Table 9-3 describes the expressions you can use with the `AscB()` function.

Syntax `AscB(expression)`

Table 9-3 Argument of the AscB() function

Argument	Description
expression	Any valid string expression

Description The `AscB()` function returns the byte value of the first character in a string. This function returns an error if it receives an empty variable; therefore, it is important to make sure a variable contains a value before calling the `AscB()` function.

Listing 9-2 uses the `AscB()` function to determine the byte value of the first character in the string typed in the `InputValue` field. The `MsgBox()` function displays the results of the `AscB()` function, as illustrated in Figure 9-2. The `Left()` function retrieves the first character in the string so it can be displayed in the message box.

Listing 9-2 Using the AscB() function

```
<HTML>

<HEAD>
<TITLE>AscB Example</TITLE>

<SCRIPT LANGUAGE="VBScript">
<!--
'............................................................
' AscCByte_OnClick()
' Determines the byte value of the first element
' in the string typed in the InputValue field.
'.............................................................
SUB AscByte_OnClick()
```

```
  Dim UserValue

  UserValue=InputValue.Value

'..............................................................
' First make sure that a value was typed in the InputValue field.
' If so, display the byte value of the first letter. Use the Left
' function to retrieve the first character in the string.
'..............................................................
  If Not IsNull(UserValue) Then

      MsgBox "The byte value of " & Left(InputValue.Value,1) & " is " & AscB(UserValue)

  Else

'........................................................
' Display this message if the field is empty.
'........................................................
    MsgBox "Type a value in the field"

  End If

END SUB
-->

</SCRIPT>
</HEAD>

<BODY>

<CENTER>

<FONT SIZE=6>Byte Value<P>
</CENTER>
<HR>

<FONT SIZE=4>

<PRE>Type a value: <INPUT NAME=InputValue SIZE=20></PRE>

<HR>
<CENTER>
<INPUT TYPE=BUTTON VALUE="Determine Byte" NAME="AscByte">
</CENTER>
</FONT>

</BODY>

</HTML>
```

Comments You can use the `IsNull()` function to verify that the variable contains a string value prior to calling the `AscB()` function. For more information about the `IsNull()` function, refer to Chapter 4, Data Validation.

See Also `Asc()`, `AscW()`

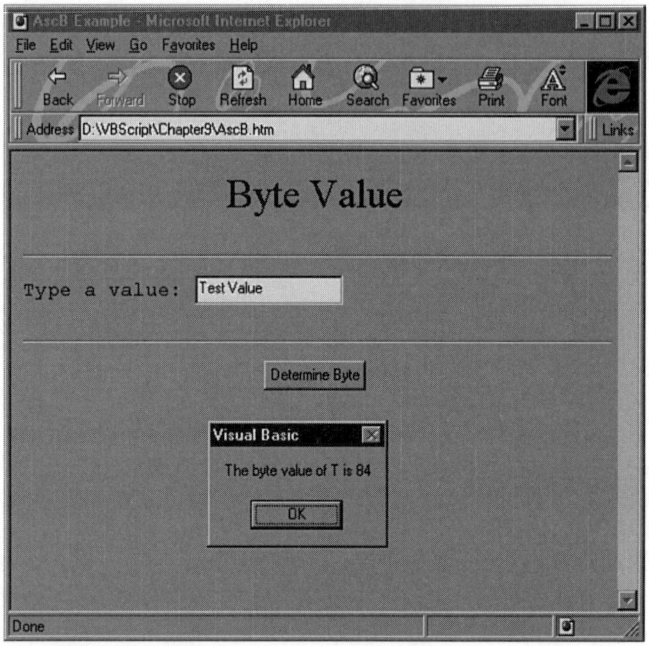

Figure 9-2 The `AscB()` function returns the byte value for the first character in the specified string

AscW Function

Purpose Use the `AscW()` function to determine the Unicode value of the first character in the specified string. Use this function when working with 32-bit platforms that use Unicode characters. Table 9-4 describes the expressions you can use with the `AscW()` function.

Syntax `AscW(expression)`

Table 9-4 Argument of the `AscW()` function

Argument	Description
`expression`	Any valid string expression

Description The `AscW()` function returns the Unicode (wide) value for the first character in a string. This function is available for 32-bit platforms.

Listing 9-3 uses the `AscW()` function to determine the Unicode value for the first character in the specified string. The `MsgBox()` function displays the results of the `AscW()` function, as illustrated in Figure 9-3.

Listing 9-3 Using the `AscW()` *function*

```
<HTML>

<HEAD>
<TITLE>AscW Example</TITLE>

<SCRIPT LANGUAGE="VBScript">
<!--
'..........................................................
' AscUnicode_OnClick()
' Determines the Unicode value of the first element
' in the string typed in the InputValue field.
'..........................................................
SUB AscUnicode_OnClick()

  Dim UserValue

  UserValue=InputValue.Value

'................................................................
' First make sure that a value was typed in the InputValue field.
' If so, display the Unicode value of the first character, and use the
' Left() function to retrieve the first character so it can also
' display in the message box.
'................................................................
  If Not IsNull(UserValue) Then

      MsgBox "The Unicode value of " & Left(InputValue.Value, 1) & " is " & AscW(UserValue)

  Else

'..........................................................
' Display this message if the field is empty.
'..........................................................
    MsgBox "Type a value in the field"

  End If

END SUB
-->

</SCRIPT>
</HEAD>

<BODY>

<CENTER>

<FONT SIZE=6>Unicode Value<P>
</CENTER>
<HR>

<FONT SIZE=4>

<PRE>Type a value: <INPUT NAME=InputValue SIZE=20></PRE>
```

continued on next page

continued from previous page

```
<HR>
<CENTER>
<INPUT TYPE=BUTTON VALUE="Determine Unicode Value" NAME="AscUnicode">
</CENTER>
</FONT>

</BODY>

</HTML>
```

Comments

Use of the `AscW()` function eliminates the need to convert from ANSI to Unicode.

You can use the `IsNull()` function to verify that the variable contains a string value prior to calling the `AscW()` function. For more information about the `IsNull()` function, refer to Chapter 4, Data Validation.

See Also

`Asc()`, `AscB()`

Chr FUNCTION

Purpose

Use the `Chr()` function to determine the character associated with the specified ANSI character code. You can use this function to display

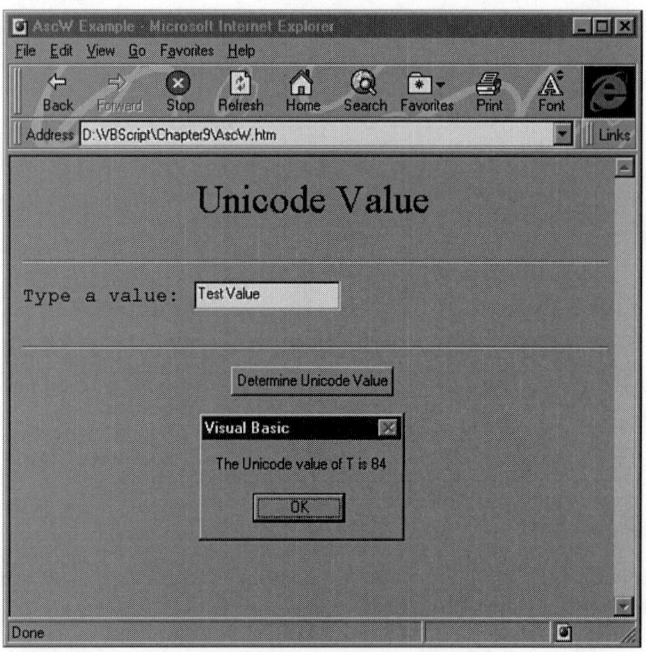

Figure 9-3 The `AscW()` function returns the Unicode value of the first character in the specified string

characters that cannot be typed on the keyboard. Table 9-5 describes the expressions you can use with the `Chr()` function.

Syntax `Chr(expression)`

Table 9-5 Argument of the `Chr()` function

Argument	Description
expression	Any numeric expression between 0 and 255 that identifies an ANSI character code

Description The `Chr()` function determines the character that has the specified ANSI character code value. The `Chr()` function only accepts values between 0 and 255; therefore, it is important to perform some type of data validation on the expression before passing it to the `Chr()` function.

Listing 9-4 uses the `Chr()` function to convert the value typed in the `InputValue` field to the corresponding ANSI character. The `MsgBox()` function displays the results of the `Chr()` function on the screen, as illustrated in Figure 9-4.

Listing 9-4 Using the `Chr()` function

```
<HTML>

<HEAD>
<TITLE>Chr Example</TITLE>

<SCRIPT LANGUAGE="VBScript">
<!--
'...........................................................
' ANSIChar_OnClick()
' Determines the ANSI character value for the character code
' value typed in the InputValue field.
'...........................................................
SUB ANSIChar_OnClick()

  Dim UserValue

  UserValue=InputValue.Value

'...........................................................................
' First make sure the value that was typed in the InputValue field is numeric.
'...........................................................................
   If IsNumeric(InputValue.Value) Then

      MsgBox "The ASCII character for " & InputValue.Value & " is " & Chr(UserValue)

   Else

'..........................................................
' Display this message if the value is not numeric.
'..........................................................
```

continued on next page

continued from previous page

```
      MsgBox "Type a numeric value in the field"

    End If

END SUB
-->

</SCRIPT>
</HEAD>

<BODY>

<CENTER>

<FONT SIZE=6>ANSI Character Value<P>
</CENTER>
<HR>

<FONT SIZE=4>

<PRE>Type a value: <INPUT NAME=InputValue SIZE=20></PRE>

<HR>
<CENTER>
<INPUT TYPE=BUTTON VALUE="Determine ANSI Character" NAME="ANSIChar">
</CENTER>
</FONT>

</BODY>

</HTML>
```

Comments The `Chr()` function can be used when you want to display double quotes (“) on the screen. Since VBScript uses double quotes to indicate the beginning and the end of a string, the quotes do not display on the screen unless you use `Chr(34)` to display double quotes.

You can use the `IsNumeric()` function to make sure that the value is numeric before passing it to the `Chr()` function. If the `Chr()` function receives a nonnumeric value, a run-time error will occur, as illustrated in Figure 9-5. For more information about using the `IsNumeric()` function, refer to Chapter 4, Data Validation.

See Also `ChrB()`, `ChrW()`

ChrB Function

Purpose Use the `ChrB()` function to determine the character value that corresponds to the specified byte value. This function only works with a 16-bit operating system, such as Windows 3.x. Table 9-6 describes the expressions you can use with the `ChrB()` function.

Syntax `ChrB(expression)`

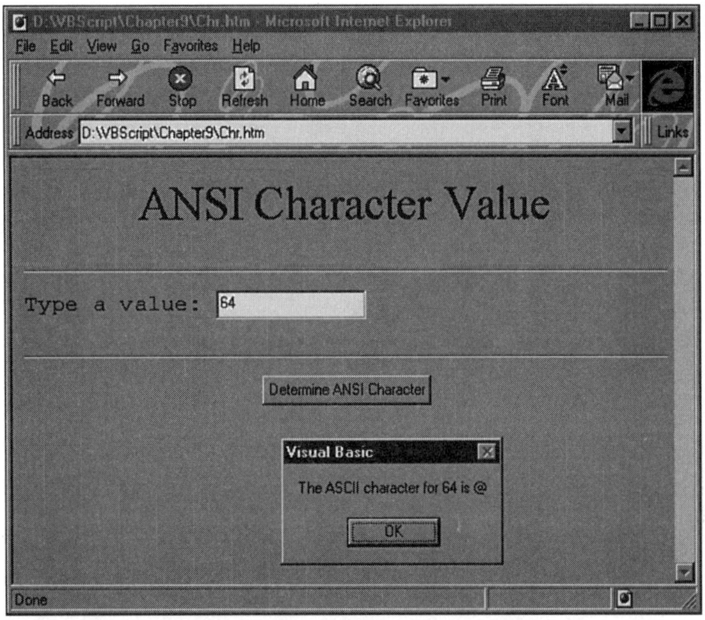

Figure 9-4 The `Chr()` function returns the ANSI character that corresponds to the numeric value

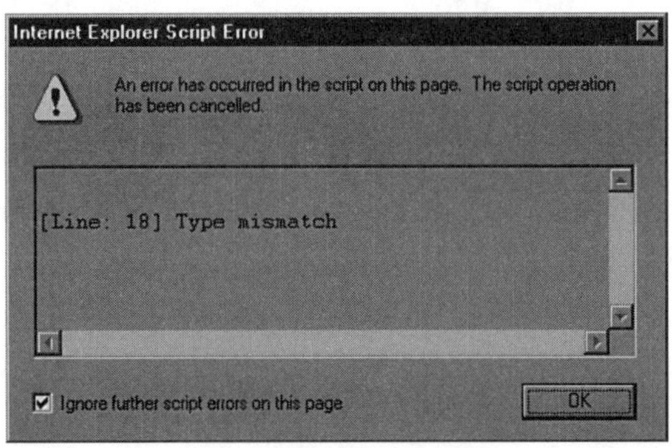

Figure 9-5 The `Chr()` function requires a numeric value; otherwise, a run-time error occurs

Table 9-6 Argument of the `ChrB()` function

Argument	Description
`expression`	Any numeric expression with a value between 0 and 255

Description The `ChrB()` function determines the character that has the specified byte value. The `ChrB()` function only accepts numeric values; therefore, it is

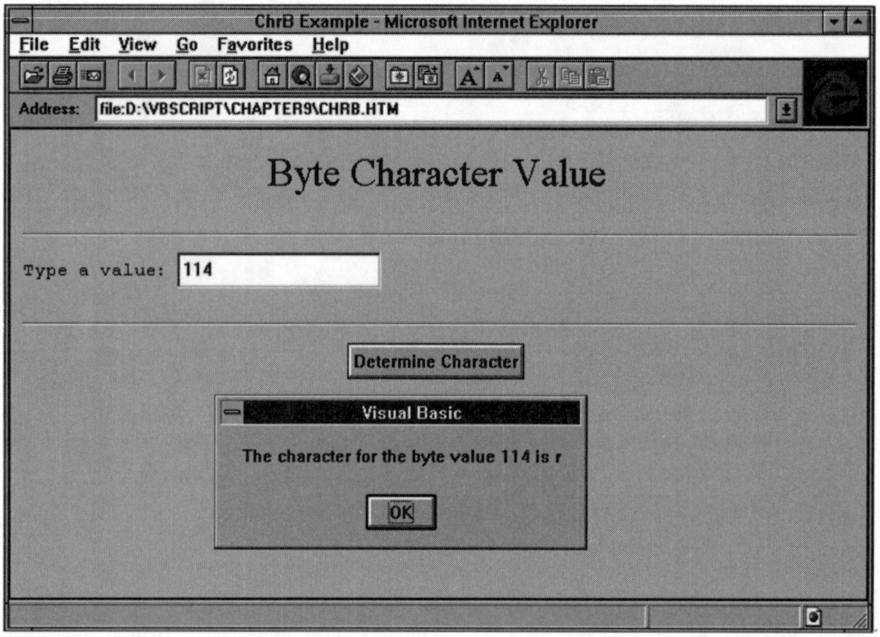

Figure 9-6 The `ChrB()` function

important to perform some type of data validation prior to calling the `ChrB()` function.

Listing 9-5 uses the `ChrB()` function to convert the byte value typed in the `InputValue` field to the corresponding character. The `MsgBox()` function displays the results of the `ChrB()` function on the screen, as illustrated in Figure 9-6. If the user does not type a value in the field before pressing the Determine Character button, a message displays informing the user that he or she must type a value.

Listing 9-5 Using the `ChrB()` *function*

```
<HTML>

<HEAD>
<TITLE>ChrB Example</TITLE>

<SCRIPT LANGUAGE="VBScript">
<!--
'.............................................................
' ByteChar_OnClick()
' Determines the byte value for the character code
' value typed in the InputValue field.
'.............................................................
SUB ByteChar_OnClick()
```

```
  Dim UserValue
  Dim Test

  UserValue=InputValue.Value

'.................................................................
' First make sure a value was typed in the InputValue field.
'.................................................................
  If IsNumeric(UserValue) Then

    If (UserValue >= 0) AND (UserValue <= 255) Then

      MsgBox "The character for the byte value " & InputValue.Value & " is " &
ChrB(UserValue)

    Else
'...............................................................
' Display this message if the value is not between 0 and 255.
'...............................................................
      MsgBox "Type a value between 0 and 255 in the field"

    End If

  Else
'...............................................................
' Display a message if nonnumeric value typed.
'...............................................................

    MsgBox "Type a numeric value in the field."

  End If

END SUB
-->

</SCRIPT>
</HEAD>

<BODY>

<CENTER>

<FONT SIZE=6>Byte Character Value<P>
</CENTER>
<HR>

<FONT SIZE=4>

<PRE>Type a value: <INPUT NAME=InputValue SIZE=20></PRE>

<HR>
<CENTER>
<INPUT TYPE=BUTTON VALUE="Determine Character" NAME="ByteChar">
</CENTER>
</FONT>

</BODY>

</HTML>
```

Comments You can use the `IsNumeric()` function to make sure a value is numeric before calling the `ChrB()` function. For more information about the `IsNumeric()` function, refer to Chapter 4, Data Validation.

See Also `Chr()`, `ChrW()`

ChrW Function

Purpose Use the `ChrW()` function to determine the character value for the specified Unicode numeric value. Table 9-7 describes the expressions you can use with the `ChrW()` function.

Syntax `ChrW(expression)`

Table 9-7 Argument of the `ChrW()` function

Argument	Description
`expression`	Any valid numeric expression

Description The `ChrW()` function determines the character that has the specified Unicode character code value. The `ChrW()` function only accepts numeric values; therefore, it is important to perform some type of data validation prior to calling the `ChrW()` function.

Listing 9-6 uses the `ChrW()` function to convert the Unicode value typed in the `InputValue` field to the corresponding character. The `MsgBox()` function displays the results of the `ChrW()` function on the screen, as illustrated in Figure 9-7.

Listing 9-6 Using the `ChrW()` function

```
<HTML>

<HEAD>
<TITLE>ChrW Example</TITLE>

<SCRIPT LANGUAGE="VBScript">
<!--
'..............................................................
' UnicodeChar_OnClick()
' Determines the character value for the Unicode value
' typed in the InputValue field.
'..............................................................
SUB UnicodeChar_OnClick()

  Dim UserValue

  UserValue=InputValue.Value

'..................................................................
```

```
' First make sure a numeric value was typed in the InputValue field.
'.................................................................
   If IsNumeric(InputValue.Value) Then

      MsgBox "The character for " & InputValue.Value & " is " & ChrW(UserValue)

   Else

'...............................................................
' Display this message if the field contains a nonnumeric field.
'...............................................................
      MsgBox "Type a numeric value is the field"

    End If

END SUB
-->

</SCRIPT>
</HEAD>

<BODY>

<CENTER>

<FONT SIZE=6>Unicode Character Conversion<P>
</CENTER>
<HR>

<FONT SIZE=4>

Type a value: <INPUT NAME=InputValue SIZE=20>

<HR>
<CENTER>
<INPUT TYPE=BUTTON VALUE="Determine the Character" NAME="UnicodeChar">
</CENTER>

</FONT>

</BODY>

</HTML>
```

Comments You can use the `IsNumeric()` function to make sure a value is numeric before calling the `ChrW()` function. For more information about the `IsNumeric()` function, refer to Chapter 4, Data Validation.

See Also `Chr()`, `ChrB()`

`Instr()` Function

Purpose Use the `Instr()` function to determine the location of one string within another string. This function is useful when comparing string values. Table 9-8 describes the expressions you can use with the `Instr()` function.

Syntax **`Instr(startloc, firststring, secondstring, comparetype)`**

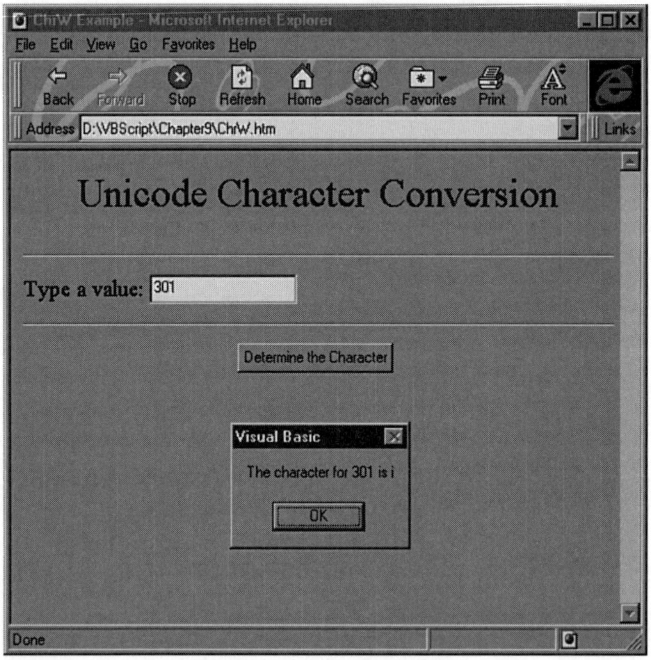

Figure 9-7 The `ChrW()` function returns the character value that corresponds to the specified Unicode value

Table 9-8 Arguments of the `Instr()` function

Argument	Description
`startloc`	A numeric expression that indicates the location in first string where the search should start. This is an optional argument for the `Instr()` function; if it is omitted, the search begins at the beginning of the string. If a `comparetype` argument is specified, the `startloc` argument is required.
`firststring`	A valid string expression identifying the string to be searched.
`secondstring`	A valid string expression to be located in the first string.
`comparetype`	A value of `0` or `1` indicating the type of string comparison that should be used. This argument is optional; if it is omitted, the default value of `0` is used. A value of `0` performs a binary comparison of the strings. A value of `1` performs a textual, case-insensitive comparison of the strings.

Description The `Instr()` function is used to determine if a string contains another string. If the second string is located in the first string, the `Instr()` function returns the location of the first character matched in the string. Table 9-9 indicates the return values for the `Instr()` function.

Table 9-9 Values returned by Instr()

If the...	The Instr Function Returns...
firststring is zero-length	0
firststring is NULL	A NULL value
secondstring is zero-length	The value of startloc
secondstring is NULL	A NULL value
secondstring is not found	0
secondstring is found	The location of the second string within the first string
startloc > secondstring	0

In Listing 9-7 the **Instr()** function is used to determine the location of the value typed in **InputString1** within the value typed in the **InputString2** field. If the string is located, the **MsgBox()** displays the result of the **Instr()** function, as illustrated in Figure 9-8. If the string is not located, the **MsgBox()** displays a message indicating the string was not found.

Listing 9-7 Using the Instr() function

```
<HTML>

<HEAD>
<TITLE>Instr Example</TITLE>

<SCRIPT LANGUAGE="VBScript">
<!--
'.............................................................
' LocateString_OnClick()
' Determines the location of the first string within the
' second string.
'.............................................................
SUB LocateString_OnClick()

  Dim UserString1
  Dim UserString2
  Dim Result

  UserString1 = InputString1.Value
  UserString2 = InputString2.Value

'.............................................................
' Determine location of the string. If the return value of the
' Instr function is greater than zero, display the result.
' Otherwise, indicate that the string was not located.
'.............................................................

  Result = Instr(1, UserString1, UserString2)

  If Result > 0 Then
```

continued on next page

continued from previous page

```
     MsgBox "The string is at character location " & Result

  Else

    MsgBox "String was not located"

  End If

END SUB
-->

</SCRIPT>
</HEAD>

<BODY>

<CENTER>

<FONT SIZE=6>String Location<P>
</CENTER>
<HR>

<FONT SIZE=4>

<PRE>         Type a string: <INPUT NAME=InputString1 SIZE=20>
Type the second string: <INPUT NAME=InputString2 SIZE=20></PRE>

<HR>
<INPUT TYPE=BUTTON VALUE="Locate String" NAME="LocateString">

</FONT>

</BODY>

</HTML>
```

Comments The `InstrB()` function can be used to determine the byte location of the string, instead of the character location returned by the `Instr()` function.

See Also `InstrB()`

`InstrB` FUNCTION

Purpose Use the `InstrB()` function to determine the byte location of one string within another string. This function is useful when comparing string values. Table 9-10 describes the expressions you can use with the `InstrB()` function.

Syntax **`InstrB(startloc, firststring, secondstring, comparetype)`**

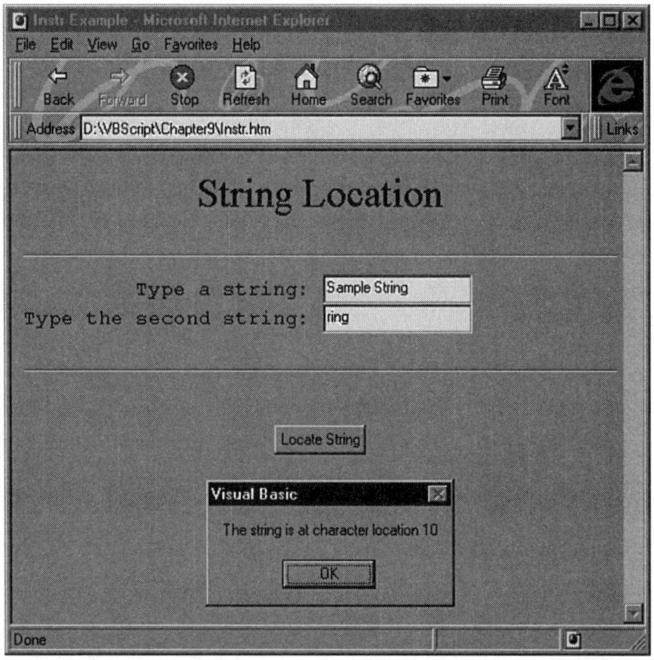

Figure 9-8 The `Instr()` function determines the character location of one string within another string

Table 9-10 Arguments of the `InstrB()` function

Argument	Description
`startloc`	A numeric expression that indicates the byte location in first string where the search should start. This is an optional argument for the `InstrB()` function; if it is omitted, the search begins at the beginning of the string. If a `comparetype` argument is specified, the `startloc` argument is required.
`firststring`	A valid string expression identifying the string to be searched.
`secondstring`	A valid string expression to be located in the first string.
`comparetype`	A value of `0` or `1` indicating the type of string comparison that should be used. This argument is optional; if it is omitted, the default value of `0` is used. A value of `0` performs a binary comparison of the strings. A value of `1` performs a textual, case-insensitive comparison of the strings.

Description

The `InstrB()` function is used to determine if a string contains another string. If the second string is located in the first string, the `InstrB()` function returns the byte location of the first character matched in the string. Table 9-11 indicates the return values for the `InstrB()` function.

Table 9-11 Values returned by `InstrB()`

If the...	The `InstrB` Function Returns...
`firststring` is zero-length	0
`firststring` is NULL	A NULL value
`secondstring` is zero-length	The value of `startloc`
`secondstring` is NULL	A NULL value
`secondstring` is not found	0
`secondstring` is found	The byte location of the second string within the first string
`startloc` > `secondstring`	0

In Listing 9-8 the **`InstrB()`** function is used to determine the byte location of the value typed in **`InputString1`** within the value typed in the **`InputString2`** field. If the string is located, the **`MsgBox()`** displays the result of the **`InstrB()`** function, as illustrated in Figure 9-9. If the string is not located, the **`MsgBox()`** displays a message indicating the string was not found.

Listing 9-8 Using the `InstrB()` function

```
<HTML>

<HEAD>
<TITLE>InstrB Example</TITLE>

<SCRIPT LANGUAGE="VBScript">
<!--
'..............................................................
' LocateString_OnClick()
' Determines the byte location of the first string within the
' second string.
'..............................................................
SUB LocateString_OnClick()

  Dim UserString1
  Dim UserString2
  Dim Result

  UserString1 = InputString1.Value
  UserString2 = InputString2.Value

'..............................................................
' Determine location of the string. If the return value of the
' Instr function is greater than zero, display the result.
' Otherwise, indicate that the string was not located.
'..............................................................

  Result = InstrB(1, UserString1, UserString2)
```

```
  If Result > 0 Then

     MsgBox "The string is at byte location " & Result

  Else

    MsgBox "String was not located"

  End If

END SUB
-->

</SCRIPT>
</HEAD>

<BODY>

<CENTER>

<FONT SIZE=6>String Byte Location<P>
</CENTER>
<HR>

<FONT SIZE=4>

<PRE>         Type a string: <INPUT NAME=InputString1 SIZE=20>
Type the second string: <INPUT NAME=InputString2 SIZE=20></PRE>

<HR>
<CENTER>
<INPUT TYPE=BUTTON VALUE="Locate String" NAME="LocateString">
</CENTER>
</FONT>

</BODY>

</HTML>
```

Comments The `Instr()` function can be used to determine the character location of the string, instead of the byte location returned by the `InstrB()` function.

See Also `Instr()`

LCase() Function

Purpose Use the `LCase()` function to convert any uppercase characters to lowercase. This is useful when working with strings that were input by the user. Use of the function ensures that the string contains lowercase characters. Table 9-12 describes the expressions you can use with the `LCase()` function.

Syntax `LCase(expression)`

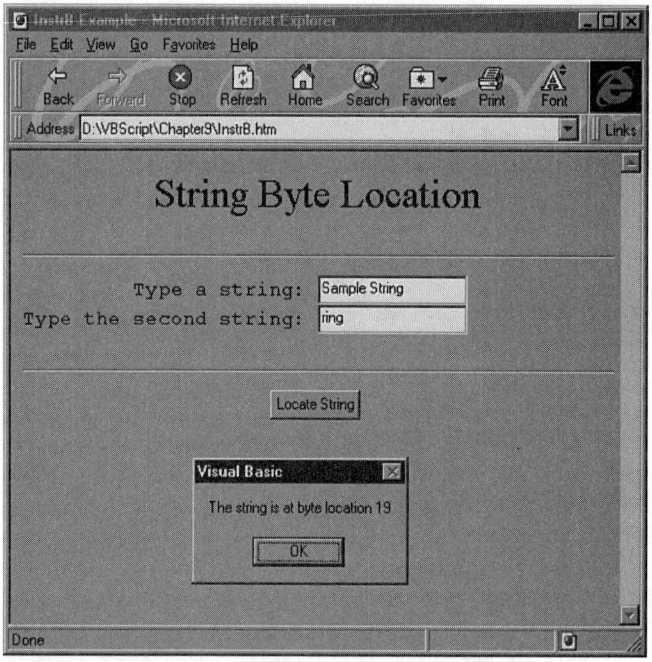

Figure 9-9 The `InstrB()` function determines the byte location of one string within another string

Table 9-12 Argument of the `LCase()` function

Argument	Description
`expression`	Any valid string expression, or `NULL`

Description The `LCase()` function converts all uppercase letters in the specified string to lowercase. This function is useful when you want to maintain consistency in the data.

In Listing 9-9 the `LCase()` function is used to convert the string typed in the `InputValue` field. The `MsgBox()` function is used to display the results of the `LCase()` function, as illustrated in Figure 9-10.

Listing 9-9 Using the `LCase()` function

```
<HTML>

<HEAD>
<TITLE>LCase Example</TITLE>
```

```
<SCRIPT LANGUAGE="VBScript">
<!--
'..........................................................
' ConvertLower_OnClick()
' Converts the string typed in the InputValue field to
' lowercase.
'..........................................................
SUB ConvertLower_OnClick()

  Dim UserValue

  UserValue=InputValue.Value

  MsgBox "The converted string is " & LCase(UserValue)

END SUB
-->

</SCRIPT>
</HEAD>

<BODY>

<CENTER>

<FONT SIZE=6>Lowercase Converter<P>
</CENTER>
<HR>

<FONT SIZE=4>

Type a value: <INPUT NAME=InputValue SIZE=20>

<HR>
<CENTER>
<INPUT TYPE=BUTTON VALUE="Convert to Lowercase" NAME="ConvertLower">
</CENTER>
</FONT>

</BODY>

</HTML>
```

Example The String Manipulation project, at the end of this chapter, uses the `LCase()` function to convert the string typed by the user to lowercase characters. By converting the string to all lowercase characters, it can easily be compared with the correct answer to determine if the strings match.

Comments The `LCase()` function only converts uppercase letters. If the string contains lowercase letters or numeric values, those characters remain unchanged in the string.

See Also `UCase()`

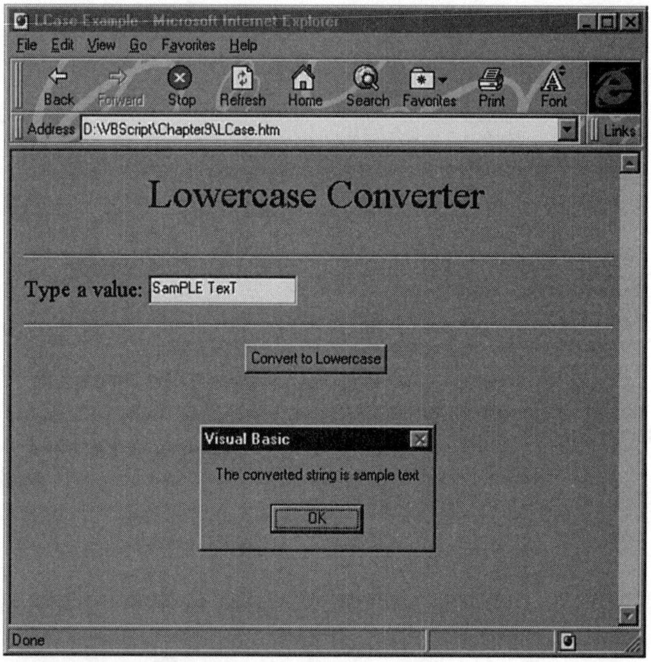

Figure 9-10 The `LCase()` function converts all uppercase letters to lowercase letters

`Left` FUNCTION

Purpose Use the `Left()` function to return a specified number of characters starting at the left, or beginning, of the string. Table 9-13 describes the expressions you can use with the `Left()` function.

Syntax `Left(expression, stringlength)`

Table 9-13 Arguments of the `Left()` function

Argument	Description
`expression`	Any valid string expression, or `NULL`
`stringlength`	A numeric expression that identifies the number of characters the function should return

Description The `Left()` function returns the specified number of characters in the string. The values are returned starting at the left side, or beginning, of the string.

In Listing 9-10 the **Left()** function is used to return the first character in each string, or name. This example illustrates how to capture a person's initials using the **Left()** function. The **MsgBox()** function is used to display the results of the three **Left()** functions, as illustrated in Figure 9-11.

Listing 9-10 Using the Left() *function*

```
<HTML>

<HEAD>
<TITLE>Left Example</TITLE>

<SCRIPT LANGUAGE="VBScript">
<!--
'..............................................................
' GetInitials_OnClick()
' Determines the initials of the name typed in the InputFirst,
' InputMiddle, and InputLast fields.
'..............................................................
SUB GetInitials_OnClick()


  MsgBox "The initials are " & Left(InputFirst.Value, 1) & Left(InputMiddle.Value, 1) &
Left(InputLast.Value, 1)


END SUB
-->

</SCRIPT>
</HEAD>

<BODY>

<CENTER>

<FONT SIZE=6>Determine Initials<P>
</CENTER>
<HR>

<FONT SIZE=4>

<PRE> Type your first name: <INPUT NAME=InputFirst SIZE=20>
Type your middle name: <INPUT NAME=InputMiddle SIZE=20>
       Type last name: <INPUT NAME=InputLast SIZE=20> </PRE>

<HR>
<CENTER>
<INPUT TYPE=BUTTON VALUE="Determine Initials" NAME="GetInitials">
</CENTER>
</FONT>

</BODY>

</HTML>
```

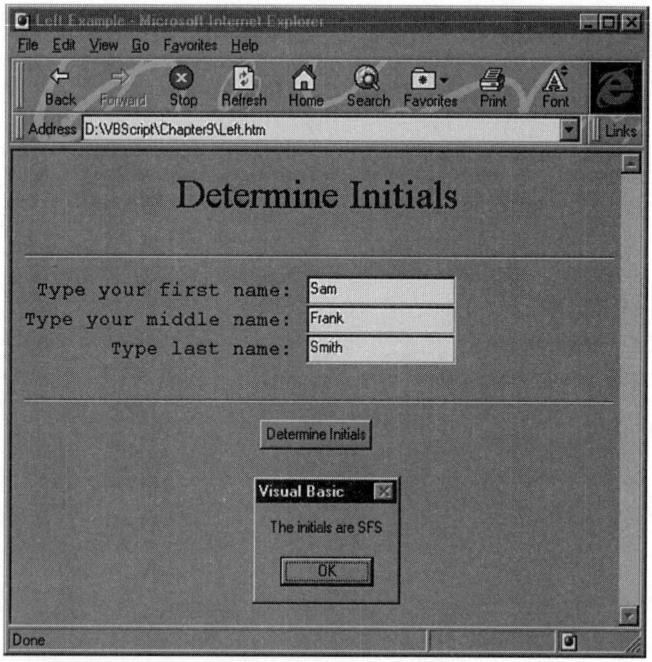

Figure 9-11 The `Left()` function returns the specified number of characters from the left side of the string

Example The String Manipulation project, at the end of this chapter, uses the `Left()` function to determine the first character in the desired string. The `MsgBox()` function displays the value returned by the `Left()` function on the screen as a hint to the user when trying to solve the puzzle.

Comments If `0` is specified for `stringlength`, a zero-length string is returned. If the length value is greater than or equal to the actual number of characters in the string, the `Left()` function returns the entire string.

See Also `LeftB()`, `Mid()`, `Right()`

`LeftB()` Function

Purpose Use the `LeftB()` function to return a specified number of bytes starting at the left, or beginning, of the string. Table 9-14 describes the expressions you can use with the `LeftB()` function.

Syntax `LeftB(expression, stringbytes)`

Table 9-14 Arguments of the LeftB() function

Argument	Description
expression	Any valid string expression, or NULL
stringbytes	A numeric expression that identifies the number of bytes the function should return

Description

The LeftB() function returns the specified number of bytes of the string. The values are returned starting at the left side, or beginning of the string.

In Listing 9-11 the LeftB() function is used to return the first two bytes in each string or name. Since it takes two bytes to store a character, the first character in each field is returned. This example is similar to Listing 9-10, for the Left() function. The only difference is that the LeftB() function returns the specified number of bytes, not characters. It illustrates how to capture a person's initials using the LeftB() function. The MsgBox() function displays the results of the three LeftB() functions, as illustrated in Figure 9-12.

Listing 9-11 Using the LeftB() function

```
<HTML>

<HEAD>
<TITLE>LeftB Example</TITLE>

<SCRIPT LANGUAGE="VBScript">
<!--
'..............................................................
' GetInitials_OnClick()
' Determines the initials of the name typed in the InputFirst,
' InputMiddle, and InputLast fields.
'..............................................................
SUB GetInitials_OnClick()

  MsgBox "The initials are " & LeftB(InputFirst.Value, 2) & LeftB(InputMiddle.Value, 2) &
LeftB(InputLast.Value, 2)

END SUB
-->

</SCRIPT>
</HEAD>

<BODY>

<CENTER>

<FONT SIZE=6>Determine Initials<P>
</CENTER>
<HR>
```

continued on next page

continued from previous page

```
<FONT SIZE=4>

<PRE>
 Type your first name: <INPUT NAME=InputFirst SIZE=20>
Type your middle name: <INPUT NAME=InputMiddle SIZE=20>
       Type last name: <INPUT NAME=InputLast SIZE=20>
</PRE>

<HR>
<CENTER>
<INPUT TYPE=BUTTON VALUE="Determine Initials" NAME="GetInitials">
</CENTER>

</FONT>

</BODY>
```

Comments If `0` is specified for `stringbytes`, a zero-length string is returned. If the length value is greater than or equal to the actual number of characters in the string, the `LeftB()` function returns the entire string.

See Also `Left()`, `MidB()`, `RightB()`

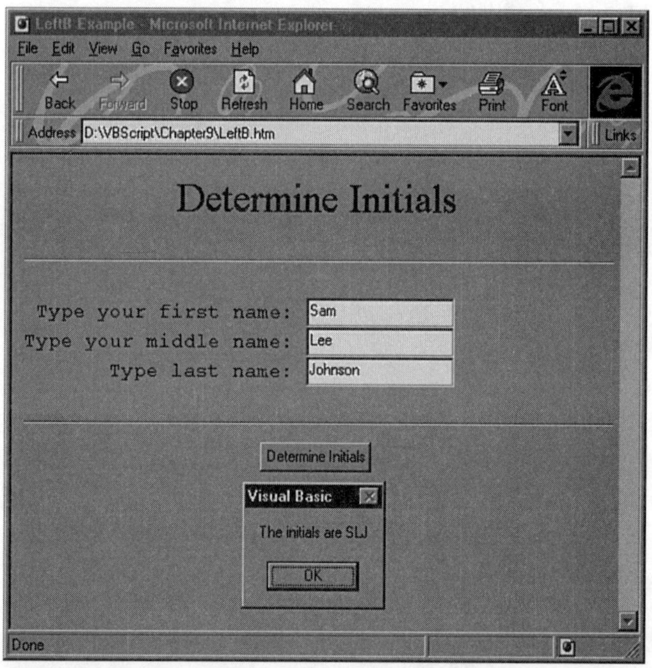

Figure 9-12 The `LeftB()` function returns the specified number of bytes from the left side of the string

Len FUNCTION

Purpose Use the `Len()` function to determine the number of characters in the specified string. Table 9-15 describes the expressions you can use with the `Len()` function.

Syntax `Len(expression)`

Table 9-15 Argument of the `Len()` function

Argument	Description
`expression`	Any valid string expression, or `NULL`

Description The `Len()` function determines the number of characters in the specified string. If the string contains spaces, including leading and trailing spacing, the spaces are counted as characters. If the string contains a `NULL` value, the `Len()` function returns a `NULL()` value.

In Listing 9-12 the `Len()` function is used to determine the length of the string typed in the `InputValue` field. The `MsgBox()` function displays the results of the `Len()` function, as illustrated in Figure 9-13.

Listing 9-12 Using the `Len()` function

```
<HTML>

<HEAD>
<TITLE>Len Example</TITLE>

<SCRIPT LANGUAGE="VBScript">
<!--
'.............................................................
' GetLength_OnClick()
' Determines the length of the string typed in the
' InputValue field.
'.............................................................
SUB GetLength_OnClick()

  MsgBox "The length is " & Len(InputValue.Value)

END SUB
-->

</SCRIPT>
</HEAD>

<BODY>

<CENTER>
```

continued on next page

continued from previous page

```
<FONT SIZE=6>Determine Length<P>
</CENTER>
<HR>

<FONT SIZE=4>

Type a value: <INPUT NAME=InputValue SIZE=20>

<HR>
<CENTER>
<INPUT TYPE=BUTTON VALUE="Determine Length" NAME="GetLength">
</CENTER>
</FONT>

</BODY>

</HTML>
```

Example

The String Manipulation project, at the end of this chapter, uses the `Len()` function to compare the length of the value typed in the `InputValue.Value` field with the correct answer. If the lengths are the same, the comparison procedure continues; otherwise, the user receives a message that not enough characters were typed.

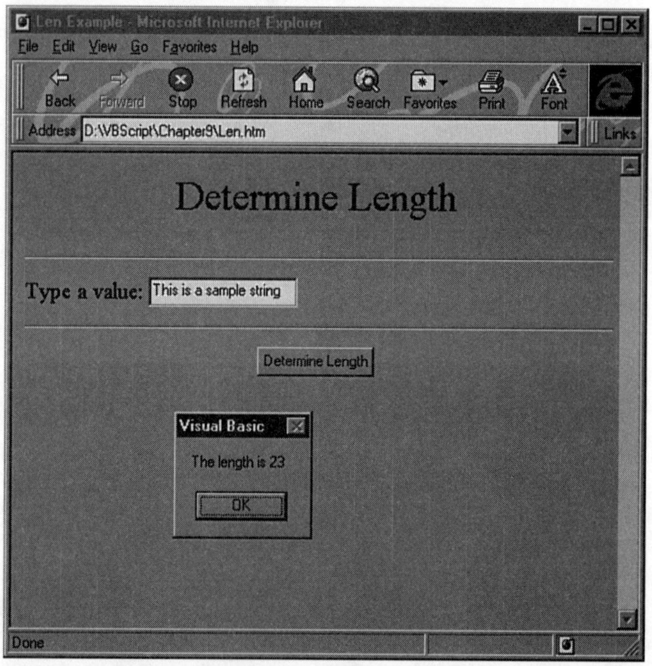

Figure 9-13 The `Len()` function determines the number of characters in the specified string

Comments The `LenB()` function can be used to determine the number of bytes needed to store a variable. This function can be used with all variable types.

See Also `LenB()`

LenB Function

Purpose Use the `LenB()` function to determine the number of bytes in the specified string. Table 9-16 describes the expressions you can use with the `LenB()` function.

Syntax `LenB(expression)`

Table 9-16 Argument of the `LenB()` function

Argument	Description
`expression`	Any valid string expression, or `NULL`

Description The `LenB()` function determines the number of bytes needed to store the specified characters. If the variable contains spaces, including leading and trailing spacing, the spaces are counted as characters. If the string contains a `NULL` value, the `LenB()` function returns a `NULL` value.

In Listing 9-13 the `LenB()` function is used to determine the number of bytes needed to store the value typed in the `InputValue` field. The `MsgBox()` function displays the results of the `LenB()` function, as illustrated in Figure 9-14.

Listing 9-13 Using the `LenB()` function

```
<HTML>

<HEAD>
<TITLE>LenB Example</TITLE>

<SCRIPT LANGUAGE="VBScript">
<!--
'...........................................................
' GetByteLength_OnClick()
' Determines the number of bytes needed to store the value typed
' in the InputValue field.
'...........................................................
SUB GetByteLength_OnClick()

  MsgBox "The byte size is " & LenB(InputValue.Value)

END SUB
-->
```

continued on next page

continued from previous page

```
</SCRIPT>
</HEAD>

<BODY>

<CENTER>

<FONT SIZE=6>Determine Byte Size<P>
</CENTER>
<HR>

<FONT SIZE=4>

Type a value: <INPUT NAME=InputValue SIZE=20>

<HR>
<CENTER>
<INPUT TYPE=BUTTON VALUE="Determine Size" NAME="GetByteLength">
</CENTER>
</FONT>

</BODY>

</HTML>
```

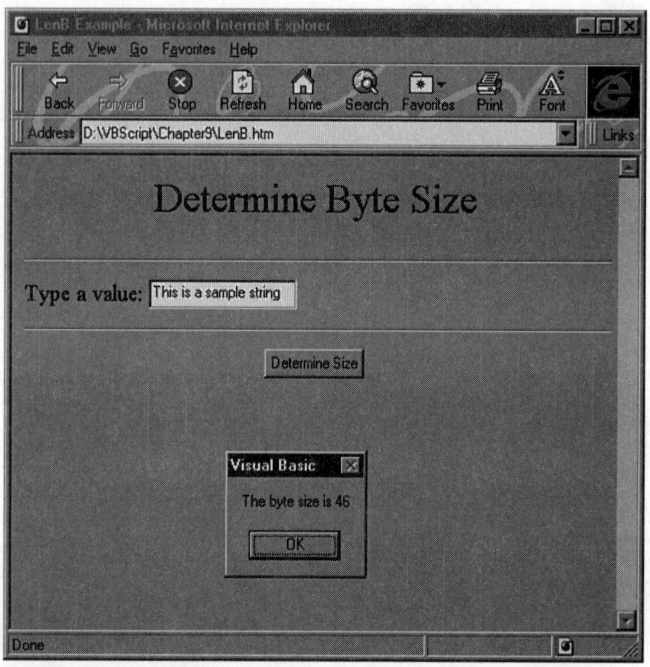

Figure 9-14 The `LenB()` function determines the number of bytes needed to store the specified string

Comments The `Len()` function can be used to determine the actual number of characters in a string.

See Also `Len()`

LTrim FUNCTION

Purpose Use the `LTrim()` function to remove the leading spaces of the specified string. Table 9-17 describes the expressions you can use with the `LTrim()` function.

Syntax `LTrim(expression)`

Table 9-17 Argument of the LTrim() function

Argument	Description
expression	Any valid string expression, or NULL

Description The `LTrim()` function removes any excess spaces at the beginning of the specified string. This is useful when you want to eliminate any characters that may have been added to the beginning of the string.

Listing 9-14 uses the `LTrim()` function to remove the extra spacing at the beginning of the string typed in the `InputValue` field. The `MsgBox()` function displays the results of the `LTrim()` function, as illustrated in Figure 9-15.

Listing 9-14 Using the LTrim() function

```
<HTML>

<HEAD>
<TITLE>LTrim Example</TITLE>

<SCRIPT LANGUAGE="VBScript">
<!--
'..................................................
' LeftTrimString_OnClick()
' Trims any leading spaces in a string.
'..................................................
SUB LeftTrimString_OnClick()

  Dim UserValue

  UserValue=InputValue.Value

  MsgBox "The string is " & LTrim(UserValue)

END SUB
-->
```

continued on next page

continued from previous page

```
</SCRIPT>
</HEAD>

<BODY>

<CENTER>

<FONT SIZE=6>Trim Leading Spaces<P>
</CENTER>
<HR>

<FONT SIZE=4>

Type a value: <INPUT NAME=InputValue SIZE=20>

<HR>
<CENTER>
<INPUT TYPE=BUTTON VALUE="Trim Leading Spacing" NAME="LeftTrimString">
</CENTER>

</FONT>

</BODY>

</HTML>
```

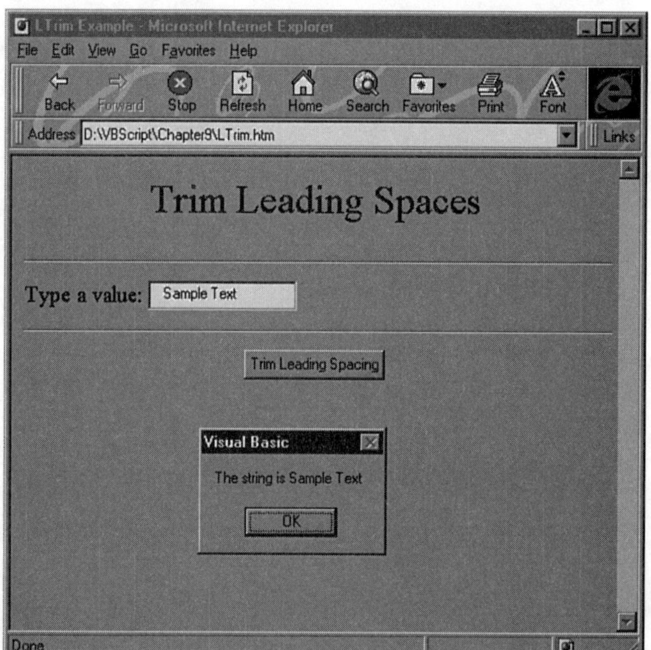

Figure 9-15 The `LTrim()` function removes the beginning spaces in a string

Comments Any spacing that exists at the end of the string remains when you use the `LTrim()` function. To remove spacing at the end of a string, use either the `RTrim()` or `Trim()` function. If you only want to eliminate spaces at the ending of the string, use the `RTrim()` function. To eliminate spacing at the beginning and end of the string, use the `Trim()` function. None of the trim functions eliminate spacing within the string.

See Also `RTrim()`, `Trim()`

`Mid()` Function

Purpose Use the `Mid()` function to return a specific number of characters from the specified string. The `Mid()` function allows you to specify the starting location of the characters. Table 9-18 describes the expressions you can use with the `Mid()` function.

Syntax `Mid(expression, startlocation, charlength)`

Table 9-18 Arguments of the `Mid()` function

Argument	Description
`expression`	Any valid string expression, or `NULL`.
`startlocation`	The character location in the string of the first character that you would like to return.
`charlength`	The number of characters to return from the string. This argument is optional; if it is omitted, all characters from the `startlocation` to the end of the string are returned.

Description The `Mid()` function provides you with the ability to select only specific characters in a string. By simply specifying the start location in the string for the desired characters and the number of characters to return, the `Mid()` function returns only those characters. If a `NULL` value is passed to the `Mid()` function, it returns a `NULL` value.

Listing 9-15 illustrates how to use the `Mid()` function. In this example, the `Mid()` function is used to return the third, fourth, and fifth characters in the string typed in the `InputValue` field. The `MsgBox()` function displays the results of the `Mid()` function on the screen, as illustrated in Figure 9-16.

Listing 9-15 Using the `Mid()` function

```
<HTML>

<HEAD>
<TITLE>Mid Example</TITLE>

<SCRIPT LANGUAGE="VBScript">
```

continued on next page

continued from previous page

```
<!--
'..........................................................
' GetChars_OnClick()
' Returns the third, fourth, and fifth characters in the
' string typed in the InputValue field.
'..........................................................
SUB GetChars_OnClick()

  MsgBox "The third, fourth, and fifth characters in " & InputValue.Value &  " are " &
Mid(InputValue.Value, 3, 3)

END SUB
-->

</SCRIPT>
</HEAD>

<BODY>

<CENTER>

<FONT SIZE=6>Return a Portion of a String<P>
</CENTER>
<HR>

<FONT SIZE=4>

Type a string: <INPUT NAME=InputValue SIZE=20>

<HR>
<CENTER>
<INPUT TYPE=BUTTON VALUE="Determine Characters" NAME="GetChars">
</CENTER>
</FONT>

</BODY>

</HTML>
```

Example The String Manipulation project, at the end of this chapter, uses the **`Mid()`** function to return various characters of the answer for the puzzle. The **`MsgBox()`** function displays the result of the **`Mid()`** function.

Comments If the **`startlocation`** value is larger than the total number of characters in the string, the **`Mid()`** function returns a zero-length string. If the **`charlength`** value is either omitted or greater than the characters in the string from the specified **`startlocation`**, the remaining characters in the string are returned.

The **`MidB()`** function can be used to locate specific bytes in the string.

See Also **`Left()`**, **`Len()`**, **`LTrim()`**, **`MidB()`**, **`Right()`**, **`RTrim()`**, **`Trim()`**

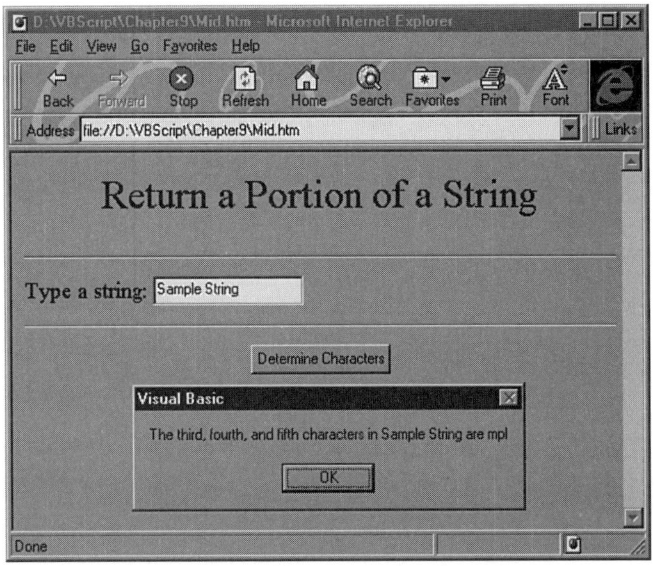

Figure 9-16 The `Mid()` function returns the specified number of characters from a specific location in a string

`MidB` Function

Purpose Use the `MidB()` function to return specific bytes within a string. When you use this function, you specify the starting byte and the number of bytes to return from that location. Table 9-19 describes the expressions you can use with the `MidB()` function.

Syntax `MidB(expression, startbyte, bytenumber)`

Table 9-19 Arguments of the `MidB()` function

Argument	Description
`expression`	Any valid string expression, or `NULL`.
`startbyte`	The byte location in the string of the first byte that you would like to return.
`bytenumber`	The number of bytes to return from the string. This argument is optional; if it is omitted, all bytes from the `startbyte` to the end of the string are returned.

Description The `MidB()` function provides you with the ability to select only specific bytes in a string. By simply specifying the first byte in the string for the desired characters and the number of bytes to return, the `MidB()` function returns only those bytes. If a `NULL` value is passed to the `MidB()` function, it returns a `NULL` value.

Listing 9-16 illustrates how to use the **MidB()** function. In this example, the **MidB()** function is used to return the third through the sixth bytes in the string typed in the **InputValue** field. Since it takes two bytes to save each character, the second and third characters in the string are returned. The **MsgBox()** function displays the results of the **MidB()** function on the screen, as illustrated in Figure 9-17.

Listing 9-16 Using the MidB() *function*

```
<HTML>

<HEAD>
<TITLE>MidB Example</TITLE>

<SCRIPT LANGUAGE="VBScript">
<!--
'...........................................................
' GetBytes_OnClick()
' Returns the third through the sixth bytes in the
' string typed in the InputValue field.
'...........................................................
SUB GetBytes_OnClick()

  MsgBox "The third - sixth bytes in " & InputValue.Value &  " are " &
MidB(InputValue.Value, 3, 4)

END SUB
-->

</SCRIPT>
</HEAD>

<BODY>

<CENTER>

<FONT SIZE=6>Return Bytes of a String<P>
</CENTER>
<HR>

<FONT SIZE=4>

Type a string: <INPUT NAME=InputValue SIZE=20>

<HR>
<CENTER>
<INPUT TYPE=BUTTON VALUE="Determine Bytes" NAME="GetBytes">
</CENTER>
</FONT>

</BODY>

</HTML>
```

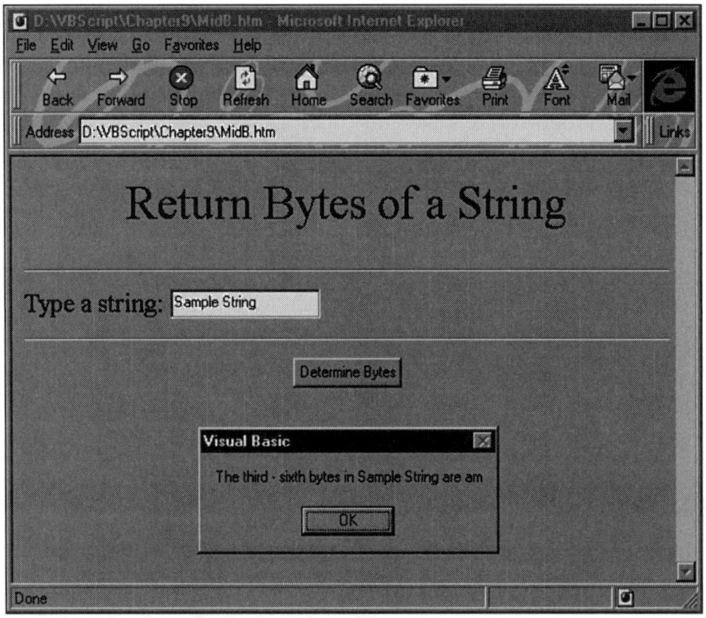

Figure 9-17 The `MidB()` function returns the specified number of bytes from a specific byte location in a string

Comments If the **`startbyte`** value is larger than the total number of bytes in the string, the **`MidB()`** function returns a zero-length string. If the **`bytenumber`** value is either omitted or greater than the number of bytes in the string from the specified **`startbyte`**, the remaining bytes in the string are returned.

The **`Mid()`** function can be used to locate specific characters in a string by specifying a starting character location and the number of characters to return from that location.

See Also `LeftB()`, `LenB()`, `MidB()`, `RightB()`

`Right` FUNCTION

Purpose Use the **`Right()`** function to return a specified number of characters from the right side (the end) of a string. This function is useful when you only want certain characters at the end of a string, not the entire string. Table 9-20 describes the expressions you can use with the **`Right()`** function.

Syntax **`Right(expression, stringlength)`**

Table 9-20 Arguments of the `Right()` function

Argument	Description
`expression`	Any valid string expression, or `NULL`
`stringlength`	A numeric expression that identifies the number of characters the function should return

Description

The **`Right()`** function returns the specified number of characters in the string. The values are returned starting at the right side, or end, of the string. If a **`NULL`** value is passed to the **`Right()`** function, it returns a **`NULL`** value.

In Listing 9-17 the **`Right()`** function is used to return the last two characters in the string typed in the **`InputValue`** field. The **`MsgBox()`** function is used to display the results of the **`Right()`** function, as illustrated in Figure 9-18.

Listing 9-17 Using the `Right()` function

```
<HTML>

<HEAD>
<TITLE>Right Example</TITLE>

<SCRIPT LANGUAGE="VBScript">
<!--
'..........................................................
' GetLastChars_OnClick()
' Determines the last two characters of the string typed in
' the InputValue field.
'..........................................................
SUB GetLastChars_OnClick()

  MsgBox "The last two characters of " & InputValue.Value & " are " &
Right(InputValue.Value, 2)

END SUB
-->

</SCRIPT>
</HEAD>

<BODY>

<CENTER>

<FONT SIZE=6>Determine Last Two Characters<P>
</CENTER>
<HR>
```

```
<FONT SIZE=4>

Type a value: <INPUT NAME=InputValue SIZE=20>

<HR>
<CENTER>
<INPUT TYPE=BUTTON VALUE="Determine Characters" NAME="GetLastChars">
</CENTER>
</FONT>

</BODY>

</HTML>
```

Example The String Manipulation project, at the end of this chapter, uses the `Right()` function to determine the last character in the answer string. The results of the `Right()` function are displayed on the screen using the `MsgBox()` function.

Comments If `0` is specified for `stringlength`, a zero-length string is returned. If the length value is greater than or equal to the actual number of characters in the string, the `Right()` function returns the entire string.

See Also `Left()`, `Mid()`, `RightB()`

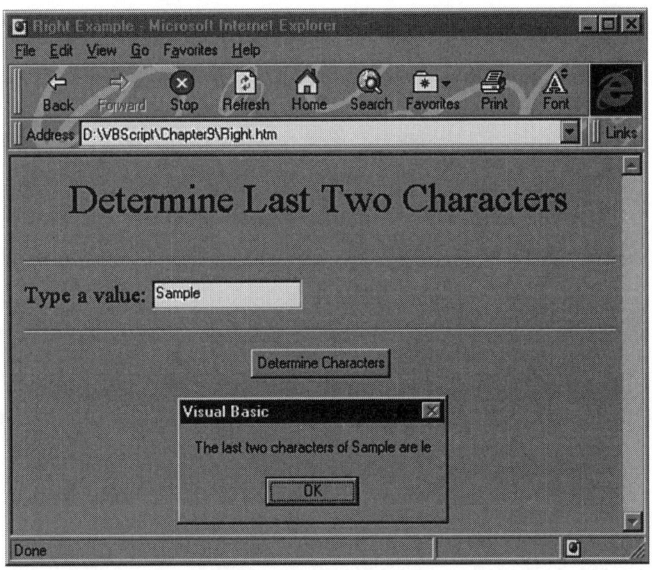

Figure 9-18 The `Right()` function returns the specified number of characters from the right side of the string

RightB Function

Purpose Use the `RightB()` function to return a specified number of bytes from the right side (the end) of a string. This function is useful when you only want a certain number of bytes from the end of a string, not the entire string. Table 9-21 describes the expressions you can use with the `RightB()` function.

Syntax `RightB(expression, stringbytes)`

Table 9-21 Arguments of the RightB() function

Argument	Description
expression	Any valid string expression, or NULL
stringbytes	A numeric expression that identifies the number of bytes the function should return

Description The `RightB()` function returns the specified number of bytes from the string. The values are returned starting at the right side, or end, of the string. If a `NULL` value is passed to the `RightB()` function, it returns a `NULL` value.

In Listing 9-18 the `RightB()` function is used to return the last four bytes in the string typed in the `InputValue` field. Since a character takes two bytes to store, only two characters are returned. The `MsgBox()` function is used to display the results of the `RightB()` function, as illustrated in Figure 9-19.

Listing 9-18 Using the RightB() function

```
<HTML>

<HEAD>
<TITLE>RightB Example</TITLE>

<SCRIPT LANGUAGE="VBScript">
<!--
'..............................................................
' GetLastBytes_OnClick()
' Determines the last four bytes of the string typed in
' the InputValue field.
'..............................................................
SUB GetLastBytes_OnClick()

  MsgBox "The last four bytes of " & InputValue.Value & " are " & ⇐
RightB(InputValue.Value, 4)

END SUB
-->

</SCRIPT>
</HEAD>
```

```
<BODY>

<CENTER>

<FONT SIZE=6>Determine Last Four Bytes<P>
</CENTER>
<HR>

<FONT SIZE=4>

Type a value: <INPUT NAME=InputValue SIZE=20>

<HR>
<CENTER>
<INPUT TYPE=BUTTON VALUE="Determine Bytes" NAME="GetLastBytes">
</CENTER>

</FONT>

</BODY>

</HTML>
```

Comments If `0` is specified for **`stringbytes`**, a zero-length string is returned. If the length value is greater than or equal to the actual number of bytes in the string, the **`RightB()`** function returns the entire string.

See Also `LeftB()`, `MidB()`, `Right()`

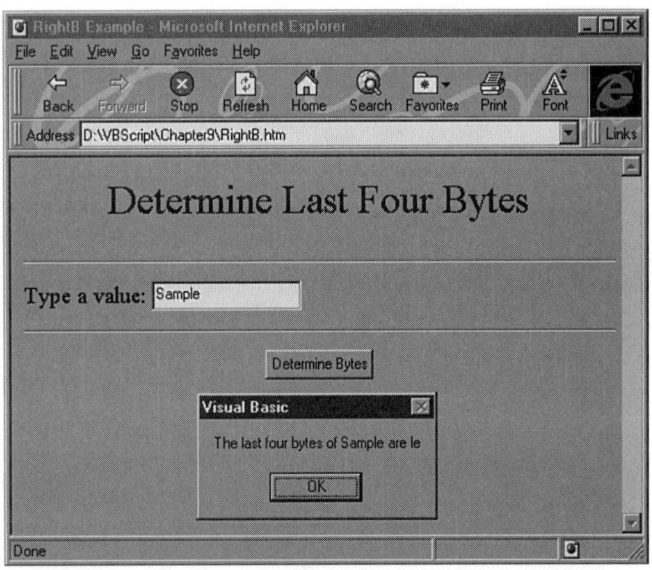

Figure 9-19 The **`RightB()`** function returns the specified number of bytes from the right side of the string

RTrim FUNCTION

Purpose Use the RTrim() function to remove the trailing spaces of the specified string. Table 9-22 describes the expressions you can use with the RTrim() function.

Syntax `RTrim(expression)`

Table 9-22 Argument of the RTrim() function

Argument	Description
expression	Any valid string expression, or NULL

Description The RTrim() function removes any excess spaces at the end of the specified string. This is useful when you want to eliminate any characters that may have been added to the end of the string.

Listing 9-19 uses the RTrim() function to remove the extra spacing at the end of the string typed in the InputValue field. The MsgBox() function displays the results of the RTrim() function, as illustrated in Figure 9-20.

Listing 9-19 Using the RTrim() function

```
<HTML>

<HEAD>
<TITLE>RTrim Example</TITLE>

<SCRIPT LANGUAGE="VBScript">
<!--
'...........................................................
' RightTrimString_OnClick()
' Trims any trailing spaces in a string.
'...........................................................
SUB RightTrimString_OnClick()

  Dim UserValue

  UserValue=InputValue.Value

  MsgBox "The string is " & RTrim(UserValue)

END SUB
-->

</SCRIPT>
</HEAD>

<BODY>
```

```
<CENTER>

<FONT SIZE=6>Trim Trailing Spaces<P>
</CENTER>
<HR>

<FONT SIZE=4>

Type a value: <INPUT NAME=InputValue SIZE=20>

<HR>
<CENTER>
<INPUT TYPE=BUTTON VALUE="Trim Trailing Spacing" NAME="RightTrimString">
<CENTER>
</FONT>

</BODY>

</HTML>
```

Comments Any spacing that exists at the beginning of the string remains when you use the `RTrim()` function. To remove spacing at the beginning of a string, use either the `LTrim()` or `Trim()` function. If you only want to eliminate spaces at the beginning of the string, use the `LTrim()` function. To eliminate spacing at the beginning and end of the string, use the `Trim()` function. None of the trim functions eliminate spacing within the string.

See Also `LTrim()`, `Trim()`

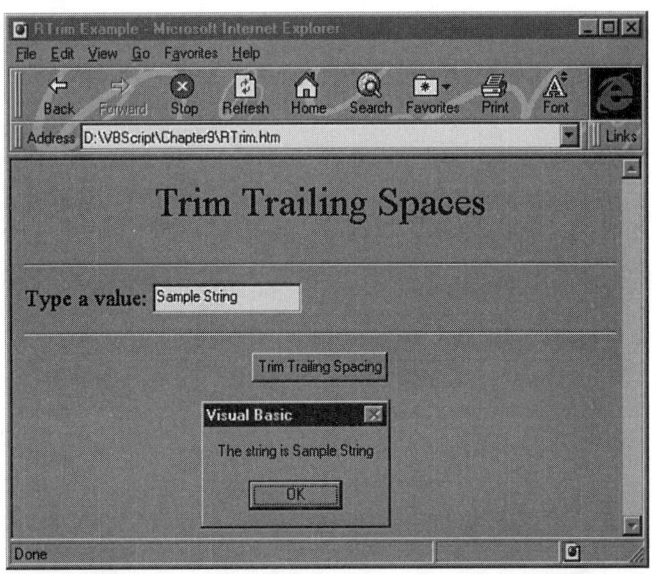

Figure 9-20 The `RTrim()` function removes the ending spaces in a string

Space FUNCTION

Purpose Use the `Space()` function to create a string containing the specified number of spaces. You can use this function when you need to add padding between fields to ensure that values line up properly. Table 9-23 describes the expressions you can use with the `Space()` function.

Syntax `Space(expression)`

Table 9-23 Argument of the Space() function

Argument	Description
expression	Any numeric expression, greater than zero, that identifies the number of spaces for the string

Description The `Space()` function allows you to create a string containing the desired number of spaces. This function is normally used when you need to add padding between fields so that they appear to be displayed in columns.

In Listing 9-20 the `Space()` function creates a string using the value typed in the `InputValue` field as the string length. The `MsgBox()` function displays the results of the `Space()` function, as illustrated in Figure 9-21. The `Chr(34)` function is used to display double quotes at the beginning and ending of the string value.

Listing 9-20 Using the Space() function

```
<HTML>

<HEAD>
<TITLE>Space Example</TITLE>

<SCRIPT LANGUAGE="VBScript">
<!--
'.........................................................
' SpaceString_OnClick()
' Creates a string containing the specified number of spaces.
'.........................................................
SUB SpaceString_OnClick()

  Dim UserValue

  UserValue=InputValue.Value

'.........................................................
' Make sure the value is numeric and greater than zero.
'.........................................................
  If IsNumeric(UserValue) Then
```

```
    If UserValue > 0 Then

      MsgBox "The string " & Chr(34) & Space(UserValue) & Chr(34) & " has " & UserValue & "
spaces."

    Else

      MsgBox "Type a numeric value greater than zero."

    End If

   Else

    MsgBox "You must type a numeric value greater than zero."

   End If
END SUB
-->

</SCRIPT>
</HEAD>

<BODY>

<CENTER>

<FONT SIZE=6>String Containing Spaces<P>
</CENTER>
<HR>

<FONT SIZE=4>

Indicate the number of spaces: <INPUT NAME=InputValue SIZE=20>

<HR>
<CENTER>
<INPUT TYPE=BUTTON VALUE="Create String" NAME="SpaceString">
</CENTER>
</FONT>

</BODY>

</HTML>
```

Comments

If the `Space()` function receives either a value that is not numeric or a negative value, a run-time error occurs, as illustrated in Figure 9-22. To eliminate errors, you need to check the value prior to calling the `Space()` function. The `IsNumeric()` function can be called to make sure the value is numeric. For more information about the `IsNumeric()` function, refer to Chapter 4, Data Validation. You should also make sure that the value is greater than zero by using an `If` statement, as illustrated in Listing 9-20.

See Also

`String()`

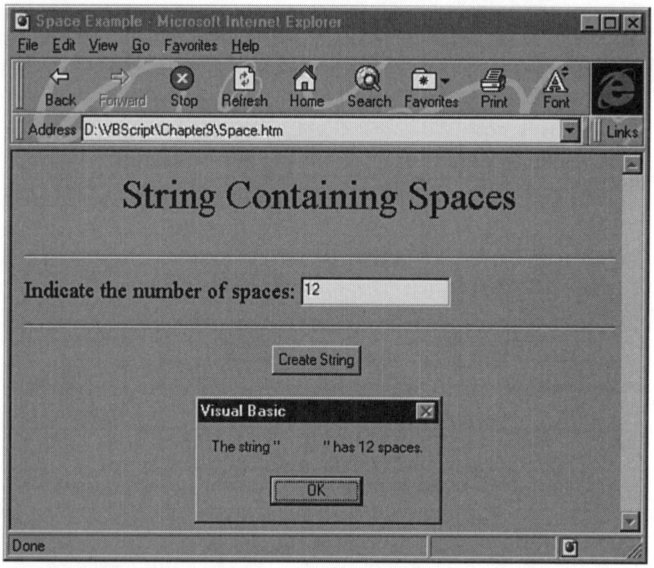

Figure 9-21 The `Space()` function creates a string containing the specified number of spaces

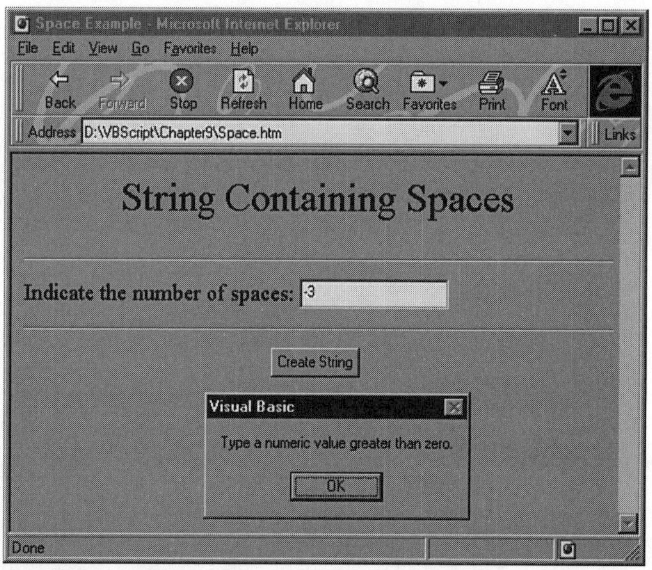

Figure 9-22 The `Space()` function requires a numeric value greater than zero; otherwise, it returns an error

StrComp FUNCTION

Purpose Use the **StrComp()** function to compare two strings to determine if they are the same. If they are not the same, the **StrComp()** function returns a value indicating which string is larger. Table 9-24 describes the expressions you can use with the **StrComp()** function.

Syntax **StrComp(firststring, secondstring, comparetype)**

Table 9-24 Arguments of the StrComp() function

Argument	Description
firststring	A valid string expression identifying the string to be compared.
secondstring	A valid string expression identifying the second string to be compared.
comparetype	A value of 0 or 1 indicating the type of string comparison that should be used. This argument is optional; if it is omitted, the default value of 0 is used. A value of 0 performs a binary comparison of the strings. A value of 1 performs a textual, case-insensitive comparison of the strings.

Description The **StrComp()** function is used to compare two strings to determine if the strings are the same, or if one string is greater than the other string. Table 9-25 indicates the return values for the **StrComp()** function.

Table 9-25 Values returned by StrComp()

If the...	The StrComp Function Returns...
firststring < secondstring	-1
firststring = secondstring	0
firststring > secondstring	1
firststring = NULL	A NULL value
secondstring = NULL	A NULL value

In Listing 9-21 the **StrComp()** function is used to compare the values typed in the **InputString1** and **InputString2** fields. Once a comparison is made, the **Select Case** statement uses the result of the comparison to determine the message that should display on the screen. The **MsgBox()** displays the result of the **StrComp()** function, as illustrated in Figure 9-23.

Listing 9-21 Using the StrComp() function

```
<HTML>

<HEAD>
```

continued on next page

continued from previous page

```
<TITLE>StrComp Example</TITLE>

<SCRIPT LANGUAGE="VBScript">
<!--
'.............................................................
' CompareString_OnClick()
' Compares the two strings.
'.............................................................
SUB CompareString_OnClick()

  Dim UserString1
  Dim UserString2
  Dim Result

  UserString1 = InputString1.Value
  UserString2 = InputString2.Value

'.............................................................
' Compare the strings. Use the Select Case statement to
' determine the message to display.
'.............................................................

  Result = StrComp(UserString1, UserString2)

  Select Case Result

    Case -1

      MsgBox "The first string is smaller than the second string."

    Case 0

      MsgBox "The strings are the same."

    Case 1

      MsgBox "The first string is larger than the second string"

    Case NULL

      MsgBox "One of the strings has a NULL value."

  End Select

 END SUB
-->

</SCRIPT>
</HEAD>

<BODY>

<CENTER>

<FONT SIZE=6>String Comparison<P>
</CENTER>
<HR>
```

```
<FONT SIZE=4>

<PRE>
        Type a string: <INPUT NAME=InputString1 SIZE=20>
Type the second string: <INPUT NAME=InputString2 SIZE=20>
</PRE>

<HR>
<CENTER>
<INPUT TYPE=BUTTON VALUE="Compare String" NAME="CompareString">
</CENTER>
</FONT>

</BODY>

</HTML>
```

Example The String Manipulation project, at the end of this chapter, uses the `StrComp()` function to determine if the value typed by the user in the `InputValue.Value` field is the correct response. The `StrComp()` function compares the value typed by the user to the correct response and returns a numeric value indicating the result. A `Select Case` statement evaluates the result of the `StrComp()` function and determines the message that should be displayed for the user.

See Also `Instr()`, `InstrB()`

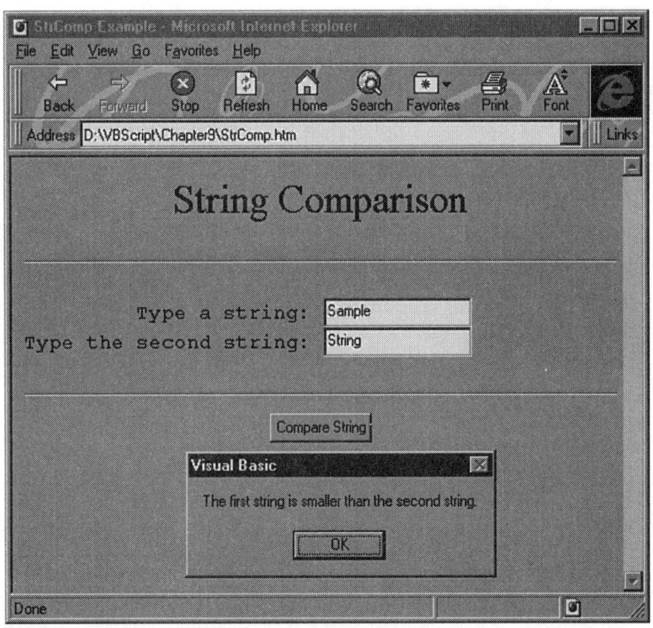

Figure 9-23 The `StrComp()` function compares two different string values

`String` Function

Purpose Use the `String()` function to create a string containing the specified number of a desired character. Table 9-26 describes the expressions you can use with the `String()` function.

Syntax `String(charnumber, character)`

Table 9-26 Arguments of the `String()` function

Argument	Description
`charnumber`	A value greater than zero indicating the length of the string. This argument can also be `NULL`.
`character`	A character or string expression whose first character should be used in the string. This argument can also be `NULL`.

Description The `String()` function creates a string containing the number of values indicated by `charnumber`. The `character` argument indicates the ASCII character that is placed in the string.

In Listing 9-22 the `String()` function is used to create a string using the two input values. The `InputNumber.Value` value indicates the number of characters in the string, and the `InputChar.Value` value indicates the character that is placed in the string. The `MsgBox()` function displays the results of the `String()` function, as illustrated in Figure 9-24.

Listing 9-22 Using the `String()` function

```
<HTML>

<HEAD>
<TITLE>String Example</TITLE>

<SCRIPT LANGUAGE="VBScript">
<!--
'..............................................................
' CreateString_OnClick()
' Creates a string containing the specified number of the
' character.
'..............................................................
SUB CreateString_OnClick()

  Dim UserNumber
  Dim UserChar

  UserNumber = InputNumber.Value
  UserChar = InputChar.Value

'..............................................................
' Make sure the number value is numeric and greater than zero.
'..............................................................
  If IsNumeric(UserNumber) Then
```

```
    If UserNumber > 0 Then

      MsgBox "The string is " & Chr(34) & String(UserNumber, UserChar) & Chr(34)

    Else

      MsgBox "Type a numeric value greater than zero."

    End If

  Else

    MsgBox "You must type a numeric value greater than zero."

  End If
END SUB
-->

</SCRIPT>
</HEAD>

<BODY>

<CENTER>

<FONT SIZE=6>String Creation<P>
</CENTER>
<HR>

<FONT SIZE=4>

<PRE>
Indicate the number of items in string: <INPUT NAME=InputNumber SIZE=10>
             Indicate value for string: <INPUT NAME=InputChar SIZE=10>
</PRE>

<HR>
<CENTER>
<INPUT TYPE=BUTTON VALUE="Create String" NAME="CreateString">
</CENTER>
</FONT>

</BODY>

</HTML>
```

Comments

To help eliminate run-time errors, it is important to check the value passed to the `charnumber` argument. Although the function will accept a `NULL` value, for Listing 9-22 only a numeric value greater than zero is allowed to be passed to the `String()` function. You can use the `IsNumeric()` function to make sure the value is numeric. For more information about the `IsNumeric()` function, refer to Chapter 4, Data Validation.

Listing 9-22 also contains an `If` statement to make sure the value was positive, greater than zero.

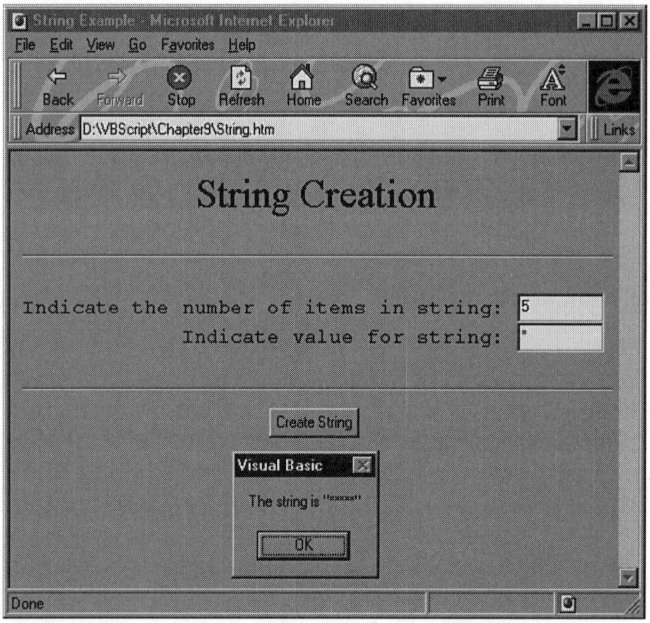

Figure 9-24 The `String()` function creates a string containing the specified number of the character

If either one of the arguments passed to the `String()` function is `NULL`, the `String()` function returns a `NULL` value.

See Also `Space()`

`Trim` FUNCTION

Purpose Use the `Trim()` function to remove the leading and trailing spaces within a string. Table 9-27 describes the expressions you can use with the `Trim()` function.

Syntax `Trim(expression)`

Table 9-27 Argument of the `Trim()` function

Argument	Description
`expression`	Any valid string expression, or `NULL`

Description The `Trim()` function removes any excess spaces at the beginning or ending of the specified string. This is useful when you want to display only the actual characters in the string and eliminate any characters that may have been added to the beginning or end of the string.

Listing 9-23 uses the **Trim()** function to remove the extra spacing at the beginning or end of the string typed in the **InputValue()** field. The **MsgBox()** function displays the results of the **Trim()** function, as illustrated in Figure 9-25.

Listing 9-23 Using the Trim() *function*

```
<HTML>

<HEAD>
<TITLE>Trim Example</TITLE>

<SCRIPT LANGUAGE="VBScript">
<!--
'..............................................................
' TrimString_OnClick()
' Trims any leading or trailing spaces in a string.
'..............................................................
SUB TrimString_OnClick()

  Dim UserValue

  UserValue=InputValue.Value

  MsgBox "The string is " & Trim(UserValue)

END SUB
-->

</SCRIPT>
</HEAD>

<BODY>

<CENTER>

<FONT SIZE=6>Trim Spaces<P>
</CENTER>
<HR>

<FONT SIZE=4>

Type a value: <INPUT NAME=InputValue SIZE=20>

<HR>
<CENTER>
<INPUT TYPE=BUTTON VALUE="Trim Spacing" NAME="TrimString">
</CENTER>
</FONT>

</BODY>

</HTML>
```

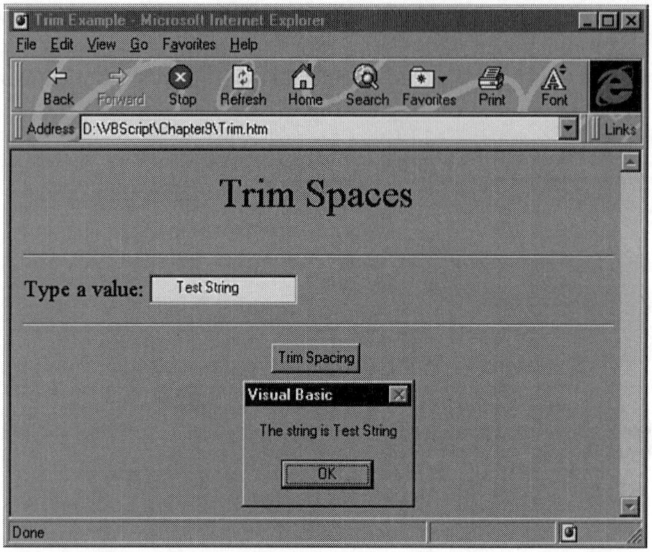

Figure 9-25 The `Trim()` function removes the beginning and ending spaces in a string

Example The String Manipulation project, at the end of this chapter, uses the `Trim()` function to eliminate any spaces the user may have typed at the beginning or end of the value in the `InputValue.Value` field. Use of this function ensures that only the intended characters are used for the comparison, and eliminates a wrong response due to extra spaces.

Comments The `Trim()` function does not eliminate the spacing within a string. If you only want to eliminate the spacing at the beginning of the string, use the `LTrim()` function. To eliminate the spacing at the end of the string, use the `RTrim()` function.

See Also `LTrim()`, `RTrim()`

UCase FUNCTION

Purpose Use the `UCase()` function to convert lowercase characters to uppercase. This is useful when working with strings that were input by the user. Use of this function ensures that the string contains only uppercase characters. Table 9-28 describes the expressions you can use with the `UCase()` function.

Syntax `UCase(expression)`

Table 9-28 Argument of the `UCase()` function

Argument	Description
expression	Any valid string expression, or NULL

Description

The `UCase()` function converts all lowercase characters in the specified string to uppercase. This function is useful when you want to maintain consistency in the data.

In Listing 9-24 the `UCase()` function is used to convert the string typed in the `InputValue` field. The `MsgBox()` function displays the results of the `UCase()` function, as illustrated in Figure 9-26.

Listing 9-24 Using the `UCase()` *function*

```
<HTML>

<HEAD>
<TITLE>UCase Example</TITLE>

<SCRIPT LANGUAGE="VBScript">
<!--
'............................................................
' ConvertUpper_OnClick()
' Converts the string typed in the InputValue field to
' uppercase.
'............................................................
SUB ConvertUpper_OnClick()

  Dim UserValue

  UserValue=InputValue.Value

  MsgBox "The converted string is " & UCase(UserValue)

END SUB
-->

</SCRIPT>
</HEAD>

<BODY>

<CENTER>

<FONT SIZE=6>Uppercase Converter<P>
</CENTER>
<HR>

<FONT SIZE=4>
```

continued on next page

continued from previous page

```
Type a value: <INPUT NAME=InputValue SIZE=20>

<HR>
<CENTER>
<INPUT TYPE=BUTTON VALUE="Convert to Uppercase" NAME="ConvertUpper">
</CENTER>

</FONT>
</BODY>
</HTML>
```

Example The String Manipulation project, at the end of this chapter, uses the `UCase()` function to convert characters of the `ScrambleWord` string to uppercase characters before displaying them. This is used when a single character is displayed as a hint.

Comments The `UCase()` function only converts lowercase letters. If the string contains uppercase letters or numeric values, those characters remain unchanged in the string.

See Also `LCase()`

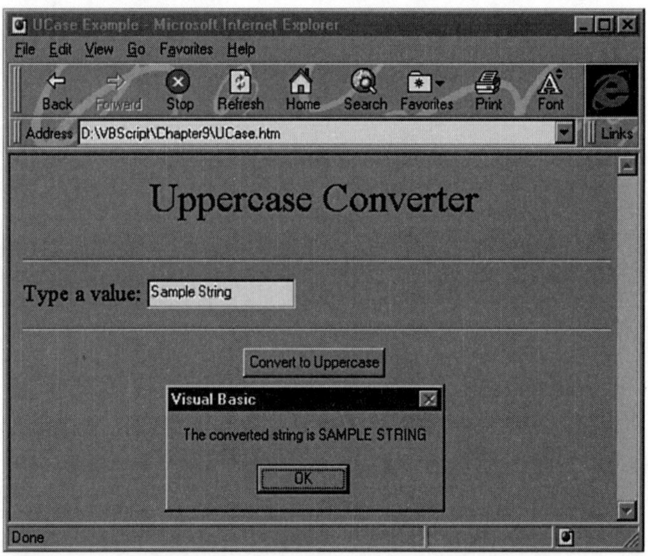

Figure 9-26 The `UCase()` function converts all lowercase letters to uppercase characters

String Manipulation Project

The String Manipulation project provides the opportunity to use several of the functions related to string values covered in this chapter. This project creates a small word game in which the user tries to unscramble a string of letters.

Building the Project

1. Start the project by setting up the standard HTML template used for all VBScript examples in this book. Place the VBScript code in the **<HEAD>** section of the HTML code to keep everything consistent. Remember to place the HTML comment tags **<!--** and **-->** around the VBScript code so that it will be ignored by browsers that cannot interpret the **<SCRIPT>** tag.

```
<HTML>

<HEAD>
<TITLE>String Manipulation Project</TITLE>

<SCRIPT LANGUAGE="VBScript">

<!--

-->

</SCRIPT>

</HEAD>

<BODY>

</BODY>

</HTML>
```

2. In the **<HEAD>** section, prior to the **<SCRIPT>** section, place the title information for the page. You are placing the title here to ensure that it displays at the top of the page. You are going to use a **Document.Write** statement in the **<SCRIPT>** section, and you want the title to display before that information.

```
<CENTER>
<FONT SIZE=6>Unscramble Word<P>
</CENTER>
<HR>
```

3. In the **<SCRIPT>** section, declare two global variables. The first variable, **Hint**, will monitor the number of times the user requests a hint for the answer. This variable is a flag to identify the type of clue that should be displayed. The second variable is **ScrambleWord**. This variable contains the answer to the puzzle.

```
Dim Hint
Dim ScrambleWord

Hint = 1
ScrambleWord = "computer"
```

4. Also in the <SCRIPT> section, outside of any procedures or functions, create a **Document.Write** statement that writes the scrambled word to the screen. Remember that you can only write to the **Document** object during the loading of the page; therefore, this is placed outside of the subroutines so that it will be executed as the page loads.

```
Document.Write "precumot"
```

5. In the <BODY> section, create an input field where the user can type the response to the scrambled word. Figure 9-27 illustrates the input field placed next to the scrambled word.

```
<FONT SIZE=4>

<INPUT NAME=InputValue SIZE=20>
```

6. In the <BODY> section, create a button that the user can press to get a hint about the scrambled word. The button name is Get Hint. When the button is pressed, the VBScript procedure **GetHint_OnClick()** is called. You can use the <HR> tag to place a horizontal line on the screen, as illustrated in the code sample.

```
<HR>
<INPUT TYPE=BUTTON VALUE="Get Hint" NAME="GetHint">
```

7. In the <SCRIPT> section, create a procedure a called **GetHint_OnClick()**. Use the **Hint** variable to determine the type of hint that you provide the user. This procedure increments the **Hint** variable each time the procedure is called; therefore,

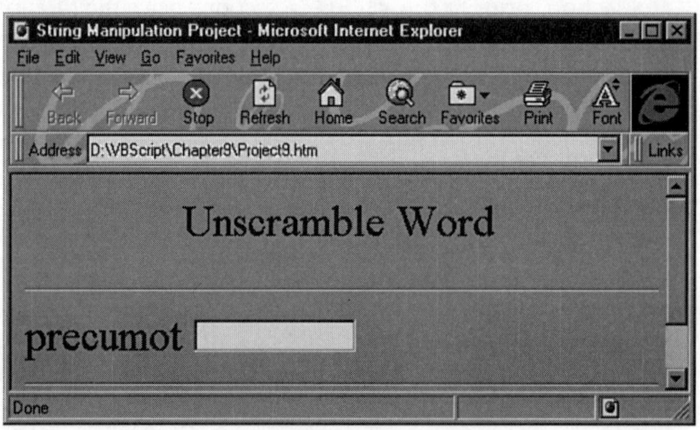

Figure 9-27 The **InputValue** field accepts the input from the user

you can provide a different type of clue to the user each time. Use a **Select Case** statement to determine which clue should display on the screen, based on the value of the **Hint** variable. Use the **Asc()** function to provide the ASCII value of the first character in the string, the **Left()** function to display the first character, the **Right()** function to display the last character, and the **Mid()** function to display each of the remaining characters in the string. Figure 9-28 illustrates the message that displays when the user requests a hint for the third time.

```
SUB GetHint_OnClick()

  Select Case Hint

    Case 1

      MsgBox "The ASCII character code for the first letter is " & Asc(ScrambleWord)

    Case 2

      MsgBox "The first letter is " & UCase(Left(ScrambleWord, 1))

    Case 3

      MsgBox "The last letter is " & UCase(Right(ScrambleWord, 1))

    Case 4

      MsgBox "The second letter is " & UCase(Mid(ScrambleWord, 2, 1))

    Case 5

      MsgBox "The third letter is " & UCase(Mid(ScrambleWord, 3, 1))

    Case 6

      MsgBox "The fourth letter is " & UCase(Mid(ScrambleWord, 4, 1))

    Case 7

      MsgBox "The fifth letter is " & UCase(Mid(ScrambleWord, 5, 1))

    Case 8

      MsgBox "The sixth letter is " & UCase(Mid(ScrambleWord, 6, 1))

    Case 9

      MsgBox "The seventh letter is " & UCase(Mid(ScrambleWord, 7, 1))

    Case 10

      MsgBox "The word is " & UCase(ScrambleWord)

  End Select

  Hint = Hint + 1

END SUB
```

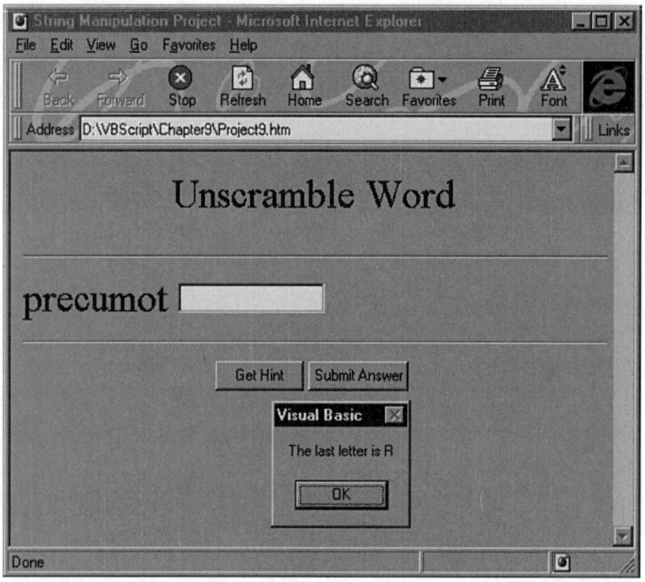

Figure 9-28 The third hint displayed when the Get Hint button is selected

8. In the `<BODY>` section, create a button that users can press when they think they have solved the puzzle. This button, called Submit Answer, calls the `CheckAnswer_OnClick()` procedure to see if the user typed the correct answer.

```
<INPUT TYPE=BUTTON VALUE="Submit Answer" NAME="CheckAnswer">
```

9. In the `<SCRIPT>` section, create a procedure called `CheckAnswer_OnClick()`. Use the `Trim()` function to remove any extra characters that may have been typed before or after the value in the `InputValue.Value` field. Compare the length of the input value to the length of the correct answer. If the lengths are the same, continue checking for the correct answer; otherwise, display a message. Convert the value typed in the `InputValue.Value` field to lowercase characters, using the `LCase()` function, so that you can easily compare it to the correct answer. Assign the return value of the `StrComp()` function to the `Result` variable and then use a `Case` statement to determine the message that displays on the screen. If the correct answer was typed, display a message indicating so, as illustrated in Figure 9-29. Otherwise, indicate that the answer is incorrect.

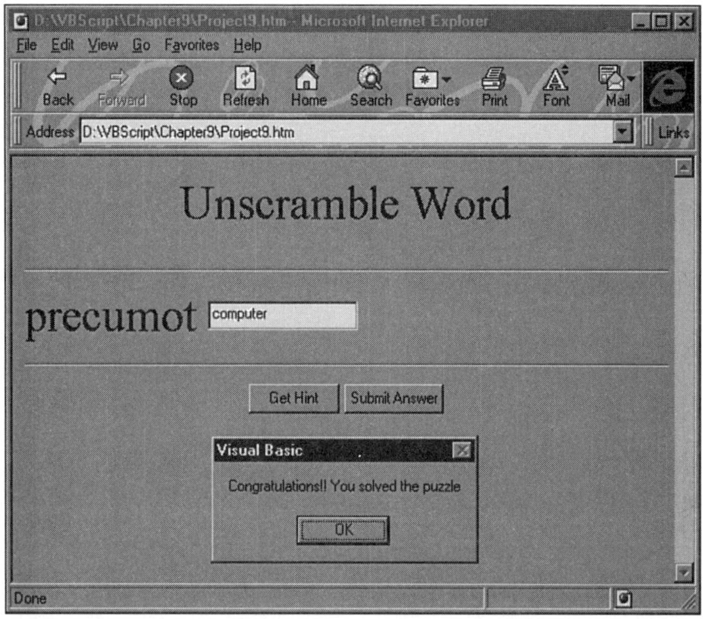

Figure 9-29 The `CheckAnswer_OnClick()` procedure displays this message if the correct answer was typed

```
SUB CheckAnswer_OnClick()

  Dim UserValue
  Dim Result

  UserValue=InputValue.Value

  Trim(UserValue)

  If Len(UserValue) = Len(ScrambleWord) Then

    LCase(UserValue)

    Result = StrComp(UserValue, ScrambleWord)

      Select Case Result

        Case -1

         MsgBox "That is not the right answer. Try again."

        Case 0
```

continued on next page

continued from previous page

```
        MsgBox "Congratulations!! You solved the puzzle"

       Case 1

        MsgBox "That is not the right answer. Try again."

       Case NULL

        MsgBox "Type an answer before selecting the button."

      End Select

    Else

MsgBox "You did not type enough characters. Try again."

   End If

END SUB
```

How It Works

The String Manipulation project is designed to illustrate how to use the functions covered in this chapter to create a small word game. A scrambled word is displayed on the screen and the user is given the opportunity to determine the correct answer for the puzzle, as illustrated in Figure 9-30.

The Get Hint button provides a hint about the correct answer for the puzzle. Each time the button is pressed, a different clue is displayed about the scrambled word. The `Hint` variable is used to monitor the number of times the Get Hint button has been pressed, so that the `Select Case` statement can determine which message to display for the hint.

When users think they have solved the puzzle, they can type the response in the field and select the Submit Answer button. This button calls the `CheckAnswer_OnClick()` procedure, which determines if the answer typed is the correct response. Listing 9-25 shows the complete source code for the project.

Listing 9-25 Complete source for the String Manipulation project

```
<HTML>

<HEAD>
<TITLE>String Manipulation Project</TITLE>

<CENTER>

<FONT SIZE=6>Unscramble Word<P>
</CENTER>
<HR>

<SCRIPT LANGUAGE="VBScript">
<!--
```

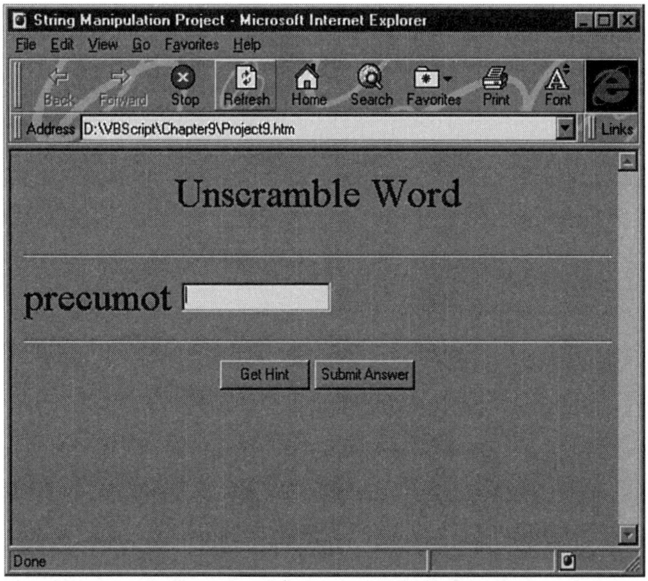

Figure 9-30 The completed String Manipulation project

```
'..........................................
' Declare global variables for the number of
' times the hint option was selected, and
' to hold the correct answer.
'..........................................
 Dim Hint
 Dim ScrambleWord

 Hint = 1
 ScrambleWord = "computer"

'..........................................
' Write the scrambled word to the screen.
' Since you are using the Document.Write
' option, this must be placed in the
' script so that it executes during the
' loading of the page.
'...........................................
 Document.Write "precumot"

'..................................................
' GetHint_OnClick()
' Provides a hint each time the Get Hint button
' is selected. The Asc(), Left(), Right(), and Mid()
' functions are used to provide clues about
' the correct answer.
'...................................................
SUB GetHint_OnClick()

  Select Case Hint
```

continued on next page

continued from previous page

```
    Case 1

      MsgBox "The ASCII character code for the first letter is " & Asc(ScrambleWord)

    Case 2

      MsgBox "The first letter is " & UCase(Left(ScrambleWord, 1))

    Case 3

      MsgBox "The last letter is " & UCase(Right(ScrambleWord, 1))

    Case 4

      MsgBox "The second letter is " & UCase(Mid(ScrambleWord, 2, 1))

    Case 5

      MsgBox "The third letter is " & UCase(Mid(ScrambleWord, 3, 1))

    Case 6

      MsgBox "The fourth letter is " & UCase(Mid(ScrambleWord, 4, 1))

    Case 7

      MsgBox "The fifth letter is " & UCase(Mid(ScrambleWord, 5, 1))

    Case 8

      MsgBox "The sixth letter is " & UCase(Mid(ScrambleWord, 6, 1))

    Case 9

      MsgBox "The seventh letter is " & UCase(Mid(ScrambleWord, 7, 1))

    Case 10

      MsgBox "The word is " & UCase(ScrambleWord)

  End Select

  Hint = Hint + 1

END SUB

'......................................................
' CheckAnswer_OnClick()
' Checks to see if the user typed the correct answer
' when the Submit Answer button is selected. First
' eliminate any excess spaces, then check the length of the
' answer; if correct see if the answer is correct.
'......................................................
SUB CheckAnswer_OnClick()

  Dim UserValue
  Dim Result
```

```
  UserValue=InputValue.Value

  Trim(UserValue)

  If Len(UserValue) = Len(ScrambleWord) Then

'........................................
' Convert all letters to lowercase, and then
' compare answer typed in InputValue.Value
' field to the correct answer. If it is
' correct, display a message. Otherwise,
' display a message indicating that
' the user should make another attempt.
'........................................
    LCase(UserValue)

    Result = StrComp(UserValue, ScrambleWord)

      Select Case Result

        Case -1

         MsgBox "That is not the right answer. Try again."

        Case 0

         MsgBox "Congratulations!! You solved the puzzle"

        Case 1

         MsgBox "That is not the right answer. Try again."

        Case NULL

         MsgBox "Type an answer before selecting the button."

       End Select

     Else

'...........................................................
' Display this message if they did not type enough
' characters in the InputValue.Value field.
'...........................................................
    MsgBox "You did not type enough characters. Try again."

    End If

END SUB
-->

</SCRIPT>
</HEAD>

<BODY>

<FONT SIZE=4>
```

continued on next page

continued from previous page

```
<INPUT NAME=InputValue SIZE=20>

<HR>
<CENTER>
<INPUT TYPE=BUTTON VALUE="Get Hint" NAME="GetHint"><INPUT TYPE=BUTTON VALUE=⇐
"Submit Answer" NAME="CheckAnswer">
</CENTER>
</FONT>

</BODY>

</HTML>
```

10

USER INTERACTION

10

USER INTERACTION

VBScript provides two different functions that can be used to either supply information to the user or request additional information from the user. Since VBScript is so compatible with HTML, the HTML tags for interacting with users are also very valuable tools.

HTML User Interaction Tags

HTML allows you to easily gather information from the user by including the `<INPUT>` tag. This tag can take several different forms. It can be used to create an input field, a button, radio buttons, or checkboxes to gather information from the user. Since these controls are placed directly on the document using the `<INPUT>` tag, this tag is often used with VBScript.

Once the `<INPUT>` tag is used to gather the information, VBScript can access the value of the controls and use it to perform calculations or data manipulations. For example, if you have the following `<INPUT>` tag, an input field is displayed on the document. VBScript can access any value typed in the field by simply using the reference `SampleInput.Value`.

```
<INPUT NAME=SampleInput VALUE=0 SIZE=10>
```

For more information about using the `<INPUT>` tag, refer to Chapter 14, HTML Features Supported by Internet Explorer 3.0.

Using the Window Object

Microsoft Internet Explorer 3.0 provides an object model that allows your VBScript code to directly access different portions of the actual Web page. A `Window` object method called `Alert` allows you to display a message to the user. Although you place this statement within your script, it is not a VBScript function. In fact, this statement can be used with any scripting language supported by Microsoft Internet Explorer 3.0.

The following sample code segment produces a message box similar to the one illustrated in Figure 10-1. For more information about the **Alert** method of the **Window** object, refer to Chapter 15, Internet Explorer Object Model for Scripting.

```
<SCRIPT LANGUAGE="VBScript">
Alert "This is a sample message"
</SCRIPT>
```

VBScript Options

VBScript provides a function called **InputBox()** that displays a dialog box requesting input from the user. Another function, **MsgBox()**, produces a dialog box that displays a message to the user. Each of these functions can be interchanged with the options available within HTML for interacting with the user.

One thing to remember about these functions is that they always display information in a dialog box. If you want to display information directly on the document, you need to use the HTML **<INPUT>** tag.

Summary of User Interaction Functions

Table 10-1 summarizes the user interaction functions covered in this chapter. A detailed description of each function follows this table. Each of these functions is also used in the User Interaction project at the end of the chapter.

Table 10-1 User interaction function summary

Use...	To Do This...
InputBox	Display a dialog box in which the user inputs a string of information.
MsgBox	Display a dialog box that contains a message for the user.

InputBox FUNCTION

Purpose

Use the **InputBox()** function to display a prompt in a dialog box. The **InputBox()** function waits for the user to either input text or select a button, and then returns the contents of the text box. Table 10-2 describes the expressions you can use with the **InputBox()** function.

Figure 10-1 The **Alert** method displays a dialog box that contains a message

Syntax

```
InputBox(userprompt, boxtitle, defaultvalue, xpos, ypos,
helpfile, contextID)
```

Table 10-2 Arguments of the `InputBox()` function

Argument	Description
`userprompt`	The string expression that displays as the message in the dialog box. This string can be a maximum length of approximately 1024 characters, depending on the width of the characters used. If you want the prompt to be more than one line, you can separate the lines using either a carriage return character (`Chr(13)`), a linefeed character (`Chr(10)`), or a carriage return–linefeed character combination (`Chr(13) & Chr(10)`) between each line.
`boxtitle`	The string expression that displays in the title bar of the dialog box. This argument is optional; if you omit it, the application name is placed in the title bar.
`defaultvalue`	The string expression that displays initially as the default value in the text box. This is an optional argument; if you omit it, the text box initially displays empty.
`xpos`	A numeric expression that specifies, in twips, the horizontal distance from the left edge of the screen to the left edge of the dialog. This is an optional argument; if you omit it, the dialog box is horizontally centered.
`ypos`	A numeric expression that specifies, in twips, the vertical distance from the top of the screen to the upper edge of the dialog box. This is an optional argument; if you omit it, the dialog box is vertically positioned approximately one-third of the way down the screen.
`helpfile`	A string expression identifying the name of the help file to use to provide context-sensitive help for the dialog box. This is an optional argument; if you specify a help file name, you must also specify a context ID.
`contextID`	A numeric expression identifying the context ID of the context-sensitive help that should display from the specified help file. This is an optional argument; if you specify a context ID number, you must also specify the help file name.

Description

The **`InputBox()`** function displays on the screen a window containing a text box requesting information from the user. The window displays on the screen until the user either selects the OK button or presses the [ENTER] key on the keyboard.

When the user either selects the OK button or presses the [ENTER] key on the keyboard, the **`InputBox()`** function returns whatever value is contained in the text box. If the text box is empty or the user selects the Cancel button, the **`InputBox()`** function returns a zero-length string.

Listing 10-1 uses the **`InputBox()`** function to request the desired number of each item from the user. The value returned by the **`InputBox()`** function is assigned to a variable and then used to calculate the total cost of the item. Figure 10-2 illustrates the use of the **`InputBox()`** function to request the total number of hamburgers desired by the user.

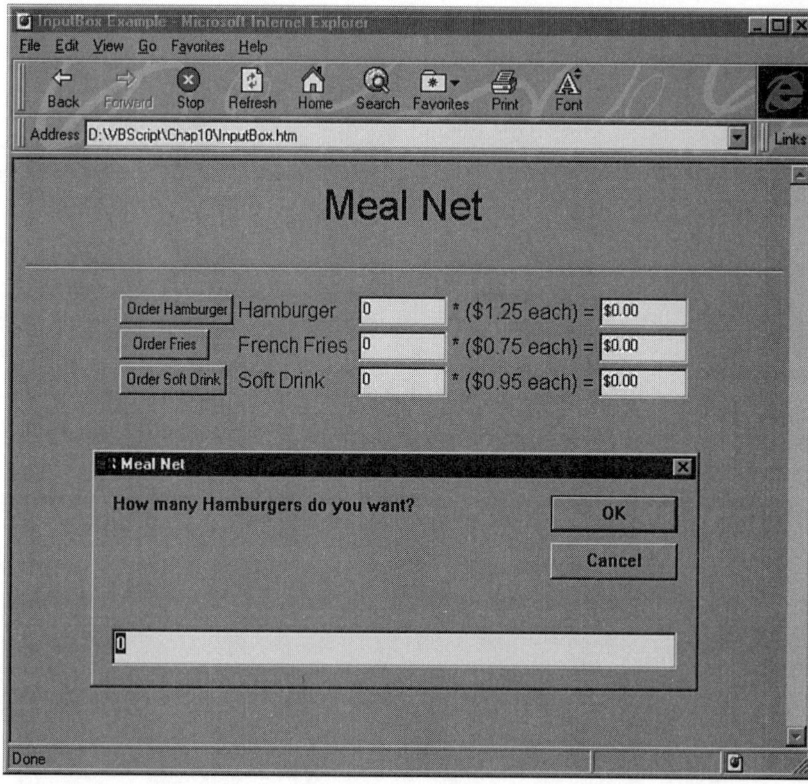

Figure 10-2 The `InputBox()` function requests a value from the user

Listing 10-1 Using the `InputBox()` *function*

```
<HTML>

<HEAD>
<TITLE>InputBox Example</TITLE>

<SCRIPT LANGUAGE="VBScript">

'...............................................
' OrderHam_OnClick()
' Called when the Order Hamburger button is
' selected. Requests the number of hamburgers
' desired, then displays number in Burger.Value
' field and total cost in BurgerSum.Value field.
'...............................................

SUB OrderHam_OnClick()

  Dim Hamburger
```

```
  Hamburger = InputBox("How many Hamburgers do you want?", "Meal Net", 0)

  If IsNumeric(Hamburger) Then

     Burger.Value = Hamburger
     BurgerSum.Value=Hamburger * 1.25
  Else
     MsgBox "You must type a Numeric value for your Hamburger order.", 0, "Meal Net"
  End If

END SUB

'.............................................
' OrderFries_OnClick()
' Called when the Order Fries button is
' selected. Requests the number of French fries
' desired, then displays number in Fries.Value
' field and total cost in FriesSum.Value field.
'.............................................

SUB OrderFries_OnClick()

  Dim FrenchFries

  FrenchFries = InputBox("How many French Fries do you want?", "Meal Net", 0)

  If IsNumeric(FrenchFries) Then

     Fries.Value = FrenchFries
     FriesSum.Value=FrenchFries * .75
  Else
     MsgBox "You must type a Numeric value for your French Fry order.", 0, "Meal Net"
  End If

END SUB

'.............................................
' OrderSoda_OnClick()
' Called when the Order Soft Drink button is
' selected. Requests the number of soft drinks
' desired, then displays number in Soda.Value
' field and total cost in SodaSum.Value field.
'.............................................

SUB OrderSoda_OnClick()

  Dim SoftDrink

  SoftDrink = InputBox("How many Soft Drinks do you want?", "Meal Net", 0)

  If IsNumeric(SoftDrink) Then

     Soda.Value = SoftDrink
     SodaSum.Value=SoftDrink * .95
  Else
     MsgBox "You must type a Numeric value for your Soft Drink order.", 0, "Meal Net"
  End If

END SUB
```

continued on next page

continued from previous page

```
</SCRIPT>

</HEAD>

<BODY>
<FONT FACE="Arial" SIZE=2>

<CENTER>
   <FONT SIZE=6>Meal Net<P>
</CENTER>

<HR>

<CENTER>

<TABLE>

<BR>

<TR><TD><INPUT TYPE=BUTTON VALUE="Order Hamburger" NAME=OrderHam></TD>
    <TD> Hamburger </TD>
    <TD><INPUT NAME=Burger VALUE=0 SIZE=10> * ($1.25 each) = <INPUT NAME=BurgerSum⇐
VALUE="$0.00" SIZE=10</TD></TR>

<TR><TD><INPUT TYPE=BUTTON VALUE="Order Fries" NAME="OrderFries"></TD>
    <TD>French Fries </TD>
    <TD><INPUT NAME=Fries VALUE=0 SIZE=10> * ($0.75 each) = <INPUT NAME=FriesSum
VALUE="$0.00" SIZE=10 </TD></TR>

<TR><TD><INPUT TYPE=BUTTON VALUE="Order Soft Drink" NAME="OrderSoda"></TD>
    <TD>Soft Drink </TD>
    <TD><INPUT NAME=Soda VALUE=0 SIZE=10>  * ($0.95 each) = <INPUT NAME=SodaSum
VALUE="$0.00" SIZE=10 </TD></TR>

</TABLE>

</CENTER>

</BODY>

</HTML>
```

Example The User Interaction project, at the end of this chapter, uses the `InputBox()` function to display an equation for the user to solve. The `InputBox()` function waits for the user to type the answer in the dialog box.

Comments As indicated in Table 10-2, it is not necessary to use all of the arguments listed for the `InputBox()` function. If you omit an argument, such as the `boxtitle` argument, but you still want to indicate a value for the `defaultvalue` argument, you must leave a space for the argument(s) you omit, as illustrated in the following code fragment. In it, arguments are only specified for the `userprompt` and `defaultvalue` arguments. Since the `boxtitle` argument comes between those arguments, you must place a comma there indicating you are not specifying a value for those arguments. If you choose to eliminate the other arguments after the **defaultvalue**, as this code does, you do not have to specify anything for those. Since they are at the end of the argument list, if they are not specified, VBScript assumes you are not using them.

```
SampleValue = InputBox("Type a value", ,10)
```

If you specify an argument value for both the **helpfile** and **contextID** arguments, a Help button is placed on the window, as illustrated in Figure 10-3. If you use these two arguments, the **InputBox()** function requires the path of a valid Microsoft Windows online help file.

See Also `MsgBox()`

MsgBox Function

Purpose Use the **MsgBox()** function to display a message in a dialog box. This function is very useful when you need to display information to users, such as instructing them to type a value in a field. Table 10-3 describes the expressions you can use with the **MsgBox()** function.

Syntax **MsgBox(userprompt, buttons, boxtitle, helpfile, contextID)**

Table 10-3 Arguments of the MsgBox() function

Argument	Description
userprompt	The string expression that displays as the message in the dialog box. This string can be a maximum length of approximately 1024 characters, depending on the width of the characters used. If you want the prompt to be more than one line, you can separate the lines using either a carriage return character (Chr(13)), a linefeed character (Chr(10)), or a carriage return–linefeed character combination (Chr(13)& Chr(10)) between each line.

continued on next page

Figure 10-3 The **InputBox()** function displays a Help button if a help file and context ID are specified

continued from previous page

Argument	Description
`buttons`	A numeric expression that is a combination of values added together from Tables 10-4, 10-5, 10-6, and 10-7, which specifies the number and type of buttons to display, the icon style to use, the identity of the default button, and the modality of the message box. This is an optional argument; if you omit this argument, the default value for `buttons` is 0.
`boxtitle`	A string expression that displays in the title bar of the dialog box. This is an optional argument; if you omit this argument, the application name displays in the title bar.
`helpfile`	A string expression that identifies the help file to use to provide context-sensitive help for the dialog box. This argument needs to be the path of an HLP file (a Microsoft Windows online help file). This is an optional argument; if you use this argument to specify a help file, you must also use the `contextID` argument to specify the context ID of the topic from the help file.
`contextID`	A numeric expression that identifies the context ID of the topic to display from the specified help file. This is an optional argument; if you used this argument to specify the context ID of a topic, you must also use the `helpfile` argument to specify the name of the help file that contains the topic.

Description

The **`MsgBox()`** function displays a dialog box on the screen containing the specified text. Once the dialog box displays, the **`MsgBox()`** function waits for the user to select one of the buttons displayed on the screen. The **`MsgBox()`** function returns a value indicating which one of the buttons was pressed.

The **`MsgBox()`** function provides the ability to specify the number and type of buttons to display, the icon style to use, the identity of the default button, and the modality of the message box. This information about the dialog box is specified by adding values from Tables 10-4, 10-5, 10-6, and 10-7 and placing the resulting value in the **`buttons`** argument of the **`MsgBox()`** function.

Table 10-4 Values of the `buttons` argument for specifying the types of buttons in the dialog box

If the `buttons` Argument Is...	The Dialog Box Contains...
0	An OK button
1	OK and Cancel buttons
2	Abort, Retry, and Ignore buttons
3	Yes, No, and Cancel buttons
4	Yes and No buttons
5	Retry and Cancel buttons

Table 10-5 Values of the `buttons` argument for specifying the icon style to use in the dialog box

If the `buttons` Argument Is...	The Dialog Box Contains...
16	The Critical Message icon
32	The Warning Query icon
48	The Warning Message icon
64	The Information Message icon

Table 10-6 Values of the `buttons` argument for specifying the default button for the dialog box

If the `buttons` Argument Is...	The Default Button in the Dialog Box Is...
0	The first button.
256	The second button.
512	The third button. If there are not three buttons, the last button is the default.
768	The fourth button. If there are not four buttons, the last button is the default.

Table 10-7 Values of the `buttons` argument for specifying the modality of the dialog box

If the `buttons` Argument Is...	The Modality of the Dialog Box Is...
0	The application. The user must respond to the message box before continuing work in the current application.
4096	The system. All applications are suspended until the user responds to the message box.

Listing 10-2 uses the **MsgBox()** function in several places. Initially the **MsgBox()** function is called if the user types a nonnumeric value in the **Burger.Value**, **Fries.Value**, or **Soda.Value** fields, as illustrated in Figure 10-4. In each of these circumstances, it is not important to get the return value from the **MsgBox()** function, since the only button displayed is an OK button; therefore, the **MsgBox()** function is not assigned to a variable.

Listing 10-2 Using the `MsgBox()` *function*

```
<HTML>

<HEAD>
<TITLE>MsgBox Example</TITLE>

<SCRIPT LANGUAGE="VBScript">

'.............................................
' PlaceOrder_OnClick()
```

continued on next page

continued from previous page

```
' Called when the Place Order button is selected.
' Determines if numeric values were typed in each
' field and then totals the fields to determine a
' total cost. Provides the total cost to the user and
' gives him or her the opportunity to accept or reject
' the order.
'...............................................

SUB PlaceOrder_OnClick()

  Dim Hamburger
  Dim FrenchFries
  Dim SoftDrink
  Dim TotalPrice
  Dim UserResponse

'..................................................
' Make sure values typed in Burger.Value, Fries.Value,
' are numeric and determine the total cost for each
' item.
'..................................................
  If IsNumeric(Burger.Value) Then

    Hamburger = Burger.Value * 1.25
    BurgerSum.Value = Hamburger

  Else

    MsgBox "Type a numeric value in the Hamburger field", 16, "Order Taker"

  End If

  If IsNumeric(Fries.Value) Then

    FrenchFries = CInt(Fries.Value) * .75
    FriesSum.Value = FrenchFries

  Else

    MsgBox "Type a numeric value in the French Fries field", 16, "Order Taker"

  End If

  If IsNumeric(Soda.Value) Then

    SoftDrink = CInt(Soda.Value) * .95
    SodaSum.Value = SoftDrink

  Else

    MsgBox "Type a numeric value in the Soft Drink field", 16, "Order Taker"

  End If

'......................................................
' Determine the total cost by adding the cost of each item.
'......................................................
  TotalPrice = Hamburger + FrenchFries + SoftDrink
```

```
'.............................................................
' Inform user of total cost and ask if he or she wants to complete
' the order. Assign user response value to the UserResponse
' variable.
'.............................................................
   UserResponse = MsgBox("The total cost is " & "$" & TotalPrice & "  Do you want to⇐
place order?", 67, "Order Taker")

'.........................................................
' Use the value of the UserResponse variable to determine
' whether or not the order is processed.
'.........................................................
   If UserResponse = 6 Then

     MsgBox "Order has been placed", 64, "Order Taker"

   Else

     MsgBox "Order has been canceled", 64, "Order Taker"

   End If

END SUB

</SCRIPT>
</HEAD>

<BODY>
<FONT FACE="Arial" SIZE=2>

<CENTER>
   <FONT SIZE=6>Order Taker<P>
</CENTER>

<HR>

<CENTER>

<TABLE>

<BR>

<TR><TD><INPUT NAME=Burger VALUE=0 SIZE=10></TD>
    <TD> Hamburger ($1.25 each)</TD>
    <TD> <INPUT NAME=BurgerSum VALUE="$0.00" SIZE=10</TD></TR>

<TR><TD><INPUT NAME=Fries VALUE=0 SIZE=10></TD>
    <TD>French Fries ($0.75 each)</TD>
    <TD><INPUT NAME=FriesSum VALUE="$0.00" SIZE=10 </TD></TR>

<TR><TD><INPUT NAME=Soda VALUE=0 SIZE=10></TD>
    <TD>Soft Drink ($0.95 each)</TD>
    <TD><INPUT NAME=SodaSum VALUE="$0.00" SIZE=10 </TD></TR>

</TABLE>

<HR>

<INPUT TYPE=BUTTON VALUE="Place Order" NAME="PlaceOrder">
```

continued on next page

continued from previous page

```
</CENTER>

</BODY>
</HTML>
```

If each of the three input fields contains a numeric value, the **MsgBox()** function displays a message indicating the total cost for the items ordered, and asks if the user would like to continue the order, as illustrated in Figure 10-5. Since the user response determines whether or not the order is processed, the return value of the **MsgBox()** function is assigned to the **UserResponse** variable.

The **MsgBox()** function returns a numeric value that indicates which button the user selected in the dialog box. Table 10-8 lists the values returned by the **MsgBox()** function.

Figure 10-4 The **MsgBox()** function displays a message instructing the user to type a numeric value

Figure 10-5 The **MsgBox()** function displays a Yes, No, or Cancel dialog box to determine if the user wants to process the order

Table 10-8 Return values of the `MsgBox()` function

If the `MsgBox` Function Returns...	The User Selected...
1	OK
2	Cancel
3	Abort
4	Retry
5	Ignore
6	Yes
7	No

Depending on how you have designed your code, it may be useful to determine which button was selected before proceeding. This can be accomplished by assigning the return value of the **MsgBox()** function to a variable, as illustrated by the following code fragment:

```
ButtonSelected = MsgBox("Do you want to continue?", "Sample Message Box", 3)
```

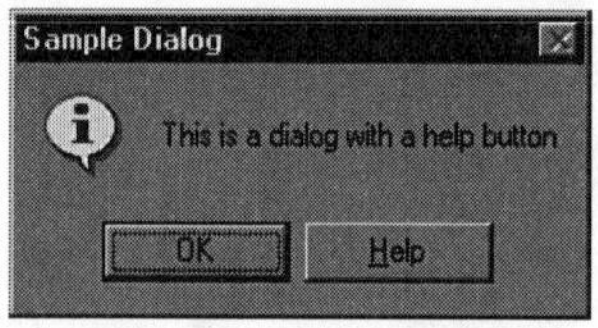

Figure 10-6 The **MsgBox()** function displays a Help button if a help file and context ID are specified

Example The User Interaction project, at the end of this chapter, uses the **MsgBox()** function to indicate whether or not the user typed the correct answer to the equation that was displayed by the **InputBox()** function. The **MsgBox()** function then displays a dialog box with three buttons: Yes, No, and Cancel. If the user selects the Yes button, the program displays a new equation for the user to solve.

Comments As indicated in Table 10-3, it is not necessary to use all of the arguments listed for the **MsgBox()** function. If you omit an argument, such as the **buttons** argument, but you still want to indicate a value for the **boxtitle** argument, you must leave a space for the argument(s) you omit, as illustrated in the code fragment below. In it, arguments are only specified for the **userprompt** and **boxtitle** arguments. Since the **buttons** argument comes between those arguments, you must place a comma there indicating you are not specifying a value for that argument. If you choose to eliminate the arguments that come after **boxtitle**, as the code here does, you do not have to specify anything for them. Since they are at the end of the argument list, if they are not specified, VBScript assumes you are not using them.

```
SampleValue = MsgBox("Type a value", ,"Sample Dialog")
```

If you specify an argument value for both the **helpfile** and **contextID** arguments, a Help button is placed on the window, as illustrated in Figure 10-6. The **MsgBox()** function requires the path of a valid Windows online help file.

See Also **InputBox()**

User Interaction Project

The User Interaction project creates a page where the user can practice solving addition, subtraction, multiplication, and division equations.

Building the Project

1. Start the project by setting up the standard HTML template used for all VBScript examples in this book. Place the VBScript code in the **<HEAD>** section of the HTML code to keep everything consistent. Remember to place the HTML

comment tags <!-- and --> around the VBScript code so that it will be ignored by browsers that cannot interpret the <SCRIPT> tag.

```
<HTML>

<HEAD>
<TITLE>String Manipulation Project</TITLE>

<SCRIPT LANGUAGE="VBScript">

<!--

-->

</SCRIPT>

</HEAD>

<BODY>

</BODY>

</HTML>
```

2. In the <BODY> section, place the title information for the page. You are creating a page that allows students to practice solving mathematical equations, so call it Practice Math Facts.

```
<BODY>
<FONT FACE="Arial" SIZE=2>

<CENTER>
   <FONT SIZE=6>Practice Math Facts<P>
</CENTER>

<HR>
```

3. In the <BODY> section, create buttons that the user can select to indicate the type of mathematical equation he or she would like to solve, as illustrated in Figure 10-7.

```
<CENTER>

<INPUT TYPE=BUTTON VALUE="  Add two numbers    " NAME=Addition>

<INPUT TYPE=BUTTON VALUE="Multiply two numbers" NAME=Multiply>

<BR>
<INPUT TYPE=BUTTON VALUE="Subtract two numbers" NAME=Subtract>

<INPUT TYPE=BUTTON VALUE=" Divide two numbers " NAME=Divide>

</CENTER>

</BODY>

</HTML>
```

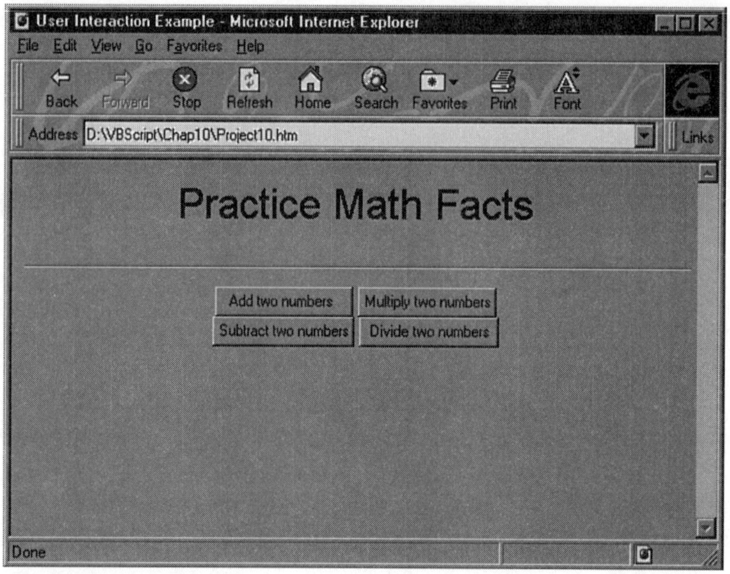

Figure 10-7 Create HTML buttons to select the type of equation that should display on the screen

4. In the `<SCRIPT>` section, create a procedure called `Addition_OnClick()` for adding two random numbers. This procedure is called each time the Add two numbers button is selected. You need to declare variables for the upper and lower limit (the range that the two numbers should be in), the first number, the second number, a variable that keeps track of whether the user wishes to continue, and the variable that contains the actual sum of the two numbers. Initially the `UserContinue` variable should be set to `6`. This variable is used by a `While Wend` statement to determine if the user wants another equation; therefore, it needs to be `6` initially so that the statement will execute. The `UpperLimit` variable should be `100`, and the `LowerLimit` variable should be `1`, specifying that you want the two numbers to be between 1 and 100.

```
SUB Addition_OnClick()

  Dim UpperLimit
  Dim LowerLimit
  Dim FirstNumber
  Dim SecondNumber
  Dim UserResponse
  Dim UserContinue
  Dim ActualSum

  UserContinue = 6
  UpperLimit = 100
  LowerLimit = 1

END SUB
```

5. In the **Addition_OnClick()** procedure, add the **Randomize** statement to initialize the random number generator so that you can use the **Rnd()** function. Create a **While Wend** statement that will continue to execute as long as the user selects the Yes button. Since the **MsgBox()** function returns a value of **6** for the Yes button, the statement executes as long as the **UserContinue** variable equals **6**. Generate two random numbers within the range of 1 to 100 using the formulas in the sample code. Use the **InputBox()** function to display the first equation for the user, as illustrated in Figure 10-8. Then use an **If** statement to see if the correct value was typed. If the value is correct, give the user the opportunity to request another equation to solve. If the value is not correct, provide the correct answer, and let the user continue if desired.

```
Randomize

  While UserContinue = 6

    FirstNumber = CInt((UpperLimit - LowerLimit + 1) * Rnd + LowerLimit)

    SecondNumber = CInt((UpperLimit - LowerLimit + 1) * Rnd + LowerLimit)

    UserResponse = InputBox("What is the sum of " & FirstNumber & " + " & SecondNumber,⇐
"Math Facts")

    ActualSum = FirstNumber + SecondNumber

    If CInt(UserResponse) = ActualSum Then

      UserContinue = MsgBox("That is correct!  Do you want do more addition?", 259, "Math⇐
Facts")

    Else

      UserContinue = MsgBox("INCORRECT! The sum of " & FirstNumber & " + " & SecondNumber⇐
& " is " & ActualSum & " Do you want to try another?", 259, "Math Facts")

    End If

  Wend

END SUB
```

6. In the **<SCRIPT>** section, create a procedure called **Multiply_OnClick()** for multiplying two random numbers. This procedure is called each time the Multiply two numbers button is selected. You need to declare variables for the upper and lower limit (the range that the two numbers should be in), the first number, the second number, a variable that keeps track of whether the user wishes to continue, and the variable that contains the actual result of multiplying the two numbers. Initially the **UserContinue** variable should be set to **6**. This variable is used by a **While Wend** statement to determine if the user wants another equation; therefore, it needs to be **6** initially so that the statement will execute. The **UpperLimit** variable should be **100**, and the **LowerLimit** variable should be **1**, specifying that you want the two numbers to be between 1 and 100.

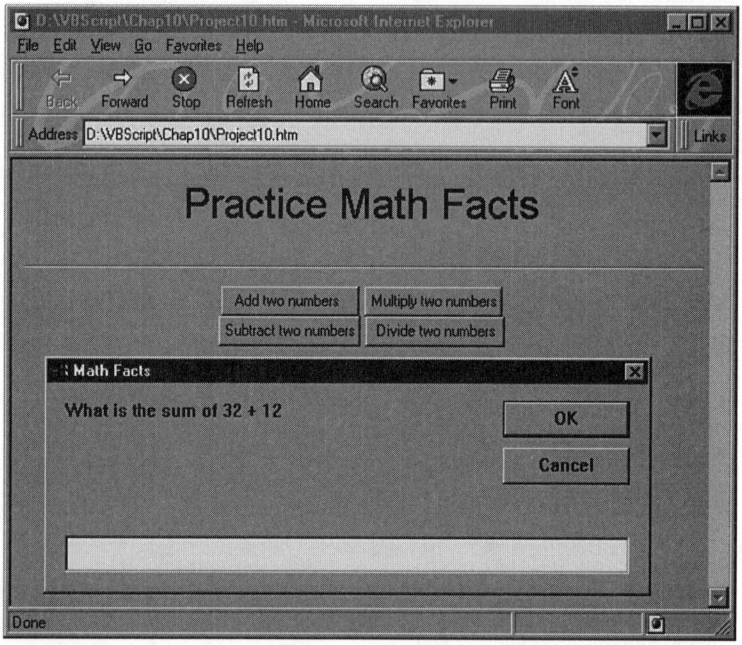

Figure 10-8 Use the `InputBox()` function to display the equation and request that the user type the correct value

```
SUB Multiply_OnClick()

  Dim UpperLimit
  Dim LowerLimit
  Dim FirstNumber
  Dim SecondNumber
  Dim UserResponse
  Dim UserContinue
  Dim ActualResult

  UserContinue = 6
  UpperLimit = 100
  LowerLimit = 1

END SUB
```

7. In the `Multiply_OnClick()` procedure, add the `Randomize` statement to initialize the random number generator so that you can use the `Rnd()` function. Create a `While Wend` statement that will continue to execute as long as the user selects the Yes button. Since the `MsgBox()` function returns a value of `6` for the Yes button, the statement executes as long as the `UserContinue` variable equals `6`. Generate two random numbers within the range of 1 to 100 using the formulas in the sample code. Use the `InputBox()` function to display the first equation for the user. Then use an `If` statement to see if he or she typed the correct value. If the value is correct, give the user the opportunity to request another equation to solve, as

illustrated in Figure 10-9. If the value is not correct, provide the correct answer, and let the user continue if desired.

```
Randomize

  While UserContinue = 6

    FirstNumber = CInt((UpperLimit - LowerLimit + 1) * Rnd + LowerLimit)

    SecondNumber = CInt((UpperLimit - LowerLimit + 1) * Rnd + LowerLimit)

    UserResponse = InputBox("What is the result of " & FirstNumber & " * " &⇐
SecondNumber, "Math Facts")

    ActualResult = FirstNumber * SecondNumber

    If CInt(UserResponse) = ActualResult Then

      UserContinue = MsgBox("That is correct!  Do you want do more multiplication?", 259,⇐
"Math Facts")

    Else

      UserContinue = MsgBox("INCORRECT! The result of " & FirstNumber & " * " &
SecondNumber & " is " & ActualResult & " Do you want to try another?", 259, "Math Facts")

    End If

  Wend

END SUB
```

8. In the `<SCRIPT>` section, create a procedure called **Subtract_OnClick()** for subtracting two random numbers. This procedure is called each time the Subtract two numbers button is selected. You need to declare variables for the upper and lower limit (the range that the two numbers should be in), the first number, the second number, a variable that keeps track of whether the user wishes to continue, and the variable that contains the actual result of subtracting one number from the other number. Initially the **UserContinue** variable should be set to **6**. This variable is used by a **While Wend** statement to determine if the user wants another equation; therefore, it needs to be **6** initially so that the statement will execute. The **UpperLimit** variable should be **100**, and the **LowerLimit** variable should be **1**, specifying that you want the two numbers to be between 1 and 100.

```
SUB Subtract_OnClick()

  Dim UpperLimit
  Dim LowerLimit
  Dim FirstNumber
  Dim SecondNumber
  Dim UserResponse
  Dim UserContinue
  Dim ActualResult

  UserContinue = 6
  UpperLimit = 100
  LowerLimit = 1

END SUB
```

Figure 10-9 Use the `MsgBox()` function to indicate that the value typed was correct and see if the user would like to try another equation

9. In the `Subtract_OnClick()` procedure, add the `Randomize` statement to initialize the random number generator so that you can use the `Rnd()` function. Create a `While Wend` statement that will continue to execute as long as the user selects the Yes button. Since the `MsgBox()` function returns a value of **6** for the Yes button, the statement executes as long as the `UserContinue` variable equals **6**. Generate two random numbers within the range of 1 to 100 using the formulas in the sample code. Use the `InputBox()` function to display the first equation for the user. Then use an `If` statement to see if the correct value was typed. If the value is correct, give the user the opportunity to request another equation to solve. If the value is not correct, provide the correct answer and let the user continue, if desired, as illustrated in Figure 10-10.

```
Randomize

  While UserContinue = 6

    FirstNumber = CInt((UpperLimit - LowerLimit + 1) * Rnd + LowerLimit)

    SecondNumber = CInt((UpperLimit - LowerLimit + 1) * Rnd + LowerLimit)

    UserResponse = InputBox("What is the result of " FirstNumber & " + " & SecondNumber,⇐
"Math Facts")

    ActualResult = FirstNumber - SecondNumber

    If CInt(UserResponse) = ActualResult Then
```

```
      UserContinue = MsgBox("That is correct!  Do you want do more subtraction?", 259,⇐
"Math Facts")

    Else

      UserContinue = MsgBox("INCORRECT! The sum of " & FirstNumber & " - " & SecondNumber⇐
& " is " & ActualResult & " Do you want to try another?", 259, "Math Facts")

    End If

  Wend

END SUB
```

10. In the `<SCRIPT>` section, create a procedure called `Divide_OnClick()` for subtracting two random numbers. This procedure is called each time the Divide two numbers button is selected. You need to declare variables for the upper and lower limit (the range that the two numbers should be in), the first number, the second number, a variable that keeps track of whether the user wishes to continue, and the variable that contains the actual result of dividing one number into the other number. Initially the `UserContinue` variable should be set to **6**. This variable is used by a `While Wend` statement to determine if the user wants another equation; therefore, it needs to be **6** initially so that the statement will execute. The

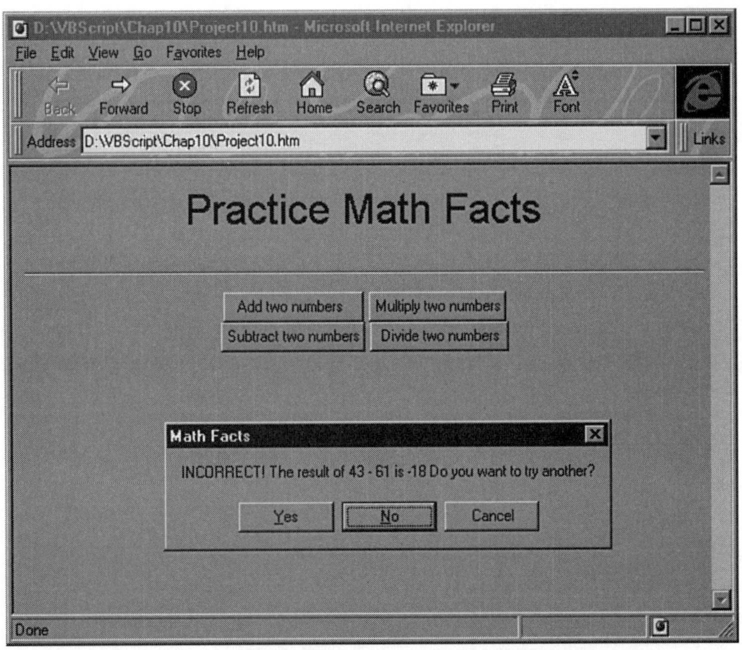

Figure 10-10 Use the `MsgBox()` function to display the correct answer to the equation and provide the opportunity for the user to solve another equation

UpperLimit variable should be 100, and the LowerLimit variable should be 1, specifying that you want the two numbers to be between 1 and 100.

```
SUB Divide_OnClick()

  Dim UpperLimit
  Dim LowerLimit
  Dim FirstNumber
  Dim SecondNumber
  Dim UserResponse
  Dim UserContinue
  Dim ActualResult

  UserContinue = 6
  UpperLimit = 100
  LowerLimit = 1

END SUB
```

11. In the Divide_OnClick() procedure, add the Randomize statement to initialize the random number generator so that you can use the Rnd() function. Create a While Wend statement that will continue to execute as long as the user selects the Yes button. Since the MsgBox() function returns a value of 6 for the Yes button, the statement executes as long as the UserContinue variable equals 6. Generate two random numbers within the range of 1 to 100 using the formulas in the sample code. Use the InputBox() function to display the first equation for the user. Then use an If statement to see if the correct value was typed. If the value is correct, give the user the opportunity to request another equation to solve. If the value is not correct, provide the correct answer and let the user continue, if desired.

```
Randomize

  While UserContinue = 6

    FirstNumber = CInt((UpperLimit - LowerLimit + 1) * Rnd + LowerLimit)

    SecondNumber = CInt((UpperLimit - LowerLimit + 1) * Rnd + LowerLimit)

    UserResponse = InputBox("What is the result of " - FirstNumber & " / " &⇐
SecondNumber, "Math Facts")

    ActualResult = FirstNumber / SecondNumber

    If CInt(UserResponse) = ActualResult Then

      UserContinue = MsgBox("That is correct!  Do you want do more division?", 259, "Math⇐
Facts")

    Else

      UserContinue = MsgBox("INCORRECT! The sum of " & FirstNumber & " / " & SecondNumber⇐
& " is " & ActualResult & " Do you want to try another?", 259, "Math Facts")

    End If
```

```
  Wend

END SUB
```

How It Works

The User Interaction project is designed to illustrate how to use the **InputBox()** and **MsgBox()** functions to interact with the user by displaying and gathering data. This project creates a small game that allows the user to practice adding, multiplying, subtracting, and dividing numeric values between 1 and 100.

The page contains four different buttons. Each one allows users to practice something different. For example, if they want to practice adding numbers, they select the Add two numbers button. They can continue practicing addition until they select the No or Cancel button on the dialog displayed by the **MsgBox()** function. Each of the four buttons calls a different procedure that either adds, multiplies, subtracts, or divides numbers.

Each procedure is designed the same. The procedure uses a **While Wend** statement that continues to execute as long as the user selects the Yes button on the dialog box. If the Yes button is selected, the **MsgBox()** function returns a value of **6**. The **While Wend** statement checks to see if a value of **6** was returned by the last dialog box.

The complete source code for the User Interaction project is shown in Listing 10-3.

Listing 10-3 Complete source for the User Interaction project

```
<HTML>

<HEAD>
<TITLE>User Interaction Example</TITLE>

<SCRIPT LANGUAGE="VBScript">

'.....................................................
' Addition_OnClick()
' Called when the Add two numbers button is selected.
' Generates two random numbers and requests that the
' user indicate the sum of the numbers. Continues to
' display additional addition equations until the user
' selects the No or Cancel button.
'.....................................................
SUB Addition_OnClick()

  Dim UpperLimit
  Dim LowerLimit
  Dim FirstNumber
  Dim SecondNumber
  Dim UserResponse
  Dim UserContinue
  Dim ActualSum

'.....................................................
' Initially set UserContinue to 6. A 6 is the value
' returned by the MsgBox() function when the user selects
```

continued on next page

continued from previous page

```
' the Yes button. Specify the lower and upper limits
' for the random values created for each equation.
'.....................................................
  UserContinue = 6
  UpperLimit = 100
  LowerLimit = 1

  Randomize

'.....................................................
' Continue to create new addition equations as long as
' the user selects the Yes button.
'.....................................................
   While UserContinue = 6

'.....................................................
' Generate two random values between 1 and 100
'.....................................................
     FirstNumber = CInt((UpperLimit - LowerLimit + 1) * Rnd + LowerLimit)

     SecondNumber = CInt((UpperLimit - LowerLimit + 1) * Rnd + LowerLimit)

'.....................................................
' Display equation for user to solve.
'.....................................................
     UserResponse = InputBox("What is the sum of " & FirstNumber & " + " & SecondNumber,⇐
"Math Facts")

'.....................................................
' Determine the actual sum of the equation.
'.....................................................
     ActualSum = FirstNumber + SecondNumber

'.....................................................
' Compare actual sum to the response typed by the user.
' If response is correct, display a message and see if
' the user wants to continue; otherwise, indicate that
' the response was incorrect and see if he or she wants to
' try another equation.
'.....................................................
     If CInt(UserResponse) = ActualSum Then

        UserContinue = MsgBox("That is correct!  Do you want do more addition?", 259,⇐
"Math Facts")

     Else

        UserContinue = MsgBox("INCORRECT! The sum of " & FirstNumber & " + " &⇐
SecondNumber & " is " & ActualSum & " Do you want to try another?", 259, "Math Facts")

     End If

   Wend

END SUB

'.....................................................
' Multiply_OnClick()
```

```
' Called when the Multiply two numbers button is selected.
' Generates two random numbers and requests that the
' user indicate the result of multiplying the numbers.
' Continues to display additional multiplication equations
' until the user selects the No or Cancel button.
'..........................................................
SUB Multiply_OnClick()

  Dim UpperLimit
  Dim LowerLimit
  Dim FirstNumber
  Dim SecondNumber
  Dim UserResponse
  Dim UserContinue
  Dim ActualResult

'.......................................................
' Initially set UserContinue to 6. A 6 is the value
' returned by the MsgBox() function when the user selects
' the Yes button. Specify the lower and upper limits
' for the random values created for each equation.
'........................................................
  UserContinue = 6
  UpperLimit = 100
  LowerLimit = 1

  Randomize

'........................................................
' Continue to create new multiplication equations as
' as long as the user selects the Yes button.
'........................................................
   While UserContinue = 6

'........................................................
' Generate two random values between 1 and 100
'........................................................
     FirstNumber = CInt((UpperLimit - LowerLimit + 1) * Rnd + LowerLimit)

     SecondNumber = CInt((UpperLimit - LowerLimit + 1) * Rnd + LowerLimit)

'........................................................
' Display equation for user to solve.
'........................................................
     UserResponse = InputBox("What is the result of " & FirstNumber & " * " &
SecondNumber,"Math Facts")

'........................................................
' Determine the actual result of the equation.
'........................................................
     ActualResult = FirstNumber * SecondNumber

'........................................................
' Compare actual result to the response typed by the user.
' If response is correct, display a message and see if
' the user wants to continue; otherwise, indicate that
' the response was incorrect and see if he or she wants to
' try another equation.
'.........................................................
```

continued on next page

continued from previous page

```
    If CInt(UserResponse) = ActualResult Then

        UserContinue = MsgBox("That is correct!  Do you want do more multiplication?",⇐
259, "Math Facts")

     Else

        UserContinue = MsgBox("INCORRECT! The sum of " & FirstNumber & " * " &⇐
SecondNumber & " is " & ActualResult & " Do you want to try another?", 259, "Math Facts")

     End If

   Wend

END SUB

'.........................................................
' Subtract_OnClick()
' Called when the Subtract two numbers button is selected.
' Generates two random numbers and requests that the
' user indicate the result of subtracting one number from
' the other number. Continues to display additional
' subtraction equations until the user selects the No or
' Cancel button.
'.........................................................
SUB Subtract_OnClick()

  Dim UpperLimit
  Dim LowerLimit
  Dim FirstNumber
  Dim SecondNumber
  Dim UserResponse
  Dim UserContinue
  Dim ActualResult

'.......................................................
' Initially set UserContinue to 6. A 6 is the value
' returned by the MsgBox() function when the user selects
' the Yes button. Specify the lower and upper limits
' for the random values created for each equation.
'.......................................................
  UserContinue = 6
  UpperLimit = 100
  LowerLimit = 1

  Randomize

'.......................................................
' Continue to create new subtraction equations as long as
' the user selects the Yes button.
'.......................................................
   While UserContinue = 6

'.......................................................
' Generate two random values between 1 and 100
'.......................................................
     FirstNumber = CInt((UpperLimit - LowerLimit + 1) * Rnd + LowerLimit)
```

```
    SecondNumber = CInt((UpperLimit - LowerLimit + 1) * Rnd + LowerLimit)

'.......................................................
' Display equation for user to solve.
'.......................................................
    UserResponse = InputBox("What is the result of " & FirstNumber & " - " &
SecondNumber,"Math Facts")

'.......................................................
' Determine the actual result of the equation.
'.......................................................
    ActualResult = FirstNumber - SecondNumber

'.......................................................
' Compare actual result to the response typed by the user.
' If response is correct, display a message and see if
' the user wants to continue; otherwise, indicate that
' the response was incorrect and see if he or she wants to
' try another equation.
'.......................................................
    If CInt(UserResponse) = ActualResult Then

      UserContinue = MsgBox("That is correct!  Do you want do more subtraction?", 259,⇐
"Math Facts")

    Else

      UserContinue = MsgBox("INCORRECT! The result of " & FirstNumber & " - " &
SecondNumber & " is " & ActualResult & " Do you want to try another?", 259, "Math Facts")

    End If

  Wend

END SUB

'.......................................................
' Divide_OnClick()
' Called when the Divide two numbers button is selected.
' Generates two random numbers and requests that the
' user indicate the result when one number is divided
' by the second number. Continues to display additional
' division equations until the user selects the No or
' Cancel button.
'.......................................................
SUB Divide_OnClick()

  Dim UpperLimit
  Dim LowerLimit
  Dim FirstNumber
  Dim SecondNumber
  Dim UserResponse
  Dim UserContinue
  Dim ActualResult

'.......................................................
' Initially set UserContinue to 6. A 6 is the value
' returned by the MsgBox() function when the user selects
' the Yes button. Specify the lower and upper limits
```

continued on next page

· continued from previous page

```
' for the random values created for each equation.
'.......................................................
  UserContinue = 6
  UpperLimit = 100
  LowerLimit = 1

  Randomize

'.......................................................
' Continue to create new division equations as long as
' the user selects the Yes button.
'.......................................................
   While UserContinue = 6

'.......................................................
' Generate two random values between 1 and 100
'.......................................................
     FirstNumber = CInt((UpperLimit - LowerLimit + 1) * Rnd + LowerLimit)

     SecondNumber = CInt((UpperLimit - LowerLimit + 1) * Rnd + LowerLimit)

'.......................................................
' Display equation for user to solve.
'.......................................................
     UserResponse = InputBox("What is the result of " & FirstNumber & " / " &
SecondNumber,"Math Facts")

'.......................................................
' Determine the actual result of the equation.
'.......................................................
     ActualResult = FirstNumber / SecondNumber

'.......................................................
' Compare actual result to the response typed by the user.
' If response is correct, display a message and see if
' the user wants to continue; otherwise, indicate that
' the response was incorrect and see if he or she wants to
' try another equation.
'.......................................................
     If CDbl(UserResponse) = ActualResult Then

        UserContinue = MsgBox("That is correct!  Do you want do more division?", 259,⇐
"Math Facts")

     Else

        UserContinue = MsgBox("INCORRECT! The result of " & FirstNumber & " / " &⇐
SecondNumber & " is " & ActualResult & " Do you want to try another?", 259, "Math Facts")

     End If

   Wend

END SUB

</SCRIPT>

</HEAD>
```

```
<BODY>
<FONT FACE="Arial" SIZE=2>

<CENTER>
   <FONT SIZE=6>Practice Math Facts<P>
</CENTER>

<HR>

<CENTER>


<INPUT TYPE=BUTTON VALUE="  Add two numbers    " NAME=Addition>

<INPUT TYPE=BUTTON VALUE="Multiply two numbers" NAME=Multiply>

<BR>
<INPUT TYPE=BUTTON VALUE="Subtract two numbers" NAME=Subtract>

<INPUT TYPE=BUTTON VALUE=" Divide two numbers " NAME=Divide>

</CENTER>

</BODY>

</HTML>
```

11

ERROR HANDLING

11

ERROR HANDLING

Unfortunately, no matter how well you validate the data passed to your VBScript functions, it is not always possible to anticipate every circumstance. Therefore, a run-time error may still occur when the user accesses your Web page. VBScript provides the `On Error Resume Next` statement and the `Err` object to allow you to design your code to be able to not only bypass a run-time error, but also determine why the error occurred.

Handling Run-Time Errors

If VBScript encounters a run-time error, the processing may not continue, depending upon the error it encounters. To keep the user from receiving a run-time error, you can use the `On Error Resume Next` statement.

The `On Error Resume Next` statement indicates how VBScript should handle a run-time error. When you include this statement in your code, the user does not receive a run-time error. Execution continues with the statement following the statement that caused the error.

Although the `On Error Resume Next` statement prevents the user from seeing run-time errors, if one does occur there is still a problem that may require attention during the execution of the code. VBScript provides the `Err` object so you can monitor any errors that have occurred. It is your responsibility when designing your code, to determine where an error could potentially occur and to check the `Err` object at that location. For example, if you are performing a mathematical calculation, you should make sure that the value is calculated without any errors.

On Error Resume Next STATEMENT

Purpose Use the `On Error Resume Next` statement to keep run-time errors from displaying on the screen. When an error is encountered, program execution continues with the statement that immediately follows the statement that caused the run-time error.

Syntax `On Error Resume Next`

Description The `On Error Resume Next` statement causes the program to skip the statement that caused the run-time error and continue execution with the line following that statement. Although this ensures that the user will not be bothered with run-time error messages, it does not ensure that the user will receive the right results. For example, if the program skips a statement that is calculating values, obviously the correct value will not be returned.

Listing 11-1 illustrates how to place the `On Error Resume Next` statement in a simple program designed to convert a numeric value to an integer value. As illustrated in Figure 11-1, if a nonnumeric value is typed, the conversion does not occur. Since the conversion did not occur, the `UserValue` variable is empty, as indicated by the text in the dialog box.

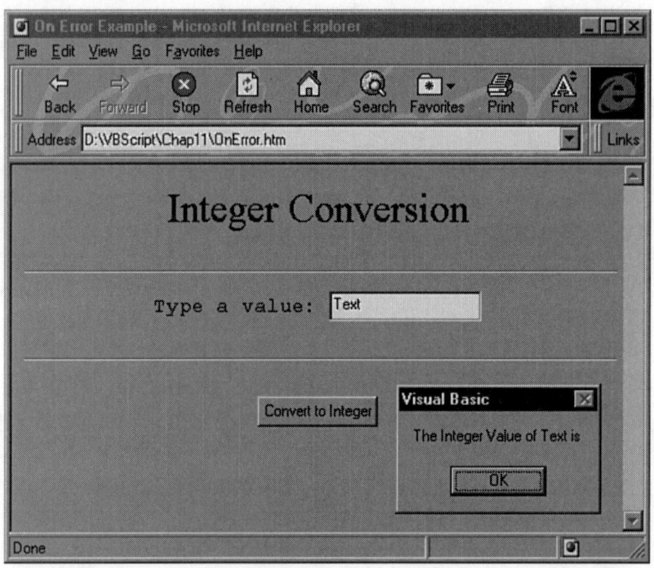

Figure 11-1 The `On Error Resume Next` statement causes VBScript to ignore the statement that caused a run-time error

Listing 11-1 Using the `On Error Resume Next` *statement*

```
<HTML>

<HEAD>
<TITLE>On Error Example</TITLE>

<SCRIPT LANGUAGE="VBScript">
<!--
'..........................................................
' ConvertInteger_OnClick()
' Converts the value typed by the user to an integer value.
'..........................................................
SUB ConvertInteger_OnClick()

  Dim UserValue

  On Error Resume Next

  UserValue = CInt(InputValue.Value)

  MsgBox "The Integer Value of " & InputValue.Value & " is " & UserValue

END SUB
-->

</SCRIPT>

</HEAD>

<BODY>

<CENTER>

<FONT SIZE=6>Integer Conversion<P>
</CENTER>
<HR>

<FONT SIZE=4>

<CENTER>
<PRE>Type a value: <INPUT NAME=InputValue SIZE=20>

<HR>
<INPUT TYPE=BUTTON VALUE="Convert to Integer" NAME="ConvertInteger">
</CENTER>

</FONT>

</BODY>

</HTML>
```

Example The Error Handling project, at the end of this chapter, uses the **`On Error Resume Next`** statement to make sure that any errors that occur do not display on the screen.

Comments If you don't use an `On Error Resume Next` statement in your code, any run-time error will cause an error message to display on the screen and execution of the program will stop.

The `On Error Resume Next` statement becomes inactive when another procedure is called; therefore, you should execute an `On Error Resume Next` statement in each called routine to ensure that error handling occurs within that routine.

Inline Error Handling

In order to use the `On Error Resume Next` statement, it is necessary to monitor the `Err` object so you can determine when an error has occurred and the type of the error. One way to monitor the `Err` object is to look at the `Err.Number` property; if it contains a value other than zero, an error has occurred. This checking should be performed at any location in the code where you anticipate a run-time error may occur. The method of handling errors as they occur is known as inline error handling.

Checking Error Results

The `Err` object maintains information about the last run-time error that occurred during the execution of your VBScript program. It is important to monitor the `Err` object to determine whether an error has occurred so that the appropriate steps can be taken to remedy the situation.

In order to gather information from the `Err` object, you need to use one of its associated properties or methods. The `Err` object and the properties and methods that can be used with it are covered in detail in the following sections.

`Err` OBJECT

Purpose The `Err` object maintains information about the last run-time error that occurred during execution of the VBScript code. Table 11-1 summarizes the properties that can be used with the `Err` object. Table 11-2 summarizes the methods that can be used with the `Err` object. A detailed description of each property and method follows the discussion of the `Err` object.

Syntax `Err.property` or `Err.method`

Table 11-1 Properties of the `Err` object

Use...	To Do This...
`Description`	Get a string expression that contains a description of the error.
`HelpContext`	Automatically display a topic from a specific help file.
`HelpFile`	Display a help file if the user presses the help button.
`Number`	Return or set a numeric value that specifies the error.
`Source`	Return or set the name of the application or object that generated the run-time error.

Table 11-2 Methods of the `Err` object

Use...	To Do This...
`Clear`	Clear the `Err` object after handling the error.
`Raise`	Use the `Err` object to generate a run-time error.

Description

The `Err` object maintains information about the last run-time error that occurred during the execution of the code. Each of the properties listed in Table 11-1 contains different information about the error. When a run-time error occurs, each of the properties of the `Err` object is filled with information that uniquely identifies the error.

You can use the `Raise` method if you want to generate a specific run-time error in your code. This may be necessary if you want to ensure that a specific type of information is passed to your procedure.

The `Clear` method is used to clear all the properties of the `Err` object after you have handled the error situation. This should be done each time you resolve an error situation. This ensures that all properties are empty if another error occurs.

The `Err` object's properties are also reset to `0` or zero-length strings (`""`) after an `On Error Resume Next` statement and after an `Exit Sub` or `Exit Function` statement occurs within an error-handling routine.

Example

The Error Handling project, at the end of this chapter, demonstrates how to use all of the properties and methods of the `Err` object.

Comments

The `Err` object properties and methods are covered in alphabetical order on the following pages. Examples are provided that illustrate how to use each of the properties and methods.

Clear Method

Purpose Use the `Clear` method to clear all the property settings of the `Err` object after handling an error.

Syntax `Err.Clear`

Description The `Clear` method allows you to clear all the properties of the `Err` object after a run-time error has occurred in your script. The properties of the `Err` object are set each time a run-time error occurs. It is necessary to clear the properties of the `Err` object once you have handled the error.

Listing 11-2 illustrates how to use the `Clear` method after a run-time error has occurred. The `MsgBox()` function initially displays the `Description` property, as illustrated in Figure 11-2. After the `Clear` method is called, the `MsgBox()` function displays the `Description` property to illustrate that it is now empty, as shown in Figure 11-3.

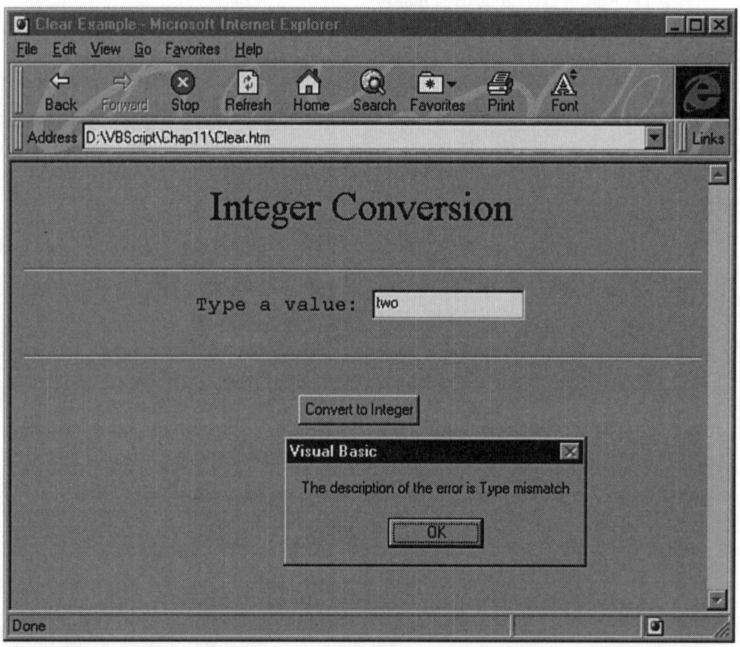

Figure 11-2 The `Err` object maintains information about the run-time error

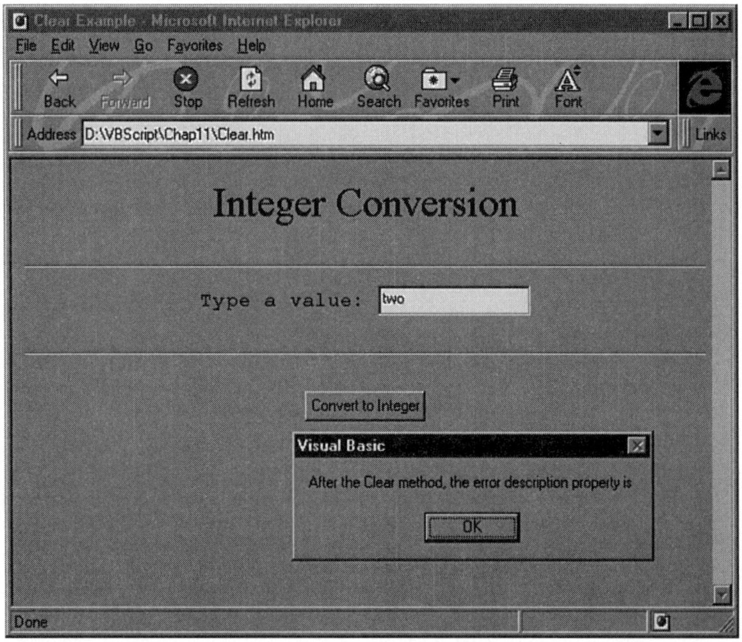

Figure 11-3 The `Clear` method clears all properties of the `Err` object

Listing 11-2 Using the `Clear` method

```
<HTML>

<HEAD>
<TITLE>Clear Example</TITLE>

<SCRIPT LANGUAGE="VBScript">
<!--
'.............................................................
' ConvertInteger_OnClick()
' Converts the value typed by the user to an integer value.
'.............................................................
SUB ConvertInteger_OnClick()

  Dim UserValue

  On Error Resume Next

  UserValue = CInt(InputValue.Value)

  MsgBox "The description of the error is " & Err.Description

  MsgBox "The Integer Value of " & InputValue.Value & " is " & UserValue

  Err.Clear

  MsgBox "After the Clear method, the error description property is " & Err.Description
```

continued on next page

continued from previous page

```
END SUB
-->

</SCRIPT>

</HEAD>

<BODY>

<CENTER>

<FONT SIZE=6>Integer Conversion<P>
</CENTER>
<HR>

<FONT SIZE=4>

<CENTER>
<PRE>Type a value: <INPUT NAME=InputValue SIZE=20></PRE>

<HR>
<INPUT TYPE=BUTTON VALUE="Convert to Integer" NAME="ConvertInteger">
</CENTER>

</FONT>

</BODY>

</HTML>
```

Example The Error Handling project, at the end of this chapter, uses the `Clear` method to clear all the properties of the `Err` object after resolving the run-time error.

Comments VBScript automatically executes the `Clear` method whenever it encounters an `On Error Resume Next`, `Exit Sub`, or `Exit Function` statement.

Objects Affected `Err`

`Description` PROPERTY

Purpose Use the `Description` property to either return or set the string associated with a run-time error. Although a description is automatically assigned to the `Description` property of the `Err` object when an error occurs, you may want to assign a more descriptive string to the property, as outlined in Table 11-3.

Syntax `Err.Description = expression`

Table 11-3 Argument of the `Description` property

Argument	Description
`expression`	A string expression that describes the error. This is an optional argument; if it is omitted, VBScript automatically assigns a string to this property.

Description

The **`Description`** property receives a string that describes the run-time error. Since this message may not always be the message you would like to display to the user, you can assign another message to the **`Description`** property of the **`Err`** object.

Listing 11-3 illustrates how to use the **`Description`** property to display the message assigned by VBScript for an error message, and to assign a different string to the **`Description`** property. The **`MsgBox()`** function first displays the error message that is placed in the **`Description`** property when a nonnumeric value is passed to a function that expects a numeric value, as illustrated in Figure 11-4. Then an **`If`** statement is used to see whether the type mismatch error occurred. Because this is error number 13, the **`Err.Number`** property is checked to see if it is **`13`**. If it is, the **`Err.Description`** property is changed to contain a string of text that is more descriptive, as illustrated in Figure 11-5.

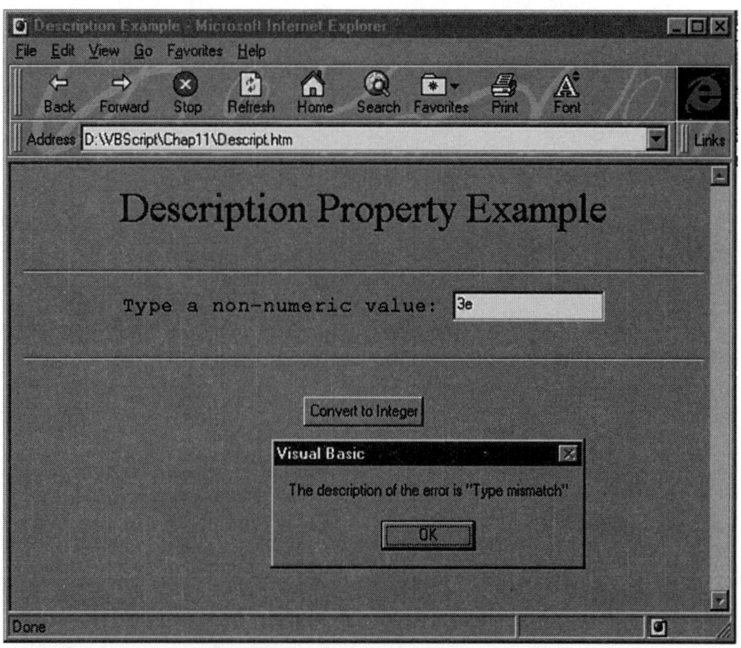

Figure 11-4 The **`Description`** property receives a string that describes the run-time error

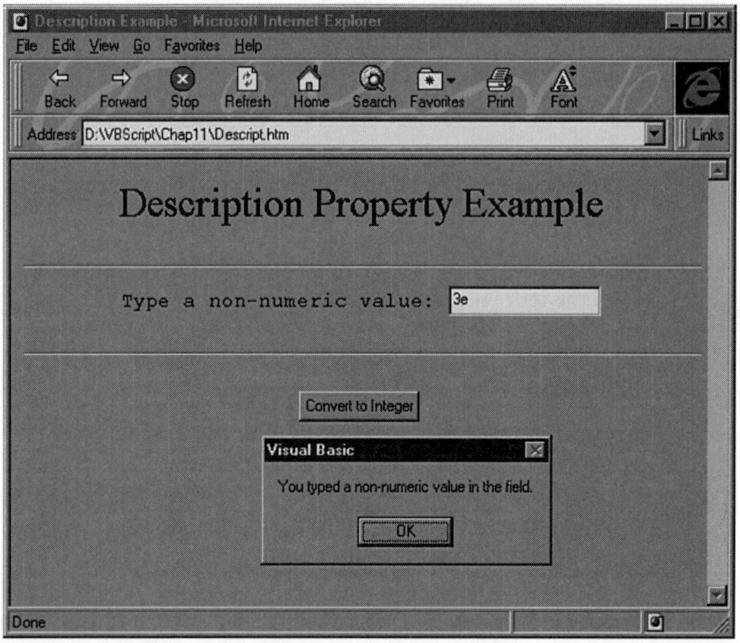

Figure 11-5 The `MsgBox()` function displays the error description that is assigned to the `Err.Description` property

Listing 11-3 Using the `Description` *property*

```
<HTML>

<HEAD>
<TITLE>Description Example</TITLE>

<SCRIPT LANGUAGE="VBScript">
<!--
'............................................................
' ConvertInteger_OnClick()
' Converts the value typed by the user to an integer value.
'............................................................
SUB ConvertInteger_OnClick()

  Dim UserValue

  On Error Resume Next

  UserValue = CInt(InputValue.Value)

  MsgBox "The description of the error is " & Chr(34) & Err.Description & Chr(34)

  If Err.Number = 13 Then

Err.Description = "You typed a non-numeric value in the field."
```

```
    MsgBox Err.Description
  Else

    MsgBox "The Integer Value of " & InputValue.Value & " is " & UserValue

  End If

END SUB
-->

</SCRIPT>

</HEAD>

<BODY>

<CENTER>

<FONT SIZE=6>Description Property Example<P>
</CENTER>
<HR>

<FONT SIZE=4>

<CENTER>
<PRE>Type a non-numeric value: <INPUT NAME=InputValue SIZE=20></PRE>

<HR>
<INPUT TYPE=BUTTON VALUE="Convert to Integer" NAME="ConvertInteger">
</CENTER>

</FONT>

</BODY>

</HTML>
```

Example The Error Handling project, at the end of this chapter, uses the `Description` property to both set and return the description of the run-time error that occurred.

Comments Use the `Description` property to alert the user about an error that you cannot or do not want to handle. When generating a user-defined error, assign a short description of your error to the `Description` property. If you do not assign a value to the `Description` property, and the value of the `Number` property corresponds to a VBScript run-time error, the string that corresponds to the run-time error is placed in the `Description` property when the error is generated.

Objects Affected `Err`

HelpContext PROPERTY

Purpose Use the `HelpContext` property to either return or set the context ID from the Microsoft Windows online help file that should display for the specified error. Table 11-4 identifies the optional argument that is used to set the context ID.

Syntax `Err.HelpContext = expression`

Table 11-4 Argument of the `HelpContext` property

Argument	Description
`expression`	A numeric expression that identifies the context ID of the topic in the Microsoft Windows online help file specified by the `HelpFile` property. This is an optional argument used when you want to set the context ID of a topic.

Description The `HelpContext` property keeps track of the context ID of the topic in the Microsoft Windows online help file that contains additional information about the specified error. You can use this property anytime you want to either return or set the context ID.

Listing 11-4 uses the `HelpContext` property to set the context ID for each of the error messages selected by the user. Once the property is set, the error description and number display in a dialog box using the `MsgBox()` function, as illustrated in Figure 11-6. The dialog box contains a Help button that can be selected to display the online help topic that describes this error, as illustrated in Figure 11-7.

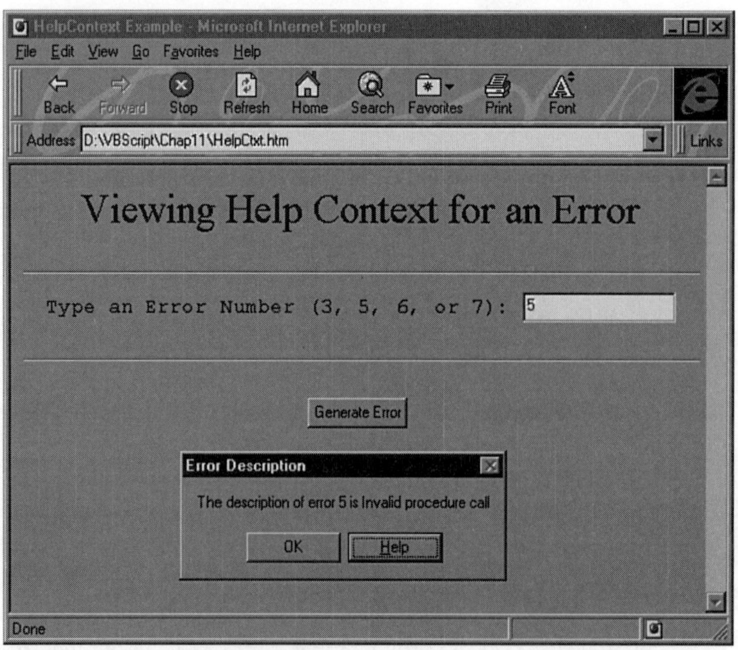

Figure 11-6 The dialog box identifies the error and contains a Help button that is pressed to view an online help description of the error

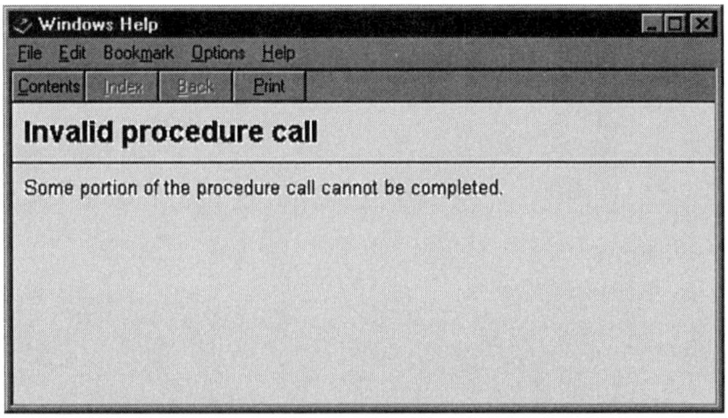

Figure 11-7 The topic specified by the `HelpContext` property displays when the Help button is pressed

Listing 11-4 Using the `HelpContext` *property*

```
<HTML>

<HEAD>
<TITLE>HelpContext Example</TITLE>

<SCRIPT LANGUAGE="VBScript">
<!--
'..........................................................
' GenerateError_OnClick()
' Creates the specified error, if it is one of the four errors
' the help file and context ID values are assigned.
'..........................................................
SUB GenerateError_OnClick()

  On Error Resume Next

  Err.Raise(InputValue.Value)

  Err.HelpFile = "d:\vbscript\chap11\ErrHelp.hlp"

  Select Case InputValue.Value

    Case 3
      Err.HelpContext = 1001

    Case 5
      Err.HelpContext = 1002

    Case 6
      Err.HelpContext = 1003

    Case 7
      Err.HelpContext = 1004

   End Select
```

continued on next page

continued from previous page

```
  MsgBox "The description of error " & Err.Number & " is " & Err.Description, 0, "Error ⇐
Description", Err.HelpFile, Err.HelpContext

  Err.Clear

END SUB
-->

</SCRIPT>

</HEAD>

<BODY>

<CENTER>

<FONT SIZE=6>Viewing Help Context for an Error<P>
</CENTER>
<HR>

<FONT SIZE=4>

<CENTER>
<PRE>Type an Error Number (3, 5, 6, or 7): <INPUT NAME=InputValue SIZE=20></PRE>

<HR>
<INPUT TYPE=BUTTON VALUE="Generate Error" NAME="GenerateError">
</CENTER>

</FONT>

</BODY>

</HTML>
```

Example The Error Handling project, at the end of this chapter, uses the `HelpContext` property to identify the context ID of the topic that describes the run-time error.

Comments If a help file and context ID are specified in the `HelpFile` and `HelpContext` properties for the error, the help file automatically displays when the user either selects the Help button in the error message dialog box or presses F1 on the keyboard.

Objects Affected `Err`

HelpFile PROPERTY

Purpose Use the `HelpFile` property to either return or set the path of the Microsoft Windows online help file that contains information about the error. Table 11-5 identifies the optional argument that can be used to set the path.

Syntax `Err.HelpFile = expression`

Table 11-5 Argument of the `HelpFile` property

Argument	Description
`expression`	A string expression that identifies the path of the Microsoft Windows online help file. This is an optional argument used when you want to set the path of the help file.

Description

The `HelpFile` property keeps track of the path and name of a Microsoft Windows online help file that contains additional information about the specified error. You can use this property anytime you want to either return the path and name of the help file or set the path and name of the help file.

Listing 11-5 uses the `HelpFile` property to assign a help file that is used when the user clicks the Help button requesting more information about the specified error. Figure 11-8 illustrates the Help button displayed on the dialog box that describes the error. When the Help button is selected, the specified help context in the help file displays on the screen, as illustrated in Figure 11-9.

Listing 11-5 Using the `HelpFile` property

```
<HTML>

<HEAD>
<TITLE>HelpFile Example</TITLE>

<SCRIPT LANGUAGE="VBScript">
<!--
'............................................................
' GenerateError_OnClick()
' Creates the specified error and assigns a help file and
' context ID.
'............................................................
SUB GenerateError_OnClick()

  On Error Resume Next

  Err.Raise(InputValue.Value)

  Err.HelpFile = "d:\vbscript\chap11\ErrHelp.hlp"

  Err.HelpContext = 1005

  MsgBox "The description of error " & Err.Number & " is " & Err.Description, 0,⇐
"Error Description", Err.HelpFile, Err.HelpContext

  Err.Clear

END SUB
-->

</SCRIPT>
```

continued on next page

continued from previous page

```
</HEAD>

<BODY>

<CENTER>

<FONT SIZE=6>Viewing Help Files for Error<P>
</CENTER>
<HR>

<FONT SIZE=4>

<CENTER>
<PRE>Type an Error Number: <INPUT NAME=InputValue SIZE=20>

<HR>
<INPUT TYPE=BUTTON VALUE="Generate Error" NAME="GenerateError">
</CENTER>

</FONT>

</BODY>

</HTML>
```

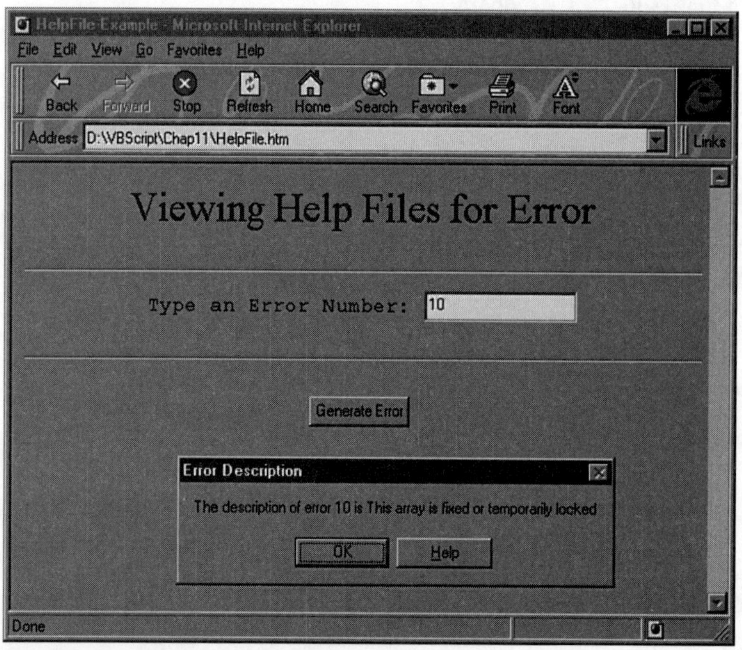

Figure 11-8 The dialog box contains a Help button

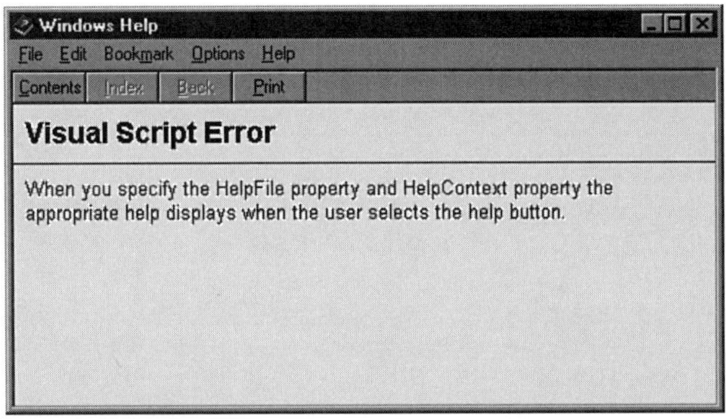

Figure 11-9 The `HelpFile` property identifies the name of the Microsoft Windows help file that displays when the user selects the Help button

Example The Error Handling project, at the end of this chapter, uses the `HelpFile` property to specify location of the Microsoft Windows online help file that contains information about the errors.

Comments If a help file is specified in the `HelpFile` property for the error, the help file automatically displays when the user either selects the Help button in the error message dialog box, or presses the F1 key on the keyboard. A valid context ID must also be specified in the `HelpContext` property.

Objects Affected `Err`

Number PROPERTY

Purpose Use the `Number` property to either return or set the error number associated with a run-time error. Although a number is automatically assigned to the `Number` property of the `Err` object when an error occurs, you may find that there are occasions when you want to assign an error number. The argument for assigning an error number is outlined in Table 11-6.

Syntax `Err.Number = expression`

Table 11-6 Argument of the Number property

Argument	Description
`expression`	An integer value that corresponds to either a VBScript error number or an OLE `SCode` error value. This is an optional argument; if it is omitted, VBScript automatically assigns the number that corresponds to the error to this property.

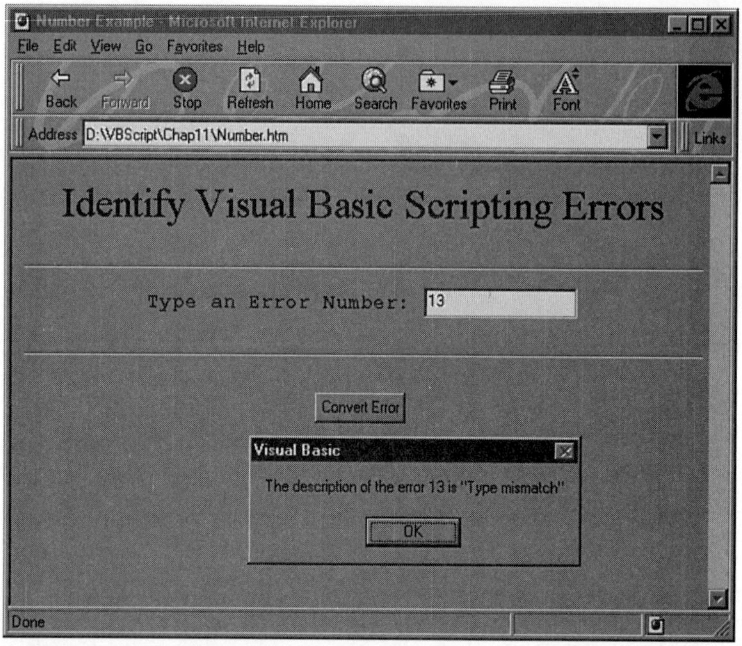

Figure 11-10 The **MsgBox()** function displays a description of the error number typed by the user

Description

The **Number** property identifies the run-time error number. This number can be any value within the range of 0 to 65,535. You can change the error number assigned to this property by using the argument expression outlined in Table 11-6 and assigning a valid VBScript or OLE **SCode** (status code) to the property.

Listing 11-6 uses the **Number** property to change the error number. The number is initially set to **2** using the **Raise** method. The **Number** property takes the error number input by the user and assigns it to the **Err** object as the new error. The **MsgBox()** displays the results of the **Number** property as illustrated in Figure 11-10.

Listing 11-6 Using the Number *property*

```
<HTML>

<HEAD>
<TITLE>Number Example</TITLE>

<SCRIPT LANGUAGE="VBScript">
<!--
```

```
'.............................................................
' ConvertError_OnClick()
' Identifies the error that was specified by the user.
'.............................................................
SUB ConvertError_OnClick()

  On Error Resume Next

  Err.Raise(2)

  Err.Number = CInt(InputValue.Value)

  MsgBox "The description of the error " & Err.Number & " is " & Chr(34) & ⇐
Err.Description & Chr(34)


END SUB
-->

</SCRIPT>

</HEAD>

<BODY>

<CENTER>

<FONT SIZE=6>Identify VBScript Errors<P>
</CENTER>
<HR>

<FONT SIZE=4>

<CENTER>
<PRE>Type an Error Number: <INPUT NAME=InputValue SIZE=20>

<HR>
<INPUT TYPE=BUTTON VALUE="Convert Error" NAME="ConvertError">
</CENTER>

</FONT>

</BODY>

</HTML>
```

Example The Error Handling project, at the end of this chapter, uses the `Number` property to identify the number of the error that occurred. The `Number` property is also used as a flag to determine whether or not an error occurred when the value was converted to an integer.

Comments When returning a user-defined error from an OLE automation object, set the `Number` property of the `Err` object by adding the error number to the constant `vbObjectError`. For example, you use the following code to return the number `1051` as an error code:

```
Err.Raise(vbObjectError + 1051)
```

An OLE `SCode` (status code) is a long integer value that you can use to pass detailed information to the caller of an interface member or API function. The status codes for OLE interfaces and APIs are defined in `FACILITY_ITF`.

Objects Affected `Err`

`Raise` METHOD

Purpose Use the `Raise` method with the `Err` object to generate the desired run-time error during execution of your VBScript code. Table 11-7 describes the arguments for the `Raise` method.

Syntax `Err.Raise(number, source, description, helpfile, helpcontext)`

Table 11-7 Arguments of the `Raise` method

Argument	Description
`number`	A long integer value that identifies the nature of the error. This value is assigned to the `Number` property of the `Err` object. All VBScript errors (including user-defined errors) are in the range of 0 to 65,535. This is a required argument for the `Raise` method.
`source`	A string expression that identifies the object or application that originally generated the error. This value is assigned to the `Source` property of the `Err` object. When setting this property for an OLE automation object, use the form `project.class`. This is an optional argument; if a value is not specified for the `source` argument, the programmatic ID of the current VBScript project is used.
`description`	A string expression that describes the specified error. This value is assigned to the `Description` property of the `Err` object. This is an optional argument; if a value is not specified for the `description` argument, VBScript checks the `number` argument. If the `number` argument identifies a valid VBScript run-time error code, the string provided by VBScript is assigned to the `Description` property. If there is not a VBScript error that corresponds to the `number` argument, a generic error message is assigned to the `Description` property.
`helpfile`	A string that identifies the path of the Microsoft Windows help file that contains online help about this error. This argument is assigned to the `HelpFile` property of the `Err` object. This is an optional argument.
`helpcontext`	The context ID of the topic within the help file specified by the `helpfile` argument that provides help for the error. This is an optional argument; if this argument is omitted, VBScript uses the context ID for the error specified by the `number` argument, if one exists.

Description

The **Raise** method allows you to generate a run-time error within your VBScript code. This allows you to create circumstances in which you require a specific type of data to be passed to your procedure. Although VBScript may not recognize a specific type of data as not valid, you can generate an error to inform the user that you will not accept that type of data.

Listing 11-7 uses the **Raise** method to generate the error specified by the user. The **MsgBox()** function displays the results of the **Raise** method by indicating the number and description of the error that was created, as illustrated in Figure 11-11.

Figure 11-11 The **MsgBox()** function displays the number and description of the error

Listing 11-7 Using the `Raise` method

```
<HTML>

<HEAD>
<TITLE>Raise Example</TITLE>

<SCRIPT LANGUAGE="VBScript">
<!--
'.............................................................
' ConvertError_OnClick()
' Identifies the error that was specified by the user.
'.............................................................
SUB ConvertError_OnClick()

  On Error Resume Next

  Err.Raise(InputValue.Value)

  MsgBox "The description of the error " & Err.Number & " is " & Chr(34) &⇐
Err.Description & Chr(34)

  Err.Clear

END SUB
-->

</SCRIPT>

</HEAD>

<BODY>

<CENTER>

<FONT SIZE=6>Identify VBScript Errors<P>
</CENTER>
<HR>

<FONT SIZE=4>

<CENTER>
<PRE>      Type an Error Number: <INPUT NAME=InputValue SIZE=20></PRE>

<HR>
<INPUT TYPE=BUTTON VALUE="Convert Error" NAME="ConvertError">
</CENTER>

</FONT>

</BODY>

</HTML>
```

Example The Error Handling project, at the end of this chapter, uses the `Raise` method to create a user-defined error when the user fails to type a value in the field before selecting the Check Answer button. The `Raise` method is used to generate an error informing the user that a value needs to be typed in the field.

Comments All the arguments for the `Raise` method are optional except the `number` argument. If you use the `Raise` method without previously using the `Clear` method to clear the properties of the `Err` object, any properties that are not reset by the `Raise` method will be part of the new error.

When returning a user-defined error from an OLE automation object, set the `Number` property of the `Err` object by adding the error number to the constant `vbObjectError`. For example, you use the following code to return the number `1051` as an error code:

```
Err.Raise(vbObjectError + 1051)
```

Objects Affected `Err`

Source PROPERTY

Purpose Use the `Source` property to either return or set the object or application that generated a run-time error. The argument for assigning the source of the error at run time is outlined in Table 11-8.

Syntax `Err.Source = expression`

Table 11-8 Argument of the Source property

Argument	Description
expression	A string expression that identifies the application or object that generated the error. This is an optional argument.

Description The `Source` property identifies the object or application that generated the run-time error. The `Source` property specifies a string expression that is usually the class name of the object that caused the error or the programmatic ID of the program code that caused the error.

Listing 11-8 uses the `Source` property to identify the application that generated the run-time error. Since the error that is generated is identified by the user, the `Source` property identifies the application that generated the error, as illustrated in Figure 11-12.

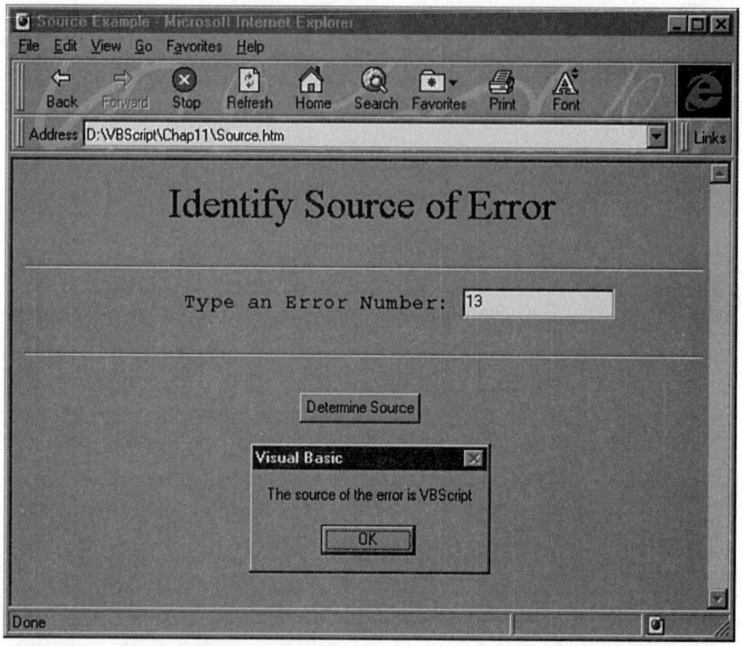

Figure 11-12 The `MsgBox()` function displays contents of the `Source` property after the error is generated

Listing 11-8 Using the `Source` *property*

```
<HTML>

<HEAD>
<TITLE>Source Example</TITLE>

<SCRIPT LANGUAGE="VBScript">
<!--
'..............................................................
' DetermineSource_OnClick()
' Identifies the source of an error when the error generated
' is specified by the user.
'..............................................................
SUB DetermineSource_OnClick()

  On Error Resume Next

  Err.Raise(InputValue.Value)

  MsgBox "The source of the error is " & Err.Source

  Err.Clear

END SUB
-->
```

```
</SCRIPT>

</HEAD>

<BODY>

<CENTER>

<FONT SIZE=6>Identify Source of Error<P>
</CENTER>
<HR>

<FONT SIZE=4>

<CENTER>
<PRE>     Type an Error Number: <INPUT NAME=InputValue SIZE=20>

<HR>
<INPUT TYPE=BUTTON VALUE="Determine Source" NAME="DetermineSource">
</CENTER>

</FONT>

</BODY>

</HTML>
```

Example The Error Handling project, at the end of this chapter, uses the `Source` property as the title of each dialog box that displays information about the error encountered.

Comments You can use the `Source` property to provide your users with information when your code is unable to handle an error generated in an accessed object. For example, if you access Microsoft Excel and it generates a division by zero error, Microsoft Excel sets the `Err.Number` property to its error code for that error and sets the `Source` property to `Excel.Application`. But if the error is generated in another object called by Microsoft Excel, Microsoft Excel intercepts the error and sets `Err.Number` to its own code for division by zero; however, the other `Err` object properties retain the values generated by the object that caused the error. In other words, the `Source` property of the `Err` object always contains the name of the object that originally generated the error.

When generating an error from within your VBScript code, the `Source` property is your application's programmatic ID. For OLE automation class modules, the `Source` property should contain a name having the form `project.class`.

Objects Affected `Err`

Error Handling Project

The Error Handling project creates a page where users can practice adding two numbers. The error handling statement, object, methods, and properties covered in this chapter are used to handle any errors that occur in this program.

Building the Project

1. Start the project by setting up the standard HTML template used for all VBScript examples in this book. Place the VBScript code in the **<HEAD>** section of the HTML code to keep everything consistent. Remember to place the HTML comment tags **<!--** and **-->** around the VBScript code so that it will be ignored by browsers that cannot interpret the **<SCRIPT>** tag.

```
<HTML>

<HEAD>
<TITLE>Error Handling Project</TITLE>

<SCRIPT LANGUAGE="VBScript">

<!--

-->

</SCRIPT>

</HEAD>

<BODY>

</BODY>

</HTML>
```

2. In the **<BODY>** section, create a title for the Web page. Because you are creating a page where the user can practice adding two numbers, call the page Adding Two Values. Use the **<HR>** tag to place a horizontal line under the title.

```
<BODY>
<FONT FACE="Arial" SIZE=2>

<CENTER>
   <FONT SIZE=6>Adding Two Values<P>
</CENTER>

<HR>
```

3. In the **<BODY>** section, create a table that contains two input fields where VBScript can place the two values to add. Be sure to place the addition sign (+) on the screen to remind users that they should add the values. The table should be similar to the one illustrated in Figure 11-13.

```
<CENTER>
<TABLE>
<TR><TD></TD><INPUT NAME=InputValue SIZE=10></TD></TR>
<TR><TD> + </TD><INPUT NAME=InputValue2 SIZE=10></TD></TR>
</TABLE>
</CENTER>
```

4. Also in the `<BODY>` section, create a table with one input field that will be used to receive the user's response to the equation. Use the `BORDER` and `FRAME` options to make the option stand out on the screen.

```
<CENTER>
<TABLE BORDER = 4 FRAME=BOX>
<TR><TD></TD><INPUT NAME=InputValue3 SIZE=10></TD></TR>
</TABLE>
</CENTER>
```

5. In the `<BODY>` section, create a button called Create Equation that will call the VBScript procedure `CreateEquation_OnClick()` when the user selects the button. Create another button called Check Answer that will call the `CheckAnswer_OnClick()` procedure when the button is pressed.

```
<BR>
<CENTER>
<INPUT TYPE=BUTTON VALUE=" Create Equation " NAME=CreateEquation>
<INPUT TYPE=BUTTON VALUE=" Check Answer " NAME=CheckAnswer>
</CENTER>

</BODY>

</HTML>
```

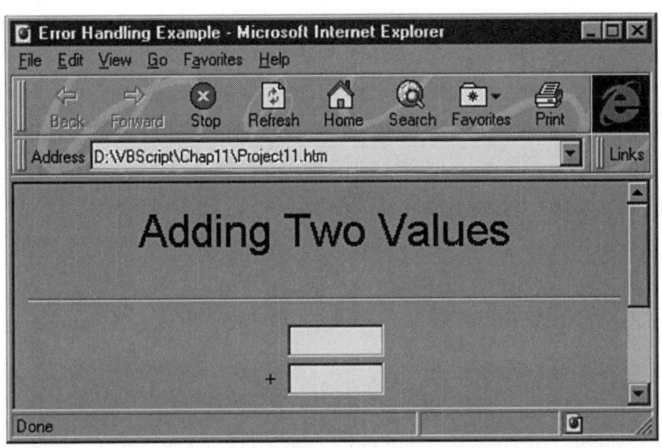

Figure 11-13 Create a table with input fields for the values

6. In the <SCRIPT> section, create a VBScript procedure called `CreateEquation_OnClick()`. This procedure executes when the Create Execute button is pressed, or when it is called from the `CheckAnswer_OnClick()` procedure. This procedure places a random number in input fields in the first table (`InputValue` and `InputValue2`). The `InputValue3.Value` field is cleared; this ensures that the field does not continue to hold the answer to a previous equation. To create the random numbers, use the `Randomize` statement to initialize the random number generator. Specify an upper and lower range limit for the random numbers created. In this program, you are creating numbers between 1 and 100. Then use the formulas below to create two random numbers and assign them to the appropriate field.

```
SUB CreateEquation_OnClick()

  Dim UpperLimit
  Dim LowerLimit

  UpperLimit = 100
  LowerLimit = 1

  Randomize

  InputValue.Value = CInt((UpperLimit - LowerLimit + 1) * Rnd + LowerLimit)

  InputValue2.Value = CInt((UpperLimit - LowerLimit + 1) * Rnd + LowerLimit)

  InputValue3.Value = " "

END SUB
```

7. Create a procedure called `CheckAnswer_OnClick()` that is executed when the Check Answer button is selected. This procedure is designed to see if the correct answer was given for the equation. Since there are several parts to this procedure, you are going to build it in steps. First, determine the actual sum of the two values displayed on the screen. Next, convert the user's response to an integer value and assign it to the variable `UserResponse`. Check to see whether the response is correct and notify the user of the results.

```
SUB CheckAnswer_OnClick()

  Dim UserContinue
  Dim UserResponse
  Dim ActualSum
.
.
.
     ActualSum = CInt(InputValue.Value) + CInt(InputValue2.Value)

     UserResponse = CInt(InputValue3.Value)

     If UserResponse = ActualSum Then

        UserContinue = MsgBox("That is correct!  Do you want do more addition?", 259,⇐
"Math Facts")
```

```
     Else

         UserContinue = MsgBox("INCORRECT! The sum is " & ActualSum & " Do you want to try
another?", 259, "Math Facts")

     End If
.
.
.
END SUB
```

8. At the end of the `CheckAnswer_OnClick()` procedure, add an `If` statement that checks to see whether the user responded Yes to the dialog boxes. If so, the `CreateEquation_OnClick()` procedure is called to generate two new values.

```
SUB CheckAnswer_OnClick()
.
.
.
If UserContinue = 6 Then

        Call CreateEquation_OnClick

     End If

END SUB
```

9. Now the only thing missing from the `CheckAnswer_OnClick()` procedure is error handling. Unfortunately, you cannot guarantee that the user will always type a numeric value in the field, so you need to create some error handling routines. At the top of the procedure, after the variable declarations, add the `On Error Resume Next` statement. Next, you want to create a special error type when the user leaves the `InputValue3.Value` field blank. Check to see whether the field contains a blank string. If so, use the `Raise` method to create an error with a value of `1`. Assign a description to the `Description` property, and make the appropriate `HelpFile` and `HelpContext` property assignments, if you have a help file. Use the `MsgBox()` function to display a message about the error, as illustrated in Figure 11-14. If you have a valid help file and context ID, the Help button displays so that the user can get additional information about the error, as illustrated in Figure 11-15. Remember to use the `Clear` method to clear the properties of the `Err` object and then exit the procedure. You are exiting the procedure at this point so that the user has the opportunity to type a value in the field before processing occurs.

```
SUB CheckAnswer_OnClick()

   Dim UserContinue
   Dim UserResponse
   Dim ActualSum

   On Error Resume Next

   If InputValue3.Value = " " Then
```

continued on next page

continued from previous page

```
    Err.Raise(1)
    Err.Description = "A value was not typed."
    Err.HelpFile = "d:\vbscript\chap11\proj11.hlp"
    Err.HelpContext = 1001
    MsgBox "Error " & Err.Number & " occurred. This means " & Err.Description, 0,⇐
Err.Source, Err.HelpFile, Err.HelpContext

    Err.Clear

    Exit Sub

  End If

.
.
.
END SUB
```

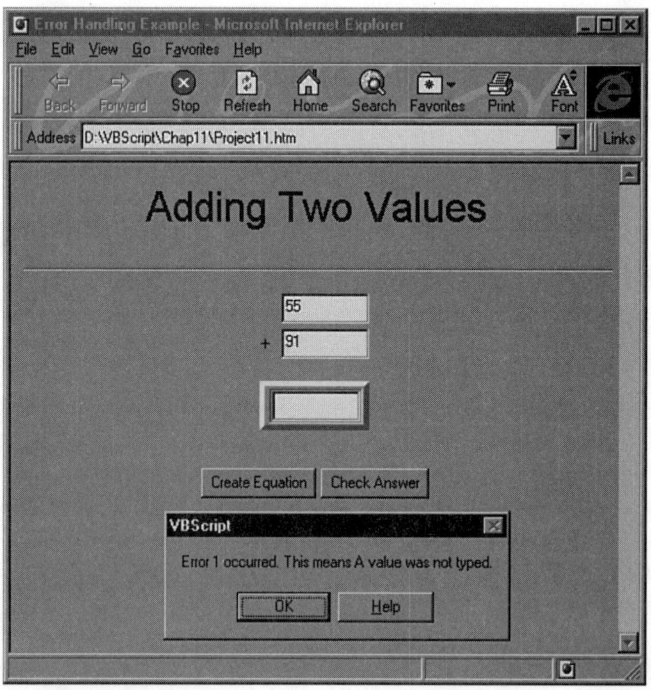

Figure 11-14 The error number and message display in the dialog box with the option to view the online help

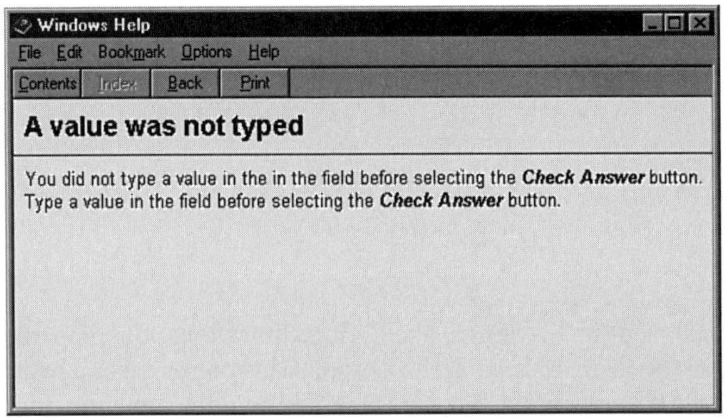

Figure 11-15 The online help for an error code of `1`

10. Now you want to add the ability to check for other types of error messages. After the statement where the value typed by the user is converted to an integer, you need to check for errors. Use an `If` statement to see whether the `Number` property of the `Err` object has a value other than `0`. If so, an error has occurred and you need to check it. The most common error that occurs at this location is number 13, a type mismatch error. This occurs when a nonnumeric value is typed in the field. A special help topic that describes this error is created, so if `13` is the value of the `Number` property, a value `1002` is assigned to the `HelpContext` property. Otherwise, `1003` is assigned to the `HelpContext` property. Display a dialog box that describes the error, as illustrated in Figure 11-16. Remember to use the `Clear` method to clear the properties of the `Err` object before exiting the procedure.

```
SUB CheckAnswer_OnClick()
.
.
.
     UserResponse = CInt(InputValue3.Value)

     If Err.Number <> 0 Then

       Err.HelpFile = "d:\vbscript\chap11\proj11.hlp"

       If Err.Number = 13 Then

         Err.HelpContext = 1002

       Else

         Err.HelpContext = 1003

       End If

       MsgBox "Error " & Err.Number & " occurred. This means " & Err.Description, 0,⇐
Err.Source, Err.HelpFile, Err.HelpContext
```

continued on next page

continued from previous page

```
        Err.Clear
        Exit Sub

    End If
.
.
.
END SUB
```

How It Works

The Error Handling project is designed to illustrate how to use the properties and methods of the **Err** object covered in this chapter. This project takes a basic program designed to have the user type a numeric value, and uses the properties of the **Err** object to determine when the user entered the wrong type of information. Figure 11-17 illustrates the completed Error Handling project, and Listing 11-9 shows the complete source code.

The first error handling routine illustrates how to create a user-defined error using the **Raise** method. The **If** statement checks to see whether the user typed a value in the field; if it is blank, an error is created. All of the properties of the **Err** object are used to display information about the error that occurred. The **Number** and **Description** properties are displayed in the message. The **Source** property is the title of the dialog box, and the **HelpFile** and **HelpContext** properties identify the help file topic that displays when the user selects the Help button.

The second error handling routine is placed after VBScript attempts to convert the value typed by the user to an integer. This **If** statement checks to see whether an error occurred during the conversion, by checking the value of the **Number** property. If the value of the property is not **0**, an error occurred. Another **If** statement checks to see whether the error is **13**. Since the most common error that will occur at this location is a type mismatch error (error 13), you are checking for that error. If the **Number** property equals **13**, the **HelpContext** property is assigned the value of **1002**, because this topic describes how to deal with a type mismatch. Otherwise, the **HelpContext** property is assigned the value of **1003**, a topic about other run-time errors.

Remember to use the **Clear** method after dealing with each error. This resets all of the properties of the **Err** object. Also, each time an error is encountered, the **Exit Sub** statement is used to exit the procedure. If an error occurs, you do not want to continue processing the values.

This project also uses a Windows online help file for displaying additional help information about the error that occurred. Several applications on the market can be used to create these files. The RTF and project files for the help files are included with the sample code on the CD.

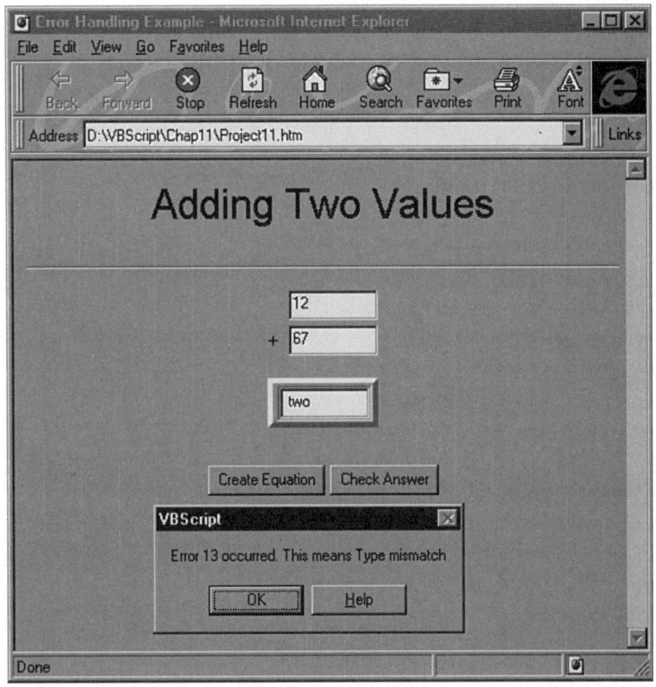

Figure 11-16 The dialog box displays the error message encountered after the attempt to convert the value to an integer

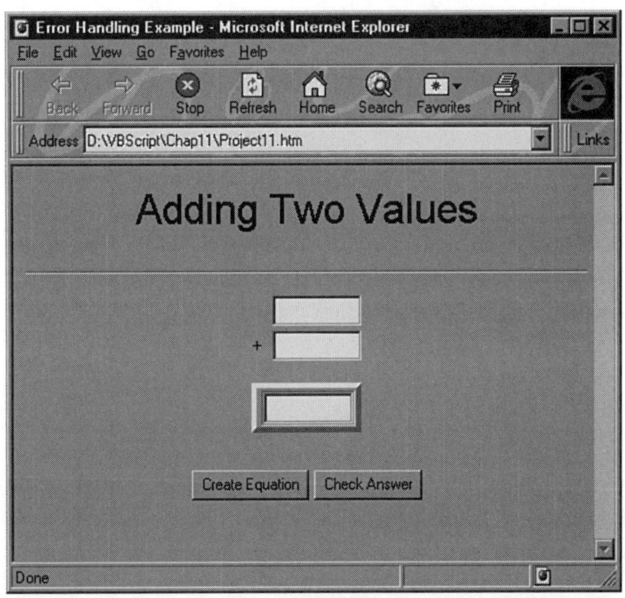

Figure 11-17 The completed Error Handling project

Listing 11-9 Complete source code for the Error Handling project

```
<HTML>

<HEAD>
<TITLE>Error Handling Example</TITLE>

<SCRIPT LANGUAGE="VBScript">

'...................................................
' CreateEquation_OnClick()
' Called when the Create Equation button is pressed.
' This procedure generates the two values used to
' create the equation.
'...................................................
SUB CreateEquation_OnClick()

  Dim UpperLimit
  Dim LowerLimit

'...................................................
' Specify the upper and lower range for the random
' numbers.
'...................................................
  UpperLimit = 100
  LowerLimit = 1

  Randomize

'...................................................
' Generate the random numbers. Be sure to clear any
' value that may have been typed in the result field
' (InputValue3).
'...................................................
  InputValue.Value = CInt((UpperLimit - LowerLimit + 1) * Rnd + LowerLimit)

  InputValue2.Value = CInt((UpperLimit - LowerLimit + 1) * Rnd + LowerLimit)

  InputValue3.Value = " "

END SUB
'...................................................
' CheckAnswer_OnClick()
' Called when the Check Answer button is pressed. This
' procedure checks for any errors, and then determines
' if the correct value was typed in the result field.
'...................................................
SUB CheckAnswer_OnClick()

  Dim UserContinue
  Dim UserResponse
  Dim ActualSum

'...................................................
' Remember to use the On Error Resume Next statement to
' ensure that the user does not receive a system
' run-time error message. Check for errors and
' notify the user at the appropriate location.
'...................................................
```

```
  On Error Resume Next

'.......................................................
' Use the Raise method to create a user-
' defined error of 1, if the result field is left blank.
' If this condition occurs, notify the user and
' exit the procedure.
'........................................................
  If InputValue3.Value = " " Then

    Err.Raise(1)
    Err.Description = "A value was not typed."
    Err.HelpFile = "d:\vbscript\chap11\proj11.hlp"
    Err.HelpContext = 1002
    MsgBox "Error " & Err.Number & " occurred. This means " & Err.Description, 0,⇐
Err.Source, Err.HelpFile, Err.HelpContext

    Err.Clear

    Exit Sub

  End If

'.......................................................
' Determine the actual sum of the equation.
'.......................................................
     ActualSum = CInt(InputValue.Value) + CInt(InputValue2.Value)

'.......................................................
' Convert the value typed in the result field to an
' integer value.
'.......................................................
     UserResponse = CInt(InputValue3.Value)

'.......................................................
' Check for an error condition. If one occurred, identify
' the proper error topic to display from the help file
' and then notify the user of the error. Remember to
' use the Clear method to clear the Err object before
' exiting the procedure.
'.........................................................
     If Err.Number <> 0 Then

       Err.HelpFile = "d:\vbscript\chap11\proj11.hlp"

       If Err.Number = 13 Then

         Err.HelpContext = 1002

       Else

         Err.HelpContext = 1003

       End If

       MsgBox "Error " & Err.Number & " occurred. This means " & Err.Description, 0,⇐
Err.Source, Err.HelpFile, Err.HelpContext
```

continued on next page

continued from previous page

```
        Err.Clear
        Exit Sub

      End If

'............................................
' If there are no errors, check to see if the
' answer is correct and notify the user.
'............................................
      If UserResponse = ActualSum Then

         UserContinue = MsgBox("That is correct!  Do you want to do more addition?", 259,⇐
"Math Facts")

      Else

         UserContinue = MsgBox("INCORRECT! The sum is " & ActualSum & " Do you want to try⇐
another?", 259, "Math Facts")

      End If

'............................................
' If the user selected the Yes button on the
' dialog box, call the CreateEquation_OnClick
' procedure to create a new equation.
'.............................................
      If UserContinue = 6 Then

         Call CreateEquation_OnClick

      End If

END SUB


</SCRIPT>

</HEAD>

<BODY>
<FONT FACE="Arial" SIZE=2>

<CENTER>
   <FONT SIZE=6>Adding Two Values<P>
</CENTER>

<HR>

<CENTER>
<TABLE>
<TR><TD></TD><INPUT NAME=InputValue SIZE=10></TD></TR>
<TR><TD> + </TD><INPUT NAME=InputValue2 SIZE=10></TD></TR>
</TABLE>
</CENTER>

<CENTER>
<TABLE BORDER = 4 FRAME=BOX>
<TR><TD></TD><INPUT NAME=InputValue3 SIZE=10></TD></TR>
```

```
</TABLE>
</CENTER>

<BR>
<CENTER>
<INPUT TYPE=BUTTON VALUE=" Create Equation " NAME=CreateEquation>
<INPUT TYPE=BUTTON VALUE=" Check Answer " NAME=CheckAnswer>
</CENTER>

</BODY>

</HTML>
```

12

ADDING OBJECTS

12

ADDING OBJECTS

One of the most powerful features of VBScript is the ability it gives you to work with objects. This chapter shows you how to use VBScript to modify at run time the properties of objects such as ActiveX controls and Java applets.

What Is an Object?

The word *object* is probably one of the most widely used terms when dealing with Web pages. Several different elements are referred to as objects:

- An OLE object, such as an ActiveX control or OLE document.
- A Java applet.
- A media file, such as an AVI or a GIF file.
- The elements that make up the actual Web page (that is, `Window`, `Document`, `Location`, and so on). For more information about these types of objects, refer to Chapter 15, Internet Explorer Object Model for Scripting.

The first two object types, ActiveX (OLE) controls and Java applets, are forms of application objects. These types of objects are basically just self-contained applications that provide specific functionality when called by another application. Use of these objects allows you to give some specific functionality to your Web page without extensive coding.

For example, Microsoft has developed an ActiveX control that allows you to rotate text on the screen. You can simply embed this ActiveX control within your HTML page and modify its parameters to make the desired text rotations instead of developing your own code to accomplish the same result.

ActiveX Controls

ActiveX is a set of technologies developed by Microsoft that help you add interactive content to your HTML Web pages. ActiveX builds upon Microsoft's previous object linking and embedding (OLE) technology, so current Visual Basic and Visual C++ programmers will have no problem working with ActiveX.

By using ActiveX controls, you can add multimedia effects and interactive objects, and embed other applications directly into your Web page.

An ActiveX control is a precompiled application that exists on the user's machine. When you create your Web page, you can specify a URL for the control, so that if it does not already exist on the user's machine, it will be downloaded when he or she accesses your page the first time. Once the control exists on the user's machine, it is used each time he or she accesses a Web page that requires it.

Embedding ActiveX Controls

ActiveX controls are embedded into your HTML page using the `<OBJECT>` and `<PARAM>` elements. The `<OBJECT>` element is used to identify the name of the control. The `<PARAM>` element is used to indicate the initial parameters for the control. The attributes in Table 12-1 can be set for each object, although each object may not use all of these attributes.

Table 12-1 Attributes of the `<OBJECT>` element

Attribute	Description
`CLASSID = "CLSID: id"`	Identifies the object that is being inserted into the HTML document. This attribute is a unique identifier for the control that is based upon the Component Object Model (COM) "class id" URL naming scheme. When embedding an ActiveX control, the attribute always resembles the following: `CLASSID="CLSID:79176FB0-B7F2-11CE-97EF-00AA006D2776"` (the string of values after the colon is unique to identify the object); otherwise, the `CLSID` value is not used with other types of controls.
`CODEBASE = "URL"`	Identifies the codebase for the object. The syntax of the URL depends on the object. Some URL schemes require an additional URL, other than the one specified by the `CLASSID` attribute, to identify the implementation.
`DECLARE`	Used to declare but not instantiate the object.
`ID = "objectID"`	A unique name that can be used to reference the object. For example, to modify an object value using VBScript, you use the `ID` attribute to reference the object.
`CODETYPE = "codetype"`	Specifies the Internet media type for the code specified by the `CLASSID` attribute.
`DATA = "objectdata"`	Points to the address of the data stream that is used to initialize the state of the object.
`TYPE = "datatype"`	Specifies the Internet media type for the data specified by the `DATA` attribute.
`STANDBY = "waittext"`	A string of text that displays while the browser loads the object.
`WIDTH = "widthvalue"`	Specifies the width of the object.

<table>
<tr><th>Attribute</th><th>Description</th></tr>
<tr><td><code>HEIGHT = "heightvalue"</code></td><td>Specifies the height of the object.</td></tr>
<tr><td><code>ALIGN = "alignment"</code></td><td>Specifies the alignment of the object on the page. The following alignment values can be used with this attribute:
<table>
<tr><th>Value</th><th>Description</th></tr>
<tr><td><code>TEXTTOP</code></td><td>The object is aligned with the top of the current font.</td></tr>
<tr><td><code>MIDDLE</code></td><td>The middle of the object is vertically aligned with the baseline.</td></tr>
<tr><td><code>TEXTMIDDLE</code></td><td>The middle of the object is vertically aligned with the position that is midway between the baseline and the height of a lowercase x in the current font.</td></tr>
<tr><td><code>BASELINE</code></td><td>The bottom of the object is vertically aligned with the baseline of the line of text.</td></tr>
<tr><td><code>TEXTBOTTOM</code></td><td>The bottom of the object is vertically aligned with the bottom of the current font.</td></tr>
<tr><td><code>LEFT</code></td><td>The object is moved down and over to the current left margin.</td></tr>
<tr><td><code>CENTER</code></td><td>The object is moved down and centered between the right and left margins.</td></tr>
<tr><td><code>RIGHT</code></td><td>The object is moved down and over to the current right margin.</td></tr>
</table></td></tr>
<tr><td><code>BORDER = "bordervalue"</code></td><td>The size of the border that displays around the object.</td></tr>
<tr><td><code>HSPACE = "hvalue"</code></td><td>Specifies the horizontal spacing for the object.</td></tr>
<tr><td><code>VSPACE = "vvalue"</code></td><td>Specifies the vertical spacing for the object.</td></tr>
<tr><td><code>USEMAP = "URL"</code></td><td>The uniform resource locator of the client-side image map. This attribute is used with static images.</td></tr>
<tr><td><code>SHAPES</code></td><td>Indicates that the object contains anchors with hypertext links.</td></tr>
<tr><td><code>NAME = "URL"</code></td><td>Specifies the name of the object when submitted as part of a form.</td></tr>
</table>

ActiveX Control Properties

The HTML **<PARAM>** element is used to set the initial values of the properties for the ActiveX control. The **<PARAM>** element has two attributes, shown in Table 12-2, which are used to specify a name and an initial value for the parameter.

Table 12-2 Attributes of the <PARAM> element

Attribute	Description
`NAME = "property name"`	Specifies the name of the property whose initial value is being defined
`VALUE = "initial value"`	Specifies the initial value for the specified property

Listing 12-1 illustrates how an ActiveX control is embedded within an HTML page. The control used in this example is the Microsoft Label control, as illustrated in Figure 12-1. This control allows you to rotate text that is displayed on the screen. The **<PARAM>** elements indicate the initial values for the properties. The property values of an ActiveX control cannot be modified by HTML; that requires a scripting language, such as VBScript.

Listing 12-1 Embedding an ActiveX control in HTML

```
<HTML>
<HEAD>

<OBJECT
       classid="clsid:99B42120-6EC7-11CF-A6C7-00AA00A47DD2"
       id=lblActiveLbl
       width=100
       height=850
       align=left
       hspace=20
       vspace=0
>
<PARAM NAME="_extentX" VALUE="550">
<PARAM NAME="_extentY" VALUE="700">
<PARAM NAME="Angle" VALUE="45">
<PARAM NAME="Alignment" VALUE="2">
<PARAM NAME="BackStyle" VALUE="0">
<PARAM NAME="Caption" VALUE="Text">
<PARAM NAME="FontName" VALUE="Arial">
<PARAM NAME="FontSize" VALUE="20">
<PARAM NAME="FontBold" VALUE="1">
<PARAM NAME="FrColor" VALUE="0">
</OBJECT>

</HEAD>

<BODY>

</BODY>

</HTML>
```

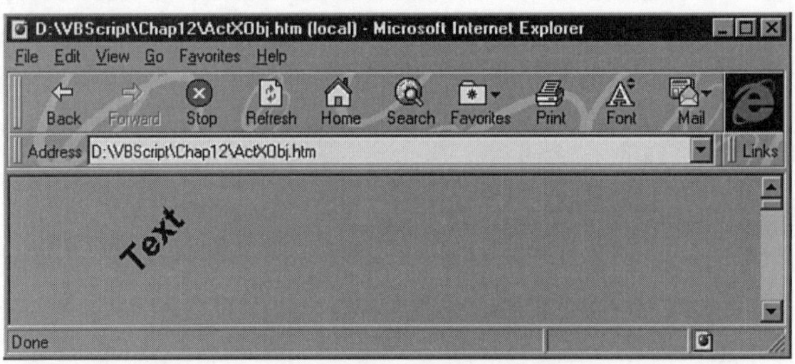

Figure 12-1 The Label control rotates text that displays on the screen

Using the ActiveX Control Pad

You can use any text editor to create an HTML page and add ActiveX controls to the page. To simplify the process of working with ActiveX controls, Microsoft has created a tool called the Microsoft ActiveX Control Pad. This tool is available from the Microsoft Web site or on the CD included with this book.

The ActiveX Control Pad allows you to easily select an ActiveX control to be placed on your Web page. This tool locates all of the controls on your machine and places them in a list to select from, as illustrated in Figure 12-2.

Once you select a control, a window displays the properties that you can set for the control. Another window illustrates how the object will look on the screen. For example, the same label that is used in Listing 12-1 is illustrated in Figure 12-3. Once you specify the values for the properties, the control is added to the Web page.

As mentioned earlier, the ActiveX Control Pad is an optional tool that you can use to create Web pages with ActiveX controls. It is not necessary to use this tool; you can easily type the necessary control information into your Web page.

Java Applets

Because it adds sophistication to your Web page not available with basic HTML, Java has recently become one of the most popular development languages. Originally developed by Sun Microsystems, there are now several different Java development environments on the market. For example, Microsoft has recently released its own Java environment called J++.

A Java applet is a compiled Java program that can be referenced by an HTML page and executed if the page is loaded by a Java-compatible browser. An applet is similar

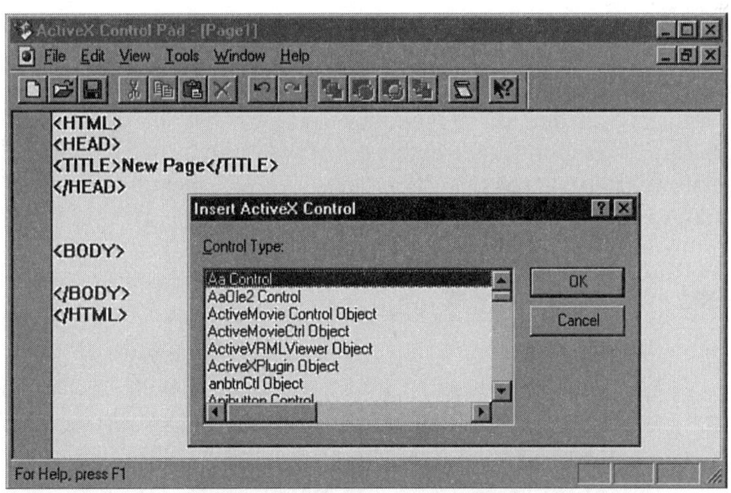

Figure 12-2 The Microsoft ActiveX Control Pad can be used to quickly add an ActiveX control to your HTML code

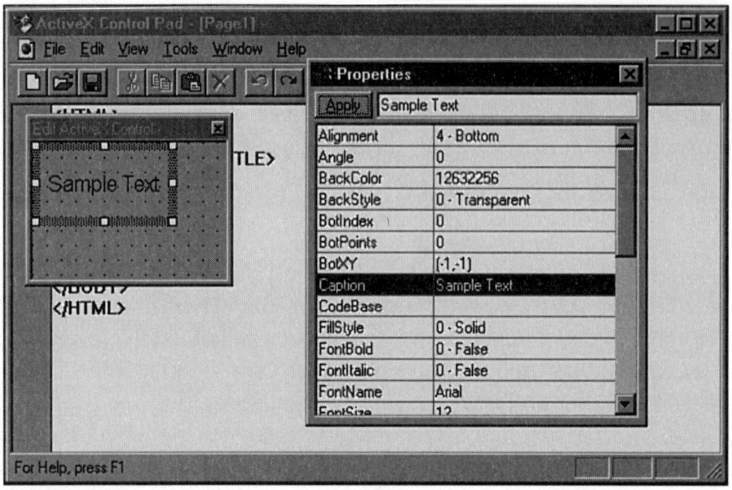

Figure 12-3 The Microsoft ActiveX Control Pad provides the ability to quickly adjust the properties of a control

to an ActiveX control in that it also allows you to add interactive content to your HTML Web pages. The main difference is that the Java applet is downloaded from the server each time the page is viewed. When you use a Java applet, the user does not store it on his or her machine like an ActiveX control. Downloading the applet every time it is run allows the code to remain up to date and does not require the client to manage any storage space. The disadvantage of an applet is the time required for downloading each time the page is viewed. For users accessing the page with slower modems, this could become a great frustration.

Inserting Applets into HTML

Java applets are embedded into your HTML page using the `<APPLET>` element. The `<APPLET>` element is used to identify the name and location of the applet. The `<PARAM>` element, the attributes of which are outlined in Table 12-2, is used with this element to indicate the initial parameters for the applet. Table 12-3 identifies the attributes that can be set for each applet using the `<APPLET>` element.

Table 12-3 Attributes of the <APPLET> element

Attribute	Description
CODEBASE = "URL"	Specifies the location of the applet. If this attribute is not specified, the URL of the HTML document is used.
CODE = "filename"	Identifies the name of the file that contains the applet subclass. This is a required attribute. The file should be located in the location specified by the CODEBASE attribute.
ALT = "text"	Identifies the text that should be displayed if the browser cannot run Java applets.
NAME = "appletname"	Specifies a name for the applet, so that other applets on the same page can locate it.
WIDTH = "pixels"	Specifies the initial width of the applet display area. This is a required attribute.

Attribute	Description
HEIGHT = "pixels"	Specifies the initial height of the applet display area. This is a required attribute.
ALIGN = alignment	Specifies the alignment of the applet with respect to other information on the page. This is a required attribute. The following values can be used with this attribute: **Value** — **Description** TOP — Text is aligned to the top of the applet. MIDDLE — Text is aligned to the middle of the applet. BOTTOM — Text is aligned to the bottom of the applet. LEFT — The applet is left aligned, and text flows around it. RIGHT — The applet is right aligned, and text flows around it.
VSPACE = "pixels"	Specifies the number of pixels above and below the applet.
HSPACE = "pixels"	Specifies the number of pixels on each side of the applet.

Listing 12-2 illustrates how a Java applet is embedded within an HTML page using the **<APPLET>** element. The applet used in this example is a bar chart applet developed by Sun Microsystems. Figure 12-4 illustrates how this applet displays on an HTML page.

Listing 12-2 Embedding a Java applet

```
<HTML>
<HEAD>
<TITLE>Java Applet</TITLE>

<applet code="chart.class" name="BarChart" width=251 height=125>

<param name=c2_color value="green">
<param name=c2_label value="Q2">
<param name=c1_style value="striped">
<param name=c4 value="30">
<param name=c3 value="5">
<param name=c2 value="20">
<param name=c4_color value="yellow">
<param name=c1 value="10">
<param name=c4_label value="Q4">
<param name=title value="Performance">
<param name=c3_style value="striped">
<param name=columns value="4">
<param name=c1_color value="blue">
<param name=c1_label value="Q1">
<param name=c3_color value="magenta">
<param name=c3_label value="Q3">
<param name=c2_style value="solid">
<param name=orientation value="horizontal">
<param name=c4_style value="solid">
<param name=scale value="5">

</applet>
</HEAD>
<BODY>


</BODY>
</HTML>
```

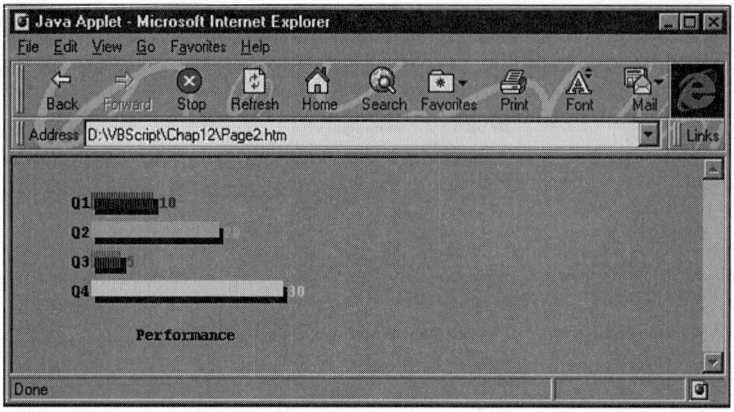

Figure 12-4 Java applets are embedded using the `<APPLET>` element

Changing Object Properties with VBScript

Unfortunately, with HTML you are unable to modify the properties of an object after it has been loaded on your Web page. This is where VBScript becomes a very valuable tool. By using VBScript you can easily modify the properties of an ActiveX control or a Java applet after the Web page is loaded.

In order to change the property value of an object, the control must have been defined with the following items:

- The `ID` attribute must be used with the `<OBJECT>` element to assign a name to the control.
- The `NAME` attribute must be used with the `<PARAM>` element to identify the name of the attribute so that VBScript can reference it.

Using VBScript with your objects can make your Web pages come alive. For example, you can modify the code in Listing 12-1 so that the user can specify the angle for the text, as illustrated in Listing 12-3. When the user types a new value in the field and then presses the button, the text is rotated to the specified angle, as illustrated in Figure 12-5.

Listing 12-3 Changing the properties of an ActiveX control

```
<HTML>

<HEAD>

<SCRIPT LANGUAGE="VBScript">
<!--
```

```
'.......................................................
' RotText_OnClick()
'
' Rotates the text to the specified angle.
'......................................................

SUB RotText_OnClick()

'......................................................
' Make sure that the value typed by the user is numeric.
'......................................................
  If IsNumeric(NewAngle.Value) Then

    lblActiveLbl.Angle = NewAngle.Value

  Else
    MsgBox "Enter a Numeric Value"
  End If

END SUB

</SCRIPT>

<OBJECT
       classid="clsid:99B42120-6EC7-11CF-A6C7-00AA00A47DD2"
       id=lblActiveLbl
       width=200
       height=850
       align=left
       hspace=20
       vspace=0
>
<PARAM NAME="_extentX" VALUE="550">
<PARAM NAME="_extentY" VALUE="700">
<PARAM NAME="Angle" VALUE="45">
<PARAM NAME="Alignment" VALUE="2">
<PARAM NAME="BackStyle" VALUE="0">
<PARAM NAME="Caption" VALUE="Sample Text">
<PARAM NAME="FontName" VALUE="Arial">
<PARAM NAME="FontSize" VALUE="20">
<PARAM NAME="FontBold" VALUE="1">
<PARAM NAME="FrColor" VALUE="0">
</OBJECT>

</HEAD>

<BODY>

<INPUT TYPE="TEXT" NAME="NewAngle" SIZE=10>
<INPUT TYPE="BUTTON" NAME="RotText" VALUE="Rotate Text">

</BODY>

</HTML>
```

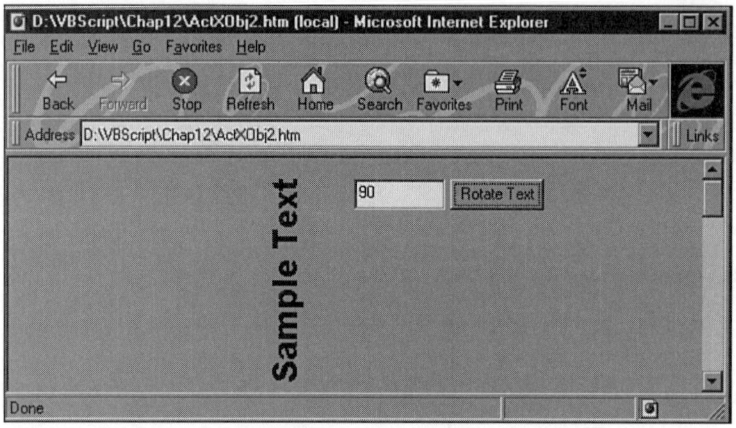

Figure 12-5 The angle of the text is changed based on the value typed by the user

You can use the same techniques to the modify the properties of the applet used in Listing 12-3. Listing 12-4 illustrates how to use VBScript to change the **Scale** property for the Java applet. Figure 12-6 illustrates the results when the Change Scale button is selected.

Listing 12-4 Changing the attributes of a Java applet

```
<HTML>
<HEAD>
<SCRIPT language = "VBScript">
<!--
'...............................................
' ChangeScale_OnClick()
' This procedure is called when the user selects
' the Change Scale button. This procedure changes
' the scale of the graph from 5 to 20.
'...............................................
Sub ChangeScale_OnClick()

  document.BarChart.scale = "20"

End Sub
-->
</SCRIPT>

<applet code="chart.class" id=BarChart width=500 height=125>

  <param name=c2_color value="green">
  <param name=c2_label value="Q2">
  <param name=c1_style value="striped">
  <param name=c4 value="30">
  <param name=c3 value="5">
  <param name=c2 value="20">
  <param name=c4_color value="yellow">
```

```
  <param name=c1 value="10">
  <param name=c4_label value="Q4">
  <param name=title value="Performance">
  <param name=c3_style value="striped">
  <param name=columns value="4">
  <param name=c1_color value="blue">
  <param name=c1_label value="Q1">
  <param name=c3_color value="magenta">
  <param name=c3_label value="Q3">
  <param name=c2_style value="solid">
  <param name=orientation value="horizontal">
  <param name=c4_style value="solid">
  <param name=scale value="5">

</applet>
</HEAD>
<BODY>
<HR>
<CENTER>
<INPUT TYPE=button VALUE="Change Scale" NAME="ChangeScale">
</CENTER>
</BODY>
</HTML>
```

Summary of Adding Objects Functions

Table 12-4 identifies the VBScript function that can be used with objects. A brief description of the function follows this table. More information about this function is available in Chapter 4, Data Validation.

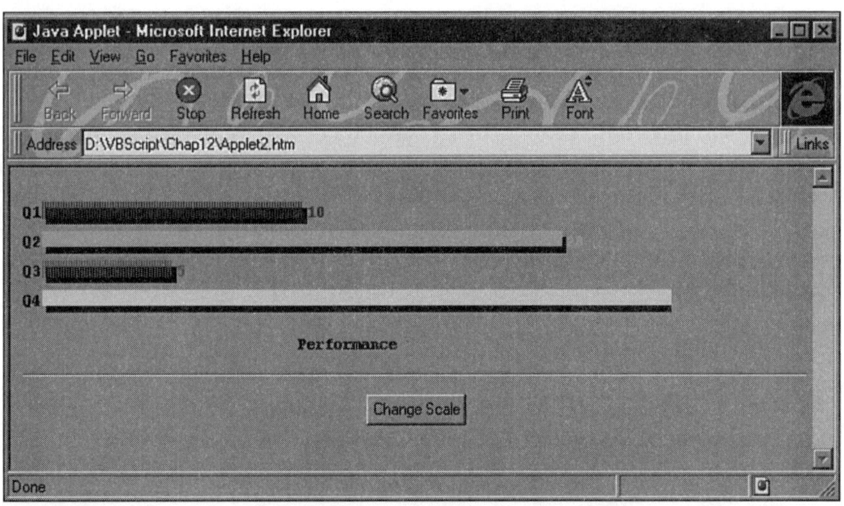

Figure 12-6 VBScript can be used to modify the properties of a Java applet

Table 12-4 Adding Objects function summary

Use...	To Do This...
`IsObject`	Determine if a variable references an OLE object

IsObject Function

Purpose Use the `IsObject()` function to determine if an expression references a valid OLE automation object.

Syntax `IsObject(expression)`

Description The `IsObject()` function returns a Boolean value of `TRUE` if the specified variant expression has an object subtype or is a user-defined object; otherwise, a value of `FALSE` is returned.

For more information about the `IsObject()` function, refer to Chapter 4, Data Validation.

Adding Objects Project

The Adding Objects project uses the information covered in this chapter. This project illustrates how to use VBScript to modify the properties of an object by creating a page where the user can graph six values and specify the type of graph that is displayed. The Microsoft ActiveX Chart control is used for this example.

Building the Project

1. Start the project by setting up the standard HTML template used for all VBScript examples in this book. Place the VBScript code in the **<HEAD>** section of the HTML code to keep everything consistent. Remember to place the HTML comment tags **<!--** and **-->** around the VBScript code so that it will be ignored by browsers that cannot interpret the **<SCRIPT>** tag.

```
<HTML>

<HEAD>
<TITLE>Adding Objects Project</TITLE>

<SCRIPT LANGUAGE="VBScript">

<!--

-->

</SCRIPT>
```

```
</HEAD>

<BODY>

</BODY>

</HTML>
```

2. In the <HEAD> section, create a title for the Web page. Since the ActiveX control you are using will be embedded on the page as it is loaded, you want the title to be loaded first. You are creating a page on which the user can graph up to six values, so title this example Graphing Values. Use the <HR> tag to place a horizontal line under the title.

```
<CENTER>
<FONT SIZE=5>Graphing Values<P>
</FONT>
</CENTER>
```

3. In the <HEAD> section, use the <OBJECT> and <PARAM> elements to embed the ActiveX control. This Chart control from Microsoft has several different properties that can be specified using the <PARAM> tags. For simplicity, you are creating a graph with one row and six columns of values; therefore, there are only seven data values listed. Remember, when working with ActiveX controls, you need to refer to the documentation to determine the properties that you can set and modify. Figure 12-7 illustrates the control you are adding to the page.

```
<OBJECT ID="iechart1" WIDTH=507 HEIGHT=253 ALIGN = "TEXTMIDDLE"
 CLASSID="CLSID:FC25B780-75BE-11CF-8B01-444553540000">
    <PARAM NAME="_ExtentX" VALUE="13414">
    <PARAM NAME="_ExtentY" VALUE="6694">
    <PARAM NAME="Rows" VALUE="1">
    <PARAM NAME="Columns" VALUE="6">
    <PARAM NAME="ChartType" VALUE="11">
    <PARAM NAME="Data[0][0]" VALUE="9">
    <PARAM NAME="Data[0][1]" VALUE="15">
    <PARAM NAME="Data[0][2]" VALUE="7">
    <PARAM NAME="Data[0][3]" VALUE="12">
    <PARAM NAME="Data[0][4]" VALUE="3">
    <PARAM NAME="Data[0][5]" VALUE="19">
    <PARAM NAME="HorizontalAxis" VALUE="0">
    <PARAM NAME="VerticalAxis" VALUE="0">
    <PARAM NAME="hgridStyle" VALUE="1">
    <PARAM NAME="vgridStyle" VALUE="0">
    <PARAM NAME="ColorScheme" VALUE="0">
    <PARAM NAME="BackStyle" VALUE="1">
    <PARAM NAME="Scale" VALUE="100">
    <PARAM NAME="DisplayLegend" VALUE="0">
    <PARAM NAME="BackColor" VALUE="16777215">
    <PARAM NAME="ForeColor" VALUE="32768">
</OBJECT>
```

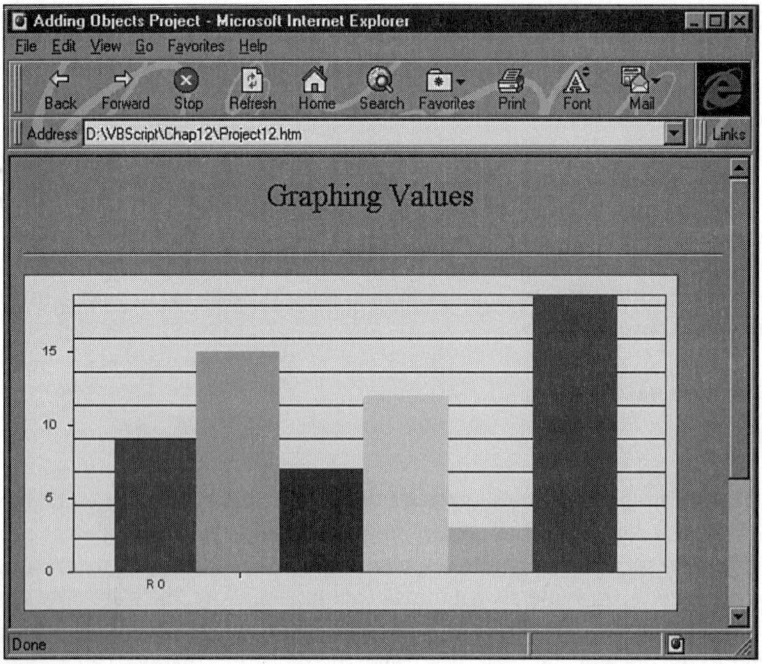

Figure 12-7 Embed the ActiveX control in the <HEAD> section for consistency

4. In the <BODY> section, create a table to contain the information that will be selected by the user. You need to create radio buttons that allow users to select the type of graph they want to display. Although this control allows you to create several different types of graphs, you are only going to use three types for this example. Also, create six input fields in which the user can enter the desired graph values.

```
<TABLE BORDER = 10>
  <TR><TD ALIGN="CENTER"><B>Chart Type</B></TD>
      <TD COLSPAN = 6 ALIGN = "CENTER"><B>Chart Values</B></TD></TR>

  <TR><TD><INPUT TYPE=RADIO ONCLICK="SelectColumn" NAME="GraphType">Column Graph</TD>
       <TD>Value 1</TD><TD>Value 2</TD><TD>Value 3</TD>
       <TD>Value 4</TD><TD>Value 5</TD><TD>Value 6</TD></TR>

  <TR><TD><INPUT TYPE=RADIO ONCLICK="SelectRow" NAME="GraphType">Row Graph</TD>
      <TD><INPUT TYPE=TEXTBOX VALUE="9" SIZE=8 NAME="Value1"></TD>
      <TD><INPUT TYPE=TEXTBOX VALUE="15" SIZE=8 NAME="Value2"></TD>
      <TD><INPUT TYPE=TEXTBOX VALUE="7" SIZE=8 NAME="Value3"></TD>
      <TD><INPUT TYPE=TEXTBOX VALUE="12" SIZE=8 NAME="Value4"></TD>
      <TD><INPUT TYPE=TEXTBOX VALUE="3" SIZE=8 NAME="Value5"></TD>
      <TD><INPUT TYPE=TEXTBOX VALUE="19" SIZE=8 NAME="Value6"></TD></TR>

<TR><TD><INPUT TYPE=RADIO ONCLICK="SelectPie" NAME="GraphType">Pie Chart</TD>

</TABLE>
```

5. Add a button to the table that updates the graph when the user types new values in the input fields. Name the button ChangeChart so that the VBScript procedure `ChangeChart_OnClick()` will execute when users select this button.

```
<TD COLSPAN = 6 ALIGN = "CENTER">
    <INPUT TYPE=BUTTON VALUE="Change Chart Values" NAME="ChangeChart"></TD></TR>
```

6. In the `<SCRIPT>` section, create three procedures called `SelectColumn()`, `SelectRow()`, and `SelectPie()`. These procedures are called when the user selects the corresponding radio button. Each procedure changes the value of the `ChartType` property for the control.

```
SUB SelectColumn()

  iechart1.ChartType = "11"

END SUB

SUB SelectRow()

  iechart1.ChartType = "14"

END SUB

SUB SelectPie()

  iechart1.ChartType = "0"

END SUB
```

7. Create another procedure called `ChangeChart_OnClick()`. This procedure executes when the user selects the Change Chart Values button. It updates the graph with the new values typed in the fields. Since this control has a multidimensional array that contains the data values, you need to specify the corresponding array index values as you update the array. You are only going to use six values from one dimension of the array, so leave the `RowIndex` value at `0`. Set the `ColumnIndex` value for each element you are changing in the array.

If you look at the properties initially listed for this array, you will notice that there are properties that appear as `Data[0][0]`, `Data[0][1]`, and so forth; these are the array values for the control. VBScript does not allow you to reference the array in the format listed above; that is why you are using the method illustrated below to assign the index values and then the column value.

```
SUB ChangeChart_OnClick()
     iechart1.ColumnIndex=0
     iechart1.DataItem = Value1.Value

     iechart1.ColumnIndex=1
     iechart1.DataItem = Value2.Value

     iechart1.ColumnIndex=2
     iechart1.DataItem = Value3.Value
```

continued on next page

continued from previous page

```
     iechart1.ColumnIndex=3
     iechart1.DataItem = Value4.Value

     iechart1.ColumnIndex=4
     iechart1.DataItem = Value5.Value

     iechart1.ColumnIndex=5
     iechart1.DataItem = Value6.Value
END SUB
```

How It Works

The Adding Objects project is designed to illustrate how to add an object to an HTML page and then change the properties of the control during the execution of the Web page. This example allows the user to select the type of graph displayed, and specify the data values that display on the selected graph. Figure 12-8 illustrates the completed Adding Objects project, and Listing 12-5 shows the complete source code.

This example uses the Microsoft ActiveX Chart control. When the user selects one of the radio buttons in the graph, the **GraphType** property of the control is modified so that the specified graph type displays on the screen.

If the user selects the Change Chart Values button, the control is updated to display the values in the input boxes.

Listing 12-5 Complete source for the Adding Objects project

```
<HTML>
<HEAD>
<TITLE>Adding Objects Project</TITLE>

<CENTER>
<FONT SIZE=5>Graphing Values<P>
</FONT>
</CENTER>

<HR>
<SCRIPT LANGUAGE="VBScript">
<!--
'.................................................................
' SelectColumn()
' This procedure is called when the user selects the Column Graph option
' in the table. This selects a simple column graph as the graph type.
'.................................................................
SUB SelectColumn()

  iechart1.ChartType = "11"

END SUB

'.................................................................
' SelectRow()
' This procedure is called when the user selects the Row Graph option
' in the table. This selects a simple row graph as the graph type.
'.................................................................
```

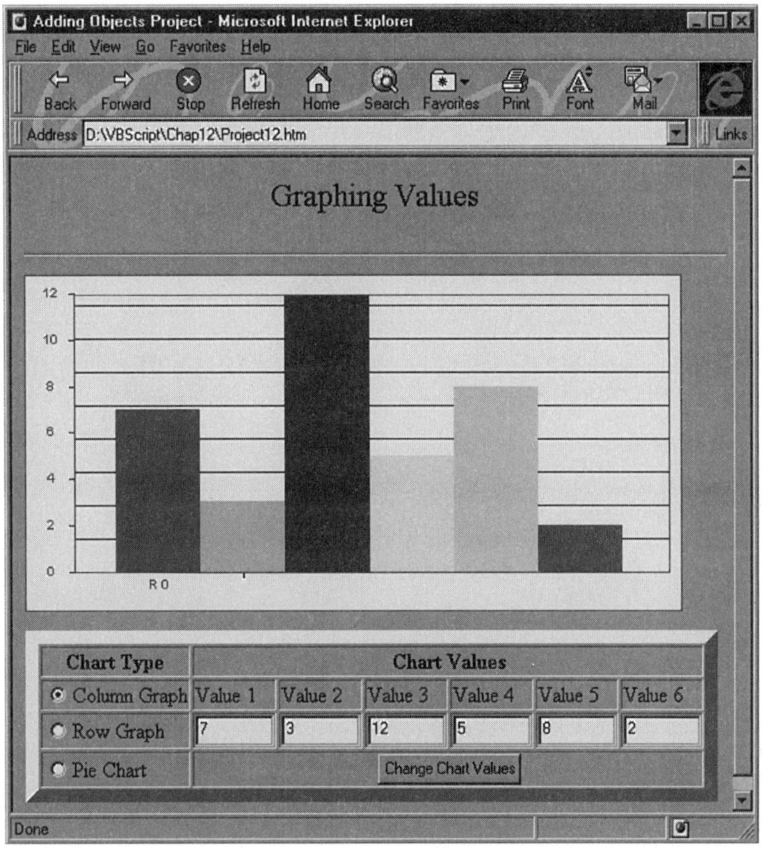

Figure 12-8 The completed Adding Objects project

```
SUB SelectRow()

  iechart1.ChartType = "14"

END SUB

'.......................................................................
' SelectPie()
' This procedure is called when the user selects the Pie Chart option
' in the table. This selects a pie chart as the graph type.
'.......................................................................
SUB SelectPie()

  iechart1.ChartType = "0"

END SUB

'.......................................................................
' ChangeChart_OnClick()
' This procedure is called when the user selects the Change Chart Values
' button on the table. This procedure changes the values
```

continued on next page

continued from previous page

```
' for the graph. Notice that since the ActiveX control is storing the
' chart values in an array, you need to specify the column index value
' for each array element. (You are only using one set of values, so
' you do not need to change the row index.)
'.........................................................................
SUB ChangeChart_OnClick()
     iechart1.ColumnIndex=0
     iechart1.DataItem = Value1.Value

     iechart1.ColumnIndex=1
     iechart1.DataItem = Value2.Value

     iechart1.ColumnIndex=2
     iechart1.DataItem = Value3.Value

     iechart1.ColumnIndex=3
     iechart1.DataItem = Value4.Value

     iechart1.ColumnIndex=4
     iechart1.DataItem = Value5.Value

     iechart1.ColumnIndex=5
     iechart1.DataItem = Value6.Value
END SUB
-->

</SCRIPT>

<OBJECT ID="iechart1" WIDTH=507 HEIGHT=253 ALIGN = "TEXTMIDDLE"
 CLASSID="CLSID:FC25B780-75BE-11CF-8B01-444553540000">
    <PARAM NAME="_ExtentX" VALUE="13414">
    <PARAM NAME="_ExtentY" VALUE="6694">
    <PARAM NAME="Rows" VALUE="1">
    <PARAM NAME="Columns" VALUE="6">
    <PARAM NAME="ChartType" VALUE="11">
    <PARAM NAME="Data[0][0]" VALUE="9">
    <PARAM NAME="Data[0][1]" VALUE="15">
    <PARAM NAME="Data[0][2]" VALUE="7">
    <PARAM NAME="Data[0][3]" VALUE="12">
    <PARAM NAME="Data[0][4]" VALUE="3">
    <PARAM NAME="Data[0][5]" VALUE="19">
    <PARAM NAME="HorizontalAxis" VALUE="0">
    <PARAM NAME="VerticalAxis" VALUE="0">
    <PARAM NAME="hgridStyle" VALUE="1">
    <PARAM NAME="vgridStyle" VALUE="0">
    <PARAM NAME="ColorScheme" VALUE="0">
    <PARAM NAME="BackStyle" VALUE="1">
    <PARAM NAME="Scale" VALUE="100">
    <PARAM NAME="DisplayLegend" VALUE="0">
    <PARAM NAME="BackColor" VALUE="16777215">
    <PARAM NAME="ForeColor" VALUE="32768">
</OBJECT>

</HEAD>

<BODY>

<BR>
<BR>
```

```
<TABLE BORDER = 10>
  <TR><TD ALIGN="CENTER"><B>Chart Type</B></TD>
      <TD COLSPAN = 6 ALIGN = "CENTER"><B>Chart Values</B></TD></TR>

  <TR><TD><INPUT TYPE=RADIO ONCLICK="SelectColumn" NAME="GraphType">Column Graph</TD>
       <TD>Value 1</TD><TD>Value 2</TD><TD>Value 3</TD>
       <TD>Value 4</TD><TD>Value 5</TD><TD>Value 6</TD></TR>

  <TR><TD><INPUT TYPE=RADIO ONCLICK="SelectRow" NAME="GraphType">Row Graph</TD>
      <TD><INPUT TYPE=TEXTBOX VALUE="9" SIZE=8 NAME="Value1"></TD>
      <TD><INPUT TYPE=TEXTBOX VALUE="15" SIZE=8 NAME="Value2"></TD>
      <TD><INPUT TYPE=TEXTBOX VALUE="7" SIZE=8 NAME="Value3"></TD>
      <TD><INPUT TYPE=TEXTBOX VALUE="12" SIZE=8 NAME="Value4"></TD>
      <TD><INPUT TYPE=TEXTBOX VALUE="3" SIZE=8 NAME="Value5"></TD>
      <TD><INPUT TYPE=TEXTBOX VALUE="19" SIZE=8 NAME="Value6"></TD></TR>

<TR><TD><INPUT TYPE=RADIO ONCLICK="SelectPie" NAME="GraphType">Pie Chart</TD>
    <TD COLSPAN = 6 ALIGN = "CENTER">
    <INPUT TYPE=BUTTON VALUE="Change Chart Values" NAME="ChangeChart"></TD></TR>

</TABLE>

</BODY>
</HTML>
```

13

ADVANCED VBSCRIPT PROGRAMMING

13

ADVANCED VBSCRIPT PROGRAMMING

VBScript was designed to enhance your Web page development by giving you the ability to create dynamic Web pages. As discussed in Chapter 12, Adding Objects, one of the most powerful features of VBScript is that it lets you change the properties of an ActiveX control during the execution of the Web page.

This chapter illustrates some of the things that can be done when VBScript is used to interact with various ActiveX controls. The main purpose of the chapter is to show how to use the major features of VBScript along with ActiveX controls to create a fully interactive Web page that contains graphics. That page, created step by step in the chapter project, will be an interactive blackjack game.

VBScript Functionality

The project in this chapter makes use of many of the VBScript functions that were covered in earlier chapters in this book. Table 13-1 describes the VBScript functionality that has been added to the project.

Table 13-1 VBScript elements used in the Advanced VBScript Programming project

Functionality	Description
Data validation	The value typed by the user in the `Bet` field is validated using the `IsNumeric()` function covered in Chapter 4, Data Validation. Use of the function ensures that the user types a numeric value in this field before an attempt is made to perform a numeric calculation using the value.
Array handling	Several different arrays are used in this project. For example, the `DeckShoe` array contains all of the cards in the deck.
Computing values	The `Randomize` statement and `Rnd()` function are used to create a series of random cards for the deck. Each of these is covered in Chapter 8, Computing Values.
Data conversion	The `CDbl()` function is used to convert the `PlayerBet` to a numeric value so that it can be properly added. This function is covered in Chapter 7, Data Conversion.
User interaction	The `MsgBox()` function is used in several locations to display a message to the user. This function is covered in Chapter 10, User Interaction.
Error handling	The `On Error Resume Next` statement is used to ensure that an error message, if it occurs, is not displayed on the screen for the user. This statement is covered in Chapter 11, Error Handling.
Adding objects	The information presented in Chapter 12, Adding Objects, is used to change the properties of several ActiveX controls that have been used.
Operators and statements	Various different operators and statements, covered in Chapter 2, VBScript Basics, are used in this project. This includes program flow statements such as the `Do While` loop statement.

Advanced VBScript Programming Project

The Advanced VBScript Programming project illustrates how to use the features of VBScript to interact with a series of ActiveX controls and create an interactive blackjack game.

Building the Project

1. Start the project by setting up the standard HTML template used for all VBScript examples in this book. You are going to alter the template slightly for this example so that the game can be coded more efficiently. Place the VBScript code in the **<BODY>** section of the HTML code after the ActiveX controls you are using. Remember to place the HTML comment tags **<!--** and **-->** around the VBScript code so that it will be ignored by browsers that cannot interpret the **<SCRIPT>** tag.

```
<HTML>

<HEAD>
<TITLE>Advanced VBScript Programming Project</TITLE>

</HEAD>

<BODY>
```

```
<SCRIPT LANGUAGE="VBScript">

<!--

-->

</SCRIPT>

</BODY>

</HTML>
```

2. In the <BODY> section, add the title for the page. Since you are creating a blackjack game, simply title the page Blackjack and place a horizontal line under the title. Create section titles for both you and the dealer. Use the <H3> tags so that these titles will display in a smaller font on the page.

```
<BODY>
<H1>Blackjack</H1>

<HR>
<H3>Dealer</H3>
<BR>

<HR>
<H3>You</H3>
<BR>
```

3. You are going to use the Microsoft ActiveX Image control to display the card images on the page. Place eight of these controls under the Dealer title in the <BODY> section. You are setting up eight of these objects for the dealer; this should accommodate all the cards that need to display for the dealer. The objects will only display a bitmap object when the VBScript passes the appropriate value. Remember to assign an `ID` value to each control so that you can change the value of the object during the execution of the page. Name the controls `Dealer1`, `Dealer2`, `Dealer3`, `Dealer4`, `Dealer5`, `Dealer6`, `Dealer7`, and `Dealer8`.

```
<OBJECT ID="Dealer1" WIDTH=96 HEIGHT=96
    CLASSID="CLSID:D4A97620-8E8F-11CF-93CD-00AA00C08FDF">
    <PARAM NAME="BorderStyle" VALUE="0">
    <PARAM NAME="SizeMode" VALUE="3">
    <PARAM NAME="Size" VALUE="2540;2540">
    <PARAM NAME="PictureAlignment" VALUE="0">
    <PARAM NAME="VariousPropertyBits" VALUE="19">
</OBJECT>

<OBJECT ID="Dealer2" WIDTH=96 HEIGHT=96
     CLASSID="CLSID:D4A97620-8E8F-11CF-93CD-00AA00C08FDF">
     <PARAM NAME="BorderStyle" VALUE="0">
     <PARAM NAME="SizeMode" VALUE="3">
     <PARAM NAME="Size" VALUE="2540;2540">
     <PARAM NAME="PictureAlignment" VALUE="0">
     <PARAM NAME="VariousPropertyBits" VALUE="19">
</OBJECT>
```

continued on next page

continued from previous page

```
<OBJECT ID="Dealer3" WIDTH=96 HEIGHT=96
     CLASSID="CLSID:D4A97620-8E8F-11CF-93CD-00AA00C08FDF">
     <PARAM NAME="BorderStyle" VALUE="0">
     <PARAM NAME="SizeMode" VALUE="3">
     <PARAM NAME="Size" VALUE="2540;2540">
     <PARAM NAME="PictureAlignment" VALUE="0">
     <PARAM NAME="VariousPropertyBits" VALUE="19">
</OBJECT>

<OBJECT ID="Dealer4" WIDTH=96 HEIGHT=96
     CLASSID="CLSID:D4A97620-8E8F-11CF-93CD-00AA00C08FDF">
     <PARAM NAME="BorderStyle" VALUE="0">
     <PARAM NAME="SizeMode" VALUE="3">
     <PARAM NAME="Size" VALUE="2540;2540">
     <PARAM NAME="PictureAlignment" VALUE="0">
     <PARAM NAME="VariousPropertyBits" VALUE="19">
</OBJECT>

<OBJECT ID="Dealer5" WIDTH=96 HEIGHT=96
     CLASSID="CLSID:D4A97620-8E8F-11CF-93CD-00AA00C08FDF">
     <PARAM NAME="BorderStyle" VALUE="0">
     <PARAM NAME="SizeMode" VALUE="3">
     <PARAM NAME="Size" VALUE="2540;2540">
     <PARAM NAME="PictureAlignment" VALUE="0">
     <PARAM NAME="VariousPropertyBits" VALUE="19">
</OBJECT>

<OBJECT ID="Dealer6" WIDTH=96 HEIGHT=96
     CLASSID="CLSID:D4A97620-8E8F-11CF-93CD-00AA00C08FDF">
     <PARAM NAME="BorderStyle" VALUE="0">
     <PARAM NAME="SizeMode" VALUE="3">
     <PARAM NAME="Size" VALUE="2540;2540">
     <PARAM NAME="PictureAlignment" VALUE="0">
     <PARAM NAME="VariousPropertyBits" VALUE="19">
</OBJECT>

<OBJECT ID="Dealer7" WIDTH=96 HEIGHT=96
     CLASSID="CLSID:D4A97620-8E8F-11CF-93CD-00AA00C08FDF">
     <PARAM NAME="BorderStyle" VALUE="0">
     <PARAM NAME="SizeMode" VALUE="3">
     <PARAM NAME="Size" VALUE="2540;2540">
     <PARAM NAME="PictureAlignment" VALUE="0">
     <PARAM NAME="VariousPropertyBits" VALUE="19">
</OBJECT>

<OBJECT ID="Dealer8" WIDTH=96 HEIGHT=96
     CLASSID="CLSID:D4A97620-8E8F-11CF-93CD-00AA00C08FDF">
     <PARAM NAME="BorderStyle" VALUE="0">
     <PARAM NAME="SizeMode" VALUE="3">
     <PARAM NAME="Size" VALUE="2540;2540">
     <PARAM NAME="PictureAlignment" VALUE="0">
     <PARAM NAME="VariousPropertyBits" VALUE="19">
</OBJECT>
```

4. Add an additional eight Microsoft ActiveX Image controls under the You title on the Web page. These objects are used to display the card images for the user.

```
<OBJECT ID="You1" WIDTH=96 HEIGHT=96
     CLASSID="CLSID:D4A97620-8E8F-11CF-93CD-00AA00C08FDF">
     <PARAM NAME="BorderStyle" VALUE="0">
     <PARAM NAME="SizeMode" VALUE="3">
     <PARAM NAME="Size" VALUE="2540;2540">
     <PARAM NAME="PictureAlignment" VALUE="0">
     <PARAM NAME="VariousPropertyBits" VALUE="19">
</OBJECT>

<OBJECT ID="You2" WIDTH=96 HEIGHT=96
     CLASSID="CLSID:D4A97620-8E8F-11CF-93CD-00AA00C08FDF">
     <PARAM NAME="BorderStyle" VALUE="0">
     <PARAM NAME="SizeMode" VALUE="3">
     <PARAM NAME="Size" VALUE="2540;2540">
     <PARAM NAME="PictureAlignment" VALUE="0">
     <PARAM NAME="VariousPropertyBits" VALUE="19">
</OBJECT>

<OBJECT ID="You3" WIDTH=96 HEIGHT=96
     CLASSID="CLSID:D4A97620-8E8F-11CF-93CD-00AA00C08FDF">
     <PARAM NAME="BorderStyle" VALUE="0">
     <PARAM NAME="SizeMode" VALUE="3">
     <PARAM NAME="Size" VALUE="2540;2540">
     <PARAM NAME="PictureAlignment" VALUE="0">
     <PARAM NAME="VariousPropertyBits" VALUE="19">
</OBJECT>

<OBJECT ID="You4" WIDTH=96 HEIGHT=96
     CLASSID="CLSID:D4A97620-8E8F-11CF-93CD-00AA00C08FDF">
     <PARAM NAME="BorderStyle" VALUE="0">
     <PARAM NAME="SizeMode" VALUE="3">
     <PARAM NAME="Size" VALUE="2540;2540">
     <PARAM NAME="PictureAlignment" VALUE="0">
     <PARAM NAME="VariousPropertyBits" VALUE="19">
</OBJECT>

<OBJECT ID="You5" WIDTH=96 HEIGHT=96
     CLASSID="CLSID:D4A97620-8E8F-11CF-93CD-00AA00C08FDF">
     <PARAM NAME="BorderStyle" VALUE="0">
     <PARAM NAME="SizeMode" VALUE="3">
     <PARAM NAME="Size" VALUE="2540;2540">
     <PARAM NAME="PictureAlignment" VALUE="0">
     <PARAM NAME="VariousPropertyBits" VALUE="19">
</OBJECT>

<OBJECT ID="You6" WIDTH=96 HEIGHT=96
     CLASSID="CLSID:D4A97620-8E8F-11CF-93CD-00AA00C08FDF">
     <PARAM NAME="BorderStyle" VALUE="0">
     <PARAM NAME="SizeMode" VALUE="3">
     <PARAM NAME="Size" VALUE="2540;2540">
     <PARAM NAME="PictureAlignment" VALUE="0">
     <PARAM NAME="VariousPropertyBits" VALUE="19">
</OBJECT>

<OBJECT ID="You7" WIDTH=96 HEIGHT=96
     CLASSID="CLSID:D4A97620-8E8F-11CF-93CD-00AA00C08FDF">
     <PARAM NAME="BorderStyle" VALUE="0">
     <PARAM NAME="SizeMode" VALUE="3">
     <PARAM NAME="Size" VALUE="2540;2540">
```

continued on next page

continued from previous page

```
      <PARAM NAME="PictureAlignment" VALUE="0">
      <PARAM NAME="VariousPropertyBits" VALUE="19">
</OBJECT>

<OBJECT ID="You8" WIDTH=96 HEIGHT=96
      CLASSID="CLSID:D4A97620-8E8F-11CF-93CD-00AA00C08FDF">
      <PARAM NAME="BorderStyle" VALUE="0">
      <PARAM NAME="SizeMode" VALUE="3">
      <PARAM NAME="Size" VALUE="2540;2540">
      <PARAM NAME="PictureAlignment" VALUE="0">
      <PARAM NAME="VariousPropertyBits" VALUE="19">
</OBJECT>
```

5. Use the Microsoft Forms 2.0 Label control to create buttons that the user can select to deal, hit, double, and stand. Remember to assign an `ID` value to each button so you can create a corresponding VBScript procedure that is executed when the button is selected. For example, when the button with the `ID` value of `DealBtn` is selected, the VBScript procedure of `DealBtn_Click()` is executed. Use the `<HR>` tags before and after the button controls to set them off by placing horizontal lines around the buttons. Please note that this control is included with the Microsoft ActiveX Control Pad; if you do not have this control installed, you will want to install the Microsoft Control Pad, included on the CD with this book, before running this project.

```
<HR>
<OBJECT ID="DealBtn" WIDTH=96 HEIGHT=32
      CLASSID="CLSID:D7053240-CE69-11CD-A777-00DD01143C57">
      <PARAM NAME="Caption" VALUE="Deal">
      <PARAM NAME="Size" VALUE="2540;847">
      <PARAM NAME="FontEffects" VALUE="1073750016">
      <PARAM NAME="FontCharSet" VALUE="0">
      <PARAM NAME="FontPitchAndFamily" VALUE="2">
      <PARAM NAME="ParagraphAlign" VALUE="3">
</OBJECT>

<OBJECT ID="HitBtn" WIDTH=96 HEIGHT=32
      CLASSID="CLSID:D7053240-CE69-11CD-A777-00DD01143C57">
      <PARAM NAME="Caption" VALUE="Hit">
      <PARAM NAME="Size" VALUE="2540;847">
      <PARAM NAME="FontEffects" VALUE="1073750016">
      <PARAM NAME="FontCharSet" VALUE="0">
      <PARAM NAME="FontPitchAndFamily" VALUE="2">
      <PARAM NAME="ParagraphAlign" VALUE="3">
</OBJECT>

<OBJECT ID="DoubleBtn" WIDTH=96 HEIGHT=32
      CLASSID="CLSID:D7053240-CE69-11CD-A777-00DD01143C57">
      <PARAM NAME="Caption" VALUE="Double">
      <PARAM NAME="Size" VALUE="2540;847">
      <PARAM NAME="FontEffects" VALUE="1073750016">
      <PARAM NAME="FontCharSet" VALUE="0">
      <PARAM NAME="FontPitchAndFamily" VALUE="2">
      <PARAM NAME="ParagraphAlign" VALUE="3">
</OBJECT>
```

```
<OBJECT ID="StandBtn" WIDTH=96 HEIGHT=32
     CLASSID="CLSID:D7053240-CE69-11CD-A777-00DD01143C57">
     <PARAM NAME="Caption" VALUE="Stand">
     <PARAM NAME="Size" VALUE="2540;847">
     <PARAM NAME="FontEffects" VALUE="1073750016">
     <PARAM NAME="FontCharSet" VALUE="0">
     <PARAM NAME="FontPitchAndFamily" VALUE="2">
     <PARAM NAME="ParagraphAlign" VALUE="3">
</OBJECT>
<HR>
```

6. Use the Microsoft Forms 2.0 Label control to create a static text field titled Bet. This field is used as a title for the field that contains the user's bet. Please note that this control is included with the Microsoft ActiveX Control Pad, included on the CD with this book.

```
<OBJECT ID="Label1" WIDTH=39 HEIGHT=20
     CLASSID="CLSID:978C9E23-D4B0-11CE-BF2D-00AA003F40D0">
     <PARAM NAME="Caption" VALUE="Bet:  ">
     <PARAM NAME="Size" VALUE="1000;529">
     <PARAM NAME="FontHeight" VALUE="240">
     <PARAM NAME="FontCharSet" VALUE="0">
     <PARAM NAME="FontPitchAndFamily" VALUE="2">
</OBJECT>
```

7. Use the Microsoft Forms 2.0 Textbox control to create an input field where the user can type the bet for each hand. Please note that this control is included with the Microsoft ActiveX Control Pad, included on the CD with this book.

```
<OBJECT ID="BetEdt" WIDTH=96 HEIGHT=24
     CLASSID="CLSID:8BD21D10-EC42-11CE-9E0D-00AA006002F3">
     <PARAM NAME="VariousPropertyBits" VALUE="746604571">
     <PARAM NAME="Size" VALUE="2540;635">
     <PARAM NAME="FontEffects" VALUE="1073741825">
     <PARAM NAME="FontHeight" VALUE="200">
     <PARAM NAME="FontCharSet" VALUE="0">
     <PARAM NAME="FontPitchAndFamily" VALUE="2">
     <PARAM NAME="ParagraphAlign" VALUE="2">
     <PARAM NAME="FontWeight" VALUE="700">
</OBJECT>
```

8. Use the Microsoft Forms 2.0 Label control to create a static text field titled `Balance:`. This field is used as a title for the field that contains the user's balance. Please note that this control is included with the Microsoft ActiveX Control Pad, included on the CD with this book.

```
<OBJECT ID="Label2" WIDTH=93 HEIGHT=23
     CLASSID="CLSID:978C9E23-D4B0-11CE-BF2D-00AA003F40D0">
     <PARAM NAME="Caption" VALUE="      Balance:  ">
     <PARAM NAME="Size" VALUE="2455;600">
     <PARAM NAME="FontHeight" VALUE="240">
     <PARAM NAME="FontCharSet" VALUE="0">
     <PARAM NAME="FontPitchAndFamily" VALUE="2">
</OBJECT>
```

9. Use the Microsoft Forms 2.0 Label control to create a text field that contains the user's balance. Please note that this control is included with the Microsoft ActiveX Control Pad included on the CD with this book. Figure 13-1 illustrates the initial screen that displays when the project is loaded.

```
<OBJECT ID="Balance" WIDTH=115 HEIGHT=24
     CLASSID="CLSID:978C9E23-D4B0-11CE-BF2D-00AA003F40D0">
     <PARAM NAME="Caption" VALUE="$ 0.00">
     <PARAM NAME="Size" VALUE="3037;635">
     <PARAM NAME="SpecialEffect" VALUE="2">
     <PARAM NAME="FontEffects" VALUE="1073741825">
     <PARAM NAME="FontHeight" VALUE="240">
     <PARAM NAME="FontCharSet" VALUE="0">
     <PARAM NAME="FontPitchAndFamily" VALUE="2">
     <PARAM NAME="ParagraphAlign" VALUE="2">
     <PARAM NAME="FontWeight" VALUE="700">
</OBJECT>
```

10. As stated in step 1, you are placing the VBScript in the **<BODY>** section, after the ActiveX controls that are embedded on the page. By placing the code in this location, you can have the VBScript reference properties of the ActiveX controls as the page is loaded.

Declare the global variables that will be used by all of the procedures. Table 13-2 outlines the global variables that need to be declared for this project.

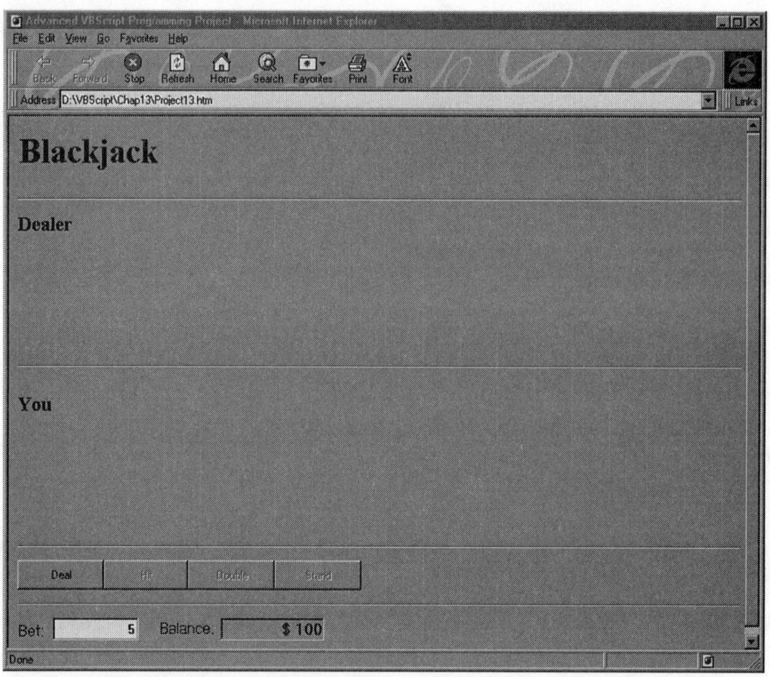

Figure 13-1 The buttons, input fields, and images are displayed using ActiveX controls

Table 13-2 Global variables for the Advanced VBScript Programming project

Variable	Description
`DeckShoe(312)`	This is an array with 312 elements that will contain all of the cards. When the decks are shuffled, the cards are placed in this array.
`DealerCards(8)`	This array keeps track of the eight cards that can be dealt to the dealer.
`PlayerCards(8)`	This array keeps track of the eight cards that can be dealt to the player.
`PlayerCard`	Indicates the number of cards that the player has.
`DealerCard`	Indicates the number of cards that the dealer has.
`CurrentCard`	Indicates the number of cards that have been dealt.
`PlayerBalance`	Contains the balance of the player. This value is set to `100` when the page is loaded.
`PlayerBet`	Contains the current bet for the player. This value is set to `5` when the page is loaded, but it can be modified by the player.

Call the `UpdateBalance()` procedure to format the balance and write it to the Balance ActiveX control. Disable the Hit, Double, and Stand buttons by setting the `Enabled` property of each ActiveX control to `FALSE`. Finally, call the `ShuffleCards()` procedure to create the array that contains a random list of the 312 cards (six decks of 52 cards).

```
<SCRIPT LANGUAGE="VBScript">
<!--
   Dim DeckShoe(312)
   Dim DealerCards(8)
   Dim PlayerCards(8)
   Dim PlayerCard
   Dim DealerCard
   Dim CurrentCard
   Dim PlayerBalance
   Dim PlayerBet

    PlayerBalance = 100
    PlayerBet = 5

    BetEdt.Value=PlayerBet
    Call UpdateBalance()

    HitBtn.Enabled=False
    DoubleBtn.Enabled=False
    StandBtn.Enabled=False

    Call ShuffleCards()
```

11. Create a procedure called `UpdateBalance()` that updates the `Caption` property of the Balance ActiveX control. Take the value of the `PlayerBalance` variable and create a string by adding a `$` character to the front of the value.

```
Sub UpdateBalance()
       Balance.Caption="$ " & PlayerBalance
    End Sub
```

12. Create a procedure called `ShuffleCards()`. This procedure, called initially when the page is loaded, creates an array that contains a random list of card values. It is also called when the array gets low on cards, so that a new array can be created. This array contains 312 card values, or six decks of 52 cards. The **Randomize** statement is used to create the random seed for the cards.

    Use the **DeckOfCards** array to keep track of the number of times a specific card has been added to the **DeckShoe** array. You do not want to have more than six of one card in the array. For example, there should only be six Queen of Hearts in the array.

```
Sub ShuffleCards()
       Dim DeckOfCards(52)
       Dim Card

       CurrentCard = 0

       Randomize()

       For i = 0 to 51
          DeckOfCards(i) = 0
       Next

       For i = 0 to 311
          Do
            Card = CINT( 51 * Rnd() )
          Loop While DeckOfCards( Card ) > 5

          DeckOfCards( Card ) = DeckOfCards( Card ) + 1
          DeckShoe( i ) = Card+1
       Next
    End Sub
```

13. Create a procedure called `DealBtn_Click()` that is called when the Deal button is selected. This procedure is designed to deal the initial cards to the user and the dealer. Figure 13-2 illustrates how the screen appears when the player selects the Deal button. Before any cards are dealt, do the following things:

    - Check the player bet to make sure it is numeric.
    - Check the player bet to make sure it is greater than five.
    - Update the player balance by subtracting the current player bet.
    - Set the paths for the card images to a **NULL** string.
    - Check the **CurrentCard** variable to see if the deck needs to be shuffled again. If more than 250 cards have been dealt, shuffle the decks again by calling the `ShuffleCards()` procedure.

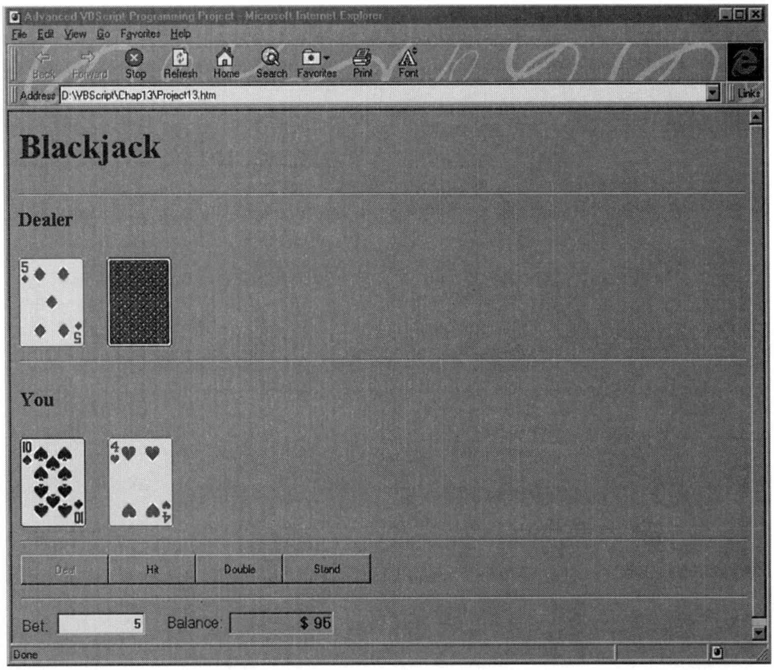

Figure 13-2 The Deal button deals the first two cards to the dealer and player

Deal the initial cards to the player and dealer and display the appropriate images for each card. Enable the Hit, Double, and Stand buttons by setting the `Enabled` property to `TRUE`, and disable the Deal button.

Check the dealer's cards. If the first card dealt to the dealer is an ace, give the player the opportunity to purchase insurance, as illustrated in Figure 13-3. After the user responds to the `MsgBox()` function, check to see if the other card of the dealer is a ten. If the dealer has blackjack, check the player's cards to see if he or she also has blackjack. If the player also has blackjack, call the `SetCard()` procedure to turn over the other card of the dealer and then call the `PayOff()` procedure to give the player back both the bet and insurance amounts.

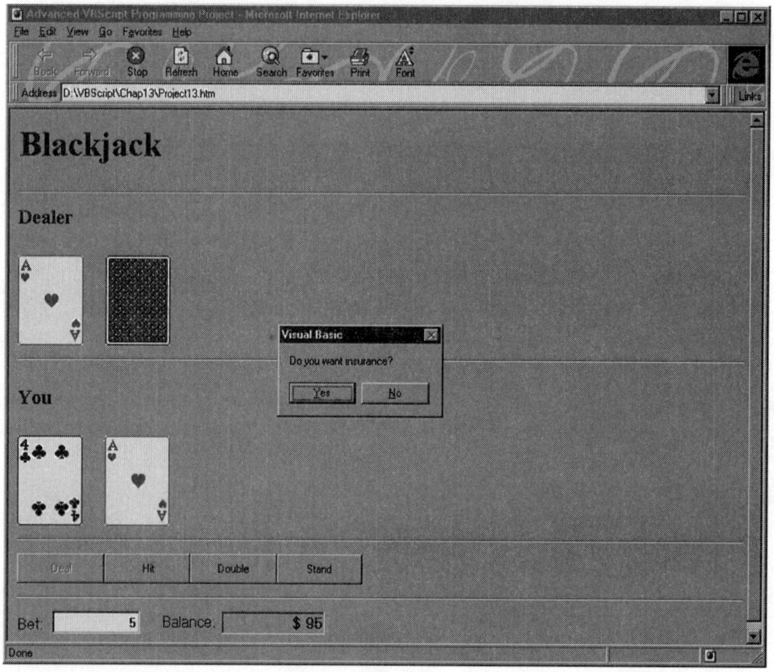

Figure 13-3 If the dealer has an ace showing, the player has the opportunity to purchase insurance

```
Sub DealBtn_Click()

       On Error Resume Next

'.........................................
' Get player bet and check it for minimum
'.........................................
       PlayerBet=BetEdt.Value
       If (Not IsNumeric(PlayerBet)) Then
         MsgBox "You must type a numeric value in the Bet field."
         Exit Sub
       End If

       If PlayerBet < 5 Then
          MsgBox( "Minimum bet is $5.00.")
          Exit Sub
      End If

'......................................
' Update balance to reflect current bet
'......................................
       PlayerBalance=PlayerBalance-PlayerBet
       Call UpdateBalance()

'.........................
' Clear all the card images
'.........................
```

```
    Dealer3.PicturePath=""
    Dealer4.PicturePath=""
    Dealer5.PicturePath=""
    Dealer6.PicturePath=""
    Dealer7.PicturePath=""
    Dealer8.PicturePath=""

    You3.PicturePath=""
    You4.PicturePath=""
    You5.PicturePath=""
    You6.PicturePath=""
    You7.PicturePath=""
    You8.PicturePath=""

'..............................
' Check if you need to shuffle.
'..............................
    if CurrentCard > 250 then
        MsgBox( "The cards are being shuffled." )
        Call ShuffleCards()
    end if

'....................
' Assign dealt cards
'....................
    PlayerCards(0)=DeckShoe(CurrentCard)
    PlayerCards(1)=DeckShoe(CurrentCard+2)
    DealerCards(0)=DeckShoe(CurrentCard+1)
    DealerCards(1)=DeckShoe(CurrentCard+3)

'......................................
' Bump counters to reflect dealt cards.
'......................................
    CurrentCard=CurrentCard+4
    PlayerCard=2
    DealerCard=2

'......................................
' Set the card images that were dealt
'......................................
    Call SetCard( Dealer1, DealerCards(0) )
    Call SetCard( Dealer2, 0 )
    Call SetCard( You1, PlayerCards(0) )
    Call SetCard( You2, PlayerCards(1) )

'.............................
' Enable buttons to play game.
'.............................
    DealBtn.Enabled=False
    HitBtn.Enabled=True
    DoubleBtn.Enabled=True
    StandBtn.Enabled=True

'................................
' Refresh the blank images
'................................
    Call Refresh( Dealer3 )
    Call Refresh( Dealer4 )
    Call Refresh( Dealer5 )
```

continued on next page

continued from previous page

```
        Call Refresh( Dealer6 )
        Call Refresh( Dealer7 )
        Call Refresh( Dealer8 )

        Call Refresh( You3 )
        Call Refresh( You4 )
        Call Refresh( You5 )
        Call Refresh( You6 )
        Call Refresh( You7 )
        Call Refresh( You8 )

'..............................
' Handle dealer showing an ace.
'..............................
        If CardValue( DealerCards(0) ) =  1 Then
           If MsgBox( "Do you want insurance?", 4 ) = 6 then
              If CardValue( DealerCards(1)  ) <> 10 Then
                 PlayerBalance=PlayerBalance-(PlayerBet/2)
                 Call UpdateBalance()
                 MsgBox( "No, the dealer didn't have a Blackjack." )
              End If
           End If

           If CardValue( DealerCards(1) ) = 10 Then
              Call SetCard( Dealer2, DealerCards(1) )
              DealBtn.Enabled=True
              HitBtn.Enabled=False
              DoubleBtn.Enabled=False
              StandBtn.Enabled=False
           End If
        End If

        If CardValue( PlayerCards(0) ) = 1 or CardValue( PlayerCards(1) ) = 1 Then
           If CardValue( PlayerCards(0) ) = 10 or CardValue( PlayerCards(1) ) = 10 Then
              MsgBox( "You got a Blackjack!" )
              Call SetCard( Dealer2, DealerCards(1) )
              Call PayOff()
           End If
        End If
    End Sub
```

14. Create a procedure called `Refresh()` that is used to refresh the images that are displayed by the ActiveX controls. Unfortunately, although you can easily modify the path of the image displayed by the ActiveX controls, the image is not refreshed until the screen is resized, or other properties, such as borders for the image, change. To ensure that the image is updated appropriately, simply add and remove borders for the specified image. The name of the image that is changed is passed to the `Refresh()` procedure when it is called.

```
Sub Refresh( Image )

    Image.SpecialEffect=1
    Image.SpecialEffect=0
End Sub
```

15. Create another procedure called **SetCard()**. This procedure is used to determine the name of the bitmap that is displayed by the specified ActiveX control. The names of all the bitmaps used by the program are numeric, so you can select the bitmap by simply using the value of the **Card** variable and adding the **.bmp** extension to create the file name.

```
Sub SetCard( Image, Card )
       Dim CardName

       CardName = Card & ".bmp"
       Image.PicturePath=CardName

       Call Refresh( Image )
    End Sub
```

16. Create a procedure called **HitBtn_Click()** that is called whenever the Hit button is selected. Add a new card to the player's current hand. Use a **Select Case** statement to see which card this is for the dealer (the third, fourth, or more) and call the **SetCard()** procedure with the appropriate values so that the bitmap image is assigned to the appropriate ActiveX control.

    After the card is dealt, check the total of the player's cards. If the total is greater than 21, display a message, turn over the dealer's card, and call the **PayOff()** procedure, as illustrated in Figure 13-4.

```
Sub HitBtn_Click()
       PlayerCards(PlayerCard)=DeckShoe(CurrentCard)

       Select Case PlayerCard
          Case 2
            Call SetCard( You3, PlayerCards(PlayerCard) )
          Case 3
            Call SetCard( You4, PlayerCards(PlayerCard) )
          Case 4
            Call SetCard( You5, PlayerCards(PlayerCard) )
          Case 5
            Call SetCard( You6, PlayerCards(PlayerCard) )
          Case 6
            Call SetCard( You7, PlayerCards(PlayerCard) )
          Case 7
            Call SetCard( You8, PlayerCards(PlayerCard) )
       End Select

       CurrentCard=CurrentCard+1
       PlayerCard=PlayerCard+1

       DoubleBtn.Enabled=False

       If CardTotal( PlayerCards, PlayerCard ) > 21 Then
          MsgBox( "Bust!" )

          Call SetCard( Dealer2, DealerCards(1) )
          Call PayOff()
       End If
    End Sub
```

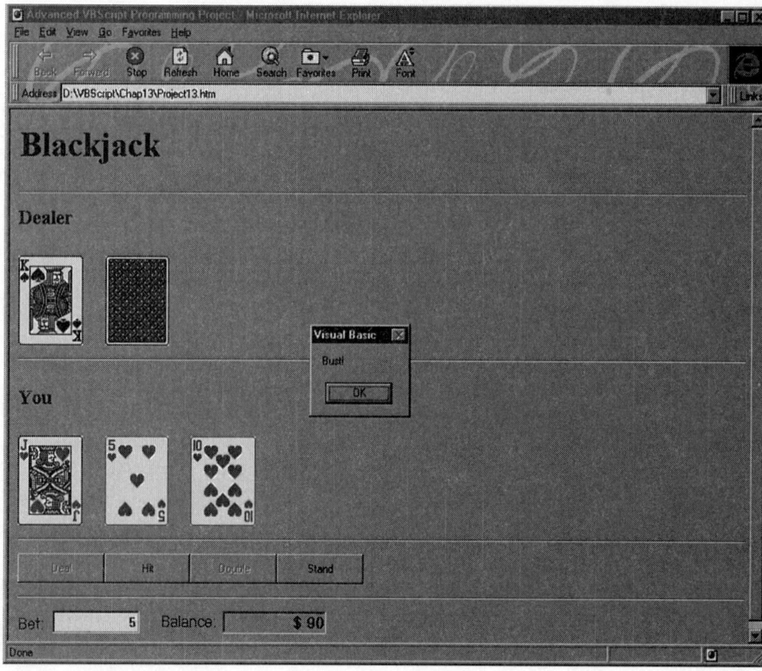

Figure 13-4 If the player total is greater than 21, a message indicates that the player busted

17. Create a procedure called `DoubleBtn_Click()` that is called when the Double button is selected. Double the player's bet and deal him or her one more card. Call the `UpdateBalance()` function to update the player's balance and then the `PlayDealer()` function to determine the hand of the dealer.

```
Sub DoubleBtn_Click()
       PlayerBalance=PlayerBalance-PlayerBet
       PlayerBet=CDbl(PlayerBet)+CDbl(PlayerBet)

       PlayerCards(2) = DeckShoe( CurrentCard )
       PlayerCard = PlayerCard+1
       CurrentCard = CurrentCard+1

       Call SetCard( You3, PlayerCards(2) )

       Call UpdateBalance()
       Call PlayDealer()
   End Sub
```

18. Create a procedure called `StandBtn_Click()` that is called when the Stand button is selected. This procedure calls the `PlayDealer()` procedure to determine the dealer's cards.

```
Sub StandBtn_Click()
       Call PlayDealer()
    End Sub
```

19. Create a procedure called **PlayDealer()** that determines the dealer's hand. Create a **Do Loop** that continues to deal a new card to the dealer as long as the card total is less than 17. When the dealer's total is equal to or greater than 17, check to see whether the dealer total is greater than 21; if so, display a message indicating that the dealer busted, as illustrated in Figure 13-5. Call the **PayOff()** procedure to determine the amount paid to the player.

```
Sub PlayDealer()
       Call SetCard( Dealer2, DealerCards(1) )

       Do While CardTotal( DealerCards, DealerCard ) < 17
          DealerCards( DealerCard ) = DeckShoe( CurrentCard )

          Select Case DealerCard
            Case 2
              Call SetCard( Dealer3, DealerCards(DealerCard) )
            Case 3
              Call SetCard( Dealer4, DealerCards(DealerCard) )
            Case 4
              Call SetCard( Dealer5, DealerCards(DealerCard) )
            Case 5
              Call SetCard( Dealer6, DealerCards(DealerCard) )
            Case 6
              Call SetCard( Dealer7, DealerCards(DealerCard) )
            Case 7
              Call SetCard( Dealer8, DealerCards(DealerCard) )
          End Select

          CurrentCard = CurrentCard + 1
          DealerCard = DealerCard + 1
       Loop

       If CardTotal( DealerCards, DealerCard ) > 21 Then
          MsgBox( "Dealer Busted!, You Win!" )
       End If

       Call PayOff()
    End Sub
```

20. Create a function called **CardValue()** that determines the actual numeric value of the card. Since the cards are numbered 1 through 52, you need to determine the actual face value. To do this, use the **Mod** operator to determine whether the card is divisible by 13. If the value of the **Card** variable is divisible by 13, the card is a king and should have an actual value of **10**. If the return value of the **Mod** operator is greater than 10, it is a face card and should have a value of **10**. Assign the value to the **CardValue** variable.

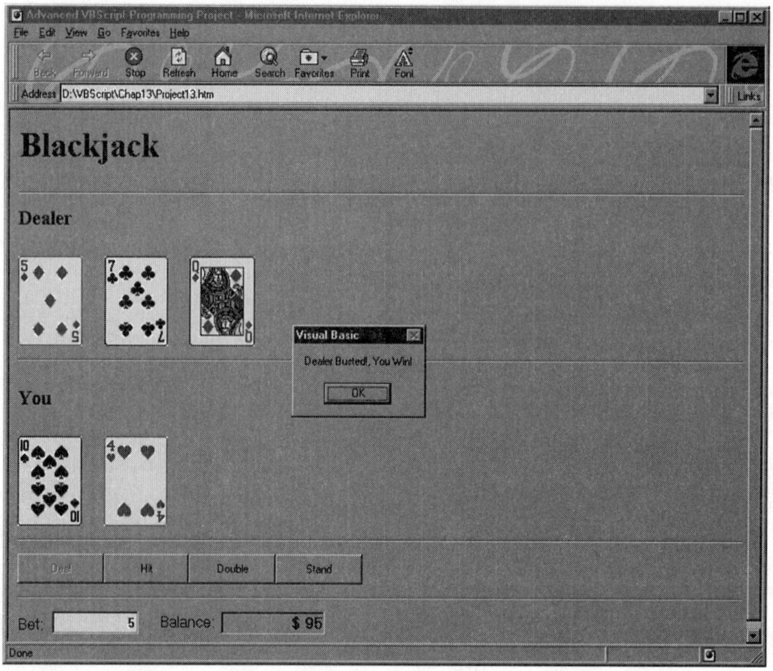

Figure 13-5 If the dealer total is greater than 21, the player wins

```
Function CardValue( ByVal Card )
       If Card > 13 Then
          Card=(Card mod 13)
       End If

       If Card = 0 Then
          Card = 10
       End If

       If Card > 10 then
          Card=10
       End If

       CardValue = Card

    End Function
```

21. Create a function called `CardTotal()` that is called to determine the value of the hand. This function is called for both the player and the dealer. Create a `For Next` statement that checks to see whether any of the cards is an ace. If there is an ace, change the value of the card to `11`. Add up all of the cards in the hand. Next, you need to check to see if there are any soft hands (hands in which the value of the ace should be counted as 1 instead of 11). If the total of the cards is greater than 21, and there is an ace, subtract 10 from the `CardValue` variable. Continue to do this until the total is less than 21, or there are no more aces in the hand.

```
Function CardTotal( Cards, NumCards )
       Dim Total
       Dim Value

       For i = 0 to NumCards-1
          Value = CardValue( Cards(i) )

          If Value = 1 Then
             Value = 11
          End If

          Total=Total+Value
       Next

       i = 0
       Do While ( Total > 21 ) and ( i < NumCards )
          If CardValue( Cards(i) ) = 1 Then
             Total=Total-10
          End If
             i=i+1
       Loop

       CardTotal = Total
    End Function
```

22. Create a procedure called **PayOff()** that determines the amount paid, if any, to the player. Reset the buttons so that the Hit, Double, and Stand buttons are disabled. Check the player total to determine whether it is less than or equal to 21. Make the appropriate adjustments to the player's balance based on the total for the dealer. If the dealer and player totals are the same, and they are both less than or equal to 21, then the player pushes, meaning he or she does not win anything but does get the original bet back, as illustrated in Figure 13-6.

```
Sub PayOff()
       Dim PlayerTotal
       Dim DealerTotal

'........................
' Reset buttons.
'........................
       HitBtn.Enabled = False
       DoubleBtn.Enabled = False
       StandBtn.Enabled = False
       DealBtn.Enabled = True

       PlayerTotal = CardTotal( PlayerCards, PlayerCard )
       DealerTotal = CardTotal( DealerCards, DealerCard )

       If PlayerTotal <= 21 Then
          If PlayerTotal = DealerTotal Then
             MsgBox( "You pushed!" )
             PlayerBalance = PlayerBalance + PlayerBet
          Else
             If DealerTotal > 21 Then
                PlayerBalance = PlayerBalance + (PlayerBet*2)
             Else
                If PlayerTotal = 21 and PlayerCard = 2 Then
```

continued on next page

continued from previous page

```
                PlayerBalance = PlayerBalance + (PlayerBet*2.5)
            Else
                If PlayerTotal > DealerTotal Then
                    PlayerBalance = PlayerBalance + (PlayerBet*2)
                    MsgBox( "You win!" )
                End If
            End If
        End If
    End If
End If

Call UpdateBalance()

End Sub
```

How It Works

The Advanced VBScript Programming project is designed to illustrate how you can use VBScript and ActiveX controls to create an interactive game or Web page. This project uses most of the information discussed in this book to illustrate the power of VBScript by creating a blackjack game, as illustrated in Figure 13-7.

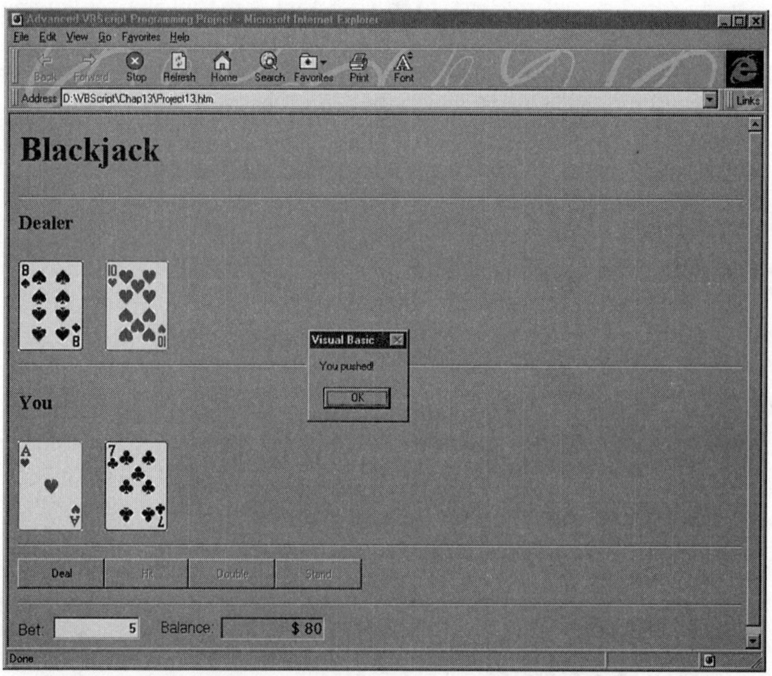

Figure 13-6 If the dealer total and player total are the same and less than or equal to 21, there is a push

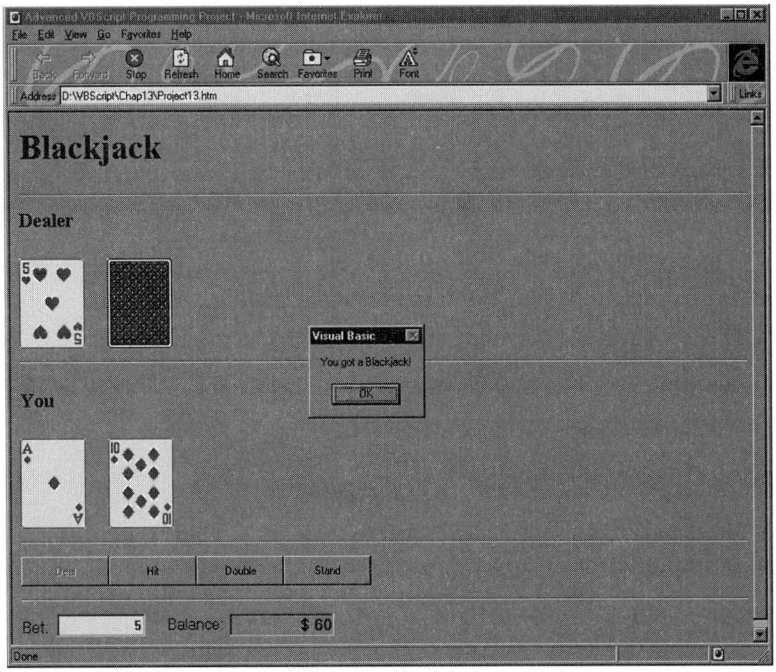

Figure 13-7 This project illustrates how to create an interactive blackjack game

This project uses a series of bitmap images that are displayed using the Microsoft ActiveX Image control that is distributed with Internet Explorer 3.0. This control allows you to embed images on your Web page, and then use VBScript to modify the properties of the control. There are also three other ActiveX controls that are used with this project; the Microsoft Forms 2.0 Command Button control is used to create buttons that are pressed by the player, the Microsoft Forms 2.0 Label control is used to display the static text labels and a balance field, and the Microsoft Forms 2.0 Textbox control in used to create the input field for the bet. These controls are distributed with the ActiveX Control Pad that is included on the CD for this book. If you do not have these controls installed, you should install the Control Pad before running this project.

The buttons could also be created using the HTML `<INPUT>` element, but by using the ActiveX control you have greater flexibility to change the properties of the button. For example, you can enable and disable the buttons depending on whether or not the player should press the button at that point in the game.

When the page is loaded, the cards are shuffled by randomly placing the card values in an array. You are working with six decks of 52 cards (312 cards total). The `Randomize` statement and `Rnd()` function create the random array of cards. To ensure that each card only appears in the array six times, you count the number of times the card has been added to the array before adding it.

When the user selects the Deal button, the first two cards are dealt for the player and the dealer. The second card for the dealer is dealt face down. At this time, the player has the option to Hit (receive another card), Double (double the bet and receive only one more card), or Stand (keep the current cards and see what the dealer has).

As the player makes his or her selection, VBScript keeps a running total of the number of cards dealt to both the player and dealer, the player bet, the balance, the number of cards in the deck, and the value of the current card. All of this information is used to calculate whether or not the player wins the hand.

Listing 13-1 contains the complete source code for the Advanced VBScript Programming project.

Listing 13-1 Complete source for the Advanced VBScript Programming project

```
<HTML>
<HEAD>
<TITLE>Advanced VBScript Programming Project</TITLE>

</HEAD>
<BODY>
<H1>Blackjack</H1>

<HR>
<H3>Dealer</H3>
<BR>
<OBJECT ID="Dealer1" WIDTH=96 HEIGHT=96
    CLASSID="CLSID:D4A97620-8E8F-11CF-93CD-00AA00C08FDF">
    <PARAM NAME="BorderStyle" VALUE="0">
    <PARAM NAME="SizeMode" VALUE="3">
    <PARAM NAME="Size" VALUE="2540;2540">
    <PARAM NAME="PictureAlignment" VALUE="0">
    <PARAM NAME="VariousPropertyBits" VALUE="19">
</OBJECT>

<OBJECT ID="Dealer2" WIDTH=96 HEIGHT=96
     CLASSID="CLSID:D4A97620-8E8F-11CF-93CD-00AA00C08FDF">
     <PARAM NAME="BorderStyle" VALUE="0">
     <PARAM NAME="SizeMode" VALUE="3">
     <PARAM NAME="Size" VALUE="2540;2540">
     <PARAM NAME="PictureAlignment" VALUE="0">
     <PARAM NAME="VariousPropertyBits" VALUE="19">
</OBJECT>

<OBJECT ID="Dealer3" WIDTH=96 HEIGHT=96
     CLASSID="CLSID:D4A97620-8E8F-11CF-93CD-00AA00C08FDF">
     <PARAM NAME="BorderStyle" VALUE="0">
     <PARAM NAME="SizeMode" VALUE="3">
     <PARAM NAME="Size" VALUE="2540;2540">
     <PARAM NAME="PictureAlignment" VALUE="0">
     <PARAM NAME="VariousPropertyBits" VALUE="19">
</OBJECT>

<OBJECT ID="Dealer4" WIDTH=96 HEIGHT=96
     CLASSID="CLSID:D4A97620-8E8F-11CF-93CD-00AA00C08FDF">
     <PARAM NAME="BorderStyle" VALUE="0">
     <PARAM NAME="SizeMode" VALUE="3">
```

```
    <PARAM NAME="Size" VALUE="2540;2540">
    <PARAM NAME="PictureAlignment" VALUE="0">
    <PARAM NAME="VariousPropertyBits" VALUE="19">
</OBJECT>

<OBJECT ID="Dealer5" WIDTH=96 HEIGHT=96
    CLASSID="CLSID:D4A97620-8E8F-11CF-93CD-00AA00C08FDF">
    <PARAM NAME="BorderStyle" VALUE="0">
    <PARAM NAME="SizeMode" VALUE="3">
    <PARAM NAME="Size" VALUE="2540;2540">
    <PARAM NAME="PictureAlignment" VALUE="0">
    <PARAM NAME="VariousPropertyBits" VALUE="19">
</OBJECT>

<OBJECT ID="Dealer6" WIDTH=96 HEIGHT=96
    CLASSID="CLSID:D4A97620-8E8F-11CF-93CD-00AA00C08FDF">
    <PARAM NAME="BorderStyle" VALUE="0">
    <PARAM NAME="SizeMode" VALUE="3">
    <PARAM NAME="Size" VALUE="2540;2540">
    <PARAM NAME="PictureAlignment" VALUE="0">
    <PARAM NAME="VariousPropertyBits" VALUE="19">
</OBJECT>

<OBJECT ID="Dealer7" WIDTH=96 HEIGHT=96
    CLASSID="CLSID:D4A97620-8E8F-11CF-93CD-00AA00C08FDF">
    <PARAM NAME="BorderStyle" VALUE="0">
    <PARAM NAME="SizeMode" VALUE="3">
    <PARAM NAME="Size" VALUE="2540;2540">
    <PARAM NAME="PictureAlignment" VALUE="0">
    <PARAM NAME="VariousPropertyBits" VALUE="19">
</OBJECT>

<OBJECT ID="Dealer8" WIDTH=96 HEIGHT=96
    CLASSID="CLSID:D4A97620-8E8F-11CF-93CD-00AA00C08FDF">
    <PARAM NAME="BorderStyle" VALUE="0">
    <PARAM NAME="SizeMode" VALUE="3">
    <PARAM NAME="Size" VALUE="2540;2540">
    <PARAM NAME="PictureAlignment" VALUE="0">
    <PARAM NAME="VariousPropertyBits" VALUE="19">
</OBJECT>

<HR>
<H3>You</H3>
<BR>
<OBJECT ID="You1" WIDTH=96 HEIGHT=96
    CLASSID="CLSID:D4A97620-8E8F-11CF-93CD-00AA00C08FDF">
    <PARAM NAME="BorderStyle" VALUE="0">
    <PARAM NAME="SizeMode" VALUE="3">
    <PARAM NAME="Size" VALUE="2540;2540">
    <PARAM NAME="PictureAlignment" VALUE="0">
    <PARAM NAME="VariousPropertyBits" VALUE="19">
</OBJECT>

<OBJECT ID="You2" WIDTH=96 HEIGHT=96
    CLASSID="CLSID:D4A97620-8E8F-11CF-93CD-00AA00C08FDF">
    <PARAM NAME="BorderStyle" VALUE="0">
    <PARAM NAME="SizeMode" VALUE="3">
    <PARAM NAME="Size" VALUE="2540;2540">
    <PARAM NAME="PictureAlignment" VALUE="0">
```

continued on next page

continued from previous page

```
     <PARAM NAME="VariousPropertyBits" VALUE="19">
</OBJECT>

<OBJECT ID="You3" WIDTH=96 HEIGHT=96
     CLASSID="CLSID:D4A97620-8E8F-11CF-93CD-00AA00C08FDF">
     <PARAM NAME="BorderStyle" VALUE="0">
     <PARAM NAME="SizeMode" VALUE="3">
     <PARAM NAME="Size" VALUE="2540;2540">
     <PARAM NAME="PictureAlignment" VALUE="0">
     <PARAM NAME="VariousPropertyBits" VALUE="19">
</OBJECT>

<OBJECT ID="You4" WIDTH=96 HEIGHT=96
     CLASSID="CLSID:D4A97620-8E8F-11CF-93CD-00AA00C08FDF">
     <PARAM NAME="BorderStyle" VALUE="0">
     <PARAM NAME="SizeMode" VALUE="3">
     <PARAM NAME="Size" VALUE="2540;2540">
     <PARAM NAME="PictureAlignment" VALUE="0">
     <PARAM NAME="VariousPropertyBits" VALUE="19">
</OBJECT>

<OBJECT ID="You5" WIDTH=96 HEIGHT=96
     CLASSID="CLSID:D4A97620-8E8F-11CF-93CD-00AA00C08FDF">
     <PARAM NAME="BorderStyle" VALUE="0">
     <PARAM NAME="SizeMode" VALUE="3">
     <PARAM NAME="Size" VALUE="2540;2540">
     <PARAM NAME="PictureAlignment" VALUE="0">
     <PARAM NAME="VariousPropertyBits" VALUE="19">
</OBJECT>

<OBJECT ID="You6" WIDTH=96 HEIGHT=96
     CLASSID="CLSID:D4A97620-8E8F-11CF-93CD-00AA00C08FDF">
     <PARAM NAME="BorderStyle" VALUE="0">
     <PARAM NAME="SizeMode" VALUE="3">
     <PARAM NAME="Size" VALUE="2540;2540">
     <PARAM NAME="PictureAlignment" VALUE="0">
     <PARAM NAME="VariousPropertyBits" VALUE="19">
</OBJECT>

<OBJECT ID="You7" WIDTH=96 HEIGHT=96
     CLASSID="CLSID:D4A97620-8E8F-11CF-93CD-00AA00C08FDF">
     <PARAM NAME="BorderStyle" VALUE="0">
     <PARAM NAME="SizeMode" VALUE="3">
     <PARAM NAME="Size" VALUE="2540;2540">
     <PARAM NAME="PictureAlignment" VALUE="0">
     <PARAM NAME="VariousPropertyBits" VALUE="19">
</OBJECT>

<OBJECT ID="You8" WIDTH=96 HEIGHT=96
     CLASSID="CLSID:D4A97620-8E8F-11CF-93CD-00AA00C08FDF">
     <PARAM NAME="BorderStyle" VALUE="0">
     <PARAM NAME="SizeMode" VALUE="3">
     <PARAM NAME="Size" VALUE="2540;2540">
     <PARAM NAME="PictureAlignment" VALUE="0">
     <PARAM NAME="VariousPropertyBits" VALUE="19">
</OBJECT>

<HR>
```

```
<OBJECT ID="DealBtn" WIDTH=96 HEIGHT=32
     CLASSID="CLSID:D7053240-CE69-11CD-A777-00DD01143C57">
     <PARAM NAME="Caption" VALUE="Deal">
     <PARAM NAME="Size" VALUE="2540;847">
     <PARAM NAME="FontEffects" VALUE="1073750016">
     <PARAM NAME="FontCharSet" VALUE="0">
     <PARAM NAME="FontPitchAndFamily" VALUE="2">
     <PARAM NAME="ParagraphAlign" VALUE="3">
</OBJECT>

<OBJECT ID="HitBtn" WIDTH=96 HEIGHT=32
     CLASSID="CLSID:D7053240-CE69-11CD-A777-00DD01143C57">
     <PARAM NAME="Caption" VALUE="Hit">
     <PARAM NAME="Size" VALUE="2540;847">
     <PARAM NAME="FontEffects" VALUE="1073750016">
     <PARAM NAME="FontCharSet" VALUE="0">
     <PARAM NAME="FontPitchAndFamily" VALUE="2">
     <PARAM NAME="ParagraphAlign" VALUE="3">
</OBJECT>

<OBJECT ID="DoubleBtn" WIDTH=96 HEIGHT=32
     CLASSID="CLSID:D7053240-CE69-11CD-A777-00DD01143C57">
     <PARAM NAME="Caption" VALUE="Double">
     <PARAM NAME="Size" VALUE="2540;847">
     <PARAM NAME="FontEffects" VALUE="1073750016">
     <PARAM NAME="FontCharSet" VALUE="0">
     <PARAM NAME="FontPitchAndFamily" VALUE="2">
     <PARAM NAME="ParagraphAlign" VALUE="3">
</OBJECT>

<OBJECT ID="StandBtn" WIDTH=96 HEIGHT=32
     CLASSID="CLSID:D7053240-CE69-11CD-A777-00DD01143C57">
     <PARAM NAME="Caption" VALUE="Stand">
     <PARAM NAME="Size" VALUE="2540;847">
     <PARAM NAME="FontEffects" VALUE="1073750016">
     <PARAM NAME="FontCharSet" VALUE="0">
     <PARAM NAME="FontPitchAndFamily" VALUE="2">
     <PARAM NAME="ParagraphAlign" VALUE="3">
</OBJECT>
<HR>

<OBJECT ID="Label1" WIDTH=39 HEIGHT=20
     CLASSID="CLSID:978C9E23-D4B0-11CE-BF2D-00AA003F40D0">
     <PARAM NAME="Caption" VALUE="Bet:  ">
     <PARAM NAME="Size" VALUE="1000;529">
     <PARAM NAME="FontHeight" VALUE="240">
     <PARAM NAME="FontCharSet" VALUE="0">
     <PARAM NAME="FontPitchAndFamily" VALUE="2">
</OBJECT>

<OBJECT ID="BetEdt" WIDTH=96 HEIGHT=24
     CLASSID="CLSID:8BD21D10-EC42-11CE-9E0D-00AA006002F3">
     <PARAM NAME="VariousPropertyBits" VALUE="746604571">
     <PARAM NAME="Size" VALUE="2540;635">
     <PARAM NAME="FontEffects" VALUE="1073741825">
     <PARAM NAME="FontHeight" VALUE="200">
     <PARAM NAME="FontCharSet" VALUE="0">
     <PARAM NAME="FontPitchAndFamily" VALUE="2">
     <PARAM NAME="ParagraphAlign" VALUE="2">
```

continued on next page

continued from previous page

```
     <PARAM NAME="FontWeight" VALUE="700">
</OBJECT>


<OBJECT ID="Label2" WIDTH=93 HEIGHT=23
     CLASSID="CLSID:978C9E23-D4B0-11CE-BF2D-00AA003F40D0">
     <PARAM NAME="Caption" VALUE="      Balance:  ">
     <PARAM NAME="Size" VALUE="2455;600">
     <PARAM NAME="FontHeight" VALUE="240">
     <PARAM NAME="FontCharSet" VALUE="0">
     <PARAM NAME="FontPitchAndFamily" VALUE="2">
</OBJECT>

<OBJECT ID="Balance" WIDTH=115 HEIGHT=24
     CLASSID="CLSID:978C9E23-D4B0-11CE-BF2D-00AA003F40D0">
     <PARAM NAME="Caption" VALUE="$ 0.00">
     <PARAM NAME="Size" VALUE="3037;635">
     <PARAM NAME="SpecialEffect" VALUE="2">
     <PARAM NAME="FontEffects" VALUE="1073741825">
     <PARAM NAME="FontHeight" VALUE="240">
     <PARAM NAME="FontCharSet" VALUE="0">
     <PARAM NAME="FontPitchAndFamily" VALUE="2">
     <PARAM NAME="ParagraphAlign" VALUE="2">
     <PARAM NAME="FontWeight" VALUE="700">
</OBJECT>

<SCRIPT LANGUAGE="VBScript">
<!--
   Dim DeckShoe(312)
   Dim DealerCards(8)
   Dim PlayerCards(8)
   Dim PlayerCard
   Dim DealerCard
   Dim CurrentCard
   Dim PlayerBalance
   Dim PlayerBet

'.............................................................
' Set the initial balance and bet variables. Then assign the bet
' to the BetEdt object and call the UpdateBalance procedure to set
' the balance. Of course the bet value can be changed by the user,
' but it must be at least 5.
'.............................................................
    PlayerBalance = 100
    PlayerBet = 5

    BetEdt.Value=PlayerBet
    Call UpdateBalance()

'.............................................................
' Disable the Hit, Double, and Stand buttons. These buttons are not
' active until the hand is dealt.
'.............................................................
    HitBtn.Enabled=False
    DoubleBtn.Enabled=False
    StandBtn.Enabled=False

    Call ShuffleCards()
```

```
'..................................................................
' ShuffleCards()
' This procedure creates a random array of cards. You are using six
' decks of cards, so you have to ensure that the array does not
' contain more than six of a specific card. The DeckOfCards array keeps
' track of the number of times a card has been added to the DeckShoe
' array.
'..................................................................
    Sub ShuffleCards()
       Dim DeckOfCards(52)
       Dim Card

       CurrentCard = 0

       Randomize()
'..................................................................
' Initialize the array with 0; you have six decks of cards.
'..................................................................
       For i = 0 to 51
          DeckOfCards(i) = 0
       Next

'..................................................................
' Shuffle the cards. You are randomly placing the cards in the
' DeckShoe array. You ensure that there are less than six of the
' specified card in the array.
'..................................................................
       For i = 0 to 311
          Do
            Card = CINT( 51 * Rnd() )
          Loop While DeckOfCards( Card ) > 5

          DeckOfCards( Card ) = DeckOfCards( Card ) + 1
          DeckShoe( i ) = Card+1
       Next
    End Sub

'..................................................................
' Refresh()
' This procedure causes the image to repaint so that the new card
' displays on the screen. The ActiveX control does not refresh the
' image if you only change the image name; you need to change the
' sizing or special effects to get it to repaint.
'..................................................................

    Sub Refresh( Image )

       Image.SpecialEffect=1
       Image.SpecialEffect=0
    End Sub

'...................................................................
' SetCard()
' This procedure sets the bitmap file that is displayed for the card
' image. Since all of the bitmap files have a numeric name, simply
' take the random number generated and add the .bmp suffix to identify
' the name of the image file.
'...................................................................
```

continued on next page

continued from previous page

```
    Sub SetCard( Image, Card )
       Dim CardName

       CardName = Card & ".bmp"
       Image.PicturePath=CardName

       Call Refresh( Image )
    End Sub

'.......................................................................
' HitBtn_Click()
' This procedure is called when the user presses the Hit button. This
' procedure deals a new card to the user, and then checks to make sure
' the user has not busted.
'.......................................................................
    Sub HitBtn_Click
       PlayerCards(PlayerCard)=DeckShoe(CurrentCard)

       Select Case PlayerCard
          Case 2
            Call SetCard( You3, PlayerCards(PlayerCard) )
          Case 3
            Call SetCard( You4, PlayerCards(PlayerCard) )
          Case 4
            Call SetCard( You5, PlayerCards(PlayerCard) )
          Case 5
            Call SetCard( You6, PlayerCards(PlayerCard) )
          Case 6
            Call SetCard( You7, PlayerCards(PlayerCard) )
          Case 7
            Call SetCard( You8, PlayerCards(PlayerCard) )
       End Select

       CurrentCard=CurrentCard+1
       PlayerCard=PlayerCard+1

'............................................................
' Disables the Double button; the user can only double before
' he or she requests an additional card. Then check to see if the
' user has busted (total is greater than 21).
'............................................................
       DoubleBtn.Enabled=False

       If CardTotal( PlayerCards, PlayerCard ) > 21 Then
          MsgBox( "Bust!" )

          Call SetCard( Dealer2, DealerCards(1) )
          Call PayOff()
       End If
    End Sub


'..............................................................
' PlayDealer()
' This procedure is called by either the StandBtn_Click() procedure
' or the DoubleBtn_Click() procedure to determine the dealer
' cards. The procedure continues to deal cards to the dealer
' as long as the dealer total is less than 17.
```

```
'.............................................................
    Sub PlayDealer
       Call SetCard( Dealer2, DealerCards(1) )

       Do While CardTotal( DealerCards, DealerCard ) < 17
          DealerCards( DealerCard ) = DeckShoe( CurrentCard )

          Select Case DealerCard
            Case 2
              Call SetCard( Dealer3, DealerCards(DealerCard) )
            Case 3
              Call SetCard( Dealer4, DealerCards(DealerCard) )
            Case 4
              Call SetCard( Dealer5, DealerCards(DealerCard) )
            Case 5
              Call SetCard( Dealer6, DealerCards(DealerCard) )
            Case 6
              Call SetCard( Dealer7, DealerCards(DealerCard) )
            Case 7
              Call SetCard( Dealer8, DealerCards(DealerCard) )
          End Select

          CurrentCard = CurrentCard + 1
          DealerCard = DealerCard + 1
       Loop

       If CardTotal( DealerCards, DealerCard ) > 21 Then
          MsgBox( "Dealer Busted!, You Win!" )
       End If

       Call PayOff()
    End Sub

'.................................................................
' StandBtn_Click()
' This procedure is called when the user clicks the Stand button.
' It calls the PlayDealer() procedure to determine the dealer's
' hand.
'.................................................................
    Sub StandBtn_Click()
       Call PlayDealer()
    End Sub

'.................................................................
' DoubleBtn_Click()
' This procedure is called when the user clicks the Double button.
' The player's bet is doubled, and he or she receives one more card. The
' The UpdateBalance() procedure is called to update the player's balance,
' and the PlayDealer() procedure is called.
'.................................................................
    Sub DoubleBtn_Click()
       PlayerBalance=PlayerBalance-PlayerBet
       PlayerBet=CDbl(PlayerBet)+CDbl(PlayerBet)

       PlayerCards(2) = DeckShoe( CurrentCard )
       PlayerCard = PlayerCard+1
       CurrentCard = CurrentCard+1

       Call SetCard( You3, PlayerCards(2) )
```

continued on next page

continued from previous page

```
      Call UpdateBalance()
      Call PlayDealer()
   End Sub

'..........................................................
' UpdateBalance()
' This procedure is called to update the user balance.
'..........................................................
   Sub UpdateBalance()
      Balance.Caption="$ " & PlayerBalance
   End Sub

'..........................................................
' CardValue()
' This function determines the numeric value of the card displayed.
' Since there are six decks of 52 cards, you need to determine the actual
' numeric value of the card. If the value of the card is greater
' than 13, use the Mod operator to divide the value by 13 and
' determine the remainder. Since the king is always the
' thirteenth card in the suit, the equation will return a value
' of 0. Assign a value of 10 for that card. All values greater
' than 13 are also face cards, so we give them a value of 10.
'..........................................................
   Function CardValue( ByVal Card )
      If Card > 13 Then
         Card=(Card mod 13)
      End If

'..............................................................
' All kings are divisible by 13, so if you have 0 then it must be a king.
'..............................................................
      If Card = 0 Then
         Card = 10
      End If

'..................................
' All face cards have a value of 10
'..................................
      If Card > 10 then
         Card=10
      End If

      CardValue = Card

   End Function

'..............................................................
' CardTotal()
' This function totals the cards in the hand.
'..............................................................
   Function CardTotal( Cards, NumCards )
      Dim Total
      Dim Value

      For i = 0 to NumCards-1
         Value = CardValue( Cards(i) )

         If Value = 1 Then
```

```
            Value = 11
         End If

         Total=Total+Value
      Next

'..................................
' Account for soft hands with aces.
'..................................
      i = 0
      Do While ( Total > 21 ) and ( i < NumCards )
         If CardValue( Cards(i) ) = 1 Then
            Total=Total-10
         End If
            i=i+1
      Loop

      CardTotal = Total
   End Function

'.......................................................
' DealBtn_Click()
' This procedure is called when the Deal button is
' selected. This procedure deals the first two
' cards for the dealer and player. The On Error
' Resume Next statement is used to assure that any
' errors that occur are not displayed to the user.
'.......................................................
   Sub DealBtn_Click()

      On Error Resume Next

'........................................
' Get player bet and check it for minimum.
'........................................
      PlayerBet=BetEdt.Value
      If (Not IsNumeric(PlayerBet)) Then
        MsgBox "You must type a numeric value in the Bet field."
        Exit Sub
      End If

      If PlayerBet < 5 Then
         MsgBox( "Minimum bet is $5.00.")
         Exit Sub
     End If

'......................................
' Update balance to reflect current bet.
'......................................
      PlayerBalance=PlayerBalance-PlayerBet
      Call UpdateBalance()

'.........................
' Clear all the card images
'.........................
      Dealer3.PicturePath=""
      Dealer4.PicturePath=""
      Dealer5.PicturePath=""
      Dealer6.PicturePath=""
```

continued on next page

continued from previous page

```
        Dealer7.PicturePath=""
        Dealer8.PicturePath=""

        You3.PicturePath=""
        You4.PicturePath=""
        You5.PicturePath=""
        You6.PicturePath=""
        You7.PicturePath=""
        You8.PicturePath=""

'..............................
' Check if you need to shuffle.
'..............................
        if CurrentCard > 250 then
            MsgBox( "The cards are being shuffled." )
            Call ShuffleCards()
        end if

'....................
' Assign dealt cards
'....................
        PlayerCards(0)=DeckShoe(CurrentCard)
        PlayerCards(1)=DeckShoe(CurrentCard+2)
        DealerCards(0)=DeckShoe(CurrentCard+1)
        DealerCards(1)=DeckShoe(CurrentCard+3)

'......................................
' Bump counters to reflect dealt cards.
'......................................
        CurrentCard=CurrentCard+4
        PlayerCard=2
        DealerCard=2

'......................................
' Set the card images that were dealt.
'......................................
        Call SetCard( Dealer1, DealerCards(0) )
        Call SetCard( Dealer2, 0 )
        Call SetCard( You1, PlayerCards(0) )
        Call SetCard( You2, PlayerCards(1) )

'.............................
' Enable buttons to play game.
'.............................
        DealBtn.Enabled=False
        HitBtn.Enabled=True
        DoubleBtn.Enabled=True
        StandBtn.Enabled=True

'................................
' Refresh the blank images.
'................................
        Call Refresh( Dealer3 )
        Call Refresh( Dealer4 )
        Call Refresh( Dealer5 )
        Call Refresh( Dealer6 )
        Call Refresh( Dealer7 )
        Call Refresh( Dealer8 )
```

```
        Call Refresh( You3 )
        Call Refresh( You4 )
        Call Refresh( You5 )
        Call Refresh( You6 )
        Call Refresh( You7 )
        Call Refresh( You8 )

'..............................
' Handle dealer showing an ace.
'..............................
        If CardValue( DealerCards(0) ) =  1 Then
           If MsgBox( "Do you want insurance?", 4 ) = 6 then
              If CardValue( DealerCards(1)  ) <> 10 Then
                 PlayerBalance=PlayerBalance-(PlayerBet/2)
                 Call UpdateBalance()
                 MsgBox( "No, the dealer didn't have a Blackjack." )
              End If
           End If

           If CardValue( DealerCards(1) ) = 10 Then
              Call SetCard( Dealer2, DealerCards(1) )
              DealBtn.Enabled=True
              HitBtn.Enabled=False
              DoubleBtn.Enabled=False
              StandBtn.Enabled=False
           End If
        End If

        If CardValue( PlayerCards(0) ) = 1 or CardValue( PlayerCards(1) ) = 1 Then
           If CardValue( PlayerCards(0) ) = 10 or CardValue( PlayerCards(1) ) = 10 Then
              MsgBox( "You got a Blackjack!" )
              Call SetCard( Dealer2, DealerCards(1) )
              Call PayOff()
           End If
        End If
     End Sub

'..............................................
' PayOff()
' This procedure is called to determine the payoff
' for the player.
'..............................................
     Sub PayOff()
        Dim PlayerTotal
        Dim DealerTotal

'.......................
' Reset buttons.
'.......................
        HitBtn.Enabled = False
        DoubleBtn.Enabled = False
        StandBtn.Enabled = False
        DealBtn.Enabled = True

        PlayerTotal = CardTotal( PlayerCards, PlayerCard )
        DealerTotal = CardTotal( DealerCards, DealerCard )

        If PlayerTotal <= 21 Then
```

continued on next page

continued from previous page

```
            If PlayerTotal = DealerTotal Then
               MsgBox( "You pushed!" )
               PlayerBalance = PlayerBalance + PlayerBet
            Else
               If DealerTotal > 21 Then
                  PlayerBalance = PlayerBalance + (PlayerBet*2)
               Else
                  If PlayerTotal = 21 and PlayerCard = 2 Then
                     PlayerBalance = PlayerBalance + (PlayerBet*2.5)
                  Else
                     If PlayerTotal > DealerTotal Then
                        PlayerBalance = PlayerBalance + (PlayerBet*2)
                        MsgBox( "You win!" )
                     End If
                  End If
               End If
            End If
         End If

         Call UpdateBalance()

      End Sub
-->
</SCRIPT>

</BODY>

</HTML>
```

14

HTML FEATURES SUPPORTED BY INTERNET EXPLORER 3.0

14

HTML FEATURES SUPPORTED BY INTERNET EXPLORER 3.0

Internet Explorer 3.0 supports all of the standard HTML 3.0 elements. It also introduces some new HTML tags, such as the **<OBJECT>** element, which is used to embed an ActiveX object in a page.

This chapter is designed to provide a brief overview of the HTML elements that are available for use with Internet Explorer 3.0. Since many of these elements are used throughout this book, this chapter provides a brief description of each element and its associated attributes.

HTML Document Layout

An HTML document must always begin and end with an **<HTML>** tag. This notifies the browser that the code between the tags is HTML, so that it knows how to interpret it appropriately. Within the **<HTML>** tags, the document is divided into two sections: the header and the body.

The header section is identified by the **<HEAD>** element. This section contains specific information about the document, such as the document title (the **<TITLE>** element). Normally, for the sake of consistency, the VBScript code is placed in this section of the document.

The body section is identified by the **<BODY>** element. This section contains all the information, such as the text and images, that displays on the page. Most of the HTML elements covered in this chapter are placed within the **<BODY>** section.

HTML Colors

Internet Explorer 3.0 allows you to specify a color value for items, such as the color of the font that displays. The colors are specified by either indicating the color name or the RGB value for the color. Table 14-1 indicates the color names and associated RGB values that are available for use within Internet Explorer 3.0.

Table 14-1 Internet Explorer 3.0 color values

Color Name	RGB Value
aqua	#00FFFF
black	#000000
blue	#0000FF
fuchsia	#FF00FF
gray	#808080
green	#008000
lime	#00FF00
maroon	#800000
navy	#000080
olive	#808000
purple	#800080
red	#FF0000
silver	#C0C0C0
teal	#008080
white	#FFFFFF
yellow	#FFFF00

HTML Reference

The remaining portion of this chapter provides a description of the HTML elements that can be used within Internet Explorer 3.0. The elements are listed in the chapter in alphabetical order so that you can quickly locate the desired element.

A brief description is provided for each element, along with a description of the associated attributes for the element. Examples have been provided to illustrate how to use several of the elements.

<!> Element

Purpose Use the <!> element to specify comments within your HTML file.

Syntax `<!-- comment text -->`

Description The <!> element is used to provide comments within your HTML code. Any text that is placed between the comment tags will not print on the page.

Since VBScript code is not recognized by all browsers, it is also recommended that you use this element around your VBScript code.

Source Internet Explorer 3.0

<!DOCTYPE> Element

Purpose Use the <!DOCTYPE> element to specify the HTML version used within the document.

Syntax `<!DOCTYPE HTML PUBLIC "-//W3C//DTD HTML 3.2//EN">`

Description The <!DOCTYPE> element is used to specify the version of HTML that is used within the document. This is a required element when creating an HTML 3.2-compliant document.

Source Internet Explorer 3.0

<A> Element

Purpose Use the <A> element to specify a hypertext link on your HTML page. One of the attributes in Table 14-2 must be used with the <A> element.

Syntax `<A attribute> </A>`

Table 14-2 Attributes of the <A> element

Attribute	Description
HREF = address	Specifies the destination of the hypertext link. When the user clicks the text between the <A> and </A>, the page at the specified address will be displayed. The address can either be a URL address or the name of another file in the same directory as the current page. For example, to specify a URL address, you would type `<A HREF = "http://www.waite.com">Display Waite Group Press</A>`.
NAME = name	Identifies the name of an anchor within an HTML page. Once an anchor has been specified, you can use the HREF attribute to specify a jump to this anchor location.

Description The <A> element is probably one of the most widely used HTML elements. With this element you can specify the location of a page that should display when the user selects the specified text. This is accomplished by using the HREF attribute.

You can also use the <A> element to specify an anchor location on a page, by using the NAME attribute. The anchor is like a bookmark; once the anchor is set, another page can use the HREF attribute to jump directly to that location on the page.

Listing 14-1 indicates how to use the <A> element to jump to another page, as illustrated in Figure 14-1.

Listing 14-1 Using the <A> element

```
<HTML>

<HEAD>

</HEAD>

<BODY>

   <A:HREF = "A2.htm">Click here to display the second page.</A>

</BODY>

</HTML>
```

Source HTML 2.0

<ADDRESS> ELEMENT

Purpose Use the <ADDRESS> element to identify information, such as an address, that should be placed in italics.

Syntax `<ADDRESS> text </ADDRESS>`

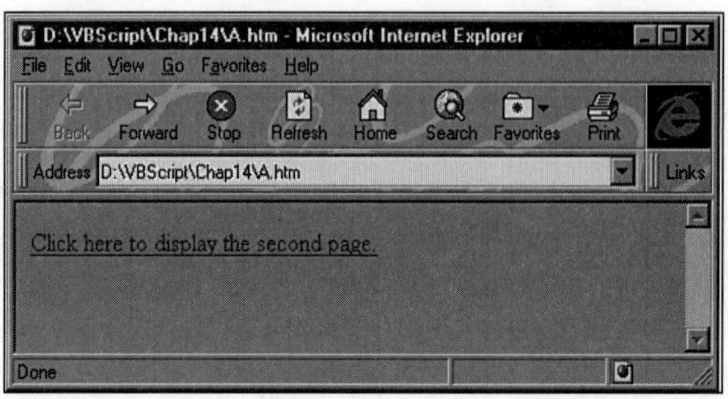

Figure 14-1 The <A> element allows you to specify a link to another location

Description The <ADDRESS> element places the specified text in italics on your HTML page. A paragraph break occurs before the initial <ADDRESS> tag and after the closing </ADDRESS> tag.

Source HTML 2.0

Related HTML Elements <CITE>, <DFN>, <EM>, <I>

<APPLET> Element

Purpose Use the <APPLET> element to embed a Java applet into your HTML page. The attributes in Table 14-3 are used with the <APPLET> element.

Syntax `<APPLET attribute>    </APPLET>`

Table 14-3 Attributes of the <APPLET> element

Attribute	Description	
ALIGN = alignment	Specifies the alignment of the applet with respect to other information on the page. This is a required attribute. The following values can be used with this attribute:	
	Value	**Description**
	BOTTOM	Text is aligned with the bottom of the applet.
	LEFT	The applet is left-aligned and text flows around it.
	MIDDLE	Text is aligned with the middle of the applet.
	RIGHT	The applet is right-aligned and text flows around it.
	TOP	Text is aligned with the top of the applet.
ALT = "text"	Identifies the text that should be displayed if the browser cannot run Java applets.	
CODE = "filename"	Identifies the name of the file that contains the Applet subclass. This is a required attribute. The file should be located in the location specified by the CODEBASE attribute.	
CODEBASE = "URL"	Specifies the location of the applet. If this attribute is not specified, the URL of the HTML document is used.	
HEIGHT = "pixels"	Specifies the initial height of the applet display area. This is a required attribute.	
HSPACE = "pixels"	Specifies the number of pixels on each side of the applet.	
NAME = "appletname"	Specifies a name for the applet, so that other applets on the same page can locate it.	
VSPACE = "pixels"	Specifies the number of pixels above and below the applet.	
WIDTH = "pixels"	Specifies the initial width of the applet display area. This is a required attribute.	

Description The <APPLET> element is used to embed an applet into an HTML page. Depending upon the applet you are adding, you may not use all of the attributes listed in Table 14-3. The <PARAM> element is also used within the <APPLET> tags to identify initial property values for the applet.

Source Netscape

Related HTML Elements <OBJECT>, <PARAM>

<AREA> ELEMENT

Purpose Use the <AREA> element to specify the shape of a "hot spot" on an image map on the HTML page. The attributes in Table 14-4 are used with the <AREA> element.

Syntax `<AREA attribute>`

Table 14-4 Attributes of the <AREA> element

Attribute	Description
COORDS = "a, b, c, d, .."	Specifies the coordinates of the hot spot on the specified image map.
HREF = "URL"	Indicates the address of the hot spot.
NOHREF	Indicates that a hot spot location does not exist for clicks in the region just specified by the COORDS attribute.
SHAPE = "shape"	Indicates the type of shape created by the COORDS attribute. The possible shape values are as follows: **Value** — **Description** RECT — Specifies a rectangle. RECTANGLE — Specifies a rectangle.

Description The <AREA> element is used to specify a hot spot location on an image map. An image map is a picture that displays on the HTML page. When the user clicks over the hot spot location on the specified image map, the appropriate page is loaded. You can place multiple hot spots on one image map by assigning different regions of the image map to each hot spot.

Source Internet Explorer 3.0

Related HTML Elements <MAP>

<B> ELEMENT

Purpose Use the <B> element to place the specified text in a bold font.

Syntax `<B> text </B>`

Description The <B> element places the specified text in bold on your HTML page, where available. In other words, if the browser does not support bold, or there is not a bold version of the font, the text will appear in the normal font.

Source HTML 2.0

Related HTML Elements <STRONG>

<BASE> Element

Purpose Use the <BASE> element to specify the URL of the HTML document. Table 14-5 describes the attribute that is used with the <BASE> element.

Syntax `<BASE attribute>`

Table 14-5 Attribute of the <BASE> element

Attribute	Description
HREF = URL	The full URL of the HTML document. This is an important element to add to your HTML page; if the document is read out of context, placing the <BASE> element allows the user to refer to the original.

Description The <BASE> element identifies the URL of the HTML document. This element must be specified within the <HEAD> section of your HTML document.

Source HTML 2.0

<BASEFONT> Element

Purpose Use the <BASEFONT> element to set the base font attributes for the HTML page. One of the attributes in Table 14-6 must be used with the <BASEFONT> element.

Syntax `<BASEFONT attribute>`

Table 14-6 Attributes of the <BASEFONT> element

Attribute	Description
SIZE = n	Specifies a value between 1 and 7 (7 is the largest) that indicates the base font size for the page. The default value is 3.

Description The <BASEFONT> element specifies changes for the base font used on the HTML page. The base font settings are the basis for all <FONT> element changes.

The FACE and COLOR attributes are only supported by Internet Explorer 3.0.

Source Netscape, Internet Explorer 3.0 (FACE and COLOR attributes)

<BGSOUND> ELEMENT

Purpose Use the **<BGSOUND>** element to specify a background sound for your HTML page. Table 14-7 specifies the attributes of the **<BGSOUND>** element.

Syntax **<BGSOUND SRC = filename, LOOP = loopvalue>**

Table 14-7 Attributes of the <BGSOUND> element

Attribute	Description
LOOP = loopvalue	This attribute of the <BGSOUND> element is optional. It specifies the number of times the sound file should play when your HTML page is accessed. If this attribute is omitted, the sound file will play once, after it is loaded. The loopvalue attribute can either be a numeric value greater than zero, which indicates the number of times to play, or INFINITE, indicating the sound file is to be repeated continuously until the user exits the page.
SRC = filename	Indicates the name and address of the sound file. The sound file can be a wave (WAV), audio (AU), or Midi (MIDI) format. This is a required attribute for the <BGSOUND> element.

Description The **<BGSOUND>** element allows you to specify a sound file that will be played each time your HTML page is accessed. The **<BGSOUND>** element has two attributes. The **SRC** attribute specifies the name and location of the sound file that should be played. The **LOOP** value is used to indicate the number of times that the file should continue to play when the page is accessed.

Source Internet Explorer 3.0

<BIG> ELEMENT

Purpose Use the **<BIG>** element to place the specified text in a bigger font than the current font.

Syntax **<BIG> text </BIG>**

Description The **<BIG>** element places the specified text in a font size larger than the currently selected font for your HTML page. The exact appearance of the text using the **<BIG>** element is based on the **<FONT>** and **<BASEFONT>** settings.

Source HTML 3.0

Related HTML Elements **<SMALL>**, **<SUB>**, **<SUP>**

<BLOCKQUOTE> Element

Purpose Use the `<BLOCKQUOTE>` element to set apart a quotation in the text of the HTML page.

Syntax `<BLOCKQUOTE> text </BLOCKQUOTE>`

Description The `<BLOCKQUOTE>` element is used to set apart text that you want to have appear as a quotation on your page. Normally the text is indented at the left and right margins and placed in italics. The `<BLOCKQUOTE>` element also causes a paragraph break and extra space above and below the quote.

Source HTML 2.0

<BODY> Element

Purpose Use the `<BODY>` element to identify the beginning and ending of the body section of your HTML code. The optional attributes in Table 14-8 can be used with the `<BODY>` element.

Syntax `<BODY attribute> </BODY>`

Table 14-8 Attributes of the <BODY> element

Attribute	Description
BACKGROUND = filename	Specifies the name and location of the file that should be used as the background graphic for the page. The graphic in this file is tiled behind the text and graphics on the HTML page.
BGCOLOR = colorvalue	Specifies either the name or the RGB value of the background color for the HTML page. This can be any one of the color names or RGB values listed in Table 14-1.
BGPROPERTIES = FIXED	Indicates that the background graphic specified by the BACKGROUND attribute specifies a water mark. This keeps the graphic from scrolling on the screen when the text and graphics on the page are scrolled. This attribute is only available in Internet Explorer 3.0.
LEFTMARGIN = number	A numeric value that specifies the left margin of the page. This setting overrides the default margin setting. If this value is set to 0, the left margin is exactly on the left side of the screen. This attribute is only available in Internet Explorer 3.0.
LINK = colorvalue	Specifies either the name or the RGB value of the links listed on the HTML page that have not been visited. This can be any one of the color names or RGB values listed in Table 14-1.
TEXT = colorvalue	Specifies either the name or the RGB value of the color of the text for the HTML page. This can be any one of the color names or RGB values listed in Table 14-1.
TOPMARGIN = number	A numeric value that specifies the top margin of the page. If this value is set to 0, the top margin is the very top edge. This option is only available in Internet Explorer 3.0.
VLINK = colorvalue	Specifies either the name or the RGB value of the links listed on the HTML page that have been visited by the user. This can be any one of the color names or RGB values listed in Table 14-1.

Description The <BODY> element is used to identify the beginning and ending of the body section of the HTML code. The body section contains the text and images that make up the HTML page. This element can be used alone to simply identify the start and end of the body section, or with one or more of the attributes in Table 14-8, to indicate specific information about the body section.

Listing 14-2 indicates how the <BODY> element can be used to specify a watermark for your page, as illustrated in Figure 14-2.

Listing 14-2 Using the <BODY> *element*

```
<HTML>

<HEAD>

</HEAD>

<BODY BACKGROUND = BODY.GIF>

<B>This is an HTML page with a watermark background.</B>

</BODY>

</HTML>
```

Source HTML 2.0 (although the **BGPROPERTIES**, **LEFTMARGIN**, and **TOPMARGIN** attributes are only available in Internet Explorer 3.0)

Related HTML Elements <HEAD>, <HTML>

Figure 14-2 The <BODY> element attributes allow you to specify additional information about the body of the document

 Element

Purpose Use the `<BR>` element to insert a line break in your HTML page. This element can be used alone or with the attribute specified in Table 14-9.

Syntax `<BR attribute>`

Table 14-9 Attribute of the <BR> element

Attribute	Description
`CLEAR = value`	This attribute is used after a floating image is specified to indicate that the text that follows the attribute statement will be placed below the image. The following values can be specified for this attribute: **Value** — **Description** `ALL` — Text will be placed after the image. `LEFT` — Text will be left-justified below the image. `RIGHT` — Text will be right-justified below the image.

Description The `<BR>` element is used to specify a line break within the text of your HTML document. If you do not specify a break, HTML will continue to place the text together on the screen. In other words, even though you may have spaced the text out appropriately in your code, HTML does not recognize the hard returns in it. If you want to break up the text, you need to specify a break using the `<BR>` element.

If you have text that should be placed after a floating image, you need to use the `<BR>` element with the `CLEAR` attribute. If the floating image is left-justified, you should use the `CLEAR = LEFT` attribute to have the text placed at the left margin under the image. If the image is right-justified, use the `CLEAR = RIGHT` attribute to right-justify the text under the image.

Source HTML 2.0 (the `CLEAR` attribute is in HTML 3.0)

<CAPTION> Element

Purpose Use the `<CAPTION>` element to specify a caption for a table on your HTML page. The attributes in Table 14-10 can be used with the `<CAPTION>` element to specify the alignment and location of the caption.

Syntax `<CAPTION attribute> text </CAPTION>`

Table 14-10 Attributes of the <CAPTION> element

Attribute	Description
ALIGN = alignment	Indicates how the caption is aligned with respect to the left and right margins of the table. The following values can be used with the ALIGN attribute: **Value** — **Description** CENTER — Centers the caption. LEFT — Left-justifies the caption. RIGHT — Right-justifies the caption.
VALIGN = location	Indicates the location of the caption with respect to the table. The following values can be used with the VALIGN attribute: **Value** — **Description** BOTTOM — Caption is placed below the table. TOP — Caption is placed above the table.

Description The <CAPTION> element is used to indicate a caption for a table. This element is placed inside of the <TABLE> tags, but outside of the <TD> and <TR> tags that specify the table rows and columns. The default alignment centers the caption at the top of the table; you can change the defaults by using the attributes in Table 14-10.

Source HTML 3.0

Related HTML Elements <TABLE>, <TBODY>, <TD>, <TFOOT>, <THEAD>, <TR>

<CENTER> Element

Purpose Use the <CENTER> element to center the specified text.

Syntax **<CENTER> text </CENTER>**

Description The <CENTER> element centers the specified lines of text between the left and right margins.

Source Netscape

Related HTML Elements <P>

<CITE> Element

Purpose Use the <CITE> element to identify citation information that should be placed in italics.

Syntax **<CITE> text </CITE>**

Description The <CITE> element places the specified text in italics on your HTML page. The citation text does not have a paragraph break before or after it.

Source HTML 2.0

Related HTML Elements <ADDRESS>, <DFN>, <EM>, <I>

<CODE> Element

Purpose Use the `<CODE>` element to identify sample code.

Syntax **`<CODE> text </CODE>`**

Description The `<CODE>` element places the specified text in a smaller, fixed-width font on your HTML page. This element is used with sample code that you want to place on the page.

Source HTML 2.0

Related HTML Elements `<SAMP>`

<COL> Element

Purpose Use the `<COL>` element to specify the alignment of text within columns of a table on your HTML page. The attributes in Table 14-11 can be used with the `<COL>` element.

Syntax **`<COL attribute>`**

Table 14-11 Attributes of the <COL> element

Attribute	Description
ALIGN = alignment	Indicates how the text in the column is aligned with respect to the left and right margins of the table. The following values can be used with the ALIGN attribute: **Value** — **Description** CENTER — Centers the text in the column. JUSTIFY — Fully justifies the text within the column. LEFT — Left-justifies the text in the column. RIGHT — Right-justifies the text in the column.
SPAN = value	Indicates the number of columns for which the ALIGN attribute should be used.

Description The `<COL>` element is used to specify the alignment of text within columns of a table. This element is placed within the `<TABLE>` tags, normally within the `<TD>` and `<TR>` tags that specify the table rows and columns. If you have multiple `<COL>` statements, they will be applied to the columns in the order they appear. For example, the first `<COL>` statement would be applied to the first column, or the number of columns specified by the `SPAN` attribute.

Source Internet Explorer 3.0

Related HTML Elements `<COLSPAN>`, `<TABLE>`, `<TD>`, `<TR>`

<COLGROUP> Element

Purpose Use the <COLGROUP> element to group columns of a table together so that you can set their alignment properties. The attributes in Table 14-12 can be used with the <COLGROUP> element.

Syntax `<COLGROUP attribute>`

Table 14-12 Attributes of the <COLGROUP> element

Attribute	Description
ALIGN = alignment	Indicates how the text in the column group is aligned with respect to the left and right margins of the table. The following values can be used with the ALIGN attribute: **Value** / **Description** CENTER — Centers the text in the column. JUSTIFY — Fully justifies the text within the column. LEFT — Left-justifies the text in the column. RIGHT — Right-justifies the text in the column.
VALIGN = alignment	Indicates how the text in the column group is aligned vertically in the cells of the table. The following values can be used with the VALIGN attribute: **Value** / **Description** BASELINE — Justifies text near the baseline of the cell. BOTTOM — Justifies text toward the bottom of the cell. MIDDLE — Centers the text vertically. TOP — Justifies the text toward the top of the cell.
SPAN = value	Indicates the number of columns for which the ALIGN attribute should be used.

Description The <COLGROUP> element is used to specify the alignment of text within a group of columns in a table. This element is placed within the <TABLE> tags, normally within the <TD> and <TR> tags that specify the table rows and columns. If you have multiple <COLGROUP> statements, they will be applied to the columns in the order they appear. For example, the first <COLGROUP> statement would be applied to the first column, or the number of columns specified by the SPAN attribute.

The <COLGROUP> element is similar to the <COL> element. The main difference is that the <COLGROUP> element allows you to also set the vertical alignment for the text.

Source Internet Explorer 3.0

Related HTML Elements <COLSPAN>, <TABLE>, <TD>, <TR>

<COMMENT> Element

Purpose Use the `<COMMENT>` element to place a comment in the HTML code.

Syntax `<COMMENT> text </COMMENT>`

Description The `<COMMENT>` element is used to specify a comment within your HTML code. This element is used to document your code. Any text placed between the beginning and ending `<COMMENT>` tags will not display on the HTML page.

Source HTML 2.0

<DD> Element

Purpose Use the `<DD>` element to specify a definition within a definition list.

Syntax `<DD> text`

Description The `<DD>` element identifies the description of the term indicated by the `<DT>` element. The text specified by the `<DD>` element is placed in the right column of the definition list.

Listing 14-4, under the `<DL>` element, illustrates how to use the `<DD>` element to create a description for a term in a definition list.

Source HTML 2.0

Related HTML Elements `<DL>`, `<DT>`

<DFN> Element

Purpose Use the `<DFN>` element to indicate the first time a term appears in a paragraph.

Syntax `<DFN> text </DFN>`

Description The `<DFN>` element identifies the first time a term appears within a paragraph, the defining instance of the term. The selected text is displayed in italics on your HTML page.

This element is currently supported only by Internet Explorer 3.0.

Source Internet Explorer 3.0

Related HTML Elements `<ADDRESS>`, `<CITE>`, `<EM>`, `<I>`

<DIR> Element

Purpose Use the `<DIR>` element to specify a directory list.

Syntax `<DIR> list </DIR>`

Description The `<DIR>` element identifies the beginning and end of a directory list. The `<LI>` element is used to identify each element of the list. Each item in the list can have up to 20 characters.

Listing 14-3 illustrates how to use the **<DIR>** element to create a directory list, as shown in Figure 14-3.

Listing 14-3 Using the <DIR> *element*

```
<HTML>

<HEAD>

</HEAD>

<BODY>

<DIR>
  <LI>Item 1
  <LI>Item 2
  <LI>Item 3
</DIR>

</BODY>

</HTML>
```

Source HTML 2.0

Related HTML Elements <LI>

<DIV> Element

Purpose Use the **<DIV>** element to enclose a group of items so that specific formatting can be applied to the items. Table 14-13 outlines the attributes that are used with the <DIV> element.

Syntax **<DIV ALIGN** = alignment, **CLASS** = classtype> text **</DIV>**

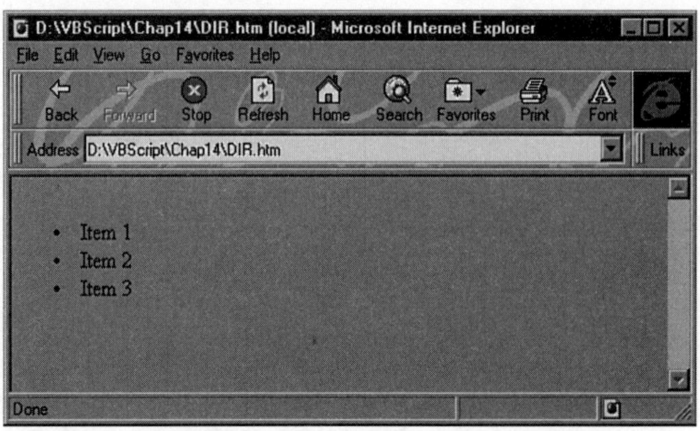

Figure 14-3 The **<DIR>** element creates a directory list

Table 14-13 Attributes of the <DIV> element

Attribute	Description
ALIGN = alignment	Indicates the default horizontal alignment for the contents of the <DIV> element. The following values can be used with the ALIGN attribute: **Value** — **Description** CENTER — Centers the contents. JUSTIFY — Fully justifies the contents. LEFT — Left-justifies the contents. RIGHT — Right-justifies the contents.
CLASS = classtype	Identifies a section of text as being a certain style based on the styles in the style sheet. This could be a chapter, section, abstract, appendix, and so on.
SIZE = n	Specifies a value between 1 and 7 (7 is the largest) that indicates the font size for this location on the page. The default value is 3.

Description The <DIV> element identifies different kinds of groups that should be given a distinctive style.

Source Netscape

<DL> Element

Purpose Use the <DL> element to specify a definition list.

Syntax **<DL> list </DL>**

Description The <DL> element identifies the beginning and end of a definition list. The <DT> element is used to identify each term in the list, and the <DD> element identifies the associated description for each term.

Listing 14-4 uses the <DL> element to create a definition list, as illustrated in Figure 14-4.

Listing 14-4 Using the <DL> element

```
<HTML>

<HEAD>

</HEAD>

<BODY>

<DL>
  <DT><B>Deluxe Pizza</B></DT><DD>Contains pepperoni, olives, green peppers, onions, ⇐
ham, and sausage
```

continued on next page

continued from previous page

```
   <DT><B>Meat Only Pizza</B></DT><DD>Contains pepperoni, ham, and sausage.</DD>
   <DT><B>Hawaiian Pizza</B></DT><DD>Contains ham and pineapple.</DD>
   <DT><B>Vegetarian Pizza</B></DT><DD>Contains olives, green peppers, onions, and ⇐
tomatoes.</DD>

</DL>

</BODY>

</HTML>
```

Source HTML 2.0

Related HTML Elements <DD>, <DT>

<DT> Element

Purpose Use the <DT> element to specify a term within a definition list.

Syntax `<DT> text`

Description The <DT> element identifies a term within your definition list. The specified term is placed in the left column of the definition list; any definition specified by a <DD> element is placed in the right column.

Listing 14-4, under the <DL> element, illustrates how to use the <DT> element to specify a term in a definition list.

Source HTML 2.0

Related HTML Elements <DD>, <DL>

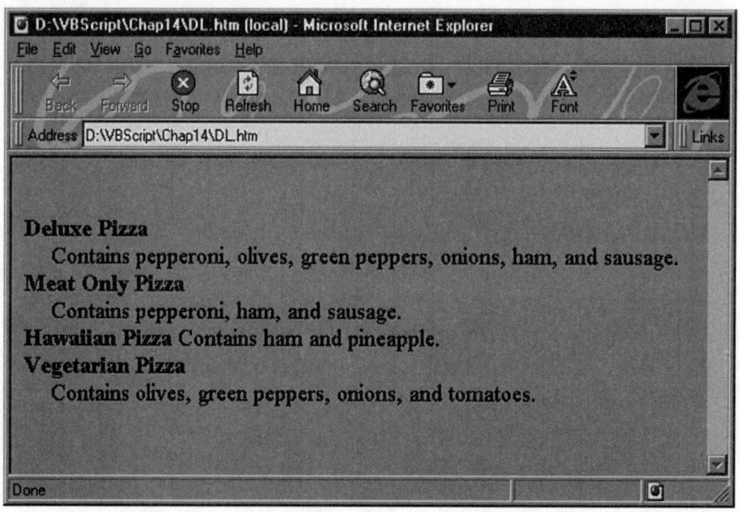

Figure 14-4 The <DL> element creates a definition list

<EM> Element

Purpose Use the `<EM>` element to identify information that should be emphasized in the text by placing it in italics.

Syntax `<EM> text </EM>`

Description The `<EM>` element places the specified text in italics on your HTML page. This tag is designed to be used when you want to emphasize a section of text.

Source HTML 2.0

Related HTML Elements `<ADDRESS>`, `<CITE>`, `<I>`

<FONT> Element

Purpose Use the `<FONT>` element to change the font attributes for the HTML page. One of the attributes in Table 14-14 must be used with the `<FONT>` element.

Syntax `<FONT attribute>`

Table 14-14 Attributes of the <FONT> element

Attribute	Description
`COLOR = color`	Specifies either the name or the RGB value of the color for the font. This can be any one of the color names or RGB values listed in Table 14-1.
`FACE = fontname`	Specifies the font that should be used at this location on the page. The specified font must already be installed on the user's computer; otherwise, the default font used by the browser to display normal text is used. You can specify a substitute font to be used, if Internet Explorer 3.0 cannot locate the specified font. For example, `<FONT FACE = Arial, Times New Roman>` uses the Arial font, if it exists on the machine; otherwise, the Times New Roman font is used.
`SIZE = n`	Specifies a value between 1 and 7 (`7` is the largest) that indicates the font size for this location on the page. The default value is `3`.

Description The `<FONT>` element specifies changes for the font used at that location on the HTML page. The element can be used anytime you want to modify the font settings for your page. Once the settings are changed, the new settings remain in effect until another `<FONT>` element statement is used.

The `FACE` and `COLOR` attributes are only supported by Internet Explorer 3.0.

Source Netscape, Internet Explorer 3.0 (`FACE` and `COLOR` attributes)

<FORM> ELEMENT

Purpose Use the `<FORM>` element to specify an HTML input form on the page. One of the attributes in Table 14-15 can be used with the `<FORM>` element.

Syntax `<FORM attribute> </FORM>`

Table 14-15 Attributes of the <FORM> element

Attribute	Description
ACTION = "URL"	Identifies the address that should be used to carry out actions specified by the form. If the ACTION attribute is not specified, the base URL of the page is used.
METHOD = method	Indicates how data from the form should be sent to the server. This attribute has two values, GET and POST. The GET value appends arguments to the URL specified by the ACTION attribute and opens it as if it were an anchor. The POST value sends the form data to the server using an HTTP post transaction.

Description The `<FORM>` element is used to specify the start and end of an input form. You can create several different forms on a page, but the forms cannot be nested.

The `<FORM>` element can use two different attributes. The **ACTION** attribute specifies the location where the contents of the form should be sent when a submit action occurs. The **METHOD** attribute specifies how the contents of the form should be sent to the server. This attribute must be used if the data is being sent to an HTTP URL.

Source HTML 2.0

<FRAME> ELEMENT

Purpose Use the `<FRAME>` element to specify a frame on your HTML page. The attributes in Table 14-16 can be used with the `<FRAME>` element.

Syntax `<FRAME attribute> </FRAME>`

Table 14-16 Attributes of the <FRAME> element

Attribute	Description
FRAMEBORDER = "response"	Specifies whether or not a border is placed around the frame. A response of Yes places a border around the frame; No displays the frame without a border.
FRAMESPACING = "value"	A pixel value that specifies the amount of additional spacing to be placed between frames.
MARGINWIDTH = "value"	A pixel value that specifies the width of the margin for the frame.
MARGINHEIGHT= "value"	A pixel value that specifies the height of the margin for the frame.
NAME = "framename"	Indicates the name of the frame.

Attribute	Description
NORESIZE	Indicates that the user cannot manually resize the frame.
SCROLLING = "response"	Specifies whether or not the frame should be scrolled when the user scrolls the page. A response of Yes scrolls the frame; No does not allow the frame to scroll.
SRC = "source"	Identifies the location of the source file to be placed in this frame.

Description

The **<FRAME>** element allows you to divide the page into more than one region. Each subregion, or frame, has the following properties:

- It can load its own URL, independently of the other frames.
- It can be assigned a **NAME**, so that other URLs can target it.
- It is resized dynamically due to changes in the size of the visible client area of the page.
- It can either allow or not allow the user to manually resize it.

Using frames allows you to design an HTML page for which certain information remains constant and visible on the page at all times, such as toolbar options, messages, and graphics. The information in the static frame remains on the screen as the user scrolls through another frame of information.

Usually, when you are working with frames, the **<BODY>** section element is replaced with the **<FRAMESET>** element.

Listing 14-5 uses the **<FRAME>** and **<FRAMESET>** elements to create an HTML page with frames. Figure 14-5 illustrates the results of creating a page with two frames.

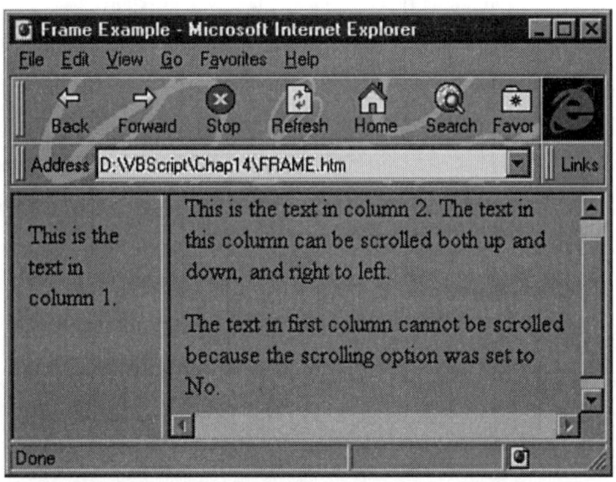

Figure 14-5 The **<FRAME>** element creates a frame on a page

Listing 14-5 Using the <FRAME> element

```
<HTML>
<HEAD>
<TITLE>Frame Example</TITLE></HEAD>

<FRAMESET FRAMEBORDER="3" FRAMESPACING="3" COLS="100,*">

<FRAME SRC="FRAME1.htm" NAME="Frame1" SCROLLING="no">
<FRAME SRC="FRAME2.htm" NAME="Frame2" SCROLLING="yes">
</FRAMESET>

</HTML>
```

Source Netscape

Related HTML Elements <FRAMESET>

<FRAMESET> Element

Purpose Use the <FRAMESET> element to specify that the HTML page contains more than one frame. The attributes in Table 14-17 are used with the <FRAMESET> element.

Syntax **<FRAMESET** attribute**>** **</FRAMESET>**

Table 14-17 Attributes of the <FRAMESET> element

Attribute	Description
COLS = "values"	Creates a frame document with the number of columns specified by a comma-separated list. The size of each column is specified and separated from the other row sizes by a comma. These values can be absolute pixel values, percentage values between 1 and 100, or relative scaling values (*). If the asterisk is specified for a column size, it receives the remaining space for its size. If the COLS attribute is not specified, a single column is arbitrarily sized to fit.
ROWS = "values"	Creates a frame document with the number of rows specified by a comma-separated list. The size of each row is specified and separated from the other row sizes by a comma. These values can be absolute pixel values, percentage values between 1 and 100, or relative scaling values (*). If the asterisk is specified for a row size, it receives the remaining space for its size. If the ROWS attribute is not specified, a single row is arbitrarily sized to fit.

Description The <FRAMESET> element replaces the <BODY> element when you have a page that contains several frames. The <FRAMESET> element specifies the number of rows and columns that make up the entire set of frames. The <FRAMESET> element must precede any of the tags that are normally placed within the <BODY> section.

By using frames, you can divide the page into more than one region. You can have regions that are scrollable and other regions that remain static.

Listing 14-5 illustrates how to use the <FRAME> and <FRAMESET> elements to create an HTML page with frames.

Source Netscape

Related HTML Elements <FRAME>

<H> Element

Purpose Use the <H> element to specify a heading level for the HTML page. One of the attributes in Table 14-18 must be used with the <H> element.

Syntax `<Hvalue ALIGN = CENTER>   </Hvalue>`

Table 14-18 Attributes of the <H> element

Attribute	Description
ALIGN = CENTER	This is an optional attribute that centers the specified heading horizontally on the page.
value	A numeric value between 1 and 6 that indicates the heading level number. Each heading level has a different font size and style. A heading with a value of <H1> has the largest font size.

Description The <H> element is used to indicate a heading level. A numeric value between 1 and 6 must be specified with the <H> element.

Listing 14-6 illustrates how to use the <H> element to specify your heading levels on an HTML page with frames. Figure 14-6 illustrates how each of the heading levels appears on an HTML page.

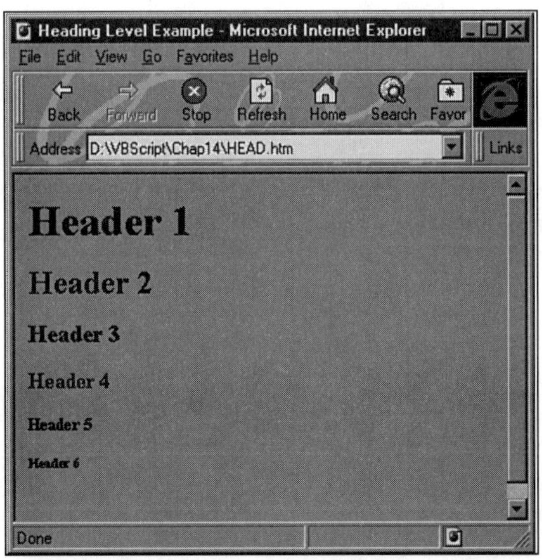

Figure 14-6 The <H> element creates heading levels for the page

Listing 14-6 Using the <H> element

```
<HTML>
<HEAD>
<TITLE>Heading Level Example</TITLE></HEAD>

<BODY>

<H1>Header 1</H1>
<H2>Header 2</H2>
<H3>Header 3</H3>
<H4>Header 4</H4>
<H5>Header 5</H5>
<H6>Header 6</H6>

</HTML>
```

Source HTML 2.0 (`ALIGN` attribute is HTML 3.0)

<HEAD> Element

Purpose Use the `<HEAD>` element to identify the beginning and ending of the head section of your HTML code.

Syntax `<HEAD attribute>    </HEAD>`

Description The `<HEAD>` element is used to identify the beginning and ending of the head section of the HTML code. The head section contains the information about your HTML page. For example, the title of the page, ActiveX controls, Java applets, and VBScript information are placed in the head section.

Source HTML 2.0

<HR> Element

Purpose Use the `<HR>` element to draw a horizontal rule on the HTML page. The attributes in Table 14-19 can be used with the `<HR>` element to change the appearance of the horizontal rule.

Syntax `<HR attribute>`

Table 14-19 Attributes of the <HR> element

Attribute	Description
`ALIGN = alignment`	Draws a horizontal rule that is justified based upon the alignment value that is specified. The possible alignment values are as follows: **Value** — **Description** `CENTER` — Horizontal rule is centered. `LEFT` — Horizontal rule is left-justified. `RIGHT` — Horizontal rule is right-justified.
`COLOR = colorvalue`	Specifies either the name or the RGB value of the color for the horizontal rule. This can be any one of the color names or RGB values listed in Table 14-1.
`NOSHADE`	Indicates that the horizontal rule should not have 3D shading.
`SIZE = value`	Sets the pixel height of the horizontal rule.
`WIDTH = value`	Sets the pixel width of the horizontal rule.

Description The **<HR>** element is used to create a horizontal rule (line) to separate sections of the HTML page. The attributes outlined in Table 14-19 can be used to change the look of the horizontal rule by adding color or changing the height or justification.

Source HTML 2.0

<HTML> Element

Purpose Use the **<HTML>** element to specify that the file is an HTML document.

Syntax `<HTML> document </HTML>`

Description The **<HTML>** element is used to specify the beginning and end of an HTML document. This element must be placed in an HTML document so that the browser will be able to interpret the HTML codes.

The HTML document is divided into two sections: the header, specified by the **<HEAD>** element, which contains information about the document, such as objects and VBScript code, and the body, specified by the **<BODY>** element, which contains the text and graphics that display on the page.

Source HTML 2.0

Related HTML Elements **<BODY>**, **<HEAD>**

<I> Element

Purpose Use the **<I>** element to place the selected text in italics.

Syntax `<I> text </I>`

Description The **<I>** element places the specified text in an italicized font on your HTML page.

Source HTML 2.0

Related HTML Elements <ADDRESS>, <CITE>, <DFN>, <EM>

<IFRAME> Element

Purpose Use the <IFRAME> element to define a floating frame. Table 14-20 outlines the attributes that can be used with the <IFRAME> element.

Syntax `<IFRAME attribute > </IFRAME>`

Table 14-20 Attributes of the <DIV> element

Attribute	Description
ALIGN = alignment	Specifies the alignment of the frame or the surrounding text. The following values can be used with the ALIGN attribute:
	Value — **Description**
	BOTTOM — Align the surrounding text with the bottom of the frame.
	LEFT — Draw the frame left-flushed and flow the text around it.
	MIDDLE — Align the surrounding text with the middle of the frame.
	RIGHT — Draw the frame right-flushed and flow the text around it.
	TOP — Align the surrounding text with the top of the frame.
FRAMEBORDER = value	Indicates whether a 3-D edge border is placed around the frame. The following values can be specified for the FRAMEBORDER attribute:
	Value — **Description**
	0 — Inserts a border. This is the default if the attribute is not specified.
	1 — Displays frame without a border.
HEIGHT = height	Specifies the height, in pixels, of the frame.
MARGINHEIGHT = height	Specifies the height, in pixels, of the margin for the frame.
MARGINWIDTH = width	Specifies the width, in pixels, of the margin for the frame.
NAME = name	Specifies the target name of the frame.
NORESIZE	Prevents the user from resizing the frame.
SCROLLING = value	Indicates whether or not the information should be scrolled in the frame. The following values can be used with the SCROLLING attribute:
	Value — **Description**
	YES — Creates a scrolling frame.
	NO — Creates a non-scrolling frame.
SRC = "location"	Indicates the address of the information to be placed in the frame.
WIDTH = width	Specifies the width, in pixels, of the frame.

Description The <IFRAME> element is used to create a floating frame on a page.

Source Internet Explorer 3.0

<IMG> Element

Purpose Use the `<IMG>` element to embed images in your HTML page. Internet Explorer 3.0 provides the capability to embed AVI video clips on the page by adding some new attributes to the `<IMG>` element. The attributes listed in Table 14-21 are used with the `<IMG>` element.

Syntax `<IMG attribute>`

Table 14-21 Attributes of the <IMG> element

Attribute	Description
ALIGN = alignment	Specifies the alignment of the surrounding text with respect to the image. The following alignment values are available: **Value** — **Description** BOTTOM — Text is aligned with the bottom of the picture. LEFT — The image is left-aligned, and text flows around it. MIDDLE — Text is aligned with the middle of the picture. RIGHT — The image is right-aligned, and text flows around it. TOP — Text is aligned with the top of the picture.
ALT = "text"	Specifies the text that will display on the HTML document if the user has turned off the option to display pictures.
BORDER = "value"	Indicates the size of the border that is placed around the image if it is a hyperlink.
CONTROLS	If the image is a video clip, a set of controls display under the clip. This option is only available in Internet Explorer 3.0.
DYNSRC = "URL"	Indicates the address of the video clip. This option is only available in Internet Explorer 3.0.
HEIGHT = value	Specifies the height of the image.
HSPACE = value	Specifies the size of the horizontal margins for the image.
ISMAP	Indicates that the image is a server-side image map. This means that if the image is clicked, the coordinates of the click location are sent back to the server. The server sends the address of the new page to display.
LOOP = value	Specifies the number of times the video clip should play when it is activated. This can either be a numeric value that indicates the desired number of times, or INFINITE, to continuously play the clip. This option is only available in Internet Explorer 3.0.
SRC = "location"	Indicates the address of the image to insert.
START = "startvalue"	Indicates when the video clip should start playing. This option is only available in Internet Explorer 3.0. There are two start value options: **Value** — **Description** FILEOPEN — Plays the clip when the file is opened. MOUSEOVER — Plays the clip when the mouse cursor is moved over the video clip location.
USEMAP = "mapname"	Indicates that the image is a client-side image map and identifies the name of the map group to use when the user clicks the appropriate location on the image.
VSPACE = value	Specifies the size of the vertical margins for the image.
WIDTH = value	Specifies the width of the image.

Description	The <IMG> element is used to embed a picture in the HTML page. This element can also be used with Internet Explorer 3.0 to embed a video clip (AVI file) in the page.
Source	HTML 2.0

<INPUT> Element

Purpose	Use the <INPUT> element to create a form control whose contents can be modified by the user. Table 14-22 outlines the attributes that you can use with the <INPUT> element.
Syntax	`<INPUT attribute>`

Table 14-22 Attributes of the <INPUT> element

Attribute	Description
`ALIGN = alignment`	This attribute is used when the value of the TYPE attribute is IMAGE. The ALIGN attribute specifies how the next line of text should be aligned with regard to the image. The following alignment values are available: **Value** — **Description** BOTTOM — Aligns text with bottom of the image. MIDDLE — Aligns text with middle of the image. TOP — Aligns text with top of the image.
`CHECKED = response`	This attribute is used when the value of the TYPE attribute is CHECKBOX. The CHECKED attribute indicates how the checkbox is selected. The following response values are available: **Value** — **Description** FALSE — If selected, value is false. TRUE — If selected, value is true.
`MAXLENGTH = value`	Specifies the maximum number of characters that can be typed in a text field.
`NAME = name`	A unique identifier for the input control.
`SIZE = "value"`	Specifies the size of the control in characters. If the TYPE attribute has a value of TEXTAREA, the height and width of the control can be specified by separating the values with a comma.
`SRC = "address"`	Specifies the location of the image file when the TYPE attribute has a value of IMAGE.
`TYPE = inputtype`	Identifies the type of input accepted by the input control. The following values are available: **Value** — **Description** CHECKBOX — Used for simple Boolean attributes, or for attributes that can take multiple values at the same time. The default value is for CHECKBOX to be selected. HIDDEN — This field is not visible to the user. The content of the field is sent to the server when the form is submitted. IMAGE — An image field that submits the form when it is selected. The coordinates of the selected point are measured in pixels from the upper-left corner of the image, and are returned (along with the other contents of the form) in two name/value pairs.

Attribute	Description	
	Value	**Description**
	PASSWORD	The text typed by the user is not displayed on the page.
	RADIO	Used to provide a list of attributes when only one should be selected. Each button in the group has the same name. Each button requires a VALUE attribute.
	RESET	When the button is clicked, all the fields are reset to the original values.
	SUBMIT	When the button is clicked, the values of the fields on the page are submitted to the server.
	TEXT	Creates a text entry field for a single line of text.
	TEXTAREA	Creates a text entry field for multiple lines of text.
VALUE = "value"	Specifies the default value of the control for textual and numerical controls. For Boolean controls, this attribute specifies the return value of the control.	

Description

The **<INPUT>** element is used to create form controls for your HTML page. These controls are used to gather information from the user. You can create text boxes, radio buttons, checkboxes, and so forth. The attributes used to create the controls are listed in Table 14-22.

Listing 14-7 illustrates how to use the **<INPUT>** element to create a text box in which the user can type information. Figure 14-7 illustrates how a text box displays on the HTML page with a default value.

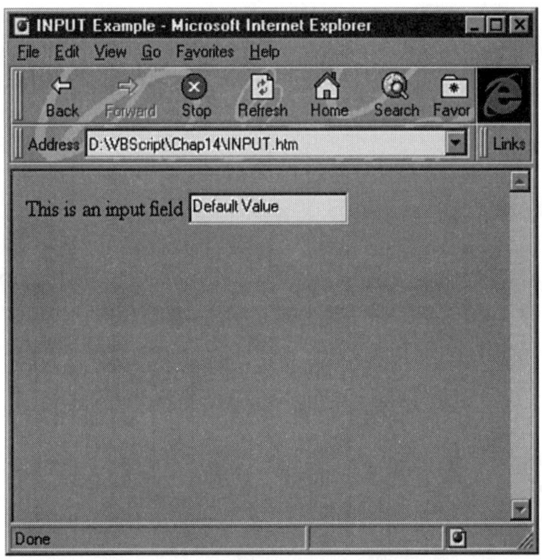

Figure 14-7 The **<INPUT>** element allows you to create different controls to gather information from the user

Listing 14-7 Using the `<INPUT>` *element*

```
<HTML>
<HEAD>
<TITLE>INPUT Example</TITLE>
</HEAD>

<BODY>

This is an input field  <INPUT TYPE=TEXT, NAME="InputBox", VALUE="Default Value">

</BODY>
</HTML>
```

Source HTML 2.0

<ISINDEX> Element

Purpose Use the `<ISINDEX>` element to indicate that the HTML document is a searchable index. The attributes listed in Table 14-23 can be used with the `<ISINDEX>` element.

Syntax `<ISINDEX attribute>`

Table 14-23 Attributes of the `<ISINDEX>` element

Attribute	Description
`ACTION = "filename"`	Specifies the name of either a CGI script or program in which the text box should pass the string typed by the user.
`PROMPT = "text"`	Changes the default prompt displayed for the user to type the search string.

Description The `<ISINDEX>` element is used to specify a searchable index. The element displays the message `You can search this index. Type the keyword(s) you want to search for:` along with a text box. When the user types the desired text and presses ENTER, the text is submitted to the page's URL as a query.

Note: The `<ISINDEX>` element is usually generated automatically by a server. If you add the element to an HTML document manually, the HTML user agent assumes that the server has a search engine that supports this element.

Source HTML 2.0

<KBD> Element

Purpose Use the <KBD> element to place text in a monospaced font.

Syntax `<KBD> text </KBD>`

Description The <KBD> element places the specified text in a bold, fixed-width (monospaced) font on your HTML page. This element is normally used to identify information that you want users to type at the keyboard. For example, you can use it to instruct them to type the word YES in a specified field. By using this element, the text that the user should type is emphasized on the page so that he or she can easily determine the correct response.

Source HTML 2.0

<LI> Element

Purpose Use the <LI> element to identify a directory list, menu, ordered list, or bulleted list item.

Syntax `<LI> text`

Description The <LI> element identifies an item within your directory, menu, ordered list, or bulleted list on the HTML page. Each item is specified by an <LI> element. The text of the directory item should not be more than 20 characters. The <DIR> element indicates the beginning and end of a directory list, the <OL> element indicates the beginning and end of an ordered list, and the <UL> element indicates the beginning and end of an unordered list.

Source HTML 2.0

Related HTML Elements <DIR>, <OL>, <MENU>, <UL>

<LISTING> Element

Purpose Use the <LISTING> element to place the specified text in a fixed-width font with a line break before and after the text.

Syntax `<LISTING> text </LISTING>`

Description The <LISTING> element places the specified text in a fixed-width font on your HTML page, with a line break before and after the text. This element is normally used to display blocks of text.

Internet Explorer 3.0 interprets any special characters that are placed within the <LISTING> element tags.

Source HTML 2.0

Related HTML Elements <PRE>, <TT>, <XMP>

<MAP> Element

Purpose Use the <MAP> element to specify a collection of hot spots for an image map. The attribute in Table 14-24 is used with the <MAP> element.

Syntax `<MAP attribute> </MAP>`

Table 14-24 Attribute of the <MAP> element

Attribute	Description
NAME = "name"	Specifies the name of the map so that you can refer to it from other locations within your HTML code

Description The <MAP> element is used to identify a group of hot spots. This element allows you to group together a series of related hot spots; for example, all the hot spots for one image. Normally, a series of <AREA> elements, which actually describe each hot spot, are placed inside the <MAP> tags.

Source Internet Explorer 3.0

Related HTML Elements <AREA>

<MARQUEE> Element

Purpose Use the <MARQUEE> element to create a scrolling text marquee on your HTML page. Table 14-25 outlines the attributes you can use with the <MARQUEE> element.

Syntax `<MARQUEE attribute> </MARQUEE>`

Table 14-25 Attributes of the <MARQUEE> element

Attribute	Description	
ALIGN = alignment	Specifies the alignment for the text around the marquee. The following alignment values are available:	
	Value	**Description**
	BOTTOM	Aligns text with bottom of the marquee.
	MIDDLE	Aligns text with middle of the marquee.
	TOP	Aligns text with top of the marquee.
BEHAVIOR = behavior	Specifies how the text should move within the marquee. The default value is SCROLL. The following behavior values are available:	
	Value	**Description**
	ALTERNATE	Bounces the text back and forth from one side of the screen to the other.
	SCROLL	Scrolls text completely across the screen and off the other side before starting again.
	SLIDE	Starts with text off screen, scrolls across screen, and stops when text touches the other side of the screen.

Attribute	Description
BGCOLOR = colorvalue	Specifies either the name or the RGB value of the color for the background of the marquee. This can be any one of the color names or RGB values listed in Table 14-1.
DIRECTION = direction	Specifies the default scroll direction for the text. The default value is LEFT. The following direction values are available: **Value** — **Description** LEFT — Scrolls text from the right side of the screen to the left side of the screen. RIGHT — Scrolls text from the left side of the screen to the right side of the screen.
HEIGHT = value	Specifies the height of the marquee. This can either be a percentage of the screen or a pixel value.
HSPACE = value	Specifies the top margin for the marquee text, in pixels.
LOOP = value	Indicates the number of times the text should scroll across the screen. This can be either a numeric value or INFINITE, to scroll the text continuously while the user views the page.
SCROLLAMOUNT = value	Indicates the number of pixels that should be between each successive draw of the marquee text.
SCROLLDELAY = value	Indicates the number of milliseconds between each successive draw of the marquee text.
VSPACE = value	Specifies the bottom margin for the marquee text, in pixels.
WIDTH = value	Specifies the width of the marquee. This can either be a percentage of the screen or a pixel value.

Description

The `<MARQUEE>` element is used to create a scrolling text marquee on the HTML page. The marquees have a wide variety of options, as specified in Table 14-25. Currently only Internet Explorer 3.0 supports the `<MARQUEE>` element.

Listing 14-8 illustrates how to place a marquee on your HTML page, as shown in Figure 14-8.

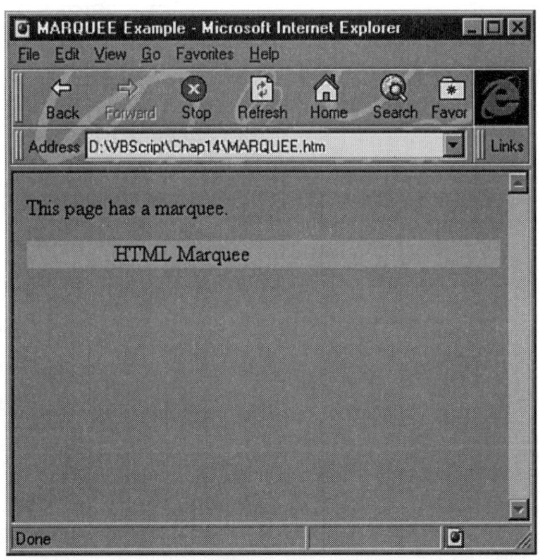

Figure 14-8 The `<MARQUEE>` element allows you to place a marquee on an HTML page

Listing 14-8 Using the <MARQUEE> element

```
<HTML>
<HEAD>
<TITLE>MARQUEE Example</TITLE>
</HEAD>

<BODY>

This page has a marquee.
<BR>
<BR>
<MARQUEE BEHAVIOR="ALTERNATE", BGCOLOR="#00FF00", LOOP=INFINITE> HTML Marquee </MARQUEE>
</BODY>
</HTML>
```

Source Internet Explorer 3.0

<MENU> Element

Purpose Use the <MENU> element to specify a list of items.

Syntax `<MENU> list </MENU>`

Description The <MENU> element identifies the beginning and end of a list of items. The <LI> element is used to identify each element of the list.

Source HTML 2.0

Related HTML Elements <LI>

<META> Element

Purpose Use the <META> element to specify client-pull information. The attributes in Table 14-26 are used with the <META> element.

Syntax `<META attribute>`

Table 14-26 Attributes of the <META> element

Attribute	Description
CONTENTS = "value; URL = URL"	Specifies the number of seconds that should elapse before the browser reloads the HTML document. If a URL is specified, the browser will reload that location when the time has elapsed; otherwise, the browser will reload the same document.
HTTP-EQUIV = REFRESH	Specifies that the document should be reloaded when the number of seconds indicated by the CONTENTS attribute have elapsed. This refreshing of the document continues on a regular basis.

Description The `<META>` element is used to specify information about when and from where the HTML document is reloaded. This tag must be placed within the `<HEAD>` section of the HTML document.

Source Netscape

<NOBR> Element

Purpose Use the `<NOBR>` element to prevent line breaks in the specified text on the page.

Syntax `<NOBR> text </NOBR>`

Description The `<NOBR>` element is used to eliminate any line breaks that may occur in the specified text. Although the `<NOBR>` element is essential for handling character sequences that you don't want to be broken, be aware that long text strings placed inside of `<NOBR>` elements will look strange if the user alters the window size.

Source Netscape

<NOFRAMES> Element

Purpose Use the `<NOFRAMES>` element to specify the HTML code that should be used in place of frames by browsers that do not support frames.

Syntax `<NOFRAMES> statements </NOFRAMES>`

Description The `<NOFRAMES>` element is used to specify the HTML code that should be used by a browser that does not support `<FRAMES>`. Since not all browsers support frames, if you have used frames in the design of the page you should consider using the `<NOFRAMES>` element. By using this element, you know exactly how the page will display for a user whose browser does not support the frames you have created.

Source Netscape

<OBJECT> Element

Purpose Use the `<OBJECT>` element to embed an ActiveX control or other media into your HTML page. The attributes in Table 14-27 are used with the `<OBJECT>` element.

Syntax `<OBJECT attribute>   </OBJECT>`

Table 14-27 Attributes of the `<OBJECT>` element

Attribute	Description
`ALIGN = alignment`	Specifies the alignment object on the page. The following values can be used with the `ALIGN` attribute: **Value** — **Description** `BASELINE` — Align the bottom of the object with the baseline of the surrounding text. `CENTER` — Center the object between left and right margins. Start subsequent text on the next line after the object. `LEFT` — Align the object with the left margin, and wrap the subsequent text along the right side of the object. `MIDDLE` — Align the middle of the object with the baseline of the surrounding text. `RIGHT` — Align the object with the right margin, and wrap subsequent text along the left side of the object. `TEXTBOTTOM` — Align the bottom of the object with the bottom of the surrounding text. `TEXTMIDDLE` — Align the middle of the object with the midpoint between the baseline and the height of the surrounding text. `TEXTTOP` — Align the top of the object with the top of surrounding the text.
`BORDER = value`	Specifies the width of the border if the object is a hyperlink.
`CLASSID = "CLSID: id"`	Identifies the object that is being inserted into the HTML document. This attribute, based upon the Component Object Model (COM) "class id" URL naming scheme, is a unique identifier for the control. The attribute always resembles the following: `CLASSID="CLSID:79176FB0-B7F2-11CE-97EF-00AA006D2776"` (the string of values after the colon is unique to identify the object).
`CODE`	A value required by some objects so that you can reference them.
`CODEBASE = location`	Identifies the URL of the code base for the object. The syntax of the URL depends upon the object.
`CODETYPE = codetype`	Specifies the Internet media type for the code.
`DATA = location`	Points to the address of the data stream that is used to initialize the state of the object.
`DECLARE`	Declares the object without instantiating it.
`HEIGHT`	Specifies the height of the object.
`HSPACE`	Specifies the horizontal spacing for the object.
`ID`	A unique name that can be used to reference the object. For example, to modify an object value using VBScript, you use the `ID` attribute to reference the object.
`NAME = location`	Sets the name of the object when submitted as part of a form.
`SHAPES`	Specifies that the object has shaped hyperlinks.
`STANDBY = message`	Sets the message to show while loading the object.
`TYPE = type`	Specifies the Internet media type for data.
`USEMAP = location`	Specifies the URL of the image map to use with the object.
`VSPACE`	Specifies the vertical spacing for the object.
`WIDTH`	Specifies the width of the object.

Description The <OBJECT> element allows you to add ActiveX controls and other media to your HTML page. Unlike the <IMG> element, you can add images that are not static to the page.

Depending upon the object that you are adding, you may not use all of the attributes listed in Table 14-27. The <PARAM> element is also used within the <OBJECT> tags to identify initial property values for the object.

Currently only Internet Explorer 3.0 supports the use of the <OBJECT> element.

Source Internet Explorer 3.0

Related HTML Elements <PARAM>

<OL> Element

Purpose Use the <OL> element to specify an ordered list of items. Table 14-28 indicates the attributes that can be used with the <OL> element.

Syntax `<OL> list </OL>`

Table 14-28 Attributes of the <OL> element

Attribute	Description
START = value	Specifies a starting number for the first item in the list.
TYPE = type	Changes the type of numbering used with the list. This attribute can be used with both the <OL> and <LI> elements. In other words, the numbering type can be changed within the list. The following numbering types are available:

Type	Description
A	Use uppercase letters.
a	Use lowercase letters.
I	Use large Roman numerals.
i	Use small Roman numerals.
1	Use numeric values.

Description The <OL> element identifies the beginning and end of an ordered list. If one of the attributes in Table 14-28 is not used, the items in the list are numbered starting at one. The <LI> element is used to identify each element of the list.

Listing 14-9 creates a numbered list on your HTML page using the <OL> element, as illustrated in Figure 14-9.

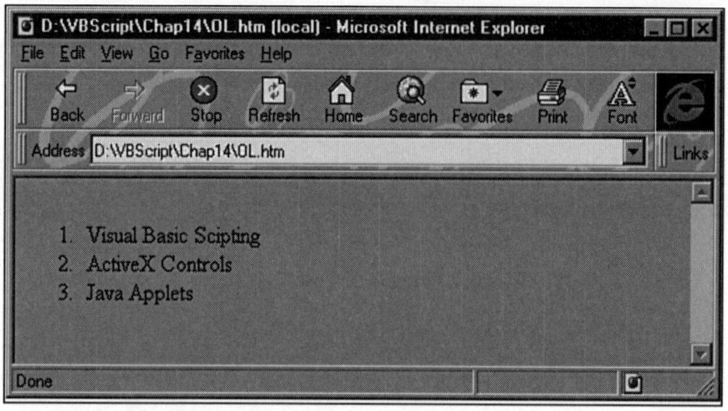

Figure 14-9 The <OL> element allows you to create a numbered list on an HTML page

Listing 14-9 Using the <OL> element

```
<HTML>
<HEAD>

</HEAD>

<BODY>

<OL>
<LI>Visual Basic Scipting
<LI>ActiveX Controls
<LI>Java Applets
</OL>
</BODY>
</HTML>
```

Source HTML 2.0

Related HTML Elements <LI>

<OPTION> Element

Purpose Use the <OPTION> element to identify each item that should be placed in the list box specified by the <SELECT> element. The attributes in Table 14-29 can be used with the <OPTION> element.

Syntax `<OPTION attribute> text`

Table 14-29 Attributes of the <OPTION> element

Attribute	Description
SELECTED	Indicates that this item will be selected as the default item for the list. If you do not identify an item as the default, the first item in the list is the default selection.
VALUE = "value"	This indicates the value that will be returned if this item is selected.

Description The <OPTION> element is used with the <SELECT> element to identify the items for a list box. Each of the items that is preceded by an <OPTION> tag displays as selections for the list box when the user selects the down arrow button.

You can use the SELECTED attribute to identify the item that should be selected as the default item in the list. The item selected as the default displays as the highlighted item in the list. You can also use the VALUE attribute to specify a value that is returned if the user selects the item. This attribute allows you to determine which item was selected by the user.

Listing 14-10, under the <SELECT> element, illustrates how to use the <OPTION> element to identify the options to display on a list box created with the <SELECT> element.

Source HTML 2.0

Related HTML Elements <SELECT>

<P> Element

Purpose Use the <P> element to specify a paragraph on your HTML page. The attribute in Table 14-30 can be used with the <P> element.

Syntax `<P attribute>   </P>`

Table 14-30 Attribute of the <P> element

Attribute	Description
ALIGN = alignment	Specifies the alignment of the paragraph on the HTML page. The following alignment values are available: **Value** — **Description** CENTER — Centers the text on the page. LEFT — Left-justifies the paragraph on the page. RIGHT — Right-justifies the paragraph on the page. This is an optional attribute that can be used to center the paragraph on the HTML page.

Description	The <P> element is used to specify a paragraph. A paragraph break occurs before the initial <P> tag and after the closing </P> tag. The end tag is optional with this attribute.
Source	HTML 3.2

<PARAM> ELEMENT

Purpose Use the <PARAM> element to specify the initialization values for an object embedded using the <OBJECT> element. The attributes in Table 14-31 are used with the <PARAM> element.

Syntax `<PARAM attribute>`

Table 14-31 Attributes of the <PARAM> element

Attribute	Description
NAME = "property name"	Specifies the name of the property whose initial value is being defined
VALUE = "initial value"	Specifies the initial value for the specified property

Description The <PARAM> element is used to identify the initial values for the property of an object that was embedded using either the <OBJECT> or the <APPLET> element. The <PARAM> tags are placed within the initial and ending <OBJECT> tags.

Currently only Internet Explorer 3.0 supports the use of the <OBJECT> and <PARAM> elements.

Source Internet Explorer 3.0

Related HTML Elements <OBJECT>, <APPLET>

<PLAINTEXT> ELEMENT

Purpose Use the <PLAINTEXT> element to indicate the text that should be shown in a fixed-width font type.

Syntax `<PLAINTEXT> text </PLAINTEXT>`

Description The <PLAINTEXT> element places all text between the initial and ending <PLAINTEXT> tags in a fixed-width font type. All HTML parsing is turned off until the </PLAINTEXT> tag is encountered.

Source HTML 2.0

<PRE> ELEMENT

Purpose Use the <PRE> element to place the specified text in a fixed-width font.

Syntax `<PRE> text </PRE>`

Description The <PRE> element places the specified text in a fixed-width font on your HTML page. This element is normally used with preformatted text or text that you want to display in a monospaced font.

Source HTML 2.0

Related HTML Elements <LISTING>, <TT>, <XMP>

<S> Element

Purpose Use the <S> element to place the specified text in a strikethrough font.

Syntax `<S> text </S>`

Description The <S> element places the specified text in a strikethrough font style on your HTML page. This means that the text is displayed with a horizontal line through the center.

Source HTML 2.0

Related HTML Elements <STRIKE>

<SAMP> Element

Purpose Use the <SAMP> element to identify sample code.

Syntax `<SAMP> text </SAMP>`

Description The <SAMP> element places the specified text in a smaller, fixed-width font on your HTML page. This element is used with sample code that you want to place on the page.

Source HTML 2.0

Related HTML Elements <CODE>

<SCRIPT> Element

Purpose Use the <SCRIPT> element to indicate the inclusion of a script within the HTML document. The attribute listed in Table 14-32 is used with the <SCRIPT> element.

Syntax `<SCRIPT LANGUAGE = scriptlanguage> scriptcode </SCRIPT>`

Table 14-32 Attribute of the <SCRIPT> element

Attribute	Description
LANGUAGE = "scriptlanguage"	Indicates the scripting language in which the enclosed script was written. Examples of scripting language are "VBScript" and "JScript".

Description The <SCRIPT> element is used to indicate that a section of the HTML document contains a scripting language, such as VBScript.

Source Internet Explorer 3.0

<SELECT> Element

Purpose Use the <SELECT> element to specify a list box control on your HTML page. The attributes listed in Table 14-33 can be used with the <SELECT> element.

Syntax `<SELECT attribute>   </SELECT>`

Table 14-33 Attributes of the <SELECT> element

Attribute	Description
MULTIPLE	Indicates that the user can select multiple items in the list.
NAME ="listname"	Indicates the name of the list box. This is the name used when you want to reference the list box within your code; for example, if you want to determine which value was selected for the list box.
SIZE = "value"	Specifies the height of the list box control.

Description The <SELECT> element is used to create a list box control on your HTML page. Normally users can only select one item from the list. If you use the MULTIPLE attribute, they have the ability to select multiple items within the list.

Listing 14-10 creates a list box using the <SELECT> element, as illustrated in Figure 14-10.

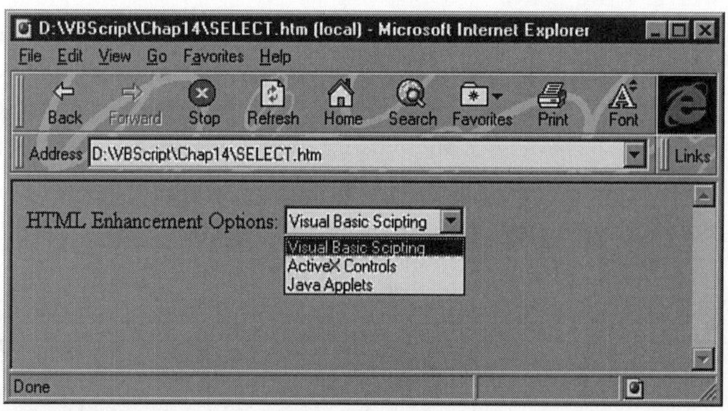

Figure 14-10 The <SELECT> element allows you to create a list box control

Listing 14-10 Using the `<SELECT>` *element*

```
<HTML>
<HEAD>

</HEAD>

<BODY>

HTML Enhancement Options:

<SELECT NAME="HTMLENHANCE">
  <OPTION VALUE=1>Visual Basic Scipting
  <OPTION VALUE=2>ActiveX Controls
  <OPTION VALUE=3>Java Applets
</SELECT>

</BODY>
</HTML>
```

Source HTML 2.0

Related HTML Elements <OPTION>

<SMALL> Element

Purpose Use the <SMALL> element to place the specified text in a font smaller than the current font.

Syntax **<SMALL>** text **</SMALL>**

Description The <SMALL> element places the specified text in a font size smaller than the currently selected font for your HTML page. The exact appearance of the text using the <SMALL> element is based on the <FONT> and <BASEFONT> settings.

Source HTML 3.2

Related HTML Elements <BIG>, <SUB>, <SUP>

<STRIKE> Element

Purpose Use the <STRIKE> element to place the specified text in a strikethrough font style.

Syntax **<STRIKE>** text **</STRIKE>**

Description The <STRIKE> element places the specified text in a strikethrough font style on your HTML page. This means that the text is displayed with a horizontal line through the center.

Source HTML 2.0

Related HTML Elements <S>

<STRONG> Element

Purpose Use the <STRONG> element to place the specified text in a bold font.

Syntax

```
<STRONG> text </STRONG>
```

Description The <STRONG> element places the specified text in a bold font on your HTML page. This element is used to identify text that should have a strong emphasis.

Source HTML 2.0

Related HTML Elements <B>

<SUB> Element

Purpose Use the <SUB> element to display the specified text as subscript.

Syntax

```
<SUB> text </SUB>
```

Description The <SUB> element places the specified text in a subscript font on your HTML page. This element can be combined with the <SMALL> element to use a smaller font than the font that would ordinarily be used to place the text in subscript.

It can also be used with the <BIG> element to force the same font size to be used for the subscript text as was used for the preceding text.

Source HTML 3.2

Related HTML Elements <BIG>, <SMALL>, <SUP>

<SUP> Element

Purpose Use the <SUP> element to display the specified text as superscript.

Syntax

```
<SUP> text </SUP>
```

Description The <SUP> element places the specified text in a superscript font on your HTML page. This element can be combined with the <SMALL> element so that a smaller font is used when the text is placed in superscript.

It can also be used with the <BIG> element to force the same font size to be used for the superscript text as was used for the preceding text.

Source HTML 3.2

Related HTML Elements <BIG>, <SMALL>, <SUB>

<TABLE> Element

Purpose Use the <TABLE> element to specify a table on your HTML page. The attributes in Table 14-34 can be used with the <TABLE> element.

Syntax

```
<TABLE attribute>  </TABLE>
```

Table 14-34 Attributes of the <TABLE> element

Attribute	Description
`ALIGN = alignment`	Specifies the alignment for the text in the table. The default is to left-justify the text. The following alignment values are available: **Value** — **Description** `LEFT` — Left-justifies the text. `RIGHT` — Right-justifies the text.
`BACKGROUND = "location"`	Specifies the URL location of a picture to display as the background for the table. The image is tiled behind the cells of the table.
`BGCOLOR = colorvalue`	Specifies either the name or the RGB value of the color for the background color of the table. This can be any one of the color names or RGB values listed in Table 14-1.
`BORDERCOLOR = colorvalue`	Specifies either the name or the RGB value of the color for the table border. This can be any one of the color names or RGB values listed in Table 14-1.
`BORDERCOLORDARK = colorvalue`	Specifies either the name or the RGB value of the dark color portion of the 3D border. This can be any one of the color names or RGB values listed in Table 14-1. This attribute must be used with the `BORDERCOLOR` attribute.
`BORDERCOLORLIGHT = colorvalue`	Specifies either the name or the RGB value of the light color portion of the 3D border. This can be any one of the color names or RGB values listed in Table 14-1. This attribute must be used with the `BORDERCOLOR` attribute.
`VALIGN = alignment`	Changes the vertical alignment of the text within the table cells. The default is to center-align the text. The values for this attribute are as follows: **Value** — **Description** `BOTTOM` — Aligns the text with the bottom of the cell. `TOP` — Aligns the text with the top of the cell.
`FRAME = "value"`	Specifies the sides of the table that have a frame. The following frame values are available: **Value** — **Description** `above` — Displays a border at the top of the table frame. `below` — Displays a border under the table frame. `border` — Displays a border on all sides of the table frame. `box` — Displays a border on all sides of the table frame. `hsides` — Displays a border at the top and bottom of the table. `lhs` — Displays a border on the left side of the table frame. `rhs` — Displays a border on the right side of the table frame. `void` — Removes all table borders. `vsides` — Displays a border on the right and left sides.
`RULES = "value"`	Specifies additional information about the rules for the table. You can only make use of this attribute with tables that have the `<THEAD>`, `<TBODY>`, and `<TFOOT>` elements. One of the following values can be specified for the `RULES` attribute:

continued on next page

continued from previous page

Attribute	Description	
	Value	**Description**
columns	`all`	Displays a border on all rows and columns.
	`basic`	Displays horizontal borders between the <THEAD>, <TBODY>, and <TFOOT> elements.
	`cols`	Displays vertical borders between all table columns.
	`groups`	Displays horizontal borders between all table groups. Groups are specified by the <THEAD>, <TBODY>, <TFOOT> and <COLGROUP> elements.
	`none`	Removes all interior table borders.
	`rows`	Displays horizontal borders between all table rows.

Description

The **<TABLE>** element is used to indicate a table that should be placed on the HTML page. The initial and ending **<TABLE>** tags mark the start and end of the table. Within these tags, additional elements such as the **<COL>**, **<COLGROUP>**, **<TD>**, **<TH>**, **<TR>**, **<THEAD>**, **<TBODY>**, and **<TFOOT>** elements specify additional information about the table.

Listing 14-11 creates a table using the **<TABLE>** element. Figure 14-11 illustrates the results of the table created in Listing 14-11.

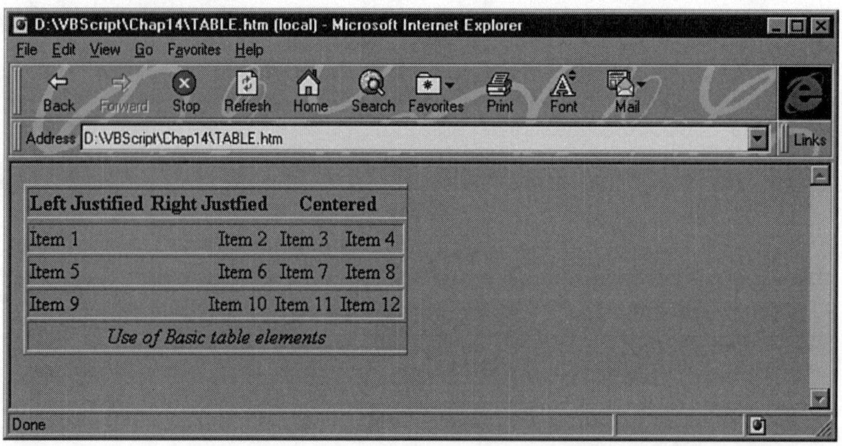

Figure 14-11 The **<TABLE>** element allows you to create a table on your HTML page

Listing 14-11 Using the `<TABLE>` *element*

```
<HTML>

<HEAD>

</HEAD>

<BODY>

<TABLE BORDER width=50% RULES = rows>

<COL ALIGN=left>
<COL ALIGN=right>

<COLGROUP SPAN=2 ALIGN = CENTER VALIGN=middle>
<THEAD>
<TD><B>Left Justified</B></TD><TD><B>Right Justified</B></TD><TD COLSPAN = ⇐
2><B>Centered</B></TD> </TR>
</THEAD>
<TR>
<TBODY>
<TD>Item 1</TD><TD>Item 2</TD> <TD>Item 3</TD> <TD>Item 4</TD></TR>

<TR>
<TD>Item 5</TD><TD>Item 6</TD> <TD>Item 7</TD> <TD>Item 8</TD></TR>

<TR>
<TD>Item 9</TD><TD>Item 10</TD> <TD>Item 11</TD> <TD>Item 12</TD></TR>

</TBODY>
<TFOOT>
<TR><TD COLSPAN = 4><I> Use of Basic table elements</I></TD></TR>
</TFOOT>
</TABLE>

</BODY>

</HTML>
```

Source HTML 3.0

Related HTML Elements `<COL>`, `<COLGROUP>`, `<TBODY>`, `<TD>`, `<TFOOT>`, `<TH>`, `<THEAD>`, `<TR>`

<TBODY> ELEMENT

Purpose Use the <TBODY> element to specify a body section in a table on your HTML page.

Syntax **<TBODY> </TBODY>**

Description The <TBODY> element specifies the body section of the table. This element is only required if you use the RULES attribute with the <TABLE> element. This element is supported only by Internet Explorer 3.0.

Listing 14-11, under the `<TABLE>` element, illustrates how to use the `<TBODY>` element in a table.

Source Internet Explorer 3.0

Related HTML Elements `<THEAD>`, `<TFOOT>`

<TD> Element

Purpose Use the `<TD>` element to specify a cell in a table on your HTML page. The attributes in Table 14-35 can be used with the `<TD>` element.

Syntax `<TD attribute>   </TD>`

Table 14-35 Attributes of the <TD> element

Attribute	Description
`ALIGN = alignment`	Specifies the alignment for the text in the cell. The default is to left-justify the text. The following alignment values are available: **Value** / **Description** `LEFT` Left-justifies the text. `RIGHT` Right-justifies the text.
`BACKGROUND = "location"`	Specifies the URL location of a picture to display as the background for the cell.
`BGCOLOR = colorvalue`	Specifies either the name or the RGB value of the color for the background color of the cell. This can be any one of the color names or RGB values listed in Table 14-1.
`BORDERCOLOR = colorvalue`	Specifies either the name or the RGB value of the color for the cell border. This can be any one of the color names or RGB values listed in Table 14-1.
`BORDERCOLORDARK = colorvalue`	Specifies either the name or the RGB value of the dark color portion of the 3D border. This can be any one of the color names or RGB values listed in Table 14-1. This attribute must be used with the `BORDERCOLOR` attribute.
`BORDERCOLORLIGHT = colorvalue`	Specifies either the name or the RGB value of the light color portion of the 3D border. This can be any one of the color names or RGB values listed in Table 14-1. This attribute must be used with the `BORDERCOLOR` attribute.
`VALIGN = alignment`	Changes the vertical alignment of the text within the table cell. The default is to center-align the text. The values for this attribute are as follows: **Value** / **Description** `BOTTOM` Aligns the text with the bottom of the cell. `TOP` Aligns the text with the top of the cell.

Description The `<TD>` element is used to specify a cell of a table. All table cells must be placed within table rows (`<TR>` element). All of the standard HTML body elements can be placed in a cell.

Listing 14-11, under the <TABLE> element, illustrates how to use the <TD> element to indicate a cell in a table.

Source HTML 3.0

Related HTML Elements <COL>, <COLGROUP>, <TABLE>, <TBODY>, <TFOOT>, <TH>, <THEAD>, <TR>

<TFOOT> Element

Purpose Use the <TFOOT> element to specify a footer section in a table on your HTML page.

Syntax <TFOOT> </TFOOT>

Description The <TFOOT> element specifies the footer section of the report. This element is only required if you use the RULES attribute with the <TABLE> element. This element is supported only by Internet Explorer 3.0.

Listing 14-11, under the <TABLE> element, illustrates how to use the <TFOOT> element in a table.

Source Internet Explorer 3.0

Related HTML Elements <TBODY>, <THEAD>

<TH> Element

Purpose Use the <TH> element to specify a header cell in a table on your HTML page. The attributes in Table 14-36 can be used with the <TH> element.

Syntax <TH attribute> </TH>

Table 14-36 Attributes of the <TH> element

Attribute	Description
ALIGN = alignment	Specifies the alignment for the text in the header cell. The default is to center-justify the text. The following alignment values are available: **Value** / **Description** LEFT — Left-justifies the text. RIGHT — Right-justifies the text.
BACKGROUND = "location"	Specifies the URL location of a picture to display as the background for the header cell.
BGCOLOR = colorvalue	Specifies either the name or the RGB value of the color for the background color of the header cell. This can be any one of the color names or RGB values listed in Table 14-1.
BORDERCOLOR = colorvalue	Specifies either the name or the RGB value of the color for the header cell border. This can be any one of the color names or RGB values listed in Table 14-1.

continued on next page

continued from previous page

Attribute	Description
BORDERCOLORDARK = colorvalue	Specifies either the name or the RGB value of the dark color portion of the 3D border. This can be any one of the color names or RGB values listed in Table 14-1. This attribute must be used with the BORDERCOLOR attribute.
BORDERCOLORLIGHT = colorvalue	Specifies either the name or the RGB value of the light color portion of the 3D border. This can be any one of the color names or RGB values listed in Table 14-1. This attribute must be used with the BORDERCOLOR attribute.
VALIGN = alignment	Changes the vertical alignment of the text within the table header cell. The default is to center-align the text. The values for this attribute are as follows: **Value** — **Description** BOTTOM — Aligns the text with the bottom of the cell. TOP — Aligns the text with the top of the cell.

Description The <TH> element is used to specify a header cell of a table. Header cells are identical to data cells in most respects, with the exception that the text in header cells is in a bold font, and has a default alignment of the text centered within the cell. All of the standard HTML body elements can be placed in a header cell.

Source HTML 3.0

Related HTML Elements <COL>, <COLGROUP>, <TABLE>, <TBODY>, <TD>, <TFOOT>, <THEAD>, <TR>

<THEAD> Element

Purpose Use the <THEAD> element to specify a header section in a table on your HTML page.

Syntax <THEAD> </THEAD>

Description The <THEAD> element specifies the header section of the report. This element is only required if you use the RULES attribute with the <TABLE> element. This element is supported only by Internet Explorer 3.0.

Listing 14-11, under the <TABLE> element, illustrates how to use the <THEAD> element in a table.

Source Internet Explorer 3.0

Related HTML Elements <TBODY>, <TFOOT>

<TITLE> Element

Purpose Use the <TITLE> element to specify the title for your HTML page.

Syntax <TITLE> text </TITLE>

Description The `<TITLE>` element specifies the title that displays at the top of your HTML page. The text that you specify with this element is placed in the title bar of Internet Explorer 3.0.

Source HTML 2.0

<TR> Element

Purpose Use the `<TR>` element to specify a row in a table on your HTML page. The attributes in Table 14-37 can be used with the `<TR>` element.

Syntax `<TR attribute> </TR>`

Table 14-37 Attributes of the <TR> element

Attribute	Description
ALIGN = alignment	Specifies the alignment for the text in the row. The default is to left-justify the text. The following alignment values are available: **Value** — **Description** LEFT — Left-justifies the text. RIGHT — Right-justifies the text.
BACKGROUND = "location"	Specifies the URL location of a picture to display as the background for the row.
BGCOLOR = colorvalue	Specifies either the name or the RGB value of the color for the background color of the row. This can be any one of the color names or RGB values listed in Table 14-1.
BORDERCOLOR = colorvalue	Specifies either the name or the RGB value of the color for the row border. This can be any one of the color names or RGB values listed in Table 14-1.
BORDERCOLORDARK = colorvalue	Specifies either the name or the RGB value of the dark color portion of the 3D border. This can be any one of the color names or RGB values listed in Table 14-1. This attribute must be used with the BORDERCOLOR attribute.
BORDERCOLORLIGHT = colorvalue	Specifies either the name or the RGB value of the light color portion of the 3D border. This can be any one of the color names or RGB values listed in Table 14-1. This attribute must be used with the BORDERCOLOR attribute.
VALIGN = alignment	Changes the vertical alignment of the text within the table row. The default is to center-align the text. The values for this attribute are as follows: **Value** — **Description** BOTTOM — Aligns the text with the bottom of the cell. TOP — Aligns the text with the top of the cell.

Description The `<TR>` element is used to specify a row of a table. All tables cells are placed within the table rows using the `<TD>` element. All of the standard HTML body elements can be placed in a cell.

Listing 14-11, under the <TABLE> element, illustrates how to use the <TR> element to specify a row in a table.

Source HTML 3.0

Related HTML Elements <COL>, <COLGROUP>, <TABLE>, <TBODY>, <TD>, <TFOOT>, <TH>, <THEAD>

<TT> Element

Purpose If available, use the <TT> element to place the specified text in a fixed-width font that resembles typewriter script.

Syntax `<TT> text </TT>`

Description The <TT> element places the specified text in a fixed-width font that resembles the type produced by a typewriter.

Source HTML 2.0

Related HTML Elements <PRE>, <LISTING>, <XMP>

<U> Element

Purpose Use the <U> element to underline the specified text.

Syntax `<U> text </U>`

Description The <U> element places the specified text in an underline font on your HTML page, where available. In other words, if the browser does not support underlining, the text will appear in the normal font.

Source HTML 2.0

<UL> Element

Purpose Use the <UL> element to specify a bulleted list of items.

Syntax `<UL> list </UL>`

Description The <UL> element identifies the beginning and end of an unordered list. The <LI> element is used to identify each element of the list.

Source HTML 2.0

Related HTML Elements <LI>, <DIR>

<VAR> Element

Purpose Use the <VAR> element to specify text that should display in a small, fixed-width font.

Syntax `<VAR> text </VAR>`

Description The <VAR> element identifies text that should be displayed in a small, fixed-width font on the HTML page. This element is normally used to identify a variable name.

Source HTML 2.0

<WBR> Element

Purpose Use the <WBR> element to specify a soft line break within a block of text between two <NOBR> tags.

Syntax `<WBR> text </WBR>`

Description The <WBR> element is used within the <NOBR> element to identify a location where a line break could occur if required by the browser. In other words, the break will only occur if the text will not otherwise display on the browser.

Source Netscape

Related HTML Elements <NOBR>

<XMP> Element

Purpose Use the <XMP> element to place the specified text in a fixed-width font.

Syntax `<XMP> text </XMP>`

Description The <XMP> element places the specified text in a fixed-width font.

Source HTML 2.0

Related HTML Elements <LISTING>, <PRE>, <TT>

15

INTERNET EXPLORER OBJECT MODEL FOR SCRIPTING

15

INTERNET EXPLORER OBJECT MODEL FOR SCRIPTING

The Microsoft Internet Explorer scripting object model is a structure for embedding VBScript and JavaScript into your HTML documents. This chapter provides an overview of the objects that make up the scripting model and their associated properties, methods, and events.

What Is the Object Model?

The Microsoft Internet Explorer scripting object provides you with the ability to interact with the various objects that make up the HTML document. The Internet Explorer model is compatible with the Netscape Navigator object model used in the JavaScript language. The Microsoft Internet Explorer object model can be used with any scripting language that is compatible with the ActiveX scripting framework, such as VBScript.

Keep in mind that all properties and methods that modify the HTML contents of a page must be called during HTML parse time (when the document is loaded). The code must reside in a script block that runs inline during the loading of the HTML document. This includes many of the properties and methods for the `Document` object.

Object Model Structure

The Internet Explorer object model is made up of nine different objects. Figure 15-1 illustrates how the different objects relate to one another. The **`Window`** object is the main object, which contains all of the other objects.

Object Model Reference

The remaining portion of this chapter provides a description of each of the objects in the Internet Explorer object model and their associated properties, methods, and events.

`Window` Object

Purpose The **`Window`** object represents the Internet Explorer window. Table 15-1 summarizes the properties that can be used with the **`Window`** object, Table 15-2 summarizes the methods that can be used with the **`Window`** object, and Table 15-3 summarizes the events that can be used with the **`Window`** object. A detailed description of each property, method, and event follows this section, in alphabetical order.

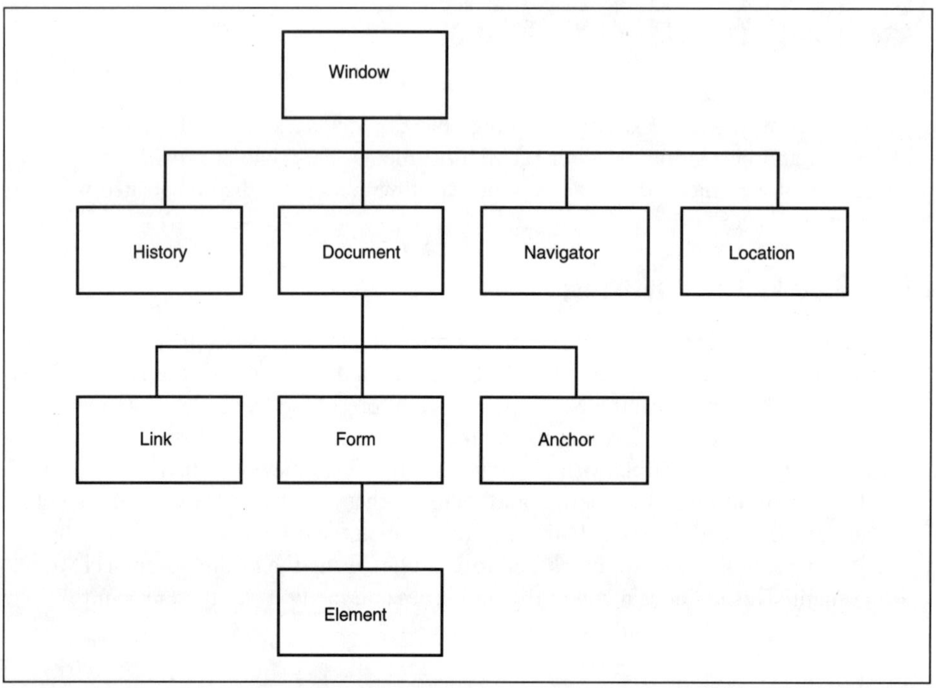

Figure 15-1 Internet Explorer object model

Syntax

```
Window.property
```

or

```
Window.method
```

or

```
Window.event
```

Table 15-1 Properties of the `Window` object

Use...	To Do This...
`DefaultStatus`	Either set or get the default status text that appears in the lower left portion of the status bar.
`Document`	Return the `Document` object for the current window.
`Frames`	Return an array of the frames in the current window.
`History`	Return the `History` object for the current window.
`Location`	Return the location object for the current window.
`Name`	Return the name of the current window.
`Navigator`	Return the `Navigator` object for the current window.
`Parent`	Return the name of the parent window.
`Self`	Return a pointer to the current window.
`Status`	Either set or get the status text that appears in the lower-left portion of the status bar.
`Top`	Return a pointer to the top window.

Table 15-2 Methods of the `Window` object

Use...	To Do This...
`Alert`	Display a message box on the HTML page.
`ClearTimeout`	Clear a specific timer.
`Close`	Close the window.
`Confirm`	Display a message box with both OK and Cancel buttons.
`Navigate`	Display another URL in the current window.
`Prompt`	Prompt the user for information.
`Open`	Create a new window.
`SetTimeout`	Create a timer so that a function is called within a specified amount of time.

Table 15-3 Events of the `Window` object

Use...	To Do This...
`OnLoad`	Specify a function that runs when the page is loaded.
`OnUnload`	Specify a function that runs when the page is unloaded.

Description

The **Window** object is used to access the properties, methods, and events of the actual browser window. These properties, methods, and events can be called by any scripting language.

Each **Window** object contains the elements in Table 15-4.

Table 15-4 `Window` object elements

Element	Description
Frame	An array of frame windows contained by a parent window. Each frame is a window that has its own properties, including a document.
`Document object`	The document in the current window.
`History` object	This object is used to access the history list of the browser application.
`Location` object	This object provides information about the location of the window's URL.
`Navigator` object	The navigator object contains information about the browser application.
Script	A scripting function defined using the `<SCRIPT>` element in the window scope.

Listing 15-1 illustrates how to use the **Alert** method of the Window object to display a message to the user. The results of the **Alert** method are illustrated in Figure 15-2.

Figure 15-2 The **Alert** method of the Window object displays a message on the active window

Listing 15-1 Using the `Alert` method with the Window object

```
<HTML>

<HEAD>

<SCRIPT LANGUAGE="VBScript">
<!--
  Alert "Click OK to view page"

-->
</SCRIPT>

</HEAD>

<B>This is a sample HTML page that uses the Alert method.</B>

</BODY>

</HTML>
```

Comments The **`Window`** object's properties, methods, and events are covered in alphabetical order on the following pages.

`Alert` METHOD

Purpose Use the **`Alert`** method to display an Alert message box on the page. Table 15-5 displays the attribute that is used with the **`Alert`** method.

Syntax **`Window.Alert`** `"alertmessage"`

Table 15-5 `Alert` method attribute

Attribute	Description
`alertmessage`	A text message that displays on the screen.

Description The **`Alert`** method is used to display a message on the HTML page. The message that is specified must be enclosed in quotes. If the **`Window`** object is omitted, the current active window is used.

Objects Affected `Window`

`ClearTimeout` METHOD

Purpose Use the **`ClearTimeout`** method to clear a specific timer. Table 15-6 describes the attribute that is used with the **`ClearTimeout`** method.

Syntax **`Window.ClearTimeout`** `"timerID"`

Table 15-6 `ClearTimeout` method attribute

Attribute	Description
`timerID`	The name of the timer that should be cleared.

Description The `ClearTimeout` method is used to clear a timer that was set using the `SetTimeout` method. The timer identification that is specified must be enclosed in quotes. If the `Window` object is omitted, the current active window is used.

Objects Affected `Window`

`Close` METHOD

Purpose Use the `Close` method to close the current window.

Syntax **`Window.Close`**

Description The `Close` method is used to close the current window. If the `Window` object is omitted, the current active window is used.

Objects Affected `Window`

`Confirm` METHOD

Purpose Use the `Confirm` method to display a message box with both OK and Cancel buttons. Table 15-7 describes the attribute that is used with the `Confirm` method.

Syntax **`Window.Confirm`** `"confirmmessage"`

Table 15-7 `Confirm` method attribute

Attribute	Description
`confirmmessage`	A text message that displays on the screen.

Description The `Confirm` method is used to display a message on the HTML page. The message box displays with both an OK and a Cancel button. A value of `TRUE` is returned if the user presses the OK button; otherwise, a value of `FALSE` is returned.

The message that is specified in the message box must be enclosed in quotes. If the `Window` object is omitted, the current active window is used.

Objects Affected `Window`

DefaultStatus PROPERTY

Purpose Use the `DefaultStatus` property to either set or get the default status of the HTML page. Table 15-8 describes the attribute that is used with the `DefaultStatus` method.

Syntax `Window.DefaultStatus = "statustext"`

Table 15-8 DefaultStatus method attribute

Attribute	Description
statustext	The text string to appear as the default status in the lower-left portion of the status bar. This attribute is only used when setting the status.

Description The `DefaultStatus` method is used to either set or capture the default status that displays in the lower-left portion of the status bar on the HTML page.

Objects Affected `Window`

Document PROPERTY

Purpose Use the `Document` property to return the document object for the current window.

Syntax `Window.Document`

Description The `Document` property is used to return the document object for the current window. If the `Window` object is omitted, the current active window is used.

Objects Affected `Window`

Frames PROPERTY

Purpose Use the `Frames` property to return the array of frames for the current window. Table 15-9 describes the attribute that is used with the `Frames` property.

Syntax `Window.Frames(value)`

Table 15-9 Frames property attribute

Attribute	Description
value	A numeric value used to identify a specific frame number.

Description The `Frames` property is used to return the array of frames for the current window. A numeric value can be used to access a specific frame.

Objects Affected `Window`

`History` PROPERTY

Purpose Use the `History` property to return the history object for the current window.

Syntax **`Window.History`**

Description The `History` property is used to return the history object for the current window. If the `Window` object is omitted, the current active window is used.

Objects Affected `Window`

`Location` PROPERTY

Purpose Use the `Location` property to return the location object for the current window.

Syntax **`Window.Location`**

Description The `Location` property is used to return the location object for the current window. This property is read-only. If the `Window` object is omitted, the current active window is used.

Objects Affected `Window`

`Name` PROPERTY

Purpose Use the `Name` property to return the name of the current window.

Syntax **`Window.Name`**

Description The `Name` property is used to return the name of the current window. Under the current version of Internet Explorer 3.0, the string `Microsoft Internet Explorer` is always returned. This property is read-only and cannot be used to change the window name. If the `Window` object is omitted, the current active window is used.

Objects Affected `Window`

`Navigate` METHOD

Purpose Use the `Navigate` method to display a page from a different URL in the current window. Table 15-10 describes the attribute that is used with the `Navigate` method.

Syntax **`Window.Navigate "URL"`**

Table 15-10 `Navigate` method attribute

Attribute	Description
`URL`	The location of the page to display on the window.

Description The `Navigate` method is used to specify the location of the HTML page that should display in the window. If the `Window` object is omitted, the current active window is used.

Objects Affected `Window`

Navigator PROPERTY

Purpose Use the `Navigator` property to return the navigator object for the current window.

Syntax `Window.Navigator`

Description The `Navigator` property is used to return the navigator object for the current window. If the `Window` object is omitted, the current active window is used.

Objects Affected `Window`

OnLoad EVENT

Purpose Use the `OnLoad` event to specify a function that runs when the HTML page is loaded. Table 15-11 describes the attribute that is used with the `Onload` event.

Syntax `Window.OnLoad = "functionname"`

Table 15-11 `OnLoad` event attribute

Attribute	Description
`functionname`	The name of the function that executes when the HTML page is loaded by the browser.

Description The `OnLoad` event is used to specify a function that should be executed when the HTML page is loaded. If the `Window` object is omitted, the current active window is used.

Objects Affected `Window`

OnUnLoad EVENT

Purpose Use the `OnUnLoad` event to specify a function that runs when the HTML page is unloaded. Table 15-12 describes the attribute that is used with the `OnUnLoad` event.

Syntax `Window.OnUnLoad = "functionname"`

Table 15-12 OnUnLoad event attribute

Attribute	Description
`functionname`	The name of the function that executes when the HTML page is unloaded by the browser.

Description The `OnUnLoad` event is used to specify a function that should be executed when the HTML page is unloaded. If the `Window` object is omitted, the current active window is used.

Objects Affected `Window`

Open METHOD

Purpose Use the `Open` method to open a new browser window. Table 15-13 contains the attributes for the `Open` method.

Syntax

```
Window.Open "windowlocation", "targetwindow", ⇐
"windowproperties"
```

Table 15-13 Open method attributes

Attribute	Description
`windowlocation`	The URL of the window that should be opened.
`targetwindow`	The name of the window in which the new window should be opened. If a window exists with the same name, that window is used; otherwise, a new window is created.

`windowproperties`	The desired window properties are specified in a comma-separated list surrounded by quotation marks. Each item in the list, with the exception of the `Width` and `Height` values, must be assigned a Boolean value of either `Yes` or `No`, or `1` or `2`, to identify whether or not the specified property should be available on the new window. The `Width` and `Height` properties should be assigned a pixel value specifying the desired size. The following properties can be specified for the new window:
	`toolbar = boolvalue`
	`location = boolvalue`
	`directories = boolvalue`
	`status = boolvalue`
	`menubar = boolvalue`

Attribute	Description
	`scrollbars = boolvalue`
	`resizeable = boolvalue`
	`width = pixelvalue`
	`height = pixelvalue`

Description The `Open` method is used to open a new HTML window. When you use the open window you need to specify the location of the window to open and the target window where it should be opened. You can specify additional information about the window by using the window properties in Table 15-13. For example, if you want to open a window and have a toolbar at the top of the window, use the statement `Open "file.htm", "New Window", "toolbar = Yes"`. If the `Window` object is omitted, the current active window is used.

Objects Affected `Window`

`Parent` Property

Purpose Use the `Parent` property to return the name of the parent window.

Syntax `Window.Parent`

Description The `Parent` property is used to identify the name of the window that contains all of the frames. If there are no frames on the current window, the parent window is the current window. This property is read-only. If the `Window` object is omitted, the current active window is used.

Objects Affected `Window`

`Prompt` Method

Purpose Use the `Prompt` method to prompt the user for specific information.

Syntax `Window.Prompt`

Description The `Prompt` method is used to display a message box that prompts the user for information. You can assign both the message that displays in the box and the default value for the input field. If the `Window` object is omitted, the current active window is used.

Objects Affected `Window`

`Self` Property

Purpose Use the `Self` property to return the window object of the current window.

Syntax `Window.Self`

Description The `Self` object is used to return a pointer to the current window. This property is read-only. If the `Window` object is omitted, the current active window is used.

Objects Affected `Window`

SetTimeout METHOD

Purpose Use the `SetTimeout` method to set a time that calls a function after a specified amount of time. Table 15-14 describes the attribute that is used with the `SetTimeout` method.

Syntax

```
timerID = Window.SetTimeout functionname timevalue
```

Table 15-14 `SetTimeout` method attributes

Attribute	Description
`timerID`	The name of the timer that should be created
`functionname`	The name of the function that should execute when the specified amount of time elapses
`timevalue`	The number of milliseconds that should elapse before the function is executed

Description The `SetTimeout` method is used to create a timer that executes a specific function when the specified number of milliseconds have elapsed. If the `Window` object is omitted, the current active window is used.

Objects Affected `Window`

Status PROPERTY

Purpose Use the `Status` property to either set or get the status of the HTML page. Table 15-15 lists the attribute that is used with the `Status` property.

Syntax

```
Window.Status = "statustext"
```

Table 15-15 `Status` method attribute

Attribute	Description
`statustext`	The text string to appear as the status in the lower-left portion of the status bar. This attribute is only used when setting the status.

Description The `Status` method is used to either set or capture the status that displays in the lower-left portion of the status bar on the HTML page.

Objects Affected `Window`

Top PROPERTY

Purpose Use the `Top` property to return a pointer to the top window.

Syntax **`Window.Top`**

Description The `Top` property is used to return a pointer to the top window on the HTML page. This is the window that contains all frames on the page. This property is read-only. If the `Window` object is omitted, the current active window is used.

Objects Affected `Window`

Document OBJECT

Purpose The `Document` object refers to the HTML document currently displayed by the browser and the associated objects on the page. Table 15-16 summarizes the properties that can be used with the `Document` object, and Table 15-17 summarizes the methods that can be used with the `Document` object. A detailed description of each property and method follows this section, in alphabetical order.

Syntax **`Document`**`.property`

or

`Document``.method`

Table 15-16 Properties of the `Document` object

Use...	To Do This...
`aLinkColor`	Set or get the color of the active link text.
`Aanchors`	Return an array of the anchors in the HTML document.
`BgColor`	Set or get the background color of the HTML document.
`Cookie`	Get or set the cookie for the current HTML document.
`FgColor`	Set or get the foreground color of the HTML document.
`Forms`	Return an array of the forms in the HTML document.
`LastModified`	Return last date that page was modified.
`LinkColor`	Set or get the color of the link text.
`Links`	Return an array of the links in the HTML document.
`Location`	Return the location object.
`Referrer`	Get the URL of the referring document for the current HTML document.
`Title`	Return the title of the current HTML document.
`vLinkColor`	Set or get the color of the visited links.

Table 15-17 Methods of the `Document` object

Use...	To Do This...
`Clear`	Close the document output string and write the data to the screen.
`Close`	Update screen with all of the strings written since the last `Open` method.
`Open`	Open a document stream for output.
`Write`	Place the specified string on the current document.
`WriteLn`	Place the specified string on the current document with a line break at the end of the string.

Description

The **`Document`** object HTML is used to refer to the document currently in the browser and the objects on the page, such as links, forms, buttons, and ActiveX objects. The methods and properties of the **`Document`** object must be called using a script, such as VBScript, by placing **`Document`** first in the statement.

Each **`Document`** object contains the elements in Table 15-18.

Table 15-18 `Document` object elements

Element	Description
`Anchor` object	An array of anchors found in the specified document.
`Form` object	An array of forms found in the specified document.
`Link` object	An array of hyperlinks found in the specified document.

Listing 15-2 illustrates how to use the **`Write`** method, of the **`Document`** object, to write the current date and time on the document when it is loaded. The results of the **`Write`** method are illustrated in Figure 15-3.

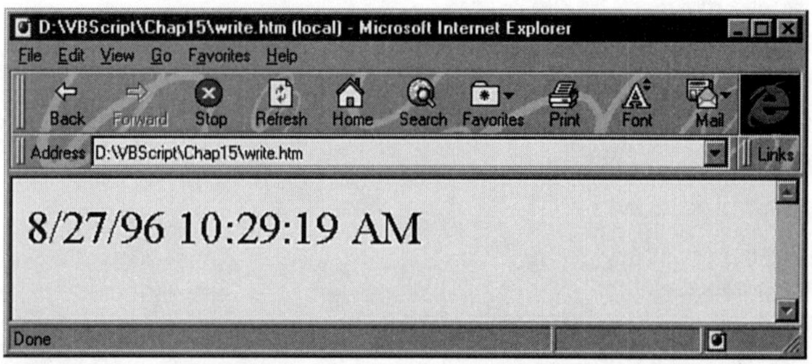

Figure 15-3 The **`Write`** method, of the Document object, writes the specified text to the document when it is loaded

Listing 15-2 Using the `Write` method with the Document object

```
<HTML>

<HEAD>

<BODY BGCOLOR="White">
<FONT SIZE=6>

<SCRIPT LANGUAGE="VBScript">
<!--
  document.write Now()

-->
</SCRIPT>

</HEAD>

<BODY>

</BODY>

</HTML>
```

Comments The `Document` object's properties and methods are covered in alphabetical order on the following pages.

ALinkColor PROPERTY

Purpose Use the `aLinkColor` property to set or get the color of the active link on the HTML document. Table 15-19 describes the attribute that is used with the `aLinkColor` property.

Syntax `Document.aLinkColor = linkcolor`

Table 15-19 `aLinkColor` property attribute

Attribute	Description
`linkcolor`	Either the RGB value for the desired color or a string that represents the color.

Description The `aLinkColor` property is used to either get or set the current color of the active links in an HTML document. A link on an HTML document is active when the mouse pointer is held down over the link but not released. Be aware that Internet Explorer does not have this feature; therefore, the `aLinkColor` property does not have an effect. This property is supported by the object model to make it compatible with other browsers. This property must be set at parse time, when the document is read.

Objects Affected `Document`

Anchors PROPERTY

Purpose Use the **Anchors** property to return an array containing the anchors in the current HTML document. Table 15-20 contains the attribute that can be used with the **Anchors** property to access a specific anchor.

Syntax `Document.Anchors(value)`

Table 15-20 Anchors property attribute

Attribute	Description
value	A numeric value that can be used to specify a specific anchor value in the array. For example, use a value of 0 to access the first anchor on the document.

Description The **Anchors** property is used to return an array of the anchors on the current HTML document. If you use the numeric value with the property, you can return the value of a specific anchor on the page.

Objects Affected Document

BgColor PROPERTY

Purpose Use the **bgColor** property to set or get the current color of the background for the document. Table 15-21 describes the attribute that is used with the **bgColor** property.

Syntax `Document.bgColor = linkcolor`

Table 15-21 bgColor property attribute

Attribute	Description
linkcolor	Either the RGB value for the desired color or a string that represents the color.

Description The **bgColor** property is used to either get or set the current color of the background for an HTML document. This property must be set at parse time, when the document is read.

Objects Affected Document

Clear METHOD

Purpose Use the **Clear** method to close the document output string and update the screen with all of the strings that have been written since the last **Open** method.

Syntax `Document.Clear`

Description The `Clear` statement is used to close the document output string and update the screen so that all strings that were written since the last `Open` message display on the document.

Objects Affected `Document`

Close METHOD

Purpose Use the `Close` method to update the screen with all of the strings that have been written since the last `Open` method.

Syntax `Document.Close`

Description The `Close` statement is used to update the screen so that all strings that were written since the last `Open` message display on the document.

Objects Affected `Document`

Cookie PROPERTY

Purpose Use the `Cookie` property to either get or set the cookie for the current HTML document. Table 15-22 describes the attribute that is used with the `Cookie` property.

Syntax `Document.Cookie = "newcookie"`

Table 15-22 Cookie property attribute

Attribute	Description
newcookie	A string of text that contains the new cookie information. This is an optional attribute that is only used when you want to change the cookie for a document.

Description The `Cookie` property is used to either return a string containing the cookie for the current document or set a new cookie for the document. The cookie is a string expression that is stored for the HTML document. It can contain any type of information. For example, you could use the cookie to store the number of times that a user has visited your Web page.

Objects Affected `Document`

FgColor PROPERTY

Purpose Use the `fgColor` property to set or get the current color of the foreground for the document. Table 15-23 describes the attribute that is used with the `fgColor` property.

Syntax `Document.fgColor = linkcolor`

Table 15-23 `fgColor` property attribute

Attribute	Description
`linkcolor`	Either the RGB value for the desired color or a string that represents the color.

Description The `fgColor` property is used to either get or set the current color of the foreground for an HTML document. This property must be set at parse time, when the document is read.

Objects Affected `Document`

Forms PROPERTY

Purpose Use the `Forms` property to return an array containing the forms in the current HTML document. Table 15-24 contains the attribute that can be used with the `Forms` property to access a specific form.

Syntax `Document.Forms(value)`

Table 15-24 `Forms` property attribute

Attribute	Description
`value`	A numeric value that can be used to specify a specific form value in the array. For example, use a value of `0` to access the first form on the document.

Description The `Forms` object is used to return an array of the forms on the current HTML document. If you use the numeric value with the property, you can access a specific frame on the page.

Objects Affected `Document`

LastModified PROPERTY

Purpose Use the `LastModified` property to determine the date when the current page was last modified.

Syntax `Document.LastModified`

Description The `LastModified` property is used to determine when the current page was last modified. This property returns a string that contains a date indicating when the page was modified.

Objects Affected `Document`

LinkColor PROPERTY

Purpose Use the `LinkColor` property to set or get the color of the links on the HTML document. Table 15-25 describes the attribute that is used with the `LinkColor` property.

Syntax `Document.LinkColor = linkcolor`

Table 15-25 `LinkColor` property attribute

Attribute	Description
`linkcolor`	Either the RGB value for the desired color or a string that represents the color.

Description The `LinkColor` property is used to either get or set the current color of the links in an HTML document. This property must be set at parse time, when the document is read.

Objects Affected `Window`

Links PROPERTY

Purpose Use the `Links` property to return an array containing the links in the current HTML document. Table 15-26 contains the attribute that can be used with the `Links` property to access a specific link.

Syntax `Document.Links(value)`

Table 15-26 `Links` property attribute

Attribute	Description
`value`	A numeric value that can be used to specify a specific link value in the array. For example, use a value of `0` to access the first link on the document.

Description The `Links` object is used to return an array of the links on the current HTML document. If you use the numeric value with the property, you can return the value of a specific link on the page.

Objects Affected `Document`

Location PROPERTY

Purpose Use the `Location` property to return the location object.

Syntax `Document.Location`

Description The `Location` property is used to return a read-only representation of the `Location` object for the HTML document.

Objects Affected `Document`

`Open` METHOD

Purpose Use the `Open` method to open a document stream for output.

Syntax **`Document.Open`**

Description The `Open` method is used to open a document stream for output. This method normally precedes the `Write`, `WriteLn`, and `Close` methods.

Objects Affected `Document`

`Referrer` PROPERTY

Purpose Use the `Referrer` property to retrieve the URL of the referring document.

Syntax **`Document.Referrer`**

Description The `Referrer` property is used to return a string that contains the URL location of the referring document. If there was no referring document, a `NULL` value is returned. A referring document is that document containing the link to the current document.

Objects Affected `Document`

`Title` PROPERTY

Purpose Use the `Title` property to return the title of the document.

Syntax **`Document.Title`**

Description The `Title` property is used to return the title of the current HTML document. The value returned by this property is read-only; therefore, this property cannot be used to modify the title of a document.

Objects Affected `Document`

`VLinkColor` PROPERTY

Purpose Use the `vLinkColor` property to set or get the color of the visited links on the HTML document. Table 15-27 describes the attribute that is used with the `vLinkColor` method.

Syntax **`Document.vLinkColor`** `= linkcolor`

Table 15-27 `vLinkColor` property attribute

Attribute	Description
`linkcolor`	Either the RGB value for the desired color or a string that represents the color.

Description The `vLinkColor` property is used to either get or set the current color of the visited links in an HTML document. This property must be set at parse time, when the document is read.

Objects Affected `Document`

`Write` METHOD

Purpose Use the **`Write`** method to place the specified string on the current document. Table 15-28 describes the attribute that is used with the **`Write`** method.

Syntax **`Document.Write`** `(textstring)`

Table 15-28 `Write` method attribute

Attribute	Description
`textstring`	A string of text that is placed on the HTML document.

Description The **`Write`** method is used to write a string of text to the current document. Since the string is added directly to HTML, it must be formatted as HTML. This method must be executed during the parsing of the page.

Objects Affected `Document`

`WriteLn` METHOD

Purpose Use the **`WriteLn`** method to place the specified string on the current document with a line break at the end of the string. Table 15-29 describes the attribute that is used with the **`WriteLn`** method.

Syntax **`Document.WriteLn`** `(textstring)`

Table 15-29 `WriteLn` method attribute

Attribute	Description
`textstring`	A string of text that is placed on the HTML document.

Description

The `WriteLn` method is used to write a string of text to the current document. When the string is written to the document, a line break is placed at the end of the string. HTML will ignore the line break character unless the script containing the `WriteLn` method is surrounded by `<PRE>` tags. Since the string is added directly to HTML, it must be formatted as HTML. This method must be executed during the parsing of the page.

Objects Affected

`Document`

Form OBJECT

Purpose

The `Form` object represents a form in the HTML document. Table 15-30 summarizes the properties that can be used with the `Form` object, Table 15-31 summarizes the method that can be used with the `Form` object, and Table 15-32 summarizes the event that can be used with the `Form` object. A detailed description of each property, method, and event follows this section, in alphabetical order.

Syntax

```
Form.property
```

or

```
Form.method
```

or

```
Form.event
```

Table 15-30 Properties of the `Form` object

Use...	To Do This...
`Action`	Set or get the address that is used to carry out actions on the form.
`Elements`	Return an array of the elements in the form.
`Encoding`	Set or get the encoding for the form.
`Method`	Specify how the form data should be sent to the server.
`Target`	Specify the name of the window where the form results should be displayed.

Table 15-31 Method of the `Form` object

Use...	To Do This...
`Submit`	Submit the form data to the server.

Table 15-32 Event of the `Form` object

Use...	To Do This...
`OnSubmit`	Specify a function that executes when the form is submitted.

Description

The **`Form`** object is used to reference an HTML form in a document. Forms are stored in the document as an array of forms and by name. A form object is always referenced through the document object. Each **`Form`** object contains the element in Table 15-33.

Table 15-33 `Form` object element

Element	Description
`Element` object	An array of objects and intrinsic controls contained in the form.

Listing 15-3 illustrates how to use the **`Target`** property, of the Form object, to set and then return the target window for the form. Remember that you must use the **`Document`** object with the **`Form`** object. The results of the **`Target`** property are illustrated in Figure 15-4.

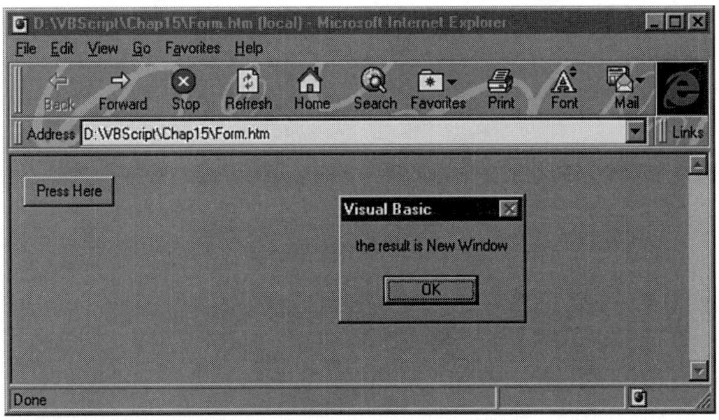

Figure 15-4 The **`Target`** property sets or gets the target window for the form

Listing 15-3 Using the `Target` property with the Form object

```
<HTML>

<HEAD>

<FONT SIZE=6>

<SCRIPT LANGUAGE="VBScript">
<!--
 SUB FormButton_onClick()

   Dim result

   document.Form1.target = "New Window"

   result = document.Form1.target

   MsgBox "the result is " & result

 END SUB
-->
</SCRIPT>

</HEAD>

<BODY>

 <FORM NAME="Form1">
   <INPUT TYPE="Button" NAME = "FormButton" VALUE = "Press Here">
 </FORM>
</BODY>

</HTML>
```

Comments The `Form` object properties, method, and event are covered in alphabetical order on the following pages.

`Action` PROPERTY

Purpose Use the `Action` property to set or get the address that is used to carry out actions on the form. Table 15-34 contains the attribute that can be used with the `Action` property.

Syntax **`Form.Action = "URL"`**

Table 15-34 `Action` property attribute

Attribute	Description
URL	A string containing the URL that should be used for actions on the form. This attribute is only used when you are setting the `Action` property.

Description The **Action** property is used to either get or set the address that is used to carry out the actions on the form. If you are setting the **Action** property, use the **URL** attribute to specify the new address to be used for the actions.

If an address is not specified, the base address of the form is used for all actions.

Objects Affected Form

Elements PROPERTY

Purpose Use the **Elements** property to return an array of the elements in the form.

Syntax **Form.Elements**

Description The **Elements** property is used to return an array of the elements for the form. These elements include intrinsic elements and objects that are embedded in the form using the **<INPUT>** and **<OBJECT>** tags.

Objects Affected Form

Encoding PROPERTY

Purpose Use the **Encoding** property to set or get the encoding for the form. Table 15-35 describes the attribute that can be used with the **Encoding** property.

Syntax **Form.Encoding = †encodestring"**

Table 15-35 Encoding property attribute

Attribute	Description
encodestring	A string containing the encoding for the form. This attribute is only used when setting the encoding for the form. The value of this attribute must be a valid MIME type; text/html is the default type.

Description The **Encoding** property is used to either get or set the encoding that is used on the form. If you are setting the **Encoding** property, use the **encodestring** attribute to specify the new encoding type to be used.

Using the **Encoding** property has the same results as using the **ENCTYPE** attribute of the **<FORM>** element.

Objects Affected Form

method PROPERTY

Purpose Use the **Method** property to specify how the form sends data to the server. Table 15-36 describes the attribute that can be used with the **Method** property.

Syntax **Form.Method = †sendmethod"**

Table 15-36 `Method` property attribute

Attribute	Description
`sendmethod`	A string specifying how the form sends data back to the server. The following two values are valid for this attribute:
	Value / **Description**
	`GET` Append the arguments to the action URL and open it as if it were an anchor.
	`POST` Send the data via an HTTP post transaction.

Description The `Method` property is used to specify how the data on the form is sent to the server. Using the `Method` property has the same results as using the `METHOD` attribute of the `<FORM>` element.

Objects Affected `Form`

onSubmit EVENT

Purpose Use the `onSubmit` event to specify a function that executes when the form is submitted. Table 15-37 describes the attribute that is used with the `onSubmit` event.

Syntax `Form.onSubmit = †submitaction"`

Table 15-37 `onSubmit` event attribute

Attribute	Description
`submitaction`	A string identifying a scripting function call.

Description The `onSubmit` event is used to specify a function that should be executed when the form is submitted. This can be a function that runs either prior to submitting the form, or in place of submitting the form.

Objects Affected `Form`

Submit METHOD

Purpose Use the `Submit` method to send the form data to the server.

Syntax `Form.Submit`

Description The `Submit` method is used to send the form data to the server. This method is the same as having the value of the `TYPE` attribute of the HTML `<INPUT>` element set to `SUBMIT`.

Objects Affected `Form`

Target PROPERTY

Purpose Use the `Target` property to specify the name of the window where the form results should be displayed. Table 15-38 describes the attribute that can be used with the `Target` property.

Syntax `Form.Target = twindowname"`

Table 15-38 Target property attribute

Attribute	Description
windowname	A string specifying the name of the window.

Description The `Target` property is used to specify the name of the window in which the results from the form should be displayed. Using the `Target` property has the same results as using the `TARGET` attribute of the `<FORM>` element.

Objects Affected `Form`

Location OBJECT

Purpose The `Location` object maintains information about the current URL. Table 15-39 summarizes the properties that can be used with the `Location` object. A detailed description of each property follows this section, in alphabetical order.

Syntax `Location.property`

Table 15-39 Properties of the Location object

Use...	To Do This...
hash	Get or set the hash portion of the URL.
host	Get and set the host and port portion of the URL.
hostname	Get or set the host portion of the URL.
href	Get or set the complete URL for the location.
pathname	Get or set the name of the path for the URL.
port	Get or set the port portion of the URL.
protocol	Get or set the protocol portion of the URL.
search	Get or set the search portion of the URL.

Description The `Location` object maintains information about the current URL for the HTML document. You can access or modify the location information by using the properties associated with the `Location` object. If you use any of

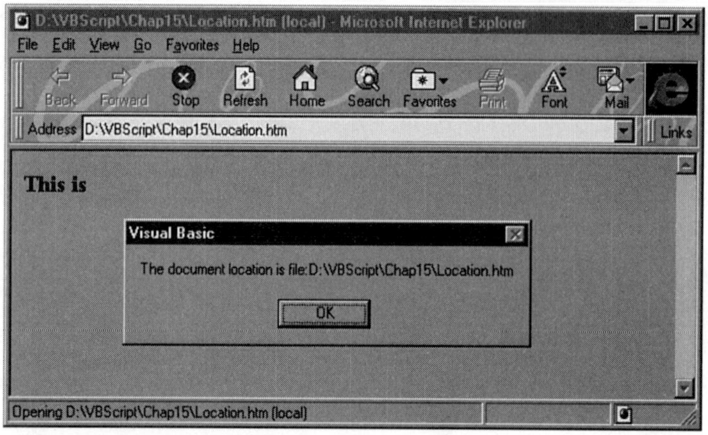

Figure 15-5 The Href property of the `Location` object sets or gets the location of the current HTML document

the `Location` object properties to modify the URL settings, the browser will navigate to the new URL settings. Always use the `Document` object with the `Location` object.

Listing 15-4 illustrates how to use the `Location` object to return the location of the current HTML document. The results of the `Location` property are illustrated in Figure 15-5.

Listing 15-4 Using the `Location` *object*

```
<HTML>

<HEAD>

<FONT SIZE=4>

<SCRIPT LANGUAGE="VBScript">
<!--

   Dim result

result = location.href
   MsgBox "The document location is " & result

-->
</SCRIPT>

</HEAD>

<BODY>

 <B>This is a sample HTML document.<B>
</BODY>

</HTML>
```

Comments The `Location` object properties are covered in alphabetical order on the following pages.

Hash PROPERTY

Purpose Use the `Hash` property to either get or set the hash portion of the URL. Table 15-40 describes the attribute that can be used with the `Hash` property.

Syntax `Location.Hash = †hashvalue"`

Table 15-40 Hash property attribute

Attribute	Description
hashvalue	A string specifying the hash value for the URL. This is an optional string used only when setting the hash value.

Description The `Hash` property is used to either get or set the hash value for the current URL. If you are setting the hash value, you assign it an optional string value, as outlined in Table 15-40. Under Internet Explorer 3.0, a value of `#` is always returned as the hash value.

Objects Affected `Location`

Host PROPERTY

Purpose Use the `Host` property to either get or set the host and port portion of the URL. Table 15-41 describes the attribute that can be used with the `Host` property.

Syntax `Location.Host = †hostvalue"`

Table 15-41 Host property attribute

Attribute	Description
hostvalue	A string specifying the host and port values for the URL. This is an optional string used only when setting the host and port values.

Description The `Host` property is used to either get or set the host and port values for the current URL. If you are setting values, you assign the property an optional string value, as outlined in Table 15-41.

Objects Affected `Location`

`Hostname` PROPERTY

Purpose Use the **`Hostname`** property to either get or set the host name portion of the URL. Table 15-42 describes the attribute that can be used with the **`Hostname`** property.

Syntax **`Location.Hostname`** `= ┼hostname"`

Table 15-42 `Hostname` property attribute

Attribute	Description
`hostname`	A string specifying the new name or IP address for the URL. This is an optional string used only when setting the host name value.

Description The **`Hostname`** property is used to either get or set the host name value for the current URL. If you are setting the host value, you assign it an optional string value specifying the new host value, as outlined in Table 15-42.

Objects Affected `Location`

`Href` PROPERTY

Purpose Use the **`Href`** property to either get or set the complete URL for the current location. Table 15-43 describes the attribute that can be used with the **`Href`** property.

Syntax **`Location.Href`** `= "hrefvalue"`

Table 15-43 `Href` property attribute

Attribute	Description
`hrefvalue`	A string specifying the complete URL. This is an optional string used only when setting the URL for the location.

Description The **`Href`** property is used to either get or set the complete URL for the location. If you are setting the URL, you assign it an optional string value, as outlined in Table 15-43.

Objects Affected `Location`

`Pathname` PROPERTY

Purpose Use the **`Pathname`** property to either get or set the name of the path in the URL. Table 15-44 describes the attribute that can be used with the **`Pathname`** property.

Syntax `Location.Pathname = †path"`

Table 15-44 `Pathname` property attribute

Attribute	Description
`path`	A string specifying the path for the URL. This is an optional string used only when setting the URL.

Description The `Pathname` property is used to either get or set the name of the path for the current URL. If you are setting the path, you assign it an optional string value, as outlined in Table 15-44.

Objects Affected `Location`

`Port` PROPERTY

Purpose Use the `Port` property to either get or set the port portion of the URL. Table 15-45 describes the attribute that can be used with the `Port` property.

Syntax `Location.Port = †portvalue"`

Table 15-45 `Port` property attribute

Attribute	Description
`portvalue`	A string specifying the port value for the URL. This is an optional string used only when setting the port value.

Description The `Port` property is used to either get or set the port value for the current URL. If you are setting the port value, you assign it an optional string value, as outlined in Table 15-45.

Objects Affected `Location`

`Protocol` PROPERTY

Purpose Use the `Protocol` property to either get or set the protocol portion of the URL. Table 15-46 describes the attribute that can be used with the `Protocol` property.

Syntax `Location.Protocol = †protocol"`

Table 15-46 `Protocol` property attribute

Attribute	Description
`protocol`	A string specifying the protocol value for the URL. This is an optional string used only when setting the protocol value.

Description The `Protocol` property is used to either get or set the protocol value for the current URL. If you are setting the protocol value, you assign it an optional string value, as outlined in Table 15-46.

Objects Affected `Location`

`Search` Property

Purpose Use the `Search` property to either get or set the search portion of the URL. Table 15-47 describes the attribute that can be used with the `Search` property.

Syntax `Location.Search = tsearchvalue"`

Table 15-47 `Search` property attribute

Attribute	Description
`searchvalue`	A string specifying the search value for the URL. This is an optional string used only when setting the search value.

Description The `Search` property is used to either get or set the search value for the current URL. If you are setting the search value, you assign it an optional string value, as outlined in Table 15-47.

Objects Affected `Location`

`Link` Object

Purpose The `Link` object contains an array of the links in the current HTML document. Table 15-48 summarizes the properties that can be used with the `Link` object, and Table 15-49 summarizes the events that can be used with the `Link` object. A detailed description of each property and event follows this section, in alphabetical order.

Syntax `Link.property`

or

`Link.event`

Table 15-48 Properties of the `Link` object

Use...	To Do This...
`Hash`	Get the hash portion of the URL for the link.
`Href`	Get the complete URL for the link.
`Host`	Get the host and port portion of the URL for a link.

Use...	To Do This...
`Hostname`	Get the host portion of the URL for the link.
`Pathname`	Get the path name portion of the URL for the link.
`Port`	Get the port portion of the URL for the link.
`Protocol`	Get the protocol for a URL.
`Search`	Get the search portion of the URL for the link.
`Target`	Return the target of the link.

Table 15-49 Events of the `Link` object

Use...	To Do This...
`MouseMove`	Perform a specified event when the cursor moves over a link.
`onClick`	Perform an event if the cursor clicks on the specified link.
`onMouseOver`	Perform an event if the cursor moves over the specified link.

Description

The `Link` object is an array of the links that exist on the current HTML document. This object is read-only; therefore, the properties and events cannot be used to modify the object.

Listing 15-5 illustrates how to use the MouseMove event with the `Link` object to launch an event when the cursor passes over a link. The events for the `Link` object are always used with the `<SCRIPT> FOR EVENT` tags, as illustrated in Listing 15-5. The results of the `Link` event are illustrated in Figure 15-6.

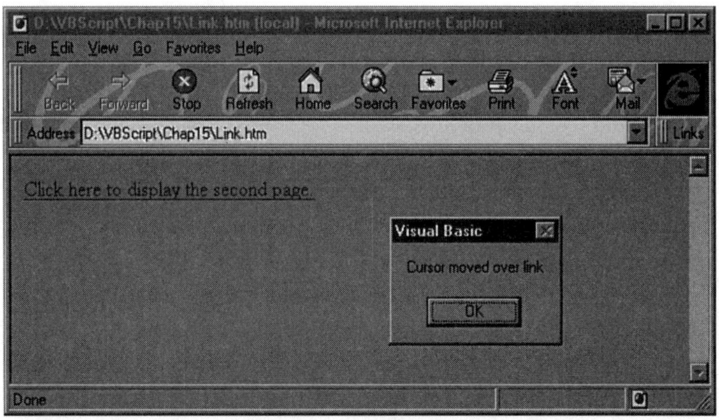

Figure 15-6 The MouseMove event of the `Link` object launches an event when the cursor moves over the link

Listing 15-5 Using the `Link` object

```
<HTML>

<HEAD>

<SCRIPT LANGUAGE="VBScript" FOR="Link1" EVENT="mouseMove(shift, button, x, y)">

  MsgBox "Cursor moved over link"

</SCRIPT>
</HEAD>

<BODY>

<A:HREF = "Link2.htm" Name = "Link1">Click here to display the second page.</A>

</BODY>

</HTML>
```

Comments The `Link` object's properties and events are covered in alphabetical order on the following pages.

`Hash` PROPERTY

Purpose Use the `Hash` property to return the hash portion of the link.

Syntax **`Link.Hash`**

Description The `Hash` property is used to get the hash portion of the URL for the link. Under Internet Explorer 3.0, the value that follows the `#` is always returned as the hash value; if a hash value does not exist, a `NULL` value is returned.

Objects Affected `Link`

`Host` PROPERTY

Purpose Use the `Host` property to return the host and port portion of the URL for the link.

Syntax **`Link.Host`**

Description The `Host` property is used to get the host and port portion of the URL for the link. You cannot modify the host or port values for a link.

Objects Affected `Link`

`Hostname` PROPERTY

Purpose Use the `Hostname` property to return the host portion of the URL for the link.

Syntax `Link.Hostname`

Description The `Hostname` property is used to get the host portion of the URL for the link. This value can either be a name or an IP address. You cannot modify the host or port values for a link.

Objects Affected `Link`

Href Property

Purpose Use the `Href` property to return the complete URL for the link.

Syntax `Link.Href`

Description The `Href` property is used to get the complete URL for the link. You cannot modify the URL value for a link.

Objects Affected `Link`

MouseMove Event

Purpose Use the `MouseMove` event to perform an event if the cursor moves over the specified link. Table 15-50 describes the attributes of the `MouseMove` event.

Syntax `Link.MouseMove shift button, x, y`

Table 15-50 MouseMove event attributes

Attribute	Description
shift	Indicates the status of the shift key.
button	Indicates the button that was pressed, if any.
x	Indicates the horizontal position of the cursor, in pixels.
y	Indicates the vertical position of the cursor, in pixels.

Description The `MouseMove` event is used to identify an event that occurs when the cursor moves over the top of the specified link. This event keeps track of the status of the shift key, the button that was pressed, and the coordinates of the cursor. Use the `<SCRIPT>` element in the following format to attach a script to this event.

```
<script language=script-engine for=linkname event="mouseMove(shift, button, x, y)">
```

Objects Affected `Link`

onClick Event

Purpose Use the `onClick` event to perform an event if the cursor clicks on the specified link.

Syntax `Link.OnClick`

Description The `OnClick` event is used to identify an event that occurs when the cursor clicks on the specified link. Use one of the following methods to attach a script to this event. Either use the `<SCRIPT>` element:

```
<script language=script-engine for=link-name event="onClick">
```

or attach a script directly in the HTML using this format:

```
<A HREF="http://www.samplesite.com" onClick="ClickFunction">Sample Site</A>
```

Objects Affected `Link`

onMouseOver EVENT

Purpose Use the `onMouseOver` event to perform an event if the cursor moves over the specified link.

Syntax `Link.OnMouseOver`

Description The `OnMouseOver` event is used to identify an event that occurs when the cursor moves over the specified link. Use one of the following methods to attach a script to this event. Either use the `<SCRIPT>` element:

```
<script language=script-engine for=link-name event="onMoveOver">
```

or attach a script directly in the HTML using this format:

```
<A HREF="http://www.samplesite.com" onMouseOver="OverFunction">Sample Site</A>
```

Objects Affected `Link`

Pathname PROPERTY

Purpose Use the `Pathname` property to return the path name portion of the URL for the link.

Syntax `Link.Pathname`

Description The `Pathname` property is used to get the path name portion of the URL for the link. You cannot modify the path name values for a link.

Objects Affected `Link`

Port PROPERTY

Purpose Use the `Port` property to return the port portion of the URL for the link.

Syntax `Link.Port`

Description The `Port` property is used to get the port portion of the URL for the link. You cannot modify the port value for a link.

Objects Affected `Link`

Protocol PROPERTY

Purpose Use the **Protocol** property to return the protocol portion of the URL for the link.

Syntax **Link.Protocol**

Description The **Protocol** property is used to get the protocol portion of the URL for the link. You cannot modify the protocol value for a link.

Objects Affected Link

Search PROPERTY

Purpose Use the **Search** property to return the search portion of the URL for the link.

Syntax **Link.Search**

Description The **Search** property is used to get the search portion of the URL for the link. You cannot modify the search value for a link.

Objects Affected Link

Target PROPERTY

Purpose Use the **Target** property to return the target of a link.

Syntax **Link.Target**

Description The **Target** property is used to return the target of a link, if one exists.

Objects Affected Link

Anchor OBJECT

Purpose The **Anchor** object specifies an array of anchors for a given document. Table 15-51 summarizes the property that can be used with the **Anchor** object. A detailed description of the property follows this section.

Syntax **Anchor.property**

Table 15-51 Property of the Anchor object

Use...	To Do This...
name	Get or set the name of the anchor.

Description The **Anchor** object is used to specify an array of anchors for a given document. Each entry in this array corresponds to an **<A>** tag that is found in the corresponding document. The anchors are only accessible through an indexed array.

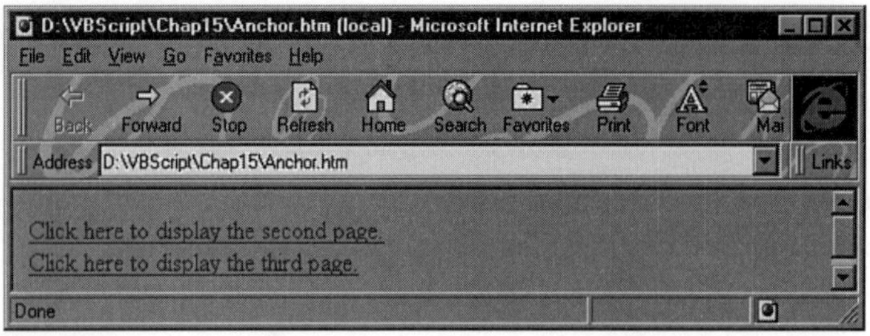

Figure 15-7 Use the **Name** property of the Anchor object to return the name of an anchor

Listing 15-6 illustrates how to use the **Name** property of the Anchor object to get the name of the anchor. The results of using the **Name** property are illustrated in Figure 15-7.

Listing 15-6 Using the Anchor *object*

```
<HTML>

<HEAD>

</HEAD>

<BODY>

<A:HREF = "Link2.htm" Name = "Link1">Click here to display the second page.</A>
<BR>
<A:HREF = "Link2.htm" Name = "Link2">Click here to display the third page.</A>

<SCRIPT LANGUAGE="VBScript">

 Dim anchortext

 anchortext = document.anchor(1).name

 MsgBox anchortext

</SCRIPT>

</BODY>

</HTML>
```

Name Property

Purpose Use the **Name** property to set or get the name of the anchor. Table 15-52 describes the attribute that can be used with the **Name** property.

Syntax `Anchor.Name = "anchorname"`

Table 15-52 Name property attribute

Attribute	Description
anchorname	The new name of the anchor. This attribute is only used to set the anchor name.

Description The `Name` property is used to either get or set the name of an anchor on the current HTML document. If you are setting the anchor name, you can use the optional attribute described in Table 15-52.

Objects Affected `Anchor`

Element OBJECT

Purpose The `Element` object represents an intrinsic HTML control or object. Table 15-53 summarizes the properties that can be used with the `Element` object, Table 15-54 summarizes the methods that can be used with the `Element` object, and Table 15-55 summarizes the events that can be used with the `Element` object. A detailed description of each property, method, and event follows this section, in alphabetical order.

Syntax

```
Element.property
```

or

```
Element.method
```

or

```
Element.event
```

Table 15-53 Properties of the Element object

Use...	To Do This...
Checked	Get or set the checked state of either a checkbox or a radio button.
DefaultChecked	Get or set the default checked state of a checkbox.
DefaultValue	Get or set the default value of an element.
Enabled	Get or set whether the element is enabled.
Form	Get the form object containing the element.
ListCount	Get the count of the elements in the list box.
ListIndex	Get or set the list index.
Length	Get the number of options in an element.
MultiSelect	Get or set whether multiple items can be selected in an element.
Name	Get or set the name of the element.
Options	Get the options of the element.
SelectedIndex	Get the index for the selected option.
Value	Get or set the value of the element.

Table 15-54 Methods of the `Element` object

Use...	To Do This...
`AddItem`	Add a new item to an element.
`Blur`	Clear the focus from an element.
`Clear`	Clear the contents of an item in an element.
`Click`	Click an element.
`Focus`	Set focus to an element.
`RemoveItem`	Remove an item from an element.
`Select`	Select contents of an element.

Table 15-55 Events of the `Element` object

Use...	To Do This...
`onBlur`	Fire an event when the element loses focus.
`onChange`	Fire an event when the element has changed.
`onClick`	Fire an event when the element is clicked.
`onFocus`	Fire an event when the element gets focus.
`onSelect`	Fire an event when the contents of the element are selected.

Description The `Element` object is used to interact with the intrinsic HTML controls and objects. These are items that are placed on the HTML page using either the `<INPUT>` tags or the `<OBJECT>` tags. Not all of the properties, methods, and events of the `Element` object can be used with all elements. When you use the `Element` events, there are three ways to script the event:

- You can use the `onEvent="subroutine"` syntax when working with any HTML intrinsic elements, such as forms, buttons, or links. This method does not work for items inserted using the `<OBJECT>` tag. When you use this method, the `<SCRIPT>` contains a procedure that is called when the element is selected.

```
<SCRIPT LANGUAGE="VBScript">
 SUB Selected
  alert "I've been pressed"
 END SUB
</script>

<form name="Form1">
  <INPUT TYPE="button" NAME="Button1" VALUE="Press the Button" onClick="Selected">
</form>
```

- You can use the `onEvent_ElementName` syntax when working with any HTML intrinsic elements, such as forms, buttons, or links. This method does not work for items inserted using the `<OBJECT>` tag. This method is similar to the first method described; the only difference being that the VBScript procedure is named **onClick_ElementName**, where **ElementName** equals the name assigned to the HTML element. When the element is selected, the procedure is automatically called.

```
<SCRIPT LANGUAGE="VBScript">
 SUB onClick_Selected
  alert "I've been pressed"
 END SUB
</script>

<form name="Form1">
  <INPUT TYPE="button" NAME="Button1" VALUE="Press the Button>
</form>
```

- You can use the **FOR="object" EVENT="eventname"** syntax. This method can be used for any named elements, plus any elements inserted using the **<OBJECT>** tag. The following example is the same as the first, but with a different syntax:

```
<FORM NAME="Form1">
    <INPUT TYPE="button" NAME="Button1" VALUE="Press me">
     <SCRIPT FOR="Button1" EVENT="onClick" LANGUAGE="VBScript">
     alert "I've been pressed"
</SCRIPT>
</FORM>
```

- Listing 15-7 illustrates how to use the **Value** property of the Element object to get the value of the text control. The results of using the **Value** property are illustrated in Figure 15-8.

Listing 15-7 Using the `Value` *property of the* `Element` *object*

```
<HTML>

<HEAD>
<SCRIPT LANGUAGE="VBScript">

SUB PressButton_onClick

  MsgBox "The value typed is " & InputField.value

END SUB

</SCRIPT>

</HEAD>

<BODY>

<INPUT TYPE= "Text" NAME = "InputField">
<INPUT TYPE= "Button" NAME = "PressButton" VALUE= "Press Button">

</BODY>

</HTML>
```

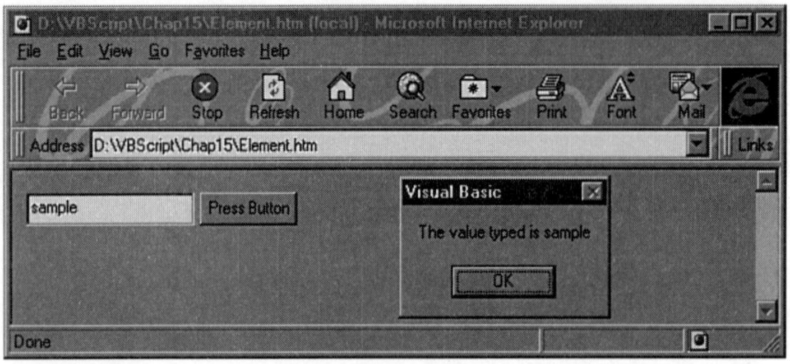

Figure 15-8 Use the **Value** property of the **Element** object to return the value of the element

Comments The **Element** object's properties, methods, and events are covered in alphabetical order on the following pages.

AddItem METHOD

Purpose Use the **AddItem** method to add a new item to an element. Table 15-56 describes the attribute that can be used with the **AddItem** method.

Syntax **Element.AddItem = "indexvalue"**

Table 15-56 AddItem method attribute

Attribute	Description
indexvalue	The index where the new item should be added.

Description The **AddItem** method is used to add a new item to an element. This item is added to the element at the location specified in the attribute described in Table 15-56. The new item is added preceding the item currently at the specified location.

Applies to Elements combo

Objects Affected Element

Blur METHOD

Purpose Use the **Blur** method to clear the focus from an element.

Syntax **Element.Blur**

Description The **Blur** method is used to clear the focus from an element.

Applies to Elements password, text, text area

Objects Affected `Element`

Checked PROPERTY

Purpose Use the `Checked` property to get or set the checked state of a checkbox or a radio button. Table 15-57 describes the attribute that can be used with the `Checked` property.

Syntax `Element.Checked = "checkedstate"`

Table 15-57 `Checked` property attribute

Attribute	Description
`checkedstate`	The checked state for the element. This attribute has a Boolean value of `TRUE` if the element is checked; otherwise, the value is `FALSE`. This is an optional attribute that is only used when changing the checked state of the element.

Description The `Checked` property is used to either change or return the checked state of an element. The attribute in Table 15-57 is used when you change the checked state of the element.

Applies to Elements check box, radio button

Objects Affected `Element`

Clear METHOD

Purpose Use the `Clear` method to clear an item in an element. Table 15-58 describes the attribute that can be used with the `Clear` method.

Syntax `Element.Clear = "indexvalue"`

Table 15-58 `Clear` method attribute

Attribute	Description
`indexvalue`	The index of the item that should be cleared.

Description The `Clear` method is used to clear the contents of an item in an element. Only the item in the element at the location specified in the attribute described in Table 15-58 is cleared.

Applies to Elements combo

Objects Affected `Element`

`Click` METHOD

Purpose	Use the `Click` method to click an element.
Syntax	**`Element.Click`**
Description	The `Click` method is used to click an element on the HTML document.
Applies to Elements	addItem, button, blur, clear, removeItem, select
Objects Affected	`Element`

`DefaultChecked` PROPERTY

Purpose	Use the `DefaultChecked` property to get or set the default checked state of a checkbox. Table 15-59 describes the attribute that can be used with the `DefaultChecked` property.
Syntax	**`Element.DefaultChecked`** `= "checkedstate"`

Table 15-59 `DefaultChecked` property attribute

Attribute	Description
`checkedstate`	The default checked state for the element. This attribute has a Boolean value of `TRUE` if the element is checked; otherwise, the value is `FALSE`. This is an optional attribute that is only used when changing the default checked state of the element.

Description	The `DefaultChecked` property is used to either change or return the default checked state of an element. The attribute in Table 15-59 is used when you change the default checked state of the element.
Applies to Elements	check box
Objects Affected	`Element`

`DefaultValue` PROPERTY

Purpose	Use the `DefaultValue` property to get or set the default value of the element. Table 15-60 describes the attribute that can be used with the `DefaultValue` property.
Syntax	**`Element.DefaultValue`** `= "elementvalue"`

Table 15-60 `DefaultValue` property attribute

Attribute	Description
`elementvalue`	The default value for the element. This is an optional attribute that is only used when changing the default value of the element.

Description The `DefaultValue` property is used to either change or return the default value of an element. The attribute in Table 15-60 is used when you change the default value of the element.

Applies to Elements password, text, text area

Objects Affected `Element`

`Enabled` PROPERTY

Purpose Use the `Enabled` property to determine whether the element is enabled. Table 15-61 describes the attribute that can be used with the `Enabled` property.

Syntax **`Element.Enabled = "enabled"`**

Table 15-61 `Enabled` property attribute

Attribute	Description
`enabled`	A Boolean value that enables or disables the element. A value of `TRUE` enables the element; otherwise, a value of `FALSE` disables the element. This is an optional attribute that is only used when enabling or disabling the element.

Description The `Enabled` property is used to either determine if an element is enabled or change an element to be enabled or disabled. The attribute in Table 15-61 is used when you are enabling or disabling the element.

Applies to Elements All elements

Objects Affected `Element`

`Focus` METHOD

Purpose Use the `Focus` method to set the focus to an element.

Syntax **`Element.Focus`**

Description The `Focus` method is used to set the focus to an element on the HTML document.

Applies to Elements All elements

Objects Affected `Element`

`Form` PROPERTY

Purpose Use the `Form` property to get the form object containing the element.

Syntax **`Element.Form`**

Description The `Form` property method is used to return the form object that contains the specified element.

Applies to Elements All elements

Objects Affected `Element`

`Length` PROPERTY

Purpose Use the `Length` property to get the number of options in an element.

Syntax **`Element.Length`**

Description The `Length` property is used to determine the number of options in the `<SELECT>` element. This property returns an integer value specifying the number of options in the element.

Applies to Elements select

Objects Affected `Element`

`ListCount` PROPERTY

Purpose Use the `listCount` property to get the count of the elements in the list.

Syntax **`Element.listCount`**

Description The `listCount` property is used to determine the number of elements in the list of a combo box.

Applies to Elements combo

Objects Affected `Element`

`ListIndex` PROPERTY

Purpose Use the `ListIndex` property to get or set the index of the selected element. Table 15-62 describes the attribute that can be used with the `ListIndex` property.

Syntax **`Element.ListIndex = "indexvalue"`**

Table 15-62 `ListIndex` property attribute

Attribute	Description
`indexvalue`	The index value to select. This is an optional attribute that is only used when setting the selected element.

Description The `ListIndex` property is used to either set or return the index of the selected element. The attribute in Table 15-62 is used when you set the selected element.

Applies to Elements combo

Objects Affected `Element`

`MultiSelect` PROPERTY

Purpose Use the `MultiSelect` property to indicate whether multiple items can be selected in a combo box. Table 15-63 describes the attribute that can be used with the `MultiSelect` property.

Syntax `Element.MultSelect = "selected"`

Table 15-63 `MultiSelect` property attribute

Attribute	Description
`selected`	A Boolean value that indicates whether or not multiple items can be selected in an element. A value of `TRUE` indicates multiple items can be selected; otherwise, the value is `FALSE` if only one item can be selected. This is an optional attribute that is only used when specifying whether or not multiple items can be selected in the element.

Description The `MultiSelect` property is used to either determine or specify whether or not a combo box can have multiple items selected. The attribute in Table 15-63 is used when you specify whether the combo box can have multiple items selected.

Applies to Elements combo

Objects Affected `Element`

`Name` PROPERTY

Purpose Use the `Name` property to get or set the name of the element. Table 15-64 describes the attribute that can be used with the `Name` property.

Syntax `Element.Name = "elementname"`

Table 15-64 Name property attribute

Attribute	Description
elementname	The new name for the element. This is an optional attribute that is only used when changing the name of the element.

Description The `Name` property is used to either change or return the name of an element. The attribute in Table 15-64 is used when you change the name of the element.

Applies to Elements All elements

Objects Affected `Element`

OnBlur Event

Purpose Use the `OnBlur` event to call an event when the element loses the focus.

Syntax **`Element.onBlur`**

Description The `OnBlur` event is used to launch the specified event when the element loses focus. Refer to the description of the `Element` object for examples of how to use events such as this.

Applies to Elements password, text, text area

Objects Affected `Element`

OnChange Event

Purpose Use the `OnChange` event to call an event when the element has changed.

Syntax **`Element.onChange`**

Description The `OnChange` event is used to launch the specified event when the element has changed. Refer to the description of the `Element` object for examples of how to use events such as this.

Applies to Elements text, text area

Objects Affected `Element`

OnClick Event

Purpose Use the `OnClick` event to call an event when the element is clicked.

Syntax **`Element.onClick`**

Description The `OnClick` event is used to launch the specified event when the element is clicked. Refer to the description of the `Element` object for examples of how to use events such as this.

Applies to Elements button, reset, submit, check box, radio, combo

Objects Affected `Element`

OnFocus EVENT

Purpose Use the `OnFocus` event to call an event when the element gets the focus.

Syntax **`Element.onFocus`**

Description The `OnFocus` event is used to launch the specified event when the element gets focus. Refer to the description of the `Element` object for examples of how to use this event.

Applies to Elements All elements

Objects Affected `Element`

OnSelect EVENT

Purpose Use the `OnSelect` event to call an event when the contents of the element are selected.

Syntax **`Element.onSelect`**

Description The `OnSelect` event is used to launch the specified event when the contents of the element are selected. Refer to the description of the `Element` object for examples of how to use events such as this.

Applies to Elements text, text area

Objects Affected `Element`

Options PROPERTY

Purpose Use the `Options` property to get the options for an element.

Syntax **`Element.Options`**

Description The `Options` property is used to return the options for the `<SELECT>` element. This property returns the options array containing the information in Table 15-65.

Table 15-65 Values of the `Options` array

Array Value	Description
`defaultSelected`	Currently selected attribute.
`index`	The index of an option.
`length`	Number of items in the element.
`name`	Name of the element.
`selected`	Used to select an option.
`selectedIndex`	Specifies the index of the selected option.
`text`	Text to be displayed for the element.
`value`	Specifies the value attribute.

Applies to Elements select

Objects Affected `Element`

`RemoveItem` Method

Purpose Use the **`RemoveItem`** method to remove an item from an element. Table 15-66 describes the attribute that can be used with the **`RemoveItem`** method.

Syntax **`Element.RemoveItem = "indexvalue"`**

Table 15-66 `RemoveItem` method attribute

Attribute	Description
`indexvalue`	The index of the location from which the item should be removed.

Description The **`RemoveItem`** method is used to remove an item from an element. This item is removed from the element at the location specified in the attribute described in Table 15-66.

Applies to Elements combo

Objects Affected `Element`

`Select` Method

Purpose Use the `Select` method to select the contents of an element.

Syntax **`Element.Select`**

Description The `Select` method is used to select the contents of an element on the HTML document.

Applies to Elements password, text, text area

Objects Affected `Element`

`SelectedIndex` PROPERTY

Purpose Use the `SelectedIndex` property to get the index of the selected option.

Syntax **`Element.SelectedIndex`**

Description The `SelectedIndex` property is used to return an integer value specifying the index of the selected option in the `<SELECT>` element.

Applies to Elements select

Objects Affected `Element`

`Value` PROPERTY

Purpose Use the `Value` property to get or set the value of the element. Table 15-67 describes the attribute that can be used with the `Value` property.

Syntax **`Element.Value`** `= "elementvalue"`

Table 15-67 `Value` property attribute

Attribute	Description
`elementvalue`	The new value for the element. This is an optional attribute that is only used when changing the value of the element.

Description The `Value` property is used to either change or return the value of an element. The attribute in Table 15-67 is used when you change the value of the element.

Applies to Elements All elements

Objects Affected `Element`

`History` OBJECT

Purpose The `History` object is used to access the current history of the browser. Table 15-68 summarizes the property that can be used with the `History` object, and Table 15-69 summarizes the methods that can be used with the `History` object. A detailed description of each property and method follows this section, in alphabetical order.

Syntax **History.**property

or

History.method

Table 15-68 Property of the `History` object

Use...	To Do This...
`length`	Return the length of the history list.

Table 15-69 Methods of the `History` object

Use...	To Do This...
`back`	Display a page from the history list that was viewed previously.
`forward`	Move forward through the history list and display a page that was viewed after the selected page.

Description The **History** object is used to work with items in the history list of the browser. For example, you can view the page that displayed two pages prior to the current page by using the **Back** method.

Listing 15-8 illustrates how to use the **Length** property to get the length of the history list. The results of the **Length** property are illustrated in Figure 15-9.

Listing 15-8 Using the `Length` property

```
<HTML>

<HEAD>
<SCRIPT LANGUAGE="VBScript">

  MsgBox "The history is " & history.length

</SCRIPT>

</HEAD>

<BODY>

Sample HTML page.
</BODY>

</HTML>
```

Comments The **History** object property and methods are covered in alphabetical order on the following pages.

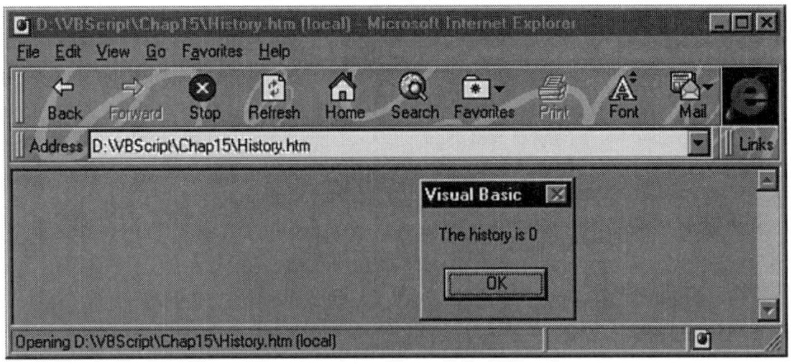

Figure 15-9 The `Length` property returns the length of the history list

`Back` METHOD

Purpose Use the **`Back`** method to display a Web page that displayed prior to the current page. Table 15-70 indicates the attribute that is used with the **`Back`** method.

Syntax **`History.Back(value)`**

Table 15-70 `Back` method attribute

Attribute	Description
`value`	A numeric value that specifies the number of Web pages

Description The **`Back`** method is used to view a specific page in the current history of the browser. The page is specified by indicating the number of pages prior to the current page. In other words, if the page was displayed two pages prior to the current page, the numeric value would be `2`. Use of this method has the same result as the user clicking the Back button on the toolbar twice.

Objects Affected `History`

`Forward` METHOD

Purpose Use the **`Forward`** method to display a Web page that was viewed after the page that currently displays. Table 15-71 describes the attribute that is used with the **`Forward`** method.

Syntax **`History.Forward(value)`**

Table 15-71 `Forward` method attribute

Attribute	Description
`value`	A numeric value that specifies the number of Web pages.

Description The `Forward` method is used to view a specific page in the current history of the browser. The page is specified by indicating the number of pages between the desired page and the page that is currently displayed on the screen. In other words, if the desired page was initially displayed two pages after the current page, the numeric value would be `2`. Use of this method has the same result as the user clicking the Forward button on the toolbar twice.

Objects Affected `History`

`Length` PROPERTY

Purpose Use the `Length` property to determine the length of the current history list of the browser.

Syntax **`History.Length`**

Description The `Length` property is used to determine how many items are in the history list of the browser. This property should be used before using the `Back` and `Forward` methods to ensure that you do not attempt to move to a history page that does not exist.

Objects Affected `History`

`Navigator` OBJECT

Purpose The `Navigator` object contains the variables that make your code compatible with the Netscape Navigator browser. Table 15-72 summarizes the properties that can be used with the `Navigator object`. A detailed description of each property follows this section, in alphabetical order.

Syntax **`Navigator.property`**

Table 15-72 Properties of the `Navigator` object

Use...	To Do This...
`appCodeName`	Return the code name of the browser application.
`AppName`	Return the name of the browser application.
`AppVersion`	Return the version of the browser application.
`userAgent`	Return the user agent of the browser application.

Description

The **Navigator** object is used to gather information about the browser that is being used to view the HTML page. Since some browsers do not support VBScript, this object can be used to determine which browser the user is using before attempting to execute your script.

Listing 15-9 illustrates how to use the **AppName** property to get the name of the current browser. The results of the **AppName** property are illustrated in Figure 15-10.

Listing 15-9 Using the AppName *property*

```
<HTML>

<HEAD>
<SCRIPT LANGUAGE="VBScript">

  MsgBox "The name of the browser is " & navigator.appName

</SCRIPT>

</HEAD>

<BODY>

Sample HTML page.
</BODY>

</HTML>
```

Comments

The **Navigator** object properties are covered in alphabetical order on the following pages.

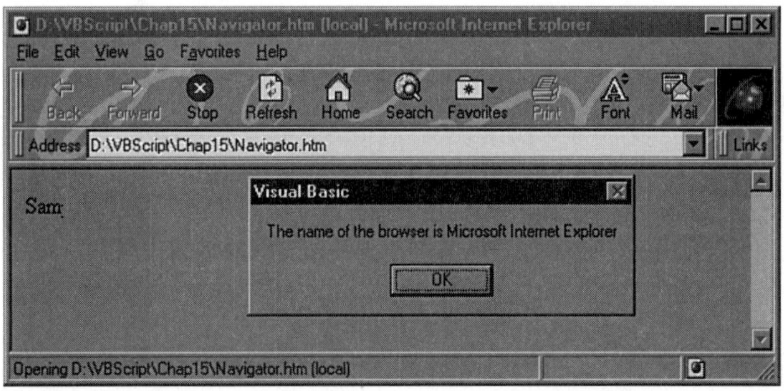

Figure 15-10 The **AppName** property returns the name of the browser

AppCodeName PROPERTY

Purpose Use the `AppCodeName` property to determine the code name of the browser.

Syntax **`Navigator.AppCodeName`**

Description The `AppCodeName` property is used with the `Navigator` object to determine the code name of the browser that is viewing the HTML page.

Objects Affected `Navigator`

AppName PROPERTY

Purpose Use the `AppName` property to determine the name of the browser.

Syntax **`Navigator.AppName`**

Description The `AppName` property is used with the `Navigator` object to determine the name of the browser that is viewing the HTML page.

Objects Affected `Navigator`

AppVersion PROPERTY

Purpose Use the `AppVersion` property to determine the version of the browser.

Syntax **`Navigator.AppVersion`**

Description The `AppVersion` property is used with the `Navigator` object to determine the version of the browser that is viewing the HTML page. This can be used to make sure the user is running a version of the browser that supports the HTML elements you have added to your page.

Objects Affected `Navigator`

UserAgent PROPERTY

Purpose Use the `UserAgent` property to determine the user agent of the browser.

Syntax **`Navigator.UserAgent`**

Description The `UserAgent` property is used with the `Navigator` object to determine the user agent of the browser that is viewing the HTML page. Currently, Internet Explorer 3.0 returns `Mozilla/2.0`.

Objects Affected `Navigator`

APPENDIX A

VBSCRIPT IN SERVER-SIDE SCRIPTS

Using VBScript in client-side scripts really activates your HTML pages. However, there's another way to use VBScript to generate exciting Web sites. It is known as server-side scripting.

At the time of this writing, Microsoft is using and testing software that expands VBScript's role into a major tool for common gateway interface (CGI) applications. CGI is the set of parameter-passing and communications conventions defined for the WWW that lets users send input to servers for further processing. VBScript can now be used to create special-purpose programs that run on the server.

This appendix looks at the power of VBScript when combined with the forthcoming Active Server technology (code-named Denali). The topics include:

- The benefits of server-side scripts over client-side scripts
- The differences in VBScript when run on the server
- How to insert server-side VBScript into HTML code
- How new Active components boost your Web programming power

What Is Active Server?

Chances are, you've already seen the results of server-side scripting, even if you haven't seen the Active Server itself. The next time you are surfing Microsoft's Web site, look at the file extensions. Instead of the familiar `.HTM` extension for HTML pages, Denali scripts use the `.ASP` extension. ASP stands for Active Server pages. When you customize views on MSN, you are using Active Server.

Microsoft developed the Active Server software to run on the Windows NT 4.0 platform with Internet Information Server. Simply put, Active Server and its add-ons interpret VBScript (or JavaScript) programs. The Web server sends out the results as HTML code.

The Benefits of Server-Side VBScript

Server-side scripts offer some advantages over client-side scripts, especially in client/server applications on the WWW. This section looks at why VBScript on the server has so much potential.

Leveraging Skills

The introduction of Active Server scripting means Visual Basic programmers no longer need to learn C-like languages such as Perl to do CGI scripting. As Microsoft points out, there's a huge base of talented VB programmers who can now leverage their skills for CGI applications.

Browser Neutral

Until Netscape adopts client-side VBScript for its highly popular Navigator browser, a large part of your potential Web audience cannot experience HTML code that uses client-side VBScript. However, with server-side VBScript, calculations and calls to functions are carried out on the server. The resulting HTML code is compatible with any browser, not just Internet Explorer. Further, by using a few lines of VBScript with an Active Server component, you can determine the type of browser and adjust your HTML output to match its capabilities.

Client/Server Programming

The designers of client-side VBScript left out commands that could read or write to the disk drive or execute programs. Unfortunately, this protection against malicious code prevents you from manipulating information stored on disk, especially databases. VBScript security doesn't need to be so strict for server-side scripts, because the Webmaster has control over the script and its rights on the server system. As a result, you can use server-side VBScript to interrogate databases, log information, and create Web pages on the fly.

Source Code Protection

With client-side VBScript, everyone with a browser can see and use your source code. By running applications on the server, you distribute only the results of your programming as pure HTML code. Even the `<SCRIPT> </SCRIPT>` tags do not appear in the code sent to the browser.

While client-side validation of data may be more efficient, for the sake of security you may need to keep calculations confidential. Figure A-1 shows an Active Server program in VBScript that validates a credit card number without revealing the validation algorithms.

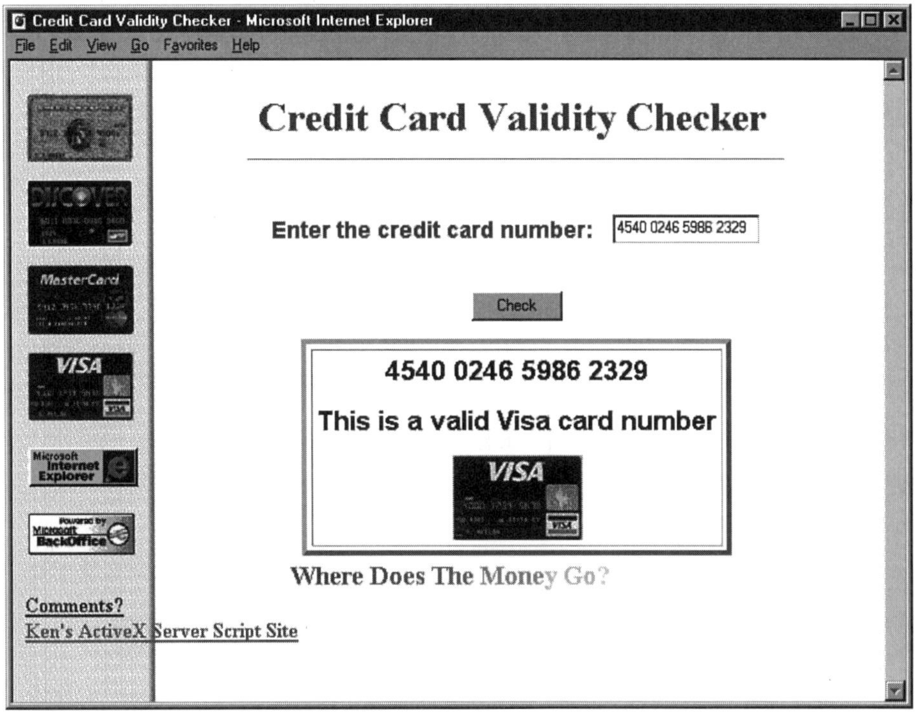

Figure A-1 Running VBScript on the server hides the source code if security is important

Differences in Server-Side VBScript

If you can code in VBScript for the client, you'll be right at home on the server side. However, there are some differences.

`InputBox()` and `MsgBox()`

Two VBScript functions are not allowed in Active Server scripts: **`InputBox()`** and **`MsgBox()`**. These will cause errors. Since the scripts run on the server, the two VBScript statements that require the Windows interface are inappropriate.

The remaining statements, functions, and methods are supported, but some may work differently. For instance, **`Date()`** and **`Time()`** in a client-side VBScript return the date and time according to the user's computer. **`Date()`** and **`Time()`** in an Active Server script return the server system date and time.

Inserting Server-Side VBScript in HTML Code

VBScript on the server can look very similar to VBScript on the client—or dramatically different. It is your choice. Listing A-1 shows the **`<SCRIPT>`** element with the addition of the **RUNAT** property. **RUNAT** ensures that the server interprets the code rather than sending the VBScript to the client for processing.

Listing A-1 RUNAT *within the* <SCRIPT> *element*

```
<SCRIPT Language="VBScript" RUNAT="server">
  NowMonth=Month(NOW)
  NowYear=Year(NOW)
  Call GenerateCalendar(NowMonth,NowYear)
</SCRIPT>
```

In the server-side version of VBScript, you can also use **<%** and **%>** to delimit your script. The **<%** delimiter replaces **<SCRIPT>** and the **%>** delimiter replaces **</SCRIPT>**. When the Active Server encounters the **<%** element, it interprets the script until it encounters the **%>** element. The **RUNAT="server"** property is assumed. Listing A-2 shows the use of the **<%** and **%>** delimiters.

Listing A-2 Using the <% and %> delimiters

```
<%
  NowMonth=Month(NOW)
  NowYear=Year(NOW)
%>
```

The Active Server script delimiters are extremely flexible. You can use them to insert VBScript code almost anywhere inside the HTML document. Listing A-3 shows the VBScript variable **Name** and the VBScript functions **Date()** and **Time()** acting as "stand-ins" for HTML code. Note the use of the equal sign (=) within the delimiters. The equal sign instructs the server to insert the value of the variable or function at the given location as HTML text.

Listing A-3 Inserting VBScript inside HTML code

```
<HTML>
<HEAD>
<BODY>
<%name = "Ken"%>
Written by <%=name%> on <%=Date%> at <%=Time%>
</BODY>
</HTML>
```

When run on the Microsoft Internet Information Server with the Active Server software, Listing A-3 creates the HTML page as shown in Figure A-2. Note that the **Date()** and **Time()** functions will produce and insert different text each time the page is refreshed.

When you view the HTML source code that created Figure A-2, you see that the VBScript output is browser neutral. Listing A-4 shows that the client (browser) sees only pure HTML, not the script that generated the page.

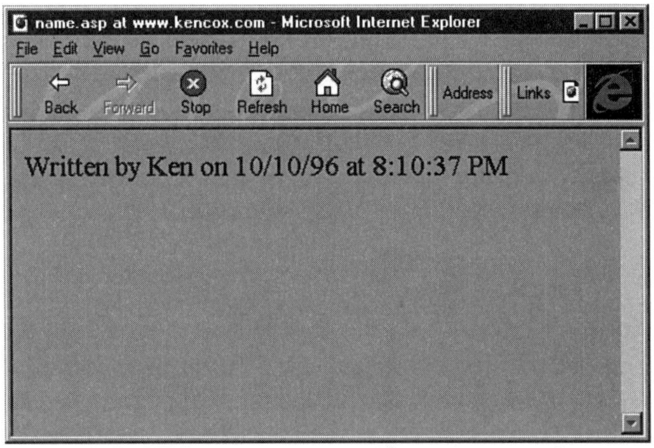

Figure A-2 VBScript in a server-side environment inserts values from variables and functions as HTML code

Listing A-4 Server-side VBScript can create browser-neutral Web pages

```
<HTML>
<HEAD>
<BODY>
Written by Ken on 10/10/96 at 8:10:37 PM
</BODY>
</HTML>
```

Active Server Components

In Chapter 12, Adding Objects, you saw how you can activate HTML pages by embedding Active (OLE) controls. Using VBScript modified the text control's parameters to rotate text on the screen. Active Server–side scripts can embed their own server objects, opening up a whole new world of CGI programming. VBScript can call on Active Server components to connect with databases. Another component lets you read the capabilities of the browser that is viewing your HTML page.

Active Server Objects

The objects that are available in the beta version of Active Server allow your VBScript program to

- Store user input and other user data throughout a session. With session variables you can create shopping baskets in virtual malls and keep a player's score in an online game.
- Read and store values passed to the script by an HTTP request, including form data.

- Write any data directly to the HTML page, including HTTP content types.
- Share information among all users of a given application.

Listing A-5 shows how VBScript receives and evaluates HTTP values that are sent from a form. The code snippet, which is part of an online perpetual calendar, uses the Active Server's **Session** variable to track the month that is currently being displayed. If the user hasn't requested a month, the VBScript defaults to the current month. The code allows the user to page through the months. Subsequent code (not shown here) uses server-side algorithms to generate the requested month's data on the fly. Figure A-3 illustrates the results of using the **Session** variable.

Listing A-5 Using Active Server's `Session` *variable to track values*

```
<HTML>
<% If Request.Form("amonth") = "" Then
      session("amonth") = Month(NOW)
   else
      session("amonth") =Request.Form("amonth")
   End If
%>
<%prevmonth=session("amonth")-1%>
<%nextmonth=session("amonth")+1%>
<TITLE>Monthly Calendar</TITLE>
```

Active Server Components

Visual Basic programmers will discover that they can substantially broaden their scripts by invoking Active Server components, formerly known as OLE automation servers.

The components included in the early versions of Active Server

- Provide read and write access to databases such as Access and SQL Server using queries and stored procedures.
- Allow you to create, read from, and write to flat ASCII text files that are stored on the server's hard disk drive.
- Automatically insert a different graphic each time a Web page is viewed. This is done by reading a display schedule from a data file.
- Log the type of browser that accessed your site and determine its capabilities.

Listing A-6 shows how a server-side VBScript uses the properties and methods of an Access database to obtain a record set. The code snippet creates an object, manipulates it, and uses an SQL query to obtain the desired records.

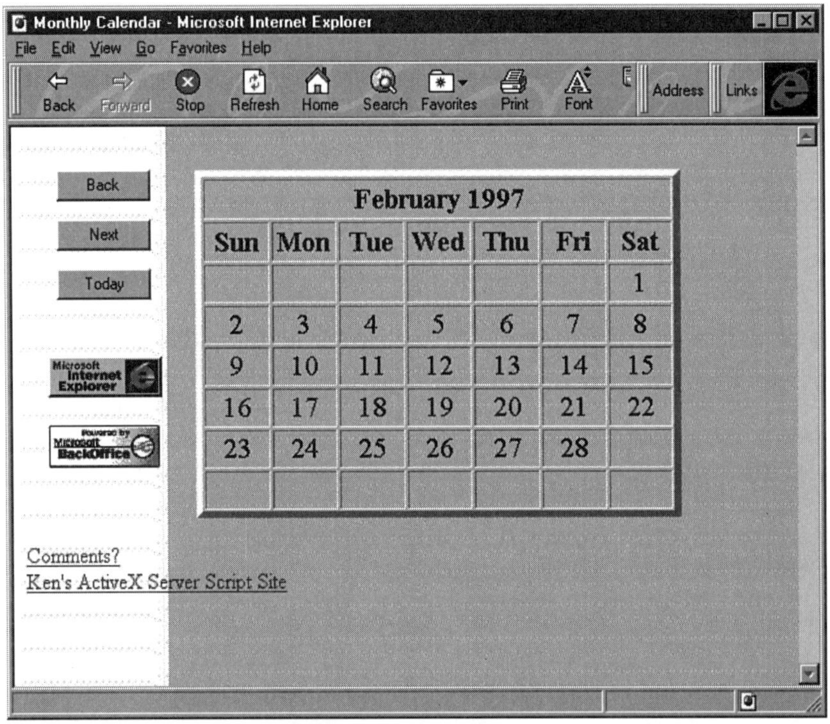

Figure A-3 In a calendar application, VBScript and Active Server generate any month on the fly

Listing A-6 Accessing server databases to fill HTML tables on the fly

```
<%
theid=request.form("theid")
if theid = "" then
  theid = 1
end if
Set cn = Server.CreateObject("ADO.Connection")
Set rs = Server.CreateObject("ADO.Recordset")
cn.Open "dsn=jobdata"
adOpenKeyset = 3
rs.CursorType = adOpenKeyset
Set rs.ActiveConnection = cn
rs.Source = "SELECT * FROM jobs Where [ID]=" & cstr(theid)
rs.Open
rs.movefirst
response.write "<P>"
 .
```

By combining VBScript, Active Server, and HTML, you can create Web pages that read and format volumes of data stored in a database. One script connected to a database can generate user-customized pages containing complex tables.

Summary

Active Server allows you to include executable VBScript directly in your HTML code. By tracking the user's input throughout a session, you can publish interactive Web pages. You can harness the power of database objects to create client-server applications across the Internet. The code you spent weeks writing and debugging remains yours to share or not to share. You can create pages that can be read by the least sophisticated browser or, better yet, adjust your page to make the most of the browser's capabilities.

The big drawback to server-side scripting in VBScript is that it requires a Windows NT host running Internet Information Server. Independent service providers will be wary of allowing "just anyone" to run scripts on their servers, and rightly so. As mentioned, the security precautions that exist in client-side VBScript don't apply on the server-side. A buggy or malicious script could crash the system and cause real damage.

That said, there's an expanding arena for those who know Visual Basic Scripting Edition. The addition of Active Server reinforces the statement made at the beginning of this book, that VBScript is one of the most valuable tools available for Web page development.

APPENDIX B

NEWLY RELEASED VBSCRIPT FUNCTIONS

With the release of the Active Server (codename Denali) discussed in Appendix A, Microsoft also added some new functions to VBScript. These functions will be available for server-side scripting with the release of the Active Server. Microsoft has indicated that these functions will also be released with future releases of Internet Explorer, with the exception of those that may pose a security issue (that is, attempting to read and write files from within a Web page).

Because this information was not available until just prior to the release of this book, the author was not able to incorporate these functions into the appropriate chapters. Within this appendix you can locate descriptions for the new functions added to VBScript.

Please keep in mind that these functions will not work with the version of Internet Explorer 3.0 that is being distributed on the CD for this book. Therefore, if you receive error messages when you attempt to use these new functions, it is because you do not have a VBScript DLL that recognizes these features.

New VBScript Features

The remaining portion of this appendix contains all of the new functions that have been added to VBScript. These functions are provided in alphabetical order.

`Array()` FUNCTION

Purpose Use the `Array()` function to return a variant containing an array. Table B-1 describes the expressions that you can use with the `Array()` function.

Syntax `Array(arglist)`

Table B-1 Argument of the `Array()` function

Argument	Description
`arglist`	A comma-delimited list of values that are intended to become the new values for the array. If a value is not specified, a zero-length array is created.

Description The `Array()` function creates a new array from a comma-delimited list of values. The values are added to the array in the order they are listed. For example, if you have the following code, the first value added to the array is `10` and this value is displayed on the document when the `Document.Write` line is executed.

```
<SCRIPT LANGUAGE = "VBSCRIPT">
<!--

  Dim NewArray

  NewArray = Array(10, 20, 30, 40, 50)

  Document.Write NewArray(0)

-->
</SCRIPT>
```

Comments The notation used to refer to an element of an array consists of the variable name followed by parentheses containing an index number indicating the desired element.

CCur() Function

Purpose Use the `CCur()` function to convert a variant to a subtype of Currency. Table B-2 describes the expressions you can use with the `CCur()` function.

Syntax `CCur(expression)`

Table B-2 Argument of the `CCur()` function

Argument	Description
`expression`	Any valid numeric expression

Description The `CCur()` function converts a variant expression to a subtype of currency.

The `CCur()` function also provides conversions from any other international data type recognized by your system to a currency subtype. For example, different values are used for decimal separators, depending upon the locale settings for your computer.

Comments To help eliminate run-time data errors, use the `IsNumeric()` function to check an expression before calling the `CCur()` function. For more information about the `IsNumeric()` function, refer to Chapter 4, Data Validation.

See Also `CBool()`, `CByte()`, `CDate()`, `CDbl()`, `CInt()`, `CLng()`, `CSng()`, `CStr()`

DateAdd() Function

Purpose Use the `DateAdd()` function to return the date that represents the addition of a specified date and a time interval. Table B-3 describes the types of expressions you must use with the `DateAdd()` function.

Syntax `DateAdd(interval, number, date)`

Table B-3 Arguments of the `DateAdd()` function

Argument	Description
`interval`	A string expression that indicates the interval of time that you want to add to the specified date. This string expression can be one of the following values: **Value** — **Description** `d` — Specifies a time interval of days. `m` — Specifies a time interval of months. `ww` — Specifies a time interval of weeks. `yyyy` — Specifies a time interval of years.
`number`	A numeric expression that indicates the number of times you want to add the specified interval to the date. This numeric expression can be positive to generate future dates, or negative to create dates in the past.
`date`	A valid date expression that represents your starting date.

Description The `DateAdd()` function creates a new date by adding a specific time interval to a date. The time interval, specified by the `interval` attribute, can be added multiple times, based on the value specified for the `number` attribute. For example, if you wanted to determine the date that is two months after Valentine's Day, you could use the following code:

```
<SCRIPT LANGUAGE = "VBSCRIPT">
<!--

Document.Write DateAdd("m",2,"2/14/96")

-->
</SCRIPT>
```

See Also `DateDiff()`, `DatePart()`

DateDiff() Function

Purpose Use the `DateDiff()` function to determine the number of intervals between two dates. Table B-4 describes the types of expressions you can use with the `DateDiff()` function.

Syntax `DateDiff(interval, date1, date2, firstdayofweek, firstweekofyear)`

Table B-4 Arguments of the DateDiff() function

Argument	Description
`interval`	A string expression that indicates the interval of time that you want to use to calculate the difference between the two dates. This is a required argument. This string expression can be one of the following values: **Value** — **Description** `d` — Specifies a time interval of days. `m` — Specifies a time interval of months. `ww` — Specifies a time interval of weeks. `yyyy` — Specifies a time interval of years.
`date1`	A valid date expression that represents the first date you want to compare. This is a required argument.
`date2`	A valid date expression that represents the first date you want to compare. This is a required argument.
`firstdayofweek`	An optional string value that can be used to specify the first day of the week. If a value is not specified, Sunday is assumed to be the first day of the week.
`firstweekofyear`	An optional string value that specifies the first week of the year. If a value is not specified, the first week is assumed to be the week that contains January 1.

Description The `DateDiff()` function determines the amount of time between two specified dates. The time value is returned based on the interval value specified for the `interval` attribute. For example, if you wanted to determine the number of days between Thanksgiving and Christmas, you could use the following code:

```
<SCRIPT LANGUAGE = "VBSCRIPT">
<!--

Document.Write DateDiff("d","11/28","12/25",SUNDAY)
-->
</SCRIPT>
```

See Also `DateAdd()`, `DatePart()`

DatePart( ) Function

Purpose Use the `DatePart()` function to return the desired portion of the specified date. Table B-5 describes the expressions used with the `DatePart()` function.

Syntax `DatePart( interval, date, firstdayofweek, firstweekofyear)`

Table B-5 Arguments of the `DatePart()` function

Argument	Description
`interval`	A string expression that indicates the interval of time that you want returned from the specified date. This is a required argument. This string expression can be one of the following values: **Value** — **Description** `d` — Specifies a time interval of days. `m` — Specifies a time interval of months. `ww` — Specifies a time interval of weeks. `yyyy` — Specifies a time interval of years.
`date`	A valid date expression that represents the first date you want to evaluate. This is a required argument.
`firstdayofweek`	An optional string value that can be used to specify the first day of the week. If a value is not specified, Sunday is assumed to be the first day of the week.
`firstweekofyear`	An optional string value that specifies the first week of the year. If a value is not specified, the first week is assumed to be the week that contains January 1.

Description The `DatePart()` function returns a specific time interval from a date. The time value is returned based on the interval value specified for the `interval` attribute. For example, if you want to know what the current year is, you could use the `DatePart()` function to return the current year out of the value returned by the `Now()` function as illustrated in the following code:

```
<SCRIPT LANGUAGE = "VBSCRIPT">
<!--

Document.Write "The current year is: " & DatePart("yyyy",Now())

-->
</SCRIPT>
```

See Also `DateAdd()`, `DateDiff()`, `Now()`

Filter() Function

Purpose Use the `Filter()` function to return a subset of a string array. Table B-6 describes the expressions used with the `Filter()` function.

Syntax `Filter(inputstrings(), value, include, compare)`

Table B-6 Arguments of the Filter() function

Argument	Description
`inputstrings`	A one-dimensional array that contains the strings to search. This is a required argument.
`value`	The value to locate in the strings contained in the `inputstrings` array. This is a required argument.
`include`	A Boolean value that indicates whether the array subset should be returned for elements of the array that contain the value or do not contain the value. If the value is TRUE, the `Filter()` function returns the subset of the array that contains the value as a substring; otherwise, if the value is FALSE, the `Filter()` function returns the subset of the array that does not contain the value as a substring.
`compare`	A numeric value that indicates the kind of string comparison to use. This is an optional argument. The following values can be used with this argument:

Value	Description
-1	Option Compare setting
0	Binary comparison
1	Case-sensitive text comparison

Description The `Filter()` function allows you to filter out elements of an array that contain or do not contain the specified value.

See Also `Replace()`

FormatDateTime() Function

Purpose Use the `FormatDateTime()` function to format a date expression with the desired format. Table B-7 describes the expressions that are used with the `FormatDateTime()` function.

Syntax `FormatDateTime(dateexpression, formattype)`

Table B-7 Arguments of the `FormatDateTime()` function

Argument	Description
`Dateexpression`	A valid date expression.
`formattype`	A numeric value that indicates the desired date format. This is an optional argument; if omitted, a value of zero is used. The following values can be used with the `FormatDateTime()` function.

Value	Date Format
0	`mm/dd/yy` + time in hh:mm:ss PM (this is the same if omitted)
1	weekday, month day, year

2	mm/dd/yy
3	time in hh:mm:ss PM
4	time in military format hh:mm

Description The `FormatDateTime()` function allows you to specify the format used to display date and time information. The format specified applies only to the specified string; therefore, if you want this format to be used multiple times, you need to use the `FormatDateTime()` function to specify the format at each location. The following code illustrates how to format the current date and time to display in the format Saturday, November 16, 1996:

```
<SCRIPT LANGUAGE = "VBSCRIPT">
<!--

Document.Write FormatDateTime(Now,1)
-->
</SCRIPT>
```

See Also `Date()`, `FormatNumber()`, `Now()`, `Time()`

FormatNumber() Function

Purpose Use the `FormatNumber()` function to format a string of numbers as a numeric expression. Table B-8 describes the values that are used with the `FormatNumber()` function.

Syntax **`FormatNumber`**`(expression, decimalplaces, decimalflag, negativeflag)`

Table B-8 Arguments of the `FormatNumber()` function

Argument	Description
`expression`	Any expression that contains numeric values.
`decimalplaces`	An integer value that indicates the number of decimal places to use when formatting the numeric expression. If this argument is omitted, the expression is formatted with two decimal places.
`decimalflag`	Indicates whether or not a decimal expression with a value between -1 and 1 should display with a zero before the decimal point. The following values are used for the `decimalflag` argument: **Value** / **Description** `True` — Displays a zero before the decimal point. For example, the value .123 displays as 0.123. `False` — Does not display a zero before the decimal point. For example, the value .123 displays as .123.
`negativeflag`	Specifies the formatting used to indicate a negative value. The following values are used for the `negativeflag` argument:

Value	Description
`True`	Places parentheses around a negative value. For example, the value -1.45 displays as (1.45).
`False`	Uses the negative sign (-) to identify a negative value. For example, a negative three displays as -3.

Description The `FormatNumber()` function allows you to format an expression that contains numeric values. The following code illustrates how to format a numeric expression to contain two decimal places:

```
<SCRIPT LANGUAGE = "VBSCRIPT">
<!--

Document.Write FormatNumber(1234.5678, 2)

-->
</SCRIPT>
```

See Also `FormatDateTime()`

GetObject() Function

Purpose Use the `GetObject()` function to return a reference to an Active object from a file. Table B-9 describes the expressions that are used with the `GetObject()` function.

Syntax **`GetObject`**`(pathname, class)`

Table B-9 Arguments of the `GetObject()` function

Argument	Description
`pathname`	A string that specifies the full path and name of the file containing the object to retrieve. If the `pathname` attribute is omitted, the `class` attribute is required. This is an optional argument.
`class`	A string that specifies the class of the object. This parameter is only required if the `pathname` attribute is omitted. The `class` argument uses the syntax `appname.objectype` and the following parts: **Part** — **Description** `appname` — A string that specifies the name of the application providing the object. This is a required part. `objectype` — A string that specifies the type or class of object to create. This is a required part.

Description The `GetObject()` function accesses an Active object from a file and assigns the object to an object variable. Use the `Set` statement to assign the object returned by the `GetObject()` function to the object variable, as illustrated in the following code.

```
Dim CADObject
Set CADObject = GetObject("C:\CAD\SCHEMA.CAD")
```

Comments

If an object with the type specified by the objectype argument does not exist, an error occurs. Some applications allow you to activate part of a file. Add an exclamation point (!) to the end of the file name and follow it with a string that identifies the part of the file you want to activate. For more information on creating this type of string, see the documentation for the application that created the object.

Use the `GetObject()` function when there is a current instance of the object or if you want to create the object with a file already loaded.

`Join()` Function

Purpose

Use the `Join()` function to join the values of an array and return a string. Table B-10 describes the expressions that are used with the `Join()` function.

Syntax

`Join(list, delimiter)`

Table B-10 Arguments of the `Join()` function

Argument	Description
`list`	A one-dimensional array that contains the substrings to be joined together.
`delimiter`	A string character used to separate each substring when they are joined together. This is an optional argument; if it is omitted, the substrings are joined together without excess spaces or characters.

Description

The `Join()` function combines multiple elements of an array into a string of characters. You can specify a character, such as a comma, to be placed between each element by using the delimiter argument.

`Mask()` Function

Purpose

Use the `Mask()` function to apply a mask to an expression. Table B-11 describes the expressions that are used with the `Mask()` function.

Syntax

`Mask(expression, mask)`

Table B-11 Arguments of the `Mask()` function

Argument	Description
`expression`	The expression to which you want to apply the mask.
`mask`	The mask to apply to the expression.

Description

The `Mask()` function applies a mask to an expression and returns the resulting string.

See Also

`UnMask()`

MonthName() FUNCTION

Description Use the **MonthName()** function to return a string indicating the specified month. Table B-12 describes the values used with the **MonthName()** function.

Syntax **MonthName**(month, abbrev)

Table B-12 Arguments of the MonthName() function

Argument	Description
month	A numeric value between 1 and 12 inclusive that specifies the desired month to be returned by the MonthName() function.
abbrev	The desired format for the date; if this argument is omitted, the full name of the month displays. The following values are used for the abbrev argument. **Value** / **Description** 0 — No value, full name of month 1 — Three character abbreviation for the month name

Description The **MonthName()** function is used to return a string that specifies the desired month. You can specify how the month displays by using the **abbrev** attribute, as described in Table B-12. By using this attribute, you can display the month name as either the entire month name or an abbreviated month name.

The following source illustrates how to use the **MonthName()** function with and without specifying a value for the **abbrev** attribute.

```
<SCRIPT LANGUAGE = "VBSCRIPT">
<!--

  Document.Write MonthName(1)

  Document.Write MonthName(4,1)

-->
</SCRIPT>
```

See Also Date(), Weekday()

Replace() FUNCTION

Purpose Use the **Replace()** to create a zero-based one-dimensional array containing a specified number of substrings. Table B-13 describes the expressions that are used with the **Replace()** function.

Syntax **Replace**(expression, delimiter, count, compare)

Table B-13 Arguments of the `Replace( )` function

Argument	Description
`expression`	A string expression that contains the desired substrings and delimiters. This is a required argument for the `Replace( )` function.
`delimiter`	A string character that identifies the substring limits. This is an optional argument; if it is omitted, the space character is assumed to be the delimiter.
`count`	The number of substrings to be returned by the `Replace( )` function. If the count argument is -1, all of the substrings are returned.
`compare`	A numeric value that indicates the kind of string comparison to use. This is an optional argument. The following values can be used with this argument: **Value** **Description** -1 Option Compare setting 0 Binary comparison 1 Case-sensitive text comparison

Description The `Replace( )` function returns a zero-based, one-dimensional array containing a number of delimited substrings.

See Also `Replace( )`

Round( ) Function

Purpose Use the `Round( )` function to a numeric value rounded to the specified number of decimal places. Table B-14 describes the expressions used with the `Round( )` function.

Syntax `Round(expression, decplaces)`

Table B-14 Arguments of the `Round( )` function

Argument	Description
`expression`	A numeric expression that contains the value to be rounded.
`decplaces`	An integer value that indicates the number of decimal places that the expression should be rounded to.

Description The `Round()` function returns a numeric value rounded to a specified number of decimal places. The following sample code illustrates how to round an expression to two decimal places.

```
<SCRIPT LANGUAGE = "VBSCRIPT">
<!--

Document.Write Round(1.555,2)

-->
</SCRIPT>
```

`Split()` Function

Purpose Use the `Split()` function to divide a string into the specified number of substrings. Table B-15 describes the values used with the `Split()` function.

Syntax `Split(expression, delimiter, count, compare)`

Table B-15 Arguments of the `Split()` function

Argument	Description
`expression`	A string expression that contains the desired substrings and delimiters. This is a required argument for the `Split()` function.
`delimiter`	A string character that identifies the substring limits. This is an optional argument; if it is omitted, the space character is assumed to be the delimiter.
`count`	The number of substrings to be returned by the `Split()` function. If the count argument is -1, all of the substrings are returned.
`compare`	A numeric value that indicates the kind of string comparison to use. This is an optional argument. The following values can be used with this argument: **Value** **Description** -1 Option Compare setting 0 Binary comparison 1 Case-sensitive text comparison

Description The `Split()` function returns a zero-based, one-dimensional array containing a number of delimited substrings.

See Also `Join()`

`StrReverse()` Function

Purpose Use the `StrReverse()` function to reverse the order of the characters in the specified string. Table B-16 describes the expressions used with the `StrReverse()` function.

Syntax `StrReverse(string)`

Table B-16 Arguments of the `StrReverse()` function

Argument	Description
`expression`	A string expression that contains the desired characters to be reversed.

Description The `StrReverse()` function reverses the specified string of characters. The following source illustrates how to reverse a string of characters.

```
<SCRIPT LANGUAGE = "VBSCRIPT">
<!--

Document.Write StrReverse("gninroM dooG")
Document.Write "<BR>"
-->
</SCRIPT>
```

TypeName() Function

Purpose Use the **TypeName()** function to determine the subtype of an expression. Table B-17 describes the expressions used with the **TypeName()** function.

Syntax **TypeName**(expression)

Table B-17 Arguments of the TypeName() function

Argument	Description
expression	An expression for which you would like to determine the subtype.

Description The **TypeName()** function determines the subtype of an expression. The following code illustrates how to determine the subtype of an expression.

```
<SCRIPT LANGUAGE = "VBSCRIPT">
<!--

Document.Write TypeName("Hello")

-->
</SCRIPT>
```

UnMask() Function

Purpose Use the **UnMask()** expression to remove the specified symbols or characters from a string. Table B-18 describes the expressions used with the **UnMask()** function.

Syntax **UnMask**(expression, mask)

Table B-18 Arguments of the UnMask() function

Argument	Description
expression	The expression to which you want to apply the mask.
mask	The mask to apply to the expression.

Description The **UnMask()** function removes the specified characters from an expression.

See Also Mask()

WeekDayName() Function

Purpose Use the **WeekDayName()** function to determine the day of the week. Table B-19 describes the expressions used with the **WeekDayName()** function.

Syntax **WeekDayName**(weekday, abbrev, firstday)

Table B-19 Arguments of the WeekDayName() function

Argument	Description
weekday	A numeric value between 1 and 7 inclusive that specifies the desired day of the week to be returned by the WeekDayName() function.
abbrev	The desired format for the day of the week; if this argument is omitted, the full name day of the week displays. The following values are used for the abbrev argument. **Value** **Description** 0 The full name of the day of the week 1 Three character abbreviation for the day of the week

Description The **WeekDayName()** function returns a string indicating the specified day of the week. The following code illustrates how to return the three-character abbreviation for Monday.

```
<SCRIPT LANGUAGE = "VBSCRIPT">
<!--

Document.Write WeekdayName(2,1)
-->
</SCRIPT>
```

See Also MonthName()

APPENDIX C

INTERNET EXPLORER 3.0: A FIELD GUIDE

A new day dawned. The sun reached its fingers over the digital outback. The mighty Navigators (*Netscapus navigatorus*)—a species that reproduced like rabbits and ran nearly as fast—covered the landscape. Yonder, on a cliff that seemed to be beyond the horizon, a trembling new creature looked out over the Internet jungle. This strange new creature, calling itself the Explorer (*Microsoftus interneticus explorus*), sniffed around, considering whether it should enter the fragile ecosystem. Netscape gators gnashed their teeth, but the Explorers were not daunted. Explorer was a formidable beast. It became a part of the jungle and thrived. And even though it began as a mere pup, it evolved, and it evolved and it evolved.

Now the jungle is rife with two intelligent species.

What follows is a guide to domesticating Internet Explorer. You will learn how to care for your Explorer and even how to teach it tricks. Before long, you shall find truth behind the old axiom that the Explorer is man's (and woman's) best friend.

INTRODUCING EXPLORER TO YOUR ECOSYSTEM

Whether you're running Windows NT or Windows 95, installing Explorer is easy. Explorer's own installation program makes setup a breeze, and you need only to select the appropriate file on the CD-ROM to launch this installer. Make sure the CD-ROM included with this book is in the CD-ROM drive; then, depending upon your system, follow the directions below for either Windows 95 or Windows NT.

Windows 95 Installation

1. Click the Start button in the lower left corner of your screen.
2. Click on the Run... option in the Start menu. A dialog box similar to the one shown in Figure C-1 appears.

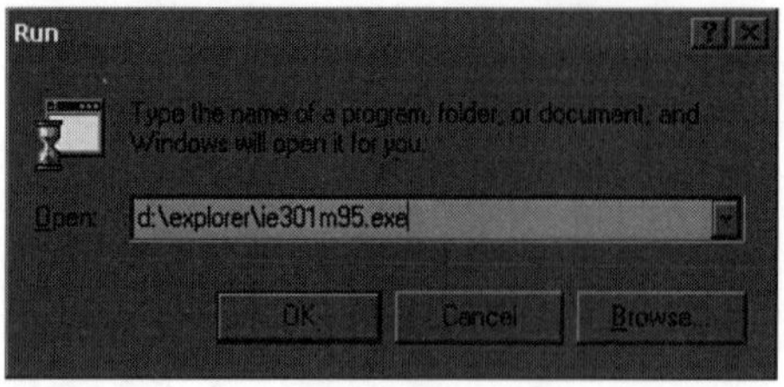

Figure C-1 The Windows 95 Run dialog box

3. Using the Run dialog box, type in a pathname and specify the location of the Explorer installation program. IE301M95.EXE is in the CD's \Explorer directory, so if your CD-ROM drive is designated as D:, you'd type

```
d:\explorer\ie301m95.exe
```

   If your CD-ROM drive has a different designation letter, type in the appropriate drive designation letter in place of `d:`.

4. After typing the proper pathname, click the OK button to start the Explorer's installation program. Depending upon your system, it may take a moment to load.
5. Once the installation program loads, follow the on-screen prompts to set up Explorer on your computer.

Windows NT 4 Installation

1. Click the Start button in the lower left corner of your screen.
2. Click on the Run... option in the Start menu. A dialog box similar to the one shown in Figure C-2 appears.

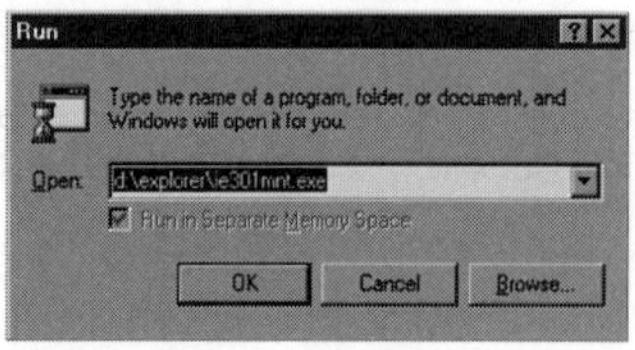

Figure C-2 The Windows NT Run dialog box

3. Using the Run dialog box, type in a pathname and specify the location of the Explorer installation program. MSIE30M.EXE is in the CD's \Explorer directory, so if your CD-ROM drive is designated as D:, you'd type:

   ```
   d:\explorer\ie301mnt.exe
   ```

   If your CD-ROM drive has a different designation letter, type in the appropriate drive designation letter in place of `d:`.

4. After typing the proper pathname, click the OK button to start the Explorer's installation program. Depending upon your system, it may take a moment to load.

5. Once the installation program loads, follow the on-screen prompts to set up Explorer on your computer.

Once you've run the installation, you'll need to restart your system. You can then click on the Internet icon on your desktop. If you've already selected an Internet provider with Windows dial-up networking, you'll be connected. If not, you'll be walked through the dial-in process. You'll need to enter the phone number of your Internet provider, your modem type, and other related information. Ultimately, you'll be taken to Microsoft's home page, where you can register your Explorer and find out about its latest features.

> **NOTE**
> The Explorer is a constantly evolving animal. For the latest updates, plug-ins, and versions, be sure to regularly check out Microsoft's neck of the woods at `http://www.microsoft.com/ie/`

Explorer Components

Explorer is more than a plain-Jane Web browser. As you work through the installation, you'll be able to choose a variety of components. You can select the following add-ons:

- Internet Mail—This is a comprehensive e-mail package. Using simple icons, you can write and read your mail off-line and then log on quickly to send and receive your latest batch of correspondence. See Figure C-3.
- Internet News—This is a window that lets you browse through thousands of newsgroups, read through the threads, and post your own messages. The News system is very easy to use. You can easily keep track of your favorite topics and automatically update with the latest news.
- ActiveMovie—This feature of Explorer lets you watch all sorts of video clips—MPEG, AVI, and QuickTime formats. It even supports a special streaming version of video that downloads movies as you watch them, letting you view video with

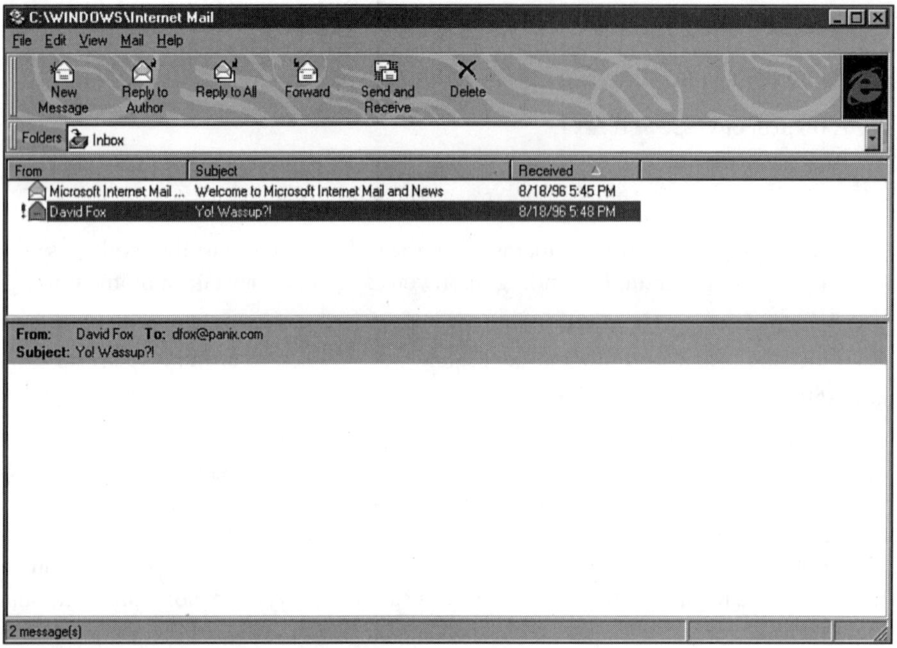

Figure C-3 The Internet Mail main window

little delay. The ActiveMovie system also lets you listen to all popular formats of audio files—AU, WAV, MIDI, MPEG, and AIFF. This makes it easy to add background sound to Web pages.

- VRML Support—This feature is a separate module that lets you download and coast through Virtual Reality Modeling Language worlds. This allows you to explore true 3D landscapes and objects.
- NetMeeting—This is a full-featured package that lets you hold entire meetings over the Internet. You can chat with one person or with dozens. If you have a microphone, you can use the Internet phone feature to hold voice conversations with other people. You can share applications. For example, you and a client can edit the same word processing document together. A whiteboard feature lets you draw on a "digital blackboard" that can be updated live across the Internet.
- HTML Layout Control—This tool lets Web page publishers create spiffy versions of HTML pages, the way professional designers would lay out a magazine page or a newspaper. Designers can choose exactly where to place elements within a Web page. You can make objects transparent and layer objects over each other, which helps make a Web page eye-catching yet uncluttered.

The Nature of the Beast

Internet Explorer features very up-to-date HTML. It supports HTML 3.2, including the following:

- Frames—These break up the Web page window into several areas. For example, you can keep an unchanging row of navigation controls along the top of the page while constantly updating the bottom. You can use *borderless frames,* which split up the page without making it seem split. A special type of frame known as the *floating frame* lets you view one Web page within another.
- Cascading Style Sheets—This allows all your Web sites to have the same general look and feel.
- Tables—You can create or view all sorts of fancy tables, with or without graphics, borders, and columns.
- Embedded Objects—Internet Explorer can handle Java applets, ActiveX controls, and even Netscape plug-ins. These objects are discussed later, in the Symbiotic Partners section of this appendix.
- Fonts—Explorer supports many fonts, allowing Web pages to have a variety of exciting designs.

From the get-go, Internet Explorer has included a few special bells and whistles. For example, it's easy to create and view marquees across Web pages. This lets you scroll a long, attention-drawing message, similar to a tickertape, that puts a great deal of information in a very small space.

Training the Explorer

By its very nature, the Explorer is a friendly beast. You can access the full range of the Explorer's talents by pushing its buttons. These buttons, which appear in the toolbar at the top of the screen as depicted in Figure C-4, are as follows:

- Back—Use this to return to the Web page you've just come from. This will help you retrace your steps as you take Explorer through the Internet maze.
- Forward—Use this after you've used the Back button, to jump forward again to the page from which you began.
- Stop—If a Web page is taking too long to load, press this button. Any text and graphics will immediately stop downloading.
- Refresh—If your Web page is missing some graphics, or if you've previously stopped its loading using the Stop button, you can reload it using Refresh.

- Home—This takes you to your pre-set home page. By default, this is Microsoft's main Web page, but you can set your home to any you'd like. See the Taming the Beast section.
- Search—This takes you to a special page that allows you to search for a Web page, using a number of cool search engines. See the Hunting Skills section.
- Favorites—This button lets you access a list of your favorite Web sites. See the Favorite Haunts section.
- Print—This allows you to print out the current Web page, allowing you to keep a perfect hard copy of it.
- Font—Find yourself squinting at a Web page? Just click here to zoom in. The font size will grow several degrees. Too big now? Click a few more times and the size will shrink once again.
- Mail—This will launch the Internet Mail program, which allows you to send and receive e-mail and to access newsgroups.

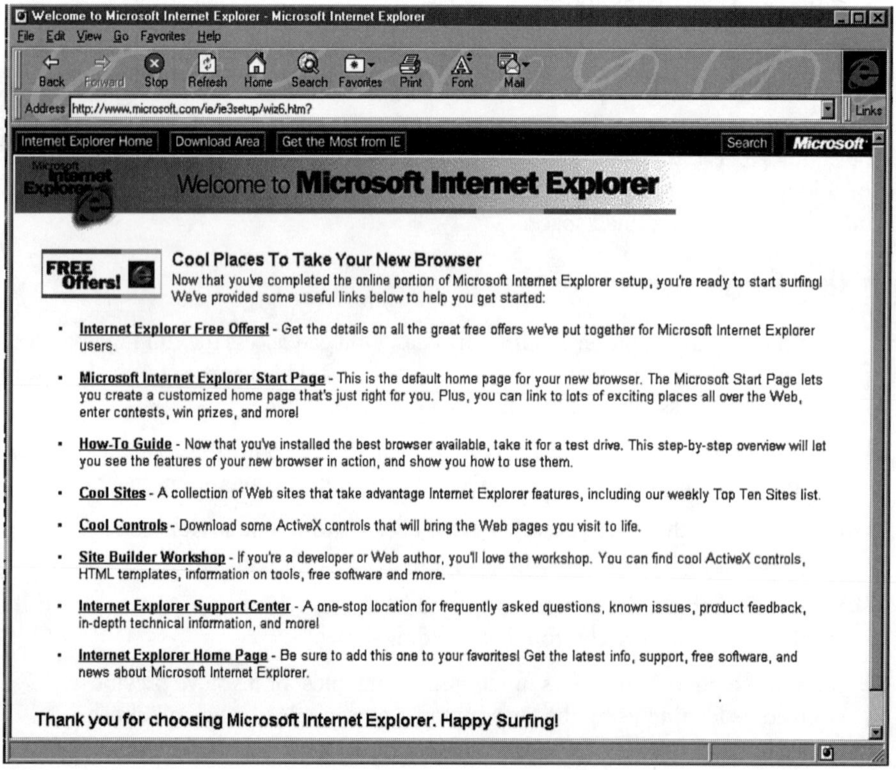

Figure C-4 A cosmetic look at Explorer

PLAYING FETCH

Your Explorer is a devoted friend. It can scamper anywhere within the Internet, bringing back exactly what you desire.

If you know where you want to go, just type the URL into Explorer's Address box at the top of the screen. If you like, you can omit the `http://` prefix. The Web page will be loaded up. You can also search for a page or load up a previously saved page.

You can now click on any *hyperlink*—an underlined or colored word or picture—to zoom to that associated Web page or Internet resource. Some hyperlinked graphics may not be obvious. Explorer will tell you when you are positioned over a valid hyperlink, because the cursor will change into a pointing finger. Continue following these links as long as you like. It's not uncommon to start researching knitting needles and end up reading about porcupines.

NOTE

If you're an aspiring Web page writer, you might want to take a peek at the HTML source code to see how that page was created. Just select View, Source.

HUNTING SKILLS

If you want to find Web pages dealing with a specific category, the Explorer makes it easy to find them. Click the Search button. The Search screen will appear, as in Figure C-5. You can search for more than Web pages. With Explorer, it's easy to find

- Phone numbers, ZIP codes, and addresses
- Information on a number of topics—health, home, education, consumer affairs, finance, weather, sports, travel, and so on
- References—maps, a dictionary, a thesaurus, quotations, and an encyclopedia
- On-line books, newspapers, and magazines

TIP

You can also quickly hunt for any idea, word, or category. Simply type GO in the Address box at the top of the screen, followed by the word or phrase you want to search for.

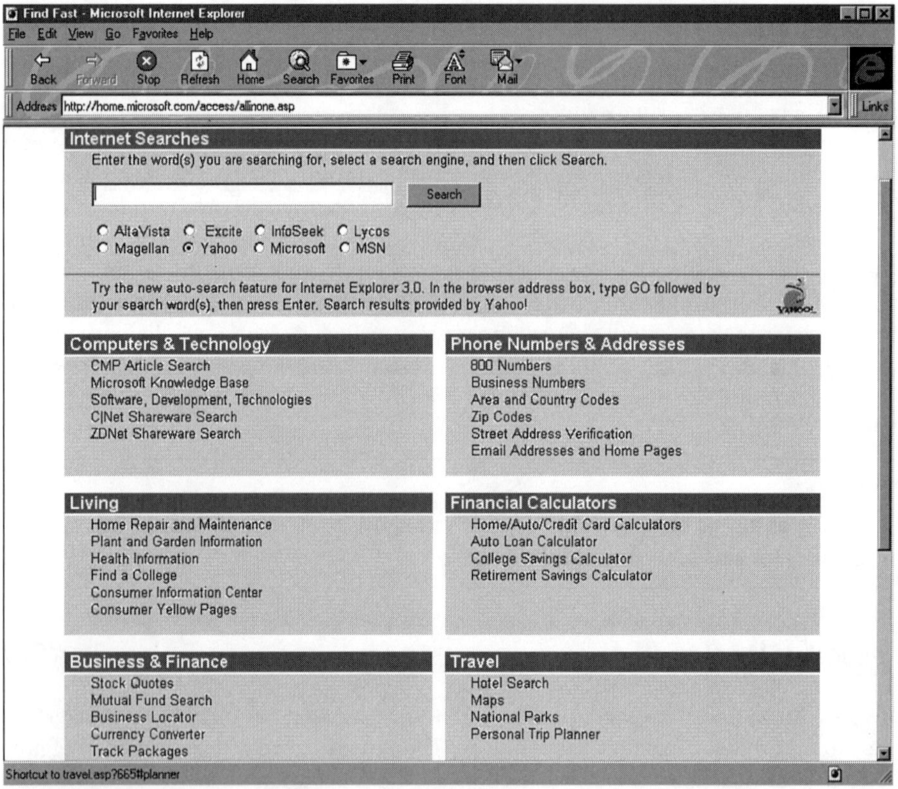

Figure C-5 The Search screen

FAVORITE HAUNTS

It's easy to keep track of the Web pages you visit most. When you want to save a page for future reference, simply click the Favorites button or choose the Favorites menu item. Select the Add To Favorites option. The current Web page will now be added to the list of favorites, which appears each time you click on the Favorites button or menu.

After a while, your list of favorites will get long and cluttered. It's simple to keep track of huge lists of favorites—just put them into separate folders. Organize your favorites, as shown in Figure C-6, by selecting Favorites, Organize Favorites.

To create a new folder, click on the New Folder icon (the folder with the little glint on it) at the top of the window. Now drag and drop your Web page bookmarks into the appropriate folders. You can also move, rename, or delete a folder by selecting it and using the corresponding buttons at the bottom of the screen.

> **TIP**
> You can even include or attach a favorite Web document within an e-mail message, the way you would attach any other file.

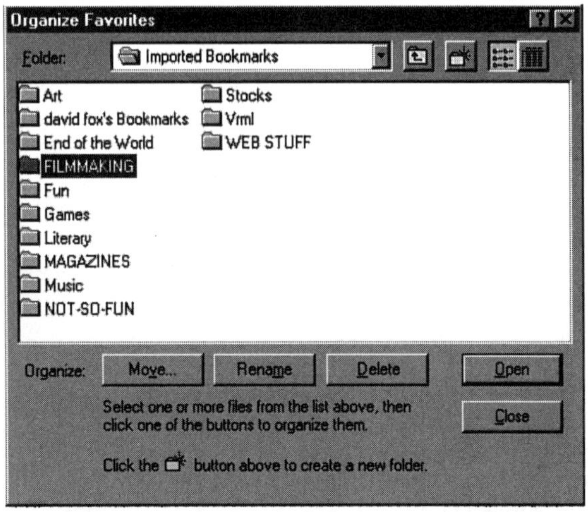

Figure C-6 Organizing the Favorites list

> **NOTE**
> On Windows systems, the Favorites list is actually a folder within your Windows directory. This reflects a Microsoft trend—treating the entire World Wide Web as just another folder to explore on your desktop. Eventually, you'll be able to drag and drop documents across the Internet as easily as you would within your own hard drive.

MEMORY

Internet Explorer keeps track of every Web page you visit. This is kept in a vast History list. You can view the entire History list, in chronological order, by clicking the View History button. Just click on any page you'd like to revisit.

> **NOTE**
> The History list is cleared every 20 days—you can set this value within the Navigation properties sheets.

TAMING THE BEAST

Now that you and your Explorer are getting acquainted, why not tame it so that it acts and looks exactly like you want? Select View, Options and pick a tab at the top of the window to customize the following properties:

- General—The general properties sheet is illustrated in Figure C-7. Since multimedia content (such as sounds, movies, and graphics) takes longer to load in Web pages, you can choose to not load certain media types. You can also easily customize the color of the text and hyperlinks. Finally, you can decide how little or how much information appears in your toolbar.

> **NOTE**
> **You can change the size and position of your toolbar simply by clicking on its borders and dragging it to a desired location.**

- Connection—You can adjust your connections settings, as shown in Figure C-8, by clicking on this tab. This lets you choose your Internet provider. If you're connecting to the Internet through a network firewall, you can also set your proxy server information here.

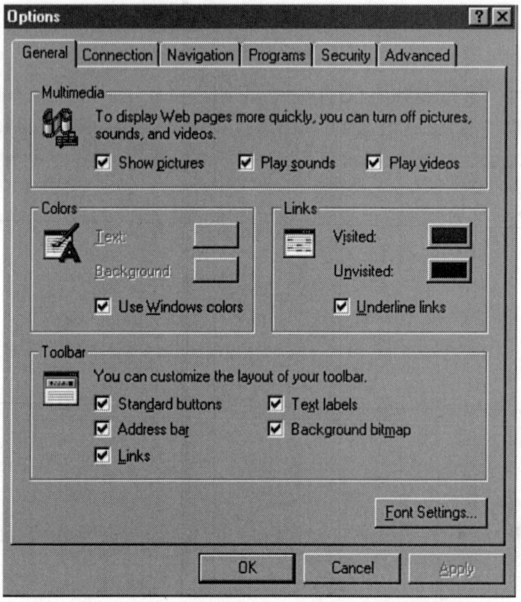

Figure C-7 The general properties sheet

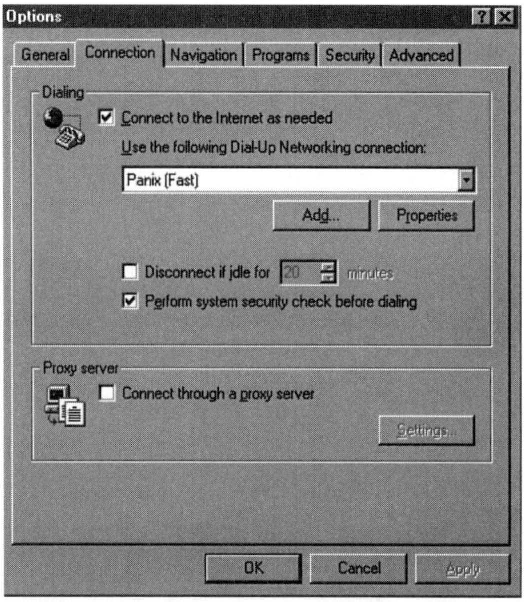

Figure C-8 The connection property sheet

- Navigation—You can customize which page you'd like to use as your starting home page. Just enter its URL in the Address box here.
- Programs—This allows you to set which programs you'd like to use for e-mail and for Usenet news. By default, you can use Microsoft's Internet Mail and Internet News, which are included with Explorer. You can also tell Explorer how to handle various types of files by selecting the File Types button. It allows you to designate which program or plug-in should be launched whenever Explorer comes across various unfamiliar file formats.
- Security—You are able to customize how securely documents will be handled by Explorer. If you want to keep your computer extremely safe, you may tell Explorer not to download possible security risks such as ActiveX controls, Java applets, or other plug-ins. Another nice feature is a Content Advisor. Click on Settings; the Content Advisor window will appear as in Figure C-9. You may now decide which Web pages to skip based on Adult Language, Nudity, Sex, or Violence. Many questionable Web pages are written with certain tags so that the pages can be weeded out by people who don't want to see them. This is a great option to use if your kids surf the Internet, or if your sensibilities are easily offended. To turn ratings on, click on the Enable Ratings button. You can also lock this window with a password.

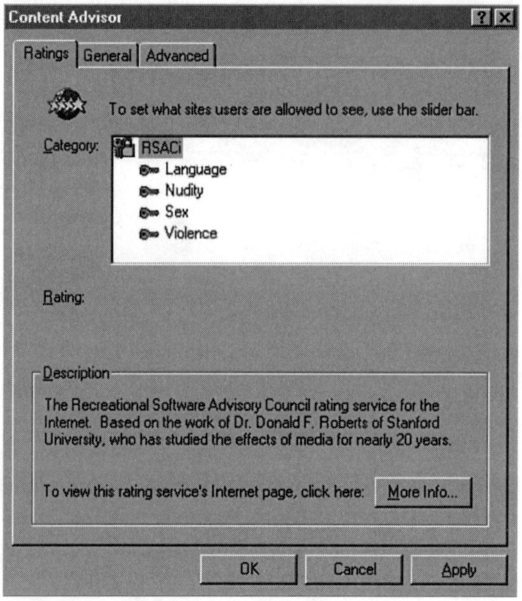

Figure C-9 The Content Advisor window

- Advanced—This properties sheet lets you customize when Internet Explorer will issue warnings. This is useful if you deal with sensitive information and want to know which Web pages are secure and which are not. You can also set a number of other advanced Java and Security options here.

SYMBIOTIC PARTNERS

Explorer includes many of the latest Web technologies. These make your Web pages sing, dance, and even act as entire applications. The line between what a computer can do in general and what a computer can do over the Internet is thinning.

ACTIVEX

Microsoft's proprietary ActiveX technology lets you drop *controls* into your Web pages. Controls are software components such as specialized buttons, input forms, graphics viewers, sound players, and so forth.

When you load a page with an ActiveX control, Explorer will check if you already have that control on your system. If not, you'll be asked whether you'd like to download it. You'll be told whether the control has been authenticated by Microsoft. If the control is secure, it'll automatically be downloaded and installed for you. The resulting Web page may look more like a software program than a Web page. Don't be surprised to find all new types of buttons, such as the up and down arrow controls in Figure C-10.

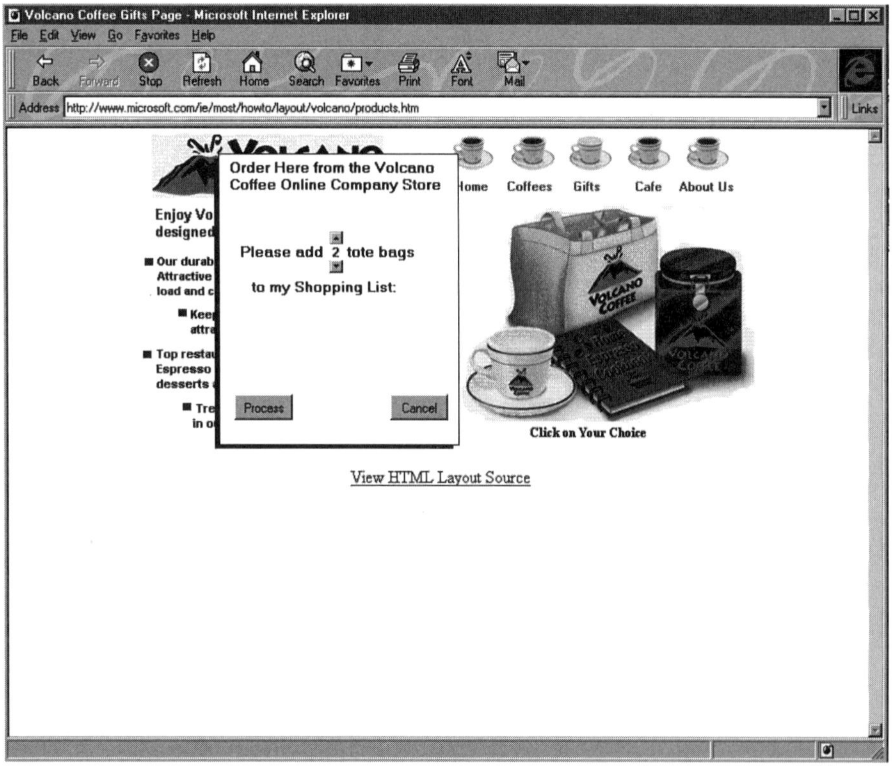

Figure C-10 Loading a page with an ActiveX control

SCRIPTS

Internet Explorer allows Web page writers to add different types of scripts right into the source code of the Web page itself. This means you can get instantaneous feedback and control of the Web browser, ActiveX controls, Java applets, and other plug-ins. This makes interactivity fast and easy. Internet Explorer supports Visual Basic, Scripting Edition and JavaScript languages.

JAVA

Finally, Explorer fully supports the popular Java language. Java is a programming language that lets you write full applications that run directly within your Web browser. Java is great for writing games, graphics demonstrations, databases, spreadsheets, and much more.

TOTAL MASTERY

Now that you are fully in control of Explorer, you can learn, work, and have fun using it with the greatest of ease. Wandering through the Internet faster than ever, you are ready to investigate new paths of adventure with your trusty, obedient Explorer guiding you every step of the way.

INDEX

Symbols

A

E

F

G-H

I

J-L

N

O

P

R-S

T-U-V

W-X-Y-Z

ENVIRONMENTAL AWARENESS

Books have a substantial influence on the destruction of the forests of the Earth. For example, it takes 17 trees to produce one ton of paper. A first printing of 30,000 copies of a typical 480-page book consumes 108,000 pounds of paper, which will require 918 trees!

Waite Group Press™ is against the clear-cutting of forests and supports reforestation of the Pacific Northwest of the United States and Canada, where most of this paper comes from. As a publisher with several hundred thousand books sold each year, we feel an obligation to give back to the planet. We will therefore support organizations that seek to preserve the forests of planet Earth.

WAITE GROUP PRESS™

JAVA 1.1 INTERACTIVE COURSE

Laura Lemay and Charles L. Perkins

This "Web-amplified" book is a complete step-by-step guide to learning Java from the ground up. Java 1.1 Interactive Course includes enrollment in the eZone (a Web-based educational site) providing a virtual classroom with real-time testing, tutoring from course "mentors," interaction with students, access to a database of FAQs, and other online resources. When you successfully complete this course, download a personalized certificate of achievement.

Available now • 500 pages
ISBN: 1-57169-083-2
U.S. $39.99 • 1 CD-ROM

PERL 5 INTERACTIVE COURSE

Jon Orwant

This customized course in Perl includes a unique Web-based component with an online "mentor" to answer your specific Perl questions, a special Internet mailing list just for readers of this book that allows students to ask questions or "meet" other students, and online quizzes and exams for immediate feedback on your progress. After successfully completing the exams, you can download a personalized certificate of achievement.

Available now • 992 pages
ISBN: 1-57169-064-6
U.S. $49.99 • 1 CD-ROM

JAVA NETWORKING AND AWT API SUPERBIBLE

Nataraj Nagaratnam, Brian Maso, Arvind Srinivasan

Acquire the most complete resource guide to the networking and windowing capabilities of Java 1.1. Hundreds of source code examples, projects, and reference entries provide complete coverage on creating high-powered Java applets and applications that run on multiple platforms simultaneously. The CD-ROM contains projects, source code, the Java Developer's Kit, prototype multimedia collage tool, and a Java-based image editor.

Available now • 1,000 pages
ISBN: 1-57169-031-X
U.S. $59.99 • 1 CD-ROM

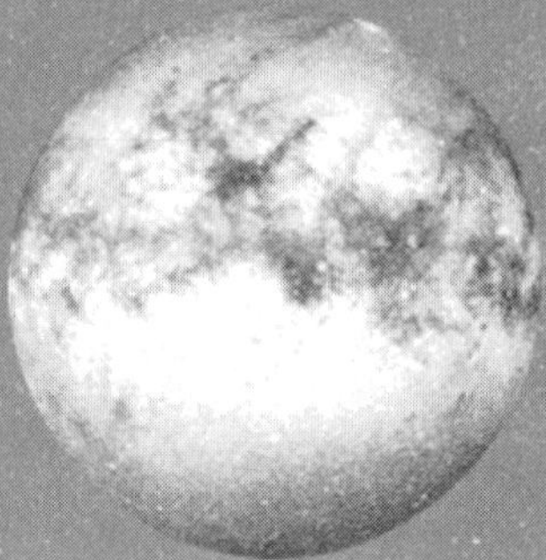

Send for our unique catalog to get more information about these books as well as our other outstanding and award-winning titles.

Message from the **Publisher**

Welcome to Our Nervous System

Some people say that the World Wide Web is a graphical extension of the information superhighway, just a network of humans and machines sending each other long lists of the equivalent of digital junk mail.

I think it is much more than that. To me, the Web is nothing less than the nervous system of the entire planet—not just a collection of computer brains connected together, but more like a billion silicon neurons entangled and recirculating electro-chemical signals of information and data, each contributing to the birth of another CPU and another Web site.

Think of each person's hard disk connected at once to every other hard disk on earth, driven by human navigators searching like Columbus for the New World. Seen this way, the Web is more of a super entity, a growing, living thing, controlled by the universal human will to expand, to be more. Yet, unlike a purposeful business plan with rigid rules, the Web expands in a nonlinear, unpredictable, creative way that echoes natural evolution.

We created our Web site not just to extend the reach of our computer book products but to be part of this synaptic neural network, to experience, like a nerve in the body, the flow of ideas and then to pass those ideas up the food chain of the mind. Your mind. Even more, we wanted to pump some of our own creative juices into this rich wine of technology.

Taste Our Digital Wine

And so we ask you to taste our wine by visiting the body of our business. Begin by understanding the metaphor we have created for our Web site—a universal learning center, situated in outer space in the form of a space station. A place where you can journey to study any topic from the convenience of your own screen. Right now we are focusing on computer topics, but the stars are the limit on the Web.

If you are interested in discussing this Web site or finding out more about the Waite Group, please send me e-mail with your comments, and I will be happy to respond. Being a programmer myself, I love to talk about technology and find out what our readers are looking for.

Sincerely,

Mitchell Waite, C.E.O. and Publisher

200 Tamal Plaza
Corte Madera, CA 94925
415-924-2575
415-924-2576 fax

Website:
http://www.waite.com/waite

Creating the Highest Quality Computer Books in the Industry

Waite Group Press

This is a legal agreement between you, the end user and purchaser, and The Waite Group®, Inc., and the authors of the programs contained in the disk. By opening the sealed disk package, you are agreeing to be bound by the terms of this Agreement. If you do not agree with the terms of this Agreement, promptly return the unopened disk package and the accompanying items (including the related book and other written material) to the place you obtained them for a refund.

SOFTWARE LICENSE

1. The Waite Group, Inc. grants you the right to use one copy of the enclosed software programs (the programs) on a single computer system (whether a single CPU, part of a licensed network, or a terminal connected to a single CPU). Each concurrent user of the program must have exclusive use of the related Waite Group, Inc. written materials.

2. The program, including the copyrights in each program, is owned by the respective author and the copyright in the entire work is owned by The Waite Group, Inc. and they are therefore protected under the copyright laws of the United States and other nations, under international treaties. You may make only one copy of the disk containing the programs exclusively for backup or archival purposes, or you may transfer the programs to one hard disk drive, using the original for backup or archival purposes. You may make no other copies of the programs, and you may make no copies of all or any part of the related Waite Group, Inc. written materials.

3. You may not rent or lease the programs, but you may transfer ownership of the programs and related written materials (including any and all updates and earlier versions) if you keep no copies of either, and if you make sure the transferee agrees to the terms of this license.

4. You may not decompile, reverse engineer, disassemble, copy, create a derivative work, or otherwise use the programs except as stated in this Agreement.

GOVERNING LAW

This Agreement is governed by the laws of the State of California.

LIMITED WARRANTY

The following warranties shall be effective for 90 days from the date of purchase: (i) The Waite Group, Inc. warrants the enclosed disk to be free of defects in materials and workmanship under normal use; and (ii) The Waite Group, Inc. warrants that the programs, unless modified by the purchaser, will substantially perform the functions described in the documentation provided by The Waite Group, Inc. when operated on the designated hardware and operating system. The Waite Group, Inc. does not warrant that the programs will meet purchaser's requirements or that operation of a program will be uninterrupted or error-free. The program warranty does not cover any program that has been altered or changed in any way by anyone other than The Waite Group, Inc. The Waite Group, Inc. is not responsible for problems caused by changes in the operating characteristics of computer hardware or computer operating systems that are made after the release of the programs, nor for problems in the interaction of the programs with each other or other software.

THESE WARRANTIES ARE EXCLUSIVE AND IN LIEU OF ALL OTHER WARRANTIES OF MERCHANTABILITY OR FITNESS FOR A PARTICULAR PURPOSE OR OF ANY OTHER WARRANTY, WHETHER EXPRESS OR IMPLIED.

EXCLUSIVE REMEDY

The Waite Group, Inc. will replace any defective disk without charge if the defective disk is returned to The Waite Group, Inc. within 90 days from date of purchase.

This is Purchaser's sole and exclusive remedy for any breach of warranty or claim for contract, tort, or damages.

LIMITATION OF LIABILITY

THE WAITE GROUP, INC. AND THE AUTHORS OF THE PROGRAMS SHALL NOT IN ANY CASE BE LIABLE FOR SPECIAL, INCIDENTAL, CONSEQUENTIAL, INDIRECT, OR OTHER SIMILAR DAMAGES ARISING FROM ANY BREACH OF THESE WARRANTIES EVEN IF THE WAITE GROUP, INC. OR ITS AGENT HAS BEEN ADVISED OF THE POSSIBILITY OF SUCH DAMAGES.

THE LIABILITY FOR DAMAGES OF THE WAITE GROUP, INC. AND THE AUTHORS OF THE PROGRAMS UNDER THIS AGREEMENT SHALL IN NO EVENT EXCEED THE PURCHASE PRICE PAID.

COMPLETE AGREEMENT

This Agreement constitutes the complete agreement between The Waite Group, Inc. and the authors of the programs, and you, the purchaser.

Some states do not allow the exclusion or limitation of implied warranties or liability for incidental or consequential damages, so the above exclusions or limitations may not apply to you. This limited warranty gives you specific legal rights; you may have others, which vary from state to state.

SATISFACTION REPORT CARD

Please fill out this card if you wish to know of future updates to *VBScript SuperBible*, or to receive our catalog.

First Name: ______ **Last Name:** ______

Street Address: ______

City: ______ **State:** ______ **Zip:** ______

E-Mail Address ______

Daytime Telephone: ( ) ______

Date product was acquired: Month Day Year **Your Occupation:**

Overall, how would you rate *VBScript SuperBible?*

☐ Excellent ☐ Very Good ☐ Good
☐ Fair ☐ Below Average ☐ Poor

What did you like MOST about this book? ______

What did you like LEAST about this book? ______

Please describe any problems you may have encountered with installing or using the disk: ______

How did you use this book (problem-solver, tutorial, reference...)? ______

What is your level of computer expertise?

☐ New ☐ Dabbler ☐ Hacker
☐ Power User ☐ Programmer ☐ Experienced Professional

What computer languages are you familiar with? ______

Please describe your computer hardware:

Computer ______ Hard disk ______
5.25" disk drives ______ 3.5" disk drives ______
Video card ______ Monitor ______
Printer ______ Peripherals ______
Sound Board ______ CD ROM ______

Where did you buy this book?

☐ Bookstore (name): ______
☐ Discount store (name): ______
☐ Computer store (name): ______
☐ Catalog (name): ______
☐ Direct from WGP ☐ Other ______

What price did you pay for this book? ______

What influenced your purchase of this book?

☐ Recommendation ☐ Advertisement
☐ Magazine review ☐ Store display
☐ Mailing ☐ Book's format
☐ Reputation of Waite Group Press ☐ Other

How many computer books do you buy each year? ______

How many other Waite Group books do you own? ______

What is your favorite Waite Group book? ______

Is there any program or subject you would like to see Waite Group Press cover in a similar approach? ______

Additional comments? ______

Please send to: **Waite Group Press**
200 Tamal Plaza
Corte Madera, CA 94925

☐ **Check here for a free Waite Group catalog**

SATISFACTION CARD

STOP!

BEFORE YOU OPEN THE DISK OR CD-ROM PACKAGE ON THE FACING PAGE, CAREFULLY READ THE LICENSE AGREEMENT.

Opening this package indicates that you agree to abide by the license agreement found in the back of this book. If you do not agree with it, promptly return the unopened disk package (including the related book) to the place you obtained them for a refund.